Nicholas Lee Doucet

DATA PROCESSING
Second Edition

COMPUTERS IN ACTION

Perry Edwards and Bruce Broadwell
Sierra College

Wadsworth Publishing Company
Belmont, California
A Division of Wadsworth, Inc.

To our wives, Kathleen and Celia, and to our children, Marcella, Lyman, James, Rosalie, Jennifer, Sarah, and Benjamin, who went with unanswered questions and unfinished chores, but who gave us encouragement and shared in our efforts.

Computer Science and Data Processing Editor:
    Rich Jones
Production Editor: Diane Sipes
Designer: Cynthia Bassett
Copy Editor: Carol Dondrea
Technical Illustration: John Cordies, J and R Art
    Service, Inc.
Art Editor: Sandra Howard
Photo Research: Kay James
Cartoons: Sidney Harris
Cover photograph courtesy of Melvin Prueitt, Los Alamos National Laboratory.

ISBN 0-534-01063-6

© 1982 by Wadsworth, Inc.
© 1979 by Wadsworth Publishing Company, Inc. All rights reserved. No part of this book may be reproduced, stored in a retrieval system, or transcribed, in any form or by any means, electronic, mechanical, photocopying, recording, or otherwise, without the prior written permission of the publisher, Wadsworth Publishing Company, Belmont, California 94002, a division of Wadsworth, Inc.

Printed in the United States of America

4 5 6 7 8 9 10—86 85 84 83

Library of Congress Cataloging in Publication Data
Edwards, Perry.
  Data processing.
  Bibliography: p.
  Includes indexes.
  1. Electronic data processing. 2. Electronic digital computers. 3. Basic (Computer program language) I. Broadwell, Bruce. II. Title.
QA76.E28 1982   001.64   81-12936
ISBN 0-534-01063-6   AACR2

CONTENTS

MODULE ONE INTRODUCTION 1

Chapter 1 What Is Data Processing? 9

Preview 10
The Curse 10
Definition of Data Processing 10
Types of Data 11
    Numeric Data 11
    Alphanumeric Data 11
Types of Processing 11
    Calculation 11
    Rearrangement 12
    Reading: Input 12
    Writing: Output 12
    Storage: Memory 12
Manufacturers and Sizes of Computers 13
History Capsule: George Boole and His Algebra 14
Definition of Programming 14
What Does a Computer Do? 14
Computer News: Supreme Court Decides to Join Computer Age 17

Chapter 2 Functional Parts of Computers 19

Preview 20
Inside a Computer 20
Central Processing Unit: CPU 20
    Control Unit 20
    Arithmetic/Logic Unit 20
    Memory 20
Input Devices 22
Output Devices 23
History Capsule: Charles Babbage/Ada Lovelace and the Analytic Engine 24
External or Secondary Storage: Magnetic Tape and Disk 25
Programs 26
    Languages 26
    Sample Program and Results 26
Summary 31
Computer News: Movies by Computer: No Actors, No Cameras 32

Chapter 3 Computer Programs 35

Preview 36
Programming Languages 36
Machine Languages 36
Assembly Languages 37
High-Level Languages 38
History Capsule: Steve Jobs and Steve Wozniak: Inventors of the Apple Personal Computer 40
Problem Definition: The VISA Statement 41
Summary 47
Computer News: Software Makers Losing Sales to Program Pirates 50

MODULE TWO   LANGUAGE   52

Chapter 4   Flowcharting   55

Preview   56
Computer Programs   56
Flowcharts   56

    Terminal Symbol   57
    Processing Symbol   57
    Input or Output Symbol   57
    Document Symbol   57
    Flowline   57
    Sample Flowcharts   58

Extended Example: Listing VISA Transactions   59

    Accumulating a Total   60
    Eliminating Repetitive Steps in the Transaction Listing Program   62

History Capsule: John Von Neumann   63

    Preparation Symbol   63

Decision Making in the Transaction Listing/Totaling Program   64

    Decision Symbol   65
    Off-page and On-page Connectors   67

Flowcharting Rules   67
Flowcharting Examples   71
Summary   75
Computer News: Moore's Is Not Less   80

Chapter 5   Beginning BASIC   81

Preview   82
BASIC: Background and Purpose   82
Language Rules   82

    Statements   82
    Labeling the Symbols   82
    Variable Naming Rules   83
    START and REM   83
    LET   83
    FOR Statement   84
    READ/DATA   86
    LET and Precedence Order   87
    PRINT—Captions, Values, Comma, Semicolon   88
    NEXT and END   88

History Capsule: Kemeny and Kurtz: The Founders of BASIC   90
Program Execution   91

    System Commands or Job Control Language   91
    Program RUN   91
    INPUT Statement   92

Solved Exercises with IF and GO TO   94

    Validating Dates   94
    GO TO Statement   94
    Discounting   94

Summary   100
Computer News: Computer Learns Shorthand   102

Chapter 6   More BASIC   105

Preview   106
Structured Programming   106

    Simple Sequence   106
    Selection   106
    Repetition   106

Adding Data to the Program   108
Documenting the Program with REM   112
Strings and TAB   112
IF and Boolean Operators   112
Arrays and DIM   118
IMAGE   120
Solved Exercises   125

    Counting Using an Array   126
    Calculating and Totaling Commissions   126

Summary   133
History Capsule: The Origins of Fortran   134
Computer News: Application—System Provides Useful Sales Data Fast   136

Chapter 7   Advanced BASIC   137

Preview   138
Functions   138

    Library Functions   138
    User-Defined Functions   139

Strings   140
Multidimensional Arrays   145
File Processing   146

Building the Transaction File   146
Sorting the Transaction File   146
Building a Master File   149
Updating the Master File   149

Solved Exercises   157

Simulation of Dice Rolling   157
Julian and Gregorian Calendars   159

Summary   165
History Capsule: The Julian and Gregorian Calendars   166
Computer News: The Smash Hit of Software   168

Chapter 8   Language Comparisons: FORTRAN, COBOL, Pascal, PL/1, RPG-II   169

Preview   170
Other Programming Languages   170
FORTRAN 77   170
COBOL-74   171
History Capsule: Captain Grace Hopper and the Origins of COBOL   176
Pascal   176
PL/1   177
RPG-II   177
Language Selection Criteria   180
Program Criterion   180
Comparison of Major Languages in VISA Problem   183
Summary   186
Computer News: How to Be a Superprogrammer   188

Chapter 9   Interaction of Programs and the Computer   191

Preview   192
Electricity and Circuits   192
Memory   197

Addresses and Contents   198
Destructive Input and Nondestructive Output   199

Programming   199

Operation Codes   199
Addresses   199

History Capsule: Gene Amdahl: The Man Who Took on IBM   200

The Control Unit   201

Instruction Fetch and Execute   201

Macroprogramming and Microprogramming   203
Summary   206
Computer News: Computer Commuter   208

MODULE THREE   HARDWARE   210

Chapter 10   Input to the Computer   213

Preview   214
Introduction to Input   214

Media and Machines   214
Considerations in Selecting Input Devices and Media   214

Minimizing Errors   216
Batch Processing: Input via Keyboard   216

Punched Cards   216
Magnetic Media   221
Multistation Data Preparation Devices   223

Batch Processing: Direct Input from Source Documents   225

Magnetic Ink Character Recognition   225
Optical Character Recognition   227

History Capsule: Hollerith, Billings, and Powers   228

Optical Mark Recognition   232
Digitizers   233

Transaction Processing: Input via Keyboard   234

Computer Terminals   235
Printing Terminals   236
Intelligent Terminals   236
Automated Teller Machines   237
Automatic Telephone Payments   237

Transaction Processing: Direct Input from Source Documents   238

Point-of-Sale Terminals   238

Transaction Processing: Input by Voice   241
Electronic Funds Transfer   241
Summary   243
Computer News: Magic Wand Comes of Age with New Uses   246

Chapter 11 Memory and Data Representation 251

Preview 252
Human and Computer Memories 252
Need for Primary and Secondary Storage 252
Need for Computer Memory 253
Memory Addresses 254
Decimal and Binary Systems 254

    Bridging the Decimal-Binary Gap 256
    Conversion Methods 257
    Hexadecimal Number Systems 257

Computer Data Notation Systems 258

    4-Bit BCD Notation 258
    Parity-Check Bit 259
    8-Bit Notation 259
    Fixed-Word Notation 260

Characteristics of Memory 262
History Capsule: Atanasoff and Berry's Special-Purpose Electronic Computer 263
Memory Types 263

    Semiconductor Memories 263

History Capsule: Mauchly and Eckert's General-Purpose Computer 264

    Charged-Coupled Devices 266
    Magnetic-Bubble Memories 266
    Techniques under Development 267

Summary 268
Computer News: How Magnetic-Bubble Memories Work 270

Chapter 12 Secondary Storage/Database Management Systems 271

Preview 272
Secondary Storage 272

    Magnetic Tape 272
    Magnetic Disk 275
    Drums and Cartridges 278

File Processing Methods 278

    Sequential 279
    Indexed Sequential 280
    Direct 282

History Capsule: Magnetic Tape and Disk 283

Database (DBMS) 284

    DBMS Techniques: Chains, Inverted Tables 284
    Types: Hierarchical, Network, Relational 286
    Comparing DBMSs 286

Summary 289
Computer News: IBM Drops the Other Shoe—and the Industry Relaxes 291

Chapter 13 Micros, Minis, and Mainframes 293

Preview 294
Microprocessors, Microcomputers, and Microcomputer Systems 294

    Microcomputer Functional Parts 294
    Microprocessor Functional Parts 295
    Bits Per Word 297
    Configurations 298
    Memory Capacity 298
    Processor Speed 299
    Software 299
    Space, Power, and Air Conditioning 300
    Costs 300
    Users and Uses 300

History Capsule: Ted Hoff and the Microprocessor 301

    Sources of Hardware and Software 302

Minicomputers and Minicomputer Systems 302

    Minicomputer Functional Parts 303
    Bits Per Word 303
    Configurations 303
    Memory Capacity 304
    Processor Speed 304
    Software 305
    Space, Power, and Air Conditioning 305
    Costs 305
    Users and Uses 306
    Sources of Hardware and Software 307

Mainframe Computers—Large, Medium, and Small 307

    Mainframe Computer Functional Parts 308
    Differentiating Features of Mainframes 308
    Mainframe Configurations 310
    Software 310
    Space, Power, and Air Conditioning 311

Costs   311
Users and Uses   311
Sources of Hardware and Software   311

Summary   312

Computer News: A Mainframe on Three Chips   315

Chapter 14   Data Output Devices   319

Preview   320
Introduction to Output   320
Visual Display Devices   320

Alphanumeric Terminals   320
Graphic Displays   322
Flat Panel Displays   322

Printer Output   325

Print Media   325
Impact Printers   326
Nonimpact Printers   332
Advantages and Disadvantages of Various Types of Printers   336

Other Output Devices   337

Computer Output on Microfilm   337
Plotters   342
Audio Response Devices   342

Summary   344

Computer News: Peripherals: Amoco's Credit Card Billing Coup   347

MODULE FOUR   MANAGEMENT   350

Chapter 15   Systems: Analysis, Design, and Implementation   353

Preview   354
What Are Accounts Receivable?   354
The Systems Process   354
Analysis   355

Investigation of Current System   355
Alternatives   355
Cost Factors   355
Proposal   355

Design   359

Output Requirements   359
Data Collection   360

File Design and Processing   363

Implementation   364

Programming   364
Testing   365
Training   365
Conversion   366
Auditing, Evaluating, and Documentation   366

Summary   366

Computer News: Systems Houses: An Option for Success   368

Chapter 16   Processing Modes and Data Communications   371

Preview   372
Symbol Definition   374
Processing Modes   374

Batch Processing: Single User, Remote Job Entry, Stacked Jobs   374
Time-Sharing: Partition and Swapping Methods   378
Multiprogramming: Fixed and Variable Partitioning   380
Multiprocessing   383
Virtual Memory   384

Data Communications   384

Data Communications Terminals   385
Modems   386
Acoustic Coupler   388
Interfaces   388
Carriers, Lines, and Channels   391

History Capsule: People in Communications   392

Transmission Modes   392
Multiplexing   393
Line Configurations   394
Communications Protocols   396
Data Communications Alternatives   399
Computer Networks   399
Distributed Processing   403

Off-Line, On-Line, and Real-Time Processing   404

Summary   408

Computer News: Electronic "Copy Boy" Hired by Texas Daily   410

Chapter 17 Trends and Future Developments 413

Preview 414
Computer Maid, Cook, Timer, and Tutor 414
Hardware Developments and Trends 414

  Computer Logic and Storage 415
  Secondary Storage 417
  I/0 Devices 417
  Terminals 418

Firmware Developments and Trends 419
Software Developments and Trends 419

  Operating Systems 420
  Systems Management Software 420
  Database Management Systems (DBMs) 420
  Languages and Programming Techniques 420
  Software Costs 422
  Report Generators 422

Personal Computers 422
Data Communications Developments and Trends 424

  Fiber Optics 424
  Summary 426

Computer News: Applications: Voice Mail Arrives in the Office 428

Chapter 18 Computer Industry 431

Preview 432
The Computer Industry in the United States 432

  Mainframe Computer Manufacturers 433
  Peripheral Devices Manufacturers 434
  Minicomputer Manufacturers 434

History Capsule: Thomas Watson: The "Old Man" of IBM 435

  Microcomputer Manufacturers 438
  Semiconductor Manufacturers 438
  Software Services 439
  Computing Services 440
  Facilities Management 443
  Computer Stores 444

International Computer Industry 445
Summary 448
Computer News: Small-Computer Shootout 449

MODULE FIVE SOCIAL ISSUES 452

Chapter 19 Automation and Robotics 455

Preview 456
The Doom and Gloom Prophecies 456
What Is Automation? 456
Employment Areas Impacted by Automation 457

  Robotics and the Manufacturing Industry 457
  The Office of the Future 459

Economic Impact 460

  Short-Term Impact on Employment 460
  Long-Term Impact on Employment 462
  Automation and Productivity 464

Sociopsychological Impact 465

  Work Ethic 465
  Workers' Attitudes 465
  Workers' Experience 466
  Life-styles 467

Responsibilities for Coping with Automation 467

  Government 468
  Business 468
  Education 468
  Labor 468

Summary 469
Computer News: The Latest Robot Who's Who 471

Chapter 20 Privacy 473

Preview 474
Introduction 474
What Is Privacy? 474
How Is Privacy Threatened? 475
The Information Revolution: Databanks 476
The Computer's Godlike Image 477
Examples of Computer Threats to Privacy 478

  Credit Bureaus 478
  Arrest Records 480
  Universal Identifiers 481

How Do We Meet Threats to Privacy? 482

    Laws and Government Action   482
    Business Self-Regulation   486
    Privacy Publications   486
    In-Service Education   486
    The Courts   486
    Other Organizations   487

Summary   487
Computer News: Computer Codes Get Censors Edgy   489

Chapter 21   Computer Security and Crime   493

Preview   494
Introduction   494
Lack of Security Leads to Abuse   495

    Fraud   495
    Theft   495
    Sabotage   496
    Espionage   496
    Accident   496

Improving Computer Systems Security 497

    Physical Security   497
    Internal Security Mechanisms   498
    Operational and Procedural Security   499
    Auditing Procedures   500
    Ethical Controls   500
    Legal Deterrents   501

Summary   502
Computer News: Accused Embezzler Had Record of DP Crime   504

MODULE SIX   SUPPLEMENTS   506

Supplement A   The Challenge of Programming   509

Preview   510
Problems to Solve   510
Payroll System   525
Inventory System   528

Supplement B   Decision Tables   531

Preview   532
Function and Structure of Tables   532

    Header   532
    Condition Stub   532
    Action Stub   532
    Condition Entry   533
    Action Entry   534

Some Sample Tables   534

    Testing Two Numbers   534
    Accounts Receivable—Validation Routine   535

Complex Tables   536

    Compressing the Table   537
    Types of Tables   538

Advantages and Disadvantages of Decision Tables   540
Payroll-Merging Decision Tables   541
Summary   542
Computer News: Social Security's Decrepit Computers   544

Supplement C   Summary of ANSI Minimal BASIC   545

Preview   546

ANSI Minimal BASIC   546
    Characters and Strings   546
    Programs   546
    Constants   547
    Variables   547
    Expressions   547
    Functions   547
    Statements   547

Supplement D   Careers with Computers   551

Preview   552
Role of the Computer in a Business   552
Management of the Computing Resource   552
Jobs Involved with Computing   553

Career Ladder 556
- Manager of Computing Services Department 556
- Systems Analyst 557
- Database Administrator 557
- Systems Programmer 558
- Applications Programmer 558
- Computer Operator 559
- Data Entry Operator 559

Summary 561

Computer News: A Company That Works at Home 562

A LAYPERSON'S GLOSSARY 564

GLOSSARY 567

INDEX 582

INDEX OF BUSINESS APPLICATIONS 591

PREFACE

TO THE INSTRUCTOR

Approach

Data Processing: Computers in Action, 2d edition, is designed for introductory data processing and information systems courses. It is written for students who have no prior knowledge of computing concepts, terminology, or programming languages. Its organization into modules allows maximum flexibility for use in courses of differing emphasis and organization.

With so many introductory computing texts already on the market, writing yet another might seem like processing another IBM card. However, we feel our book offers many unique features that can improve students' learning.

In hardware/software books, the opening chapters often present the history of computing. However, we decided to spread this material throughout the text so that the history can be linked to specific topics. Consequently, not only do students remember the history better (because they see how it fits in), but they also can be introduced immediately to contemporary, state-of-the-art topics.

Many textbooks treat programming in an "either/or" fashion—it is either stressed at the expense of other topics or virtually ignored. In contrast, we combine student-written programs with class material to make both more interesting and understandable. For instance, we use a program on files to illustrate the concepts of file creation, deletion, and update in a discussion of magnetic disk and tape files. Programming helps students visualize fields, records, and files.

Other texts offer a computers-in-society approach. These "computer appreciation" courses often include too little material to show how or why computers do what they do. They introduce a term like *data file,* for example, describe it, and analyze it, but only in an abstract manner. We wonder how students can relate to such concepts without actually experiencing file processing in a program. Though some might argue that writing an actual program to create and access a file is too hard for the average student, we do not think this is the case with interactive computer systems.

In essence, our approach combines the general study of the computer with a study of a specific language, so that students experience a sense of immediacy and learn about the computer directly. This has given our students the perspective and background to understand what computer use is really all about.

Organization

The text is divided into six modules: Introduction, Language, Hardware, Management, Social Issues, and four supplements, including a group of problems for programming. Since everyone teaches differently, we have written the modules and many

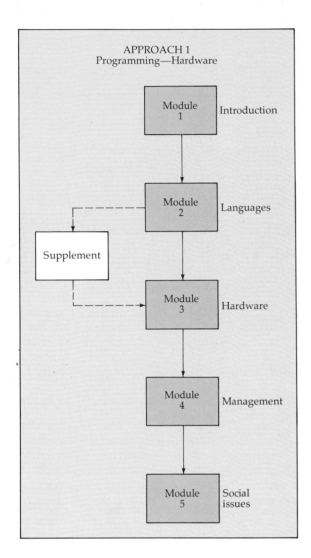 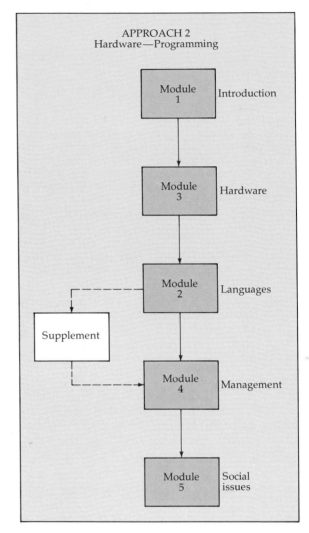

of the chapters to be used independently. Thus, you can "customize" our book to fit your favorite course structure and emphasis. If you believe that programming should be taught first, you might assign the chapters as shown in Approach 1, above left on this page. If you want to present hardware first and programming second, you might use the modules as shown in Approach 2. If you like to mix the two approaches (as we do), see the pathway through the text shown in Approach 3. Approach 4 shows you how you can use a language other than BASIC with our book. Other approaches are possible, and the module concept gives you the flexibility to develop your own.

The first module, Introduction, establishes the essential terms, definitions, and concepts. It also discusses how computer systems retrieve and process data.

The second module, Language, covers flowcharting, Job Control Language (JCL), BASIC, and an overview of FORTRAN 77, COBOL 74, RPG-II, Pascal, and PL/1. We have programmed a single application in each language to show students how the languages differ. We use a VISA statement as the

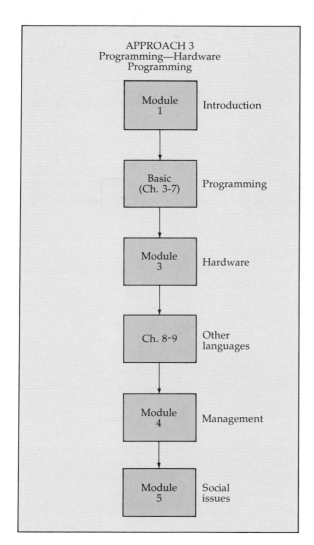

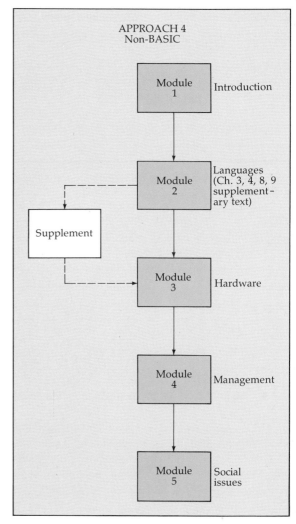

common example because so many people use this credit card system.

We emphasize BASIC because of its wide availability and its popularity on time-sharing, small business, and personal computers. Also, students can learn to use BASIC easily and quickly, thus rapidly gaining a positive first-time computer experience. The modular organization of our book does not mandate BASIC as the language, however. If you want to substitute FORTRAN, COBOL, Pascal, or RPG-II for BASIC, simply choose a supplementary text and use it in place of the BASIC material. The flowcharting chapter is designed to allow this substitution easily.

The third module, Hardware, concerns data processing equipment and functions. It explains how people enter data into the computer, how the computer stores, processes and outputs data, and how data are stored on external file devices. We also compare the various types of processors: micros, minis, and mainframes.

The fourth module, Management, begins with a study of a real system. We analyze the alternatives, design reports, calculate costs, study various data

PREFACE   **xiii**

bases, determine the proper system, and look at its implementation. Next we look at modes of processing data (on-line, real-time, batch, networks, distributed processing). The module ends with a look at trends and future developments and an overview of the computer industry, both within the United States and abroad.

The fifth module, Social Issues, discusses automation and robotics and their impact on our society. The final two chapters concern computer privacy and security. Here we look at the various laws that are in place and how people can protect themselves and the computing system.

The first supplement in the sixth module, "The Challenge of Programming," contains fifty-seven widely varied problems, all of which have been classroom tested, categorized by type, and rated for programming complexity. In addition, there are two complete systems, payroll and inventory, that students can program. The second supplement discusses decision tables as an alternative to flowcharting. The third is a summary of ANSI minimal BASIC, and the fourth describes career paths in the computer field.

The text ends with two glossaries and two indexes. The first glossary is quite unique in that it defines words and terms in a hierarchical fashion and in a layperson's vocabulary. You may want to have your students read this glossary after they have read Chapter 1. In fact, you can reproduce and distribute copies of this glossary with our permission. The second glossary is the more traditional one and uses ANSI formal definitions.

The Index of Business Applications lists the pages where a certain business term, for example, *payroll*, is discussed. The second index uses boldface page numbers to allow you to locate the definition of a term in context and to find it in the body of the text.

Features

Each chapter offers a rich assortment of teaching and learning devices:

1. a chapter outline, giving chapter content at a glance

2. a preview that introduces the topics to be discussed

3. new material, with key terms emphasized in boldface type

4. a history capsule, describing a person who or an event that had an impact on the computer industry

5. cartoons by Sidney Harris, spaced at pertinent locations

6. a summary that reinforces the concepts presented in the chapter

7. a "Computer News" article reprinted from a recent journal, newspaper, or magazine. These articles bring real people or events to the book; they vary from discussions on robots to voice mail to the Supreme Court.

8. a list of key terms

9. exercises, arranged by level of difficulty, that offer practice in chapter material

Modifications for the Second Edition

Many significant alterations are reflected in this edition. There are three new chapters: Systems: Analysis, Design, and Implementation; Micros, Minis, and Mainframes; and Careers with Computers.

The text is now divided into six rather than five modules. The language module is now in second position and the hardware module in third.

The language of the text is still BASIC, but flowcharting is not as separated from BASIC as it was. Instead, the programming material is presented in the form of a spiral. A simple flowchart and program start the spiral, and the finally developed program becomes an entire accounts receivable system. It starts with a data capture/validation program and ends with a master file update program that prints a statement almost identical to the real one used by VISA. Programming structure, style, and documentation are stressed throughout this section of the book.

General updating of all topics is a must in a new edition. You will find new material on Pascal, robotics, data communications, microprocessors, minicomputers, and structured programming.

Some material has been deleted, mostly in the areas of punched input/output devices, core storage, and internal memory codes (6 and 7 bit).

Some additional features have been developed for the second edition. There are twenty-two CAI programs you can use to reinforce the vocabulary of each chapter. The Challenge of Programming Supplement has two spirals, payroll and inventory control, which parallel the VISA accounts receivable spiral. You can have your students program in a spiral similar to the one in the text. Lastly, a computerized test bank of over one thousand multiple choice questions is available. As an adopter of the text you need to contact Wadsworth Publishing Company, 10 Davis Drive, Belmont, CA 94002 to make arrangements to use this system.

Teaching and Learning Aids

To accompany the text we have an instructor's manual and a student study guide. For each chapter the instructor's manual includes:

1. Behavioral objectives
2. A summary
3. Teaching suggestions
4. Answers to end-of-chapter exercises
5. Multiple choice and true/false questions
6. Overhead transparency masters
7. CAI vocabulary testing programs

The student study guide is written by William L. Harrison (Oregon State University) and produced by P.S. Associates. For each chapter the study guide includes:

1. Chapter objectives
2. A synopsis
3. Self-evaluation questions and a review of terminology
4. A short-answer integrative problem
5. A self-test

Acknowledgments

Many people think that a book is solely the creation of its authors. Our experience has shown how invaluable others are in such a creation. To list them all would be impossible, yet we want to acknowledge them.

Before publication of our book the following individuals also reviewed the manuscript. Our thanks to: David R. Adams, Arkansas State University; Ray V. Alford, John Carroll University; Gerald H. Anderson, Cowley County Community College; James D. Brainerd, Lansing Community College; N. D. Brammer, Colorado State University; Chuanyu E. Chen, Montclair State College; Rosemary W. Damon, Canada College; Stephen Deam, Milwaukee Area Technical College; Donald B. Distler, Jr., Belleville Area College; Robert H. Dourson, California Polytechnic State University, San Luis Obispo; Felix E. Dugger, Southwestern College; Sallyann Z. Hanson, Mercer County Community College; William L. Harrison, Oregon State University; Robert C. Hopkins, Los Angeles Pierce College; Hattie Russell Jones, Chowan College; Robert A. Marshburn, West Virginia Institute of Technology; B. Matley, Ventura College; Richard E. Matson, Schoolcraft College; Lawrence McNitt, Andrews University; Don B. Medley, Moorpark College; George L. Miller, North Seattle Community College; Michael P. O'Neill, Pacific Lutheran University; Donald J. Puro, C. S. Mott Community College; Donald J. Schaefer, Wright State University; John J. Thornton, formerly of University of South Florida; Jay-Louise Weldon, New York University; Gary A. Wicklund, University of Iowa; Dan C. Winters, Orange County Community College.

The contribution of William Harrison is particularly important to us. Bill developed the student study guide, which we feel is a great asset in helping students learn and practice the concepts we present.

For their consultations and assistance in acquiring materials, we thank Phillis Heisler, Burroughs Corp.; Frank Cravens, Hewlett-Packard Co.; Lisa Dreske and Andrew Volk, Intel Corp.; Carol Weiner, Scan-Tron Corp.; and Clifford Burns and Donald Price, Sierra College.

Rebecca Gregg, Leonard Taylor, and Steve Hunter, our colleagues at Sierra College, were particularly helpful. Besides our students and colleagues, the support provided by Wadsworth

Publishing Company has been enormous. The list of Wadsworth people is almost as long as our reviewer list. Our thanks are extended to Jon Thompson, Cynthia Bassett, Diane Sipes, Rich Jones, and Sandra Howard.

The tasks of typing and duplicating were performed by Pat Brophy, Susie Fox, and Don Skewis. They conscientiously met our deadlines without complaint.

Without support from our families we never would have made it. Many hours that could have been spent with them were sacrificed toward the creation of this book. Our acknowledgment of them should have come first, not last.

TO THE STUDENT

Among today's fastest changing fields are electronics and computers. To realize how fast they are changing, think back to the early 1970s when a handheld calculator was physically the size of this book, cost around $100, and could only add, subtract, multiply, and divide. Today a four-function calculator is small enough to fit inside a wrist watch (and still have the watch, too) and may cost as little as $3.50. In fact, the size of the calculator depends more on the size of the buttons we humans need to push than on the electronic needs of the calculator itself.

Change is a big part of our lives and computers are one reason why. We believe you should realize the capabilities and limitations of computers. We have tried here to give you knowledge on which to base a philosophy of the computer's role in business and society. This same knowledge should also give you insight into the impact of the computer in helping to shape society's future.

This course will bring you some skills and techniques in problem solving that can be transferred to other disciplines and to your everyday life. You will see how simple and logical you must be when trying to get the computer to do something. You will be forced to consider every possible alternative the computer will encounter, and plan for it.

Most colleges offer computer courses more advanced than the one you are now taking. This book will prepare you for advanced courses in computer science or data processing if you choose to take them.

Besides a computer philosophy, some insight, and technical skills, you will also receive an historical perspective of the social and technological state of the art. Since the first commercial computer was installed in the early 1950s, the history is brief, but it is also very significant.

One final word before you turn to Chapter 1 and begin your study of an exciting and unique field. We believe you will learn the most by doing. We do not think you will fully grasp the concepts in this book unless you get involved with computers. That may mean solving a problem wrong sometimes, but you can learn from that experience, too. When you write a program you will inevitably make mistakes. Just remember that only you and the computer know of these mistakes, and the computer can't tell anyone.

Perry Edwards

Bruce Broadwell

MODULE one

INTRODUCTION

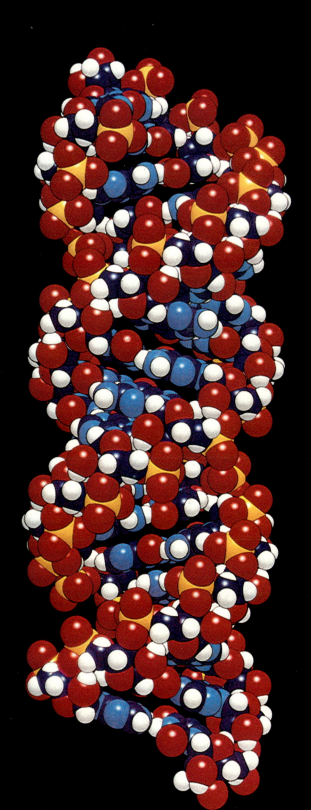

Computer-based technology is expanding our knowledge in many diverse fields. Some of this range is illustrated in the photographs on the following pages. Photo N, for example, shows a technique developed at Bell Labs that may help design yellow page ads in the future; Photo G, by contrast, is a cutaway image of the space shuttle. An industrial application of computer technology is shown in Photo H (a computer robot), a biochemical application in Photos A and P (the structures of RNA and DNA), and a meteorological application in Photo F (a model of the global atmosphere).

One of the areas that has benefited most from the expansion of computer technology is space exploration, illustrated here by computerized color enhancements of the sun taken from the Skylab solar telescope (Photos D and E) and a computer-enhanced image of Saturn taken from Pioneer 11 (Photo B). Computer technology in data communications makes the world smaller every day, particularly the business world: Photos T and U show electronic switching systems in Saudi Arabia and France, and Photo V shows the trading floor of a large New York brokerage house.

Further developments of the flat panel display in Photo L will soon enable graphic computer output to be provided in portable book-size screens, making communication through graphic illustration (the rate of which is thousands of times faster than reading) much more widely accessible. As is clear from these photographs, computers also have a substantial contribution to make in the area of aesthetics. Many computer graphics are developed purely for their design appeal, like Photos O and R; others have a specific scientific purpose, like Photo K, a computer graphics circuit design, and Photo M, which illustrates mathematical functions, and Photo Q, which illustrates—stunningly—some of the amino acids in the protein coat of the tomato bushy stunt virus.

VIKING 2, CAMERA 1, CAMERA EVENT A213, SOL 23 COLOR.
MULTBK COLOR ENHANCED VERSION SOFT COLOR STRETCH.
GRN = (((GRN/BLU+RED) * 5.62) - 488) * RED
RED = (((RED/BLU+GRN) * 2.70) - 243) * RED

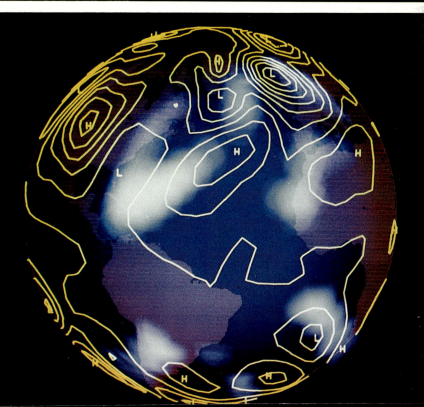

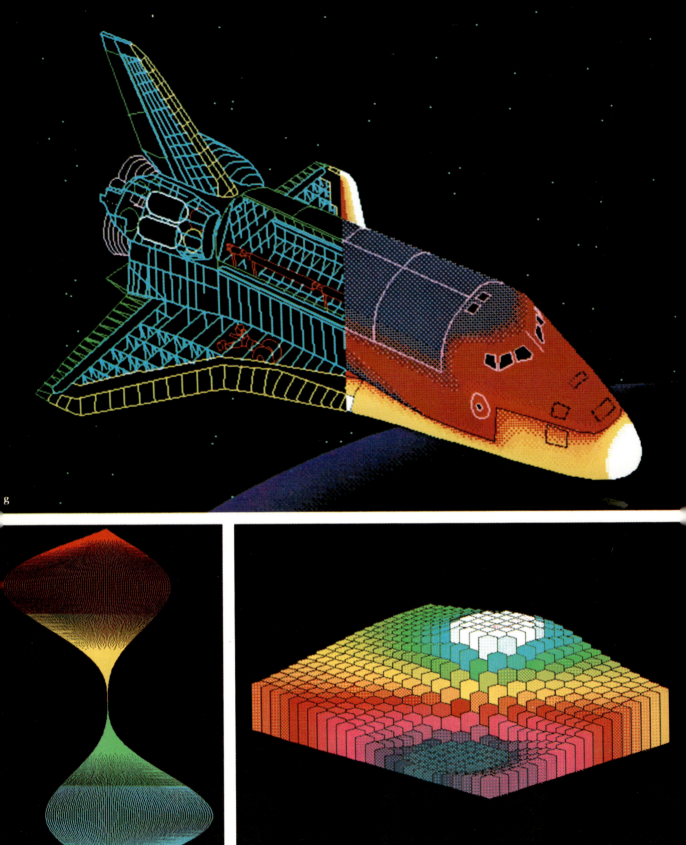

h

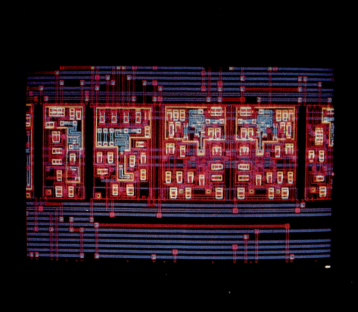

k

l

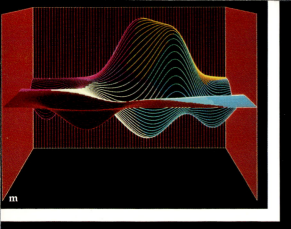
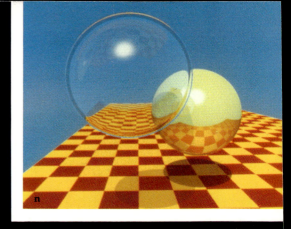
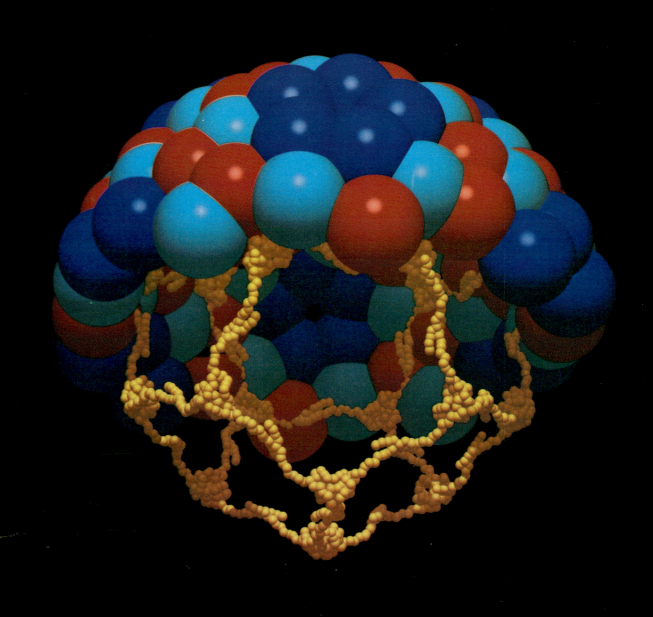

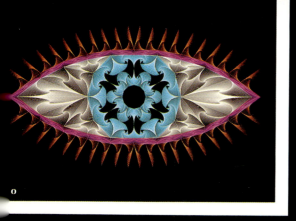

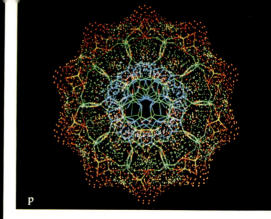

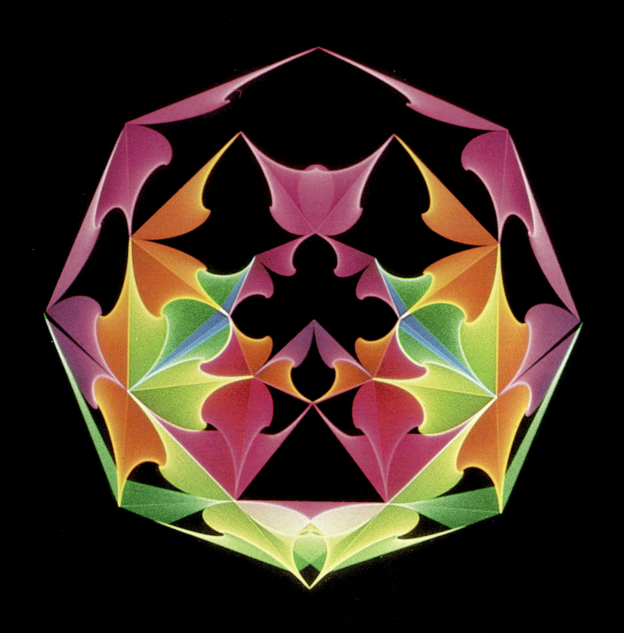

WHAT IS DATA PROCESSING?

Preview

The Curse

Definition of Data Processing

Types of Data
   Numeric Data
   Alphanumeric Data

Types of Processing
   Calculation
   Rearrangement
   Reading: Input
   Writing: Output
   Storage: Memory

Manufacturers and Sizes of Computers

History Capsule: George Boole and His Algebra

Definition of Programming

What Does a Computer Do?

Computer News:
Supreme Court Decides to Join Computer Age

PREVIEW

Computers are invading our lives more and more. They have already changed society more than the wheel, which merely extended our "muscle power." Computers have extended our "mind power." Just what is a computer? What can it do? What can it not do? What do we mean by data? This chapter answers these questions and more.

THE CURSE[1]

Most bills are now sent out on perforated business-machine cards that say in large letters DO NOT FOLD, BEND, OR MUTILATE. I have a friend who doesn't like to be told what to do with a bill, and one day, to my horror, I saw him fold, bend, and mutilate a card right in front of my eyes.

"You shouldn't have done that," I said, quivering. "There is a curse on anyone in the United States who folds, bends, or mutilates a bill."

He laughed at me. "That's an old wive's tale. This is a free country, isn't it?"

"Only if you don't fold, bend, or mutilate."

"You're chicken," he said. "No computer is going to tell me what to do."

I didn't see my friend for several months. Then I finally ran across him in a bar. He was unshaven, dirty, and obviously had been on a bender.

"What happened?" I asked.

"The curse," he croaked. "The curse got me."

Then he told me his story. He had sent back the folded, bent, and mutilated card to the company and received another card in a week, saying, "We told you not to F. B. or M. This your last chance."

"I crumpled up the card and sent it back," he said, "still thinking I had the upper hand. Then it started."

"First my telephone went out on me. I could not send or receive any messages. I went down to the phone company and they were very nice until they looked up my name. Then the woman said, 'It says here that you mutilated your bill.'"

"'I didn't mutilate my phone bill.'"

"'It doesn't make any difference what bill you mutilated. Our computer is aware of what you did to another computer and it refuses to handle your account.'"

"'How would your computer know that?'"

"'There is a master computer that informs all other computers of anyone who folds or bends or mutilates a card. I'm afraid there is nothing we can do about it.'"

My friend took another drink. "The same thing happened when my electricity was cut off, and my gas. Everyone was sorry, but they all claimed they were unable to do anything for me."

"Finally payday came, but there was no check for me. I complained to my boss and he just shrugged his shoulders and said, 'It's not up to me. We pay by machine.'"

"I was broke, so I wrote out a check on my bank. It came back marked 'Insufficient respect for IBM cards.'"

"You poor guy," I said.

"But that isn't the worst of it. One of the computers got very angry, and instead of canceling my subscription to the Reader's Digest it multiplied it. I've been getting 10,000 Reader's Digests a month."

"That's a lot of Digests," I said.

"My wife left me because she couldn't stand the scandal, and besides, she was afraid of being thrown out of the Book-of-the-Month Club."

He started crying.

"You're in bad shape," I said. "You better go to the hospital."

"I can't," he cried. "They canceled my Blue Cross, too."

---

[1] Art Buchwald, "The Curse," *Son of the Great Society* (New York: G. P. Putnam's Sons, 1966).

DEFINITION OF DATA PROCESSING

In the 60 seconds or so that it takes most people to read Art Buchwald's humorous anecdote, a modern computer can:

- Calculate and print natural gas and electric bills for 600 or more customers, or
- Make 60,000,000 computations for scientists, or
- Sort into alphabetical order 20,000 checks, or
- Print a copy of the first 120 pages of the *Bible*.

The computer can work at speeds that humans cannot. The work that people use computers for is known as data processing. Notice that the term is composed of two words: *data* and *processing*. They are inseparable. Neither by itself can describe the work of the computer. The term **data processing** means the manipulation of data to generate information.

A typical example of the use of a computer for data processing is the calculation of natural gas and/or electric utility bills. To find how much a customer owes and to create a bill for that amount, we need (1) the gas or electric usage for the month being billed, (2) the customer's name and address, and (3) a method or formula, such as a rate schedule, that dictates how the bill is to be calculated.

TYPES OF DATA

Data are the facts that relate to a certain event, task, or person. Once the data have been processed, they are called **information**. In the utility billing example two pieces of data were needed: the amount of gas or electricity used and the user's name and address.

Numeric Data

The electrical usage is an example of **numeric data** because it is expressed in numbers. Other examples of numeric data are:

- 54 (kilowatts of electricity used)
- 95677 (ZIP codes)
- 35 (age)
- 1970 (year of birth)

Numeric data, then, contain only numeric characters, or numbers.

Alphanumeric Data

The customer's name and address are alphanumeric data (sometimes called "string" data). **Alphanumeric data** are composed of combinations of letters, numbers, or special punctuation characters. Examples of alphanumeric data are:

- Chicago, Illinois, George Washington (names)
- 5000 Rocklin Road (addresses)
- July 4, 1976 (dates)

A computer can accept both alphanumeric and numeric data and store them in memory.

A definition of data would be incomplete without the idea of relatedness. The information or facts must relate (have some connection) to the problem being solved. In the utility billing example, the user's Social Security number (SSN), although data, is not required to calculate the bill; in fact, it is useless. Not all facts are data, only those that have a bearing on the information we want—in this case, the amount owed.

TYPES OF PROCESSING

Processing is what a computer does with data to make them more useful. Such manipulations or operations include calculation, rearrangement, reading (input), writing (output), and storage (memory).

Calculation

The term **calculation** simply means addition, subtraction, multiplication, division, and exponentiation (raising a quantity to a power, for example, r^2). Early computers added about 2,000 numbers per second; today's can add a million or more.

FIGURE 1-1   Large-scale computer IBM 3033.

Rearrangement

A computer **rearranges** or **sorts** data when they have been stored in one order and are to be used in another. For utility bills, for example, meters are read geographically, by city or county. However, the company will probably want the computer to process the information in some other order, for example, alphabetical by customer name.

Reading: Input

In **reading** or **inputting,** the computer takes in data, sometimes from punched cards. Many computers can read 1,200–1,500 of these cards per minute.

FIGURE 1-2   Medium-scale computer IBM 3031.

Since each card holds a maximum of 80 characters (numbers, letters, and special characters such as *, ?, *, !), a computer is inputting data at the rate of 100,000 characters per minute.

Writing: Output

Although this input speed seems lightning fast by our standards, it is slow compared to a computer's

FIGURE 1-3   Small computer NCR 8200.

output speed. Many printers run at over 1,500–2,000 lines per minute. Since each line can be 132 or more letters or digits long, this amounts to some 260,000 characters per minute—more than twice the input speed.

Storage: Memory

Finally, a computer can store data. A computer typically has two **storage** units, one internal and one external. An internal storage unit, frequently called **memory,** is limited in the amount of data it can hold, while the cheaper external storage units can hold hundreds of millions of characters. External storage is thus used as auxiliary storage to main memory. External storage has high volume capacity and is low in cost, but the speed at which the data can be recalled is slow. Data can be recalled from an external storage unit in 30 milliseconds (thirty-thousandths of a second = 0.030 sec), whereas data can be recalled from internal storage in approximately 1 microsecond (one-millionth of a second = 0.000001 sec).

MODULE ONE: INTRODUCTION

MANUFACTURERS AND SIZES OF COMPUTERS

Regardless of the speed of their input units, output units, or storage units, all computers perform the five actions of calculation, rearrangement, input, output, and storage. Among the computer companies, IBM (International Business Machines), Sperry-UNIVAC, Burroughs, and Honeywell are widely known. Data General, Digital Equipment, National Cash Register, Control Data Corporation, Prime, and Hewlett-Packard are less well known, but they have made and sold almost as many computers as IBM Corporation (although generally smaller ones).

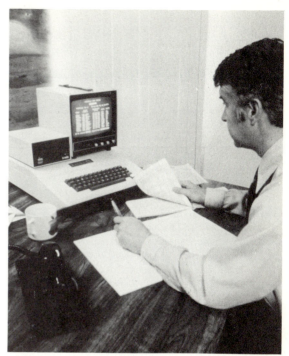

FIGURE 1–5   Home/hobby computer the Apple-II +.

FIGURE 1–4   HP 3000 minicomputer.

Computers come in sizes ranging from giants like the IBM 3033 (Figure 1–1) to medium-size computers like the IBM 3031 (Figure 1–2) to small computers such as the NCR 8200 (Figure 1–3) to minis like HP's 3000 (Figure 1–4) to home/hobby computers such as the Apple-II (Figure 1–5), and finally, to an IBM microcomputer smaller than a paper clip (Figure 1–6). The main difference among these, aside from cost, is speed. The IBM 3033 performs about 10 million additions in a second, while the microcomputer can do perhaps 500,000 additions per second. A grocery store cashier working at a rate of two additions per second every second of a 40-hour week would take 34 weeks to add 10 million items on a cash register.

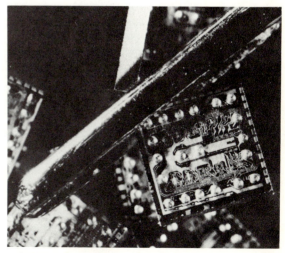

FIGURE 1–6   IBM computer on a chip.

CHAPTER 1: WHAT IS DATA PROCESSING?

GEORGE BOOLE AND HIS ALGEBRA

While the formula $x \cdot x = x$ is not correct according to our modern algebra, it is the fundamental formula upon which today's computers are designed. First postulated by George Boole in 1854 in his book *An Investigation of the Laws of Thought, on Which Are Founded the Mathematical Theories of Logic and Probabilities*, the formula remained largely a curiosity until Claude Shannon showed its practicality in 1938.

The son of a shoemaker who dropped out of school after the third grade, George Boole decided early in life to become a clergyman. He taught himself German, Latin, Greek, French, and Italian in preparation for this position. At the age of 20 he began his own school and taught himself algebra and differential equations (calculus).

The algebra that George Boole developed is now referred to simply as Boolean algebra. The algebra is really an explanation of binary, zero-one logic. In the formula $x \cdot x = x$ the only numeri solutions in modern algebra are 0 and 1; this is the same in Boolean algebra. If you represent a condition of no current flow in a circuit by 0 and a condition of current flow in the circuit by 1, then other Boolean formulas are possible:

$1 + 1 = 1 \qquad 1 \cdot 1 = 1$
$0 + 1 = 1 \qquad 0 \cdot 1 = 0$
$0 + 0 = 0$

Unfortunately, George Boole died in 1864 at the age of 49, well before the advent of computers. The famous English philosopher Bertrand Russell once said of his fellow countryman, "Pure mathematics was discovered by George Boole in his work published in 1854."

DEFINITION OF PROGRAMMING

How can a computer read, store, calculate, and print data quickly and accurately? How does it know when to read data? To calculate? To print a line of output? It doesn't! It must be instructed. A computer's essential characteristic is that it automatically and rigidly follows a given set of instructions. These **instructions, called a program, cause the computer to perform certain actions on the data.** Somehow, somewhere, someone must choose and arrange the instructions and give them to the computer so it can solve a problem. If the instructions are wrong, a computer generates the wrong answer. Did the computer make a mistake? Probably not. Computers do make mistakes, but the vast majority of errors are made by the person who instructs the computer, who improperly defines the problem in the first place, or who enters the data.

The person who creates a program is known as a programmer. Many people think programming is very complicated and difficult, but almost anyone with a proper understanding of what can and cannot be done on a computer can write simple programs.

WHAT DOES A COMPUTER DO?

A computer may do many different kinds of work. An individual may use a computer to accumulate income tax deductions or to play a space invader game. An attorney may use a computer to print monthly statements for his or her clients. A government agency may prepare employee payroll checks or direct an armed missile to a target by computer.

FIGURE 1–7	Some Accounting Uses of the Computer.
Payroll	The collecting of employee work hours and the converting of those hours into gross earnings; computing deductions; computing net pay.
Accounts Payable	The collecting of data about the goods and services *bought from* a supplier. The data are used to determine how and when to pay the supplier.
Accounts Receivable	The collecting of data about the goods and services *sold to* a customer. The data are used to prepare a statement that reflects the amounts owed and paid thus far for those goods and services.
General Ledger	The final consolidation of all financial transactions made by an organization. Transactions are totaled by various categories or accounts (which are defined by the chart of accounts each company has) and must balance, in that charges and credits must offset each other.

Businesses, of course, use computers for a variety of tasks. A manufacturer of automobiles, pencils, or sprinklers, for example, uses a computer to keep track of what was made; when it was made; who made it; how long it took to make; how much it cost to make; how many items were made; to whom the items were sold; and so on. A retailing or wholesaling business might use a computer to keep track of what they have to sell; from whom they buy the items they sell; how many items they have in stock; who sells the various items; who buys the items and how much they owe; what it costs to sell the items; and so on. Colleges and universities keep track of who is attending school; what classes they have taken; what classes they are taking; grades received; who teaches which classes; what rooms are used by which classes and during which hours; and so on.

Most businesses use their computer to do the bulk of their accounting applications (see Figure 1–7).

An engineering company may use a computer to calculate the stress on a proposed bridge, help design roadways, solve complex mathematical equations, or show the variations in temperature on the skin of the space shuttle, so that the right amount of insulation can be planned ahead of the flight.

Computers can also be used to control an operation physically. A petroleum cracking or chemical manufacturing firm may have their entire plant operated by a computer. The computers used here may be justifiable because the work may be dangerous or hazardous to humans. Furthermore, the plant's valving and piping systems may be so large and complex or the process may occur so quickly that the computer may be the only possible operator. Under computer control, the plant may operate at a lower cost or at a higher efficiency (over a number of years) than it could if operated by people.

Regardless of how a computer is being used, it must be programmed for that task. It is the program that makes the computer the valuable and indispensable tool that it has become and will continue to be in the future.

"I still think it's really magic."

TERMS

The following words or terms have been presented in this chapter.

Data processing	Sort
Data	Reading
Information	Input
Numeric data	Output
Alphanumeric data	Storage
Processing	Memory
Calculation	Program
Rearrangement	Programmer

EXERCISES

The exercises that follow are grouped by level of difficulty. Problems in the A series are the easiest; B series problems are moderately hard; and C series problems are the most difficult.

A–1 What kind of computer(s) is available for your use?

A–2 Find the names of at least four computer manufacturers other than those mentioned in the chapter.

A–3 What other types of rearrangements do you suppose a computer can do besides alphabetizing?

A–4 Most books printed today have an ISBN number printed after the copyright notification. Locate an ISBN number. Is this item or data considered numeric or alphanumeric?

A–5 List two other brands of home/hobby computers.

B–1 Is the computer that is available for your use classified as large, medium, small, or mini?

B–2 If a computer can perform one computation every one-millionth of a second, how many computations can it perform in a minute?

B–3 Figure 1–7 lists payroll, accounts payable, accounts receivable, and general ledger as applications of a computer. Make a list of three or more other business uses of a computer.

B–4 According to George Boole's algebra, what is $0 \cdot (1 + 0)$?

C–1 Most four-function ($+$, $-$, $\times$, $\div$) hand calculators are not computers. Why?

C–2 If a book has 45 lines per page, 85 characters per line, and 350 pages:
    a. how many total lines are there?
    b. how long will it take a 2,000-line-per-minute printer to produce a copy of the book?
    c. how many words are in the book (one word has five characters)?

C–3 What is the difference between accounts payable and accounts receivable?

C–4 Go to your college's business office or to a local business and ask for a copy of the chart of accounts they use for their general ledger. How are these accounts grouped?

COMPUTER NEWS

SUPREME COURT DECIDES TO JOIN COMPUTER AGE

By Stephen Wermiel
Staff Reporter of The Wall Street Journal

WASHINGTON—The Supreme Court is moving into the age of computerization.

Next October, for the first time since the Justices began issuing opinions in 1792, decisions will be printed by a computer. The changes are supported by Chief Justice Warren Burger, who recalls that when he arrived at the Supreme Court in 1969, "they didn't even have a Xerox machine in the building."

The Justices' opinions will be typed into word processors in their offices, where television-like display terminals are already in place. From there, the opinions will be transmitted by a push of a button to a typesetting computer on the court's ground floor. At the end of the line, two offset presses will turn the proofs into precedents.

The system may not sound startling. After all, computers are used every day in many offices, banks and stores.

SEAMSTRESS AND CARPENTERS

But traditions aren't discarded casually at the Supreme Court. The building still has its own seamstress to sew the Justices' robes and a woodworking shop to repair their chairs. And before Mr. Burger bought some copiers in 1969, memos were reproduced by using nine sets of carbon paper, called "flimsies."

The idea to bring in computers originated with Mr. Burger in 1972. He says he wanted some statistics from the court clerk's office and discovered that office workers had to count cases from a handwritten log. "They were doing it the way they had done it in Civil War days," the Chief Justice says, "only they used ballpoints instead of quill pens."

Some court operations are already computerized. The clerk's office began using computers in 1974 to keep track of pending cases. The Justices' law clerks and secretaries are practicing using word processors to produce draft opinions and memos, but the machines haven't been hooked up yet to the typesetting computer that makes copies.

Court officials believe that full computerization this fall will promote efficiency in the drafting of decisions and will save time and money in printing and personnel. They also hope to produce bound volumes of the court's work in less than a year; it now takes three years.

LEGAL PADS STAY

Not all customs will die, though. With one exception, the Justices will continue to write their opinions on legal pads, use Dictaphones or

---

CHAPTER 1: WHAT IS DATA PROCESSING?   17

work from drafts written by law clerks. Only Justice Byron White, who writes his opinions on a typewriter, is expected to work directly on the keyboard of a word processor.

> When Chief Justice Burger saw clerks counting cases from a handwritten log, he decided a change was needed. "They were doing it the way they had done it in Civil War days," he says.

Although the law clerks who use the machines receive computer training, mistakes have happened. In the court's last term, a clerk pressed the wrong button and lost a 40-page draft opinion. Fortunately, he already had a paper copy. Another lost a memo to his Justice about whether to grant a review of a case. He didn't have a copy and had to start over.

For the most part, says James Donovan, the court's computer specialist, the bugs have been worked out of the system. (The word processors are made by Atex Inc., in Bedford, Mass., and the printers by Xerox Corp.; the typesetting computer is a Mergenthaler L202 and the printing presses are made by Addressograph-Multigraph Corp., now called AM International Inc.)

"The Justices are delighted that something's happening to make the work easier, but other than that, they don't really get involved much," says a former Supreme Court law clerk.

REJECT TYPE STYLE

But Chief Justice Burger says the nine Justices are reviewing type styles for the computer printing. They've been using one style in test runs this year, he says, and "they don't like it." Other than type style, Mr. Burger says, "there has been no real resistance" from the Justices to converting the court to a computer operation. "By going at the word processing gradually," Mr. Burger says, "first with the secretarial pool, then one Justice's chambers and then a second, it just unfolded."

The use of computers is also spreading to federal courts. Federal district and appeals courts have been experimenting, through the Federal Judicial Center in Washington, with a system called Courtran that would provide centralized management and docketing capability.

A common concern in all the courts is the security of the computer system. The Supreme Court system, says Mr. Donovan, has codes and passwords that are supposed to prevent the work of one Justice or his clerks from ending up on the screen of another Justice's word processor.

CHAPTER two

FUNCTIONAL PARTS OF COMPUTERS

Preview

Inside a Computer

Central Processing Unit: CPU
    Control Unit
    Arithmetic/Logic Unit
    Memory

Input Devices

Output Devices

History Capsule: Charles Babbage/ Ada Lovelace and the Analytic Engine

External or Secondary Storage: Magnetic Tape and Disk

Programs
    Languages
    Sample Program and Results

Summary

Computer News: Movies by Computer: No Actors, No Cameras

PREVIEW

The word *computer* was not really defined for you in Chapter 1. Most people have seen pictures of a computer or have heard or read jokes about a computer, but if you asked them to tell you specifically what a computer is, they probably could not. This chapter tells you what a computer is, describes its functional units, and shows you a typical program that would make a computer solve a problem.

INSIDE A COMPUTER

Like the floor plan of an American home with its sleeping, food preparation, bathing, and recreation areas, the "floor plan" of today's computer is roughly divided into specialized areas. The functional parts of computers include:

1. Input devices
2. Arithmetic and logic unit
3. Memory
4. Output devices
5. External storage devices
6. Control unit

A computer floor plan would look like Figure 2–1.

The lines and arrows linking the six functional areas together represent the electric circuitry and the direction of information flow among the parts. Although the diagram looks quite simple, the actual machine is very complex. These six parts are not so easily separated. The functional areas even look much alike, as you can see from the picture of the inside of an actual computer in Figure 2–2.

CENTRAL PROCESSING UNIT: CPU

The control, memory, and arithmetic/logic units of a computer are usually grouped together and called the "central processing unit" **(CPU)**. These three areas, the most complex, fastest, and most powerful parts of the computer, are analogous to the human brain and central nervous system.

The CPU can be further subdivided. When we want to talk about the control and the arithmetic/logic units together, we call them the *processor*. The speed of the processor is sometimes used as a way of comparing different CPUs.

Control Unit

The **control unit** (CU) of a CPU keeps track of what goes on in all the functional parts. It recalls the instructions that were programmed (one at a time), sets up the internal circuitry for performing the instructions, and causes the circuits to perform the instructions. It also monitors the flow of data between the other two parts of the CPU and keeps track of which instruction is to be retrieved next.

Arithmetic/Logic Unit

The *arithmetic/logic unit* (ALU) calculates and makes decisions. If a program tells the computer to add, subtract, multiply, or divide two or more numbers, the control unit has those numbers copied into special memory areas called **registers** or **accumulators**. The ALU then manipulates these areas and returns the results to the proper memory location.

As an example of decision making, or comparison operations on data, a program may need to determine whether an employee has worked more than 40 hours. If so, he or she might be paid for overtime. The control unit would cause the total hours to be brought to the ALU, and then would have the number 40 subtracted from the total hours. If the difference were a positive number, the CU would cause the ALU to perform the overtime calculation. The ALU's decision-making power and the CU's ability to direct alternate actions makes the computer the powerful machine it is.

Memory

The third part of the CPU is **memory**. Sometimes known as primary storage, memory is the area from which the control unit recalls the instructions to be performed and the data to be processed.

MODULE ONE: INTRODUCTION

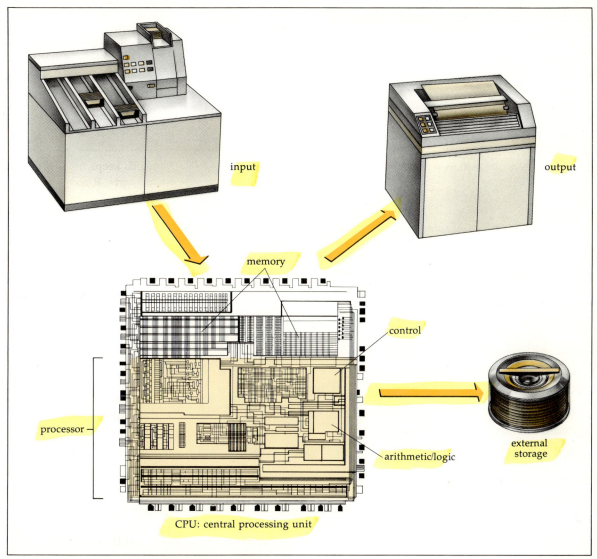

FIGURE 2–1 Functional areas of the computer.

The most widely used storage medium is the **semiconductor** memory unit (see Figure 2–3). The semiconductor memory consists of thousands of tiny transistors formed into a small (approximately ⅛ inch square) piece of silicone. Each transistor functions as a switch that represents the number one (1) when "on" and the number zero (0) when "off."

Eight of these tiny transistors are used together to store a unit of information called a **byte.** Thus, a computer with 32,768 bytes of memory has 262,144 transistors in it. A byte of memory can hold the code for a one- or two-digit decimal number (for example, 6 or 48), or for one alphabetic or special character.

In the late 1960s and early 1970s many business computers had memories of 64,000 bytes (abbreviated 64KB, where K means a thousand and B

CHAPTER 2: FUNCTIONAL PARTS OF COMPUTERS 21

FIGURE 2–2 A Data General computer opened for viewing.

stands for bytes). Today, we find many home computers like the Apple-II with 48KB, and medium-scale computers often have a million or more bytes (1MB) of memory, all of which are mounted on a memory board (see Figure 2–4). This increase in memory sizes is a direct result of the falling prices of memory devices created by the use of semiconductors.

INPUT DEVICES

The data to be processed must be brought into the computer's memory. To accomplish this, the control unit calls into use an **input device,** a piece of equipment that converts data from "human oriented" form to "machine oriented" form. A common input device is a card reader, which reads punched cards (see Figure 2–5).

Cards are normally prepared, or punched, on another machine, called a "keypunch." The information on the card may be data to be processed by a program, or it may be a program itself. The card reader can translate the cards into machine language form at up to 1,500 cards per minute.

There are many other input devices besides card readers. These include special purpose devices like those that read checks or cash register tapes, general purpose devices that can read typewritten pages,

FIGURE 2–3 IBM 64K bit memory chip.

FIGURE 2–4 Chip being mounted on circuit connectors.

and keyboards that allow direct input of data onto secondary storage.

OUTPUT DEVICES

An **output device** accepts the data sent to it from memory and converts them from machine language

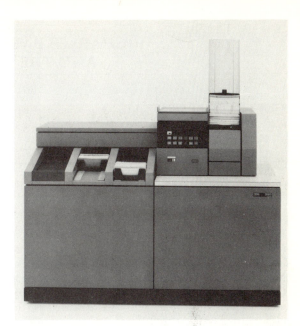

FIGURE 2–5 Card reader.

FIGURE 2–6 Line printer.

CHAPTER 2: FUNCTIONAL PARTS OF COMPUTERS   23

CHARLES BABBAGE/ADA LOVELACE AND THE ANALYTIC ENGINE

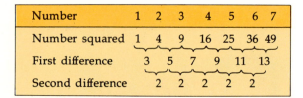

Today it is possible for you to look in many books and find tables of various mathematical formulas: squares, square roots, logarithms, sines, cosines, and so on. In the 1600s, 1700s, and 1800s tables like these were important to sailors, military men, business people, and mathematicians, to name just a few. At that time, the tables were all calculated by hand, using techniques like the first and second differences. Thus, to find 8 squared, the 49 of 7 squared was added to the last first difference (13) and the second difference (2), giving 64 (49 + 13 + 2). Producing tables in this manner was tiresome, boring, and time-consuming.

Charles Babbage (1791–1871) was the first person to attempt to mechanize the process of table construction. He visualized a machine that could be set (instructed) to calculate a given formula once the associated data from the formula were entered. Furthermore, the machine would calculate the results and display them automatically. His machine, the analytic engine, thus displayed all the functional parts of today's computers: input of data, arithmetic unit for computation, memory for data and instructions, and display of output.

Professor of Mathematics at Cambridge University by 1812, and a contemporary of Darwin and Dickens, Babbage was a man of far-ranging interests; he is credited with inventions in the mail service, railroads (cow-catcher), signaling devices, telescopic instruments, dating of archaeological finds, locks, submarines, earthquake detectors, and stage lighting.

By 1842 Babbage had been working on his protocomputers for 20 years. Both he and the British government were several thousand pounds poorer, the government was withdrawing its support, and the project needed some new blood. Enter Lady

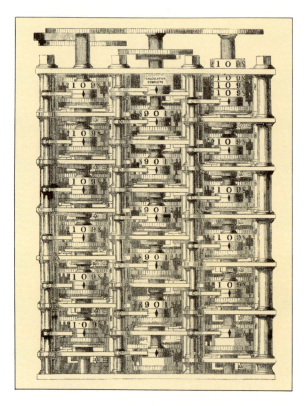

Ada Lovelace (1815–1852), the brilliant and spirited daughter of Lord Byron and Lady Annabella Milbanke. As a child she studied geometry alone (for fun), was tutored by the famous mathematician William de Morgan, and visited Babbage. He remembered her as one who, when shown the analytic engine, did not ask the usual silly questions, but understood both its working and its implications.

In 1842, after Lovelace had published her translation of an Italian engineer's paper on Babbage's machine, Babbage suggested she do an original paper. She did so at once, extending the thoughts in the engineer's paper, and correcting some serious errors in Babbage's own work. It is through this paper that we understand Babbage's machines today.

Lovelace now joined the project, first as apprentice and then as full collaborator. Among other things, she suggested using a binary system of storage instead of the decimal system Babbage was using. She also foresaw many of the computer's possibilities, predicting that it would one day compose music, and encouraging Babbage's plans for a machine to play tic-tac-toe. Today there is a new computer programming language called ADA.

Lovelace became as obsessed as Babbage with the analytic engine, devoting several hours each morning to it, and calling it "this first child of mine." Always desperate for money to continue their work, they tried to develop a system for winning at the horse races. At first they won, but then started to lose, and twice Ada had to pawn her jewels to pay their debts.

Babbage and Lovelace were never able to build a successful model of the analytic engine. Even had their funds been unlimited, and even had Ada not died of cancer at the age of 36, they probably would not have been able to do it. The technology needed to manufacture the special gears and shafts simply had not yet been developed. (IBM, with the benefit of modern technology, has now built a working model.) Nevertheless, if Charles Babbage is recognized, as he usually is, as the father of the modern computer, Lady Ada Lovelace should be recognized as its mother. As she predicted, her "child" has grown to be "a man of the first magnitude and power."

form to human language form. **Line printers** are a commonly used output device (see Figure 2–6).

A line printer prints the entire line at one time. In contrast, a typewriter prints each letter in succession across the line. It is not uncommon for a line printer to print 1,500 to 2,000 lines per minute.

Some devices are capable of both input and output. Machines like the cathode ray tube (CRT) terminal (see Figure 2–7) can display information on a TV-like screen and can accept data through a keyboard. These two-way devices are commonly called **I/O** (input/output) **devices**.

FIGURE 2–7   Hewlett-Packard 2624B CRT terminal.

EXTERNAL OR SECONDARY STORAGE: MAGNETIC TAPE AND DISK

The maximum internal memory capacity of the largest computers is about 32 million bytes (32MB). A large university, however, may need a billion bytes to store data about its students. The cost of building that much internal memory would be astronomical; to meet these large storage needs cheaply, we use an **external** or **secondary storage device**. The most widely used external storage devices are **magnetic tape** (see Figure 2–8) and **magnetic disks**. Data that are stored on tapes or disks can be recalled in thousandths of a second (milliseconds), compared with data in primary memory that can be recalled in millionths (microseconds) or billionths (nanoseconds) of a second.

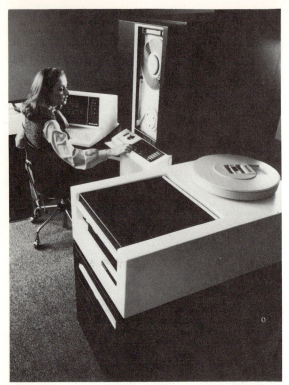

FIGURE 2–8 Magnetic disk (in foreground) and tape (in background) devices.

To process data stored on disks or tape, the program must first locate the data and then copy them into memory for processing. Data on tape are recorded sequentially; that is, to reach a desired item of data, the machine must read and examine every earlier item of data. Data recorded on disks, however, may be copied directly into memory, bypassing all other items. Computer systems usually have both tape and disk devices so programmers can take advantage of both locating procedures.

External storage media, unlike punched cards, are usually reusable. To change an item of data stored on disk or tape, the new information is simply recorded over the old, and only the new data remain.

Sometimes disk and tape are considered I/O devices. The CPU can put data onto tape or disk and then recall them at some future time. In this instance, the tape or disk first functions as an output device and then as an input device.

PROGRAMS

All computers, whether they fill a room or only your pocket, require a program. A program is a series of instructions that direct the processing of data to get the desired information; the instructions must be in the right order before the control unit can use them.

Languages

Programs can be written in several languages. Four widely used languages today are **BASIC** (*Be*ginners *A*llpurpose *S*ymbolic *I*nstruction *C*ode), **COBOL** (*CO*mmon *B*usiness *O*riented *L*anguage), **FORTRAN** (*FOR*mula *TRAN*slator), and **RPG** (*Re*port *P*rogram *G*enerator). COBOL and RPG are used primarily by businesses, FORTRAN by scientists and engineers. Computer languages, like ordinary languages, have rules of grammar. Some languages even have dialects, for example, FORTRAN 77 and COBOL-74.

Sample Program and Results

Many people buy items using plastic charge cards. They purchase groceries, gasoline, dinners in a restaurant, clothing, and many other items using this "plastic money." At the end of each month they normally receive a statement that shows their purchases and payments for the preceding month. A sample of the BankAmericard VISA statement is shown in Figure 2–9, and a portion of that statement has been shaded. While the form of a statement may vary depending on whether the statement is for Master Card, Shell, or Sears, the same kinds of data are printed: the date of the charge; a transaction, invoice, or reference number; and the dollar amount of the transaction.

The computer requires a program to print the data onto the statement. That program must be

MODULE ONE: INTRODUCTION

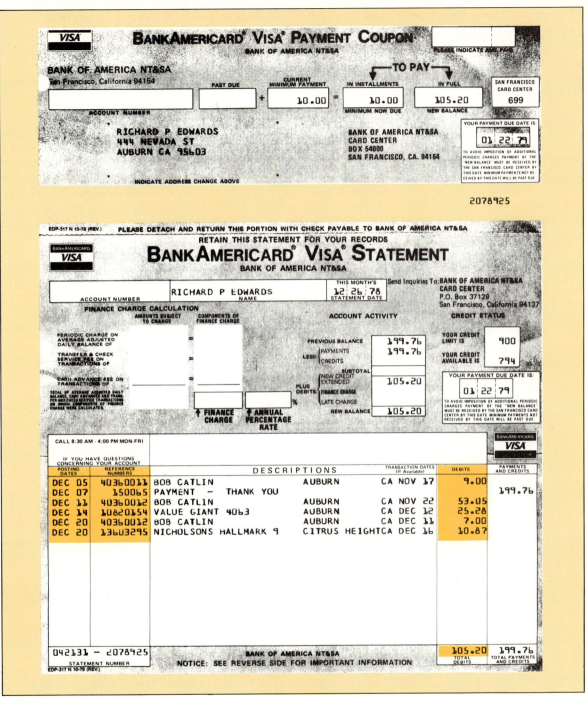

FIGURE 2-9   VISA statement.

written in a language the computer can understand. One of the easiest of all programming languages is **BASIC** (*Beginners All-purpose Symbolic Instruction Code*). BASIC is designed for beginning programmers and can be learned quickly. A sample BASIC program to print a slightly modified form of the shaded DEBIT portion of the BankAmericard VISA statement is shown in Figure 2–10.

In the BASIC programming language each line of the program is called a **statement** and has a line number. A line number is used to give the line a name and to show the order of the various lines with one another. After the line number, each line has a key word like REM, LET, FOR, or PRINT, which describes the main action of the line. After the key word, a line usually has information that is particular to the key word used.

Line numbers 10 through 90 are remark statements; they define the purpose of the program and explain what variables are being used (A, R, D, and so on). Line number 100 in Figure 2–10 tells the computer to allocate some memory space and to call that memory space T; and it tells the computer to put a zero into that memory space. Line 110 causes the computer to repeat each statement between 110 and 200 (NEXT C) five times. The repeating of a group of statements is called a loop. The FOR statement represents the beginning of the loop, and the NEXT statement, number 200, is the last statement of the loop. The C=1 TO 5 portion of FOR causes a memory space named C to be set aside and places a 1 in that space.

Line 120 of Figure 2–10 causes three numbers to be read from a DATA statement. The first number

```
10   REM
20   REM A PROGRAM TO PRINT THE DEBITS OF A VISA STATEMENT
30   REM
40   REM VARIABLES USED IN THIS PROGRAM
50   REM D: DATE OF A TRANSACTION
60   REM R: REFERENCE NUMBER OF A TRANSACTION
70   REM A: AMOUNT OF A TRANSACTION
80   REM C: LOOP COUNTER
90   REM T: TOTAL OF THE AMOUNTS
100  LET T=0
110  FOR C=1 TO 5
120  READ D,R,A
130  DATA 1205,403600.,9
140  DATA 1211,403600.,53.05
150  DATA 1214,108201.,25.28
160  DATA 1220,403600.,7
170  DATA 1220,136032.,10.87
180  LET T=T+A
190  PRINT D,R,A
200  NEXT C
210  PRINT
220  PRINT TAB(30);T
230  END
```

FIGURE 2–10   Sample BASIC program.

(1205) will be read into a memory space called D, the second number (403600) will be stored in memory space R, and the third (9) will be stored in A. These three numbers stored in memory spaces D, R, and A represent the date, reference number, and amount of a transaction.

The LET statement in line 180 causes the value stored in A (which is 9) to be added to the current value stored in memory space T (which was set equal to 0 in line 100), giving a new value to T (0+9=9). Line 190 has the values of D, R, and A (1205, 403600, and 9, respectively) printed. Since the preprinted VISA statement specifies that the date (D) is to be printed first, reference number (R) second, and amount (A) third, the values will print under the proper caption as we want them.

Line 200's NEXT C causes the loop counter C to have its value, now 1, increased by 1 to 2, and tests

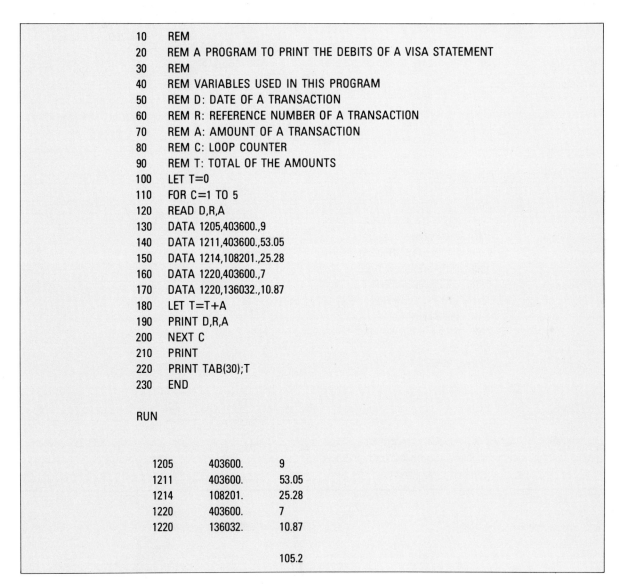

```
10    REM
20    REM A PROGRAM TO PRINT THE DEBITS OF A VISA STATEMENT
30    REM
40    REM VARIABLES USED IN THIS PROGRAM
50    REM D: DATE OF A TRANSACTION
60    REM R: REFERENCE NUMBER OF A TRANSACTION
70    REM A: AMOUNT OF A TRANSACTION
80    REM C: LOOP COUNTER
90    REM T: TOTAL OF THE AMOUNTS
100   LET T=0
110   FOR C=1 TO 5
120   READ D,R,A
130   DATA 1205,403600.,9
140   DATA 1211,403600.,53.05
150   DATA 1214,108201.,25.28
160   DATA 1220,403600.,7
170   DATA 1220,136032.,10.87
180   LET T=T+A
190   PRINT D,R,A
200   NEXT C
210   PRINT
220   PRINT TAB(30);T
230   END

RUN

      1205      403600.      9
      1211      403600.      53.05
      1214      108201.      25.28
      1220      403600.      7
      1220      136032.      10.87

                             105.2
```

FIGURE 2-11 BASIC program with RUN.

to see if the loop has been performed five times. Since the loop has only been done once, NEXT C causes the computer to cycle through the loop again starting at line 120. When the READ is done the second time, the values of D, R, and A that are read are 1211, 403600, and 53.05, respectively.

Eventually the loop is done five times and the PRINT statement of line 210 is performed. A PRINT like this causes the printing of a blank line. Line number 220 prints the value of T, 105.20, beginning in position 30. The last line, 230, causes the computer to terminate the program.

```
10    REM
20    REM A PROGRAM TO PRINT THE DEBITS OF A VISA STATEMENT
25    REM LINE NUMBER 100 IS NOW LINE NUMBER 115
30    REM
40    REM VARIABLES USED IN THIS PROGRAM
50    REM D: DATE OF A TRANSACTION
60    REM R: REFERENCE NUMBER OF A TRANSACTION
70    REM A: AMOUNT OF A TRANSACTION
80    REM C: LOOP COUNTER
90    REM T: TOTAL OF THE AMOUNTS
110   FOR C=1 TO 5
115   LET T=0
120   READ D,R,A
130   DATA 1205,403600.,9
140   DATA 1211,403600.,53.05
150   DATA 1214,108201.,25.28
160   DATA 1220,403600.,7
170   DATA 1220,136032.,10.87
180   LET T=T+A
190   PRINT D,R,A
200   NEXT C
210   PRINT
220   PRINT TAB(30);T
230   END

RUN

       1205      403600.      9
       1211      403600.      53.05
       1214      108201.      25.28
       1220      403600.      7
       1220      136032.      10.87

                              10.87
```

FIGURE 2–12   BASIC and RUN with modifications.

The program of Figure 2–10 needs one more instruction for the computer, RUN, before the computer will actually read the data, print the statement, and compute the total of the debits. RUN tells the control unit to start doing what the program says. Adding the RUN instruction to Figure 2–10 gives the results shown in Figure 2–11.

We must use the proper statement or the answer will be wrong, but, at the same time, the right statements will not work if they are in the wrong order. Figure 2–12 shows what happens with only a single change in the order of instructions in the statement printing program (line number 100 becomes 115). Note that the total debits now becomes 10.87. Putting T=0 as line 115 resets T to zero at each loop cycle.

Getting things in the right order is as important as writing correct instructions. The computer does not determine whether the sequence is right—that is the job of the programmer. The computer follows the instructions in the order given. If the order is wrong, the result is a wrong answer. The computer did not make an error—the programmer did.

"WHAT IT COMES DOWN TO IS THIS THING IS CAPABLE OF TELLING US A LOT MORE THAN WE REALLY WANT TO KNOW."

2. The arithmetic/logic unit makes computations and decisions as dictated by the program.

3. The memory unit holds the data to be processed and the program that is being executed.

4. Input devices convert data from human language form to machine language form.

5. Output devices convert data from machine language form to human language form.

6. External storage devices hold large volumes of data for later use.

The six functional units are always under the control of a program, which is written by people in a language the computer can understand.

TERMS

The following words or terms have been presented in this chapter.

CPU	I/O devices
Control unit	External or secondary
Arithmetic/logic unit	storage device
Register	Magnetic tape
Accumulator	Magnetic disk
Memory	BASIC
Semiconductor	COBOL
Byte	FORTRAN
Input device	RPG
Output device	Statement
Line printer	

EXERCISES

The exercises that follow are grouped by level of difficulty. Problems in the A series are the easiest; B series problems are moderately hard; and C series problems are the most difficult.

A–1 What kind of computer memory does your computer have?

A–2 Find the names of at least three other programming languages.

SUMMARY

Computers have six functional units or areas:

1. The control unit recalls the instructions of a program and has those instructions executed.

CHAPTER 2: FUNCTIONAL PARTS OF COMPUTERS

COMPUTER NEWS

MOVIES BY COMPUTER: NO ACTORS, NO CAMERAS

Will the day ever come, asks Rand Corp.'s Suzanne Landa, when movie films will be made totally by computer—without actors or cameras? Her answer: "An undeniable yes."

Landa, who has surveyed the use of computers in tinseltown, qualifies her statement by adding: "Whether movies produced by computer will be competitive in cost and quality with those produced by the traditional process, with computer aids, remains highly questionable." But she adds that with the use of computer technology it isn't too far-fetched to envision an actor speaking with another actor's voice, or an actor's head attached to another's body, where the body might be doing things that are totally unacceptable to the actor, but germane to the plot.

Landa leads a session at the National Computer Conference June 7 entitled, "Computer Technology in the Movie Industry," in which she will trace a study she's done of the movie industry's use of computers all the way from a movie's initial conception through exhibition, preservation, and redistribution. Her study wasn't done under a contract to the Santa Monica company, but Rand could benefit from it, she says, "because everyone in the movie industry wants to become a producer, but without having to get involved in busy paper work." Rand's knowledge of computers could help them.

For instance, she explains, the movie industry's payroll system is more complex than in any other industry because of changing regulations in the more than 60 unions and guilds to which their employees belong. And the employment figures vary widely. A studio that employs 3,500 to 7,000 persons permanently, easily could be paying 50,000 persons a year. She notes that Universal Studios, which employs between 50 and 2,000 extras a day, uses an interactive system to access a data base containing the names of available extras and information about their skills, attributes, costumes, and props.

Another studio uses computer graphic aids to help them determine the parts of each set which must be built to avoid the waste of building, say, a $3,000,000 set of which maybe only a third will appear in the final print. She says line drawn versions of sets and people are entered into an Evans & Sutherland Picture

System 2 through a tablet. For each set, camera angles and moves are executed in a way that those portions of a set that need not be built because they will never be visible can be determined.

Production cost control also is being done with the use of a computer. For example at Disney Productions, a minicomputer system soon will be used to help the location auditor explore the costs of various courses of action when an unforeseen event occurs. "For example, should a storm break, with an expected duration of two weeks, the location auditor would like to determine the costs of keeping everyone on location versus sending them home, paying required penalties, and bringing them back later."

Not until this year, Landa says, have special effects been created with the aid of computer-controlled cameras and models. Such previous science fiction movies as "2001: A Space Odyssey," and "Star Wars" have used special-purpose, hard-wired machines, not computers, "depending of course on what your conception of a computer is."

The popular movie "The China Syndrome" required the precise duplication of the interior of a nuclear power plant during the various stages of an alert. This meant the operation of 131 circuits controlling 2,500 instrument panel lights in differing sequences and in differing states, such as off, slow-flash, fast-flash or solid-on for each stage of the alert. And these had to be synchronized with live-action performances. The task was compounded by the need to restart the sequences at any point for retakes and for daily continuity.

Landa says this was done by programming a microcomputer in assembly language to allow accurate, flexible and reliable operation of the panel lights in coordination with the actors' performances.

She says digital storage of films, once they're removed from distribution, should be feasible within five years. Today's data compression techniques aren't sufficiently advanced. To store a 90-minute, high quality, color film digitally would require tens of trillions of bits of storage, and data compression techniques would reduce this amount by only 20 percent to 30 percent.

The purpose of her session is "to provide the computer-oriented audience with an understanding of the movie-making process and where each panelist fits in." Two guest speakers are Al Jerumanis, director of corporate data processing at MCA, Inc. (Universal Studios), who will discuss the use of computer technology in filmmaking from a studio's point of view, and William Dietrick of Mini-Micro Systems, Inc., Anaheim, Calif., who has developed an automated sound editing system that is used in movies and television shows. Landa says the system is considered to be the biggest technical advance in sound editing in 50 years. A third guest panelist, Larry Elin, director of animation with Magi, a New York commercial animation company, will talk from the point of view of the user of computers in filmmaking.

Landa says in her research she talked to many persons in the movie industry who weren't aware of their own extensive use of computers. "They'd tell me, 'Oh, we don't really use computers much,' and two hours later we would still be discussing their applications."

A–3 Does your computer have disk, tape, or both?

B–1 Examine line number 180 of Figure 2–10. What do you think it means?

B–2 From another book about computers, find out what the term *core stack* means. Sketch a picture of one.

C–1 How do you modify Figure 2–11 to read also the transaction dates listed in Figure 2–9?

C–2 Some computers have two different primary storage devices. Determine whether your system does and, if so, why?

C–3 Explain what would happen to the program in Figure 2–11 if line 180 read 180 LET T=T+D.

C–4 Set up a chart of numbers similar to the one shown in the Babbage/Lovelace example, except that you will cube the numbers. Find the first, second, and third differences.

CHAPTER *three*
COMPUTER PROGRAMS

Preview

Programming Languages

Machine Languages

Assembly Languages

High-Level Languages

History Capsule: Steve Jobs and Steve Wozniak: Inventors of the Apple Personal Computer

Problem Definition: The VISA Statement

Summary

Computer News:
Software Makers Losing Sales to Program Pirates

PREVIEW

In Chapter 2 you saw a computer program written in BASIC that printed a portion of a BankAmericard VISA statement. Just as there are many spoken languages, there are many different computer languages you can use. Some languages allow you to write your program rapidly, but are inefficient for a computer since they require a vast amount of the computer's time when your program is actually executed. Other languages require more thought, detail, and effort on your part, but take very little computer time. However, regardless of the language you use to write your program, the computer will probably not understand it directly. Your program will need to be translated to the "native" language of the computer.

This chapter gives you a quick glimpse at some of the languages in wide use. In addition, we will look more closely at the steps associated with printing the VISA statement.

PROGRAMMING LANGUAGES

Since the advent of computers in the late 1940s and early 1950s, one of the most time-consuming tasks faced by people was (and still is) the actual writing of the program that causes the computer to do tasks. In the early years of computers, people wrote their programs as a series of 0s and 1s (using the binary number system), and, using a set of switches, manually entered their program into the computer's memory. In 1949 programmers developed a special program that allowed the EDSAC computer to help in this programming task. This special program allowed the programmers to write their programs in a very stilted version of English and the EDSAC's special program translated this "English" program to 0s and 1s. Since that time, over 400 translators have been developed that allow programmers to write their programs in a variety of languages.

The various languages that have been developed are usually categorized as one of three types: machine, assembly or micro, and high level.

MACHINE LANGUAGES

The computer's own language is called **machine language.** Each brand of computer has its own language, which means that different brands of computers cannot understand programs written in another's machine language. This makes machine language programs **machine-dependent.**

Machine language programs, called **object programs,** consist of a series of numbers that the computer interprets to cause some action to take place. The numbers in the series consist of an **operation code** or **opcode** that tells the computer what action it is to perform, and gives the names or addresses of the memory location(s) that will be affected by this operation. For instance, if we want to have the computer add together the numbers currently stored in memory locations 7 and 9, and then store their sum in location 7, a typical machine language instruction for an IBM 360/370 computer would be:

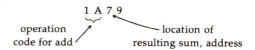

On an NCR Century 100 computer, the instruction would read:

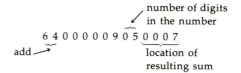

The result of both instructions is the same.

In order to program in machine languages, a programmer must keep track of which memory locations have been used and what the purpose is of each memory location. Also, the programmer must know every operation code and the action that it causes the computer to take. For very long and intricate programs it can become tedious for a programmer to keep track in his own memory of all these facts. While it is not impossible, the amount of time spent actually writing programs in this manner for even the simplest of tasks can be quite lengthy. As a result, machine languages are often called low-level languages. Very few programmers write in machine languages.

ASSEMBLY LANGUAGES

To help programmers write their instructions in less time, to relieve them of having to remember numeric opcodes and addresses, and to have programs that are still efficient for the computer to use are the objectives of an **assembly language**. Being also machine-dependent, programs written in assembly language still require the programmer to be familiar with the operation codes and addressing concepts that machine languages use.

However, instead of using a numeric operation code for each action that is to be programmed, an easily remembered word, called a **mnemonic**, is substituted. As an example, the opcode for an IBM 360/370 for "add" is 1A and its mnemonic assembler language equivalent is AR[1]. In a similar manner, the programmer can also assign a name to each memory

---

[1] For an IBM 360/370 some memory locations are called **registers**, hence, AR stands for "Add Register."

FIGURE 3–1		Single-operand instructions.
Opcode	Operand	Meaning
M	ZERO	Multiply accumulator by 0
A	P	Add value of P to accumulator
A	Q	Add value of Q to accumulator
ST	P	Store contents of accumulator in P

location. For example, we might give register 7 the name P and register 9 the name Q. The equivalent assembly language instruction for our machine language instruction 1A79 would be written: AR P,Q.

Assembly language instructions with the names of two memory locations linked by the mnemonic opcode are called "two-operand languages." In a single-operand language a special register, the accumulator, is used for arithmetic. Operations in this

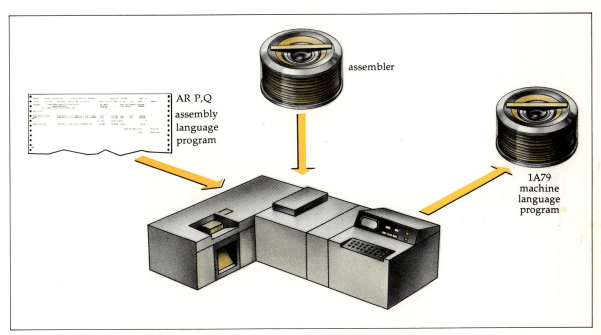

FIGURE 3–2 The assembler translation process.

CHAPTER 3: COMPUTER PROGRAMS

language automatically refer to or use the accumulator. The same series of instructions in a single-operand assembly language might be as shown in Figure 3–1. In a triple-operand assembly language instruction, the very same instructions might be written as:

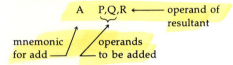

Many assembly languages are in use today, the most widely used being **BAL** (the letters *B-A-L* stand for the *B*asic *A*ssembly *L*anguage). BAL is the assembly language for IBM's 360 and 370 line of computers. Other computer manufacturers offer languages similar to BAL for use on their computers: Control Data Corporation's assembly language is called COMPASS, and NCR's is called NEAT/3. Some of the older assembly languages used by IBM are SPS and AUTOCODER.

Regardless of which assembly language is used, the computer does not "understand" the program in this abbreviated form of English. The program must, therefore, be translated into machine language. Normally, each assembly language instruction is translated into a single machine language instruction. The actual translation process is done by a special program called the **assembler**. Assemblers were first used in 1949 to automate programming. Prior to this time, programmers wrote only in machine language. This translation process for a typical program is depicted in Figure 3–2.

HIGH-LEVEL LANGUAGES

Both machine and assembly languages require programmers to construct their instructions in a form that does not follow mathematical or English language notation. In order to alleviate this problem, a third group of programming languages has been developed. These **high-level languages** or **problem-oriented languages** allow mathematicians and scientists to use algebraic notation and other lay programmers to write in sentence form.

A large number of high-level languages are in use today. The predominant high-level languages are BASIC, FORTRAN 77, COBOL-74, Pascal, RPG-II, and PL/1. High-level-language names are usually abbreviations of words; thus, the letters *R-P-G* stand for *R*eport *P*rogram *G*enerator. Many other high-level languages do exist, but they are little used compared to these six.

Every language has rules that govern how a program is actually written, and programmers must learn them. As an example, Figure 3–3 shows the same instructions—Add P and Q together and place the sum in P—in each of these six languages.

The primary disadvantage of writing programs in either machine or assembly languages is their machine dependence. With models of computers changing rapidly, programs written in either of these two language types require rewriting or, at least, major modifications to be operable on any newly acquired computer system. High-level languages, however, are **machine-independent**—that is, a program in one of these languages can be run

FIGURE 3–3	High-level language comparisons.	
Abbreviated Language Name	Language Name	Command
COBOL-74	*C*ommon *B*usiness *O*riented *L*anguage	ADD Q TO P.
FORTRAN 77	*FOR*mula *Tran*slation	P=P+Q
BASIC	*B*eginners *A*ll Purpose *S*ymbolic *I*nstruction *C*ode	LET P=P+Q
PL/1	*P*rogramming *L*anguage One	P=P+Q;
RPG-II	*R*eport *P*rogram *G*enerator	ADD Q P
Pascal	Named after Blaise Pascal, seventeenth-century mathematician and philosopher	P:=P+Q;

with very few changes on computers made by many different manufacturers. For this reason, as new computers replace older ones, programmers will not have to learn a new assembly language and will not have to rewrite all the existing programs. Since the computer understands only machine language, a new translator program is all that needs to be developed.

High-level language translator programs are usually called **compilers** or **interpreters**. They read the program, usually called a **source program,** which has been keypunched onto cards or entered from a terminal for input to the translator, and analyze each instruction in the program to ensure that it follows the rules of the language. Most compilers or interpreters provide for the programmer a

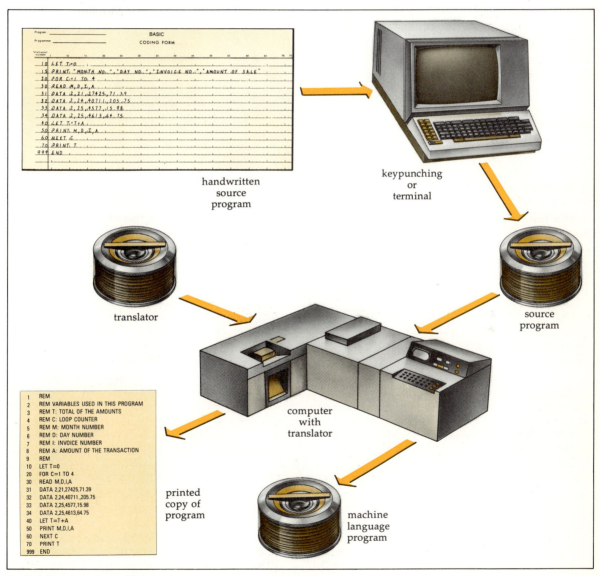

FIGURE 3-4 Compiling a source program.

STEVE JOBS AND STEVE WOZNIAK: INVENTORS OF THE APPLE PERSONAL COMPUTER

In the spring of 1981, Apple Computer, Inc. shipped its one hundred fifty thousandth personal computer—not bad for a company that was incorporated in 1977. Apple's sales of $3 million in 1977 had zoomed to $160 million by 1980.

Apple Computer began in 1976, when two young engineers collaborated on a small computing board for personal use. Steven P. Jobs (upper photograph), then 21, and Stephen G. Wozniak, then 26, took six months to design the prototype, 40 hours to build it, and soon had an order for 50 of their personal computers.

With that first order in hand, they raised about $1,200 from the sales of a used Volkswagen van and a programmable calculator and set up shop in Jobs's garage. By late 1976 they were doing well enough to form Apple Computer Company, with Jobs as business manager and Wozniak as engineer. They named their computer—and the company—Apple, because an apple represents the simplicity they were trying to achieve in the design and use of their

computers. Their first computer, sold in kit form to electronics hobbyists, was so successful that demand soon outstripped both the capacity of Jobs's garage and their capital. Believing they had a product with commercial value, Jobs and Wozniak set out to form an organization to market their computer.

Their first recruit was A. C. "Mike" Markkula, whom they met through a mutual friend. Markkula had successfully managed marketing for two semiconductor companies that had experienced dynamic growth—Intel Corporation and Fairchild Semiconductor. After researching the personal computer market and assessing Apple Computer's chances of leading the field, the three men decided what the company needed in terms of capital, management expertise, technical innovation, software development, and marketing.

Initial financing for Apple came from Markkula and a group of venture capitalists that included Venrock Associates, Arthur Rock and Associates, and Capital Management Corporation. Apple also obtained a line of credit from the Bank of America. Subsequently, retained earnings have provided most of the financing required for the company's growth.

The company's employment in 1980 rose to about 800 people, who occupied 560,000 square feet of floor space both in the U.S. and in Europe. Apple's manufacturing plants are located in Cupertino, California; Carrollton, Texas; and Cork, Ireland. In addition, there are six regional support centers in the U.S. and Europe, and Apple products are sold worldwide through a network of more than 1,200 retail dealers.

Most of Apple's professional employees have technical degrees, and more than half of this technical staff is involved in software development. Each year Apple invests about 10 percent of its total sales in research and development activities. Apple's personal computer systems are designed for use in education, business, scientific, and home applications. Its main products are the Apple II personal computer, introduced in 1977, and the Apple III computer system, introduced in 1981. Apple II is a simple-to-use, entry-level system priced at $1,200. The more sophisticated Apple III is aimed at the professional user and costs between $4,300 and $7,800, depending on system design.

In addition, Apple designs and manufactures its own disk drives and develops many of the applications software programs for its computers. Because of the large installed base of more than 200,000 units, many independent companies make equipment and write programs for Apple computers. This assures users of a wide selection of hardware and software with which to expand their systems.

In a series of Apple advertisements that appeared in *The Wall Street Journal* in April of 1981, Steve Jobs outlined his philosophy about the Apple and personal computers in general. Steve Jobs feels that the personal computer is more than just a small "big" computer. It brings intelligence directly to where it's needed: *the personal level.* It lets you use that intelligence in creative ways you never imagined. And it's a portable, easy-to-use tool that everyone can afford. Second, unlike the camera or the stereo (which are dedicated to just one function) the personal computer is truly a general purpose tool. One minute the personal computer can help educate elementary school students on math drills; the next minute, it does financial modeling; the next minute, it encourages artistic creativity via color graphics. A personal computer is not just a tool for people in business. A whole generation of kids is growing up learning how to use the personal computer as a problem-solving tool. For example, 97 percent of the students in Minnesota have the opportunity to solve problems with personal computers (more specifically, Apple computers), which aren't just being used to teach computer science courses. Students from Alaska to Mexico are learning physics, mathematics, spelling, and many other subjects on their computers. And kids who have problems learning how to read and write are actually overcoming their disabilities with the personal computer.

Jobs believes that personal computers will increase productivity because they are tools not toys. He points out, for example, that in the last 15 years, there have been only four tools that have actually increased the efficiency of the office worker: the IBM Selectric typewriter, the calculator, the Xerox machine, and the newer, advanced phone systems. Maybe the portable cassette player could be number five. Like all those inventions, the personal computer offers its power to the *individual.* The integration of personal computers into society will have an even greater effect than the calculator or the Xerox machine. By the end of the decade, Jobs predicts the personal computer will be a mystery to no one. Society will realize that the opportunity for a man-machine partnership is well within everyone's reach. In 1977 the personal computer didn't even exist. Yet by 1981 it had reached one in every 100 American households—and there are 72 million households in America! By the end of the 1980s, that figure will be one in ten.

The personal computer has even affected this textbook. The words you are now reading and most of the chapters in this second edition were written using an Apple II personal computer. We envision that the third edition will be completely written on a personal computer.

---

printed copy of the program, which shows any errors that may have been detected. The translator also converts the program to machine language and places it onto an external storage device, usually a disk. This translation process is usually called **compiling;** it is depicted in Figure 3–4.

PROBLEM DEFINITION: THE VISA STATEMENT

As you are probably aware, there are many different forms of bills like the VISA statement shown in Chapter 2. In Figure 3–5 you can see the form of the statement Pacific Gas & Electric Company uses for charging for gas and electricity used; the one EXXON Company uses for gasoline purchases; the one Bank of America uses for banking service; and that Sears Roebuck and Company uses for the wide variety of products they sell.

As a consumer you probably know that when you make a purchase you sign an invoice or sales receipt similar to the one in Figure 3–6. The data that are recorded on this statement are the date of sale, the account number of the buyer, the account number of the seller, and the amount of sale. Other data may also be recorded, like the type of gasoline purchased and the quantity purchased, but these data are not as important in generating the statement.

Periodically, the seller sends in copies of these invoices for processing. The first step in processing

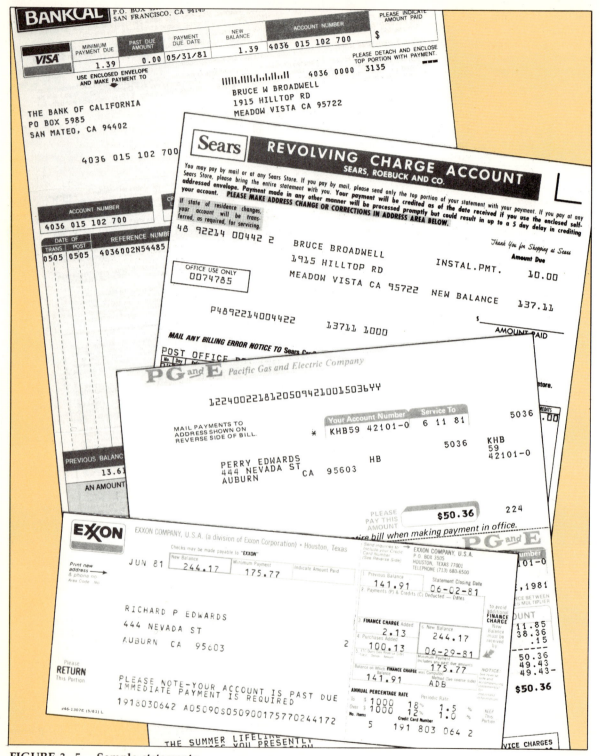

FIGURE 3–5 Sample statements.

42 MODULE ONE: INTRODUCTION

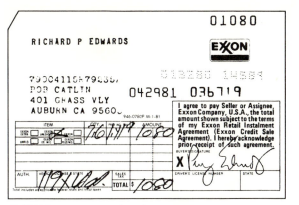

FIGURE 3–6   Receipt for gasoline purchase.

is to have the data on the invoices input to the computer. This inputting may be done in a variety of ways, ranging from keying the data using a key entry machine to directly reading the actual invoices with an optical character reader. Once the data have been input they may be stored on an external storage device like a disk or tape (see Figure 3–7).

Data that are stored on an external storage device are usually referred to as a **file**. In a file the data about a single invoice are called a **record,** and the individual pieces of data within a record are called **fields.** Our transaction file, therefore, has a field to store the buyer's account number, a field for the date of the sale, a field for the account number of the seller, and lastly, a field for the amount of the sale. Computer programs that process data files access the records and manipulate the various fields within the record.

As the weeks pass, more and more invoices are input to our disk or tape file until, finally, it is time to generate the statements or bills. Unfortunately, the invoice data now stored on the disks or tapes probably are not grouped by the buyers' account numbers, but are stored in the order in which they

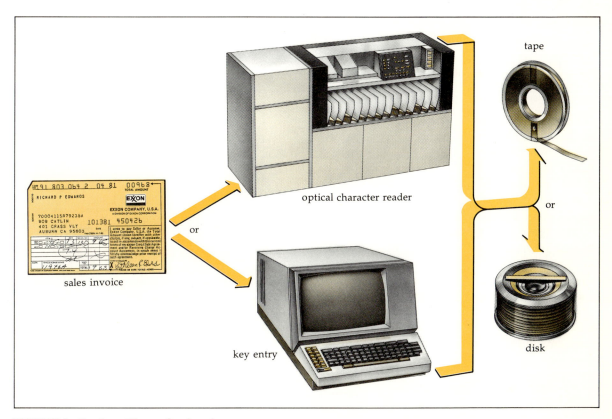

FIGURE 3–7   Inputting sales invoices.

CHAPTER 3: COMPUTER PROGRAMS   43

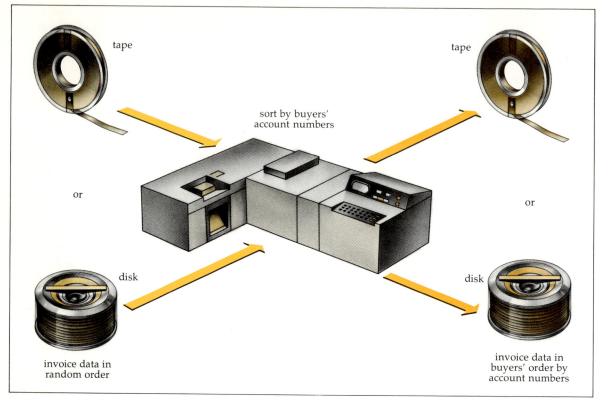

FIGURE 3-8 Sorting of invoice data.

are input. To rearrange the data into the order desired, we need to sort the invoice data by the buyers' account numbers (see Figure 3-8). In fact, it would be better to sort not only according to the buyers' account numbers but also according to the date of the sale. We would then have the invoice data in chronological order for each customer.

The sorted invoice data file is now ready to be used to generate a statement. A problem we face is to whom do we send the bill? Where do we find the name and address of our customer? Also, what is the balance? See shaded portion of Figure 3-9.

What we need is a list of our customers' names, addresses, account numbers, and balances. With these data and our invoice data, we can generate the statement. Let us assume that these additional data are stored in another disk or tape file.

The disk or tape holding the sorted invoice data is referred to as a **transaction file**, since it contains

"SAY — ACCORDING TO OUR HOME COMPUTER, WE'RE OUT OF BEER!"

MODULE ONE: INTRODUCTION

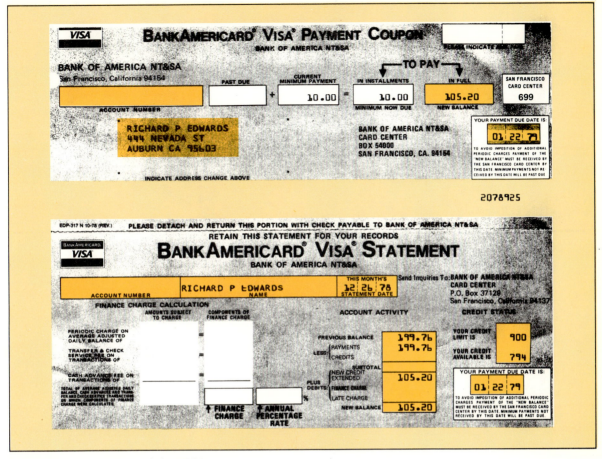

FIGURE 3-9 Portion of the VISA statement.

all of the transaction amounts that must be applied to each customer. The disk or tape holding the customers' names and addresses is called a **master file** since it holds each customer's fixed data (account number, name, and address) plus the variable data, the customer's balance.

We now want to take our transaction file and calculate the bill. Then we want to add this amount to the old balance, print a bill to send to the customer, and create a new or *updated master file*. This process is shown in Figure 3–10.

File update programs are complex. Records from old master files and transaction files must be read and their account numbers compared. If the numbers match, we can calculate the bill, add it to the old balance, print the bill, and write a record with these constant data and the new balance for the updated master file. However, some customers may make more than one purchase a month; this requires our program to read more than one transaction record for each customer's name and address record. Furthermore, we may not have a name and address record for some customer number invoices (the data entry operator may have made an error).

The diagrams drawn in Figures 3–7, 3–8, and 3–10 show the data flow and the operations for our billing or statement printing system. When combined into one diagram, Figure 3–11, we have a **systems flowchart**. The key program in Figure 3–11

CHAPTER 3: COMPUTER PROGRAMS   45

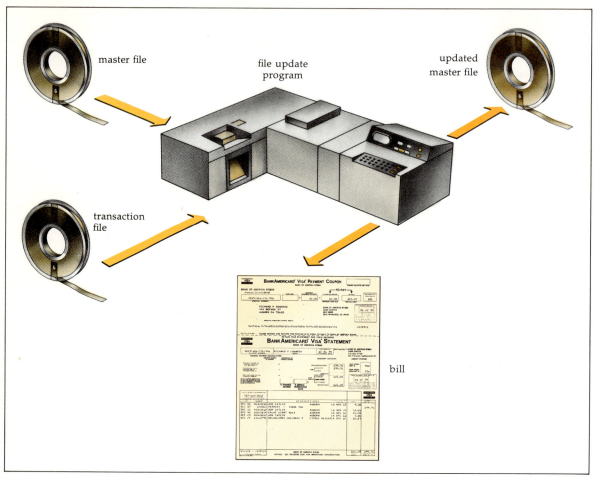

FIGURE 3–10 Master file update, using tape.

is the update program. In Chapter 2 you saw a portion of the program that prints the VISA statement. In the next four chapters we expand this program and this system until it prints a VISA statement almost identical to the one shown in Figure 3–9. Businesses that sell their goods or services on a credit basis keep track of who owes how much money. To an accountant or bookkeeper this type of computerized billing system is known as accounts receivable.

Mnemonic
Register
BAL
Assembler
High-level language
Problem-oriented language
Machine-independent
Compiler
Interpreter

Source program
Compiling
File
Record
Field
Transaction file
Master file
Systems flowchart

SUMMARY

Three distinct types of programming languages exist: machine, assembly, and high level. Since the computer only "understands" machine language, programs written in any of the others must be translated into machine language. The translation process is done by special programs called assemblers, compilers, or interpreters. These translators can detect certain programmer errors, print a copy of the program as written by the programmer, provide the machine language version of the program for reference purposes, and execute the program if the programmer desires.

Many high-level languages are in use today. The most common of these are BASIC, FORTRAN 77, COBOL-74, Pascal, RPG-II, and PL/1. To allow you to become acquainted with these languages, a problem based on the VISA statement has been developed. The next chapters will show you the program for this VISA statement written in each of the six high-level languages.

TERMS

The following words or terms have been presented in this chapter.

Machine language
Machine-dependent
Object program
Operation code
Opcode
Assembly language

EXERCISES

The exercises that follow are grouped by level of difficulty. Problems in the A series are the easiest; B series problems are moderately hard; and C series problems are the most difficult.

A–1 Go to your computer center and find the names of the high-level languages available on your computing system.

A–2 What is the name of the assembly language available on your computer system? What do the letters stand for? Is it a single-, double-, or triple-operand language?

A–3 The operation code for "subtract" for an IBM computer is 1B. Write the machine language command to subtract register 7 from 9, leaving the difference in register 7.

A–4 The mnemonic for "subtract" on an IBM computer is SR. Write an assembly language command to subtract Q from P leaving the difference in P.

B–1 Ask your computer center personnel or another student enrolled in a programming class how long it takes to translate an average program.

B–2 Using the chart of Figure 3–3, write the commands in BASIC, FORTRAN 77, COBOL-74, Pascal, RPG-II, and PL/1, to subtract Q from P leaving the difference in P.

C–1 In past issues of the newspaper *Computerworld*, much discussion has taken place concerning Pascal. Locate a past issue and write a one-paragraph synopsis of the article.

C–2 Locate a statement other than the VISA statement, and describe how it differs from the VISA statement.

CHAPTER 3: COMPUTER PROGRAMS

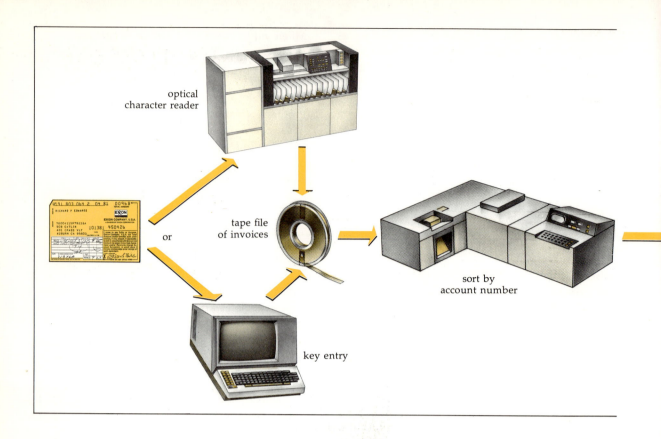

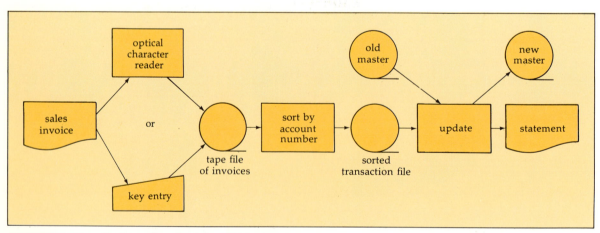

FIGURE 3–11 Systems flowchart for VISA statement.

48 MODULE ONE: INTRODUCTION

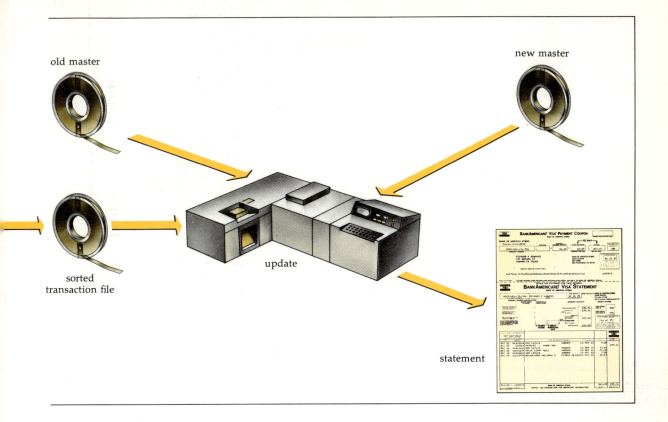

COMPUTER NEWS

SOFTWARE MAKERS LOSING SALES TO PROGRAM PIRATES

By Richard A. Shaffer
Staff Reporter of The Wall Street Journal

THE BOOMING MARKET in personal computers owes its vitality not only to the low prices of the machines themselves but also to the quality of the programs, or software, that raises the computers above the entertainment level and enables them to do work and save time for people. Thousands have bought small computers to edit text with WordStar, to file information and find it again with DB Master, or to analyze financial situations with VisiCalc.

Many in the emerging personal computing industry therefore are worried by a recent rise in what some call software piracy. Increasingly, individuals are reproducing microcomputer programs that aren't supposed to be duplicated. Most of the programs are copyrighted and the authors have used sophisticated recording techniques to guard against copying. Most people making the program duplicates seem to be doing so as insurance in case something goes wrong with their original, as it often does.

But many others are giving copies away by the dozen, and some are selling them. "Individuals are passing programs around the table like a stack of toast at breakfast," says Val J. Golding, editor of a magazine for owners of Apple computers, Call-A.P.P.L.E.

By one estimate, unauthorized copying has risen from economic insignificance to cut sales of the $200-million-a-year microcomputer software publishing industry by $12 million to $36 million annually.

SUCH COPYING WAS LIMITED until recently to the few computer buffs who understood enough electronics and programming to outwit the protection schemes. But a few months ago, "copy-all" programs were born. And now anyone with such a program can make unlimited duplicates of almost any other program.

Since last fall, at least five programs that will enable the buyers to duplicate supposedly protected software have come on the market. For the popular Apple brand of computer, they are: Locksmith, $74.95, Omega Software Products, Chicago; V-Copy, $20, Lee Meador, Arlington, Texas, and Back-It-Up, $60, Sensible Software, West Bloomfield, Mich. For the widely used Radio Shack computers: Super Utility, $49.95, Soft Sector Marketing, Garden City, Mich., and Trakcess, $24.95, The Alternate Source, Lansing, Mich.

Trakcess has become its publisher's best-selling program, and Omega, whose only product is Locksmith, says it has sold thousands of copies since the first of the year.

With the advent of such programs, retailers and makers of computers report that increasingly corporations, government agencies and educational institutions are buying several microcomputers at a time, but only one copy of certain important software. "It's clear what's going on," says Gary E. Haffer, president of Software Technology for Computers, Watertown, Mass. "Software piracy is a growing problem now in what could be the industry's two most important markets, schools and big business."

Copying also is significant outside the U.S., especially in Europe and Mexico, software publishers say.

FOR THOSE WHOSE LIVELIHOODS depend on profits from original software, what makes these developments all the more ominous is the rise of such networks as The Source and MicroNet, which connect thousands of personal computers to one another over ordinary telephone lines. Through these networks it is possible to send a program in minutes from one side of the country to the other, so that unauthorized duplicates could become widespread in an evening.

At present, the copying affects only such relatively small makers of personal data-processing equipment as Apple Computer, Commodore International and Tandy Corp. and the even smaller companies that write and publish most of the programs for such machines. But it also could hinder new ventures by the larger, traditional computer companies, such as Data General, Digital Equipment, International Business Machines and Wang Laboratories that are expected to enter the personal-computer market with product introductions at the National Computer Conference opening Monday in Chicago.

To some degree, industry observers say, software publishers brought the copying problem on themselves by failing to provide additional or replacement copies of important programs quickly. In some cases, users have come to depend on uncopyable programs that went awry, only to find that the program took weeks to replace.

"Any company that doesn't protect its users better than that deserves every bootleg copy made," says Allan Tommervik, managing editor of Softalk, a magazine for owners of Apple computers.

STILL, THE COPY PROGRAMS have created a furor in personal computing. Although a few industry magazines did publish advertisements for the programs early this year, most say they no longer will do so and have written editorials against the programs. Omega Software, for one, says it may sue the magazines for damage to its business.

Meantime, software publishers are scrambling to find new ways to protect their products.

And in the whole process, a lot of effort is wasted, says Dr. Allan Emery, an obstetrician who heads Sensible Software. "It's circular. When some people come up with bigger shields, others get bigger swords. So then you have to redesign your shield," he says.

MODULE *two*
LANGUAGE

a

Although some computers may be able to talk (like C3PO in "Star Wars"—a computer robot), the photographs on these pages illustrate a different form of communication by computer—computer graphics. Many computer graphics are produced by experimental programs that select colors and points at random (like the image on the cover of this book)—partly to see what visual results can be obtained, partly for serious research purposes.

The concentric spheres in Photo A present a visual paradox: the computer program has removed the lines on the back side of each sphere that would normally cause the surfaces to appear opaque, making them transparent to the other spheres. To produce the image in Photo B, Professor Gordon Lind of Utah State University plotted the nuclear spectra of several isotopes on one image. This type of plot enables scientists to study relationships among the isotopes. Three-dimensional plots like the one in Photo C are useful for studying topographical data.

Photo D is a double-exposure computer graphic showing two base pairs of DNA. Each exposure uses a different way of showing the atoms; one is called "ball-and-stick," the other "space-filling." The New York Power Pool in Guilderland, N.Y., collects and monitors data on the generation and transmission of electricity for several northeastern states (Photo E). The display consoles provide "real-time" data, and the map panel in the background shows where more electricity might be needed within the area. Computer scientists like Nelson Max at Lawrence Livermore Laboratories in Berkeley, California, who developed the DNA computer graphic, are aware that the visual attractiveness of these images can go a long way to help clarify the concepts they illustrate. A new relationship between science and aesthetics seems to be emerging in the field of computer graphics.

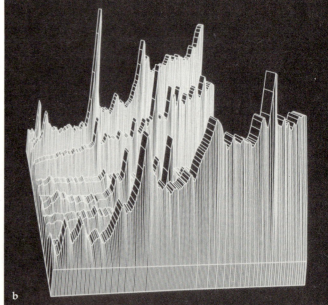

b

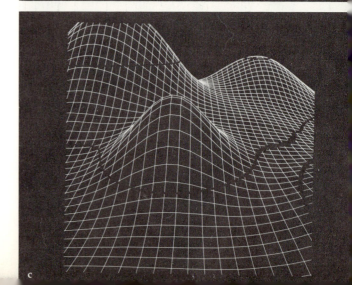

c

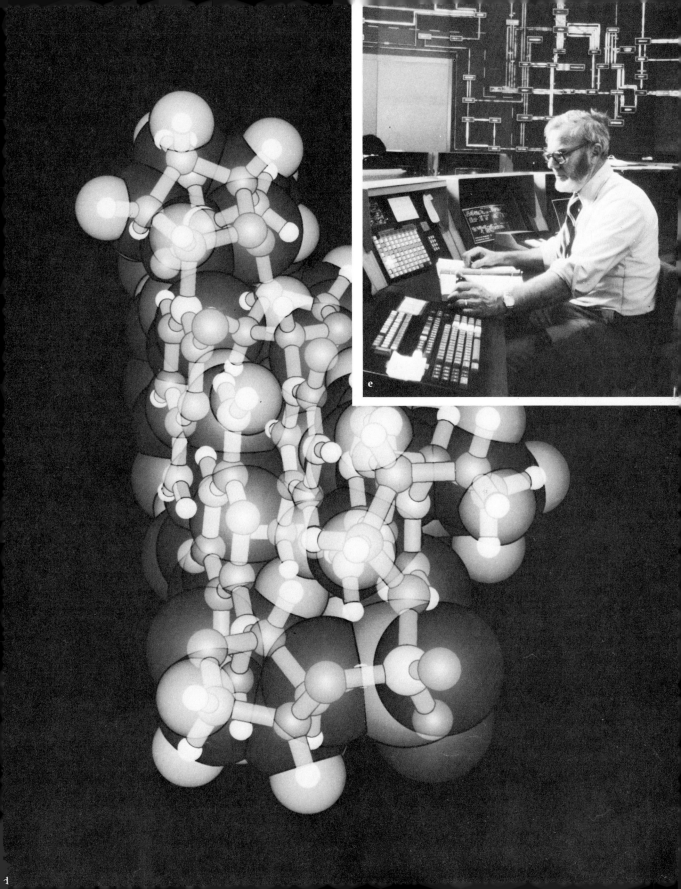

CHAPTER *four*
FLOWCHARTING

Preview

Computer Programs

Flowcharts
   Terminal Symbol
   Processing Symbol
   Input or Output Symbol
   Document Symbol
   Flowline
   Sample Flowcharts

Extended Example: Listing VISA Transactions
   Accumulating a Total
   Eliminating Repetitive Steps in
   the Transaction Listing Program
   Preparation Symbol

History Capsule: John Von Neumann

**Decision Making in the
Transaction Listing/Totaling Program**
   Decision Symbol
   Off-page and On-page Connectors

Flowcharting Rules

Flowcharting Examples

Summary

Computer News: Moore's Is Not Less

PREVIEW

In Chapter 1 a computer program was described and defined as a set of instructions. In this chapter we learn how to use the programming tool called "flowcharting" as an aid to writing the set of instructions in a program.

COMPUTER PROGRAMS

A computer program is a sequential set of instructions given to the computer to tell it how to solve a problem. The sequence of steps must be determined before the program is written. This sequence of steps is called the **algorithm** of the problem. As shown in Figure 2–12, if even a single instruction is out of sequence, the program's results will change. Also, if even one instruction is incorrect, the program will give the wrong answer and will probably be unusable until the instruction is corrected. To illustrate, let us look at the "algorithm" of setting up a camping tent. Suppose you have the tent, a bag of poles and stakes, and a list of instructions, as follows:

1. Rake ground smooth and level where you want to put the tent.

2. Unfold tent on the ground.

3. Locate tent door and move tent to face the door in desired direction.

4. Drive a stake into ground through each of the loops around the base of the tent.

5. Feed ridge pole through loops along top (ridge) of tent.

6. Insert end poles into curved end of ridge pole.

7. With one person at each ridge pole, raise ridge pole until tent canvas is taut.

Suppose you tried to pitch the tent, but you did not bother to maintain this sequence of steps, and decided to perform step 4 last. When you reached step 7, raised the ridge pole, and then let go of the poles, what would happen? Or suppose you did not carefully follow step 5 and instead fed the end poles into the loops along the ridge? What kind of camping partner would you be?

To develop an algorithm, or set of instructions, two essential processes must occur: The individual steps of the algorithm must be determined, and the steps must be arranged in a logical order. More specifically, follow this procedure to help develop an algorithm:

1. Consider what kind of answer or end result is needed. In a billing program, for example, you must know if interest charges are to be calculated and, if so, at what rate. Also, if discounts are allowed for early payment, you need to indicate the discount percentage. Such a statement is called the **problem statement.**

2. Determine what data are needed, whether they are available, and how they can be collected in a form the computer can use.

3. Write a rough list of steps using a degree of detail similar to that used in the list of steps for pitching the tent.

4. Draw a graphic plan (flowchart) of the steps in the rough list.

5. Using the flowchart as a guide, write the language instructions the computer will use in solving the problem.

FLOWCHARTS

A **flowchart** is a drawing or graphic plan of the steps required in processing data. The flowchart illustrates events or actions and the sequence in which those actions must be taken to provide the desired results. The flowchart is used to communicate graphically, hence each of the flowcharting symbols must have an agreed-upon, unique meaning. Knowing the meaning of the symbols, a reader can comprehend the function of the individual steps and of the whole flowchart without having to sift through a verbal narrative of a data processing task.

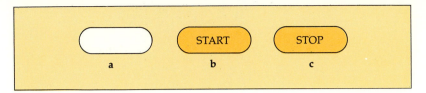

FIGURE 4–1 Terminal symbol for beginning and ending.

Terminal Symbol

The oval, called the **terminal symbol,** represents the beginning and ending steps in the sequence (Figure 4–1a). All flowcharts must show a beginning (Figure 4–1b) and at least one ending (Figure 4–1c).

Processing Symbol

The rectangular **processing symbol** depicts an arithmetic or a data movement process (Figure 4–2a). Figure 4–2b shows the adding of the value stored in memory location C and the value 7.63. The sum of the value of C and 7.63 will be stored in memory location D.

Input or Output Symbol

Input of data to the computer or output from the computer's memory may be represented by the parallelogram **input/output symbol** (Figure 4–3a). The input/output symbol of Figure 4–3b indicates either that information is being input to the computer and stored in memory location C or, conversely, that the value stored in memory location C is being output.

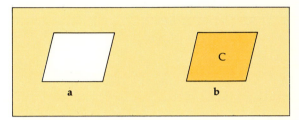

FIGURE 4–3 Input/output symbol.

Document Symbol

The printing of information on paper is represented by the **document symbol** (Figure 4–4a). Use the document symbol when you want to specify printed output; this is in contrast to using the input/output symbol when you do not wish to specify a particular output method. Figure 4–4b shows that the values stored in memory locations C and H are being printed on paper.

Flowline

The arrow, or **flowline,** shown in Figure 4–5, indicates **precedence,** the order of steps. The flowline links all the symbols together to form a flowchart.

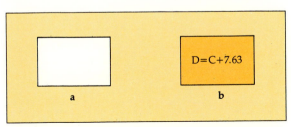

FIGURE 4–2 Processing symbol for calculations and data movement.

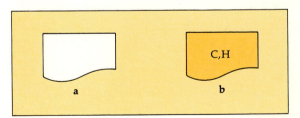

FIGURE 4–4 Document symbol for printing.

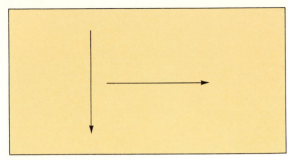

FIGURE 4-5   Flowline.

Sample Flowcharts

A flowchart generally has five major parts, as shown in the following algorithm:

1. Starting point
2. Data inputting
3. Data processing
4. Data outputting
5. Stopping point

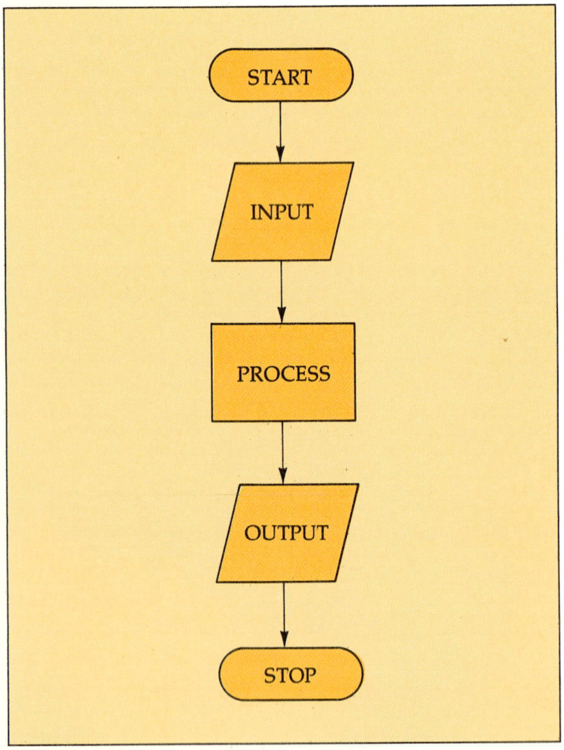

The flowchart of Figure 4-6 depicts these major steps diagrammatically. Let us look at some sample flowcharts.

Suppose you want to have the computer add two numbers together and print the sum. Assume one number is stored in memory space A, the other in memory space B, and the sum is to be stored in space C. The list of steps needed to direct the computer to find the sum is:

1. Start.
2. Read a number into A and another into B (for example, 2.15 and 6.07).
3. Add the value of A and B together, store the sum in C.
4. Print the value of C (in this example, 8.22).
5. Stop.

These sequential steps written in English language phrases are sometimes called **pseudocode**. The pseudocode may be combined with appropriate flowchart symbols as shown in Figure 4-7.

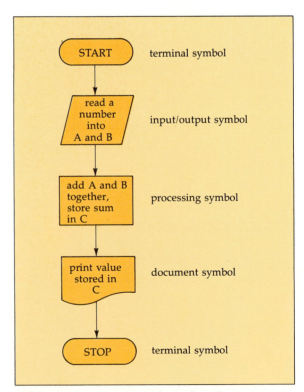

FIGURE 4-6   Major flowchart steps.

FIGURE 4-7   Pseudocode in flowchart.

MODULE TWO: LANGUAGE

A more concise notation is used in the **symbolic flowchart.** Symbolic flowcharts are usually written so that each flowchart symbol can be translated to a program instruction without further interpretation. Figure 4-8 is a symbolic flowchart form of the pseudocode flowchart of Figure 4-7. The input/output symbol (parallelogram) itself represents the reading operation, so we do not need to write READ inside it. The "A,B" notation designates the memory locations where the two numbers being read are stored. The document symbol represents the printing operation, and the notation "C" indicates that the number stored in space C is to be printed. To show that the values stored in A and B are being added together and their sum is stored in C, we simply write: C=A+B. The A, B, and C designations for the memory locations are also called **variable names.** That is, "A," "B," and "C" are names for memory locations whose values can be altered—or, in other words, whose values are variable.

Although most people have some difficulty constructing flowcharts at first, it becomes second nature after a while. A flowchart must accurately depict the problem to be solved. If the flowchart does not have all the logical steps, the computer program will not have all the logical steps and will give the wrong answer. Flowcharts should be carefully planned, drawn, and checked before they are translated into computer instructions.

EXTENDED EXAMPLE: LISTING VISA TRANSACTIONS

In Chapters 2 and 3 you saw a VISA statement that listed and totaled VISA transaction data. The data that were read for each sales transaction were the month number, day number, invoice or reference number, and the dollar amount of the transaction. Suppose we have these data for four transactions and we want to print a list of these data in columnar form.

If data are: 02, 21, 27425, $71.39, 02, 24, 40711,

One set of data items

$205.75, 02, 25, 4577, $15.98, 02, 25, 4613, $64.75, then the desired end result should be:

(Month)	(Day)	(Invoice No.)	(Amount)
02	21	27425	71.39
02	24	40711	205.75
02	25	4577	15.98
02	25	4613	64.75

Pseudocode:

1. Start.

2. Read the month, day, invoice number, and amount for the first transaction.

3. Print the month, day, invoice number, and amount for the first transaction.

4. Read the month, day, invoice number, and amount for the second transaction.

5. Print the month, day, invoice number, and amount for the second transaction.

6. Read the month, day, invoice number, and amount for the third transaction.

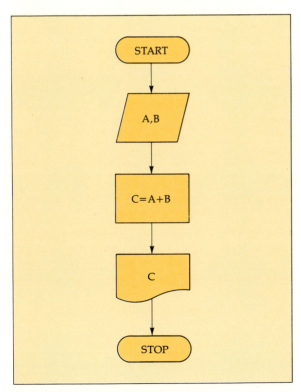

FIGURE 4-8 Symbolic flowchart.

CHAPTER 4: FLOWCHARTING

7. Print the month, day, invoice number, and amount for the third transaction.

8. Read the month, day, invoice number, and amount for the fourth transaction.

9. Print the month, day, invoice number, and amount for the fourth transaction.

10. Stop.

The pseudocode flowchart for these ten steps is given in Figure 4–9. When drawing a symbolic flowchart, you should first write the pseudocode for the problem being solved. Then draw the symbolic flowchart. Remember that a symbolic flowchart uses abbreviations called "variable names" for the words you used in your pseudocode. The variable names chosen, plus a brief description of what they represent, are listed in the upper right-hand corner of a symbolic flowchart, and are titled agreements. The agreements for our VISA listings are:

- M: Month number
- D: Day of month
- I: Invoice number
- A: Amount of transaction

In the pseudocode flowchart (Figure 4–9) the first step after the START symbol is "read first set of month, day, invoice number, and amount." In symbolic notation we simply write M, D, I, A, and the parallelogram gives the "read" meaning (Figure 4–10).

The next step in the pseudocode flowchart uses the document symbol with the notation "print first set of month, day, invoice number, and amount." In symbolic notation the variables M, D, I, A, within the document symbol mean print the values stored in memory spaces M, D, I, and A (see Figure 4–11).

The complete symbolic flowchart with agreements is drawn in Figure 4–12. Pseudocode flowcharts are not commonly drawn, but symbolic flowcharts are. From now on we will only write pseudocode and draw symbolic flowcharts.

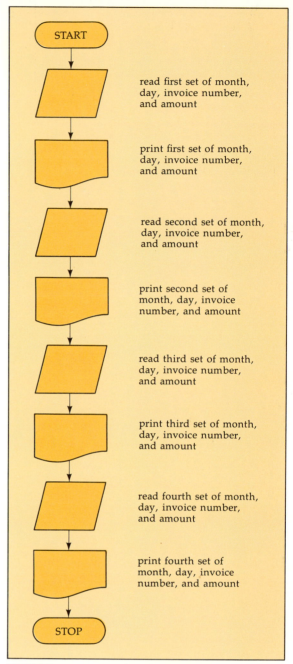

FIGURE 4–9 Pseudocode transaction listing.

Accumulating a Total

If you were asked to have the computer print the four transaction amounts and then print the total,

60 MODULE TWO: LANGUAGE

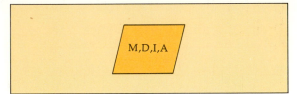

FIGURE 4–10 Reading a value into memory space M, D, I, and A.

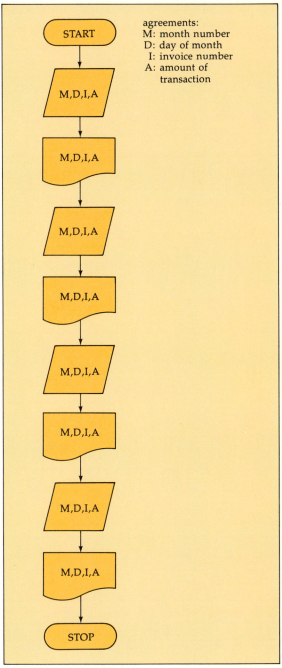

FIGURE 4–12 Symbolic program flowchart of transaction listing.

several new kinds of steps would be required. The first would be to establish a procedure for accumulating the total. Second, each transaction amount would have to be added to the total. Finally, the accumulated total would have to be printed after all four sets of data were processed.

The steps involved in totaling will now be added to both the pseudocode and the symbolic flowcharts. The first new step is inserted immediately after the start, and involves accumulating a total. The memory location within the computer that we use to store the accumulating total is called an **accumulator** or **totaler**. In pseudocode the step reads "set totaler to zero" (see Figure 4–13).

In the symbolic flowchart, we write T=0 within the block (Figure 4–14). This means "place a zero in memory space called T." We cannot assume that memory location T has a zero stored in it, so we direct the computer to place a zero in it. This establishing of a beginning value is referred to as **initializing**.

The second new step, adding, follows the read step. The transaction amount that has just been read (Figure 4–13, line 3) is added to the totaler; in pseudocode this reads "add amount to the totaler" (Figure 4–13, line 4). In symbolic flowcharting, the process of adding the transaction amount that has

FIGURE 4–11 Printing the values of M, D, I, and A.

CHAPTER 4: FLOWCHARTING

1. Start.
2. Set totaler to zero.
3. Read month, day, invoice number, and amount for the first transaction.
4. Add amount to the totaler.
5. Print the month, day, invoice number, and amount for the first transaction.
6. Read month, day, invoice number, and amount for the second transaction.
7. Add amount to the totaler.
8. Print the month, day, invoice number, and amount for the second transaction.
9. Read month, day, invoice number, and amount for the third transaction.
10. Add amount to the totaler.
11. Print the month, day, invoice number, and amount for the third transaction.
12. Read month, day, invoice number, and amount for the fourth transaction.
13. Add amount to the totaler.
14. Print the month, day, invoice number, and amount for the fourth transaction.
15. Print the total.
16. Stop.

FIGURE 4–13   Pseudocode of transaction listing with total.

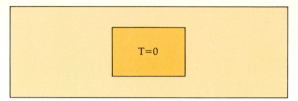

FIGURE 4–14   Initializing memory space T.

value of A. In symbolic flowcharting, all arithmetic operations are shown on the right-hand side of the equals sign because of this replacement meaning.

After reading, totaling, and printing the four transactions, a final new action in the pseudocode reads "print the total" (Figure 4–13, line 15). In symbolic flowchart notation, the variable T within a document symbol (see Figure 4–16) means print the value stored in memory space T.

The complete symbolic flowchart with agreements is drawn in Figure 4–17.

Eliminating Repetitive Steps in the Transaction Listing Program

Both the pseudocode and the symbolic flowcharts (Figures 4–13 and 4–17) are lengthy. If there were 400 transactions instead of only four, the program's length would become ridiculous. Such a repetitious program would be tedious to write, time-consuming to enter into the computer, and wasteful of memory space. To shorten the program, some of the instructions that are repetitive can be reused. For instance, the three steps shown in Figure 4–18 appear four times in Figure 4–17.

However, you can eliminate all the repetitive steps and, in this case, simply reuse the three steps illustrated, as in Figure 4–19. Returning to a preceding step and reusing that and subsequent steps is called **looping**; that portion of the program is called a **loop**. Do you see any problems resulting

just been read to the total of the amounts is illustrated by a processing symbol. The number just read, which is now stored in memory space A, is to be added to the sum, T. This is depicted as shown in Figure 4–15. While not a valid algebra formula, in symbolic flowcharting terms this step says to take the current value of T and add it to the current value of A, then to take the sum of A and T and place it in memory location T, making the sum the new value of T. The equal symbol (=) does not have the same meaning in symbolic flowcharting as it does in algebra. Here it means replace—that is, replace the current value of T with a new value of T, which is the sum of the current value of T and the current

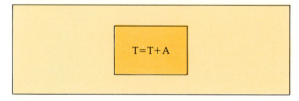

FIGURE 4–15   Adding and totaling.

JOHN VON NEUMANN

The intellectual father of flowcharting was probably John Von Neumann who, in a paper termed simply "The First Draft," first described computers by their logical functions instead of their electrical aspects. While working in June 1946 on the EDVAC, the successor to the first general purpose computer (ENIAC), Arthur W. Burks, Herman H. Goldstine, and Von Neumann described what they called "flow diagrams" in a report titled "Preliminary Discussion of the Logical Design of an Electronic Computing Instrument." In 1972 Goldstine, in his book *The Computer from Pascal to Von Neumann*, writes "In the spring of that year Von Neumann and I evolved an exceedingly crude sort of geometrical drawing . . . as a sort of tentative aid to us in programming . . . I became convinced that this type of flow diagram . . . could be used as a logically complete and precise notation . . . and that indeed this was essential to the task of programming."

Von Neumann, born in Budapest, Hungary, on December 28, 1903, educated in Budapest, Berlin, and Zurich, was a superb mathematician and a great teacher of mathematics. He also earned

degrees in chemistry and physics. Blessed with the power of absolute recall, Von Neumann was a great storyteller and combined this skill with a great sense of humor to lighten discussions that were too serious and too long. He greatly enjoyed people's company and, together with his wife, entertained young and old in their home in Princeton, New Jersey, where he was a professor of mathematics at the Institute for Advanced Study from 1933 to his untimely death in 1957.

John Von Neumann's contribution to the development of flowcharting has been overshadowed by his better known contributions to computer design—which he communicated to others in part, through flowcharts. Von Neumann is credited with being one of the first to: recommend that computer memory store programs as well as data; propose that all data and instructions be stored in binary form; understand that a computer essentially performs logical functions; and suggest that instructions be performed in a strictly serial fashion as opposed to multiple actions being performed simultaneously.

---

from using the flowchart containing the loop as it is now drawn? Are there provisions for totaling and printing the transactions total? Is an allowance made for stopping the looping process, or will it continue indefinitely?

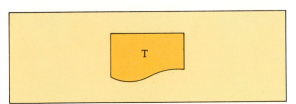

FIGURE 4–16   Printing the value of T.

Preparation Symbol

To loop effectively in the transaction totaling flowchart, we must (1) provide for stopping of the looping, and (2) include steps for accumulating the total, printing the total, and ending the program. To stop the looping and still provide for the correct number of loop cycles, we can use a preparation symbol (Figure 4–20). The **preparation symbol** signifies the initiation of a series of steps repeated a certain number of times. A memory location called an **index** or **counter** is established to keep track of the repetitions.

CHAPTER 4: FLOWCHARTING   63

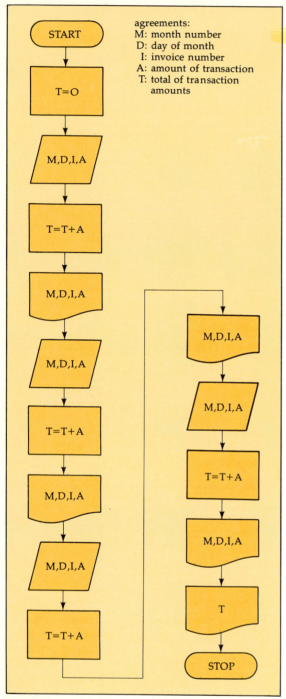

FIGURE 4–17 Symbolic flowchart of transaction listing with total.

With the preparation symbol we establish the name of the memory location we will use as the *loop counter* (see Figure 4–20a). The preparation symbol also contains the starting value of the loop counter (Figure 4–20b) and the value the counter will have reached when the looping process ceases (Figure 4–20c). Finally, within the preparation symbol we show the amount by which the counter will be altered during each pass through the loop (Figure 4–20d). The fully developed preparation symbol will show all four values (Figure 4–20e).

The preparation symbol precedes the operations that will be repeated within the loop. Following the operations within the loop, a large circle with the name of the loop counter symbolizes the bottom of the loop (see Figure 4–21). A flowline from this circle to just below the preparation symbol shows the return path of the loop. Figure 4–22 shows the modified flowchart (study the bracketed descriptions closely).

DECISION MAKING IN THE TRANSACTION LISTING/TOTALING PROGRAM

What would happen if an erroneous month number such as 13 were entered? What can be done to

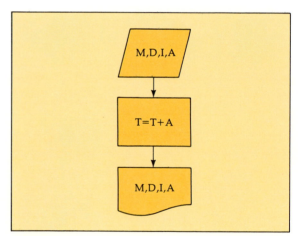

FIGURE 4–18 Three steps that are used repetitively.

MODULE TWO: LANGUAGE

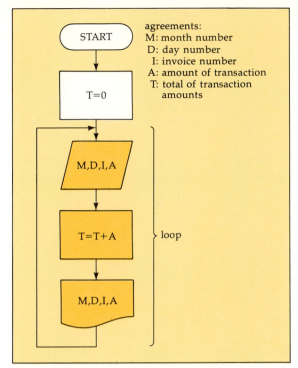

FIGURE 4–19   Accumulating transaction amounts using a loop.

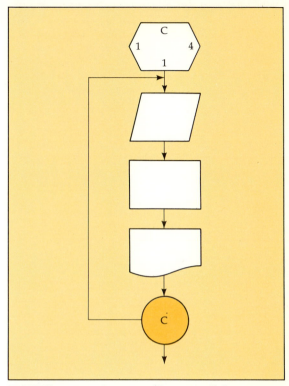

FIGURE 4–21   Bottom of loop symbol.

minimize the probability of incorrect data being entered? Within the computer program we can write instructions that direct the computer to determine if the data are within acceptable limits, are alphabetic if they should be, are numeric if they should be, are not blank, or meet several other tests. These tests are called **validations**.

To determine the acceptability of the data, we may compare them with certain agreed-upon limits. The lower limit month number is 1; the upper limit is 12. In flowcharting how do we show that the computer is deciding whether a particular month is within these limits?

Decision Symbol

The diamond-shaped **decision symbol** is used to show that a decision is being made between two alternative actions (Figure 4–23a). The decision is made on the basis of a comparison of one value with another value. In Figure 4–23b, if memory location F does in fact contain the number 10 the comparison

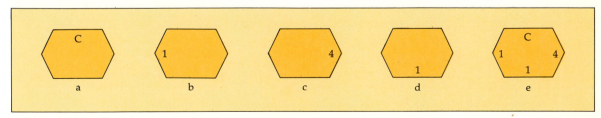

FIGURE 4–20   Preparation symbol for establishing a loop.

CHAPTER 4: FLOWCHARTING

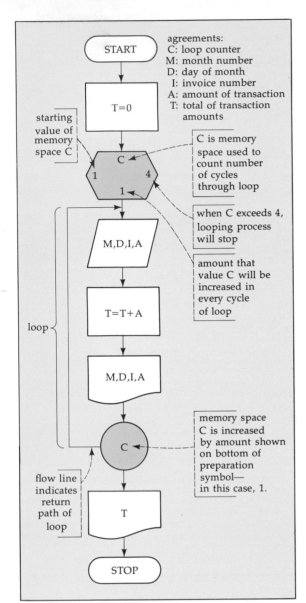

FIGURE 4-22 VISA transaction printing and totaling, using a preparation process for looping.

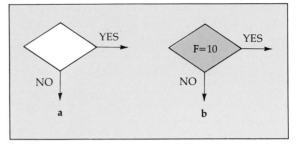

FIGURE 4-23 Decision symbol with yes and no alternatives.

To determine whether a particular month is below the lower limit of one (1), the pseudocode would be:

Is the month less than one?

A symbolic flowchart uses a symbol as shown in Figure 4-24. The symbol < means "less than" and > means "greater than."

If the month number is less than 1, what action should the computer take? Should it simply stop? Should it notify the user and then stop? Should it notify the user that it is discarding that piece of data and waiting for the correct month? If the second option is chosen, it is flowcharted as shown in Figure 4-25. We can add a decision step for upper limit, also.

The pseudocode for decision making and resulting action relating to month number is:

Is the month number less than 1?
a. Yes, print error message.
b. No, go on to next step.

The complete symbolic flowchart for the transaction listing and totaling, making use of looping and decision making, is shown in Figure 4-26.

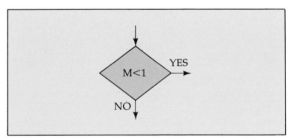

FIGURE 4-24 Decision-making portion of a flowchart.

shows an equal condition, and the YES path is taken. If memory location F contains a number other than 10, the comparison shows an unequal condition, and so the NO path is taken. The arrow from the decision symbol leads to the first step in the alternative sequence.

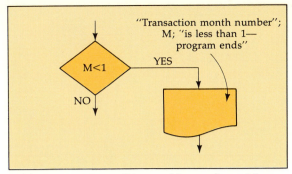

FIGURE 4–25 Decision making and resulting action.

Off-page and On-page Connectors

A flowchart is often too long to be completed in one vertical line of steps and must be continued in another column on the same page. It then flows downward, parallel to the preceding portion. The flowchart of Figure 4–12, when drawn on a page with more limited vertical space, might appear as in Figure 4–27. The upward flowlines leading from one series of steps to the next tend to clutter a flowchart and may be replaced with a pair of **connector symbols** that, by having common alphabetic characters within the small circles, tie the bottom of one flowline to the top of another (see Figure 4–28).

If the sections of a flowchart are on different pages, the connectors that join them may be further cross-referenced by having page numbers placed to their upper left (Figure 4–29). Notice that the page number of the following page is noted by the connector of the preceding page, and the page number of the preceding page is noted by the connector of the following page.

FLOWCHARTING RULES

As you might suspect, flowcharts can become very complex, with flowlines merging and crossing. For

FIGURE 4–26 Transaction listing/totaling flowchart with decisions within the loop.

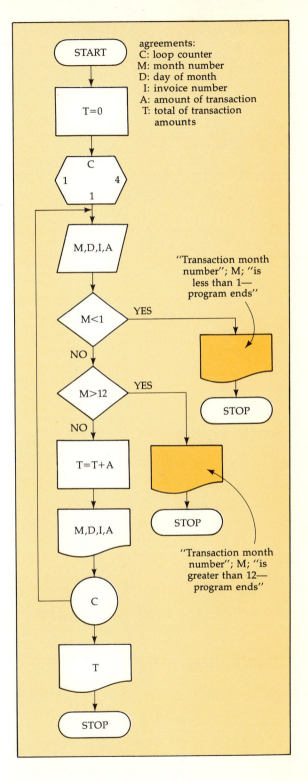

CHAPTER 4: FLOWCHARTING

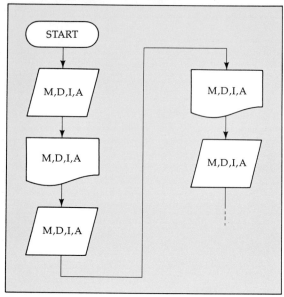

FIGURE 4–27 A flowchart broken into parallel sections.

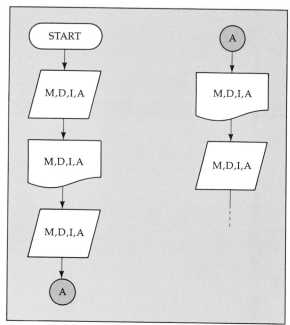

FIGURE 4–28 A flowchart with connector symbols tying parallel sections together.

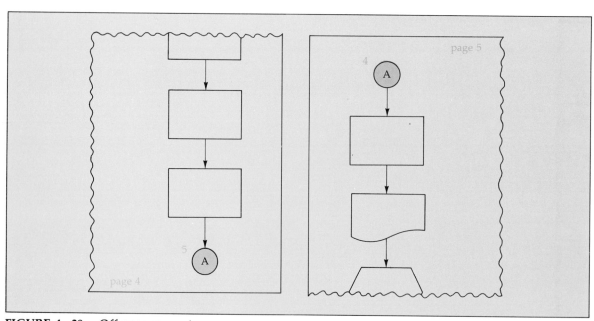

FIGURE 4–29 Off-page connectors.

Symbol	Meaning	Possible Number of Flowlines In	Possible Number of Flowlines Out
START	Indicates beginning of flowchart	None	Only One
(rectangle)	Computation or other type of process	Only one	Only one
(parallelogram)	Input/output takes place	Only one	Only one
(diamond)	Decision point; usually a comparison of magnitudes	Only one	Two (YES and NO)
(hexagon)	Indicates a preparation process—the establishing of a loop counter	Only one	Only one
(circle)	Indicates the last step within the loop—testing for the last cycle	Only one	Two
STOP	Indicates the end of the flowchart	Only one	None
A and A	Indicate a break in flowline at bottom of page and resumption at top of same page	Only one	Only one
8 A and 7 A	Indicate break in flowline at end of page and continuation on another page	Only one	Only one

FIGURE 4–30 Flowline guide.

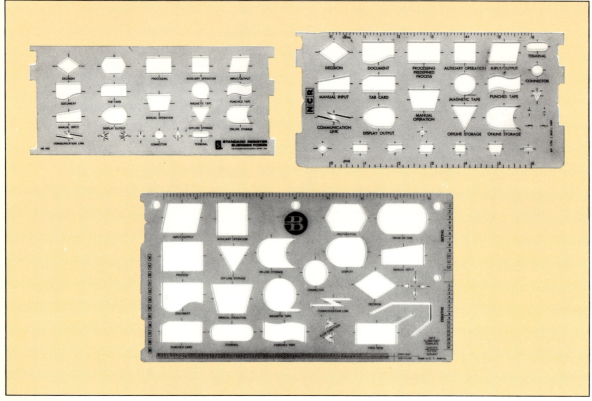

FIGURE 4–31   NCR, Standard Register, and Burroughs templates.

easily readable flowcharts, we suggest these guidelines:

1. Begin the flowchart in the upper left corner of the page.

2. Use a template for drawing symbols, so they are the same size and shape (see Figure 4–31).

3. Draw the flowchart in a vertical pattern, top down.

4. At decision points that lead to a subsequent step in the flowchart, draw a flowline to the right and downward.

5. At decision points that lead to an earlier point, draw the flowline to the left and upward.

6. Avoid crossing flowlines if possible.

7. Keep symbols the same distance from each other.

8. Write legibly, either next to the flowcharting symbol or inside it.

Figure 4–30 gives some rules about the number of flowlines that can enter or exit each of the various symbols. These flowline guides provide a check as to whether each symbol in the diagram has been used correctly. If any of the rules are violated, the flowchart will not accurately depict the problem's solution. If the symbols do follow the rules, this is still not a guarantee that the flowchart is absolutely logical, but at least it is properly constructed. Using the flowline guide, prove to yourself that the symbols in Figure 4–26 have been used correctly.

Generally, a **template** is used to draw the symbols in a flowchart because it enables the programmer to draw uniform shapes that are easily recognized. Figure 4–31 illustrates several of the widely used templates. A few variations exist, depending on the supplier of the template, but they are generally minor. Note also that there are more symbols available than those we have discussed here. Complex flowcharts may use the additional symbols for special purposes.

FLOWCHARTING EXAMPLES

To reinforce the concepts and rules of flowcharting, four solved exercises follow. Each contains a problem statement (describing the end results), data, other pertinent information, pseudocode, and the symbolic flowchart.

The first three examples deal with calculating commissions earned on sales of merchandise. Commissions are calculated by multiplying a commission rate (percentage) times the dollars worth of sales made. The fourth example finds the largest transaction amount.

Example 4–1

Calculate and print the commission earned by each of five people. The data required for input are:

Salesperson Number	Total Sales of Salesperson
1	$1250
2	1500
3	950
4	2100
5	1850

The commission rate is 10% of sales. The printout should appear as follows:

(Salesperson Number)	(Total Sales of Salesperson)	(Commission Earned)
1	1250	125
2	1500	150
3	950	95
4	2100	210
5	1850	185

Pseudocode:

1. Establish a loop that will cycle five times.
2. Read an employee number and sales amount.
3. Calculate a commission.
4. Print employee number, sales amount, and commission amount.
5. Have five commissions been calculated? If yes, go to step 6. If no, go to step 2.
6. Stop.

The symbolic flowchart for Example 4–1 is shown in Figure 4–32.

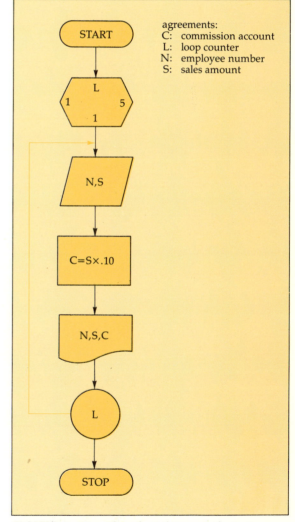

FIGURE 4–32   Flowchart for example 4–1.

Example 4-2

Calculate and print total commissions earned on the total sales of each salesperson for seven days. The last data item for each salesperson will be a zero (0); this is called an **end-of-data sentinel**. The program will test for this zero value, and when determining a zero, will assume that all the data for that salesperson have been input. The data for input are:

Salesperson Number	Amount of Sales	End-of-Data Sentinel
1	110, 400, 285, 315, 140	0
2	200, 350, 175, 221, 300, 254	0
3	175, 50, 280, 445	0
4	375, 150, 410, 527, 229, 270, 139	0
5	410, 343, 162, 520, 105, 310	0

The commission rate is 10% of sales. The printout for the first two employees would be:

(Salesperson Number)	(Amount of Sale)	(Commission Earned)
1	110	11.00
1	400	40.00
1	285	28.50
1	315	31.50
1	140	14.00

TOTAL COMMISSION: 125

2	200	20.00
2	350	35.00
2	175	17.50
2	221	22.10
2	300	30.00
2	254	25.40

TOTAL COMMISSION: 150

Pseudocode:

1. Establish a loop that cycles five times.
2. Set totaler for total commission to zero.
3. Read employee number.
4. Read sale amount.
5. Is sale amount equal to zero? If yes, go to step 10. If no, go to next step.
6. Calculate commission on the single sale.
7. Add commission to total commission.
8. Print salesperson number, sale amount, commission amount.
9. Go to step 4.
10. Print total commission for the salesperson.
11. Add 1 to loop counter and compare with five (the number of salespersons that are included in the processing). If greater than five, go to step 12. If not greater than five, add 1 to counter and go to step 2.
12. Stop.

The flowchart for Example 4-2 is shown in Figure 4-33.

Example 4-3

Modify Example 4-2 to provide the following additional output:

1. Total sales for each salesperson
2. Total sales of all salespeople combined
3. Total commissions of all salespeople combined

Use your own judgment about the placement of these additional items of output. No additional data are required for input.

The resultant output for the first two employees will be:

(Salesperson Number)	(Amount of Sale)	(Commission Earned)
1	110	11.00
1	400	40.00
1	285	28.50
1	315	31.50
1	140	14.00

TOTAL SALES: 1250
TOTAL COMMISSIONS: 125

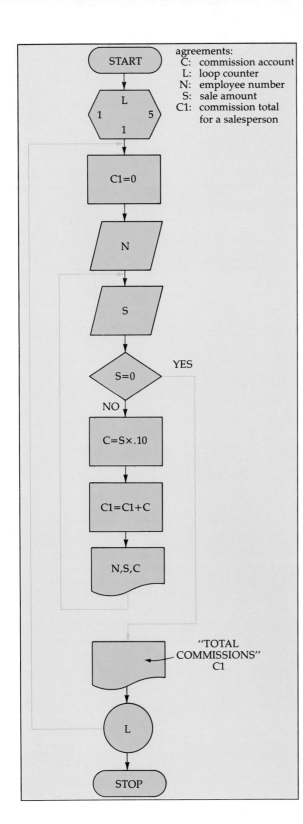

2	200	20.00
2	350	35.00
2	175	17.50
2	221	22.10
2	300	30.00
2	254	25.40

TOTAL SALES: 1500
TOTAL COMMISSIONS: 150

The summary output that follows the individual sales and commission amounts will be

- **TOTAL SALES OF ALL SALESPEOPLE COMBINED:** 7650
- **TOTAL COMMISSIONS OF ALL SALESPEOPLE COMBINED:** 765

Pseudocode:

1. Set a totaler for sales for all employees to zero.
2. Set a totaler for commissions for all employees to zero.
3. Establish a loop that cycles five times.
4. Set a totaler for individual salesperson's sales to zero.
5. Set a totaler for individual salesperson's commissions to zero.
6. Read employee number.
7. Read sales amount.
8. Is sales amount equal to zero? If yes, go to step 14. If no, go to next step.
9. Calculate commission on the single sale.
10. Add sale to individual's total sales.
11. Add commission to individual's total commission.
12. Print salesperson number, sale amount, commission amount.
13. Go to step 7.
14. Print total sales for the salesperson.
15. Print total commission for the salesperson.
16. Add total commissions for the salesperson to the all-employee commissions' total.

FIGURE 4–33 Flowchart for example 4–2.

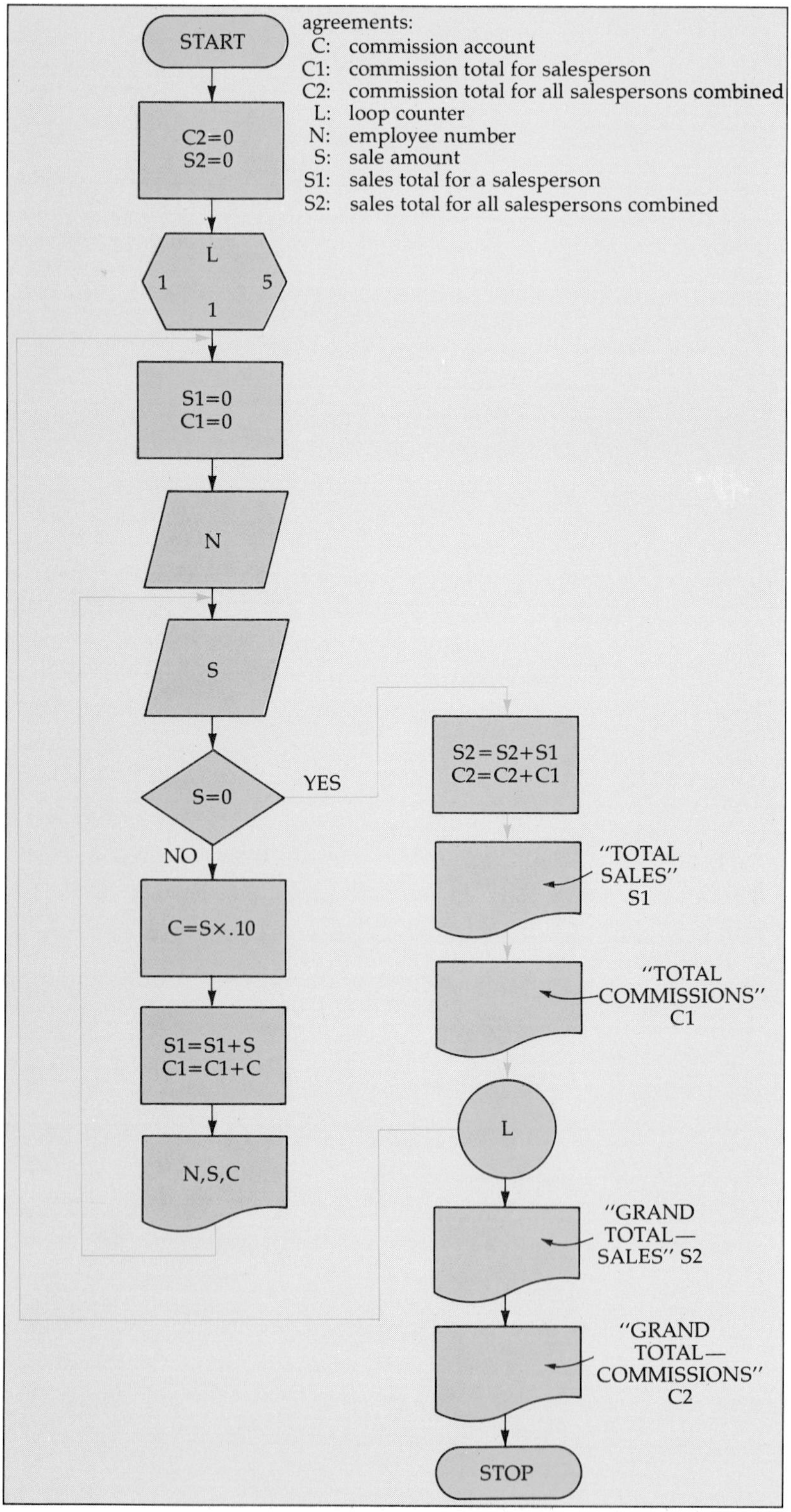
START
agreements:
C: commission account
C1: commission total for salesperson
C2: commission total for all salespersons combined
L: loop counter
N: employee number
S: sale amount
S1: sales total for a salesperson
S2: sales total for all salespersons combined
C2=0
S2=0
L
1
5
1
S1=0
C1=0
N
S
S=0
YES
NO
C=S×.10
S1=S1+S
C1=C1+C
N,S,C
S2=S2+S1
C2=C2+C1
"TOTAL
SALES"
S1
"TOTAL
COMMISSIONS"
C1
L
"GRAND
TOTAL—
SALES" S2
"GRAND
TOTAL—
COMMISSIONS"
C2
STOP

FIGURE 4–34 Flowchart for example 4–3.

17. Add total sales for the salesperson to the all-employee sales total.

18. Add 1 to loop counter and compare with five (the number of salespersons included in the processing). If equal to five, go to step 19. If not equal to five, go to step 4.

19. Print sales total of all salespersons combined.

20. Print commissions total of all salespersons combined.

21. Stop.

The flowchart for Example 4–3 is shown in Figure 4–34.

Example 4–4

Modify the flowchart shown in Figure 4–26 ("Transaction listing/totaling flowchart with decisions within the loop") to determine the largest

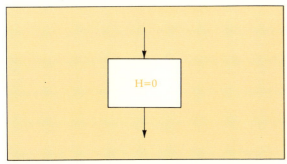

FIGURE 4–35 Setting L to zero.

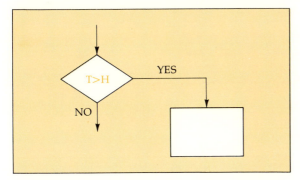

FIGURE 4–36 Comparing the first transaction amount to zero.

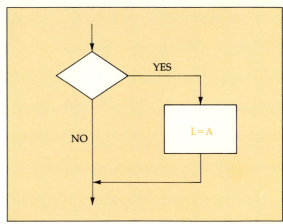

FIGURE 4–37 Current transaction amount replacing previous transaction amount.

transaction amount. Retain the tests for the upper and lower limits. The output should appear as follows:

> THE LARGEST TRANSACTION AMOUNT WAS XX

The decision process determines whether the current transaction amount (A) is larger than any previously encountered. By setting the value of L (Figure 4–35) to zero prior to reading in the first amount (A), when the first amount is compared to zero (L) (Figure 4–36), it will be found to be greater. When A is greater than L, that value of A is moved to L, replacing the old value of L (Figure 4–37). The flowchart for Example 4–4 is shown in Figure 4–38.

SUMMARY

A computer program is a set of sequentially arranged instructions written in a lnguage the computer can "understand." In writing a computer program, you must first define the desired end result in a problem statement. Next, you must determine what data you need and whether they are available. Third, you must write pseudocode, giving the list of steps for the computer to perform. Then, you must draw a flowchart that diagrammatically shows the steps and the sequence

CHAPTER 4: FLOWCHARTING

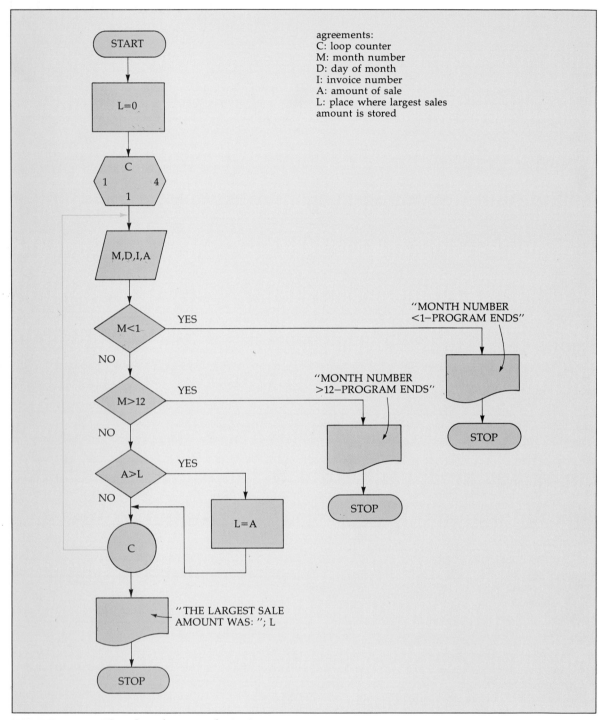

FIGURE 4-38   Flowchart for example 4-4.

that the computer must follow to accomplish the end results. Finally, as you will learn how to do in the next chapter, you must write the program in a language the computer understands.

Flowcharting uses standardized symbols and some generally accepted rules. To describe the action that will take place with each flowchart symbol concisely, a symbolic notation describes both the actions and the memory spaces being acted upon.

TERMS

The following words or terms have been presented in this chapter.

Algorithm	**Totaler**
Problem statement	**Initializing**
Flowchart	**Replace**
Terminal symbol	**Looping**
Processing symbol	**Loop**
Input/output symbol	**Preparation symbol**
Document symbol	**Index**
Flowline	**Counter**
Precedence	**Validation**
Pseudocode	**Decision symbol**
Symbolic flowchart	**Connector symbol**
Variable names	**Template**
Agreements	**End-of-data sentinel**
Accumulator	

EXERCISES

The exercises that follow are grouped by level of difficulty. Problems in the A series are the easiest; B series problems are moderately hard; and C series problems are the most difficult.

A–1 Write the pseudocode and the symbolic flowchart showing the instruction sequence that would print a list showing the gross pay that would be earned during the weekly pay period. The input for each of 80 employees would consist of:

1. employee number
2. hours worked
3. pay rate in dollars per hour

The printed output would consist of:

1. employee number
2. hours worked
3. pay rate
4. gross earnings

Assume that no overtime payrate is given for hours in excess of 8 per day or 40 per week. The algorithm for the calculation is:

$$\text{GROSS PAY} = \text{HOURLY DOLLAR RATE} \times \text{HOURS WORKED}$$

A–2 Modify exercise A–1 to pay for overtime hours at 1.5 times the regular hourly rate for any hours in excess of 40 per week.

A–3 As business property is used or gets old, its usefulness decreases. This decrease in usefulness is called "depreciation." Depreciation (by the straight-line method) can be computed if three facts are known: (1) the cost incurred in acquiring the property; (2) the estimated market value when it becomes useless (called "scrap value"); (3) the number of years the business plans to use the property. Knowing these three items, the following algorithm yields yearly depreciation:

$$\text{YEARLY DEPRECIATION} = \frac{\text{COST} - \text{SCRAP VALUE}}{\text{YEARS OF LIFE}}$$

Write the pseudocode showing the instruction sequence that would cause the computer to print the following information for one piece of property:

1. property item number
2. cost
3. scrap value
4. years of life
5. yearly depreciation

The input data consist of:

1. property item number
2. cost
3. scrap value
4. years of life

A–4 Modify exercise A–3 to compute and print the yearly depreciation for 27 pieces of equipment rather than simply one.

A–5 Employees are receiving Christmas bonuses at the rate of 5 percent of their annual earnings to date or $450, whichever is less. Write pseudocode and draw a symbolic flowchart showing an instruction sequence that would cause the computer to print the following information for each of 50 employees.

1. employee number
2. year-to-date earnings (January 1 to date of job)
3. amount of bonus

The input data for the 50 employees would include:

1. employee number
2. year-to-date earnings

A–6 Money earned on funds deposited in a savings account or loaned to another party is called "interest." Interest is really rent earned on money you have made available to someone else. The amount loaned is called the "principal." Simple interest or annual percentage rate is calculated by the following algorithm.

$$\text{INTEREST} = \text{PRINCIPAL} \times \text{RATE} \times \text{TIME IN YEARS}$$

Write pseudocode and draw a symbolic flowchart showing the instruction sequence that would cause the computer to print the following information for a single loan:

1. principal amount
2. interest rate in percentage
3. time period for which interest is being calculated
4. amount of interest earned

The input data consist of:

1. principal amount
2. interest rate in percentage
3. time period

A–7 Modify exercise A–6 to provide the same kind of output data, but for 30 loans.

B–1 The personnel and payroll information for employees is stored and ready for input into a computer program. A program is needed to print a list of employees who are approaching retirement age. Write pseudocode and draw a symbolic flowchart showing the instruction sequence that would: print a list of employees who were first employed by the company before 1948 or were born prior to 1916. The list should include: (a) employee number; (b) date of hire; (c) date of birth. The input data for the 210 employees consist of: (a) employee number; (b) date of hire; (c) date of birth.

B–2 Modify exercise A–1 to calculate and print overtime pay for overtime hours at 1.5 times the regular hourly rate for any hours in excess of 40 per week. In addition, accumulate and print totals for all employees for:

1. hours worked
2. regular gross earnings
3. overtime earnings
4. gross earnings (regular plus overtime earnings)

B–3 Modify exercise A–3 to compute and print the yearly depreciation for 27 pieces of equipment. Also, accumulate and print the amount of total depreciation for the year on all 27 pieces.

B–4 Modify exercise A–6 to provide the same kind of output plus the value of the savings account if the interest is left in the account (principal plus interest). There are 30 loans to process.

B–5 Modify exercise A–6 to provide for the printing of a check if an additional input item (code number) is equal to 1. If it is not equal to 1, the program should simply print the amount of interest as directed in exercise A–6.

B–6 Monthly sales data for a company's salespeople are available for a 12-month period. Write pseudocode and draw a symbolic flowchart showing the instruction sequence that would cause the computer to print the following information for one salesperson:

1. salesperson's number
2. the arithmetic mean (average) of the salesperson's monthly sales.

The input data for the salesperson consist of: (a) salesperson's number; (b) sales for each of the 12 months.

"MADGE, DID WE REALLY NEED A HOME COMPUTER TO MAKE SCRAMBLED EGGS?"

B–7 Monthly net income figures are available for a business. The owner wants to know the highest monthly income for the year and in which month it occurred. The average is also needed. Write pseudocode and draw a symbolic flowchart showing the instruction sequence that would cause the computer to print that information in the following order:
1. twelve monthly net income amounts
2. the number of the month (Feb., 2, Dec., 12, and so on) that had the lowest net income
3. the amount of the lowest monthly net income
4. the number of the month that had the highest net income
5. the amount of the highest monthly net income
6. the average monthly income

Hint: Refer to solved Example 4–4.

C–1 Modify exercise B–1 to print within a single program a separate list of employees who were employed before 1948 and another separate list of employees who were born prior to 1916.

C–2 Modify exercise B–6 to perform the same operations for 120 salespeople.

C–3 Modify exercise B–6 to perform the same operations for 120 salespeople and, additionally, to analyze each monthly sales figure. If the amount is less than zero or greater than $10,000, print an error comment instead of the average.

C–4 Modify exercise B–7 to perform the same task for each of five years.

C–5 Figure 4–30 has nine different flowchart symbols. Which ones are not necessary?

C–6 If John Von Neumann and his associates had not invented flow diagrams, what do you suppose would have taken their place?

COMPUTER NEWS

COMPUTER: MOORE'S IS NOT LESS

It's not uncommon for businessmen to take their work home with them, but few can match Chet Moore's dedication—and passion for systematic record keeping.

The Redding dentist, who recently underwent leg surgery, had his microcomputer installed in his hospital room so he could keep tabs on his business and his many interests, ranging from his family genealogy to his Rotary Club service work.

To show how easy it is to operate a computer, Moore made a few strokes on the keyboard.

Instantly, the screen showed a listing of his family history, 107 names and addresses of relatives, plus other related information.

The former test pilot said his computer also helps fill other needs such as compiling Christmas card lists, ham radio rosters and even his current hospital expenses.

Moore, 62, punched the keyboard again, and the video screen revealed a list of his medical costs for his recent surgery, the 17th on his legs, which were badly damaged several years ago in an accident.

Although he is pleased with the efficiency of his computer, Moore said buying one was not easy.

A few years ago, he went to several stores, but couldn't get a salesman to speak computer language in layman's terms.

Undaunted, Moore continued until he found a salesman who encouraged him, telling him about the unlimited uses that a computer offers.

He bought a microcomputer, read several books and then "wrote" his own programs.

A program is a list of instructions for a computer, and it is displayed on the video screen for the operator.

"The basic program I wrote," Moore said, "could be used for a dentist or attorney."

Incidentally, Moore has assisted other single practitioners in setting up their own programs, thus saving them several thousand dollars in software costs.

Today, his system includes a word processor "that puts out perfect letters," a video tube for putting information into the computer and giving it instructions and the computer itself.

Moore uses the system for compiling insurance records, patient data, a daily journal and a jazz group roster.

A skilled trumpet player, he belongs to All That Jazz, a local group of musicians which gives benefit performances in the area.

The computer enthusiast has found several other uses for his computer, some purely entertainment.

For instance, Moore has programs for such games as Star Wars and blackjack.

He encouraged other small businessmen to consider the advantage of having their own small computer. "Learn how to do a simple program at home—learn it as a hobby."

Redding Record Searchlight, May 21, 1981.

CHAPTER *five*
BEGINNING BASIC

Preview

BASIC: Background and Purpose

Language Rules
    Statements
    Labeling the Symbols
    Variable Naming Rules
    START and REM
    LET
    FOR Statement
    READ/DATA
    LET and Precedence Order
    PRINT—Captions, Values, Comma, Semicolon
    NEXT and END

History Capsule:
Kemeny and Kurtz: The Founders of BASIC

Program Execution
    System Commands or Job Control Language
    Program RUN
    INPUT Statement

Solved Exercises with IF and GO TO
    Validating Dates
    GO TO Statement
    Discounting

Summary

Computer News: Computer Learns Shorthand

PREVIEW

BASIC is a programming language designed for people who have no prior programming experience and is one of the easiest of all programming languages to learn. This chapter presents the rules for writing the nine BASIC commands: FOR, LET, IF, NEXT, GO TO, PRINT, READ/DATA, INPUT, END. The rules are covered using the VISA statement flowchart developed in the previous chapters.

BASIC: BACKGROUND AND PURPOSE

BASIC is a high-level programming language specifically designed for beginning programmers. The letters *B-A-S-I-C* stand for *B*eginners *A*ll-purpose *S*ymbolic *I*nstruction *C*ode. BASIC was developed at Dartmouth College in 1963. The language is "standardized," as are FORTRAN and COBOL. A synopsis of the standard for BASIC appears in Supplement C. After you have written five or six BASIC programs you might compare the version of BASIC you are using with this standard.

The intent of BASIC is to enable the student to enter a program while sitting at a computer terminal. As the program is entered, the various statements are checked by the computer for errors; these can then be corrected immediately. Once a program has been entered completely, it can be executed (RUN in BASIC) or saved on an external storage device for later use.

LANGUAGE RULES

Statements

The rules that govern the writing of a BASIC program are not as complex as those of other languages such as COBOL or FORTRAN. Let us compare BASIC with English. The rules of English are familiar to us all: Characters (letters and numbers) are combined to form words; words make sentences; sentences make paragraphs; and so on. Within these rules there are others. A sentence is usually composed of a subject, verb, and object. The equivalent of the English sentence in BASIC is the **statement.** A BASIC statement is composed of a sequence number followed by a keyword and then an expression. In the BASIC statement

20   LET A=4+C

20 is the sequence number, LET is the keyword, and A=4+C is the expression. Sequence numbers show the order in which BASIC statements appear. In addition to LET, some of the other keywords in BASIC are FOR, READ, and PRINT. **Keywords** define what the BASIC statement is going to do in the program. The exact expression in a BASIC statement depends on the keyword being used. The expression in the LET statement above causes the computer to compute a sum, while a PRINT statement tells the computer to output values from the computer's memory.

The various BASIC statements are closely linked to the symbols used in a flowchart (see Figure 5–1). This is not a complete listing of all the statements in the BASIC language, but most BASIC programs use these statements for the bulk of their programming.

After examining this flowchart and the statement categories in Figure 5–2, we see that the following BASIC statements are required:

LET   FOR   READ   PRINT   NEXT   END

A BASIC program may be written on special paper called a "coding form" before it is entered into the computer (Figure 5–3). Positions 1 to 4 of the coding form are used to enter the line number of the statement. Positions 5 to 8 are used to enter the BASIC keyword needed. Positions 9 and onward contain the expression for this particular statement.

Labeling the Symbols

Before any BASIC statement is written, each symbol in a flowchart (except START) is assigned a **line number** (see Figure 5–4). The rules of BASIC do not require that line numbers be 10, 20, 30, . . . , 999. They could just as easily have been numbered 1, 2,

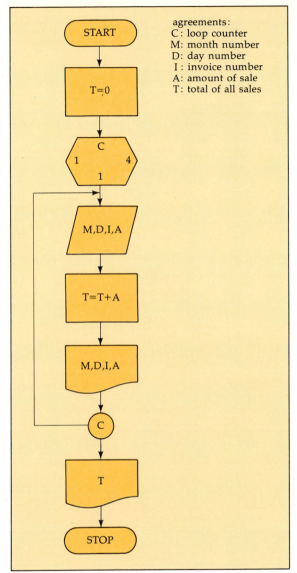

FIGURE 5–1 VISA transaction flowchart with totals.

number is above and to the right of the flowchart symbol.

Variable Naming Rules

The variable names assigned in the flowchart should conform to the BASIC rules for assigning variable names. In BASIC a **variable name** may consist of a single letter (such as M, D, I) or a letter followed by a digit (for example, $S1, S2, C1, C2$). This naming rule allows 286 unique names: A to Z, $A0$ to $A9$, $B0$ to $B9$, . . . , $Z0$ to $Z9$. Thus, the variable $C10$ is not valid for BASIC.

START and REM

When we drew our flowcharts we made a list of variables and their meanings, called "agreements"; but when we wrote the BASIC, the agreements were not part of the program. BASIC has a special statement called **REM**, short for "remark," that allows us to put our agreements into the program (see Figure 5–7). The REM statement is useful for other purposes, and these will be presented in the next chapter.

The first symbol in the flowchart in Figure 5–4 is:

In BASIC, no statements are written for this symbol.

LET

The second symbol in Figure 5–4, **LET,** sets T to zero.

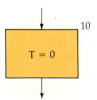

3, 4, . . . , 8 or 100, 200, 300, 400, . . . , 800 or 20, 21, 30, 45, . . . , 70. The sequence 10, 20, 30, . . . , 999 is used for convenience. Gaps in line number sequence allow you to add statements to your program if the need arises. BASIC does require that line numbers increase throughout the sequence since the computer recalls BASIC statements in line number order. A convenient place to write the line

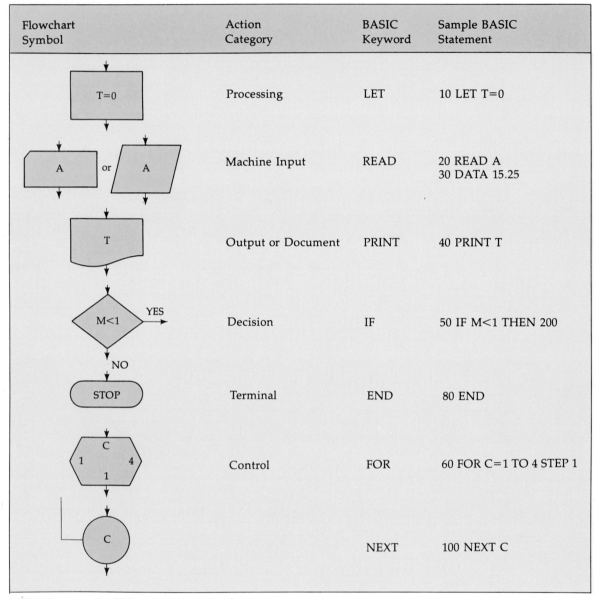

FIGURE 5–2 BASIC statement categories.

It is written in BASIC as:

10   LET T=0

The LET statement causes a zero to be placed in the memory location assigned to T.

The LET statement also is used for computations, which must be written to the right of the equal sign. That is, no computations are allowed on the left side of the equal sign.

FOR Statement

The third symbol in Figure 5–4 represents the beginning of a loop.

84 MODULE TWO: LANGUAGE

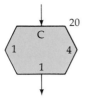

The BASIC keyword for this symbol is **FOR,** and the statement is written:

20   FOR C=1 TO 4 STEP 1

The rules governing FOR cause a loop to be established whose loop counter is C, which begins at 1. FOR causes the computer to cycle through a loop that begins with the line immediately following the FOR. A later statement in the program (line 60) tells the computer where the loop ends. During each loop cycle the value of C is changed by the quantity indicated by the STEP clause. The STEP clause may be omitted if the increment is 1; thus, the following statement is also acceptable:

20   FOR C=1 TO 4

The looping process continues until the loop counter C exceeds the value 4. The rules of FOR allow loops to go forward or backward:

18   FOR Q=16 TO 92 STEP 4   ← forward

37   FOR N=18 TO 12 STEP −2   ← backward

In backward loops the value of N in the preceding illustration will be 18, 16, 14, 12 during the various cycles. Furthermore, a FOR statement allows the beginning, ending, and increment in a FOR state-

```
10  LET T=0
15  PRINT "MONTH NO.","DAY NO.","INVOICE NO.","AMOUNT OF SALE"
20  FOR C=1 TO 4
30  READ M,D,I,A
31  DATA 2,21,27425,71.39
32  DATA 2,24,40711,205.75
33  DATA 2,25,4577,15.98
34  DATA 2,25,46131,64.75
40  LET T=T+A
50  PRINT M,D,I,A
60  NEXT C
70  PRINT T
999 END
```

FIGURE 5–3   BASIC coding form.

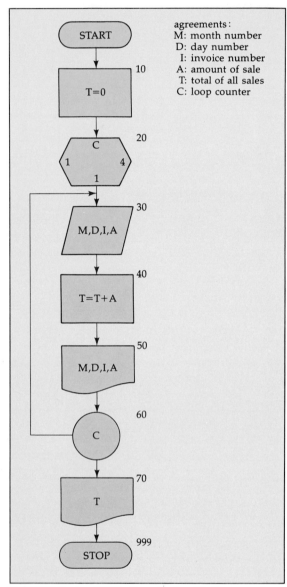

FIGURE 5–4 VISA flowchart with line numbers.

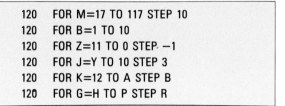

FIGURE 5–5 FOR statements.

READ/DATA

The fourth action of Figure 5–4 reads the values of M, D, I, and A.

Since BASIC is a terminal-oriented language, card readers are not usually available. (Some versions of BASIC do allow cards to be read.) In place of the card-reading symbol, a parallelogram is used for flowcharting BASIC programs.

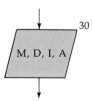

The BASIC keywords to read these values are **READ** and **DATA**. The program now appears as:

```
10   LET T=0
20   FOR C=1 TO 4 STEP 1
30   READ M,D,I,A
31   DATA 2,21,27425,71.39
```

The READ in line 30 causes four numbers to be read from the DATA statement, line 31. The first number in the DATA statement (2) is assigned to the first variable (M) in the READ statement; the second number (21) to the second variable (D); and so on.

ment to be variables or constants. Some examples of FOR statements are shown in Figure 5–5.

The FOR statement in BASIC is a powerful one since many programs have loops. The statement allows the programmer to write a loop giving the beginning, ending, and increment values for the loop counter.

FIGURE 5-6 Arithmetic operators.

Arithmetic Operators	Meaning	Example	Precedence Priority
( )	Parentheses	(F−32)	High
↑	Exponentiate	R↑2	↑
*/	Multiply, Divide	9/5*C	
+−	Add, Subtract	F+32−C	↓
=	Equals	C=5/9*(F−32)	Low

The numbers in the DATA statement must be separated by commas, and they must be in the same order as the variables in READ. For example, if the statement 30 READ A,B,C is written with the corresponding DATA statement 31 DATA 29,0.71,2.4, the value of A becomes 29, the value of B becomes 0.71, and the value of C becomes 2.4. The numbers in the DATA statement must be in decimal form (for example, 0.33) rather than in fraction form (for example, 1/3). With a second loop cycle another set of values for M, D, I, and A is needed. This requires another DATA statement with another line number:

```
32    DATA 2,24,40711,205.75
```

with the next set of values for M, D, I, and A. As the loop cycles a second time, the new values replace the old ones. For the four loop cycles, four DATA statements are needed. The DATA statements are sometimes placed after the READ statement (that's one reason line numbers are not 1, 2, 3, 4, . . .). If there are not enough DATA statements in the program for the READ statement, an error message OUT OF DATA will be printed by the computer, and more data must be placed in the program for it to run properly. DATA statements can be placed anywhere in a program.

LET and Precedence Order

The fifth symbol in Figure 5-4 requires a LET statement. It is written in BASIC as:

```
10    LET T=0
20    FOR C=1 TO 4
30    READ M,D,I,A
31    DATA 2,21,27425,71.39
32    DATA 2,24,40711.,205.75
33    DATA 2,25,4577,15.98
34    DATA 2,25,4613,64.75
40    LET T=T+A
```

This LET statement is different from the one in line number 10 because it requires a computation. A computation of variables and constants uses **arithmetic operators** to show the operations to be performed (see Figure 5-6).

The computer evaluates the portion of the arithmetic expressions to the right of the equal sign, according to the type of arithmetic operator used, in a left-to-right direction. Terms that are surrounded by parentheses have the highest priority and are calculated first. Next to be calculated are terms with exponents, then expressions with */, followed by those with +−, and lastly those with =. This is the way statements are evaluated, and the programmer must use the operators correctly in order to have the formula evaluated properly. This evaluation order is called the **precedence order.**

Using this precedence order, the LET statement for line number 40 causes the computer to add the value of A from the first loop (71.39) to T (now 0) and store this sum in T. The new value (71.39) replaces the old value (0).

To override the normal precedence order, parentheses are inserted around the expression that is to be evaluated first. For example, if you want to compute gross wages when an employee has worked for more than 40 hours in a week, and when the employer's policy is to pay at 1.5 times the regular rate for hours in excess of 40:

CHAPTER 5: BEGINNING BASIC

gross = 40*hourly + 1.5 (total hours *hourly
wages   wage rate   worked − 40)   wage rate
         ⎵_____⎵ ⎵_____⎵
           regular   overtime
           earnings   earnings

The parentheses show that 40 should be deducted from total hours worked before any other operations are executed. If any exponentiation is to be performed, it will be done next (in this example, there is no exponentiation). Then, any multiplication or division is performed, starting from the left and moving to the right. Finally, addition or subtraction is performed, again starting from the left and moving to the right. The order of evaluation for our formula would thus be:

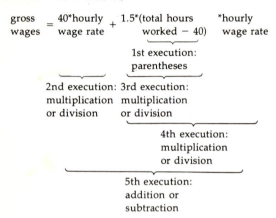

PRINT—Captions, Values, Comma, Semicolon

The sixth symbol in our flowchart directs the computer to print the values of *M, D, I,* and *A*. The

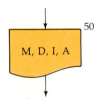

BASIC keyword to output is **PRINT**; it is written as shown in line number 50:

```
10   LET T=0
20   FOR C=1 TO 4
30   READ M,D,I,A
31   DATA 2,21,27425,71.39
32   DATA 2,24,40711.,205.75
33   DATA 2,25,4577,15.98
34   DATA 2,25,4613,64.75
40   LET T=T+A
50   PRINT M,D,I,A
```

A PRINT statement is used to output the values of variables or captions or both. Variables or captions to be printed are separated by commas or semicolons. If commas are used, the quantities will automatically be spaced across the line in intervals. The intervals are usually 15 positions or letters wide and only five values can be printed per line. At the end of a line, BASIC automatically begins a new line at the left-hand margin. The values of *M, D, I,* and *A* would be printed like this:

```
2        21       27425      71.39
2        24       40711.     205.75
```

Semicolons are used to group items closer together. If we wrote our PRINT statement like this:

```
50   PRINT M;D;I;A
```

the values of *M, D, I,* and *A* would look like this:

```
2  21  27425  71.39
2  24  40711. 205.75
```

If we mixed semicolons and commas like this:

```
50   PRINT M,D;I,A
```

the values of the variables would look like this:

```
2        21 27425   71.39
2        24 40711.             205.75
```

With bigger numbers, the spaces between variables separated by semicolons is determined by the size or magnitude of the numbers.

NEXT and END

The circle symbol of Figure 5–4 uses a **NEXT** state-

MODULE TWO: LANGUAGE

ment in BASIC and is written as shown in line number 60:

```
10    LET T=0
20    FOR C=1 TO 4
30    READ M,D,I,A
31    DATA 2,21,27425,71.39
32    DATA 2,24,40711.,205.75
33    DATA 2,25,4577,15.98
34    DATA 2,25,4613,64.75
40    LET T=T+A
50    PRINT M,D,I,A
60    NEXT C
```

A NEXT statement shows the end of the FOR loop. The word NEXT is written, followed by the name of the loop counter. This statement causes the loop counter to be incremented and tested. The testing, which occurs after the incrementing, is a "greater than" test. If the loop counter exceeds the final value of the loop counter as established in the FOR statement, the looping is terminated. Control then goes to the statement that immediately follows the NEXT. If the loop counter does not exceed the final value, another cycle is executed.

The rules for writing NEXT are simple—a NEXT is required with every FOR, and FOR/NEXT loops cannot overlap:

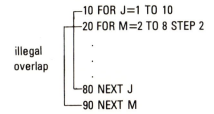

illegal overlap

A FOR/NEXT loop, however, can surround another FOR/NEXT loop. These are called **nested loops.**

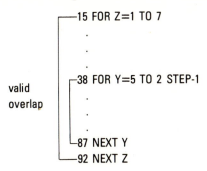

valid overlap

Finally, FOR/NEXT loops can occur separately:

```
┌─13  FOR A=7 TO 17
│      .
│      .
│      .
└─29  NEXT A

┌─32  FOR B=J TO F STEP 2
│      .
│      .
│      .
│      .
└─81  NEXT B
```

The second to the last symbol in Figure 5–4:

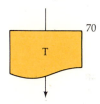

directs the computer to print the value of *T*; in BASIC this statement is written as shown on line number 70:

```
10    LET T=0
20    FOR C=1 TO 4
30    READ M,D,I,A
31    DATA 2,21,27425,71.39
32    DATA 2,24,40711.,205.75
33    DATA 2,25,4577,15.98
34    DATA 2,25,4613,64.75
40    LET T=T+A
50    PRINT M,D,I,A
60    NEXT C
70    PRINT T
```

Since this statement is outside of the loop it will not be printed until the loop has cycled four times. When the computer gets to this PRINT statement, it causes the value of *T* to be printed like this:

357.87

It would look better to have the words TOTAL OF ALL SALES printed before 357.87. To print a caption or a heading you enclose the desired caption in quotation marks like this:

```
70    PRINT "TOTAL OF ALL SALES", T
```

CHAPTER 5: BEGINNING BASIC

KEMENY AND KURTZ: THE FOUNDERS OF BASIC

In the early 1960s John G. Kemeny (right) and Thomas E. Kurtz of Dartmouth College, Hanover, New Hampshire, designed the BASIC timesharing language. Their goal was to develop a simple and powerful programming language that students of all disciplines could learn easily. The result was BASIC.

Kemeny was born in Budapest, Hungary, and immigrated to the United States in 1940. His education includes a Bachelor of Arts and a Ph.D. in mathematics from Princeton University. He has written numerous articles and books (including one on BASIC). Dr. Kemeny retired from Dartmouth College in June 1981; he was the college's president.

The second designer of BASIC is Dr. Thomas Kurtz. Dr. Kurtz also has a Ph.D. from Princeton University in mathematics. He is the coauthor (with Dr. Kemeny) of one of the original BASIC books (*BASIC Programming,* 2d ed. [New York: John Wiley, 1971]). Dr. Kurtz has been a member of the President's Science Advisory Commission (1965–66), Professor of Mathematics at Dartmouth College, and Director of Dartmouth's Kiewit Computation Center; he is now Director of the Office of Academic Computing at Dartmouth.

Doctors Kemeny and Kurtz have tried to impress upon members of the college and university community the philosophy that an understanding of computers is as necessary to life as being able to read and write. The result is that 90 percent of all Dartmouth College students use the computer while enrolled at Dartmouth. Furthermore, the two believe that computers should be as accessible as a library. At Dartmouth all students can use the library (computer) at little or no cost; are allowed to borrow books (program the computer); and use reference materials (prewritten programs). This generous, yet radical, philosophy is now being implemented in other schools across the United States.

---

and the computer will print:

TOTAL OF ALL SALES   357.87

If you had put a semicolon before the T, like this:

70   PRINT "TOTAL OF ALL SALES"; T

the computer would have printed:

TOTAL OF ALL SALES 357.87

A comma or a semicolon at the end of a PRINT statement has the effect of not returning the printing mechanism to the left-hand margin when the PRINT is completed. Further, a blank line can be printed with a statement such as

75   PRINT

The last symbol of our flowchart in Figure 5–4 is

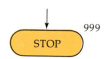

It is written in BASIC as:

```
10    LET T=0
20    FOR C=1 TO 4
30    READ M,D,I,A
31    DATA 2,21,27425,71.39
32    DATA 2,24,40711.,205.75
33    DATA 2,25,4577,15.98
34    DATA 2,25,4613,64.75
40    LET T=T+A
50    PRINT M,D,I,A
60    NEXT C
70    PRINT T
999   END
```

MODULE TWO: LANGUAGE

"I THINK WHAT WE NEED NOW IS SOMEONE CALLED A COMPUTER PROGRAMMER."

The last instruction of every BASIC program is **END**. The END statement must have the highest line number of all the statements. Many programmers ensure this by always giving the END statement line number 999 or 9999.

The seven BASIC statements that have been used are not the only ones available. BASIC programs can be written to process alphanumeric data (called **strings** in BASIC), draw pictures, and do much more, as you will see.

PROGRAM EXECUTION

System Commands or Job Control Language

The complete BASIC program, along with the four sets of data, is given in Figure 5–7. To have the computer execute this program, a special instruction, **RUN**, is used. This command is called a **system command**. It is not a BASIC statement and therefore does not have a line number. Figure 5–8 gives some system commands.

Commands to the computer to do something with a program or its data are also called **JCL (Job**

```
1    REM
2    REM VARIABLES USED IN THIS PROGRAM
3    REM T: TOTAL OF THE AMOUNTS
4    REM C: LOOP COUNTER
5    REM M: MONTH NUMBER
6    REM D: DAY NUMBER
7    REM I: INVOICE NUMBER
8    REM A: AMOUNT OF THE TRANSACTION
9    REM
10   LET T=0
20   FOR C=1 TO 4
30   READ M,D,I,A
31   DATA 2,21,27425,71.39
32   DATA 2,24,40711.,205.75
33   DATA 2,25,4577,15.98
34   DATA 2,25,4613,64.75
40   LET T=T+A
50   PRINT M,D,I,A
60   NEXT C
70   PRINT T
999  END

RUN

2         21      27425     71.39
2         24      40711.    205.75
2         25      4577      15.98
2         25      4613      64.75
357.87
```

FIGURE 5–7   BASIC source program for VISA flowchart.

Control Language). For large computers like an IBM 4300 or 3030 series, the JCL is complex and powerful. IBM's JCL is almost a programming language in its own right.

Program RUN

When the system command RUN is given, the results are as shown as in Figure 5–9.

The RUN of our VISA transactions program of Figure 5–9 would have a better appearance if we put captions across the top of the columns of numbers. The PRINT statement allows us to print variables (line 50), variables and captions (line 70), or just

CHAPTER 5: BEGINNING BASIC

FIGURE 5-8 BASIC system commands.

System Command	Meaning
RUN	Execute current program
LIST	Provide a copy of the statements comprising the current version of program
SCR or NEW	Erase the computer's primary memory
BYE	Signal end of this terminal session
SAVE	Store copy of program on external device
CATALOG	Name of all programs saved
KILL or UNSAVE	Delete program from catalog
LEN or SIZE	Provide the length of program in memory locations
TIME	Tell the amount of time used
OLD or GET	Copy program from secondary storage into memory

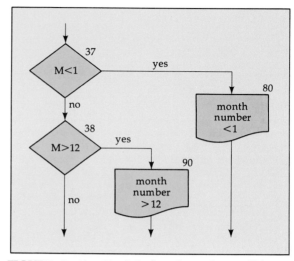

FIGURE 5-10 Partial flowchart that validates month numbers

captions. Since we want to print the caption before the column of numbers, and we want to print the caption once, we need to put this PRINT statement before the FOR statement that starts the loop. Figure 5-11 shows you the BASIC listing and program RUN with the caption PRINT statement, line 15. Notice that the order of the captions is the same as the order of the variables of the PRINT statement in line 50. It is this sameness that causes

```
RUN

2     21    27425    71.39
2     24    40711.   205.75
2     25    4577     15.98
2     25    4613     64.75
357.87
```

FIGURE 5-9 VISA program RUN.

the captions to be over their related column of numbers. Two-line captions can be programmed by having two PRINT statements following each other, as in Figure 5-12.

INPUT Statement

With a READ statement you must have the data for your program entered as lines within the program before the program is RUN. In some cases, however, you may not know the data for your program ahead of time, although you will have them ready when it is time to run the program. For such cases, BASIC has another instruction, **INPUT,** that allows you to enter these data during the program's run. The flowchart symbol for INPUT is:

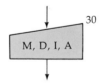

You write INPUT in BASIC as:

30   INPUT M,D,I,A

When the program is RUN, the computer responds with a question mark (?). At this point you enter the

```
1    REM
2    REM VARIABLES USED
3    REM T: TOTAL OF THE AMOUNTS
4    REM C: LOOP COUNTER
5    REM M: MONTH NUMBER OF THE TRANSACTION
6    REM D: DAY NUMBER OF THE TRANSACTION
7    REM I: INVOICE NUMBER OF THE TRANSACTION
8    REM A: AMOUNT OF THE TRANSACTION
9    REM
10   LET T=0
15   PRINT "MONTH NO.","DAY NO.","INVOICE NO.","AMOUNT OF SALE"
20   FOR C=1 TO 4
30   READ M,D,I,A
31   DATA 2,21,27425,71.39
32   DATA 2,24,40711.,205.75
33   DATA 2,25,4577,15.98
34   DATA 2,25,4613,64.75
40   LET T=T+A
50   PRINT M,D,I,A
60   NEXT C
70   PRINT T
999  END

RUN


MONTH NO.      DAY NO.        INVOICE NO.    AMOUNT OF SALE
   2              21             27425           71.39
   2              24             40711.          205.75
   2              25             4577            15.98
   2              25             4613            64.75
357.87
```

FIGURE 5–11   VISA program and RUN with captions.

values of M, D, I, and A, separating the values with commas, as you did in the DATA statement, like this:

?   2,21,27425,71.39

The INPUT thus allows you to write your program without data and vary the data during each run.

In the past, BASIC has been used primarily by educational institutions or by users who did not want to spend a lot of time programming problems. Now, with the wide use of minicomputers and home or hobby computers, BASIC's popularity is growing since the language can be provided easily on these small machines.

The major complaint that "professional" programmers have with BASIC is its limited printing capabilities. It is difficult (but not impossible) to have a number like 10721.3 printed as: $10,721.30. Further, although early versions of BASIC could not access data from card, disk, or tape, newer versions, sometimes called "super BASIC," or "EXTENDED BASIC" overcome these limitations.

SOLVED EXERCISES WITH IF AND GO TO

Validating Dates

The flowchart of Figure 5–13 shows you a routine that validates the month number and is a modified version of Figure 4–25. Line numbers are placed next to each symbol, and captions are printed before the loop. The only flowchart symbols we haven't already discussed are those used to cause a decision.

The BASIC keyword for decision making is **IF**; it is written in complete statement form as (see Figure 5–10):

```
37   IF M < 1 THEN 80
38   IF M > 12 THEN 90
```

The IF statement in line 37 tests a particular condition for true or false. If M is less than (<) 1, the computer is then to perform statement 80. If M is not less than 1, the THEN portion is ignored and the statement that follows line 37 is performed. The < in line 37 is called a **relational operator.** The relational operators in BASIC are shown in Figure 5–15. The IF, coupled with the relational operators, allows a wide variety of relationships to be tested.

GO TO Statement

The complete program listing and RUN for the flowchart of Figure 5–12 is given in Figure 5–14. Lines 71, 81 and 91 are new BASIC statements. The **GO TO** in line 81 says that line 999 is the next one to be performed and that all the statements between 81 and 999 are to be skipped. A GO TO statement is useful for branching either forward or backward in a program.

Discounting

The following problem statement shows the use of multiple IF statements within a loop, the printing of captions, and some further uses of GO TO. The problem begins with background information and continues with a problem statement, a flowchart (Figure 5–16), a listing of the program (Figure 5–17) and the RUN (Figure 5–18).

Background: Businesses, like individuals, have to plan their cash spending and inflow. An excess of cash on hand is wasteful because if it were invested or placed in a savings account it would earn dividends or interest. On the other hand, a lack of cash inflow on a timely basis limits a business in buying merchandise, supplies, or equipment as they are needed. Such a shortage may be met by borrowing cash from a bank, but that requires paying interest on the loan. To help ensure a steady, dependable inflow of cash, therefore, a business may offer a discount to purchasers who pay early. For example, many businesses sell to customers on a charge basis, with terms being that the customer will pay in full within 30 days. However, to encourage the customer to pay the bill even more quickly, a business may offer a reduction (called a "discount") in the amount owed to those who pay early.

A discount of 2 percent of the amount owed may be given if the debt is paid within five days or 1 percent if it is paid within ten days. Hence, if a charge sale of $1,000 to Alpine Markets is made on October 15, Alpine must pay the full amount by November 14 (30 days later). However, if payment is received on or before October 20 (that is, within five days of the sale: October 15 + 5), a discount of 2 percent off the purchase price is allowed ($1,000 × 0.02 = $20). If payment is received between October 21 and October 25, the 1 percent discount is allowed ($1,000 × 0.01 = $10).

```
1    REM
2    REM VARIABLES USED
3    REM T: TOTAL OF THE AMOUNTS
4    REM C: LOOP COUNTER
5    REM M: MONTH NUMBER OF THE TRANSACTION
6    REM D: DAY NUMBER OF THE TRANSACTION
7    REM I: INVOICE NUMBER OF THE TRANSACTION
8    REM A: AMOUNT OF THE TRANSACTION
9    REM
10   LET T=0
15   PRINT "MONTH","DAY","INVOICE","AMOUNT"
16   PRINT "NUMBER","NUMBER","NUMBER","OF SALE"
20   FOR C=1 TO 4
30   READ M,D,I,A
31   DATA 2,21,27425,71.39
32   DATA 2,24,40711.,205.75
33   DATA 2,25,4577,15.98
34   DATA 2,25,4613,64.75
40   LET T=T+A
50   PRINT M,D,I,A
60   NEXT C
70   PRINT T
999  END

RUN
```

MONTH	DAY	INVOICE	AMOUNT
NUMBER	NUMBER	NUMBER	OF SALE
2	21	27425	71.39
2	24	40711.	205.75
2	25	4577	15.98
2	25	4613	64.75
357.87			

FIGURE 5-12 VISA program and RUN with two-line captions.

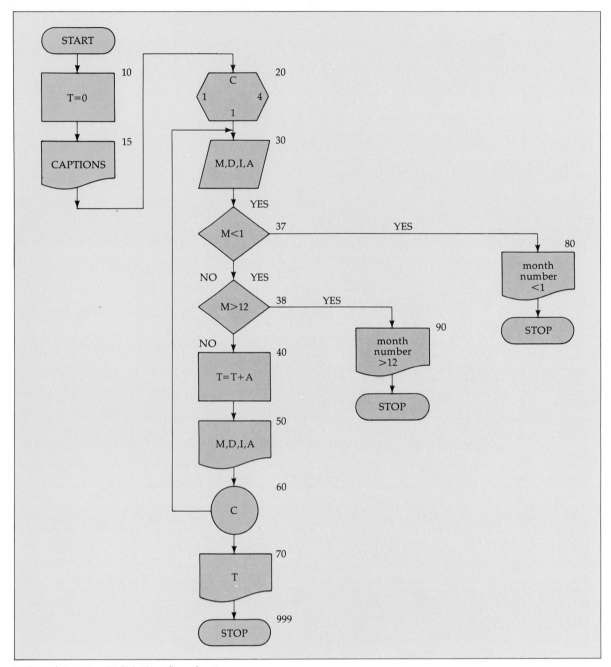

FIGURE 5–13 Validation flowchart.

```
1    REM
2    REM VARIABLES USED
3    REM T: TOTAL OF THE AMOUNTS
4    REM C: LOOP COUNTER
5    REM M: MONTH NUMBER OF THE TRANSACTION
6    REM D: DAY NUMBER OF THE TRANSACTION
7    REM I: INVOICE NUMBER OF THE TRANSACTION
8    REM A: AMOUNT OF THE TRANSACTION
9    REM
10   LET T=0
15   PRINT "MONTH","DAY","INVOICE","AMOUNT"
16   PRINT "NUMBER","NUMBER","NUMBER","OF SALE"
20   FOR C=1 TO 4
30   READ M,D,I,A
31   DATA 2,21,27425,71.39
32   DATA 2,24,40711.,205.75
33   DATA 2,25,4577,15.98
34   DATA 0,25,4613,64.75
37   IF M<1 THEN 80
38   IF M>12 THEN 90
40   LET T=T+A
50   PRINT M,D,I,A
60   NEXT C
70   PRINT T
71   GOTO 999
80   PRINT "MONTH NUMBER < 1"
81   GOTO 999
90   PRINT "MONTH NUMBER >12"
91   GOTO 999
999  END

RUN

MONTH         DAY           INVOICE       AMOUNT
NUMBER        NUMBER        NUMBER        OF SALE
  2             21            27425         71.39
  2             24            40711.        205.75
  2             25            4577          15.98
MONTH NUMBER < 1
```

FIGURE 5–14   BASIC program and RUN for validation.

FIGURE 5-15 BASIC relational operators.

Relational Operator	Meaning
=	Equals
>	Greater than
<	Less than
>=	Greater than or equal to
<=	Less than or equal to
<>	Not equal to

Problem Statement: Figures 5–16 through 5–20 show the logic of a BASIC program that calculates and prints the data input with appropriate captions, the discounts on each of the charge sales listed, and the RUN.

Invoice No.	Sale Date	Sale Amount	Payment Received
3476	1015 (Oct 15)	1000	1020 (Oct 20)
4967	1015 (Oct 15)	1000	1021 (Oct 31)
5463	1016	257	1031
5539	1017	500	1028
5541	1017	620	1020

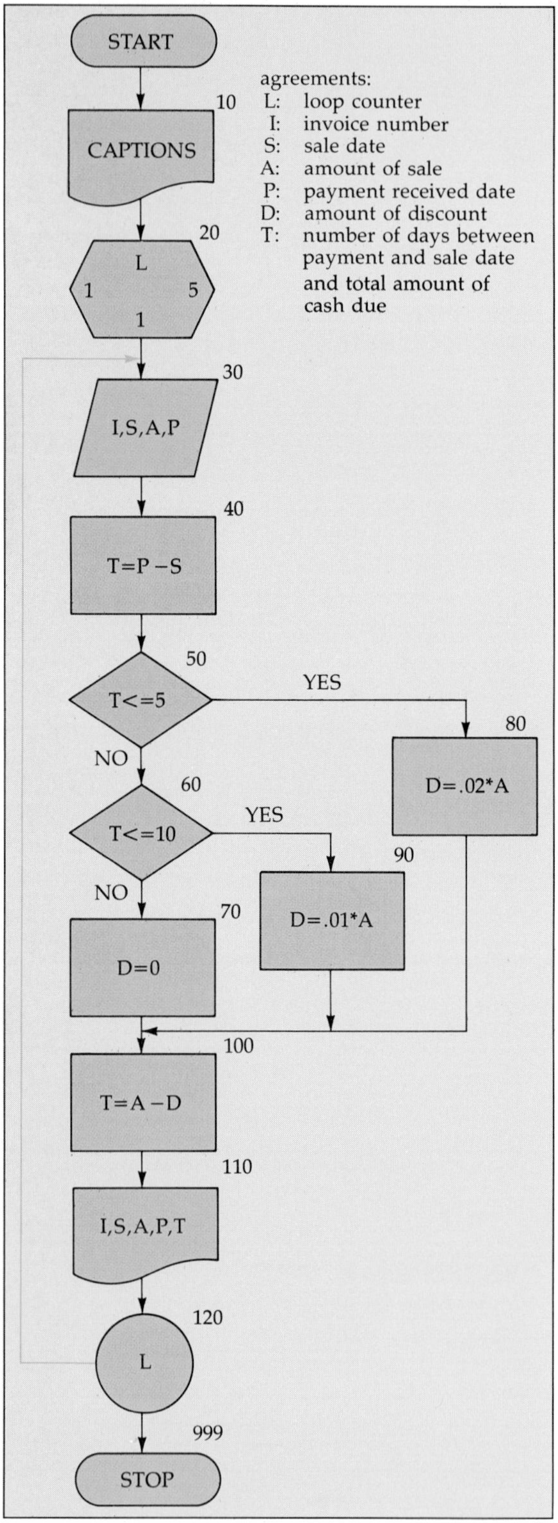

FIGURE 5-16 Discounting flowchart.

agreements:
L: loop counter
I: invoice number
S: sale date
A: amount of sale
P: payment received date
D: amount of discount
T: number of days between payment and sale date and total amount of cash due

START
10 CAPTIONS
20 L 1,1,5
30 I,S,A,P
40 T=P−S
50 T<=5 YES → 80 D=.02*A
NO
60 T<=10 YES → 90 D=.01*A
NO
70 D=0
100 T=A−D
110 I,S,A,P,T
120 L
999 STOP

MODULE TWO: LANGUAGE

```
1     REM
2     REM VARIABLES USED
3     REM L: LOOP COUNTER
4     REM I: INVOICE NUMBER
5     REM S: DATE OF THE SALE
6     REM A: AMOUNT OF THE SALE
7     REM P: POSTING DATE OF THE SALE
8     REM T: NUMBER OF DAYS BETWEEN POSTING DATE AND SALE DATE
9     REM D: AMOUNT OF THE DISCOUNT TO BE GIVEN TO THIS TRANSACTION
10    PRINT "INVOICE NO.","SALE DATE","SALE AMOUNT","SALE REC'D","TOTAL DUE"
20    FOR L=1 TO 5
30    READ I,S,A,P
31    DATA 3476,1015,1000,1020
32    DATA 4967,1015,1000,1021
33    DATA 5463,1016,257,1031
34    DATA 5539,1017,500,1028
35    DATA 5541,1017,620,1020
40    LET T=P-S
50    IF T <= 5 THEN 80
60    IF T <= 10 THEN 90
70    LET D=0
71    GOTO 100
80    LET D=.02*A
81    GOTO 100
90    LET D=.01*A
100   LET T=A-D
110   PRINT I,S,A,P,T
120   NEXT L
999   END
```

FIGURE 5–17 BASIC discounting listing.

```
RUN

INVOICE NO.    SALE DATE    SALE AMOUNT    SALE REC'D    TOTAL DUE
3476           1015         1000           1020          980
4967           1015         1000           1021          990
5463           1016         257            1031          257
5539           1017         500            1028          500
5541           1017         620            1020          607.6
```

FIGURE 5–18 Discounting program RUN.

SUMMARY

BASIC is a language originally intended for students but now also used by some businesses. Programs are entered through a terminal, and errors in the program are immediately detected and reported for correction. The most frequently used BASIC statements are:

1. FOR—Sets up a loop. Establishes the beginning, ending, and increment for the loop counter.
2. NEXT—End of loop indicator. Used in conjunction with FOR.
3. READ/DATA—Provides for entering of data for program processing.
4. LET—Defines a computational expression. Expressions are written in a form similar to an algebraic equation, using the arithmetic operators =, +, −, *, /, ↑.
5. IF—Allows transfer to another statement. Conditions are tested using the logical operators =, <, >.
6. PRINT—Provides for the output of answers, captions, or mixtures of the two.
7. END—Final statement of the program.
8. GO TO—Allows transfer to another statement, unconditionally.
9. INPUT—Allows data to be entered during the program execution.

Once the program is entered into the computer, it can be executed using the system command RUN. Other system commands are available for directing the computer to do other tasks.

TERMS

The following words or terms have been presented in this chapter.

BASIC
Statement
Keyword
Line number
Variable name
REM
LET
FOR
READ
DATA
Arithmetic operators
Precedence order
PRINT
NEXT
Nested loop
END
Strings
RUN
System command
JCL (Job Control Language)
INPUT
IF
Relational operator
GO TO

EXERCISES

The exercises that follow are grouped by level of difficulty. Problems in the A series are the easiest; B series problems are moderately hard; and C series problems are the most difficult.

A–1 Identify each of the following as a valid or invalid variable name.

a. J   d. K   g. 47   j. J27
b. Z4   e. JOKER   h. FS   k. L
c. 5K   f. AB   i. K5   l. LO

A–2 Which of the following FOR statements are correct? If a statement is incorrect write it correctly.

a. FOR K=27,1
b. FOR B=7 TO 17
c. FOR C=G TO H STEP 3
d. FOR L=1 TO 7 STEP −2
e. FOR M=9,32,2
f. FOR P=.1 TO 1.2 STEP .1
g. FOR D=P TO 12
h. FOR L=−7 TO 12
i. FOR L=L TO L

A–3 Determine if your computing system has BASIC available. If so, does it use NEW or SCR as a system command?

A–4 Using the arithmetic operators of Figure 5-6, convert the following into BASIC LET statements.

a. $F = \frac{9}{5}(C+32)$

b. $C = \frac{5}{9}F-32$

c. $S = P(1+I)^N$

d. $B = 1.27 + .07\,(U-50) + .065\,(U-75)$

e. $A = P(1+I/N)^{NR}$

MODULE TWO: LANGUAGE

f. $A = \pi R^2 \left(\dfrac{H+H1}{2}\right)$

g. $G = 40R + (H-40)\,1.5R$

A-5 Convert the following into BASIC statements:

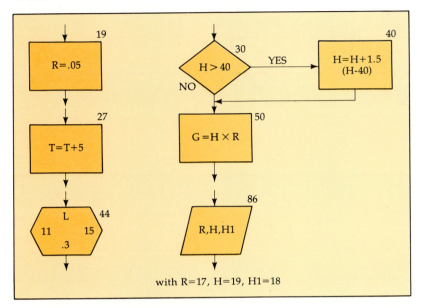

B-1 If your computer system has BASIC available, make a list of three additional system commands and state what they do.

B-2 What values would the variables have to be to cause a YES condition for the following IF statements?

    a. 17 IF A = B THEN 42
    b. 23 IF C > 2*D THEN 19
    c. 181 IF J−2 < 0 THEN 456
    d. 217 IF L <> 42 THEN 603
    e. 103 IF P>= 14 + R*2 THEN 71

B-3 For the BASIC of Figure 5–11, does the order of the sale amounts in the various DATA statements matter?

C-1 BASIC programs are sometimes compiled and other times interpreted. What is the difference in these two translation procedures? Which is best?

C-2 Go to your library or computer center and ask for a copy of the BASIC reference manual for your computer system. Does your system support card input? Is there any way you can have numbers printed with commas or $?

C-3 Enter the program shown in Figure 5–7. RUN it and see if your results match those of Figure 5–9.

C-4 Enter the program shown in Figure 5–14. RUN it and see if your results match.

C-5 At Dartmouth College, 90 percent of all students use the computer. What percentage of students at your school use a computer during their education?

COMPUTER NEWS

COMPUTER LEARNS SHORTHAND

By Steve Wright
Staff Writer

FREMONT—Computers have mastered a new language—stenographic symbols—and for two local court reporters a machine named TomCat has become a best friend.

Jenny Griffin, 24, and her 18-year-old sister, April, are the management and employees of Griffin Reporting in Fremont. As certified shorthand reporters they are responsible for taking down, word for word, exchanges among fast-talking attorneys, judges and witnesses.

Perched above stenographic machines, set on tri-pod legs, both young women have been clocked at 260 words per minute.

Sometimes their work is done in a courtroom, but as freelance court reporters they prefer the more lucrative practice of being hired by attorneys to take down sworn depositions.

They make more than $25,000 per year at the trade.

While the salary the young women earns sounds inviting, 25 percent of the money they collected went to a typist for transcribing. Like other court reporters, they had to spend part of their day deciphering the stenographic symbols and reading the material onto a tape which was then delivered to a typist.

TomCat, on the other hand, takes about 12 percent of their fee. It reads a tape of the symbols, can be kept in the office and does the work in half the time.

In the old days, the Griffins estimate it took an average of 90 minutes to dictate their notes, a half hour or so to drive to a typist and about four hours for a transcription.

The turn-around time with the $27,000 computer is only 30 minutes.

And, as in many businesses, time is money.

For a deposition the fee ranges from $2.55 to $3 per page for an original and one copy. If they fill in at court for a salaried court reporter, they are paid $92 per day, plus $1.61 per page.

"What we wanted to do is cut down on our time in the office so we could get more jobs," said Jenny, a three-year court-reporting veteran.

If everything goes as planned, the Griffins will have TomCat paid for in five years, said April, who has been in the business for eight months.

Standard stenographic machines cost approximately $400, but the ones the Griffins use come equipped with a small cassette tape attachment which electronically picks up the stenographic symbols—these machines cost almost $1,500.

At the end of an assignment, the Griffins

now put the cassette into a reading machine attached to the computer. TomCat then reads the tape, changing the symbols into words, which then show up on a screen.

After some editing, the computer is plugged into a printer which takes the edited copy from the computer screen and puts it onto paper, ready for the client.

TomCat comes complete with a standard stenographic dictionary of its own and Jenny and April also have logged their own personal shorthand into the computer's brain.

Jenny decided on court reporting as a profession after a trip to the hair dresser about five years ago.

"I had never heard of court reporting, but I was getting my hair done and the beautician said that a friend of hers was making $40,000 per year," she recalled.

After a little investigating she entered an Oakland court-reporting school and after two years of classes got her California and national certifications.

April followed in her sister's footsteps when she decided that high school was not for her. At 16, April passed the high school equivalency tests and enrolled in court-reporting classes at Ohlone College and the Oakland court-reporters school. Two years later she picked up her certifications.

Many people might have thought that the advancement of audio/video tape recordings would have spelled the end for court reporters, but the Griffins say they feel secure in their business.

"We have control over the proceedings," said Jenny. "If the district attorney, defense attorney and judge all start speaking at once we can ask them to stop and go one at a time. Or, if it's a witness or someone who has a heavy accent, we can ask for clarifications. It's just hard to get a good transcript of a tape-recorded proceeding."

"Besides," adds April, "on a tape you can't always tell who is talking."

CHAPTER six

MORE BASIC

Preview

Structured Programming
  Simple Sequence
  Selection
  Repetition

Adding Data to the Program

Documenting the Program with REM

Strings and TAB

IF and Boolean Operators

Arrays and DIM

IMAGE

Solved Exercises
   Counting Using an Array
   Calculating and Totaling Commissions

Summary

History Capsule: The Origins of FORTRAN

**Computer News: Application—
System Provides Useful Sales Data Fast**

PREVIEW

In Chapter 5 we began to develop a program to validate incoming data and to print a VISA-like statement. We saw programs that used the READ, DATA, INPUT, LET, FOR, NEXT, IF, GO TO, and END statements. In this chapter we expand our study of these statements and add some new ones. Further, we will see how we can make the computer read and process nonnumerical information called "strings"; make use of a powerful programming concept called "arrays," which can shorten programs immensely; and make our output look better by using the BASIC statement called IMAGE. We begin our study of these new concepts by first examining how we structure programs to make them correct.

STRUCTURED PROGRAMMING

Beginning programmers are always faced with the question of where to start the program. What is the correct flowchart and program? And, once the program is written, is it correct? Is there a better way it could have been written? These same questions are frequently asked by both beginning and experienced professional programmers. In 1964 Corrado Bohm and Guiseppe Jacopini, in a paper presented to an international computer science conference, proved that a program written in any programming language can be built from three basic structures: *simple sequence, selection, and repetition* (Figure 6–1). The paper went on to show that these three structures could be applied to very complex routines or very simple ones. The complexity does not matter; the three structures work all the time. Programs that are written using sequence, selection, and repetition are called **structured programs.**

Simple Sequence

The first control structure, **simple sequence,** has each processing event or action followed by the next (Figure 6–1a). There are no decisions or looping.

Selection

The second control structure is **selection** (Figure 6–1b). It shows the testing of a certain condition. As a result of this test, two possible events or actions may take place. Sometimes selection is called the

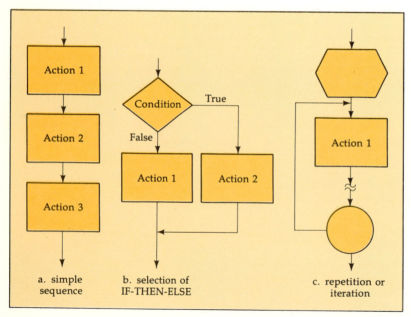

a. simple sequence
b. selection of IF-THEN-ELSE
c. repetition or iteration

FIGURE 6–1 Three control structures.

IF-THEN-ELSE structure, where IF means the test, THEN the event(s) to be processed when the test is true, and ELSE the event(s) to be processed when the test is false.

Repetition

The third control structure is **repetition** (Figure 6–1c). Repetition, sometimes called DO WHILE, is used to form a loop that is to continue cycling as long as a given condition remains true. The BASIC programming language uses the FOR/NEXT statements to cause looping. FOR/NEXT does not provide for true repetition since the NEXT specifically causes looping to continue only as long as the loop counter is less than or equal to the final value. The repetition structure may test for other conditions as well, such as input data being of a certain value, a computed value equaling a predetermined amount, or even several simultaneous conditions existing.

Along with simple sequence, selection, and repetition, structured programming embodies the concept of the **module**. A module is a group of statements in a program that perform a specific function. A module is like a chapter in a book—each chapter represents an event or some group of events, and all the chapters together make the book. If a program is modularized, there must be some interrelationship among the modules. This order or hierarchy can be shown using a **structure chart** (Figure 6–2). Structure charts are read top-down and left-to-right. In Figure 6–2 the order of the modules, therefore, is module A first, then B, and last C. Within module A the sequence is A.1, A.2, and A.3. Within modules B and C a similar pattern is followed.

Modules, as well as the three control structures, also embody the concept of single entry-single exit. We begin a module/control structure at only one point and end it only at one point. Some examples of violations of the single entry-single exit concept are shown in Figure 6–3. Here we find the P loop and the Y loop being entered in the middle of the body of the loop and not from the beginning of the loop, the FOR statement.

Some of the benefits of structured programming

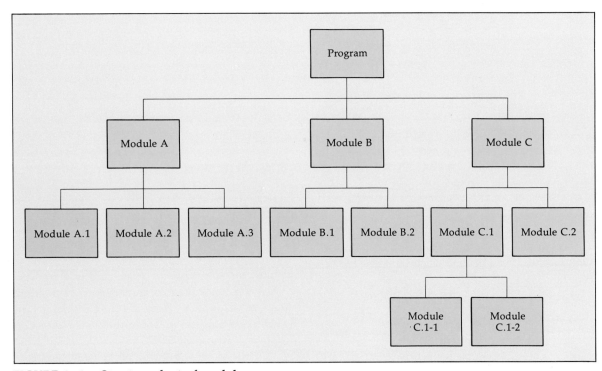

FIGURE 6–2 Structure chart of modules.

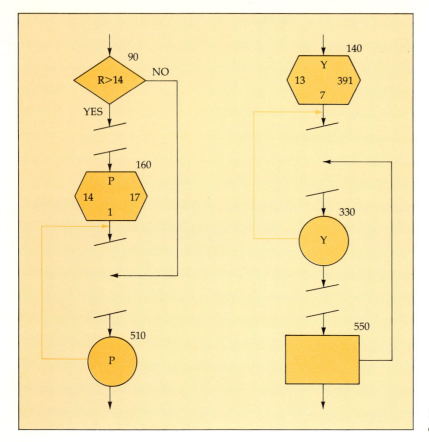

FIGURE 6-3 Unacceptable control structures.

involve increased programmer productivity. Programmers are able to write more quickly and with fewer errors. Structured programs are easier to change when the need arises, and are more likely to be correct than programs not written by this method. Finally, modularity implies that programs can be developed and tested in small pieces; modules can even be written by different programmers. The net result is a potential in cost savings from programs that cost less to write and cost less to keep running.

ADDING DATA TO THE PROGRAM

With the ideas of simple sequence, selection, and repetition as program structures, let's now look at how they are programmed in BASIC. The VISA program shown in Figure 5–11 uses FOR and NEXT to make a loop that processes four transactions. To make the program process a different number of transactions, all we have to do is modify the FOR statement and add more DATA statements (see Figure 6–4).

What do we do when we don't know how many transactions there are going to be? There are two ways to solve this problem. The first is to make the number of loop cycles a variable and read the value of the variable before the loop begins, as in Figure 6–5. The second is to use an END-OF-DATA sentinel (see Figure 4–33), and to test for the end of the loop just after the READ statement, as in Figure 6–6. Both of these methods allow us to program a loop to cycle a variable number of times.

```
1      REM
2      REM VARIABLES USED IN THIS PROGRAM
3      REM T: TOTAL OF THE AMOUNTS
4      REM C: LOOP COUNTER
5      REM M: MONTH NUMBER OF THE TRANSACTION
6      REM D: DAY NUMBER OF THE TRANSACTION
7      REM I: INVOICE NUMBER OF THE TRANSACTION
8      REM A: AMOUNT OF THE TRANSACTION
9      REM
10     LET T=0
15     PRINT "MONTH","DAY","INVOICE","AMOUNT"
16     PRINT "NUMBER","NUMBER","NUMBER","OF SALE"
20     FOR C=1 TO 6
30     READ M,D,I,A
31     DATA 2,21,27425,71.39
32     DATA 2,24,40711.,205.75
33     DATA 2,25,4577,15.98
34     DATA 2,25,4613,64.75
35     DATA 2,28,4908,67.56
36     DATA 3,12,1290,50.01
37     IF M<1 THEN 80
38     IF M>12 THEN 90
40     LET T=T+A
50     PRINT M,D,I,A
60     NEXT C
70     PRINT T
71     GOTO 999
80     PRINT "MONTH NUMBER < 1"
81     GOTO 999
90     PRINT "MONTH NUMBER >12"
91     GOTO 999
999    END
RUN
```

MONTH	DAY	INVOICE	AMOUNT
NUMBER	NUMBER	NUMBER	OF SALE
2	21	27425	71.39
2	24	40711.	205.75
2	25	4577	15.98
2	25	4613	64.75
2	28	4908	67.56
3	12	1290	50.01
475.44			

FIGURE 6-4 VISA program with extra data.

```
1    REM
2    REM VARIABLES USED IN THIS PROGRAM
3    REM T: TOTAL OF THE AMOUNTS
4    REM C: LOOP COUNTER
5    REM M: MONTH NUMBER OF THE TRANSACTION
6    REM D: DAY NUMBER OF THE TRANSACTION
7    REM I: INVOICE NUMBER OF THE TRANSACTION
8    REM A: AMOUNT OF THE TRANSACTION
9    REM L: NUMBER OF LOOP CYCLES
10   LET T=0
15   PRINT "MONTH","DAY","INVOICE","AMOUNT"
16   PRINT "NUMBER","NUMBER","NUMBER","OF SALE"
17   READ L
18   DATA 6
20   FOR C=1 TO L
30   READ M,D,I,A
31   DATA 2,21,27425,71.39
32   DATA 2,24,40711.,205.75
33   DATA 2,25,4577,15.98
34   DATA 2,25,4613,64.75
35   DATA 2,28,4908,67.56
36   DATA 3,12,1290,50.01
37   IF M<1 THEN 80
38   IF M>12 THEN 90
40   LET T=T+A
50   PRINT M,D,I,A
60   NEXT C
70   PRINT T
71   GOTO 999
80   PRINT "MONTH NUMBER < 1"
81   GOTO 999
90   PRINT "MONTH NUMBER >12"
91   GOTO 999
999  END

RUN
```

| MONTH | DAY | INVOICE | AMOUNT |
NUMBER	NUMBER	NUMBER	OF SALE
2	21	27425	71.39
2	24	40711.	205.75
2	25	4577	15.98
2	25	4613	64.75
2	28	4908	67.56
3	12	1290	50.01
475.44			

FIGURE 6–5   VISA program with variable in FOR.

```
1    REM
2    REM VARIABLES USED IN THIS PROGRAM
3    REM T: TOTAL OF THE AMOUNTS
4    REM C: LOOP COUNTER
5    REM M: MONTH NUMBER OF THE TRANSACTION
6    REM D: DAY NUMBER OF THE TRANSACTION
7    REM I: INVOICE NUMBER OF THE TRANSACTION
8    REM A: AMOUNT OF THE TRANSACTION
9    REM
10   LET T=0
15   PRINT "MONTH","DAY","INVOICE","AMOUNT"
16   PRINT "NUMBER","NUMBER","NUMBER","OF SALE"
29   READ M,D,I,A
30   IF M=0 THEN 70
31   DATA 2,21,27425,71.39
32   DATA 2,24,40711.,205.75
33   DATA 2,25,4577,15.98
34   DATA 2,25,4613,64.75
35   DATA 2,28,4908,67.56
36   DATA 0,0,0,0
37   IF M<1 THEN 80
38   IF M>12 THEN 90
40   LET T=T+A
50   PRINT M,D,I,A
60   GOTO 29
70   PRINT T
71   GOTO 999
80   PRINT "MONTH NUMBER < 1"
81   GOTO 999
90   PRINT "MONTH NUMBER >12"
91   GOTO 999
999  END

RUN

MONTH    DAY       INVOICE   AMOUNT
NUMBER   NUMBER    NUMBER    OF SALE
  2        21       27425     71.39
  2        24       40711.    205.75
  2        25       4577      15.98
  2        25       4613      64.75
  2        28       4908      67.56
425.43
```

FIGURE 6–6   VISA program with END-OF-DATA sentinel.

DOCUMENTING THE PROGRAM WITH REM

Besides using REMs to list the variables and their meanings, we can also use REM to describe what the program does, who wrote the program, and when it was written, and to explain the major portions of logic that have been programmed (see Figure 6–8). The use of REM in a program helps you to remember the program, especially if you have not looked at it for a week, a month, or a year. REM also helps you or another programmer when you examine a program that was written by someone else. This second use of REM is especially important to professional programmers who frequently have to read somebody else's program. The insertion of commentary material is called **program documentation**. Remarks placed in a program do not affect the program RUN; they are visible only when you list the source program.

STRINGS AND TAB

The VISA statement shown in earlier chapters reflects both charges and payments that a customer made during the month, as well as the balance of the account after each charge or payment is recorded. The program that printed that statement was able to: tell the difference between charges and payments; print the charge amounts in one location, and payment amounts in another; and alter the customer's balance accordingly.

To distinguish whether a particular transaction in Figure 6–8 is a charge or a payment, we could add an extra item to the DATA statement and another variable to the READ. In the DATA statement we could include the letter C or P in quotation marks to indicate the kind of transaction. In the READ statement we could write the variable K$ as the fifth variable (see Figure 6–9).

BASIC language requires a $ as the second character of a variable name if that variable is going to store nonnumeric (or **string**) data. Technically, string data can be a mixture of letters, numbers, or special characters. Thus, the variable K$ holds string data, whereas K would hold numeric data. String data can be tested using the IF statement, can be accessed with READ or INPUT, and can be output using PRINT.

In our particular case we need to test the value of K$ after it is read, and if it is a "C" we want to print the amount in the charge column and add the amount to the customer's balance. If K$ is a "P", the logic of the program should print the transaction amount in a new column, Payments, and subtract the amount from the customer's balance. Figure 6–10 shows all this logic in BASIC, with the customer's beginning balance starting at zero.

In line number 286 in Figure 6–10, there is a new BASIC command called **TAB**. TAB, short for *tabulate*, is used in a PRINT statement to override the normal comma or semicolon spacing. TAB causes the printing of the value of the variable that follows it to appear in the position number found inside the parentheses (in this example, position 60). If the number in parentheses is smaller than where the printing mechanism is located on a line, the TAB is ignored and the value of the variable is printed immediately.

The TAB command can also be used to make graphs like the one shown in Figure 6–11. In this program we read the population, P, of a particular census year. Then we divide it by 4 (to scale it to fit on a line) and use TAB to skip over to the particular location for this year. An asterisk is then printed to represent the population for this year.

IF AND BOOLEAN OPERATORS

The IF statements we have written so far have tested both month numbers to see if they are between 1 and 12 and strings to see if they are "C" or "P". In many instances, more complex decisions need to be programmed, and the flowchart and resulting BASIC are themselves complex.

In our program to validate month numbers, Figure 5–14, we might also validate day numbers. However, all months do not have the same number of days (see Figure 6–12).

```
1    REM
2    REM VARIABLES USED IN THIS PROGRAM
3    REM T: TOTAL OF THE AMOUNTS
4    REM C: LOOP COUNTER
5    REM M: MONTH NUMBER OF THE TRANSACTION
6    REM D: DAY NUMBER OF THE TRANSACTION
7    REM I: INVOICE NUMBER OF THE TRANSACTION
8    REM A: AMOUNT OF THE TRANSACTION
9    REM L: NUMBER OF LOOP CYCLES
10   LET T=0
15   PRINT "MONTH","DAY","INVOICE","AMOUNT"
16   PRINT "NUMBER","NUMBER","NUMBER","OF SALE"
17   READ L
18   DATA 6
20   FOR C=1 TO L
30   READ M,D,I,A
31   DATA 2,21,27425,71.39
32   DATA 2,24,40711.,205.75
33   DATA 2,25,4577,15.98
34   DATA 2,25,4613,64.75
35   DATA 2,28,4908,67.56
36   DATA 3,12,1290,50.01
37   IF M<1 THEN 80
38   IF M>12 THEN 90
40   LET T=T+A
50   PRINT M,D,I,A
60   NEXT C
70   PRINT T
71   GOTO 999
80   PRINT "MONTH NUMBER < 1"
81   GOTO 999
90   PRINT "MONTH NUMBER >12"
91   GOTO 999
999  END

RUN

MONTH      DAY        INVOICE    AMOUNT
NUMBER     NUMBER     NUMBER     OF SALE
  2          21        27425      71.39
  2          24        40711     205.75
  2          25         4577      15.98
  2          25         4613      64.75
  2          28         4908      67.56
  3          12         1290      50.01
475.44
```

FIGURE 6-7 VISA program with REM and agreements.

```
10    REM THIS PROGRAM READS MONTH, DAY, INVOICE NUMBERS AND THE AMOUNT OF
20    REM THE SALE AND VALIDATES THE MONTH. IT THEN PRINTS THE DATA READ.
30    REM WRITTEN BY EDWARDS AND BROADWELL      JANUARY 1982
31    REM
40    REM AGREEMENTS
50    REM M: MONTH NUMBER
60    REM D: DAY NUMBER
70    REM I: INVOICE NUMBER
80    REM A: AMOUNT OF SALE
90    REM T: TOTAL OF ALL SALES
100   REM C: LOOP COUNTER
101   REM L: NUMBER OF LOOP CYCLES
102   REM
105   REM INITIALIZATION MODULE
106   REM INITIALIZE VARIABLES, PRINT HEADINGS, READ NUMBER OF DATA ITEMS
107   REM
108   REM
110   LET T=0
120   PRINT "MONTH","DAY","INVOICE","AMOUNT"
130   PRINT "NUMBER","NUMBER","NUMBER","OF SALE"
140   READ L
150   DATA 6
160   REM
161   REM MAIN PROCESSING MODULE
162   REM SET UP LOOP, READ THE DATA, VALIDATE THE MONTH, AND PRINT
163   REM DATA READ IF VALID.
170   FOR C=1 TO L
180   READ M,D,I,A
190   DATA 2,21,27425,71.39
200   DATA 2,24,40711.,205.75
210   DATA 2,25,4577,15.98
220   DATA 2,25,4613,64.75
230   DATA 2,28,4908,67.56
240   DATA 3,12,1290,50.01
241   REM TEST MONTH TO BE IN RANGE 1 THRU 12
250   IF M<1 THEN 330
260   IF M>12 THEN 350
261   REM UPDATE TOTALS AND PRINT THE DATA
270   LET T=T+A
280   PRINT M,D,I,A
290   NEXT C
300   PRINT T
310   GOTO 370
320   REM PRINT ERROR MESSAGES FOR INVALID MONTHS
```

FIGURE 6-8   VISA program with REM and module names.

```
330    PRINT "MONTH NUMBER < 1"
340    GOTO 370
350    PRINT "MONTH NUMBER >12"
360    GOTO 370
361    REM
362    REM CLOSING MODULE
363    REM
370    END
```

FIGURE 6-8 *Continued*

```
180    READ M,D,I,A,K$
190    DATA 2,21,27425,71.39,"C"
200    DATA 2,24,40711.,205.75,"C"
210    DATA 2,25,4577,15.98,"P"
220    DATA 2,25,4613,64.75,"P"
230    DATA 2,28,4908,67.56,"C"
240    DATA 3,12,1290,50.01,"P"
```

FIGURE 6-9 READ and DATA with kind of transaction.

```
10     REM THIS PROGRAM READS MONTH, DAY, INVOICE NUMBERS AND THE AMOUNT OF
20     REM THE SALE AND VALIDATES THE MONTH. IT THEN PRINTS THE DATA READ.
30     REM WRITTEN BY EDWARDS AND BROADWELL        JANUARY 1982
31     REM
40     REM AGREEMENTS
41     REM K$: KIND OF TRANSACTION P=PURCHASE; C=CHARGE
50     REM M: MONTH NUMBER
60     REM D: DAY NUMBER
70     REM I: INVOICE NUMBER
80     REM A: AMOUNT OF SALE
90     REM T: TOTAL OF ALL SALES
100    REM C: LOOP COUNTER
101    REM --------------------------------------------------------------------------------
105    REM INITIALIZATION MODULE
106    REM --------------------------------------------------------------------------------
107    REM PRINT HEADINGS, INITIALIZE TOTALS, READ NUMBER OF LOOP CYCLES
108    REM
110    LET T=0
120    PRINT "MONTH","DAY","INVOICE","CHARGE","PAYMENT"
130    PRINT "NUMBER","NUMBER","NUMBER","AMOUNT","AMOUNT"
140    READ L
150    DATA 6
```

FIGURE 6-10 VISA program with strings.

```
160    REM----------------------------------------------------------------
161    REM MAIN PROCESSING MODULE
162    REM----------------------------------------------------------------
163    REM READ THE DATA, VALIDATE IT, AND PRINT
170    FOR C=1 TO L
180    READ M,D,I,A,K$
190    DATA 2,21,27425,71.39,"C"
200    DATA 2,24,40711.,205.75,"C"
210    DATA 2,25,4577,15.98,"P"
220    DATA 2,25,4613,64.75,"P"
230    DATA 2,28,4908,67.56,"C"
240    DATA 3,12,1290,50.01,"P"
241    REM TEST MONTH TO BE IN RANGE 1 THRU 12
250    IF M<1 THEN 330
260    IF M>12 THEN 350
261    REM TEST KIND OF TRANSACTION, UPDATE TOTALS, PRINT THE DATA
263    IF K$="P" THEN 285
270    LET T=T+A
280    PRINT M,D,I,A
281    GOTO 290
285    LET T=T-A
286    PRINT M,D,I,TAB(60);A
290    NEXT C
300    PRINT T
310    GOTO 370
320    REM PRINT ERROR MESSAGES FOR INVALID MONTHS
330    PRINT "MONTH NUMBER <1"
340    GOTO 370
350    PRINT "MONTH NUMBER >12"
360    GOTO 370
361    REM----------------------------------------------------------------
362    REM CLOSING MODULE
363    REM----------------------------------------------------------------
370    END
RUN
```

MONTH NUMBER	DAY NUMBER	INVOICE NUMBER	CHARGE AMOUNT	PAYMENT AMOUNT
2	21	27425	71.39	
2	24	40711.	205.75	
2	25	4577		15.98
2	25	4613		64.75
2	28	4908	67.56	
3	12	1290		50.01

213.96

FIGURE 6–10 *Continued*

```
10    REM A PROGRAM TO GRAPH THE POPULATION IN THE UNITED STATES
20    REM FOR CENSUS YEARS 1890 TO 1970
30    REM
40    REM WRITTEN BY EDWARDS AND BROADWELL,     JANUARY 1982
50    REM
60    REM AGREEMENTS:
70    REM P:POPULATION OF U.S. (IN MILLIONS)
80    REM L: LOCATION OF DOT FOR GRAPHING PURPOSES
90    REM Y: YEAR OF CENSUS AND LOOP COUNTER
100   REM
110   REM READ THE POPULATION AND PRINT THE GRAPH (SCALED TO ¼)
120   REM
130   FOR Y=1890 to 1970 STEP 10
140   READ P
150   DATA 67.948,75.995,91.992,105.711,122.755
160   DATA 131.669,150.697,178.464,199.208
170   PRINT TAB(P/4);"*"
180   NEXT Y
190   END

RUN

              *
               *
                *
                 *
                  *
                   *
                     *
                       *
                        *
```

FIGURE 6–11   Population in U.S. bar graph using TAB.

FIGURE 6–12	Table of months and days.				
Month Name	Month Number	Number of Days	Month Name	Month Number	Number of Days
January	1	31	July	7	31
February	2	28	August	8	31
March	3	31	September	9	30
April	4	30	October	10	31
May	5	31	November	11	30
June	6	30	December	12	31

Ignoring the fact that some years are leap years and others are not, we need to test each month number and then the number of days in that month to validate our incoming data correctly. The BASIC program to validate requires many IF statements and many GO TO statements to catch all the possible errors.

You are probably thinking that there must be an easier way, and you are right. Many versions of BASIC allow us to write IF statements using the **Boolean operators** shown in Figure 6–13. As you can see, these Boolean operators can combine many individual tests into one, and our long program of Figure 6–14 can be considerably shortened into Figure 6–15. We can write an even shorter version of Figure 6–15 if we group all the months with 31 days together in one IF and all the months with 30 days in another IF, and test for February by itself (Figure 6–16).

While the order of the IF statements is technically not important, the logic is better written with the test for February last, since only one month in twelve has 28 days, while seven in twelve have 31 days and six in twelve have 30 days. Thus, we have a probability of 7/12 of completing the validation by the first IF and a probability of 11/12 of completing the validation within two IF statements. The idea of preplanning the order of steps in a program to achieve the best possible efficiency by the computer is often overlooked by programmers. An efficient program will execute more quickly than an inefficient one, thereby saving computer time and, if computer costs are based on how much computer time is used, the efficient program will cost less to run.

ARRAYS AND DIM

Another concept that allows for more concise programs is the **array**. An array is a series of numeric values that are collectively viewed and individually accessed. An array allows a programmer to access many different counters, totalers, or reference data "automatically." An array uses two variables together to access the particular item.

FIGURE 6–13 Boolean operators in BASIC.

Boolean Operator	Example of Use
AND	IF M=12 AND D>31 THEN 80
OR	IF M<1 OR M>12 THEN 40
NOT	IF NOT M<1 THEN 55

The concept of the array surrounds us in everyday life. Your class, for instance, may meet in some room numbered W1. You would interpret this to mean building W, room 1. If building W is Wheeler Hall, you would go to that building and then to its

```
180   READ M,D,I,A,K$
190   DATA 2,21,27425,71.39,"C"
200   DATA 2,24,40711.,205.75,"C"
210   DATA 2,25,4577,15.98,"P"
220   DATA 2,25,4613,64.75,"P"
230   DATA 2,28,4908,67.56,"C"
240   DATA 3,12,1290,50.01,"P"
250   IF M=1 THEN 390
260   IF M=2 THEN 410
270   IF M=3 THEN 390
280   IF M=4 THEN 430
290   IF M=5 THEN 390
300   IF M=6 THEN 430
310   IF M=7 THEN 390
320   IF M=8 THEN 390
330   IF M=9 THEN 430
340   IF M=10 THEN 390
350   IF M=11 THEN 430
360   IF M=12 THEN 390
370   PRINT "INVALID MONTH NUMBER"
380   GOTO 700
390   IF D <= 31 THEN 600
400   GOTO 440
410   IF D <= 28 THEN 600
420   GOTO 440
430   IF D <= 30 THEN 600
440   PRINT "INVALID DAY NUMBER"
450   GOTO 700
```

FIGURE 6–14 Partial BASIC program to validate months and days.

```
180    READ M,D,I,A,K$
190    DATA 2,21,27425,71.39,"C"
200    DATA 2,24,40711.,205.75,"C"
210    DATA 2,25,4577,15.98,"P"
220    DATA 2,25,4613,64.75,"P"
230    DATA 2,28,4908,67.56,"C"
240    DATA 3,12,1290,50.01,"P"
250    IF M=1 AND D <= 31 THEN 700
260    IF M=2 AND D <= 28 THEN 700
270    IF M=3 AND D <= 31 THEN 700
280    IF M=4 AND D <= 30 THEN 700
290    IF M=5 AND D <= 31 THEN 700
300    IF M=6 AND D <= 30 THEN 700
310    IF M=7 AND D <= 31 THEN 700
320    IF M=8 AND D <= 31 THEN 700
330    IF M=9 AND D <= 30 THEN 700
340    IF M=10 AND D <= 31 THEN 700
350    IF M=11 AND D <= 30 THEN 700
360    IF M=12 AND D <= 31 THEN 700
370    PRINT "INVALID DATE"
```

FIGURE 6–15 Partial validation program using Boolean operators.

room 1. In programming, the notation used is a little different. Rather than writing the room as W1, it would be written as W(1) and read as "W SUB 1." The room number is placed in parentheses and is usually called the **index** or **subscript**; the name W associated with W(1) is called the "array name."

In general, the notation used in arrays is:

$$W(R)$$

name of array ⟶ ⟵ position in the array of a particular value

Thus, a building that has seven rooms numbered 1 through 7 consecutively might be pictured as in Figure 6–17.

The value inside the W(R) might be the number of people attending a class at a given time. It is important to note that our problem does not have a W(0) or W(8). Also, R(W) is not the same as W(R); the array name is always first, the index second and in parentheses.

One of the primary advantages to array notation is that the room number—the index—is a variable. When the index is changed, a different position is automatically referenced. This concept can be used to advantage in our validating program by having an array called N of the number of days in each month (see Figure 6–18). Thus, the number of days in August, month 8, is found in N(8) and is 31.

Before an array can be used, BASIC may require a special statement, **DIM** (short for "dimension"), which declares the number of elements or locations that the array will use. The N array has 12 elements—thus, the DIM statement would read: 1 DIM N(12). Since the DIM statement must be placed before the first usage of an array, it is good practice to place it at the beginning of your program.

```
180    READ M,D,I,A,K$
190    DATA 2,21,27425,71.39,"C"
200    DATA 2,24,40711.,205.75,"C"
210    DATA 2,25,4577,15.98,"P"
220    DATA 2,25,4613,64.75,"P"
230    DATA 2,28,4908,67.56,"C"
240    DATA 3,12,1290,50.01,"P"
250    IF (M=1 OR M=3 OR M=5 OR M=7 OR M=8 OR M=10 OR M=12) AND D <= 31 THEN 700
260    IF (M=4 OR M=6 OR M=9 OR M=11) AND D <= 30 THEN 700
270    IF M=2 AND D <= 28 THEN 700
280    PRINT "INVALID DATE"
```

FIGURE 6–16 Partial validation program with complex IF statements.

CHAPTER 6: MORE BASIC

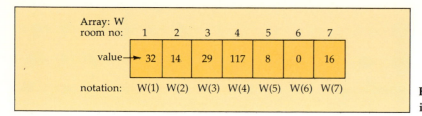

FIGURE 6–17 Array of rooms in Wheeler Hall.

If two or more arrays are required in a program, you can use a single DIM statement, such as:

1   DIM A(16),B(47)

or with two DIM statements, such as:

1   DIM A(16)
2   DIM B(47)

A frequent mistake programmers make is to DIM the index of an array rather than the array itself. Thus, for the array N, which utilizes the index W, you should write: 1 DIM N(12) and *not*: 1 DIM W(12). Another common error is to write: 1 DIM N(W). Remember that you are reserving space and that most versions of BASIC require a number rather than a variable inside the parentheses in a DIM.

After an array has been dimensioned, it must have the various constants inserted into the proper locations. This process is called **initializing** and is mandatory in programs that use arrays. Two different methods of initializing the N array are shown in Figure 6–19. Method **a** requires more BASIC commands than method **b**, but both result in the same values for the array N.

Using the N array in our validation program of Figure 6–16, enables us to replace the three IF statements with a single IF statement (line 250), using the value of *M* as the index of the N array (see Figure 6–20). The use of the array has caused this part of our validation program to shrink from 20 (line numbers 180–370) statements to 9 (line numbers 180–260). Thus, array-oriented programs like this allow the programmer to write fewer BASIC instructions; they also save memory space within the computer and run faster once they are written since fewer commands need to be executed. The two primary disadvantages of arrays are the extra initialization steps that are required (line numbers 132–135 in Figure 6–20) and the mathematical notation that arrays require, which tends to mystify the novice programmer.

IMAGE

The partial validation program with the N array, TAB, charges, payments, and REMarks, along with the RUN, is shown in Figure 6–20. As you can see, the invalid months and days are detected and printed, payments and charges are printed in different columns, and the customer's balance is adjusted correctly.

The only problem that remains is that the numbers and their decimal points are not vertically aligned with the other values of the same column. To overcome this final problem, BASIC has a statement called **IMAGE** to dress up printed output.

To use an IMAGE statement, you first modify the PRINT statement of line 286, as follows

286   PRINT USING 287; M,D,I,A,T

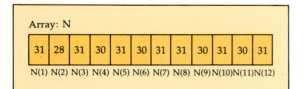

FIGURE 6–18 Number-of-days-in-the-month array.

```
10    DIM N(12)              10    DIM N(12)
20    LET N(1)=31            20    FOR M=1 TO 12
30    LET N(2)=28            30    READ N(M)
40    LET N(3)=31            40    DATA 31,28,31,30,31,30,31,31,30,31,30,31
50    LET N(4)=30            50    NEXT M
60    LET N(5)=31
70    LET N(6)=30
80    LET N(7)=31
90    LET N(8)=31
100   LET N(9)=30
110   LET N(12)=31
120   LET N(11)=30
130   LET N(12)=31

        a                            b
```

FIGURE 6–19 Initializing an array.

The "USING 287" causes BASIC to use the IMAGE statement with line number 287 to tell the computer how to print the values of *M,D,I,A,* and *T*. The IMAGE statement describes from left to right where the values of the variables should be printed and how many decimal digits are to be printed for each variable. If our IMAGE statement looked like this:

```
10    REM THIS PROGRAM READS MONTH, DAY, INVOICE NUMBERS AND THE AMOUNT OF
20    REM THE SALE AND VALIDATES THE MONTH. IT THEN PRINTS THE DATA READ.
21    REM TAB STATEMENTS ARE USED TO DRESS UP THE OUTPUT
30    REM WRITTEN BY EDWARDS AND BROADWELL        JANUARY 1982
31    REM
40    REM AGREEMENTS
41    REM K$: KIND OF TRANSACTION    P=PURCHASE, C=CHARGE
50    REM M: MONTH NUMBER
60    REM D: DAY NUMBER
70    REM I: INVOICE NUMBER
80    REM A: AMOUNT OF SALE
90    REM T: TOTAL OF ALL SALES
100   REM C: LOOP COUNTER
101   REM N: AN ARRAY OF 12 ELEMENTS THAT HOLDS THE DAYS IN A MONTH
102   REM
105   REM INITIALIZATION MODULE
106   REM INITIALIZE VARIABLES, PRINT HEADINGS, READ NUMBER OF DATA ITEMS
```

FIGURE 6–20 Validation program with an array.

```
107  REM
108  REM
109  DIM N(12)
110  LET T=0
120  PRINT "DATE","INVOICE","CHARGE","PAYMENT","BALANCE"
130  PRINT "MO/DAY","NUMBER","AMOUNT","AMOUNT"
132  FOR M=1 TO 12
133  READ N(M)
134  DATA 31,28,31,30,31,30,31,31,30,31,30,31
135  NEXT M
140  READ L
150  DATA 6
160  REM
161  REM MAIN PROCESSING MODULE
162  REM SET UP LOOP, READ THE DATA, VAIDATE THE MONTH, AND PRINT
163  REM DATA READ IF VALID.
170  FOR C=1 TO L
180  READ M,D,I,A,K$
190  DATA 2,21,27425,71.39,"C"
200  DATA 2,24,40711.,205.75,"C"
210  DATA 2,25,4577,15.98,"P"
220  DATA 2,25,4613,64.75,"P"
230  DATA 2,28,4908,67.56,"C"
240  DATA 3,12,1290,50.01,"P"
241  REM TEST MONTH TO BE IN RANGE 1 THRU 12
250  IF M>=1 and M<=12 AND D<=N(M) THEN 263
260  GOTO 330
261  REM TEST KIND OF TRANSACTION, UPDATE TOTALS, PRINT THE DATA
263  IF K$="P" THEN 285
270  LET T=T+A
280  PRINT M;"/";D,I,TAB(30);A;TAB(60);T
282  GOTO 290
285  LET T=T-A
286  PRINT M;"/";D,I;TAB(45);A,T
290  NEXT C
300  PRINT T
310  GOTO 370
320  REM PRINT ERROR MESSAGES FOR INVALID MONTHS
330  PRINT "DATE ERROR"
361  REM
362  REM CLOSING MODULE
363  REM
370  END
```

FIGURE 6–20 *Continued*

```
RUN

DATE    INVOICE   CHARGE    PAYMENT
MO/DAY  NUMBER    AMOUNT    AMOUNT    BALANCE
2  / 21  27425    71.39               71.39
   / 24  40711.   205.75              277.14
2  / 25  4577               15.98     261.16
2  / 25  4613               64.75     196.41
2  / 28  4908     67.56               263.97
3  / 12  1290               50.01     213.96
213.96
```

FIGURE 6–20 *Continued*

287   IMAGE 2X,DD,"/",DD,8X,DDDDDDD,
      23,DDDDD.DD,8X,DDDDD.DD

it would mean:

2X	Skip the first two spaces on this line.
DD	Print a two-digit decimal number; since M is the first variable, its value gets printed here.
"/"	Print a slash.
DD	Print a two-digit decimal number; the number printed would be the value of D.
8X	Skip the next eight spaces on this line.
DDDDDDD	Print a right-justified seven-digit number, the value of I.
23X	Skip the next twenty-three spaces.
DDDDD.DD	Print the value of A with two digits to the right of the decimal point and a maximum of five digits to the left of the decimal point.
8X	Skip the next eight spaces.
DDDDD.DD	Print the value of B in the same form as the value of A was printed.

The IMAGE statement could also have been written as:

287   IMAGE 2X,2D,"/",2D,8X,7D,8X,5D.DD,22X,5D.DD

In this form the 7D is the same as writing DDDDDDD, and 5D.DD is the same as DDDDD.DD. The seven and the five in front of the D's are like the numbers in the front of the X's and provide a shorthand method of writing multiple D and X fields. These numbers are called replicators.

In Figure 6–21 is the completed VISA statement printing program with the data validating logic and IMAGE statements. The RUN of the program is also shown.

CHAPTER 6: MORE BASIC

```
10   REM THIS PROGRAM READS MONTH, DAY, INVOICE NUMBERS AND THE AMOUNT OF
20   REM THE SALE AND VALIDATES THE MONTH. IT THEN PRINTS THE DATA READ.
21   REM IMAGE STATEMENTS ARE USED TO DRESS UP THE OUTPUT
30   REM WRITTEN BY EDWARDS AND BROADWELL       JANUARY 1982
31   REM
40   REM AGREEMENTS
41   REM K$: KIND OF TRANSACTION      P=PURCHASE; C=CHARGE
50   REM M: MONTH NUMBER
60   REM D: DAY NUMBER
70   REM I: INVOICE NUMBER
80   REM A: AMOUNT OF SALE
90   REM T:TOTAL OF ALL SALES
100  REM C: LOOP COUNTER
101  REM N: AN ARRAY OF 12 ELEMENTS THAT HOLDS THE DAYS IN A MONTH
102  REM
105  REM INITIALIZATION MODULE
106  REM INITIALIZE VARIABLES, PRINT HEADINGS, READ NUMBER OF DATA ITEMS
107  REM
108  REM
109  DIM N[12]
110  LET T=0
120  PRINT "DATE","INVOICE","CHARGE","PAYMENT","BALANCE"
130  PRINT "MO/DAY","NUMBER","AMOUNT","AMOUNT"
132  FOR M=1 TO 12
133  READ N(M)
134  DATA 31,28,31,30,31,30,31,31,30,31,30,31
135  NEXT M
140  READ L
150  DATA 6
160  REM
161  REM MAIN PROCESSING MODULE
162  REM SET UP LOOP, READ THE DATA, VALIDATE THE MONTH, AND PRINT
163  REM DATA READ IF VALID.
170  FOR C=1 TO L
180  READ M,D,I,A,K$
190  DATA 2,21,27425,71.39,"C"
200  DATA 2,24,40711.,205.75,"C"
```

FIGURE 6–21 Completed data validation program with IMAGE statement.

```
210   DATA 2,25,4577,15.98,"P"
220   DATA 2,25,4613,64.75,"P"
230   DATA 2,28,4908,67.56,"C"
240   DATA 2,12,1290,50.01,"P"
241   REM TEST MONTH TO BE IN RANGE 1 THRU 12
250   IF M >= 1 AND M <= 12 AND D <= N[M] THEN 263
260   GOTO 330
261   REM TEST KIND OF TRANSACTION, UPDATE TOTALS, PRINT THE DATA
263   IF K$="P" THEN 285
270   LET T=T+A
280   PRINT USING 281;M,D,I,A,T
281   IMAGE 2X,DD,"/",DD,8X,DDDDDDD,8X,DDDDD.DD,23X,DDDDD.DD
282   GOTO 290
285   LET T=T-A
286   PRINT   USING 287;M,D,I,A,T
287   IMAGE 2X,DD,"/",DD,8X,DDDDDDD,23X,DDDDD.DD,8X,DDDDD.DD
290   NEXT C
300   PRINT T
310   GOTO 370
320   REM PRINT ERROR MESSAGES FOR INVALID MONTHS
330   PRINT "DATE ERROR"
361   REM
362   REM CLOSING MODULE
363   REM
370   END

RUN

DATE     INVOICE   CHARGE    PAYMENT
MO/DAY   NUMBER    AMOUNT    AMOUNT    BALANCE
 2/21    27425      71.39               71.39
 2/24    40711     205.75              277.14
 2/25     4577               15.98     261.16
 2/25     4613               64.75     196.41
 2/28     4908      67.56              263.97
 3/12     1290               50.01     213.96
213.96
```

FIGURE 6-21 *Continued*

SOLVED EXERCISES

The two exercises that follow show some additional features of BASIC. The first is an example of an array that is used to count the number of times a certain event takes place. The second uses nested loops and an END-OF-DATA sentinel. For both exercises there are discussions of what is to be done, a flowchart, the BASIC program for the exercise, and the RUN of the program.

"You can put away your translating calculator now. I'm speaking to you in English."

Counting Using an Array

Alphanumeric string processing is not limited to captions. Many items of data are coded using alphabetic characters, and programs must process the data. A fuel wholesaler, for instance, might record sales by using the following code for fuel sales (see Figure 6–22).

A flowchart to input a product code, give the amount of sale ($), and print gross sales by product code is given in Figure 6–23. Since the number of

FIGURE 6–22	Coding of data using strings.
Product Code	Interpretation
R	Regular gasoline
E	Ethyl gasoline
U	Unleaded gasoline
D	Diesel
K	Kerosene

receipts will be unknown (unless they are counted ahead of time), the last sale amount will be followed by a zero. Figure 6–24 gives the BASIC program and the RUN.

Calculating and Totaling Commissions

In the flowcharting examples in Chapter 4, a flowchart was developed to depict the logic of calculating and totaling commissions for the sales made by various individuals. This flowchart is shown in Figure 6–25, with line numbers added. The BASIC program is given in Figure 6–26, and the RUN is given in Figure 6–27. This program is considered by professional programmers to be one of the classic programs, just as some books (*Moby Dick, Tale of Two Cities, Tom Sawyer*) are considered classic novels. The technical name for this classic program type is the **control break.** The control break program accumulates totals for one group of transactions, and when that group is completed, prints the group's total. When all the groups and their respective totals have been printed, a grand total of all the transaction amounts of all the groups is printed.

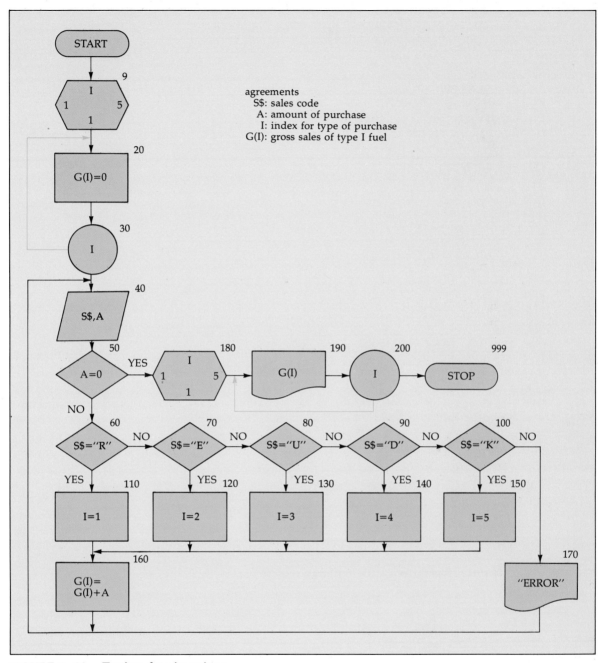

FIGURE 6–23 Testing data in strings.

```
1    REM PROGRAM FOR FIGURE 6-23 THAT TESTS DATA IN A STRING
2    REM WRITTEN BY EDWARDS AND BROADWELL.        JANUARY 1982
3    REM
4    REM AGREEMENTS
5    REM S$: SALES CODE
6    REM A: AMOUNT OF PURCHASE
7    REM I: INDEX FOR TYPE OF PURCHASE
8    REM G: AN ARRAY THAT TOTALS SALES BY FUEL TYPE
9    REM
10   REM OPENING MODULE
11   REM
12   REM DIMENSIONING AND INITIALIZATION
13   REM
18   DIM G(5)
19   FOR I=1 TO 5
20   LET G(1)=0
30   NEXT I
31   REM
32   REM PROCESSING MODULE
33   REM
34   REM INPUT THE DATA, VALIDATE IT, SET THE INDEX OF THE ARRAY,
35   REM
40   INPUT S$,A
50   IF A=0 THEN 180
60   IF S$="R" THEN 110
70   IF S$="E" THEN 120
80   IF S$="U" THEN 130
90   IF S$="D" THEN 140
100  IF S$="K" THEN 150
101  GOTO 170
110  LET I=1
111  GOTO 160
120  LET I=2
121  GOTO 160
```

FIGURE 6-24 BASIC program and RUN for array counting.

```
130    LET I=3
131    GOTO 160
140    LET I=4
141    GOTO 160
150    LET I=5
160    LET G(1)=G(I)+A
161    GOTO 40
170    PRINT "ERROR IN PRODUCT CODE"
171    GOTO 40
172    REM
173    REM CLOSING MODULE
174    REM
175    REM PRINT THE ARRAY THAT HOLDS THE TOTALS
176    REM
180    FOR I=1 TO 5
190    PRINT G(I)
200    NEXT I
999    END
RUN

?"A",34.56
ERROR IN PRODUCT CODE
?"R",45.00
?"E",12.50
?"E",22.34
?"K",5.99
?"U",12.90
?"A",0
   45
   34.84
   12.9
   0
   5.99
```

FIGURE 6–24 *Continued*

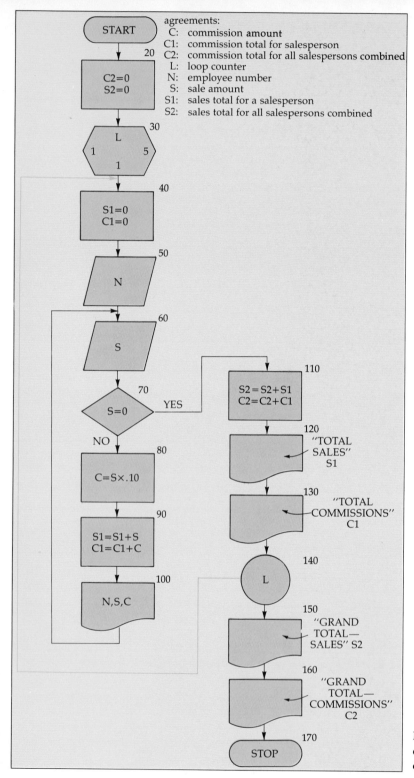

FIGURE 6-25 Flowchart for calculating and totaling sales commissions.

```
1     REM PROGRAM THAT USES A CONTROL BREAK
2     REM WRITTEN BY EDWARDS AND BROADWELL.      JANUARY 1982.
3     REM
4     REM AGREEMENTS
5     REM C: COMMISSION AMOUNT
6     REM C1: COMMISSION TOTAL FOR A SALESPERSON
7     REM C2: COMMISSION TOTAL FOR ALL SALESPERSONS COMBINED
8     REM L: LOOP COUNTER
9     REM N: EMPLOYEE NUMBER
10    REM S1: SALES TOTAL FOR A SALESPERSON
11    REM S2: SALES TOTAL FOR ALL SALESPERSONS COMBINED
12    REM
13    REM OPENING MODULE
14    REM
15    REM INITIALIZE TOTALS
16    REM
20    LET C2=0
21    LET S2=0
22    REM
23    REM PROCESSING MODULE
24    REM
30    FOR L=1 TO 5
31    PRINT "SALESPERSON","AMOUNT OF SALE","COMMISSIONS"
32    PRINT "NUMBER",TAB(30);"EARNED"
40    LET S1=0
41    LET C1=0
50    READ N
60    READ S
61    DATA 1,110,400,285,315,140,0
62    DATA 2,200,350,175,221,300,254,0
63    DATA 3,175,50,280,445,0
64    DATA 4,375,150,410,527,229,270,139,0
65    DATA 5,410,343,162,520,105,310,0
66    REM TEST FOR END OF DATA SENTINEL
70    IF S=0 THEN 110
80    LET C=S*.1
90    LET S1=S1+S
91    LET C1=C1+C
100   PRINT N,S,C
101   GOTO 60
109   REM UPDATE GRAND TOTALS AND PRINT THE TOTALS FOR THIS SALESPERSON
110   LET S2=S2+S1
111   LET C2=C2+C1
112   PRINT
```

FIGURE 6-26   BASIC program for totaling commissions.

```
120    PRINT "TOTAL SALES";S1
130    PRINT "TOTAL COMMISSIONS";C1
135    PRINT
136    PRINT
140    NEXT L
145    REM
146    REM CLOSING MODULE
147    REM
148    REM PRINT THE GRAND TOTALS
149    PRINT
150    PRINT "GRAND TOTAL OF SALES";S2
160    PRINT "GRAND TOTAL OF COMMISSIONS";C2
170    END
```

FIGURE 6–26 *Continued*

SALESPERSON NUMBER	AMOUNT OF SALE	COMMISSIONS EARNED
1	110	11
1	400	40
1	285	28.5
1	315	31.5
1	140	14

TOTAL SALES 1250
TOTAL COMMISSIONS 125

SALESPERSON NUMBER	AMOUNT OF SALE	COMMISSIONS EARNED
2	200	20
2	350	35
2	175	17.5
2	221	22.1
2	300	30
2	254	25.4

TOTAL SALES 1500
TOTAL COMMISSIONS 150

SALESPERSON NUMBER	AMOUNT OF SALE	COMMISSIONS EARNED
3	175	17.5
3	50	5
3	280	28
3	445	44.5

TOTAL SALES 950
TOTAL COMMISSIONS 95

SALESPERSON NUMBER	AMOUNT OF SALE	COMMISSIONS EARNED
4	375	37.5
4	150	15
4	410	41
4	527	52.7
4	229	22.9
4	270	27
4	139	13.9

TOTAL SALES 2100
TOTAL COMMISSIONS 210

FIGURE 6–27 RUN for totaling commissions.

SALESPERSON NUMBER	AMOUNT OF SALE	COMMISSIONS EARNED
5	410	41
5	343	34.3
5	162	16.2
5	520	52
5	105	10.5
5	310	31

TOTAL SALES 1850
TOTAL COMMISSIONS 185

GRAND TOTAL OF SALES 7650
GRAND TOTAL OF COMMISSIONS 765

FIGURE 6–27   *Continued*

4. DIM—Reserves space in memory for an array.
5. IMAGE—Describes the format or layout of a line to be printed.
6. PRINT USING—Used in conjunction with IMAGE to indicate which IMAGE is to be used.

SUMMARY

In this chapter the techniques of structured programs (simple sequence, selection, and repetition), arrays, and strings have been presented. These techniques can help the programmer write more succinct and efficient programs.

Arrays provide for multiple totals, counters, and references. This programming technique is one of the most powerful available to programmers.

Strings involve nonnumerical information. While their use may appear minimal to the novice programmer, many of the data that are captured or wanted by businesses fall into this category, and their accurate processing is just as important as number manipulation.

The new BASIC statements or constructs introduced in this chapter are:

1. REM—Provides a way for the programmer to put comments or remarks in the source program.
2. TAB—Overrides the comma and semicolon spacing in a PRINT statement and allows the quantity or captions to be printed anyplace on a line.
3. AND, OR, NOT—Boolean operators used in an IF statement to allow for the writing of complex decisional logic.

TERMS

The following words or terms have been presented in this chapter.

Structured program	Boolean operator
Simple sequence	Array
Selection	Index
Repetition	Subscript
Module	DIM
Structure chart	Initializing
Program documentation	IMAGE
String	Control break
TAB	

EXERCISES

The exercises that follow are grouped by level of difficulty. Problems in the A series are the easiest; B series problems are moderately hard; and C series problems are the most difficult.

A–1   Write a DIM statement that reserves 84 positions for an array named B.

A–2   Which of the following are valid string variables?

    a. A1$ d. F$ g. Q2$
    b. A$ e. $B   h. R$
    c. BC$ f. 1$ i. "CAB"

A–3   Correct each of the following if errors exist:

    a. PRINT B$(7,2)
    b. LET R$=T$(1)
    c. READ S$
    d. IF A$=5 THEN 142
    e. LET X$=T$="57"
    f. LET B$="OK"

THE ORIGINS OF FORTRAN

During the summer of 1954, under the sponsorship of IBM Corporation, a group of programming specialists were charged with developing a high-speed automatic programming system. The group was led by J. W. Backus and Irving Ziller. By 1957 they had developed a system that allowed rapid programming in a mathematical notation. In an early test of the programming language, a group of 47 FORTRAN statements were written in four hours and compiled to almost 1,000 machine language commands.

In spite of the advantages of FORTRAN over the more tedious assembly languages that were in use, many programmers rejected its use. Nevertheless, at Convair, a division of General Dynamics Corporation, the pro-FORTRAN programmers were encouraged to wear "FORTRAN" T-shirts to promote its acceptance.*

The translator itself normally resides on a magnetic disk and is called into the memory of the computer by special commands that precede the source program. The object program, once built by the translator, can be recalled immediately for execution if the data for the program are available, or the object program can wait until such time as the computer user decides to execute the program. A translator that provides immediate execution of the program is sometimes called a load-and-go translator.

There is normally one translator for each language. Compilers and interpreters themselves are very long, complex programs that usually are provided by the manufacturer of the computer, although in recent years some translators have been developed by nonmanufacturers. Primary among these types of translators are the WATFOR, WATFIV, and WATBOL compilers written at the University of Waterloo in Ontario, Canada.

Technically, a compiler and an interpreter are different things. A compiler translates the entire program into machine language before the program is executed. An interpreter, on the other hand, translates each instruction into machine language just before that statement is executed. A compiler then is better used on a program that is executed many times, since the translated machine language can be executed many times without recompiling. An interpreter is best used for a program that is executed only a few times, since only those instructions executed are translated; the others are not.

---

* Richard A. McLaughlin, "The IBM 704: 36 Bit Floating Point Money Maker," *Datamation*, August 1975, p. 48.

A–4 Enter the following program. What does it do?

```
10  FOR N=1 TO 20
20  PRINT TAB(N);"*"
30  NEXT N
40  END
```

A–5 Which of the following are valid uses of Boolean operators?

   a. IF M=10 AND OR M=11 THEN 702
   b. IF J< 14 OR J>14 THEN 866
   c. IF K NOT=12 THEN 607
   d. IF B AND A=15 THEN 317

B–1 Does your version of BASIC require that you use quotation marks when an INPUT is used?

B–2 What is the maximum length of a string in your version of BASIC?

B–3 What does the following program do?

```
10  FOR N=1 TO 20
20  PRINT TAB(N);"*";
30  NEXT N
40  END
```

B–4 Suppose there is an array P that has been dimensioned to 100 places. Which of the following are valid?

   a. 5   LET P(101)=17
   b. 62 PRINT P(0)
   c. 72 LET I=6
      73 PRINT P(3*I+2)
   d. 16 IF P(47)< 470 THEN 822

B–5 Modify line 100 in Figure 6–26 to use an IMAGE statement to print N, S, C in positions 1–10, 21–26, and 37–45, with zero, two, and two decimal places, respectively.

C–1 Determine if your version of BASIC will allow the following:

```
5   M=13
10  DIM J(M)
```

If it does, what does this imply?

C–2 What would happen to the program in Figure 6–24 if S$ is "L"?

C–3 Modify the IMAGE statements in Figure 6–21 to print $ before each amount and total field.

C–4 Find a copy of a program without REMs in it. Try and determine what each variable does, what the program does, and what the major logic portions in the program are.

COMPUTER NEWS

APPLICATION
System provides useful sales data fast

With the help of an IBM 3031 Processor and some field-developed programs called Inforem, County Seat Stores, Inc. has become, in less than eight years, one of the top ten chains in the country, with 237 stores. "The IBM equipment has been a factor in CSS's growth," says Lee Roberts, manager of data center operations. "It gives us an edge over our competitors without it. We are more efficient, and more profitable." In short, the 3031 Processor gathers and assimilates sales information from the stores, then Inforem (inventory forecasting and replenishment modules) is used to help resupply the stores with a diverse and complete line of the sold items. The IBM 3031 was purchased three years ago for $1.2 million. Inforem costs $18,000.

County Seat Stores, Inc. is a wholly owned subsidiary of Super Valu Stores, Inc. (Hopkins, MN). The stores, located in large shopping centers throughout the Midwest and South, specialize in mens' and boys' jeans. According to Max Harris, senior vice president, "We started when jeans were becoming popular, and we filled the geographical gaps in the competition's coverage. But as we continued to grow, these advantages weren't enough. We needed what we have now: timely, custom-tailored information in the hands of a professional staff."

That's provided by the 3031, with the help of some other equipment. Each store has a TRW 2001 electronic point-of-sale terminal and a TRW 2805 data-collection device. Together, they are a $6,000 investment per store. The information is collected each night by the 3031, which is located in Minneapolis, MN, where County Seats is based. The gathered information, which includes unit sales by stockkeeping unit (SKU) number, prices, credits, exchanges, returns, and payroll hours, is then analyzed by the 3031.

REPORTS GIVE VITAL INFO

Over 200 reports can be generated, and they are available to managers, buyers, and distribution personnel via 40 IBM 3279 color video display terminals, which are leased by CSS for $113 a month per terminal.

The information included in the reports is then processed against Inforem modules, which forecasts sales by considering seasonality, trends, lead time, past sales, and many other factors. "We believe we are providing more data in a more usable form, and faster, than anyone else in specialty retailing," says Roberts. Before the 3031 was bought, the reports were produced manually. That was not good, according to Roberts, because "retailing information is only as credible as the time in which it is reported, and the average in-store life cycle of our garments is only 13 weeks."

Generating customized information for each of the County Seat Stores has improved the workers' morale too, a source of satisfaction for Harris. "The result is synergistic," says Harris. "We have a sparking of ideas, an appreciation of the system, and constant contributions to it, too."

ADVANCED BASIC

Preview

Functions
    Library Functions
    User-Defined Functions

Strings

Multidimensional Arrays

File Processing
    Building the Transaction File
    Sorting the Transaction File
    Building a Master File
    Updating the Master File

Solved Exercises
    Simulation of Dice Rolling
    Julian and Gregorian Calendars

Summary

History Capsule: The Julian and Gregorian Calendars

Computer News: The Smash Hit of Software

PREVIEW

Chapters 3, 4, 5, and 6 have given you insight into the rules of analyzing problems, structuring your logic, drawing flowcharts, and writing BASIC programs.

The material in this chapter examines the rules of writing BASIC programs that use functions, involve the various looping structures, and process data using multidimensional arrays; it also describes how to work with more than a single character string and, finally, how to use BASIC to work with data in a file. The simpler BASIC instructions previously covered are greatly enhanced by the new instructions discussed here. The wider variety of problems you will be able to solve will allow you to write much more interesting and useful programs.

FUNCTIONS

Many programs require the computer to make complex mathematical computations. Land surveying programs, for example, often require trigonometry in order to solve for varying distances and angles. To reduce the burden of having to write all these computations in each and every program, most languages use preprogrammed computations. Routines like these are called **functions**.

To have the computer recall and use a function, the program simply cites the name of the function in a statement. For instance, if the square root of a number must be found, the routine **SQR** is used. The programmer gives the function the number whose square root is to be calculated; and the function returns the result. The use of a function is illustrated in the partial flowchart in Figure 7–1. The number to be operated on by the function is called the **argument**. In the case of Figure 7–1, the argument is B and the SQR function calculates the square root of 16. C is then used to retain the square root of B, which is calculated to be 4.

Library Functions

A function that is built into BASIC is called a **library function**. A list of the library functions available in most versions of BASIC is shown in Figure 7–2.

To write the BASIC for Figure 7–1, for example, we would say:

```
110    LET B=16
120    LET C=SQR(B)
130    PRINT C
```

Alternatively, we could write Figure 7–1 in BASIC as

```
110    LET B=16
130    PRINT SQR(B)
```

and we would get the square root of 16.

Besides the square root function, a second widely used function is **INT**. The letters INT stand for integer; they cause BASIC to discard all digits to the right of the decimal point and keep only the portion to the left. As an illustration of how INT may be used, let us reexamine the VISA program of Figure 6–21 (lines 180 and 190). Recall that we read the month and day numbers as two separate values.

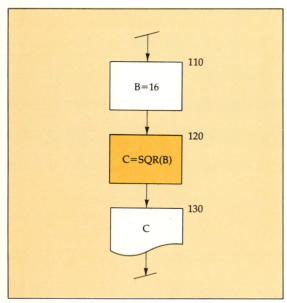

FIGURE 7–1   Functions in a flowchart.

ABS(X)		returns absolute value of X.
ATN(X)		returns arctangent of X.
BRK(X)		X<0 returns Break status.
		X=0 disables Break.
		X>0 enables Break.
CHR$(X)		returns ASCII equivalent of numeric value X.
COS(X)		returns cosine of X.
CTL(X)		controls ASCII file output devices. (See Device Control Codes for values of X.)
EXP(X)		returns value of e^X.
INT(X)		returns integer part of expression X.
ITM(X)		returns number of data items from beginning of current record in file X.
LEN(S)		returns the current length of string S.
LIN(X)		X>0 causes carriage return and X line feeds.
		X=0 causes carriage return only.
		X<0 no return and ABS(X) line feeds.
LOG(X)		returns natural logarithm ($\log_e$ x).
NUM$(S)		returns numeric ASCII equivalent of first character in string S.
POS(S_1,S_2)		returns character position in string S_1 where S_2 (if a substring of S_1) starts; else 0.
REC(X)		returns current record number in file X.
RND(X)		generates pseudo random number based on X.
SGN(X)		returns value indicating sign of X:
		-1 if X<0, 0 if X=0, +1 if x>0.
SIN(X)		returns sine of X.
SPA(X)		spaces X character positions.
SQR(X)		returns square root of X.
SYS(X)		X=0 returns last error number. (0 if none)
		X=1 returns line number of error. (0 if none)
		X=2 returns last file accessed. (-1 if none, 0 if terminal)
		If Break Key disabled, X=3 returns 1 if key was pressed or 0 if not pressed.
		X=4 returns terminal type.
TAB(X)		moves to character position X.
TAN(X)		returns tangent of X.
TIM(X)		X=0 returns current minute.
		X=1 returns hour.
		X=2 returns day.
		X=3 returns year.
		X=4 returns second.
TYP(X)		returns 1 for numeric data; 2 for string data, 3 for end of data in DATA statement (X=0) or end-of-file on file (X=file number). Returns 4 for end of record if X is negative.
UPS$(S)		upshifts lower-case characters in string S.

FIGURE 7-2   BASIC library functions.

Suppose that instead of reading February 21 as 2,21 we wrote the READ statement as:

    30   READ S,I,A,K$
    31   DATA 221,27425,71.39,"C"

where S represents the date the sale was made, 221. We can use INT to calculate M and D as follows:

    35   LET M=INT(S/100)
    36   LET D=S−M*100

When the value of S is 221, the quotient of S divided by 100 is 2.21. The use of INT in line 35 causes the .21 (the part to the right of the decimal point) to be discarded and leaves only the 2 (the part to the left of the decimal point) as the value of M. The LET statement of line 36 first multiplies M by 100 giving 200 and subtracts this product from S, 221, giving 21 as the day number.

Line 36 could also have been written as

    36   LET D=S−INT(S/100)*100

In this form the quotient of S and 100 would have been calculated first (remember that according to the precedence order of arithmetic operators the operations in parentheses are done first), then the INTeger of the quotient, then multiplication by 100, and, finally, the subtraction.

You might be wondering, "Why do all this extra work; why not just use the program as before?" The answer to both of these questions is that on some occasions the data desired are not in the most convenient form, and we have to convert the data to the form required.

User-Defined Functions

The second type of function that can be written in BASIC is the user-defined function. **User-defined functions** are constructed by the programmer to solve a particular problem and are a part of the user's program only. In general, their construction is reserved for programs that require the same calculation to be performed at two (or more) places in a program. In these instances, the calculation only has to be written once, but can be accessed at different points. When the function is required, its name is cited within the BASIC statement (like a library function), causing the computation to be performed; then the normal sequence of the program continues. The actual computational statement of the function is placed at the beginning of the program.

As an example of a user-defined function, let us suppose that we again modify the READ statement in line number 30, as follows:

    30   READ S,P,I,A
    31   DATA 221,224,27425,71.39

where S is the date of the sale and P is the date the sale was posted, or put into, the computer. We now need to extract the month and day number from both S and P. The BASIC program to do this is shown in Figure 7-3, where M1 and D1 are month and day number of the sale and M2 and D2 are the month and day number the sale was posted.

We can define a function to find the month number in statement 5 of Figure 7-4, and another func-

```
30    READ S,P,I,A
31    DATA 221,224,27425,71.39
35    LET M1=INT(S/100)
36    LET D1=S−M1*100
37    LET M2=INT(P/100)
38    LET D2=P−M2*100
```

FIGURE 7–3 Month and day numbers without a function.

tion for day number is in statement 6. The letters *D-E-F* in lines 5 and 6 indicate to BASIC that this line is a user-defined function. The FNM and FND give this user-defined function a name. The *M* and *D* inside parentheses are called "dummy arguments." They do not represent real data but are given to show their relationship in the formula that is to the right of the equal sign.

When statement 5 is executed by line 35, the value of *S*, 221, is substituted for *M* in the formula, and the value of *M1* is calculated as 2. The second time statement 5 is executed, by line 37, the value of *P*, 224, is substituted for *M*, and *M2* is calculated as 2. Similarly, when line 6 is executed by line 36, the value of *S*, 221, is substituted into FND, and *D1* is calculated as 21. Lastly, line 6 is executed a second time by line 38 and 224 is substituted for *D*, giving *D2* as 24.

Some versions of BASIC allow only a single argument, while others allow more. In either case a function is defined by

Line number   DEF FNb(a)=C

```
5     DEF FNM(M)=INT(M/100)
6     DEF FND(D)=D−INT(D/100)*100
30    READ S,P,I,A
31    DATA 221,224,27425,71.39
35    LET M1=FNM(S)
36    LET D1=FND(S)
37    LET M2=FNM(P)
38    LET D2=FND(P)
```

FIGURE 7–4 Month and day numbers with a function.

where *b* is the name of the function and must be a single letter of the alphabet, *a* is the dummy argument(s), and *C* is the computational expression to be evaluated. The line number associated with a function must place the function before its first usage. It is generally a good practice to place all functions at the beginning of your program. A user-defined function can access any of the library functions if such a need arises.

A function, then, is a special purpose miniprogram that automatically calculates some desired quantity. Most programming languages, BASIC included, have library functions, as well as provisions allowing programmers to write their own.

STRINGS

In our VISA program of Figure 6–21 we used a string (K$) to hold the kind of transaction, charge or payment, that was being processed. The value of K$ was either "C" or "P", and we used an IF statement to test the value of K$ so we could print the amount in the proper column.

Figure 7–5 shows the bottom third of our VISA statement, which has posting and transaction dates using abbreviations for month names and not the month numbers. Although the program we have developed thus far reads and prints month numbers and not month names, the computer is able to convert the numbers to names. To make this conversion we need the ability to have a string of more than one letter. In this case, we have to hold the three letters for each month's abbreviated form.

Like an array, a string of more than one letter must be dimensioned with a DIM statement. If the string G$ is to hold 26 different letters, the proper DIM statement is:

```
3    DIM G$(26)
```

To place a value into a string variable, a LET, INPUT, or READ statement can be used. When the LET is used, the value must be surrounded by quotation marks. Thus, to place the letters of the alphabet, *A* to *Z*, into G$, the following LET is used:

```
47    LET G$="ABCDEFGHIJKLMNOPQRSTUVWXYZ"
```

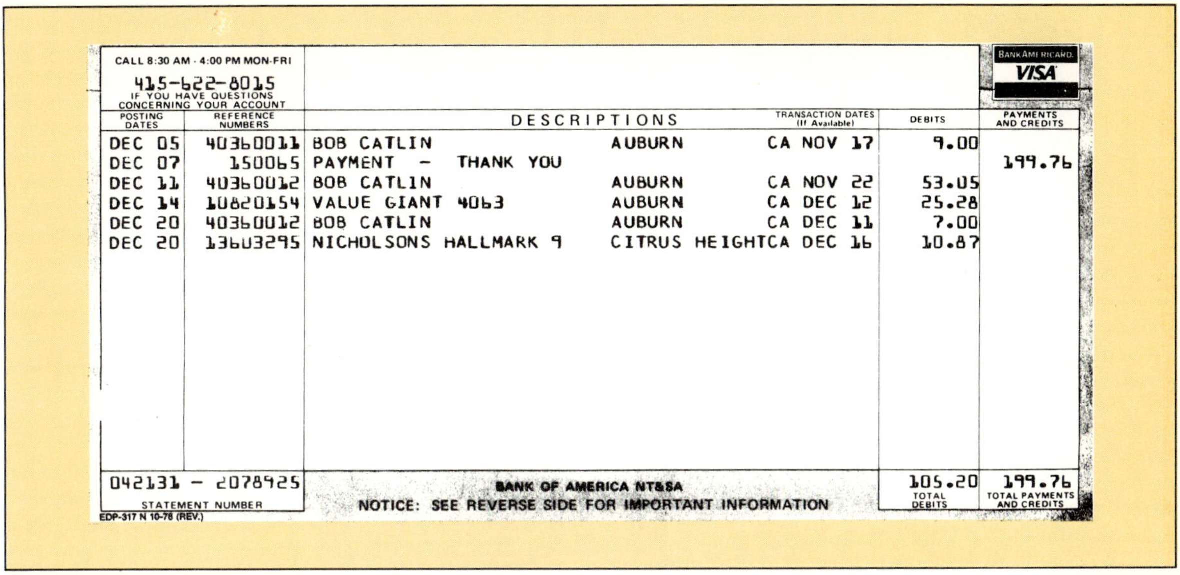

FIGURE 7–5 Bottom third of VISA statement.

To set G$ to that same value with an INPUT statement, we write:

91   INPUT G$

When the command is executed, the computer will respond with a question mark (?). At this point, we enter the values for G$ as shown:

?ABCDEFGHIJKLMNOPQRSTUVWXYZ

Some versions of BASIC may require us to surround the values by quotation marks (''):

?"ABCDEFGHIJKLMNOPQRSTUVWXYZ"

When a READ is used to set the value of the string, some versions of BASIC require that the value be enclosed in quotation marks in the DATA statement. To get G$ using READ, we write:

34   READ G$
35   DATA "ABCDEFGHIJKLMNOPQRSTUVWXYZ"

If two strings are to be set to a value in the same READ or INPUT statement, we write:

10   INPUT U$,S$
?   UNITED,STATES

or

?   "UNITED", "STATES"

or

10   READ U$,S$
20   DATA "UNITED", "STATES"

Once a string has been initialized with either a LET, INPUT, or READ, that value can be tested with an IF statement, can be output with a PRINT, or can be copied into another string variable using a LET. As an illustration, suppose a drill program were written for checking whether a person understands that the + symbol stands for addition. The person must input his or her answer in the string A$. This string is then tested to see if it contains the word ADDITION. The BASIC for this program is shown in Figure 7–6.

If we wrote line 320 as

320   IF A$(1,3)="ADD"THEN 350

the IF would examine only the first through the third characters of A$ with the word ADD. If they matched, then line 350 would be executed next. Tests of this type allow for misspelling or for vary-

CHAPTER 7: ADVANCED BASIC

```
10    DIM A$[20]
300   PRINT "WHAT DOES + STAND FOR";
310   INPUT A$
320   IF A$="ADDITION" THEN 350
330   PRINT "INCORRECT. IT STANDS FOR ADDITION."
340   GOTO 360
350   PRINT "VERY GOOD"
360   PRINT "WHAT DOES − STAND FOR";
370   INPUT A$
380   IF A$="SUBTRACTION" THEN 410
```

FIGURE 7–6   Testing a string for a known value.

ing answers beginning with the same letter or group of letters.

The notation A$(1,3) denotes a portion of or **substring** of the string A$. Strings may be subdivided for printing, testing, or for joining parts of two strings together. As an example, let us take the strings U$ and S$ defined earlier. These two strings can be combined to form a new string, V$

```
10    LET V$(1,6)=U$
15    LET V$(7,7)=" "
20    LET V$(8,13)=S$
30    PRINT V$
```

The value of V$ will be the words UNITED STATES.

If the statement:

```
40    LET T$=U$(1,4)
```

is written, the value of T$ is the first through the fourth characters in U$. The value of T$ is therefore the word UNIT. In cases where a substring is written, the position denoters of the substring must progress from lower to higher positions. The statement:

```
50    LET T$=U$(4,1)
```

is incorrect and should result in an error message to the programmer.

The position denoters of a substring do not have to be constants, but instead may be variables. If the following BASIC statements are written:

```
60    LET I=2
70    LET J=5
180   PRINT S$(I,J)
```

the word printed is TATE. The use of variables as substring position denoters allows great flexibility to the programmer.

Returning to our VISA statement, we need a string to hold the abbreviations of the month names:

```
115   DIM M$(36)
116   LET M$(1,18)="JANFEBMARAPRMAYJUN"
117   LET M$(17,36)="JULAUGSEPOCTNOVDEC"
```

When we read the value of M, and the value is a 2, we will need the fourth, fifth, and sixth characters in M$. The chart of Figure 7–7 shows the relationship between the beginning and ending characters in M$ that we will need, depending on the value of M.

The beginning character position (B) is related to M as is the ending character (E), by the following formulas:

$$B = 3*M - 2$$
$$E = 3*M$$

Thus, when the value of M is 2, the values of B and E are 4 and 6, respectively, as required.

The notation M$(B,E) represents all the characters in M$ beginning in position B and continuing to (and including) the character in position E. In order to print the month names instead of month numbers and thus resemble the VISA statement more closely, we will use M$ twice—once for the posting date and once for the transaction date (Figure 7–8). The RUN of this program is given in Figure 7–9.

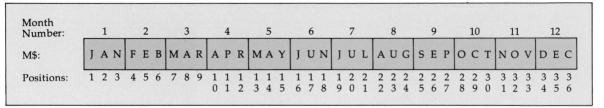

FIGURE 7–7 Character positions in M$.

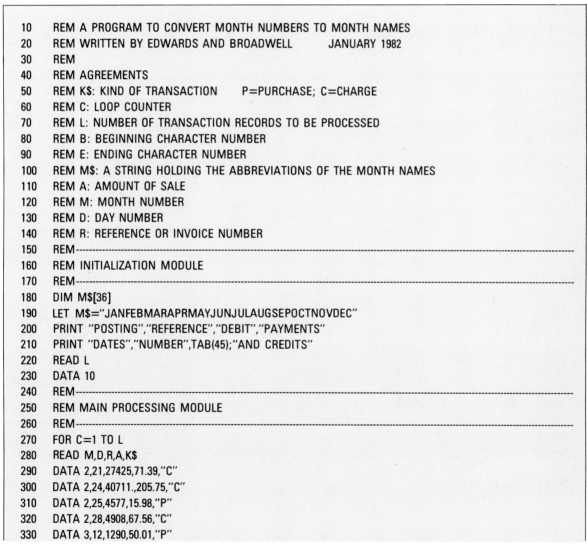

FIGURE 7–8 VISA statement with month names.

```
340    DATA 4,1,23332,4.34,"C"
350    DATA 5,7,9809,23.99,"P"
360    DATA 12,3,6744,21.88,"C"
370    DATA 10,23,6677,56,"P"
380    DATA 1,23,112233.,2.1,"C"
390    IF M >= 1 AND M <= 12 THEN 420
400    PRINT "INVALID MONTH NUMBER"
410    GOTO 520
420    REM TEST THE KIND OF TRANSACTION
430    LET B=3*M−2
440    LET E=3*M
450    IF K$="C" THEN 490
460    IF K$="P" THEN 510
470    PRINT "INVALID TYPE OF TRANSACTION"
480    GOTO 520
490    PRINT M$[B,E];D,R,A
500    GOTO 520
510    PRINT M$[B,E];D,R,TAB(45);A
520    NEXT C
530    REM--------------------------------------------------------------------------
540    REM CLOSING MODULE
550    REM--------------------------------------------------------------------------
560    END
```

FIGURE 7−8 *Continued*

POSTING DATES	REFERENCE NUMBER	DEBIT	PAYMENTS AND CREDITS
FEB 21	27425	71.39	
FEB 24	40711.	205.75	
FEB 25	4577		15.98
FEB 28	4908	67.56	
MAR 12	1290		50.01
APR 1	23332	4.34	
MAY 7	9809		23.99
DEC 3	6744	21.88	
OCT 23	6677		56
JAN 23	112233.	2.1	

FIGURE 7−9 RUN for VISA program with month names.

The program in Figure 7–8 and its RUN in Figure 7–9 illustrate the use of substrings. Like arrays, substrings can dramatically alter program length and execution time. The procedure can be ineffective, however, if the version of BASIC used does not support a string of at least 36 characters.

MULTIDIMENSIONAL ARRAYS

The array N(M) of Figure 7–7 is called a **single dimension array** since it has only a single index. In many instances, though, two or three indices are used for an array. When an array has two indices, it is called a **double dimension array** or a two-dimension array. When it has three indices, it is called a **triple dimension array**. Physically, these arrays might be thought of as shown in Figure 7–10.

The array N(M) uses 12 memory locations, N(R,M) uses 36, while N(R,M,U) requires 72. As the number of dimensions increases, and the occurrences of each index increase, the memory requirements for these arrays also increase significantly.

A double dimension array can be used to advantage to have a computer remember certain factors. For example, the San Francisco–Oakland Bay Area has a computer-controlled rapid transit system

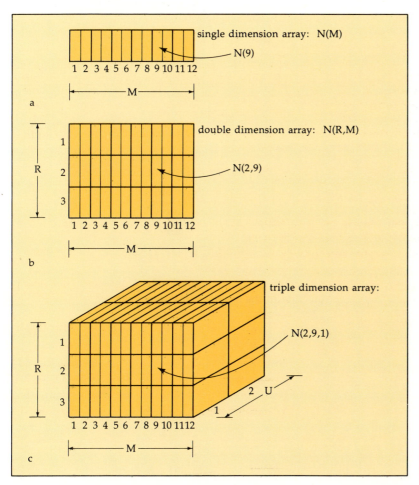

FIGURE 7–10 Single, double, triple dimension arrays.

CHAPTER 7: ADVANCED BASIC

called BART. The computer has all the fares stored away and can automatically recall the fare from any one station to any other station (see Figure 7–11). A ticket is purchased for a given amount of money, and each time the ticket is used, the fare for the trip is subtracted from the current value of the ticket. To determine the fare, a two-dimension array is used.

If a program requires a two-dimension array C with three rows and five columns, it would be DIMensioned as:

```
1    DIM C(3,5)
```

This DIM statement reserves 15 elements or storage locations for C. Two-dimension arrays are very useful for storing large tables like the tax table shown in Figure B–1.

Problems that require the use of arrays are typically those that require many simultaneous totals, that count the frequency of a given event, or that repeatedly need to reference data that are unchanging.

FILE PROCESSING

In Chapter 3 you saw a system flowchart that showed the three steps required in printing the VISA statement. The first step in the process involved reading and validating transaction data, and building a file. The second step was sorting this file, called a "transaction file," into ascending order by customer number. The third and final step involved taking the sorted transaction file and coupling it with the data in the master file in order to print the VISA statement. In this third step, we also took the customer's old balance and added the charges and payments from the transaction file to calculate the new balance. The new balance plus the other data from the master file then created a new or updated master file.

Building the Transaction File

The program to build the transaction file has to:

1. Read the customer number, transaction date, posting date, amount of sale, reference number, and kind of sale.
2. Validate the two dates and kinds of sale.
3. If all the data are correct, write these data to the transaction file, but if the data are not correct, then print an error message indicating the type of error.

Unlike most statements in BASIC, file processing statements are not standardized. One version of BASIC may have a special statement to use when writing data to a file. Another version of BASIC may not support file processing at all, while yet another version of BASIC may use a different form of an existing statement. For our purposes let us assume the last of these three methods of file processing—a modification of the PRINT statement.

To output data to a file we write

```
800    PRINT #1; N,T1,T2,P1,P2,A,R,K$
```

where #1 indicates that data are to be printed to file number 1. The variables mean:

- N: Customer number
- T1: Month number of transaction date
- T2: Day number of transaction date
- P1: Month number of posting date
- P2: Day number of posting date
- A: Amount of the sale
- R: Reference number
- K$: Kind of sale, "C"-Charge; "P"-Payment

The program to build the transaction file, along with the RUN, is in Figure 7–12.

Sorting the Transaction File

The program to sort the transaction file into ascending order by customer number is not one we are going to write.[1] Sorting is done so frequently that most computers already have a sort program. In

---

[1] A copy of a file sorting program is printed in the instructor's manual for this text.

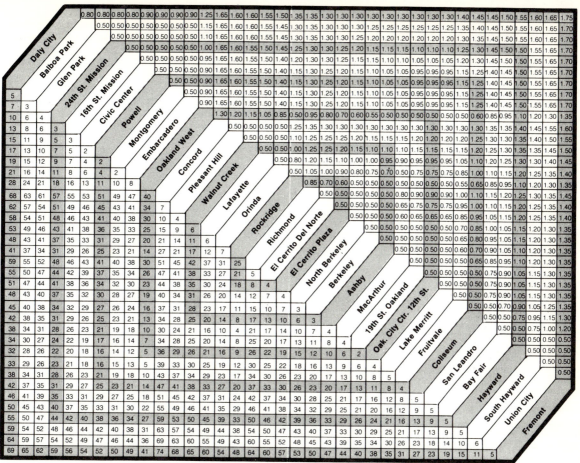
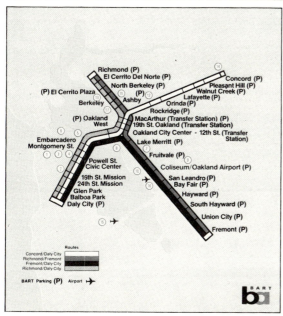

FIGURE 7–11 BART fare array.

```
10    REM A PROGRAM THAT VALIDATES AND BUILDS A TRANSACTION FILE
20    REM WRITTEN BY EDWARDS AND BROADWELL        JANUARY 1982
30    REM
40    REM AGREEMENTS
50    REM K$: KIND OF TRANSACTION      P=PURCHASE; C=CHARGE
60    REM C: LOOP COUNTER
70    REM L: NUMBER OF TRANSACTION RECORDS TO BE PROCESSED
80    REM N: CUSTOMER ACCOUNT NUMBER
90    REM T1: MONTH NUMBER OF TRANSACTION DATE
100   REM T2: DAY NUMBER OF TRANSACTION DATE
110   REM P1: MONTH NUMBER OF POSTING DATE
120   REM P2: DAY NUMBER OF POSTING DATE
130   REM A: AMOUNT OF SALE
140   REM N: AN ARRAY OF 12 ELEMENTS THAT HOLDS THE DAYS IN A MONTH
150   REM R: REFERENCE OR INVOICE NUMBER
160   REM--------------------------------------------------------------
170   REM INITIALIZATION MODULE
180   REM--------------------------------------------------------------
190   FILES TRANS
200   DIM N[12]
210   FOR M=1 TO 12
220   READ N[M]
230   DATA 31,28,31,30,31,30,31,31,30,31,30,31
240   NEXT M
250   READ L
260   DATA 10
270   REM--------------------------------------------------------------
280   REM MAIN PROCESSING MODULE
290   REM--------------------------------------------------------------
300   FOR C=1 TO L
310   READ N,T1,T2,P1,P2,R,A,K$
320   DATA 4019,2,21,2,24,27425,71.39,"C"
330   DATA 4019,2,24,2,28,40711.,205.75,"C"
340   DATA 5007,2,25,3,1,4577,15.98,"P"
350   DATA 4019,2,25,3,4,4613,64.75,"P"
360   DATA 5007,2,28,3,14,4908,67.56,"C"
370   DATA 1234,3,12,3,13,1290,50.01,"P"
380   DATA 5007,2,23,2,24,34,12,"C"
390   DATA 4019,2,26,3,14,23123,45.5,"C"
400   DATA 1234,2,22,3,1,98989.,30,"P"
410   DATA 5007,2,23,2,28,112233.,2.1,"C"
420   IF T1 >= 1 AND P1 >= 1 AND T1 <= 12 AND P1 <= 12 THEN 450
430   PRINT "INVALID MONTH NUMBER"
440   GOTO 540
```

FIGURE 7–12   BASIC program and RUN to build a transaction file.

```
450    IF T2 <= N[T1] AND P2 <= N[P1] THEN 490
460    PRINT "INVALID DAY NUMBER"
470    GOTO 540
480    REM TEST THE KIND OF TRANSACTION
490    IF K$="C" THEN 530
500    IF K$="P" THEN 530
510    PRINT "INVALID TYPE OF TRANSACTION"
520    GOTO 540
530    PRINT #1;N,T1,T2,P1,P2,R,A,K$
540    NEXT C
550    REM-------------------------------------------------------------
560    REM CLOSING MODULE
570    REM-------------------------------------------------------------
580    END
```

FIGURE 7–12   *Continued*

fact, a recent survey showed that on some computers almost 40 percent of the available computer time was spent sorting files into various orders. Since sorting is so common we will use this prewritten program to sort our transaction file.

Prewritten programs are called **utility programs**. Some of the various utility programs include programs to sort files, make copies of files, list the contents of a file, and merge files together. In Figure 7–13a you will see what the utility program to sort a file does when it is RUN. Following the RUN of the sort utility is the RUN of a utility program to list the contents of a file, Figure 7–13b.

Building a Master File

The master file in our VISA system contains the fixed data about each customer. In our example, let us suppose the master file has the following data: customer or account number, customer name, customer address, credit limit, and previous balance. Furthermore, let us assume that our master file can hold these data for each of five customers (in the real VISA system there are millions of customers).

Before we can write the program to update the master file, we need to have a master file. A program to build this file in order by customer number is found in Figure 7–14. Once this program is RUN we can proceed with the update step.

Updating the Master File

A program to update the master file is logically complex. We need to:

1. Read a record from the transaction and master files.

2. Compare the customer number from the master file with the customer number from the transaction file.

3. If the two customer numbers are equal, then we print a line on the VISA statement and add or subtract from the balance the amount of the transaction, and then read another transaction record.

4. If the customer number in the transaction is less than the master, we have an error. In this case we have a charge or a payment without a matching master record, so we print an error message and read the next transaction record.

5. If the customer number in the transaction is greater than the master, we have processed all the transaction records for this customer. We therefore print the total line, create an updated master record and write it to the new version of the master file, read the next master record, and print the headings for this next customer's VISA statement.

The BASIC program to update the master file and print the VISA statement is shown in Figure 7–15 and the RUN in Figure 7–16.

```
FILIST

INPUT NAME OF FILE TO BE LISTED: TRANS
AT WHICH RECORD # DO YOU WISH TO START? 1
    4019  ⎤
    2     |
    21    |
    2     ⎬  1st RECORD
    24    |
    27425 |
    71.39 |
C         ⎦
    4019  ⎤
    2     |
    24    |
    2     ⎬  2nd RECORD
    28    |
    40711.|
    205.75|
C         ⎦
    5007  ⎤
    2     |
    25    |
    3     ⎬  3d RECORD
    1     |
    4577  |
    15.98 |
P         ⎦
    4019  ⎤
    2     |
    25    |
    3     ⎬  4th RECORD
    4     |
    4613  |
    64.75 |
P         ⎦
    5007
    2
    28
    3
    14
    4908
    67.56
C
```

FIGURE 7–13a   Before sort file listing.

```
    1234
    3
    12
    3
    13
    1290
    50.01
P
    5007
    2
    23
    2
    24
    34
    12
C
    4019
    2
    26
    3
    14
    23123
    45.5
C
    1234
    2
    22
    3
    1
    98989.
    30
P
    5007  ⎫
    2     ⎪
    23    ⎪
    2     ⎬  LAST RECORD
    28    ⎪
    112233.⎪
    2.1   ⎭
C
ANY MORE? NO
```

FIGURE 7–13a *Continued*

```
FILIST

INPUT NAME OF FILE TO BE LISTED: TRANS
AT WHICH RECORD # DO YOU WISH TO START? 1
    1234  ⎫
    2     ⎪
    22    ⎪
    3     ⎬ 1st RECORD
    1     ⎪
    98989.⎪
    30    ⎪
P         ⎭
    1234  ⎫
    3     ⎪
    12    ⎪
    3     ⎬ 2nd RECORD
    13    ⎪
    1290  ⎪
    50.01 ⎪
P         ⎭
    4019  ⎫
    2     ⎪
    21    ⎪
    2     ⎬ 3d RECORD
    24    ⎪
    27425 ⎪
    71.39 ⎪
C         ⎭
    4019  ⎫
    2     ⎪
    24    ⎪
    2     ⎬ 4th RECORD
    28    ⎪
    40711.⎪
    205.75⎪
C         ⎭
    4019
    2
    25
    3
    4
    4613
    64.75
P
```

FIGURE 7–13b After sort file listing.

```
     4019
     2
     26
     3
     14
     23123
     45.5
C
     5007
     2
     23
     2
     28
     112233.
     2.1
C
     5007
     2
     23
     2
     24
     34
     12
C
     5007
     2
     25
     3
     1
     4577
     15.98
P
     5007  ⎫
     2     ⎪
     28    ⎪
     3     ⎬  LAST RECORD
     14    ⎪
     4908  ⎪
     67.56 ⎭
C
ANY MORE? NO
```

FIGURE 7–13b   *Continued*

```
10    REM A PROGRAM TO BUILD A MASTER FILE
20    REM WRITTEN BY EDWARDS AND BROADWELL.    JANUARY 1982
30    REM
40    REM AGREEMENTS
50    REM C: LOOP COUNTER
70    REM N$: CUSTOMER NAME
71    REM S$: CUSTOMER STREET ADDRESS
72    REM C$: CUSTOMER CITY AND STATE
73    REM Z: ZIP CODE
80    REM N: CUSTOMER ACCOUNT NUMBER
90    REM L: CREDIT LIMIT
100   REM B: CUSTOMER BALANCE
110   REM-------------------------------------------------------------
120   REM OPENING AND INITIALIZATION MODULE
130   REM-------------------------------------------------------------
140   FILES MASTER
150   DIM N$[26]
160   DIM S$[26]
161   DIM C$[30]
170   REM-------------------------------------------------------------
180   REM MAIN PROCESSING MODULE
190   REM-------------------------------------------------------------
200   FOR C=1 TO 5
210   READ N,N$,S$,C$,Z,L,B
220   DATA 1234,"PERRY EDWARDS","444 NEVADA ST.","AUBURN CA",95603.,1200,366
230   DATA 4019,"BRUCE BROADWELL","1020 HILLTOP RD.","MEADOW VISTA CA",95666.
231   DATA 1500,100
240   DATA 5007,"KRISTEN STENSAAS","RT 1 BOX 1000","WEED CA",96094.,1500
241   DATA 250
250   DATA 6786,"KAREN WILLIAMS","4405 WILLOW GLENN RD.","CONCORD CA"
251   DATA 94521.,1750,0
260   DATA 9888,"PEGGY GOODWIN","P O BOX 45","COLORADO SPRINGS CO"
261   DATA 80904.,1200,50
270   PRINT #1;N,N$,S$,C$,Z,L,B
280   NEXT C
290   REM-------------------------------------------------------------
300   REM CLOSING MODULE
310   REM-------------------------------------------------------------
320   END
```

FIGURE 7–14   BASIC program to build a master file.

```
10    REM A PROGRAM TO UPDATE A MASTER FILE AND PRINT VISA STATEMENTS
20    REM WRITTEN BY EDWARDS AND BROADWELL
30    REM
40    REM AGREEMENTS:
50    REM
60    REM C: LOOP COUNTER FOR MASTER FILE CUSTOMERS
70    REM N1: CUSTOMER ACCOUNT NUMBER IN THE TRANSACTION FILE
80    REM R: REFERENCE NUMBER
90    REM A: AMOUNT OF SALE
100   REM K$: STRING HOLDING THE KIND OF TRANSACTION
110   REM T1: MONTH OF TRANSACTION DATE
120   REM T2: DAY OF TRANSACTION DATE
130   REM P1: MONTH OF POSTING DATE
140   REM P2: DAY OF POSTING DATE
150   REM N2: CUSTOMER NUMBER IN THE MASTER FILE
170   REM N$: CUSTOMER NAME
171   REM S$: CUSTOMER STREET ADDRESS
172   REM C$: CUSTOMER CITY AND STATE
173   REM Z: ZIP CODE
180   REM B: CUSTOMER BALANCE
190   REM L: CREDIT LIMIT
200   REM T3: TOTAL OF DEBITS FOR A CUSTOMER
210   REM T4: TOTAL OF THE CREDITS FOR A CUSTOMER
220   REM M$: STRING HOLDING THE ABBREVIATIONS OF THE MONTH NAMES
300   REM --------------------------------------------------------------------------------
310   REM OPENING AND INITIALIZATION MODULE
320   REM --------------------------------------------------------------------------------
330   FILES TRANS,MASTER,NEWMAS
340   DIM N$[26],S$[26],C$[30]
341   DIM M$[36]
342   LET M$="JANFEBMARAPRMAYJUNJULAUGSEPOCTNOVDEC"
350   REM --------------------------------------------------------------------------------
360   REM MAIN PROCESSING MODULE
370   REM --------------------------------------------------------------------------------
380   FOR C=1 TO 5
385   LET T3=0
386   LET T4=0
390   READ #2;N2,N$,S$,C$,Z,L,B
400   REM PRINT THE TOP PORTION OF THE STATEMENT
410   PRINT
420   PRINT
430   PRINT "ACCOUNT NUMBER";N2
440   PRINT "CUSTOMER NAME ";N$
450   PRINT "ADDRESS         ";S$
```

FIGURE 7–15 Master file update program.

```
460    PRINT TAB(14);C$;Z
470    PRINT
480    PRINT "POSTING","REFERENCE","TRANSACTION","DEBITS","PAYMENTS"
490    PRINT "DATES","NUMBERS","    DATES",TAB(60);"AND CREDITS"
500    READ #1;N1,T1,T2,P1,P2,R,A,K$
505    IF  END #1 THEN 800
510    REM TEST THE ACCOUNT NUMBERS
520    IF N1<N2 THEN 600
530    IF N1=N2 THEN 700
540    GOTO 800
600    PRINT "ERROR IN FILES — MISSING MASTER FOR A TRANSACTION"
610    GOTO 500
700    REM CUSTOMER NUMBERS ARE EQUAL
710    REM TEST TRANSACTION TYPE
715    IF K$="C" THEN 750
720    LET T4=T4+A
730    LET B=B+A
731    PRINT   USING 732;M$[P1*3−2,P1*3],P2,R,M$[T1*3−2,T1*3],T2,A
732    IMAGE AAA,1X,DD,9X,DDDDDDD,8X,AAA,1X,DD,24X,DDDDDDD.DD
732    GOTO 500
750    LET T3=T3+A
751    LET B=B−A
752    PRINT   USING 753;M$[P1*3−2,P1*3],P2,R,M$[T1*3−2,T1*3],T2,A
753    IMAGE AAA,1X,DD,9X,DDDDDDD,8X,AAA,1X,DD,9X,DDDDDD.DD
754    GOTO 500
800    REM END OF TRANSACTIONS FOR THIS MASTER RECORD
810    REM PRINT THE NEW MASTER AND READ THE NEXT MASTER.
820    PRINT #3;N2,N$,S$,C$,Z,L,B
821    PRINT
830    PRINT   USING 840;T3,T4
840    IMAGE 44X,DDDDD.DD,10X,DDDDD.DD
850    PRINT TAB(45);"TOTAL       TOTAL PAYMENTS"
860    PRINT TAB(45);"DEBITS        AND CREDITS"
900    NEXT C
997    REM --------------------------------------------------------------------------------
998    REM CLOSING MODULE
999    REM --------------------------------------------------------------------------------
1000   END
```

FIGURE 7–15   *Continued*

The program to update the file is not only complex in a logical sense, it is also quite lengthy—82 BASIC statements. Update programs are the fundamental programs of business data processing, since so many data are stored in files. To complete our VISA system, we need another update system, one that would allow us to: add new customers, change the data (for example, the address) of existing customers, and allow us to drop customers from the file.

SOLVED EXERCISES

The two exercises that follow describe how to use functions to "roll dice" and how to change from a Gregorian calendar date to a Julian calendar date. Both exercises have a discussion of the problem, a flowchart, the program, and the RUN to illustrate the results of the program.

Simulation of Dice Rolling

The use of functions by programmers is not restricted to mathematical computations. Many real world phenomena can be analyzed and studied using a computer. The idea of programming the computer to display or behave in a manner similar to some real world event is called **simulation.**

One of the easiest events to simulate is that of rolling a die. The roll of a die is a random event, with the probability of rolling a 1 equal to the probability of rolling a 2, equal to the probability of rolling a 3, and so on. A statistician may want to simulate the roll of a die 10,000 times to test the hypothesis that these probabilities are indeed equal. To actually roll a die 10,000 times, however, and manually record the results would take many hours, and the chances of a recording error are enormous. Fortunately, many programming languages support random event processes with a function like **RND.**[2]

---

[2] If your computer does not support RND, it can easily be fabricated. See problem A-25 in Supplement A of this book.

When an RND function is used, the computer generates a number between 0 and 1. The statistician, however, wants either a 1, 2, 3, 4, 5, or 6. In addition, the statistician wants the probability of any of those numbers to be the same. The number that RND yields thus needs to be altered so that it becomes 1, 2, 3, 4, 5, or 6 with equal probability of occurrence. The alteration is done in the following manner. The number generated by RND is as likely to be 0.13 as to be 0.3966 or 0.415 or 0.71381, or any other number between 0 and 1. To simulate these 10,000 events for the statistician, the programmer needs to generate a new random number and check its value.

If the value is between 0 and $1/6$ (less than or equal to: $<=$), then the programmer might call this event a 1. If the value is between $1/6$ (0.16666) and $2/6$ (0.3333) the event is called a 2, and so on.

Each time the RND function is called by the programmer, the computer generates a new random number and the testing takes place again. Depending on the speed of the computer, simulating 10,000 rolls of a die may take a few minutes.

Since the value returned is between 0.000001 and 0.999999 (but it is never equal to 1), by multiplying the random number by 6, a number between 0.000000 and 5.99999 can be generated. If the fractional portion (in this case, 99999) of this new number is then truncated (dropping all the digits to the right of the decimal point) using the INT function, the result yields a 0, 1, 2, 3, 4, 5—six different events, but not the six—1, 2, 3, 4, 5, 6—the statistician requires. To change the range of numbers from 0 to 5 to a range of 1 to 6, the programmer simply adds 1, and a range of 1 to 6 is achieved.

This process can be represented in BASIC using the precedence order of operators, INT, and RND; it is written as:

F=INT(6*RND(4))+1

To count the number of occurrences of a 1, 2, 3, and so on, we can use an array, let us call it C, with six elements. Then when F is 2 we will want to add 1 to C(2) like this:

C(2)=C(2)+1

CHAPTER 7: ADVANCED BASIC

```
RUN

ACCOUNT NUMBER 1234
CUSTOMER NAME PERRY EDWARDS
ADDRESS        444 NEVADA ST.
               AUBURN CA 95603.

POSTING      REFERENCE      TRANSACTION      DEBITS           PAYMENTS
DATES        NUMBERS        DATES                             AND CREDITS

                                             0.00             0.00
                                             TOTAL            TOTAL PAYMENTS
                                             DEBITS           AND CREDITS

ACCOUNT NUMBER 4019
CUSTOMER NAME BRUCE BROADWELL
ADDRESS        1020 HILLTOP RD.
               MEADOW VISTA CA 95666.

POSTING      REFERENCE      TRANSACTION      DEBITS           PAYMENTS
DATES        NUMBERS        DATES                             AND CREDITS
FEB 28       40711          FEB 24           205.75

                                             205.75           0.00
                                             TOTAL            TOTAL PAYMENTS
                                             DEBITS           AND CREDITS

ACCOUNT NUMBER 5007
CUSTOMER NAME KRISTEN STENSAAS
ADDRESS        RT 1 BOX 1000
               WEED CA 96094.

POSTING      REFERENCE      TRANSACTION      DEBITS           PAYMENTS
DATES        NUMBERS        DATES                             AND CREDITS
MAR  1       4577           FEB 25                            15.98
MAR  1       4577           FEB 25           15.98

                                             15.98            15.98
                                             TOTAL            TOTAL PAYMENTS
                                             DEBITS           AND CREDITS

ACCOUNT NUMBER 6786
CUSTOMER NAME KAREN WILLIAMS
ADDRESS        4405 WILLOW GLENN RD.
```

FIGURE 7–16 Master file update RUN—partial listing of the output.

Using F in place of the 2, we can also write this counting step as

C(F)=C(F)+1

Now let us also suppose that our statistician wants to have three sets of 10,000 throws each. Two loops will exist: a loop for the 10,000 throws and a loop to repeat the 10,000 throws three times. The inner loop will simulate the 10,000 throws and the outer loop will cause the repetition of the inner loop three times. The flowchart to show this process is given in Figure 7–17, and the program with its RUN is in Figure 7–18.

Julian and Gregorian Calendars

The calendar with 12 months and varying numbers of days per month is the **Gregorian calendar.** In contrast, the **Julian calendar,** developed during the reign of Julius Caesar in 45 B.C., assigns each day a sequential number (Figure 7–19). Thus, January 1 is Julian day 1, while February 1 is Julian day 32, and December 31 is Julian day 365. A different numbering system is used for leap years, which assign Julian day 60 to February 29 rather than to March 1, as is the case for non-leap years.

In many business situations, the date a transaction occurs is recorded by Gregorian dates using their month names rather than their month numbers. Let us design a program that converts dates like August 2 to Julian 214 and February 23 to Julian 54.

A procedure to solve this problem is to place the abbreviations of each month's name as a series of substrings (just as we did in Figure 7–7 earlier). By looping through the substrings and comparing them with the desired month name until a match is made, and by storing values representing the last days of the various months in an array, the conversion can be made. The flowchart to convert Gregorian to Julian and the BASIC program with its RUN are given in Figures 7–20 and 7–21, respectively.

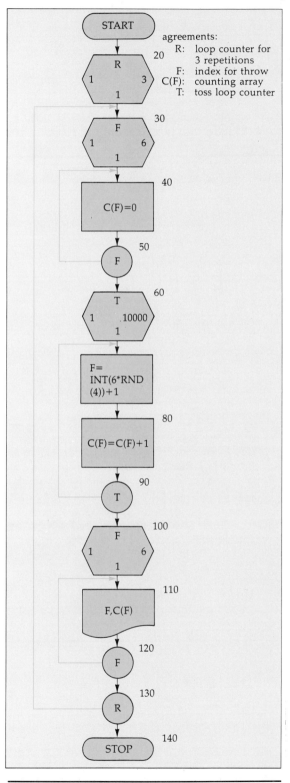

FIGURE 7–17 Flowchart to throw a die 30,000 times and print a summary of the frequences of 1s, 2s, 3s, 4s, 5s, and 6s.

```
1    REM A PROGRAM TO SIMULATE THE ROLLING OF DICE 30,000 TIMES
2    REM WRITTEN BY EDWARDS AND BROADWELL.    JANUARY 1982.
3    REM
4    REM AGREEMENTS
5    REM R: LOOP COUNTER FOR 3 REPETITIONS
6    REM F: INDEX OF THROW COUNTER ARRAY
7    REM C: AN ARRAY OF 6 ELEMENTS USED FOR COUNTING
8    REM T: LOOP COUNTER FOR TOSSES
10   REM---------------------------------------------------------------------------------
11   REM OPENING AND INITIALIZATION MODULE
12   REM---------------------------------------------------------------------------------
16   DIM C[6]
20   FOR R=1 TO 3
21   REM INITIALIZE THE C(F) ARRAY TO ZERO
30   FOR F=1 TO 6
40   LET C[F]=0
50   NEXT F
51   REM GENERATE A RANDOM THROW AND COUNT IT
60   FOR T=1 TO 10000
70   LET F=INT(6*RND(4))+1
80   LET C[F]=C[F]+1
90   NEXT T
91   REM PRINT THE TOTALS OF THE C(F) ARRAY
100  FOR F=1 TO 6
110  PRINT F,C[F]
120  NEXT F
130  NEXT R
131  REM---------------------------------------------------------------------------------
132  REM CLOSING MODULE
133  REM---------------------------------------------------------------------------------
140  END
```

FIGURE 7–18 BASIC program and RUN to throw a die 30,000 times and print a summary of the frequencies of 1s, 2s, 3s, 4s, 5s, and 6s.

RUN	
1	1635
2	1671
3	1647
4	1705
5	1620
6	1722
1	1617
2	1722
3	1641
4	1692
5	1638
6	1690
1	1661
2	1618
3	1684
4	1669
5	1661
6	1707

FIGURE 7–18 *Continued*

FIGURE 7–19 Julian/Gregorian calendar.

Day	Jan	Feb	Mar	Apr	May	June	July	Aug	Sep	Oct	Nov	Dec	Day
1	001	032	060	091	121	152	182	213	244	274	305	335	1
2	002	033	061	092	122	153	183	214	245	275	306	336	2
3	003	034	062	093	123	154	184	215	246	276	307	337	3
4	004	035	063	094	124	155	185	216	247	277	308	338	4
5	005	036	064	095	125	156	186	217	248	278	309	339	5
6	006	037	065	096	126	157	187	218	249	279	310	340	6
7	007	038	066	097	127	158	188	219	250	280	311	341	7
8	008	039	067	098	128	159	189	220	251	281	312	342	8
9	009	040	068	099	129	160	190	221	252	282	313	343	9
10	010	041	069	100	130	161	191	222	253	283	314	344	10
11	011	042	070	101	131	162	192	223	254	284	315	345	11
12	012	043	071	102	132	163	193	224	255	285	316	346	12
13	013	044	072	103	133	164	194	225	256	286	317	347	13
14	014	045	073	104	134	165	195	226	257	287	318	348	14
15	015	046	074	105	135	166	196	227	258	288	319	349	15
16	016	047	075	106	136	167	197	228	259	289	320	350	16
17	017	048	076	107	137	168	198	229	260	290	321	351	17
18	018	049	077	108	138	169	199	230	261	291	322	352	18
19	019	050	078	109	139	170	200	231	262	292	323	353	19
20	020	051	079	110	140	171	201	232	263	293	324	354	20
21	021	052	080	111	141	172	202	233	264	294	325	355	21
22	022	053	081	112	142	173	203	234	265	295	326	356	22
23	023	054	082	113	143	174	204	235	266	296	327	357	23
24	024	055	083	114	144	175	205	236	267	297	328	358	24
25	025	056	084	115	145	176	206	237	268	298	329	359	25
26	026	057	085	116	146	177	207	238	269	299	330	360	26
27	027	058	086	117	147	178	208	239	270	300	331	361	27
28	028	059	087	118	148	179	209	240	271	301	332	362	28
29	029		088	119	149	180	210	241	272	302	333	363	29
30	030		089	120	150	181	211	242	273	303	334	364	30
31	031		090		151		212	243		304		365	31

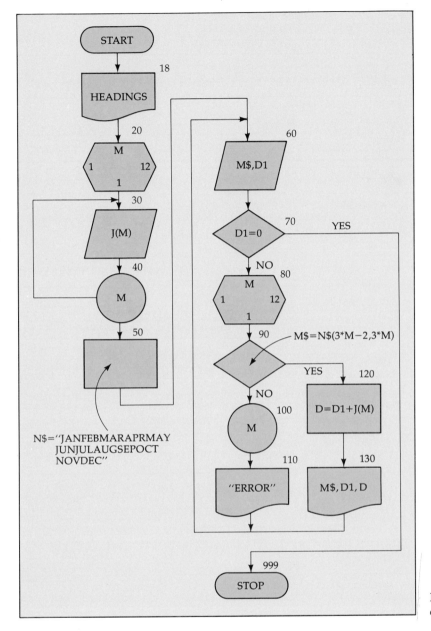

FIGURE 7–20 Flowchart to convert Gregorian dates to Julian.

```
1    REM A PROGRAM TO CONVERT GREGORIAN DATES TO JULIAN DATES
2    REM WRITTEN BY EDWARDS AND BROADWELL.     JANUARY 1982.
3    REM
4    REM AGREEMENTS
5    REM M: MONTH NUMBER
6    REM J: AN ARRAY OF 12 ELEMENTS HOLDING THE JULIAN DAYS
7    REM M$: STRING WITH THE MONTH TO BE CONVERTED
8    REM D1: DAY OF MONTH TO BE CONVERTED
9    REM D: JULIAN DAY OF CONVERTED GREGORIAN DAY
10   REM N$: A STRING HOLDING THE ABBREVIATIONS OF THE MONTH NAMES
15   REM--------------------------------------------------------------------------------
16   REM OPENING AND INITIALIZATION MODULE
17   REM--------------------------------------------------------------------------------
18   PRINT "GREGORIAN DATE",TAB(30);"JULIAN DATE"
19   DIM J[12],N$[36],M$[3]
20   FOR M=1 TO 12
30   READ J[M]
31   DATA 0,31,59,90,120,151,181,212,243,273,304,334
40   NEXT M
50   LET N$="JANFEBMARAPRMAYJUNJULAUGSEPOCTNOVDEC"
51   REM--------------------------------------------------------------------------------
52   REM PROCESSING MODULE
53   REM--------------------------------------------------------------------------------
60   READ M$,D1
61   DATA "AUG",2
62   DATA "FEB",23
63   DATA "SEP",15
64   DATA "SEP",17
65   DATA "DEC",25
66   DATA "JAN",1
67   DATA "FEB",1
68   DATA "   ",0
69   REM TEST FOR END OF DATA
70   IF D1=0 THEN 999
71   REM TEST SUBSTRING FOR A MATCH
80   FOR M=1 TO 12
90   IF M$=N$[3*M-2,3*M] THEN 120
100  NEXT M
110  PRINT "INVALID MONTH"
111  GOTO 60
112  REM CALCULATE THE JULIAN DAY AND PRINT IT
```

FIGURE 7-21   BASIC program and RUN to convert Gregorian to Julian.

```
120     LET D=D1+J[M]
130     PRINT M$;D1,"IS",D
131     GOTO 60
133     REM--------------------------------------------------------
140     REM CLOSING MODULE
141     REM--------------------------------------------------------
999     END

RUN

GREGORIAN DATE        JULIAN DATE
AUG 2           IS    214
FEB 23          IS    54
SEP 15          IS    258
SEP 17          IS    260
DEC 25          IS    359
JAN 1           IS    1
FEB 1           IS    32
```

FIGURE 7–21 *Continued*

SUMMARY

This chapter, when used with Chapter 6, provides you with the additional BASIC statements needed to write programs that allow complex looping structures, to process alphabetic and alphanumeric data, to use an array, and to construct functions.

The DEF statement is used to define a user-written function. While these statements are restricted to a single line of BASIC, they do allow that statement to be accessed from any other line in your program. Some functions are already defined for you and are called library functions.

The DIM statement is used to reserve memory for arrays and strings. It must be placed before the first use of an array or string variable. The number of BASIC commands that a programmer can save using arrays and strings is significant.

Strings can be tested using an IF statement. They can also be divided into substrings and used for a variety of purposes, for example, validating or printing.

Files are used to store data for later use. You saw two types of files used in this chapter—transaction and master. Master files are used to hold semipermanent data that may need to be changed periodically. Transaction files store data that describe the current activities that will affect the master file.

TERMS

The following words or terms have been presented in this chapter.

Function
SQR
Argument
Library function
INT
User-defined
  function
Substring
Single dimension
  array

Double dimension
  array
Triple dimension array
Utility program
Simulation
RND
Gregorian calendar
Julian calendar

THE JULIAN AND GREGORIAN CALENDARS

The first modern calendar was put into use in 45 B.C. by Julius Caesar, who decreed that henceforth there should be three years of 365 days each, and then one year of 366 days, in perpetual cycle. This became known as the Julian calendar, and began the custom we still observe today of adding one day to the month of February every fourth year—leap year.

Even though the Julian calendar was an enormous improvement over all previous systems, it still was not completely accurate. Since there are approximately 365 ¼ days in a solar year, the Julian calendar was reasonably satisfactory for many years—but there are not exactly 365 ¼ days in a year. The exact solar year consists of 365 days, 5 hours, 48 minutes, 47.8 seconds. That difference of about 11 minutes becomes appreciable over several centuries.

The final calendar correction was done in 1582 by Pope Gregory XIII, and the corrected calendar we use today is called the Gregorian calendar. First, in order to make up for all the days that had accumulated since the beginning of the Julian calendar, Pope Gregory XIII decreed the elimination of 10 days from the year 1582. This was done, and in many countries the day after October 4, 1582, became October 15, 1582.

The pope also installed the leap year rule now in effect, which will serve us for more than a thousand years. The Gregorian leap year rule provides for dropping a day from every centesimal year (those ending in 00) whose number cannot be divided by 400. Thus, a day was dropped in the years 1700, 1800, and 1900. This meant that the years 1700, 1800, and 1900 were not leap years, that is, they had 28 days in February. The day will not be dropped in the year 2000, so the month of February, 2000, will have 29 days. The error in our present calendar is less than one day every 3,000 years; even so, it is still not 100 percent accurate.

The Gregorian calendar was initially adopted in 1582, but its use was by no means universal. As might be expected, the first countries to adopt the new calendar were primarily Roman Catholic nations. Most Protestant countries did not adopt the Gregorian calendar until later.

The American colonies made the switch in 1752, when the whole British Empire changed. September 2, 1752, was followed by September 14, 1752. Note that an 11-day adjustment was now needed, the Julian calendar having added another day between 1582 and 1752. Dates preceding the change are sometimes designated OS for Old Style. Thus, George Washington's birthday is really February 11, 1732 (OS); only after the change to the Gregorian calendar was his birthday established as February 22, 1732. Most dates in American history have been converted to New Style, or Gregorian dates. Other countries were even slower in adopting the new calendar: Japan, 1873; China, 1912; Greece, 1924; Turkey, 1927.

EXERCISES

The exercises that follow are grouped by level of difficulty. Problems in the A series are the easiest; B series problems are moderately hard; and C series problems are the most difficult.

A–1   Using the list of library functions in Figure 7–2 as a guide, make a new list showing library functions that you have available in your version of BASIC.

A–2   Write a user-defined function that will convert distances measured in yards into feet.

A–3   Write a DIM statement that reserves 84 positions for an array named B.

A–4   Examine the flowchart in Figure 7–17. Is the loop single, multiple, or nested?

A–5   Examine the flowchart in Figure 7–20. Is the loop single, multiple, or nested?

A–6   How would you modify Figure 7–18 to output the result of each throw?

A–7 How many times are each of the actions that follow performed in Figure 7–17?

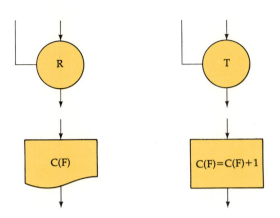

"WE PROGRAMMED IT TO SIMULATE LIVING CONDITIONS IN THE YEAR 2000, AND IT'S BECOME HYSTERICAL."

A–8 From Figure 7–10 draw a picture of a four-dimension array.

B–1 Determine if the version of BASIC you use supports one dummy argument or whether it will support more than one.

B–2 Write a user-defined function that will convert weights measured in pounds and ounces into grams.

B–3 Write a DIM statement that reserves space for an array with five rows and seven columns.

B–4 Does your version of BASIC require that you use quotation marks when an INPUT is used?

B–5 What is the maximum length of a string in your version of BASIC?

B–6 Figure 7–19 shows the Julian dates for non-leap years. How would a leap year chart differ from the one given?

B–7 The history capsule names the years in which nations changed to the Gregorian calendar. Why do you think it is imperative that all nations have the same calendar-dating procedure?

B–8 Modify Figure 7–18 to simulate the roll of two dice, adding together the faces of the two. Print the number of times each of the possible 11 outcomes occurred.

C–1 From the flowchart in Figure 7–17, describe what would happen if the initialization step were to be placed before the R loop beings.

C–2 Modify Figure 7–17 to use an array to count the number of times a 2, 3, 4, 5, . . . , 11, 12 result when two dice are tossed and their faces added together.

CHAPTER 7: ADVANCED BASIC

COMPUTER NEWS

THE SMASH HIT OF SOFTWARE

Daniel Bricklin, 29, and Robert Frankston, 31, a team of new-wave composers, have penned a dynamite disc that has grossed an estimated $8 million. It is not a punk-rock smash, but an unmelodic magnetic number called VisiCalc, the bestselling microcomputer program for business uses. The featherweight sliver of plastic is about the size of a greeting card, but when it is placed in a computer, the machine comes alive. A computer without a program, or "software," is like a $3,000 stereo set without any records or tapes.

Three years ago, Bricklin, then a first-year Harvard Business School student, conceived VisiCalc while struggling with financial-planning problems on his calculator. He enlisted the aid of Frankston, a longtime friend and an expert programmer, to develop a new piece of computer software that would make juggling all those figures easier.

The partnership paid off. Since late 1979 nearly 100,000 copies of nine different versions of VisiCalc have been ordered at prices ranging from $100 to $300. It is far ahead of other business programs like Data Factory and General Ledger, and even outsells the programs for Star Cruiser, Dogfight and other arcade-like computer games.

VisiCalc translates simple commands typed on a keyboard into computer language that the machine then uses to solve problems. It enables a businessman, for example, to manipulate labyrinthine equations to calculate financial trends for his company. If he changes one figure, the machine can tell quickly how that affects the other numbers. A firm that gives its workers a 10 percent pay hike could estimate how that action would alter its costs, sales, profits, or dividends.

The computer program is being put to a wide range of uses. It helps Allerton Cushman Jr., a New York financial analyst, to project insurance-industry profits during the week and tote up his income taxes on the weekend. The Cabot Street Cinema Theatre in Beverly, Mass., bought VisiCalc to figure out which pattern of movie show times draws the best box-office receipts. An accounting firm in Las Vegas plans to use VisiCalc to tell its gambling-house clients how to position slot machines around the floor to ensure the biggest take. VisiCalc is obviously one composition that is in no danger of fading from the charts.

Time, June 2, 1981.

CHAPTER *eight*

LANGUAGE COMPARISONS: FORTRAN, COBOL, PASCAL, PL/1, RPG-II

Preview

Other Programming Languages

FORTRAN 77

COBOL-74

History Capsule:
Captain Grace Hopper and the Origins of COBOL

Pascal

PL/1

RPG-II

Language Selection Criteria

Program Criterion

Comparison of Major Languages in VISA Problem

Summary

Computer News: How to Be a Superprogrammer

PREVIEW

In Chapter 5 you saw the VISA problem programmed in BASIC (see Figures 5–14 and 8–1). In addition to BASIC, five other languages: FORTRAN, COBOL, Pascal, RPG-II, PL/1 are in general use. There are also special purpose languages that ease the programming of unique problems.

With this wide variety of languages available, which one is best? How does one choose the most appropriate language? What factors should be considered in choosing a language? This chapter answers these questions.

OTHER PROGRAMMING LANGUAGES

Since the first programming language, it is estimated that several hundred languages have been developed and used. These languages vary from the mathematic-like languages of FORTRAN and BASIC to business-oriented COBOL and RPG. There are special languages, such as SNOBOL and LISP, for analyzing alphabetic groups of characters, and languages such as SPSS, FORTH, GPSS, and SIMSCRIPT, which can simulate various operations. Some specialized languages, such as APT, have been developed for automatically programming controlled machine tools. Figure 8–2 lists some of these other languages.

FORTRAN 77

One of the first languages developed was **FORTRAN**, which stands for "FORmula TRANslation." Most FORTRAN programmers use a version called FORTRAN 77, but the older version, FORTRAN IV, is still in use. All major manufacturers of computers

```
10     LET T=0
15     PRINT "MONTH","DAY","INVOICE","AMOUNT"
16     PRINT "NUMBER","NUMBER","NUMBER","OF SALE"
20     FOR C=1 TO 6
30     READ M,D,I,A
31     DATA 2,21,27425,71.39
32     DATA 2,24,40711,205.75
33     DATA 2,25,4577,15.98
34     DATA 2,25,4613,64.75
35     DATA 2,28,4908,67.56
36     DATA 3,12,1290,50.01
37     IF M<1 THEN 80
38     IF M>12 THEN 90
40     LET T=T+A
50     PRINT M,D,I,A
60     NEXT C
70     PRINT T
71     GO TO 999
80     PRINT "MONTH NUMBER < 1"
81     GO TO 999
90     PRINT "MONTH NUMBER >12"
999    END
```

FIGURE 8–1 BASIC program and RUN for the VISA problem.

FIGURE 8–2	Special purpose languages.	
Language	Meaning	Use
COGO	Coordinate Geometry	Surveying
ALGOL	Algorithmic Language	Mathematics
JOVIAL	Jules Own Version of IAL	Algebraic formulation
PLATO	Program Logic for Automatic Teaching Operation	Computer-assisted instruction
ATS	Administrative Terminal System	Report writer and text editor
APL	A Programming Language	Timesharing

have compilers or interpreters that allow FORTRAN programs to be processed by their computers. The language has been "standardized" by the American National Standards Institute (ANSI) and is known officially as ANSI FORTRAN 77, but is generally just called FORTRAN.

In Figure 8–3 is the FORTRAN version of our VISA program. As you can see, BASIC and FORTRAN are quite similar. In BASIC we use FOR/NEXT to form a loop, while in FORTRAN loops are written using DO/CONTINUE. To input or output data, FORTRAN uses READ and WRITE along with FORMAT; these are similar to BASIC's READ, PRINT, and IMAGE. Captions in BASIC are printed by placing the words to be printed between quotation marks. The same is true in FORTRAN except that the caption is in the FORMAT. Lastly, to terminate a BASIC program we use an END statement; in FORTRAN the statements STOP and END are used to terminate the program.

FORTRAN 77 differs from BASIC in four major ways. First, FORTRAN inputs and outputs data with the associated FORMAT statement. Second, FORTRAN variables that begin with $I, J, K, L, M,$ or N represent integer quantities, while variables that begin with the letters A to H and O to Z represent real numbers with decimal places. Third, variable names in FORTRAN can be from one to six letters long (the first letter determines whether it is real or integer).

The fourth and last major difference concerns the decision statement. In FORTRAN we use an IF statement to make a decision, as we do in BASIC. However, the FORTRAN IF may be written as:

```
IF (A .LT. B) THEN
   Statement-1
   Statement-2
   Statement-3
ELSE
   Statement-4
   Statement-5
END IF
```

The IF-THEN-ELSE lets the programmer place a series of statements after the THEN, which will be done if A is less than (.LT.) B, and a series of statements after the ELSE, which will be done if A is not less than B. This type of IF statement aids in writing more structured programs with fewer GO TO's than the BASIC IF statement.

During the 1960s FORTRAN IV was widely taught in colleges and universities. In the 1970s, however, BASIC became more popular because of its relative simplicity. With the new version of FORTRAN adopted in 1977 there has been a mild resurgence of interest in FORTRAN. We now find FORTRAN available on home/hobby computers as well as on large systems.

COBOL-74

A programming language frequently used by business and government is **COBOL**. The letters

```
        INTEGER D,C
        T=0
        WRITE(6, 1000)
1000    FORMAT( "1",T2,"MONTH",T15,"DAY",T30,"INVOICE",T45,"AMOUNT"
  *             "1", T2,"NUMBER", T15, "NUMBER", T30, "NUMBER", T45, "OF SALE")
        DO 100 C=1,6,1
            READ(5,1200) M,D,I,A
1200        FORMAT(3I10, F10.2)
            IF (M .LT. 1) GO TO 80
            IF (M .GT. 12) GO TO 90
            T=T+A
            WRITE(6, 1400) M,D,I,A
1400        FORMAT( 3I10, F10.2)
100     CONTINUE
        GO TO 999
80      WRITE(6,1600)
1600    FORMAT(T10, "MONTH NUMBER < 1")
        GO TO 999
90      WRITE(6, 1800)
1800    FORMAT(T10, "MONTH NUMBER > 12")
999     STOP
        END
```

| MONTH | DAY | INVOICE | AMOUNT |
NUMBER	NUMBER	NUMBER	OF SALE
2	21	27425	71.39
2	24	40711	205.75
2	25	4577	15.98
2	25	4613	64.75
2	25	4908	67.56
3	12	1290	50.01
475.44			

FIGURE 8–3   FORTRAN program and execution for the VISA problem.

C-O-B-O-L stand for *CO*mmon *B*usiness-*O*riented *L*anguage. The latest version is COBOL-74. Like FORTRAN and BASIC, the language has been "standardized" to the extent that a COBOL compiler, whether provided by the computer manufacturer or an independent group, can be certified to be COBOL-74. This standard language is officially known as American National Standard (ANS) COBOL 1974, but is generally referred to simply as COBOL.

The intent of COBOL is to allow business-oriented programs to be easily written by programmers in a nonmathematical form. Thus, COBOL commands are written in a modified version of English, and words like DIVIDE are used rather than mathematical operators. Because of this English orientation, COBOL programs are said to be easier to read and understand than programs written in other languages. The language, therefore, is said to be **self-documenting.** Since most business programs are concerned with the processing of data stored in files, COBOL has special features that allow programmers to define files easily. COBOL also has special provisions for processing alphanumeric data (names, addresses, descriptions, and so on).

If we compare the COBOL VISA program in Figure 8–4 with the equivalent BASIC and FORTRAN versions, Figures 8–1 and 8–3, we will see that COBOL is not at all like BASIC or FORTRAN. Every COBOL program has four **divisions:** Identification, Environment, Data, and Procedure. Each division in a COBOL program has a specific function. The **IDENTIFICATION DIVISION** gives the name of the program and the author of the program (see line numbers 1010 to 1030 in Figure 8–4). The **ENVIRONMENT DIVISION** describes the particular computer that this program is designed to run on and the files that this program uses (line numbers 2000 to 2070 in Figure 8–4).

The third division in every COBOL program is the **DATA DIVISION** (line numbers 3000 to 3960 in Figure 8–4). In this division memory locations are reserved for the variables, called **data names** in COBOL, that will be used.

The DATA DIVISION is subdivided into the FILE SECTION, WORKING-STORAGE SECTION, and the REPORT SECTION. The FILE SECTION is used to reserve memory spaces for data that are file-oriented, while the WORKING-STORAGE SECTION reserves memory spaces for variables whose values are to be calculated or for constant information that will not change, like a caption or page heading. The REPORT SECTION, not shown in Figure 8–4, is used when a programmer wants to use COBOL to automatically generate a printed report with various headings, detail lines, footing lines, and different types of totals.

The fourth and final division of every COBOL program is the **PROCEDURE DIVISION** (line numbers 4000 to 999999 in Figure 8–4). The exacting list of steps to be executed by the computer is placed in this division. Each sentence in the PROCEDURE DIVISION begins with a **reserved word.** There are hundreds of reserved words in COBOL, but those used in the procedure division all cause an action, such as MOVE, READ, WRITE, or PERFORM.

In a structured COBOL program the use of GO TO is minimized or eliminated and COBOL procedural paragraphs are PERFORMed instead. This means that the program is really a series of blocks or modules, each of which does a specific task. The modules are accessible only at their beginning and terminate with their last sentence. Modules, therefore, have hierarchy or order (see Figure 8–5). The control module, with higher order, PERFORMs the process modules with lower order. You can see this hierarchy by looking at the procedure division of our VISA program.

Studies have shown that programs can be written more quickly in structured form than in nonstructured form. These programs are easier to modify if the need arises, and provide less complex programs with fewer logic errors. Structuring programs in modules, therefore, results in straightforward programs that are more easily read and that cost less to write and maintain.

COBOL programs tend to be lengthy compared to other programming languages, but they execute rapidly on the computer despite this. The COBOL compiler itself is usually large and requires extensive amounts of computer memory. Thus, COBOL is usually available on computers with large memory capacities.

The primary advantage of COBOL is its resemblance to English. This feature minimizes the amount of supporting material, called **documentation,** that programmers must develop after their programs are completed and operational. Normally, documentation consists of a description of the program's purpose, a flowchart of the program's logic, diagrams of the input/output (I/O) files processed, and a step-by-step description of the major parts of the program itself. COBOL programs, with their

```
1010        IDENTIFICATION DIVISION.
1020        PROGRAM-ID. EDWARDS.
1030        AUTHOR. PERRY EDWARDS AND BRUCE BROADWELL.
2000        ENVIRONMENT DIVISION.
2010        CONFIGURATION SECTION.
2020        SOURCE-COMPUTER. B6800.
2030        OBJECT-COMPUTER. B6800.
2040        INPUT-OUTPUT SECTION.
2050        FILE-CONTROL.
2060            SELECT CARDS ASSIGN TO CARD-READER.
2070            SELECT LINEPRINTER ASSIGN TO PRINTER.
3000        DATA DIVISION.
3005        FILE SECTION.
3010        FD CARDS.
3020        01 CARD.
3030            03  MONTH-NUMBER PIC 9(10).
3040            03  DAY-NUMBER PIC 9(10).
3050            03  INVOICE-NUMBER PIC 9(10).
3060            03  AMOUNT PIC 9(8)V99.
3070            03  FILLER PIC X(40).
3170        FD LINEPRINTER LINAGE 66.
3180        01 PRINT-LINE PIC X(132).
3220        WORKING-STORAGE SECTION.
3700        01 LAST-LINE.
3710            03  LAST-T PIC Z,ZZZ,ZZZ.99.
3720            03  FILLER PIC X(120) VALUE SPACES.
3800        01 CAPTION-1.
3810            03  FILLER PIC X(20) VALUE "      MONTH      DAY".
3820            03  FILLER PIC X(20) VALUE "    INVOICE    AMOUNT".
3830            03  FILLER PIC X(92) VALUE SPACES.
3850        01 CAPTION-2.
3860            03  FILLER PIC X(20) VALUE "     NUMBER    NUMBER".
3870            03  FILLER PIC X(20) VALUE "     NUMBER    OF SALE".
3880            03  FILLER PIC X(92) VALUE SPACES.
3900        01 FINISHED PIC X VALUE "N".
3901            88  DONE VALUE "Y".
3902        01 T PIC 9(8)V99 VALUE ZERO.
3910        01 DETAIL-LINE.
3920            03  DETAIL-MONTH PIC Z(10).
3930            03  DETAIL-DAY PIC Z(10).
3940            03  DETAIL-INVOICE PIC Z(10).
3950            03  DETAIL-AMOUNT PIC ZZZ,ZZZ.99.
3960            03  FILLER PIC X(102) VALUE SPACES.
4000        PROCEDURE DIVISION.
```

FIGURE 8-4 COBOL program and execution for the VISA problem.

```
4010      100-MAIN-PARAGRAPH.
4020          PERFORM 200-OPENING.
4040          PERFORM 300-PROCESS-DATA UNTIL DONE.
4050          PERFORM 400-CLOSING.
4051          STOP RUN.
4060      200-OPENING.
4070          OPEN INPUT CARDS.
4080          OPEN OUTPUT LINEPRINTER.
4081          READ CARDS AT END MOVE "Y" TO FINISHED.
4082          PERFORM 500-TOP-OF-PAGE.
4090      300-PROCESS-DATA.
4091          IF MONTH-NUMBER IS LESS THAN 1 DISPLAY "MONTH NUMBER <1"
4092          ELSE IF MONTH-NUMBER > 12 DISPLAY "MONTH NUMBER > 12"
4093              ELSE
4094              ADD AMOUNT TO T
4100              MOVE MONTH-NUMBER TO DETAIL-MONTH
4110              MOVE DAY-NUMBER TO DETAIL-DAY
4115              MOVE INVOICE-NUMBER TO DETAIL-INVOICE
4120              MOVE AMOUNT TO DETAIL-AMOUNT
4700              WRITE PRINT-LINE FROM DETAIL-LINE BEFORE ADVANCING 1 LINE
4710                  AT EOP PERFORM 500-TOP-OF-PAGE.
4800          READ CARDS AT END MOVE "Y" TO FINISHED.
5000      400-CLOSING.
5040          MOVE T TO LAST-T.
5050          WRITE PRINT-LINE FROM LAST-LINE BEFORE ADVANCING 1 LINE
5060              AT EOP PERFORM 500-TOP-OF-PAGE.
5100          CLOSE CARDS.
5200          CLOSE LINEPRINTER.
5300      500-TOP-OF-PAGE.
5310          MOVE SPACES TO PRINT-LINE.
5320          WRITE PRINT-LINE AFTER ADVANCING PAGE.
5330          WRITE PRINT-LINE FROM CAPTION-1 BEFORE ADVANCING 1 LINE.
5340          WRITE PRINT-LINE FROM CAPTION-2 BEFORE ADVANCING 1 LINE.
999999    END-PROGRAM.
```

MONTH	DAY	INVOICE	AMOUNT
NUMBER	NUMBER	NUMBER	OF SALE
2	21	27425	71.39
2	24	40711	205.75
2	25	4577	15.98
2	25	4613	64.75
2	25	4908	67.56
3	12	1290	50.01

475.44

FIGURE 8-4   *Continued*

CAPTAIN GRACE HOPPER AND THE ORIGINS OF COBOL

On May 28 and 29, 1959, a meeting was held in the Pentagon to consider the desirability of establishing a common language for programming electronic computers for business-type applications. Representatives from users both in private industry and in government, from computer manufacturers, and from other interested parties were present. The group agreed that the project should be undertaken. The *COnference on DAta SYstems Languages* (CODASYL) developed out of this meeting.

The original COBOL specification resulted from the work of a CODASYL committee. By September 1959, this committee had specified a language they considered superior to existing language-compiler systems. This language specification was further modified, and by December 1959, COBOL existed as a language that was not identified with any manufacturer and, therefore, presented advantages for both government and private industry users.

One of the prime movers in the development of COBOL during the 1950s and continuing through the 1960s and 1970s was Captain Grace Hopper of the United States Navy. A Phi Beta Kappa graduate of Vassar College (1928) and Yale University (masters and doctorate), Captain Hopper has worked continuously to test various COBOL compilers. In 1969 she was the first ever recipient of Data Processing Management Association's annual "Man of the Year" award, and she is the keynote speaker for many conferences and conventions across the United States. In 1944 Captain Hopper learned to program the first large-scale computer, the Mark 1. Later she learned to program its successors, Mark II, Mark III, and UNIVAC I. She has written many technical papers, served on numerous committees, and is an active member of many computer-related organizations. The COBOL-74 of today is a direct result of the efforts of visionaries like Captain Grace Hopper.

English orientation, minimize the need for a step-by-step description of the documentation.

PASCAL

Pascal was designed by Niklaus Wirth at the Institute für Informatik in Zurich and was first published in its standard form in 1973. Thus, it is one of the most modern programming languages in widespread use today. The name Pascal is not an acronym—the letters do not stand for anything. The language was named for Blaise Pascal, a brilliant seventeenth-century mathematician and philosopher who, among other things, invented the first mechanical digital computer at the age of 19.

Pascal is a very simple language—its formal definition is only six pages long—but it is also very powerful, which leads many people to refer to it as an elegant language. A widely available version of Pascal is known as UCSD Pascal.

Pascal, like PL/1, is a free-form language, although most programmers who use it adopt a style of indentation that causes program listings to indicate graphically what control structures are in use. Each Pascal program consists of a **declarations section** and a **program body section.** Declarations are much briefer in Pascal than in COBOL. Usually the only requirement is that all the program variables be listed, along with the type of data they will contain.

In terms of control structures, Pascal is as powerful as PL/1 and is more oriented toward structured

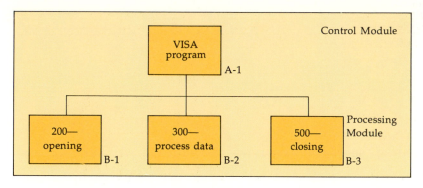

FIGURE 8–5 Hierarchy chart of paragraph modules.

programming. Pascal does lack the sophisticated editing, and complex I/O capabilities of PL/1 and COBOL, and it is also limited to working only with sequential files. Pascal is a very easy language to learn. Like BASIC it was originally designed for teaching programming concepts. It is also a very easy language to write programs in, and it is especially nice for writing large programs. In fact, several computer manufacturers use a slightly extended version of Pascal to write their operating systems and compilers. Figure 8–6 shows the VISA problem written in Pascal.

PL/1

PL/1 was developed in the middle 1960s. This language combines the mathematical structure of FORTRAN with the file processing features of COBOL. PL/1 (*Programming Language 1*) was first developed by IBM. Although it was thought that PL/1 would eventually become the dominant programming language, its use has not yet become widespread.

PL/1 is different from most other languages because of its **free-form** instructions. The programmer is not restricted to entering statements line by line, using particular words at the beginning of each statement. Statements do not have to be numbered and the entries of a given statement do not have to be placed on certain locations. The compiler is able to determine statements and desired actions.

Unlike COBOL, FORTRAN, or most other programming languages, PL/1 has **default options.** If the programmer makes minor errors or forgets to write a statement properly, the compiler in some instances will accommodate the error.

PL/1 programs are similar to COBOL with its division structure (see Figure 8–7). In the PROCEDURE OPTIONS and DECLARE statements, a PL/1 program is named, files are described, and data fields are named and types designated (numeric or alphanumeric). Procedural statements causing actions on the data fields follow the declarations. These statements are written in a hybrid FORTRAN-COBOL form; that is, IF commands can be like FORTRAN, or COBOL, or both.

The language rules of PL/1 are similar in difficulty and complexity to those of COBOL. Compiler memory requirements limit the use of PL/1 to large-memory computers. Furthermore, PL/1 is not a standardized language like FORTRAN or COBOL; this leads to variations in the language rules as compilers are written for different computing systems.

RPG-II

The **RPG-II** programming language is another of the business-oriented languages. The letters *R-P-G* stand for *R*eport *P*rogram *G*enerator, and RPG-II is specifically designed for programming business-oriented printed reports. The older version of the

CHAPTER 8: LANGUAGE COMPARISONS 177

```
PROGRAM VALIDATE (INPUT, OUTPUT);
(* VISA PROGRAM TO VALIDATE MONTH AND DAY NUMBERS*)
VAR   M, D, I: INTEGER;
      A, T: REAL;
      VALID:BOOLEAN;
BEGIN
  T: =0;
  WRITELN ('MONTH':10, 'DAY':10, 'INVOICE':10, 'AMOUNT':10);
  WRITELN ('NUMBER':10, 'NUMBER':10, 'NUMBER':10, 'OF SALE':10);
  READLN (M, D, I, A);
  VALID:=TRUE;
  WHILE NOT EOF AND VALID DO
    IF (M<1) THEN BEGIN
        WRITELN ('MONTH NUMBER <1');
        VALID:=FALSE
        END (*BEGIN*)
    ELSE IF (M > 12) THEN BEGIN
        WRITELN ('MONTH NUMBER >12');
        VALID:=FALSE
        END (*BEGIN*)
    ELSE BEGIN
        WRITELN (M:10, D:10, I:10, A:10:10:2);
        T:=T+A;
        READLN (M, D, I, A)
        END (*BEGIN AND WHILE*);
    IF EOF THEN
        WRITELN (T:10:2)
END.
```

| MONTH | DAY | INVOICE | AMOUNT |
NUMBER	NUMBER	NUMBER	OF SALE
2	21	27425	71.39
2	24	40711	205.75
2	25	4577	15.98
2	25	4613	64.75
2	25	4908	67.56
3	12	1290	50.01
475.44			

FIGURE 8–6   Pascal program and execution for the VISA problem.

language is generally used on small business computers like the IBM System/32 or IBM System/34. The newest version of the language is RPG-III, which is used on IBM System/38 computers among others. RPG-II will be discussed rather than RPG-III because of the newness of RPG-III and the wide use of RPG-II by most users of the language.

When writing a program in RPG-II the pro-

```
DP:     PROCEDURE OPTIONS(MAIN);
        DECLARE INPUTS FILE STREAM;
        DECLARE LISTING FILE STREAM;
        DECLARE T FIXED (8,2) INITIAL (0,00), C FIXED (5,0);
        DECLARE M FIXED (2,0), D FIXED (2,0), I FIXED (7,0);
        DECLARE A FIXED (7,2);
        OPEN FILE (INPUTS) STREAM;
        OPEN FILE (LISTING) PRINT;
        PUT LIST ("MONTH","DAY","INVOICE","AMOUNT");
        PUT LIST ("NUMBER","NUMBER","NUMBER","OF SALE");
        DO C = 1 TO 10 BY 1;
            GET LIST (M, D, I, A);
            IF M < 1 THEN PUT LIST ("MONTH NUMBER < 1");
            ELSE IF M > 12 THEN PUT LIST ("MONTH NUMBER > 12");
                ELSE BEGIN;
                    T = T + A;
                    PUT LIST (M, D, I, A);
                END;
        END;
        PUT LIST (T);
        END DP;
```

| MONTH | DAY | INVOICE | AMOUNT |
NUMBER	NUMBER	NUMBER	OF SALE
2	21	27425	71.39
2	24	40711	205.75
2	25	4577	15.98
2	25	4613	64.75
2	28	4908	67.56
3	12	1290	50.01
475.44			

FIGURE 8–7   PL/1 program and execution for the VISA problem.

grammer describes the files and action to be taken by completing five different specification sheets (see Figure 8–8). The first sheet, **Control Card and File Specifications,** names the program, identifies the kind of files that will be processed (card, disk, or tape), and designates the use of the file (input, output, or combined input and output).

The second of the sheets is the **Input Specifications.** This sheet names the various fields being read and describes the type of field as being numeric or alphabetic.

The **Calculation Specifications** is the third sheet of an RPG program. This form describes the operations that will be performed on the various data fields and the order of the operations.

The **Output Specifications** form shows the data to be output. The output information can be headings across the top of a page, results from computations, or a mixture of caption and results. Results can be edited in RPG-II so that dollar signs and commas are inserted as required.

The fifth sheet, **File Extension and Line Counter**

Specifications, of an RPG-II program is less frequently used. This sheet is required only for data being processed from disk or when tables are required. It is not shown in Figure 8-8.

As you can see from the VISA problem in Figure 8-9, RPG-II has limited calculation and decision features, so mathematical formulas cannot easily be written in the language. A section of a program that must be used at two or more points in the same program is also hard to write in RPG-II. To make a decision in RPG a set of indicators must be set and tested at a later time. For programming printed reports, however, RPG-II is very effective, and it has been used extensively in business for this purpose.

LANGUAGE SELECTION CRITERIA

The choice of which of the many programming languages to use can have a dramatic effect on the success or failure of the problem being solved. In many instances the choice of a particular language is made because it is the only language the programmers know. Or a particular language may be the only one available on a certain computing system. But many other factors besides these two should be considered when selecting a language.

One of the most important considerations is cost. The cost of originally writing a program and maintaining it over its lifetime is mainly a direct labor cost. Cost can be somewhat lessened by using a high-level, machine-independent language that minimizes the documentation required by the program once it is completed. Studies of programmers show that a competent programmer will correctly write 11 lines of program a day, and while this may seem very slow, this rate includes composing and testing the program to ensure its correctness, and preparing the documentation report that describes what these instructions do. Figure 8-10 gives a comparison of the programming/documenting time of each of the major languages.

A second criterion often ignored in writing programs is the amount of memory required for the resulting object program and the time it takes the object program to run. Since the computer costs money to operate, this factor can also affect the total cost of the program. For a program that is going to be run often, such as the VISA program, this cost may be more important in the long run than the cost of programming. Figure 8-11 shows the amount of memory required and the time necessary to process a single line in our VISA program in each of the six languages. The statistics of Figure 8-11 depend on the particular computer and compiler in use, but they do reflect general tendencies.

"I SIT HERE AND SOLVE MATHEMATICAL PROBLEMS, PROGRAM ELECTRONIC MUSIC, ANALYZE ARCHITECTURAL POSSIBILITIES... BUT SOMEHOW BEING A RENAISSANCE MAN ISN'T WHAT IT USED TO BE."

PROGRAM CRITERION

In addition to the criteria for language selection just discussed, the program being written may not lend itself to a particular language. FORTRAN, for instance, does not provide for easy editing of data or easy manipulation of alphanumeric characters. RPG-II does not have a sophisticated mathematical feature, but it does have editing provisions. COBOL tends to be wordy, but has excellent file-

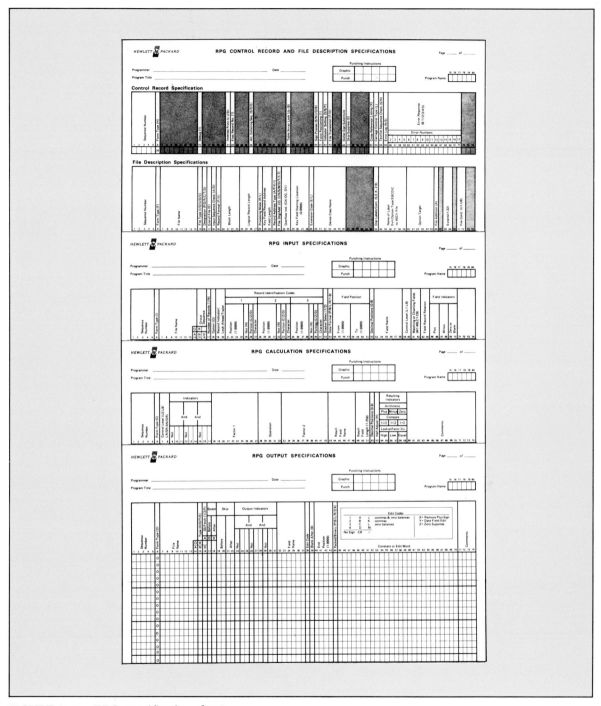

FIGURE 8-8 RPG specification sheets.

```
0001      H                                                    X           RPGPRG

0002      FRPGDATA   IPEAF 216  72              DISC
0003      FPRINTER   O  F  132  132             LP

0004      IRPGDATA   NS   10
0005      I                                      1   10MONTH
0006      I                                      2    3 DAY
0007      I                                      4    9 INVOIC
0008      I                                     11  152AMT

0009      C    10         MONTH     COMP  1                       40
0010      C    40                   GOTO  END
0011      C    10         MONTH     COMP  12                      50
0012      C    50                   GOTO  END
0013      C               AMT       ADD   TOTAMT    TOTAMT 62
0014      C               END       TAG
0015      C    40                   SETON                         LR
0016      C    50                   SETON                         LR

0017      OPRINTER   H   101    1P
0018      O                                          5  "MONTH"
0019      O                                         18  "DAY"
0020      O                                         37  "INVOICE"
0021      O                                         51  "AMOUNT"
0022      O          H   1      1P
0023      O                                          6  "NUMBER"
0024      O                                         21  "NUMBER"
0025      O                                         36  "NUMBER"
0026      O                                         52  "OF SALE"
0027      O          D   1      10N40N50
0028      O                             MONTH Z     2
0029      O                             DAY        18
0030      O                             INVOIC     37
0031      O                             AMT   3    52
0032      O          D   1      40
0033      O                                         17  "MONTH NUMBER < 1"
0034      O          D   1      50
0035      O                                         17  "MONTH NUMBER >12"
0036      O          T          LRN40N50
0037      O                             TOTAMT3     7
```

MONTH	DAY	INVOICE	AMOUNT
NUMBER	NUMBER	NUMBER	OF SALE
2	21	27425	71.39
2	24	40711.	205.75
2	25	4577	15.98
2	25	4613	64.75
2	28	4908	67.56
3	12	1290	50.01
475.44			

FIGURE 8–9 RPG program and execution for the VISA problem.

FIGURE 8–10 Language and writing time comparison.

Language	Number of Instructions	Time to Write (days)
BASIC	17	1.55
FORTRAN 77	21	1.91
COBOL-74	78	7.09
Pascal	28	2.55
PL/1	21	1.91
RPG-II	37	3.36

processing provisions. A chart comparing the various provisions of the major languages is given in Figure 8–12, and, although not all-inclusive, the major provisions are listed; you can make your own comparison.

In this chart "high" means that the language is considered to be strong in this category; "middle" means that the language is capable of this category; and "low" means that the language does not support this category or it must be specially programmed.

COMPARISON OF MAJOR LANGUAGES IN VISA PROBLEM

The VISA problem has now been programmed in each of the major languages. It has been compiled, tested, timed, and compared. The last criterion in language comparison concerns the cost of writing and running a program one time, two times, three times, a hundred times. For a business, whose goal is to minimize costs, this is an important criterion and might be the only criterion used for selecting a particular language.

If we summarize the statistics of Figures 8–10 and 8–11, and add some cost information, it is possible to calculate the overall cost of programming our VISA problem (see Figure 8–13). It is assumed in Figure 8–13 that the computer cost includes such factors as maintenance, a computer operator, heating, cooling, and supplies. The programming costs include provisions for fringe benefits, such as vacation time and sick leave.

The cost of writing a program stays the same regardless of the number of times the program is run. In business terminology this is a **fixed cost**. The fixed cost of programming the VISA problem for each of the programming languages is shown in the fourth column of Figure 8–13.

The cost of running a program depends on the computer cost and can be stated as:

cost to run = (computer cost per second)*(execution time in seconds per run)*(number of runs, N)

The computer cost is $0.016 per second and the amount of time it runs depends on the language

FIGURE 8–11 Language versus memory and time in VISA program.

Language	Amount of Memory (bytes) Needed to Process a Single Line of VISA Program	Time (in seconds) to Process a Single Line of VISA Program	Type of Computer
BASIC	8502	.20	Burroughs B6805
FORTRAN 77	11952	.20	Burroughs B6805
COBOL-74	13224	.15	Burroughs B6805
Pascal	22845	.20	Burroughs B6805
PL/1	25960	.20	Burroughs B6805
RPG-II	4722	.20	HP 3000/33

CHAPTER 8: LANGUAGE COMPARISONS

FIGURE 8–12 Language comparisons.

Division	BASIC	FORTRAN 77	COBOL-74	RPG-II	PL/1	Pascal
Mathematics	High	High	Middle	Low	High	High
Alphanumeric	Middle	Middle	Middle	Middle	High	Middle
Arrays	High	High	Middle	Middle	High	High
Subprograms	Middle	High	Low	Low	High	High
Editing	Low	Low	High	High	High	Low
File Processing	Middle	Middle	High	High	High	Middle
Multiple input forms	Low	Middle	High	High	High	High
Looping commands	Middle	High	High	High	High	High
Compiler requirements	Low	Middle	High	Low	High	Low
Easy language rules	High	Middle	Low	Middle	Low	High
Widely available	High	High	Middle	Middle	Middle	Middle
Easily readable	Middle	Middle	High	Low	Middle	Middle
Machine-independent	Low	High	High	High	Middle	Middle
Standardized	Middle	High	High	High	Middle	High
Self-documenting	Low	Low	High	Low	Middle	Middle
Tracing routines	Low	Middle	High	High	High	Middle
Structured programming	Low	Middle	High	Middle	High	High

FIGURE 8–13 Comparison and cost factors in VISA program.

Language	Time to Write (days)	Time to Validate (sec)	Cost to Write ($)	Cost to Run ($)
BASIC	1.55	.20	108.50	.0032
FORTRAN 77	1.91	.20	133.7	.0032
COBOL-74	7.09	.15	496.3	.0024
Pascal	2.55	.20	178.50	.0032
PL/1	1.91	.20	133.7	.0032
RPG-II	3.36	.20	235.20	.0032

Computer cost: $60/hr = $1/min = $0.016/sec

Programmer cost*: $1400/mo = $350/week = $70/day

* These costs taken from *Datamation* 1981 Salary Survey.

used, as you can see in the third column figure. This cost, then, varies according to the number of runs and is called a **variable cost**.

The total cost is the sum of the fixed and variable costs. For each language, the total cost is written as follows:

- BASIC = 108.50 + .0032N
- FORTRAN 77 = 133.7 + .0032N
- COBOL-74 = 496.30 + .0024N
- Pascal = 178.50 + .0032N
- PL/1 = 133.70 + .0032N
- RPG-II = 235.20 + .0032N

These six formulas predict the overall cost of programming in each of the languages. In mathematical terminology these formulas are called

FIGURE 8-14 Total cost of programming.

Number of Runs (N)	BASIC	FORTRAN 77	COBOL-74	Pascal	PL/1	RPG-II
0	108.50	133.70	496.30	126.70	133.70	223.30
1	108.50	133.70	496.30	126.70	133.70	223.30
10	108.53	133.73	496.32	126.73	133.73	223.33
100	108.82	134.02	496.54	127.02	134.02	223.62
1,000	111.70	136.90	498.70	129.90	136.90	226.50
10,000	140.50	165.70	520.30	158.70	165.70	255.30
100,000	428.50	453.70	736.30	446.70	453.70	543.30
1,000,000	3308.50	3333.70	2896.30	3326.70	3333.70	3423.30
10,000,000	32108.50	32133.70	24496.30	32126.70	32133.70	32223.30

"first-degree equations" and, when graphed, all yield a straight line. In order to draw the formulas, first substitute values for "numbers of runs" and solve (see Figure 8-14).

The graph in Figure 8-15 shows that BASIC is the least costly language up to point A. The intent of BASIC, FORTRAN, and Pascal was to write programs quickly and use them only once or infrequently. This intent is depicted by the chart, since these languages are the cheapest for programs where the number of runs is low. COBOL is more costly to write and run for only a few runs, but it becomes less costly as the number of runs increases—and in a business environment programs are often run many times. RPG-II and PL/1, with their higher fixed costs, parallel BASIC, FORTRAN, and Pascal in cost and are not the cheapest languages for a large number of runs.

Figures 8-14 and 8-15 show an interesting phenomenon. Small businesses (those with, say, 10,000 customers) need to minimize their overhead (fixed) costs since they probably do not have extra money to spend on programming. Their best programming languages, therefore, would be Pascal, BASIC, FORTRAN, or RPG since these languages have the smallest initial programming cost. If each of their customers is billed monthly, then the program would use 120,000 (12 × 10,000) runs per year. With this few runs their overall total cost would be low also.

For large businesses (say, 1 million customers) that bill monthly, COBOL is a better language choice. Although COBOL has a higher initial programming cost, the total cost for 12 million bills (12 × 1 million) will be lower than that of the other languages. Thus small businesses are more likely to use BASIC and FORTRAN and large ones to use COBOL because costs are minimized for each, respectively.

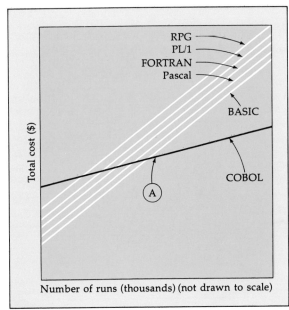

FIGURE 8-15 Graph of total cost of programming.

SUMMARY

The proper choice of which programming language to use depends on many factors. Although BASIC, FORTRAN, COBOL, Pascal, PL/1, and RPG are the major programming languages, they are not the only one from which to choose. FORTRAN, the oldest of these computer languages, uses a mathematical formula basis to express the instructions and is standardized. COBOL is English-like in structure, using sentences and paragraphs, and is widely used by businesses. PL/1 combines the mathematical features of FORTRAN with the file-processing capabilities of COBOL. RPG is a business language whose primary purpose is to generate printed reports from data on cards, disk, or tape. Pascal is the newest of the languages we have examined and is finding increased popularity in colleges, universities, businesses, and among home hobby computer users.

The major criteria for the proper choice of a computer language are:

1. Language availability
2. Language familiarity of programmers
3. Ease of program maintenance
4. Cost of programming
5. Time needed to write the program
6. Time needed to execute the program
7. Characteristics of problem

Only by considering all seven of these factors, as well as the number of times the program is going to be used, is it possible to pick the correct language.

TERMS

The following words or terms have been presented in this chapter.

FORTRAN
COBOL
Self-documenting
Division
IDENTIFICATION DIVISION
ENVIRONMENT DIVISION
DATA DIVISION
Data name
PROCEDURE DIVISION
Reserved word
Documentation
Pascal
Declarations section
Program body section
Procedures
Functions
PL/1
Free form
Default options
RPG-II
Control Card and File Specifications
Input Specifications
Calculation Specifications
Output Specifications
File Extension and Line Counter Specifications
Fixed cost
Variable cost

EXERCISES

The exercises that follow are grouped by level of difficulty. Problems in the A series are the easiest; B series problems are moderately hard; and C series problems are the most difficult.

A–1 Based on Figure 8–14, which programming language is the cheapest for: 5 runs? 50 runs? 500 runs? 5,000 runs? 50,000 runs?

A–2 Using Figure 8–12 and counting 0 points for low, 3 points for middle, and 5 points for high, which language is best? Or can the best language be computed on the basis of total points? Explain.

B–1 Using the total cost formulas that were used to graph the lines for Figure 8–15, determine the exact number of runs at which COBOL becomes cheaper than FORTRAN.

B–2 Captain Grace Hopper worked on COBOL-74. What version of COBOL does your school use? Check the COBOL reference manual in your library or computer center.

B–3 Convert the following into FORTRAN, COBOL, and Pascal:

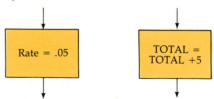

C-1 Obtain from your computer center the time it takes to compile a BASIC, FORTRAN, COBOL, Pascal, PL/1, and RPG program, the cost of the computer, and the cost of programmers and entry operators. Then redraw Figure 8–15 using the data.

C-2 Some versions of FORTRAN have a DO WHILE or DO UNTIL statement to aid in writing structured FORTRAN programs. Does the version of FORTRAN on your computer have these statements?

COMPUTER NEWS

HOW TO BE A SUPERPROGRAMMER

A great deal of the current interest in structured programming, chief programmer teams and "egoless" programming is intimately involved with the concept of a superprogrammer. It appears that the term was first introduced into the literature at the NATO Software Engineering conference by Joel Aron of IBM, who described the exploits of Dr. Harlan Mills at NASA; Dr. Mills participated in a superprogrammer experiment that became the forerunner of IBM's chief programmer team organization. However, the concept of a programmer who could "code faster than a speeding bullet" has existed for a number of years at several other computer manufacturing organizations, several universities (notably MIT's Project MAC and Stanford's Artificial Intelligence Group) and a few commercial organizations.

While the phrase superprogrammer is apparently being replaced by the phrase chief programmer, it is still recognized that there are programmers in the industry—and always will be—who are at least an order of magnitude better than the average programmer. The question is: how does one become a superprogrammer? Is one born that way? Does it come from eating Wheaties every morning? (I attribute my limited superprogrammer capabilities to the fact that I ate an entire box of Wheaties and a quart of milk for breakfast every day until I was 11 years old—by which time I reckon that my personality was pretty well established.) Is it something that can be practiced? Does it involve certain programming techniques that one can learn? In any case, does one even want to be a superprogrammer, considering that the management of most EDP organizations is unwilling to pay their programmers in a manner directly proportional to their technical productivity?

There are very few definitive answers to these questions. However, some clues concerning the personality, training, and characteristics of a superprogrammer may be obtained from a classic study by Sackman et al in the January 1968 Communications of the ACM, and from Wolfe's study of programmer aptitudes, as reported in the Proceedings of the 1971 Annual Conference of the ACM. In addition, I can make some comments on superprogrammers I have observed and known at Project MAC, DEC, General Electric, several small consulting organizations and several hundred training seminars around the world.

CHARACTERISTICS OF SUPERPROGRAMMERS

In discussions of superprogrammers, one question is raised time and again: Is one born a superprogrammer or can one learn to be a superprogrammer?

In this context, it is interesting that Sackman found, in a group of trainee programmers, that there was a strong correlation between those who were superior in coding, testing, debugging and generating efficient programs and those who had superior results in a standard programming aptitude test; on the other hand, there was no detectable correlation with experienced programmers. Sackman concluded, "This situation suggests that general programming skill may dominate early training and initial on-the-job experience, but that such skill is progressively transformed and displaced by more specialized skills with increasing experience."

All of this would seem to suggest that potential superprogrammers are born with a certain knack for programming, but that it is imperative to assemble a certain "bag of tricks" during the first few years of one's career in order to really be a superprogrammer. The real superprogrammer learns, for example, not to implicitly trust any vendor-supplied hardware manual or programming manual; he/she learns to use certain hardware features or language features with great caution, because they hardly ever work; etc.

There is another phenomenon that is enormously important if one is to understand the personality of a superprogrammer: most of them reach a critical age (usually 30, plus or minus a couple years) when they decide that they should grow up and do something constructive with their lives, rather than just playing games in a computer room. As a result, we have seen a number of brilliant superprogrammers throw it all away by becoming a manager (ugh!), getting married, having a baby or deciding to become a farmer. Conversely, those superprogrammers who do not make such a radical change at the age of 30 are often those who, because of their personality, are totally unable to do so. Hence, it should not surprise us that many of the established superprogrammers are freaks in some sense of the word: they look funny; they wear funny clothes; they refuse to work regular hours; they don't get along with normal people; and so forth.

TRAINING OF SUPERPROGRAMMERS

There is also a great deal of debate as to the type of university training one should have in order to be a superprogrammer—or whether one needs a college education at all. Throughout the 1960s the programming profession was populated (and often dominated) by a wide variety of people—philosophy majors, undertakers, dogcatchers, electrical engineers (who are often terrible programmers), mathematicians (ditto) and a few people who called themselves computer scientists. In the 1970s, however, most organizations have begun expecting that their trainee programmers will have had some training or education in programming—and will often require a bachelor's degree in computer science.

That there might be some rationale behind this was illustrated by a fascinating study conducted by Professor Jack Wolfe of Brooklyn College. After testing more than 11,000 persons in some 500 companies over a four-year period, Wolfe found that computer science majors, as a group, scored higher than any other group. Mathematics/physics majors ranked second; analysts with programming experience ranked third; programmers ranked fourth; programming trainees ranked fifth; programming instructors ranked sixth (which in itself is a fascinating commentary on the state of programming education); mathematics teachers ranked seventh; systems analysts without programming experience ranked eighth; EDP supervisors ranked ninth (which confirms what most programmers have always known); persons attending one or two courses at private EDP schools ranked tenth; persons attending private EDP schools full-time for one year ranked eleventh(!); computer operators ranked twelfth; tab operators ranked thirteenth; and keypunch operators ranked last.

Obviously, one cannot—and should not—derive any universal laws from this experiment.

TECHNIQUES OF SUPERPROGRAMMERS

What does a superprogrammer do that a normal programmer doesn't do? The superficial answer, of course, is that he writes code very quickly, gets it to work very quickly and usually has extremely clever, efficient code. These days, it is becoming more and more important that, in addition, the superprogrammer writes code that can be understood and maintained by mere mortals. Still, the question remains: What tricks does the superprogrammer have that enable him to write code quickly and get it to work quickly? Having watched several superprogrammers in a variety of environments, I offer the following suggestions:

1) Pick a programming problem that you know you can solve and whose entire dimensions you can grasp mentally. I have seen several superprogrammers tackle small- and medium-sized programming problems with blinding speed; given a problem too large to mentally visualize all at once, they become helpless.

2) Isolate yourself from the distractions normally found in an office. It is extremely difficult carrying out superprogrammer activities in a typical commercial "bullpen" office.

3) Make sure you are calm and rested and then work straight through until you have finished the project. This implies, of course, that the project is not very large. Nevertheless, I have watched several superprogrammers work 24, 36 and even 54 hours until they have finished coding a program, at which point they drop from exhaustion.

4) Don't flowchart—that's a waste of time and you should be able to carry the flowchart in your head if you are a superprogrammer. A structure chart or rough block diagram may be helpful to organize your thinking, but they should be considered working documents and thrown in the wastebasket as soon as you are finished coding.

5) Spread your papers—especially your coding sheets—out on a large table so you can see everything you have done as you write the code. Even better, paste the program up on a wall as you write it. This will allow you to see the entire program as you write it, so you can see if you've forgotten anything and so you can see how everything fits together.

6) Use very conservative programming techniques. Contrary to the popular myth, most real superprogrammers do not use clever, tricky coding sequences—unless they know the hardware and/or the language extremely well.

Because they are obsessed with getting the job done very quickly, they usually write very simple, straight-line code; they tend to use defensive programming techniques, so that if a bug does exist in their code, its scope will be limited. They are inclined to use structured programming and modular programming techniques; on the other hand, since they are capable of comprehending larger and more complex chunks of code than the average programmer, they may not design modules as small and simple as the maintenance programmer would like.

CONCLUSIONS

Most of the superprogrammers I have known were turned on to computers by the time they were 18 and tended to devote the energy and passion of their youth to absorbing everything they could find on the subject of computers. Since there is a good chance that if you are reading this magazine you are over 18, I would suggest that if you are not already a superprogrammer, it's too late; if you don't know, if you don't feel that you're a superprogrammer, then the chances are that you probably aren't. If you are a superprogrammer, you know that you are, and much of this article is probably irrelevant. However, if you're a young superprogrammer (i.e., under 30), watch out; the next few years will be critical. Assuming that you manage to avoid the urge to do something more constructive with your life, you must keep in mind that there is an enormous difference between a clever 23-year-old junior programmer and a real 35-year-old superprogrammer. Keep learning new techniques; keep reading about new approaches to programming; and keep working on new programs—if you don't, your knack for programming will gradually fade away until you, too, are forced to tell the next generation of junior programmers what it was like in the good old days of the 1401.

CHAPTER nine

INTERACTION OF PROGRAMS AND THE COMPUTER

Preview

Electricity and Circuits

Memory
   Addresses and Contents
   Destructive Input and Nondestructive Output

Programming
   Operation Codes
   Addresses

History Capsule:
Gene Amdahl: The Man Who Took on IBM

The Control Unit
   Instruction Fetch and Execute

Macroprogramming and Microprogramming

Summary

Computer News: Computer Commuter

PREVIEW

In Chapters 1 and 2, you read about computers and saw your first computer program. You were also exposed to the six functional parts of computers (control, memory, arithmetic/logic, input, output, and external storage), and to the interaction that must take place among them.

Chapters 3 through 8 discussed programming in BASIC as well as other languages. You saw that writing a program requires that you state in a very rigorous fashion all that you wish the computer to do. As you probably know, the computer does not really understand BASIC. The program must first be translated into machine-language form by a compiler or interpreter. Once in machine language, the computer takes that machine language program and the data it needs to yield the desired answers. This chapter shows you just how that is done.

ELECTRICITY AND CIRCUITS

Probably ten times a day you flip a switch that operates an electrical device. It may be a light, a shaver, a blow dryer, or a radio. When you flip the switch from "OFF" to "ON," the electricity flows through a series of wires from its source to the device you want to use. If the device is a light bulb, the electricity flows through a meter to a fuse box (which prevents too much electricity from going to the device at any one instant), then through a particular set of wires to the switch that operates the light bulb, and then to the bulb itself.

In some respects, the design of today's computers is like the circuits found in a home (see Figure 9–1). Instead of having individual rooms, though, a computer has six functional parts (see Chapter 2), which are linked together by electrical circuits. Further, computer circuits are operated not by a

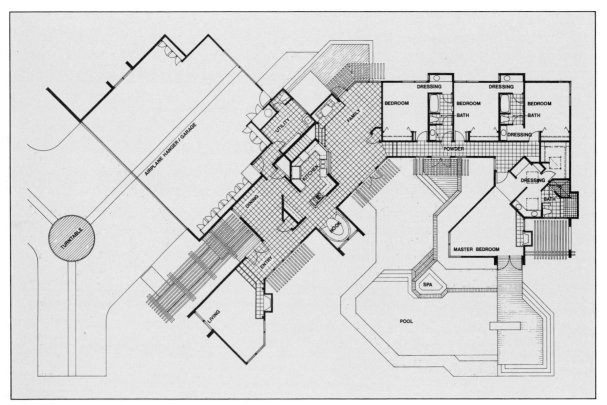

FIGURE 9–1 Circuits in a typical home.

hand switch, but by the control unit. The control unit is similar to the fuse box in that all circuits originate from it.

The number of circuits coming from the control unit is proportional to the number of individual activities that the designers or engineers of a computer want it to be able to perform. Since computers can: (1) bring an item of data from an input device into memory; (2) add, subtract, multiply, or divide a number in the arithmetic/logic unit; (3) move a number from the arithmetic/logic unit to memory; (4) take a quantity within memory and send it to an output device; and (5) compare two numbers to see which is the larger, there are one or more circuits for each of these capabilities.

The circuit that brings an item of data from an

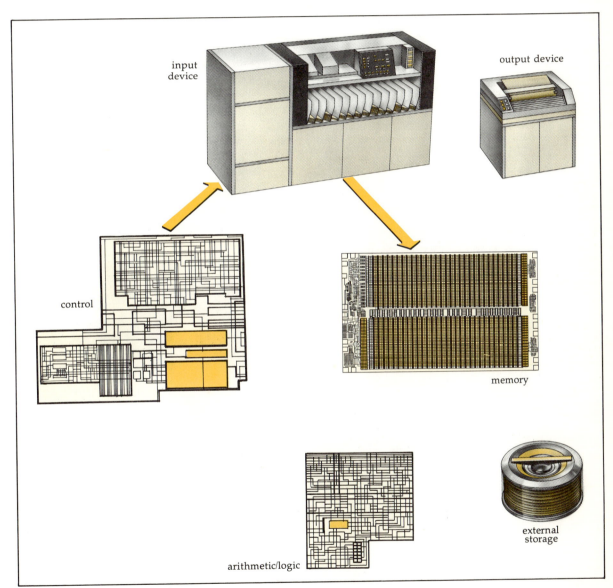

FIGURE 9-2 Circuit for input.

input device into memory must link the control unit with the input device and then with memory. Such an input circuit is shown in Figure 9–2.

The circuit for computer arithmetic links the control unit with memory and memory with the arithmetic/logic unit (see Figure 9–3). This circuit causes the number being manipulated to be brought out of memory and combined with a number already in the arithmetic/logic unit. Many computers have a circuit for each of the four arithmetic operations.

The circuit for **moving**, such as moving a number from the arithmetic/logic unit to memory, links the control unit with the arithmetic/logic unit, and

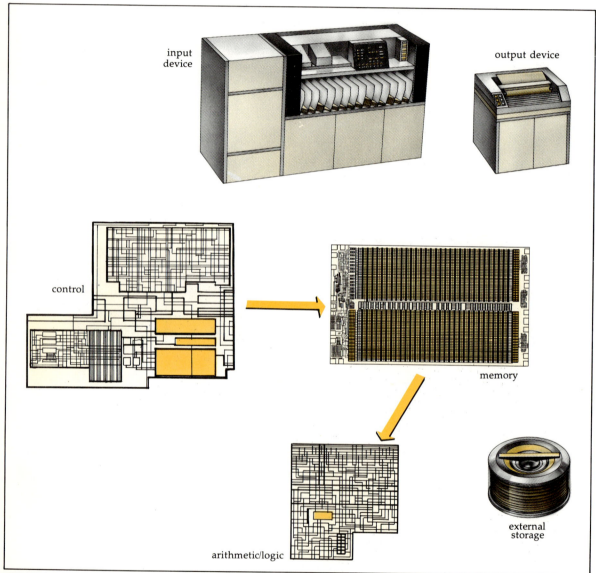

FIGURE 9–3 Circuit for arithmetic.

then with memory. This path is shown in Figure 9–4.

The output circuit, which takes a quantity within memory and sends it to an output device, links control with memory and then with the output device (Figure 9–5).

Finally, the computer is capable of a **comparison** of two numbers. To see which of the two numbers is bigger, the computer subtracts one from the other using the subtraction circuit. The comparison circuit causes a message, called an **indicator,** to be sent back to the control unit if this difference is positive (but not if negative). If positive, the first of the two numbers is larger. If the difference is negative, the

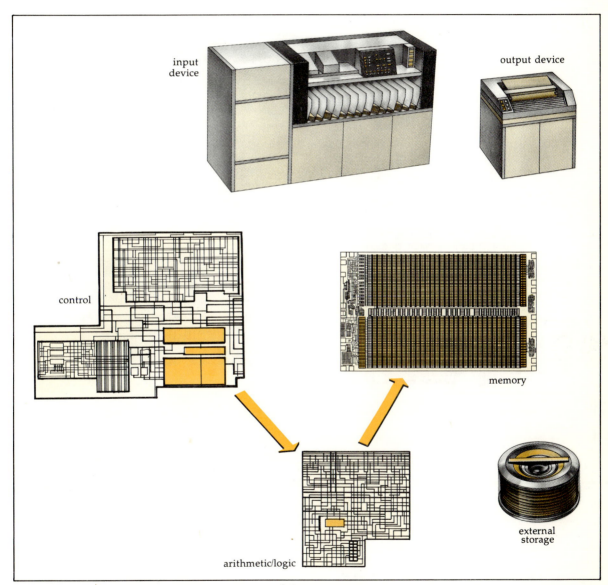

FIGURE 9–4   Circuit for internal movement of data.

second of the two numbers is larger. This circuit is shown in Figure 9–6.

Circuits not diagrammed are the ones to and from the control unit and external storage. The two circuits for these operations are similar to the input circuit (Figure 9–2) and the output circuit (Figure 9–5) in that they link control with external storage and memory. Lastly, there is a circuit to stop the computer from performing any other operations. You might picture this circuit as one that comes from the control unit and goes right back into the control unit, thereby causing no operation to take place.

The six functional parts and the circuits neces-

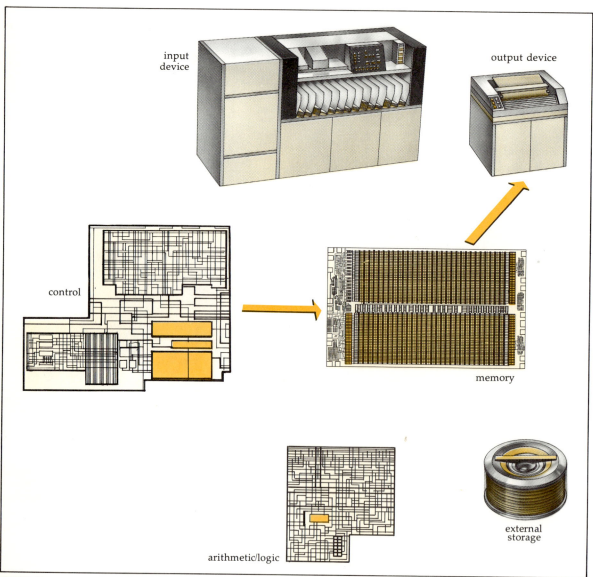

FIGURE 9–5   Circuit for output.

MODULE TWO: LANGUAGE

sary for all five capabilities are shown in Figure 9–7. For our hypothetical computer, there are circuits that will allow nine different actions (the arithmetic capability is counted as four separate actions: +, −, ×, ÷). Actions that have physical circuits are called **hardware instructions.** Some computers, like IBM's 370, have over a hundred hardware instructions.

MEMORY

All of the hardware instructions, or circuits, of Figure 9–7 cause the control unit to retrieve the data stored in memory. Memory itself is divided into individual storage cells or **locations,** each of which

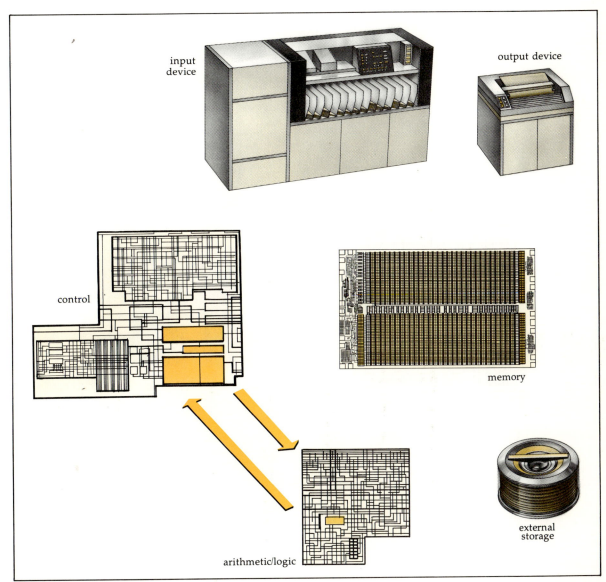

FIGURE 9–6   Circuit for comparison.

has a name called an **address.** The name of the first memory address is usually 0; the name of the last one is the highest number in the memory. Thus, a computer with 32,768 memory locations will have memory addresses from 0 to 32,767. Diagrammatically, you might think of memory as a series of mailboxes (see Figure 9–8).

Addresses and Contents

In each memory location, a computer can store a number, such as 147, or a word, such as THIS. Notice that the address tells where or which memory location; it does not tell what currently occupies that location. Thus, 6 is the address of a memory

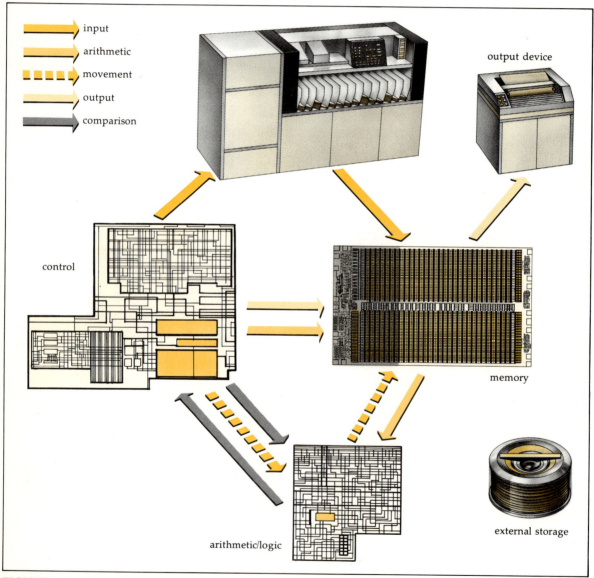

FIGURE 9–7 Functional parts and all circuits.

MODULE TWO: LANGUAGE

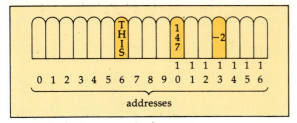

FIGURE 9–8 Mailbox analogy and memory.

location that now happens to contain the word THIS, while 10 is the address of a memory location now containing the number 147. Usually, the size of the word or number stored in a memory location is limited. For example, each memory location in a Burroughs B6805 computer can hold at most a six-letter word or a number between -10^{75} and $+10^{75}$. To have a computer store a bigger word or number, we must use two or more memory locations, each location holding portions of it.

Destructive Input and Nondestructive Output

The contents of a memory location can be changed by certain hardware instructions. The input circuit (Figure 9–2) brings a number from an input device into memory, where it replaces the current contents of a given memory location. This property is called **destructive input**. The circuits of Figure 9–7 that cause a memory location to be altered are input and movement. The arithmetic, output, and comparison instructions do not change the current value of a memory location and are called **nondestructive output**. In this sense, memory is like audio tape—it can be replayed as many times as necessary without changing what is recorded. However, if something else is recorded on that tape, the original material is lost.

PROGRAMMING

Writing a series of instructions telling the computer to do something is called **coding** or **programming**, and the series of instructions is a program. A program is a set of **messages** to the computer. Each message has two parts: (1) the circuit, or **operation**, and (2) the memory location, or address, to be used.

Operation Codes

Messages are written in a code. In other words, each circuit is given a number rather than a word name. The codes for operations for our nine circuits might be as listed in Figure 9–9.

Addresses

In a program, each message is written as a number with several digits. The leftmost digit of the number is the operation code and the rest of the digits are the address of the memory location to be used. Some sample messages are given in Figure 9–10.

If you look closely at these messages, you will notice that some of them are three-digit numbers, and others are four- or five-digit numbers. Computers, however, require that all messages be the same length. In our case, let us agree that all messages will be four-digit numbers—one digit for the operation code and three for the memory location. This agreement gives us 1,000 addressable locations within the computer's memory (locations 000 through 999), enough to hold a considerable volume of words or numbers. These four-digit messages will make up a program.

As an example of a simple program, let us have the computer input two numbers, compute their

FIGURE 9–9 Operation codes and associated circuits.

Operation Code	Hardware Circuit
1	Input
2	Arithmetic: Add
3	Arithmetic: Subtract
4	Arithmetic: Multiply
5	Arithmetic: Divide
6	Move
7	Output
8	Comparison
9	Stop

GENE AMDAHL:
THE MAN WHO TOOK ON IBM

When most people think of computers they think of IBM. The dominance of the computer industry by IBM is phenomenal. Studies have shown that IBM computers are used by as many as 70 percent of all computer users. Of course, many other companies make and successfully sell computers. Of these, none has created the interest Gene Amdahl and his computer, the Amdahl 470, has.

An IBM employee from 1952 to 1970, Gene Amdahl formed the Amdahl Corporation in 1970. Within four years he raised sufficient capital, hired a staff, and manufactured his Amdahl 470V/6 computer. His computer has been found to be twice as fast, to occupy only one-third the floor space, and to cost less than a comparable IBM 370 computer. Furthermore, the Amdahl 470V/6 can use IBM disks, tapes, card readers, printers, and other equipment. Lastly, the 470V/6 can run without change the same programs written for the IBM 370.

In 1979, Amdahl Corporation of Sunnyvale, California, had $321 million in sales. In a disagreement with other owners over future strategy, Gene Amdahl (who owned less than 3.5 percent of the stock) resigned from the company. Since that time he has formed Trilogy Corporation. This new venture focuses on smaller, faster, more economical computers that are, like the Amdahl 470V6, 470V7, and now, the 470V8, IBM-compatible.

Gene Amdahl was born in South Dakota and raised on a farm. He holds a B.A. degree from South Dakota State University and a Ph.D. from the University of Wisconsin. Amdahl is an inventor (he has at least eight patents) and a family man (married 30 years, three children). In 1976 he was named 1976 DPMA (Data Processing Management Association) Computer Science Man of the Year.

---

sum, and output the result. First, we must tell the computer to input the two numbers. Let us assume that we will put the first number into memory location 304 and the second into 879. We select these two memory locations because we already know they have not been used. To have the computer input in this fashion, the first two messages, or instructions, in our program are:

- 1304 (1 is the operation code; 304 is the address)
- 1879 (1 is the operation code; 879 is the address)

To find the sum of the numbers stored in memory locations 304 and 879, we must add them together. Unfortunately, the arithmetic circuit for addition, circuit 2, adds a number to what is currently contained in the arithmetic/logic unit. If we wrote:

- 2304
- 2879

we would add the numbers stored in memory locations 304 and 879 to whatever is already in the arithmetic/logic unit so, if there is a number other than zero in the arithmetic/logic unit, we will get the wrong answer. The easiest way to get rid of any undesirable tenants in the arithmetic/logic unit is to change them to zero before we start. To do this, we do not have to be sure they exist; we simply tell the computer to multiply by zero. Since the product of any number and zero is zero, and since the multiply circuit, circuit 4, keeps this product in the arithmetic/logic unit, we have gotten rid of the tenant. Many programs have this clearing problem, so

FIGURE 9-10	Examples of messages.
Message	Meaning
1223	Take a number from an input device and put it into memory location 223.
24135	Add to the number in the arithmetic/logic unit the number now occupying memory location 4135.
314	Subtract from the number in the arithmetic/logic unit the number now occupying memory location 14.
4175	Multiply the number in the arithmetic/logic unit by the number contained in memory location 175.
59130	Divide the number in the arithmetic/logic unit by the number contained in memory location 9130.
6173	Move the number in the arithmetic/logic unit to memory location 173.
78021	Take the number contained in memory location 8021 and send it to the output device.
8024	If the arithmetic/logic unit now contains a positive number, replace the contents of the control unit with 024.

we might set aside memory location 999 to hold a zero. To form our sum, we now write the messages:

- 4999 (4 is the operation code—here it means multiply; 999 is the address—remember memory location 999 contains 0)
- 2304
- 2879

The sum of memory locations 304 and 879 is now in the arithmetic/logic unit of the computer. Before this sum can be printed, it must first be taken into memory. To move the sum to memory, we must use circuit 6 plus a storage location. Supposing memory location 531 is available, we write:

- 6531

To output our sum, we want circuit 7 to take the contents of memory location 531 to the output device. Thus, we write:

- 7531

Our completed program for inputting two numbers, adding them, and outputting their sum, appears in Figure 9-11. Such programs are often called **machine,** or **object, language** programs. They are directly usable by the computer.

THE CONTROL UNIT

In order for the computer physically to **execute,** run, or carry out the instructions in this program, the object language program, or object program, itself is placed inside memory. Let us assume that our program will be placed in memory locations 0 to 6, as shown in Figure 9-12 (other locations except for 304 and 879 will be set to zero). Placing an object program in memory is called **loading.**

Instruction Fetch and Execute

The next step in the execution of this object program is placing the address of the first instruction of the program in the control unit of the computer.

control
0000

FIGURE 9-11 Program to add two numbers.	
Instruction Number	Instruction
1	1304
2	1879
3	4999
4	2304
5	2879
6	6531
7	7531

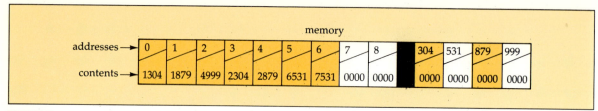

FIGURE 9–12   Program in memory.

Executing each instruction in an object program consists of two actions: the first, **instruction fetch,** brings the instruction from memory; the second, **instruction execute,** actually carries out the instruction (Figure 9–13). Fetch brings the instruction whose address is in the control unit (0000) from memory; thus, 1304 is fetched. Execute activates the circuit represented by the leftmost digit of the instruction, circuit 1. This circuit causes the input device to send the number it reads to the memory location whose address is given in the right three digits of our instruction, 304. If the number read by the input device is 1900, the memory of our computer now appears as in Figure 9–14.

As the last step in execute, the control unit is increased by 1 to point to the next command to be fetched, memory location 1.

The process of fetching, executing, and increasing the control unit by 1 continues as shown in Figure 9–15 until the computer comes to a command that means nothing to it, as when the control unit executes the 0000 stored in memory location 0007. This noninstruction, which we could also call an improper or invalid operation code, stops the program.

This program does not use a comparison instruction, but if it did and if it produced a positive number in the arithmetic/logic unit, the address of the next instruction in the control unit would not be increased by 1. Rather, the right three digits of this comparison instruction would replace the number now in the control unit. For instance, if the comparison instruction 8000 were to be executed, and if the arithmetic/logic unit had the number 1984, then the control unit would be set to 000. The next fetch cycle would retrieve the instruction occupying memory location 000. According to our chart of Figure 9–15, this instruction is 1304; it would activate the input device. The comparison command thus lets us skip from one point to another in the program. Decision making by comparing two quantities and changing the instruction to be fetched next as a result of the comparison is the main thing that differentiates a computer from a calculator and, indeed, from all other machines.

Object program instructions and the data stored in memory are indistinguishable to a computer. The number 1025 could be interpreted as the number 1025 or as the object instruction to input a number and place it in memory location 025. It is only

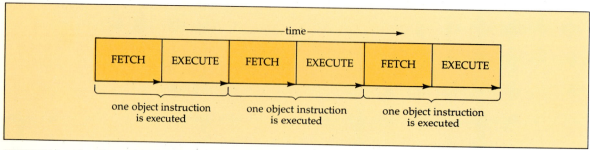

FIGURE 9–13   Executing an object command.

202   MODULE TWO: LANGUAGE

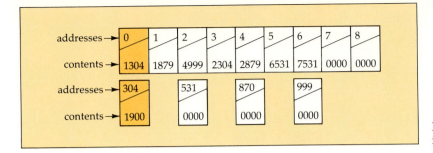

FIGURE 9–14 Executing of input command.

through the fetch-and-execute sequence that the computer can tell whether 1025 is a number or an instruction. This blindness is a very powerful programming tool, letting us change object instructions while instructions are carried out. A command might read 1013 at one point in the program and 1014 the next time it is fetched. Such changes help us program complex problems easily.

MACROPROGRAMMING AND MICROPROGRAMMING

Programming a complex problem with operation codes and addresses soon gets to be tedious. To speed things up, programmers can "invent" new instructions out of old ones. Instructions of this type are called **macroinstructions,** or "macros."

As Figure 9–11 shows, to do any type of computation you first have to multiply the contents of the arithmetic/logic unit by zero, then add a memory location. How much neater to have a single instruction that would clear and add all at once. Since operation code 9 is not being used, we might invent a new instruction, 9304. This new instruction would cause the computer to perform two actual instructions: a 4999 followed by a 2304. This double instruction would be a macroinstruction.

Macros are always combinations of existing instructions. A computer like the popular IBM 360/370, with over a hundred machine instructions, can have many macroinstructions. Each machine instruction has a separate group of circuits. Increasing the number of machine instructions increases the number of circuits required and raises the cost of making the computer, but it also increases what the computer can do in a given period of time. If, instead, the number of macros is increased, the programming will be easier, but the program will execute more slowly, which also leads to a higher cost. A proper balance between speed and ease must be achieved to get the most out of the control unit of the computer.

Some computers can use parts of the individual circuits of an instruction, called **microinstructions,** to form a "new" instruction. This concept is called **microprogramming.** Since the new microinstruction is not a new machine language instruction but a new instruction the computer can already execute,

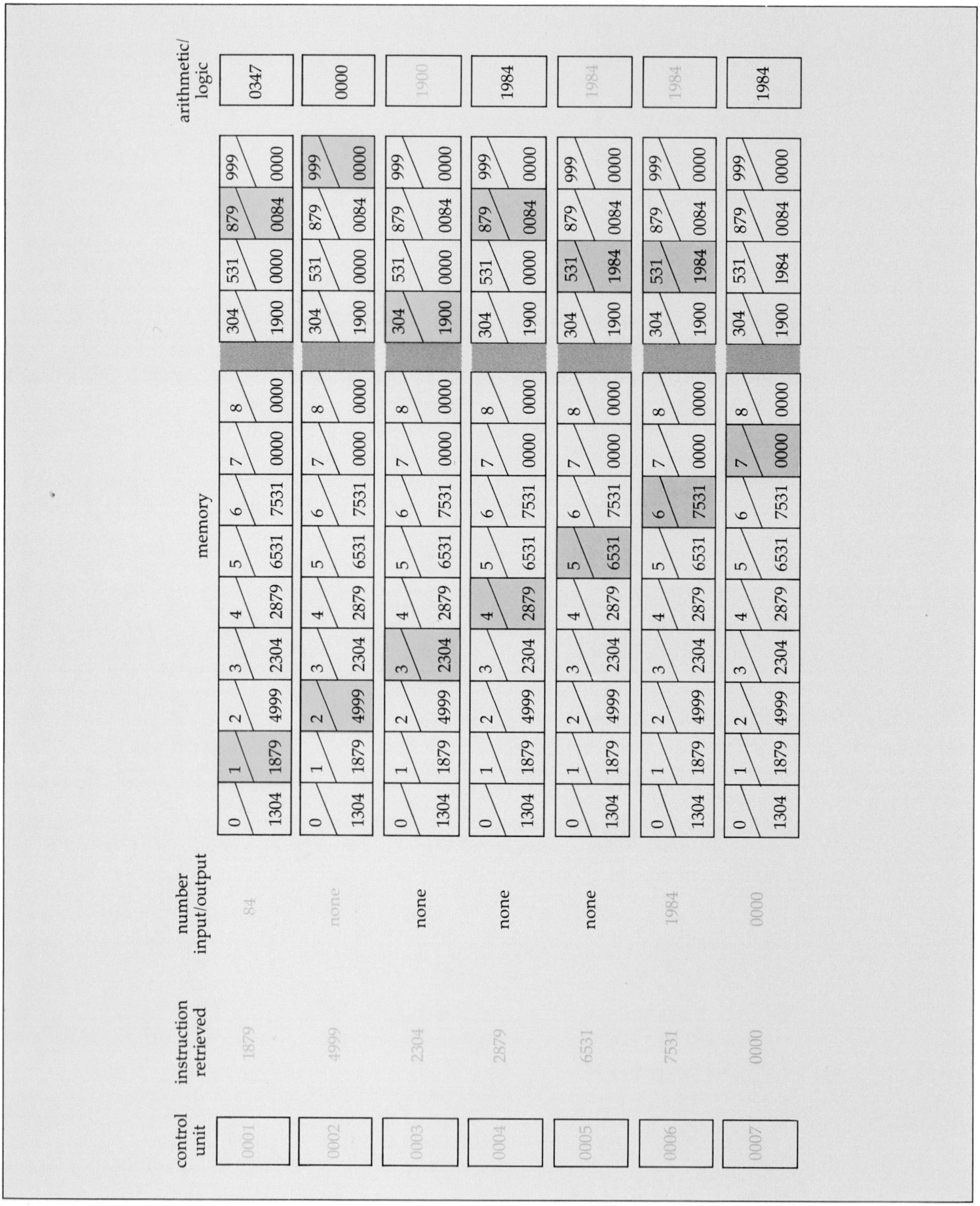

FIGURE 9–15 Fetch/execute of program.

it can be saved for later use. For this reason, microprograms are usually kept in a separate memory unit called **read-only memory** (ROM). Microprograms are usually written and placed in the read-only memory by the manufacturer of the computer, and not by the programmer.

As an example of a microprogram, suppose we wanted a "new" instruction that would take a number from the arithmetic/logic unit and put it on the output device. To construct this new instruction, we would use the microcircuits labeled A and B in Figure 9–16. This microprogram would be

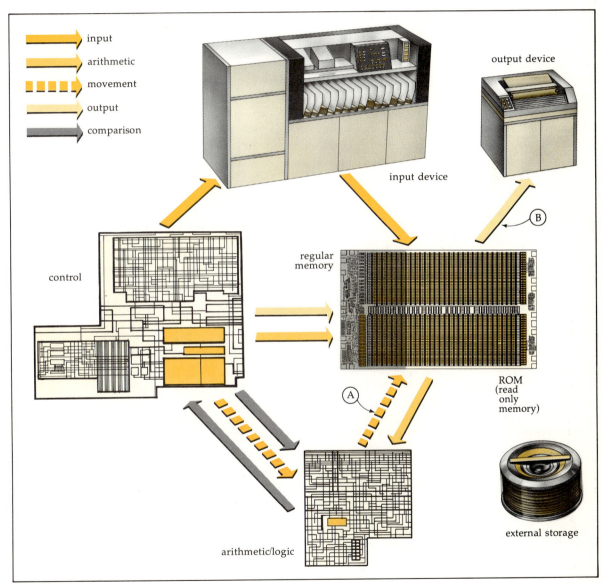

FIGURE 9–16 Microprogram.

stored in ROM and might be assigned operation code 0. Thus, when the control unit fetches an instruction with the operation code 0, the control unit will use ROM to interpret what will happen during the execute cycle.

Some microprograms enable a computer to "understand" the language of another computer. This is made possible by writing a microprogram for each of the various commands of the other computer. Thus, the costly and time-consuming task of changing a program written for one kind of computer into a program for another would not have to be done. Through a microprogram, a computer of one make and model can simulate another computer of a different make or model. Microinstructions execute faster than macros, but slower than machine-level commands.

Micro, macro, or machine language programming is difficult and is seldom done, even by experienced programmers. That is why English-oriented languages like BASIC were covered in our discussion of programming.

SUMMARY

Computer programs are a series of messages that tell the computer what to do and what memory locations to use. The messages are written in a numeric code and cause certain electrical circuits to activate one or more of the six functional parts of the computer. Messages themselves are stored in the memory of the computer and are retrieved by the control unit. Once retrieved, a message is executed by the control unit. Then the next message is retrieved. This process continues until the end of all the messages in the series.

Some types of computers allow two or more messages to be grouped together to form a macroinstruction. Instructions of this type simplify the programming task. Some computers even allow microprograms to be written by putting together pieces of two or more messages to form new instructions. Microprogramming lets a computer manufactured by one company execute a program written for a computer made by another company.

TERMS

The following words or terms have been presented in this chapter.

Moving	Operation
Comparison	Machine language
Indicator	Object language
Hardware instructions	Execute
Location	Loading
Address	Instruction fetch
Destructive input	Instruction execute
Nondestructive output	Macroinstructions
Coding	Microinstructions
Programming	Microprogramming
Message	Read-only memory

EXERCISES

The exercises that follow are grouped by level of difficulty. Problems in the A series are the easiest; B series problems are moderately hard; and C series problems are the most difficult.

A–1 Draw a circuit diagram similar to Figure 9–2 for input from external storage.

A–2 Draw a circuit diagram similar to Figure 9–5 for output to external storage.

A–3 What do the following messages mean?

    a. 5037   **c.** 9073   **e.** 6014

    b. 8491   **d.** 1001   **f.** 2213

A–4 According to Figure 9–9, how many different operation codes are possible?

B–1 Early in this chapter we agreed that all messages will have a three-digit address portion. With only three digits, why are there 1,000 individual memory locations?

B–2 Why do we think Gene Amdahl created a machine that would be compatible with IBM equipment?

B–3 Write a separate program for each of the following:

    a. Double the contents of memory location 412.

    b.   Place a zero in memory location 765.
    c.   Put a 1 in memory location 342.
    d.   Multiply the contents of memory location 213 by itself.

B-4   In the program listed in Figure 9–11, will any of the following actions affect the final outcome of the program?

    a.   reversing the instructions numbered 1 and 2
    b.   reversing the instructions numbered 4 and 5
    c.   reversing the instructions numbered 6 and 7

B-5   Write a program to:

    a.   Input two numbers, find their difference, and output this result.
    b.   Input two numbers, find their product, and output this result.
    c.   Input two numbers, find their quotient, and output this result.

C-1   Adding 1 to a memory location is a task that is frequently programmed. Write a macroprogram to add 1 to any memory location.

C-2   Which of the operation codes listed in Figure 9–9 are unnecessary?

C-3   The formula to convert temperature measured in degrees Fahrenheit to Celsius is $C = \frac{5}{9}(F - 32)$. Write a program similar to the one shown in Figure 9–11 that inputs a temperature in Fahrenheit and outputs its equivalent in Celsius.

C-4   Exponentiation is raising a number to a power. Write a program that will input values of A and N and find B for the formula $B = A^N$.

C-5   Draw a diagram similar to that in Figure 9–16 of a microprogram to take data from the input device and put them in the arithmetic/logic unit.

COMPUTER NEWS

COMPUTER COMMUTER

Terminal Bridges 150-Mile Gap Between Home, Job

KINGSTON, Okla. (AP)—Norma Posey works for an Oklahoma City bank, but her office, complete with easy chair, washer, dryer, television set and computer terminal, is in her home, 150 miles away.

"If there had to be a guinea pig, I'm glad it was me," said Posey, a computer programmer and analyst for Liberty National Bank and Trust Co.

Her office is in the den of her home in Kingston, a southern Oklahoma town near the shores of Lake Texoma. Next door, her husband Gene operates a welding business.

"I can just get out of bed and walk to the den, and I'm at work," said Norma Posey, who has worked for the bank for 18 years.

It's a lot easier than when she lived in Moore, an Oklahoma City suburb, and battled the traffic to and from the office every day.

And there were the night calls.

"If there was some sort of problem, I'd have to get out of bed, get dressed, drive 15 miles to the office, clear up the problem, drive home, get back in bed and try to get a little sleep," she said.

Now, if there is a problem at night, she pulls on a robe, sits down at her computer console—it looks like a TV with a typewriter keyboard—and works the problem out.

"I try to work a normal 9-to-5 job," Posey said. "But the other night, I got called about 11:30 p.m. I worked for over a half-hour to clear up the problem, so I'll just take 30 minutes off some day when I want to go shopping or something."

Her computer console sits in the corner of the den just inside the door. A telephone connects her with a computer at the bank in Oklahoma City.

"There are three computers at the bank, and my terminal is hooked up to one," she explained. "I can communicate with that computer, or with the other people who work in that department."

The Poseys decided to change their lifestyle after spending at least two weekends a month, summer after summer, at Lake Texoma "and meeting the friendly people around here," Norma Posey said. They grew to love the area so much, they decided to move here.

Posey intended to look for computer work in towns near the lake, but then came her going-away party at the bank.

"Someone—I'm not sure who it was, one of the auditors, I think—spoke up and said, 'Why don't you take a computer with you?'"

There were some giggles at first, she said, but the idea caught on with the bank's officials.

Among the first visitors after the Poseys arrived were a computer serviceman from the bank, who installed her terminal, and Southwestern Bell Telephone Co. workers who wired it to the telephone line.

"The telephone people said they had never done anything like that before, but they did it real quick and without any problems," she said.

Her job is to maintain and change programs

Norma Posey does job with home computer terminal.

in the bank's computer.

"If a change has to be made in a program, my bosses at the bank call me or send a written request," Posey said. "I can write a new program or make changes in current programs right here at this terminal."

Liberty National does the data processing for about 80 Oklahoma banks, including some near Kingston. "The computers work hours a day, seven days a week, all year long," she said.

A courier service goes to all member banks after the close of business to pick up the data-processing information, she said, and send it to Liberty, where the work is done overnight.

Posey said she sometimes misses seeing her co-workers, "But wouldn't trade places with them for anything.

"My family likes having me at home with them. We get to spend time together that we would otherwise spend going in separate directions.

"And if I have a particularly long program to run, I can dump a load of clothes in the washer while it's running."

CHAPTER 9: PROGRAMS AND THE COMPUTER

MODULE *three*
HARDWARE

From wafer-thin pocket calculators to desktop computers with the power of a large mainframe—computer hardware is shrinking all around us. Less than 30 years since IBM manufactured its first computer, today we can hold in the palms of our hands a computer on a chip with the same power as that first IBM mainframe. How is it possible to compress so much circuitry into such a small area? The photographs on these pages illustrate some of the stages in the making of a chip.

Photo A shows a computer-drawn mask being inspected for flaws. Different masks are used, one at a time, to build up layers of various materials and patterns on the silicon wafer, and the lines on each mask must align. During the inspection, layout errors are marked, and correcting data are then fed into the computer, which directs an automatic drawing of a corrected mask. A completed silicon wafer undergoes an ultrafine cleaning operation (Photo E). The wafer is placed under ultraviolet light to show imperfections or dust particles, while an electrostatic blowgun whisks away the foreign objects. The technician's clothing is typical of the extreme care required to ensure a clean environment; one speck of dust can make a chip useless.

Photo D shows silicon wafers, each containing 29 chips, being loaded into a vapor depositing machine. This machine vaporizes a metallic substance that is attracted to the chip and becomes one of the patterned layers of microconductors serving as data paths. Each chip has 36,000 transistors. Before being separated into chips (Photo C), the silicon wafer is scribed with a diamond-tipped stylus. After many precision manufacturing steps, the chip (Photo B) is ready for mounting in a protective cover. This 1.5-centimeter-square chip is a Bell Labs 32-bit microprocessor that is as powerful as some ten-thousand dollar minicomputers.

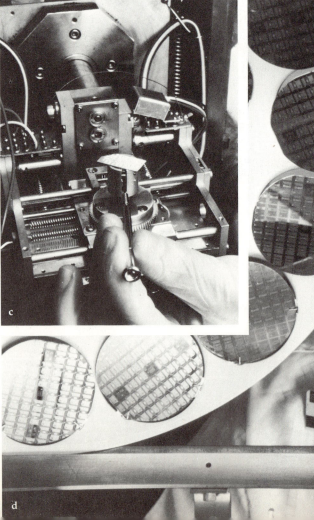

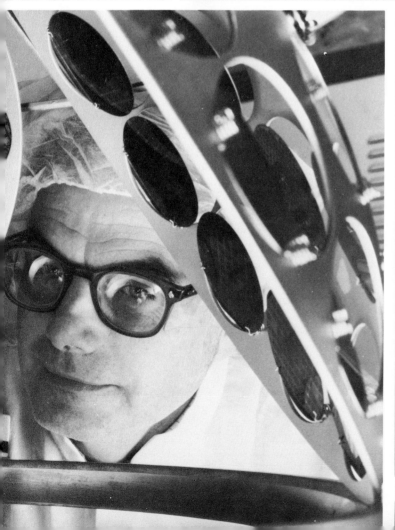
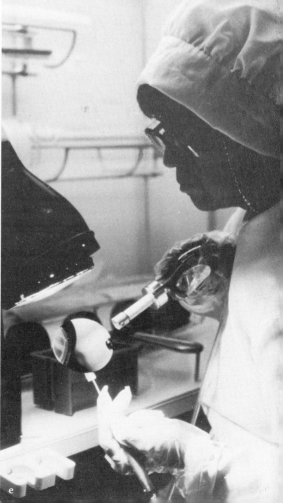

INPUT TO THE COMPUTER

Preview

Introduction to Input
    Media and Machines
    Considerations in Selecting Input Devices and Media

Minimizing Errors

Batch Processing: Input via Keyboard
    Punched Cards   Magnetic Media
    Multistation Data Preparation Devices

Batch Processing: Direct Input from Source Documents
    Magnetic Ink Character Recognition
    Optical Character Recognition
    History Capsule: Hollerith, Billings, and Powers
    Optical Mark Recognition
    Digitizers

Transaction Processing: Input via Keyboard
    Computer Terminals
    Printing Terminals
    Intelligent Terminals
    Automated Teller Machines
    Automatic Telephone Payments

Transaction Processing: Direct Input from Source Documents
    Point-of-Sale Terminals

Transaction Processing: Input by Voice

Electronic Funds Transfer

Summary

Computer News: Magic Wand Comes of Age with New Uses

PREVIEW

In Chapter 2 we briefly described the six functional parts of the computer. As we indicated, **input devices** take data and store them in memory (either primary or secondary) for subsequent processing. In this chapter we examine two basic approaches to inputting data and ways of minimizing errors that may occur in the data. We also survey the media and machines—from older punched card devices to newer methods such as optical reading and voice recognition machines.

INTRODUCTION TO INPUT

There are two basic approaches to inputting data into the computer, depending on how they are created and collected.

A traveling salesperson may return to his or her home office with a stack of sales invoices that contain data for input to the computer. That stack, along with similar collections of sales invoices from other salespersons, may be pooled together into one large batch for processing as a group. This inputting and subsequent computer processing of the collection of sales invoice data is called **batch processing.** Other information processing applications lend themselves to batch processing. For instance, in a payroll system a time card or pay sheet is collected from each employee at the end of the week. All the time cards can then be gathered into a batch that is input for computer processing.

As the alternative to batch processing, a salesperson may carry a portable computer input device similar to a small typewriter. As a sale is made, the salesperson enters the transaction data directly into the home office's computer by a terminal-telephone-computer connection. In this case, the computer acts immediately on the sale rather than having to wait until the salesperson returns with the invoices. This direct inputting to the computer of the sales data is called **on-line** or **transaction processing.**

Before looking at specific batch and on-line processing procedures, we will explain the concepts of media and machines and consider selection criteria for input methods. Then we discuss ways of preventing or minimizing errors before the main computer processes begin.

Media and Machines

Musical compositions have to be translated from notes on a printed page to sounds created by musical instruments in order to be enjoyed and appreciated. With musical instruments, musicians create vibrations that are transmitted by air to the human eardrum. The musical instrument, the device or mechanism that creates the sound, can be called an **output device.** The air, the carrier of vibrations, is called the **medium.** The ear, the mechanism that receives the vibrations, can be called an **input device.** Transmission of information from and to computers is similar to the transmission of music from an instrument to a human being. (See Figure 10-1.)

To communicate sales invoice data from invoice to computer, for instance, a device or mechanism must be used that carries data to the computer's "eardrum." This eardrum is an input device. The carrier of the data the input device receives may be a magnetic tape, punched card, or one of many other media.

Without the ability to receive information, the computer would be worthless. Thus, understanding computers and their use depends, in part, on understanding input devices and their media.

Considerations in Selecting Input Devices and Media

The selection of an input device and the medium with which it functions depends on five factors: compatibility, speed, reliability, cost, and, in some cases, human readability. Together these factors govern the choice of actual device required for the computer system.

Input devices and media vary widely with respect to the machine codes they can receive. A device can accept as input from another device only data that are in a code the device has been designed to "understand"—in other words, codes that are

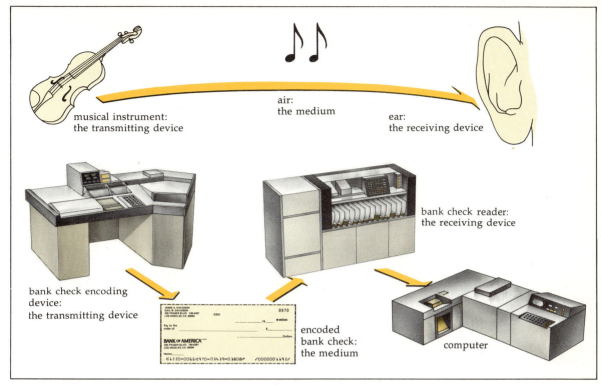

FIGURE 10–1 Relationship of output device, medium, and input device.

compatible with it. These compatible coding systems are called **protocols.** A machine that observes one protocol cannot communicate with a machine that observes a different protocol. To facilitate the connection of various input devices to computers, some industry standards are followed by many manufacturers. One, called the **RS232C standard,** is followed by many keyboard-type input devices. There are also standards based on certain widely used devices such as the popular, low-cost Teletype terminal and certain widely used IBM input devices. Since devices must be compatible if they are to be connected, many manufacturers design their input devices to be compatible with IBM's computers and to a lesser degree with those of other computer manufacturers.

An input device's speed can be viewed in several ways. It may be stated in rates—for example, an input rate of 30 **characters per second (CPS)** for a particular terminal. Or it may be viewed as the total time consumed in performing a particular function. Comparisons of speeds must be done with caution since the high speed of a certain device may be of little value if a dependent or subsequent action is much slower.

The ability of a device to continue to operate at its rated speed is its **reliability.** A device that, on the average, functions for 1,000 hours before it fails to function as designed is said to have a **mean time between failures (MTBF)** rating of 1,000 hours. MTBF ratings are especially noteworthy in information processing systems that operate under tight schedules or in systems where some ongoing process depends on the continuous functioning of a device—for example, a computer that controls the operations of a rapid transit train system.

The costs of using a particular input device must be determined on the basis of total costs incurred.

Too often, only the direct costs of rental or lease, supplies, electricity, and wages are considered. Often ignored, but very important, are the indirect costs of depreciation of the device, its maintenance, and intangible costs such as loss of customer goodwill resulting from the slow processing of an order due to device failure. A variety of costs, then, should be considered when choosing an input device.

MINIMIZING ERRORS

When people key in data to the computer there is a chance for error. For example, digits in an account number can be transposed or entered incorrectly. To minimize the probability that erroneous data will be processed, another person can rekey the same data and have the machine compare the two versions to determine that the data originally entered were correct. If the data keyed in by two different people agree, they are assumed to be correct, since the probability that two individuals would both make the same mistake in keying the character is remote. This process is called **verifying**.

Verifying will not, of course, point out an error that exists on the source document. Such an error may be discovered during the computer processing following the data's input. Most computer programs that input human-prepared data need to compare those data against predetermined upper and lower limits, see if they are the right kind of data (such as alphabetic as opposed to numeric), or if they match certain established constants. This type of accuracy check is called **validation**.

No matter what preparation device is used, verification and validation are important steps in data processing. When can they be justifiably omitted? The answer is simple: When the cost of not correcting an error is equal to or greater than the cost involved in locating and correcting it, the error locating procedure should be undertaken. The cost of not correcting an error might be undercharging a customer and, thus, losing sales dollars, or overcharging and perhaps losing a customer.

BATCH PROCESSING: INPUT VIA KEYBOARD

Batch input processing involves sending accumulated transaction data to the computer as a unit. These data must be converted into some machine-readable medium for input to the computer. This conversion process may be done by people using devices that have keyboards or directly by devices that can "read" the transaction documents.

Punched Cards

Punched cards are one medium for carrying data to the computer when the data cannot be read directly. The use of punched cards is, to a large degree, a carry-over from the precomputer era. One reason why they are still used may be that they are human-readable documents, as well as a machine-readable input medium. Punched card processing will probably persist until users become comfortable with media such as magnetic disks and tape.

Punched cards are used as the primary data entry medium for many computers. An estimated 250,000 card punch machines are still in use in the United States. There are two popular types of punched cards: the 80-column Hollerith card, developed in the 1880s, which is commonly called the "IBM card," and the 96-column card, which IBM introduced with its popular System/3 computer in 1969.

The **80-column Hollerith card** was patterned in width and height after the U.S. currency in use at that time. It measures $7\frac{3}{8} \times 3\frac{1}{4}$ inches and is 0.007 inch thick. One of the upper corners is cut angularly to aid in spotting any cards that might be upside down or backside forward. The Hollerith card is laid out in 12 horizontal **rows** and 80 vertical **columns** (see Figure 10–2). The top three rows (12, 11, and 0) are called "zone rows" and rows 0 to 9 are called "numeric rows." (Note that the 0 row is included in both categories.) Any single numeric character 0 through 9 can be recorded in a vertical column by simply punching out a rectangular hole at the row corresponding to the desired decimal number. For example, in Figure 10–3 the numeric

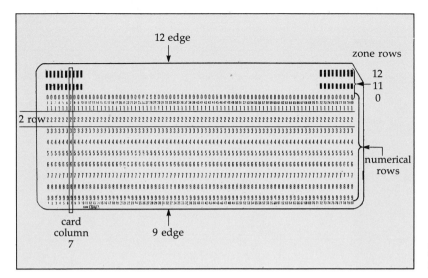

FIGURE 10-2 Format of the 80-column card.

value seven (7) is recorded in card column 20 by punching a hole in row 7 of the column. The alphabetic character *N* appears in column 40 by punching holes in one of the zone rows (11) and one of the numeric rows (5). The plus (+) sign, in column 71, has holes punched in rows 12, 6, and 8. Figure 10-4 illustrates all the punch patterns in the Hollerith code. A single card column or a group of adjacent card columns treated as a unit is called a **field** (see Figure 10-5). A card field contains one item of data. Data are keyed into cards by the **keypunch machine**, a typewriter-like device. Data are keyed in through the keyboard while a punching mechanism punches a corresponding pattern of holes into a card to represent the data (see Figure 10-6). Column-by-column punching continues serially across the card until all the desired fields are punched.

Once a batch of transactions are transcribed into punched cards, a **punched card reader** inputs the data to the computer memory. The card reader is one of the most common input devices. On some

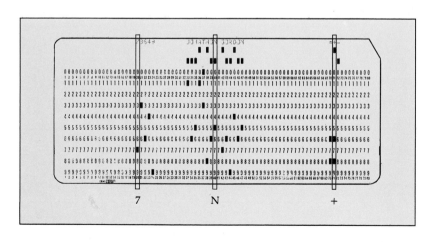

FIGURE 10-3 80-column card with numeric, alphabetic, and special symbols.

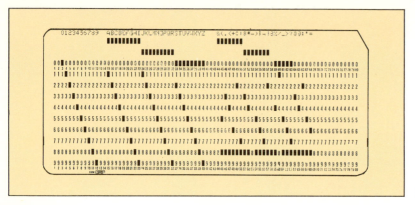

FIGURE 10-4 Hollerith code.

computers, card readers are the primary method of entering programs. Card readers translate from the card's codes into a code the computer uses within its CPU. Once in the computer, their data are usually stored on a secondary storage device to facilitate rapid access during subsequent use of the data (see Figure 10-7). Card reader speeds are generally measured by the number of **cards per minute (CPM)** the device can read. Speeds range from a low of 100 CPM to a high of 2,000 CPM, depending on make, model, and method of reading.

Punched cards have both advantages and disadvantages. The advantages of punched card input largely result from the card's being a human-oriented medium. The punched card data are human-readable, whereas other media may not be. Also, since each card is separate from the others, physical rearrangement of cards can be accom-

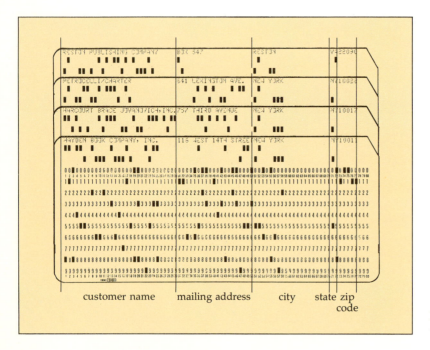

FIGURE 10-5 Cards subdivided into fields.

218 MODULE THREE: HARDWARE

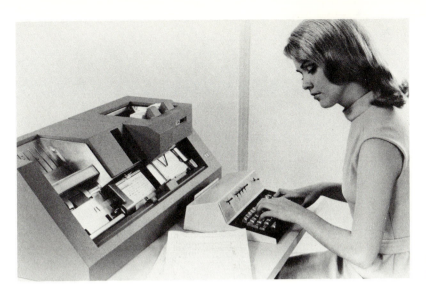

FIGURE 10-6 Card path of IBM 029 keypunch.

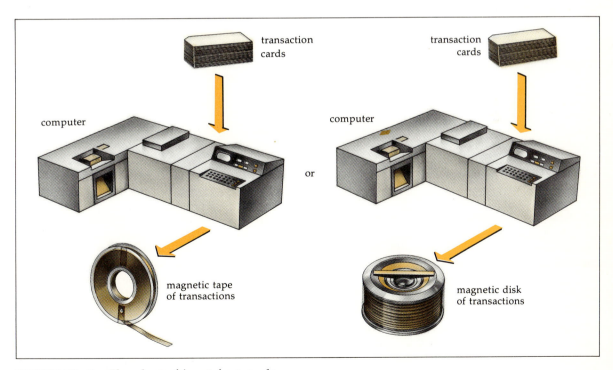

FIGURE 10-7 Flowchart of input from cards.

CHAPTER 10: INPUT TO THE COMPUTER 219

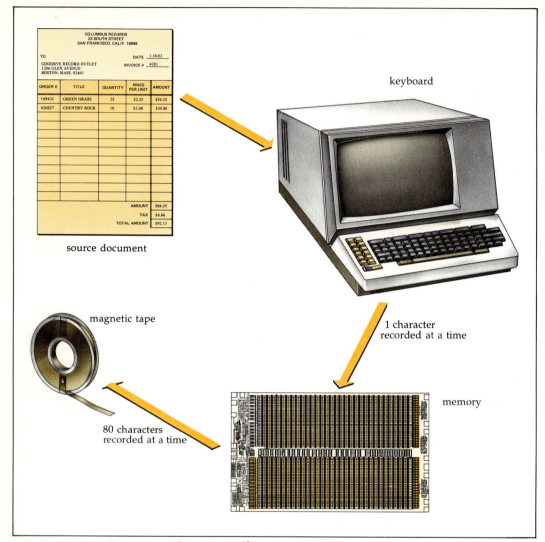

FIGURE 10-8 Key-to-tape data preparation.

plished easily. Further, each card often contains a complete record (for example, of an event or transaction, or a mailing label); such a card is called a **unit record**. Cards are easily stored, and reasonable handling does not affect readability. Finally, cards are relatively inexpensive when the volume of data being stored is moderate. Punched cards have some major disadvantages, however. First, card reading speeds are relatively slow, ranging from 100 to 2,000 CPM. Translated into **characters per second (CPS)**, this speed is equivalent to 130 to 3,200 CPS. In contrast, data on magnetic tape can be input at the rate of 2,000 to 320,000 CPS—100 times faster. Second, many input records are far longer than 80 or 96 characters and, hence, are cumbersome to process via punched cards. A third disadvantage of punched cards is that they cannot be reused once the recorded data is no longer needed, nor can an error in the card be corrected without punching a new card. Finally, punched card input is bulky; a punched card file of 2,000 cards or 160,000 characters consumes about 770 cubic inches of file space. In contrast, five reels of magnetic tape consumes the same amount of space and can hold 200,000,000 characters.

Magnetic Media

Use of magnetic media for recording batches of data has come about in part because of the disadvantages of punched card media. Magnetic media allow higher density of storage and faster reading and writing, and they are reusable. Like cards, magnetic medium devices transcribe data via a keyboard. Once on the magnetic medium the data are readable by the computer. There are three major types of magnetic medium devices: key-to-tape, key-to-flexible-disk, and key-to-cartridge/cassette tape.

The features that key-to-tape devices offer are: (1) As data are keyed in, they are stored in a memory unit rather than written directly on tape—this feature allows for easy correction. Once all the characters in the record are keyed in, the record is recorded on the tape (Figure 10–8). (2) The key-to-tape device is quiet. (3) Key-to-tape devices use tape, which is compatible with most computers. (4) As the recorded tape is read by the computer's tape reader, data are transferred to the computer at rates up to 320,000 characters per second.

There are also disadvantages to key-to-tape devices. First, the data are not human-readable, and second, records on tape cannot be sorted or merged with other records prior to computer processing.

Verification of previously keyed data is performed by using the same machine, but simply switching to the verify mode. The source document is then rekeyed, and the key-to-tape device compares the recorded data with the entered data, stopping when a verification error is encountered so the operator can intervene.

The flexible disk (often called "floppy disk") is another medium used in data preparation devices.

FIGURE 10–9   Key-to-flexible-disk device.

The disk was originally introduced to provide rapid input of software into the IBM 370 series of computers. Called the **key-to-flexible-disk device,** or simply "key-disk," the machine has the normal keyboard and viewing device, but records the keyed data on a flexible disk that can be removed and read directly into a computer (see Figure 10–9).

A variation of the key-to-tape device, the **key-to-cartridge** or **key-to-cassette device,** records data on a magnetic tape whose supply and take-up reels are both permanently encased in a single plastic

FIGURE 10–10 NCR 7200 key-to-cassette data entry terminal.

housing (Figure 10–10). These cassettes and the larger cartridge-type devices are used on data preparation machines where speed and ease of operator tape handling are high priority.

The cassette and cartridge tapes are not compatible with most computers and, therefore, require a conversion to the one-half-inch computer-compatible tape. Most suppliers of cartridge/cassette key-to-tape devices provide a converter that enables this translation to a computer-compatible tape format (Figure 10–11).

Cassettes that are used for data preparation and other computer-related uses, are generally of a higher quality than home audio recording tapes

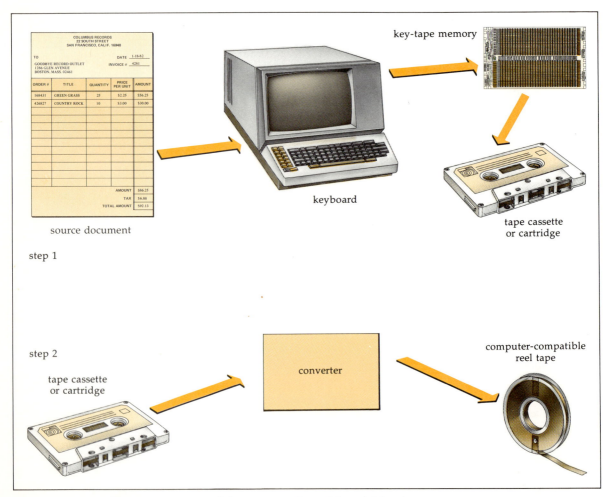

FIGURE 10–11 Two-step process of data preparation with cartridges/cassettes.

MODULE THREE: HARDWARE

(Figure 10–12). They sell for about twice the price of a high-quality audio tape.

Data preparation machines that use tape cassettes and cartridges function like those that use reel-to-reel tape. That is, they utilize a keyboard, have a display device, can back up for corrections, and can be switched to a verify mode.

Multistation Data Preparation Devices

When the volume of data being prepared for computer input is large enough to fully occupy two or more persons, a multistation data preparation device provides advantages over several individual units. In a multistation system, each separate keyboard input device is called a **keystation.** The output of such a system may be tape, disk, or both, but only one output device is needed rather than one per keystation. On some models, the records from each station are accumulated on a single removable disk assembly called a **disk pack,** which later will be physically detached and mounted on the computer's disk drive for processing (Figure 10–13). Other models transfer the data on the disk

FIGURE 10–12 Magnetic tape data cassette.

to a computer-compatible magnetic tape, which is then read by the computer's tape handler (Figure 10–14). Still others, through an **interface** device called a **communication controller,** transfer data accumulated on a disk or tape directly to the computer (see Figure 10–15). Many multistation data preparation systems include a minicomputer and use stored programs to perform formatting, validation, and accumulation of batch totals (Figure 10–16).

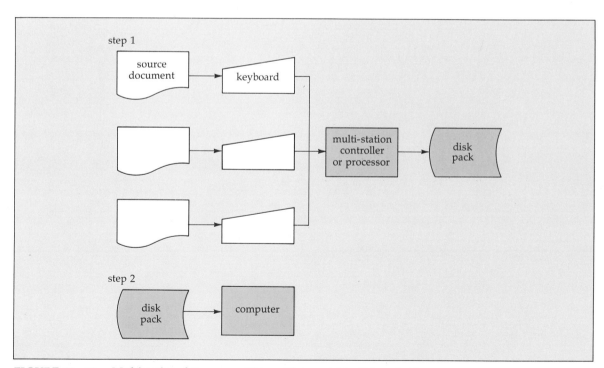

FIGURE 10–13 Multistation data preparation with magnetic disk output.

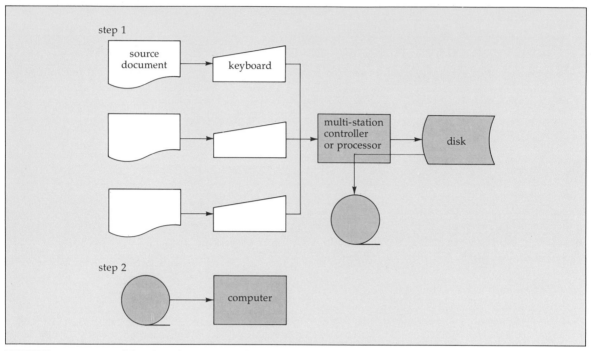

FIGURE 10-14 Multistation data preparation with magnetic tape output.

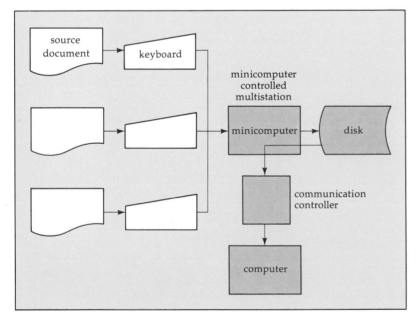

FIGURE 10-15 Direct transfer of prepared data to a computer.

FIGURE 10-16 Minicomputer-controlled multistation data preparation system.

BATCH PROCESSING: DIRECT INPUT FROM SOURCE DOCUMENTS

A growing number of media are used to input data automatically and directly into the computer, or to record the data on magnetic media for rapid entry to the computer. An example is charge tickets imprinted by the inexpensive hand-operator embosser with data from your gasoline charge card. Another example is the 1980 U.S. Census questionnaire form with the circles you marked to indicate your responses.

The objective of all direct input onto media is to eliminate the cost of human key entry and its inherent errors. The devices that read data directly from these source documents are often called **media readers**.

Magnetic Ink Character Recognition

Have you wondered what those oddly shaped characters on the bottom of checks are (see Figure 10–17)? They are magnetic numbers and special

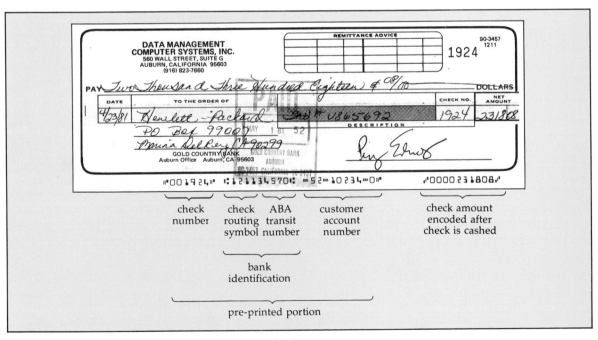

FIGURE 10-17 Magnetic ink characters on a check.

CHAPTER 10: INPUT TO THE COMPUTER 225

symbols that represent the bank's unique number and the checking account number, and they are used in processing the check. These characters are preprinted on check blanks by the printing company that supplies the blanks. Nearly 100 million checks are processed every day in United States banks by **magnetic ink character recognition (MICR)**.

The American Bankers Association (ABA) adopted the characters shown in Figure 10–18 as the standard type font for the banking industry. The characters, 14 in all, are printed with a special ink that can be magnetized for rapid machine reading. The size and thickness of the paper can vary, and the characters will still be read. Smudges and wrinkles are ignored by the magnetic reading device.

After a check is cashed and deposited with a bank, the amount of the check is encoded on the check in MICR font by a keyboard-type machine called a **magnetic ink encoder**. The checks are then read by a **magnetic ink character reader** (Figure 10–19) that reads the magnetic ink characters, verifies them, sends the data directly to the computer or to magnetic tape for input to the computer, and physically sorts them by ABA number (Figure 10–20).

FIGURE 10–18	Magnetic ink characters.
Check Character	Magnetic Symbol
Zero digit	0
One digit	1
Two digit	2
Three digit	3
Four digit	4
Five digit	5
Six digit	6
Seven digit	7
Eight digit	8
Nine digit	9
Dash symbol Q4	⑈
Transit symbol Q3	⑉
On-us symbol Q2	⑊
Amount symbol Q1	⑇

FIGURE 10–19 Magnetic ink character reader.

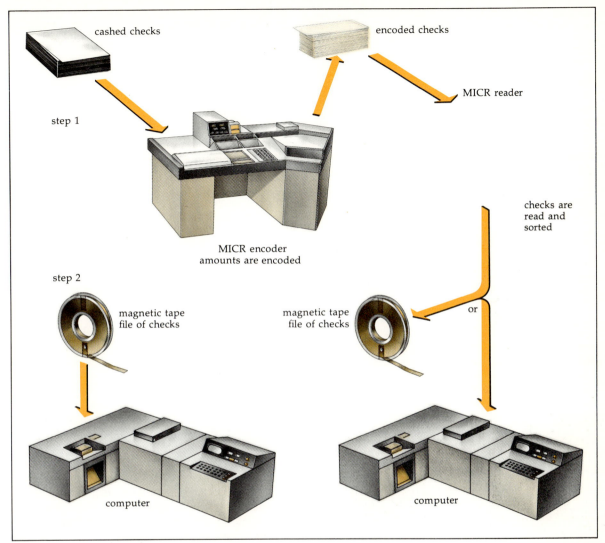

FIGURE 10-20 Data flow in MICR system.

MICR has several advantages. It provides a human-readable document that is still machine-readable. The MICR reading devices are automatic, fast, and accurate. Also, the prerecording of data in MICR minimizes human involvement, which is costly and error prone. Without MICR or some similar automatic input, it is unlikely that the banking industry could have kept up with the rapid move toward a cashless economy.

MICR is limited in usage because it has only 14 characters, which eliminates the ability to handle alphanumeric data. Also, as with many input media, it requires a human to key in some of the data on each check.

Optical Character Recognition

The reading of printed data is called **optical character recognition (OCR)**. The development of OCR was first funded by the U.S. Post Office Department, which had a plan to sort mail by reading name, street address, city, and state. However, with the infinite variations in handwriting style, size,

CHAPTER 10: INPUT TO THE COMPUTER

HOLLERITH, BILLINGS, AND POWERS

The computer owes much to the contributions of three men, whose individual efforts were all closely related. Herman Hollerith (1860–1929), son of German immigrants, was born in Buffalo, N.Y., and graduated from Columbia University's School of Mines. Hollerith was hired by the U.S. Census Office in 1879, and worked with Major John Shaw Billings, who had been assigned to the Census Office by the U.S. Army Surgeon General's office to help in the analysis of biological statistics. Billings was in charge of work on vital statistics for both the 1880 and 1890 censuses.

While discussing the need to relieve clerks of the tedious task of hand-tallying data from census sheets, Billings suggested to Hollerith that a mechanical way of tabulating census data might be possible. Billings referred to Frenchman Joseph Marie Jacquard's 1805 invention that used cards with punched holes to regulate the pattern to be woven by a loom. Billings suggested using pasteboard cards whose punched holes would represent census data; he suggested that a mechanical device could interpret the holes as representing specific data.

Besides the tediousness of hand tabulating, an increase in speed of tabulating was essential, for the Census Office faced a vexing problem. The 1880 census took eight years to tabulate, and by 1890 the U.S. population had grown by 25 percent. Without faster tabulating procedures, the 1890 census would not be completely tallied until after the 1900 census was begun, and by then the 1890 data would be obsolete.

The idea suggested by Billings and the compelling need for faster processing stimulated the talented young Hollerith to invent punched card data processing. Hollerith's machine consisted of three parts: a tabulator that used clock like counting devices that received electrical signals from reading brushes; a sorter box with 24 bins that were electrically connected to the clocklike counters in the tabulator; and a hand-operated punch. After the punched census data card was read, the operator dropped the card by hand into the bin whose door had automatically opened. Although it was hand-operated, the 1890 census count of 63,000,000 persons was reached within a month after all census sheets had reached Washington, D.C.

Building on this success, Hollerith set up the Tabulating Machine Company in 1896, and made both machines and cards. His business flourished as census takers in Western Europe and Canada acquired his machines. Although Hollerith's machines were used in the 1900 census, in 1908 the Director of the Census disagreed with Hollerith on rental rates. Thereupon the Census Bureau (as it was now called) began development work on improved tabulating machines. One of the Bureau's engineers was James Powers, who developed an automatic card-punching machine. Another new development by the Bureau's engineers was a printing device to replace the clocklike display of counters.

In 1911, Powers formed the Powers Tabulating Company and competed with Hollerith's Tabulating Machine Company. In the same year, Hollerith's company combined with a company that manufactured butcher scales and industrial time clocks. The new firm was called the Computer-

Tabulating-Recording Company, which in 1924 changed its name to International Business Machines Corporation (IBM). In 1927, Powers' firm merged with Remington-Rand Corporation; in 1955 this company merged with Sperry Gyroscop and became known as the Sperry Rand Corporation. The computer division of this company is called Sperry-Univac, using the name of Remington-Rand's most notable product, the UNIVAC computer.

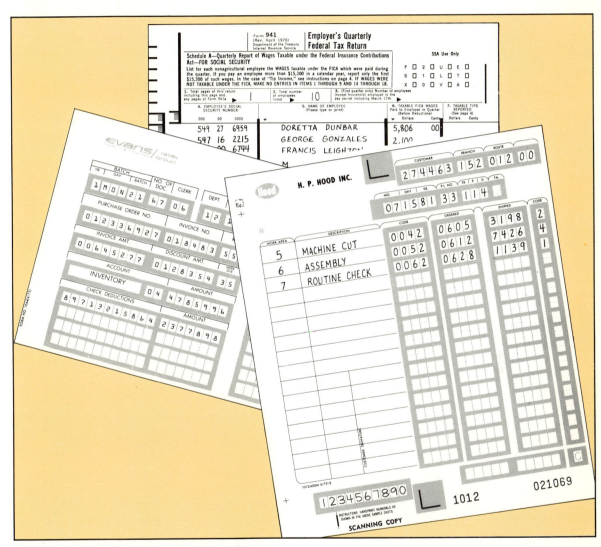

FIGURE 10-21 Examples of OCR media.

and placement on envelopes, this plan did not succeed and, instead, ZIP codes were implemented.

A wide range of media is used by OCR, ranging from retail price tags to punched cards in credit card invoices to 8½ × 11-inch forms for quarterly payroll reports that are submitted to the U.S. Treasury Department (Figure 10–21). A standard type font called **OCR-A,** consisting of slightly irregular angular characters including uppercase and lower case letters, numerals 0 through 9, and special symbols is used in most OCR applications (see Figure 10–22). However, with more flexible and more expensive OCR equipment, typewritten and even carefully handwritten characters can be read fairly reliably. This reliability depends on the quality of the images. Lightness of ink, smudges, wrinkles in the paper, and grease spots can cause rejection of the document or misinterpretation of the data.

The **OCR document reader/sorter** reads the OCR-imprinted documents at the rate of 400 documents per minute, analyzes whether the characters are valid, and rejects them if they are not (Figure 10–23). If valid, the data are transmitted to the computer or to magnetic tape, and the document is sorted into one of many pockets (see Figure 10–24). If the printed characters are not recognizable by the reader, the document falls into a reject stacker and the data are withheld from the computer. Often the

FIGURE 10–23 Typical optical character reader/sorter.

sorting process is not needed, so a device that simply reads is adequate. The flow of data is shown graphically in Figure 10–25.

Another type of OCR input device uses a hand-held reader called a **light pen** or **wand** (Figure 10–

OCR-A NUMERIC	0123456789|YHJ'
OCR-B Numeric	1234567890
Farrington 7 B	0123456789
Farrington 12F	0123456789EP-H
407	0123456789
E13B	0123456789⑊⑊⑊'
1428 Numeric	0123456789 ./-+
OCR-A ALPHA	ABCDEFGHIJKLMNOPQRSTUVWXYZ {}%?■8"*:;=
Hand Print	0 1 2 3 4 5 6 7 8 9 C S T X Z

FIGURE 10–22 Characters recognized by OCR devices.

"NOT BAD FOR A COMPUTER, BUT THE CHIMPANZEE'S WORK HAD MORE FEELING."

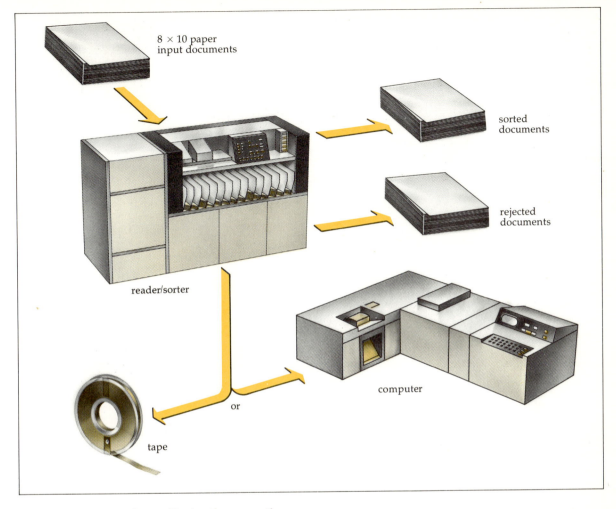

FIGURE 10–24 OCR reading/sorting operation.

26). The wand is moved across the document by hand at speeds up to 10 inches per second, which is equivalent to 100 characters per second (CPS). It can recognize handwritten numerals, OCR-A, or typewritten characters.

OCR devices generally operate by having a light shine on the printed character and then passing the lighted character under photoelectric cells. The cells convert the reflected light into electrical pulses that are fed into a recognition unit that compares the pattern of pulses to the "legal" patterns the reader was designed to recognize. If the patterns match each other, a code for the character is stored and the next character is processed. When the whole document is read, the data are transmitted to the computer or to a magnetic tape unit.

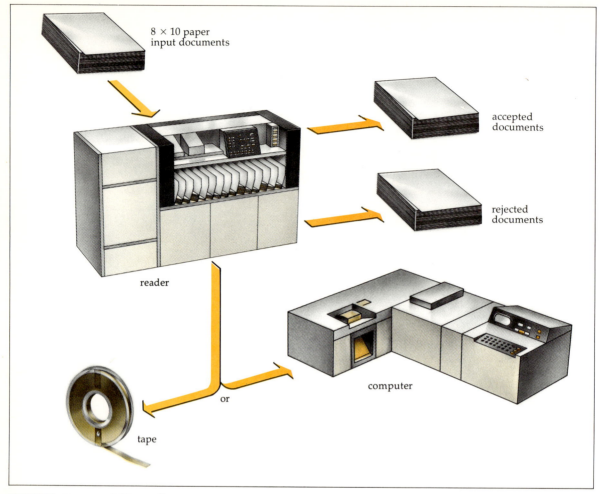

FIGURE 10–25 OCR reading operation.

The prime advantages of OCR are the elimination of manual keying-in of data, and human readability. The disadvantages include its relatively high equipment cost, highly constricted document format, the requirement of high-quality character images, and reject and error rates that are higher than for many other media.

Optical Mark Recognition

Closely related to OCR is **optical mark recognition (OMR)**, which is a simpler function because the optical reading is done in binary. That is, at each fixed location on the document, one of two conditions exists; either a pencil (or an ink) mark will exist, or the location will be unmarked. The meaning of the mark depends on its location, as shown by the markings on the Intel inventory worksheet in Figure 10–27. The data density is very low in comparison to most other media. So why use OMR? The answer is that you are eliminating manual key input and doing so at a very low cost. OMR does have another drawback in addition to its low density, however—that is, the tendency of the person completing the form to mark sloppily or incorrectly. The best use of OMR is when the person marking

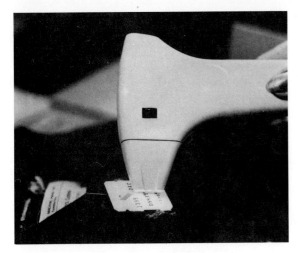

FIGURE 10-26 OCR wand reader.

the form has a stake in its accuracy, such as a student taking a test, or a salesperson who orders merchandise by marking OMR sheets.

OMR machines (Figure 10-28), like other media readers, may input data directly to the computer or, more likely, transcribe them onto magnetic tape for later computer processing.

Digitizers

Another input device, the **digitizer,** uses a handheld penlike device to send signals to a micro- or minicomputer for translation to numeric digits or alphabetical characters. The objective of digitizers is to provide faster and more accurate data entry into the computer by eliminating the time-consuming key entry of data.

FIGURE 10-28 OMR reader.

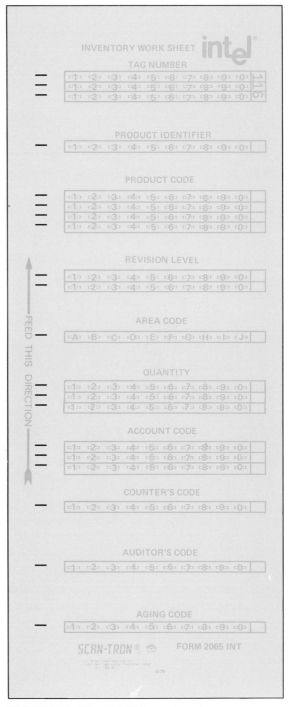

FIGURE 10-27 OMR inventory form.

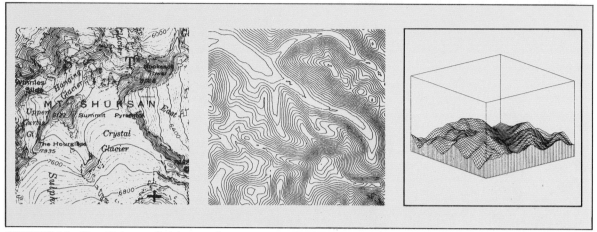

FIGURE 10–29   Using a digitizer to input a numeric description of a drawing.

In entering numeric descriptions of engineering or architectural drawings into the computer via digitizer, the operator traces over the lines in the drawings (Figure 10–29). The visual image of the lines is translated by the digitizer into a numeric description and stored in the computer. One design of the digitizer utilizes a tablet under the drawing. This tablet's surface consists of a fine grid, each point of which can detect the pen's passing. As the pen is passed over many successive points, the computer receives successive signals, which it translates into numeric descriptions of the path of the pen and, hence, of the drawing (see Figure 10–30).

TRANSACTION PROCESSING: INPUT VIA KEYBOARD

In batch processing data were accumulated over a period of time and then processed as a group. With on-line transaction processing, data are not transcribed onto a machine-readable medium prior to processing, but are entered directly into the computer for immediate processing.

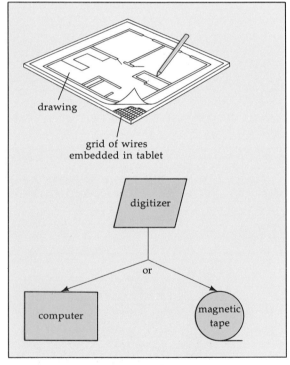

FIGURE 10–30   Tablet and pen for digitizing a drawing.

A variety of methods exist for inputting data directly to the computer. Bank tellers also use a keyboard-type device to communicate with a central computer. Even push-button telephones are now being used to key in data that direct banks to transfer checking account funds to other accounts such as a utility company, retail store, or installment loan company. Others read from media such as price tags and magnetic strips on credit cards while another accepts voice input.

Computer Terminals

One of the most popular devices for inputting data to the computer is the **computer terminal.** The most common terminal is the **cathode ray tube (CRT),** which has a TV-like display screen to show the characters as they are entered on the keyboard. The CRT can serve as both an input and output device since it can also display data and instructions sent from the computer.

CRT terminals are used in a wide variety of applications. The airline industry was one of the first large users to install CRTs as input/output for their remote ticket reservation desks (see Figure 10–31). The clerk requests reservations of the computer through a keyboard and gets a response back via the CRT. Another use of CRT devices is the direct entering of instructions or programs to a computer, called **on-line programming.** When the computer analyzes the instructions as they are entered and gives feedback to the programmer line by line it is called **interactive programming.**

IBM offered its first CRT in 1966, the 2260 Display Station, and a subsequent one in 1971, the 3270. In 1973 Teletype Corporation, a subsidiary of Bell Telephone's manufacturing arm, Western Electric, introduced its Model 40 Data Terminal to ultimately replace its old, inexpensive, mechanical character-at-a-time KSR-33 teletypewriter. These four computer terminals—the IBM 2260, IBM 3270, Teletype Model 40, and Teletype KSR-33—have become in-

FIGURE 10–31   CRT terminal used for airline reservations.

FIGURE 10–32   Printing terminal.

dustry standards. That is, most CRTs manufactured (over 80 percent) are designed to simulate these four electronically. For example, a user can unplug an KSR-33 teletypewriter and plug in a KSR-33–compatible CRT and have no compatibility problems.

The advantages of CRTs for data input are their low cost, ease of correction (simply backspace and strike over), their compact size, and their similarity to the standard typewriter keyboard. Also, since characters keyed in are displayed on an erasable screen, rather than printed, paper is not consumed.

Printing Terminals

In some situations where data are being input via keyboard, a printed copy of the input may be desirable. In that case a **printing terminal,** or **hard-copy terminal** (Figure 10–32) as it is sometimes called, is used. Printing terminals and other types of printers will be discussed in Chapter 13 when we examine output devices.

Intelligent Terminals

A computer terminal is used for input to a computer or output from a computer. An **interactive terminal** is a terminal that allows the operator to converse with the computer in a two-way conversation, such as asking questions and receiving responses, or responding to directions. A terminal that is interactive and, in addition, stores data and performs some processing within itself (such as calculating sales tax) by use of a built-in micro- or minicomputer, is an **intelligent terminal.** Its purpose is to allow as much processing and computing as possible to remain at remote locations. It enables the central computer to be free of involvement until summary, validated, or edited data are ready to be transmitted.

An intelligent terminal must have, as a minimum, the following characteristics:

1. Hardware

   a. Keyboard

   b. Electronics that code and format the data

   c. Capability of on-line communications with other terminals or a computer

   d. Output device such as a CRT

   e. Processing unit (arithmetic/logic and control units) capable of executing conventional computer instructions from an operating system, utility program, or application program (Instructions might include formatting, editing, and validation.)

   f. Random access memory for storage of data and operating programs

2. Software, including a programming language (assembler, compiler, or interpreter), utility programs, debugging aids, operating system, diagnostic programs, and a communications handling program

FIGURE 10–33   Automated teller machine.

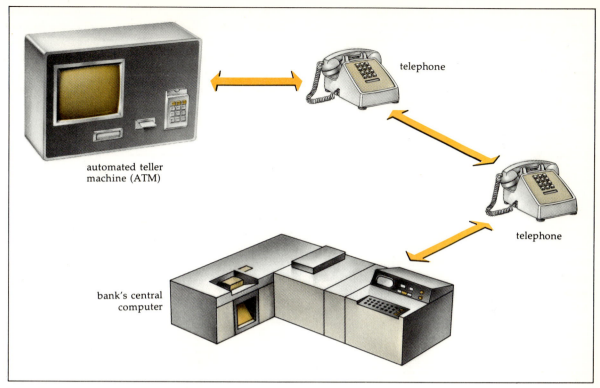

FIGURE 10-34 The ATM, communication link, and central computer.

Intelligent terminals also frequently have a secondary storage device such as a flexible disk, tape cassette, or tape cartridge.

Automated Teller Machines

An unmanned service device, either on or off bank premises, that receives and dispenses cash and handles other routine financial transactions, is called an **automated teller machine (ATM)** (see Figure 10-33).

The ATM is activated by inserting an embossed plastic card with a magnetic strip containing identifying data. The ATM then leads the customer through the transaction with illuminated function keys and/or a programmable display of instructions. A communications link ties the off-premises ATM to the bank's computer (see Figure 10-34).

ATMs allow banks to expand their services to more locations without the cost of expensive branch buildings. For retailers, ATMs relieve them of the burden of cashing customer checks. The convenience of 24-hour check cashing and other bank services will cause the use of ATMs to grow. However, in some states legal issues relating to whether or not an ATM is a branch bank or simply an extension of a bank, have held back growth.

The primary disadvantage of ATMs is that many customers prefer to deal with a human teller.

Automatic Telephone Payments

Perhaps one of the most exciting and far-reaching developments in the input of data to computers is the use of the push-button telephone to allow the user to initiate payments or transfer funds between accounts, such as from the user's account to the account of a utility company, gasoline/oil company, or to a department store. This system is called **automatic telephone payments (ATP)**.

To use ATP you call a special telephone number of either the company to whom you owe money or a company that handles their account. This step connects you to the computer. Next, you enter your identification number, transaction code, and dollar amount via the keys on your telephone. The computer routes your instructions to your bank, which then transfers your funds to your creditor's bank.

The system enables you to pay most of your bills without leaving your home or paying postage. You have precise control over when payments are made. If your account is interest-bearing, you earn interest up to the day you must make the payment. Furthermore, the ATP system allows you to make payments 24 hours a day. The primary disadvantage is that you have no physical evidence of your payment, such as you currently have with a canceled check or a receipt. Also, as with other electronic transactions, you lose the human contact that you may want.

TRANSACTION PROCESSING: DIRECT INPUT FROM SOURCE DOCUMENTS

One of the most common information processing machines is the cash register. Developed in the 1800s, this keyboard-type machine has evolved to the point that it is now often a computer input device. However, the keyboard is becoming an auxiliary input device on the cash register as scanning devices read the bulk of the input data.

Point-of-Sale Terminals

As you have made purchases at fast-food, supermarket, or department stores, you have probably noticed that your purchase is "rung up" on a special type of cash register that displays glowing numerals. This machine does not have the mechanical sound of the older, conventional cash register, but is more likely to emit tones to let the operator know it is operating. This cash register is probably connected directly to a minicomputer that is collecting sales data and performing some calculations for the sales clerk. Such a cash register is an example of what is commonly called a **point-of-sale (POS) terminal** (see Figure 10–35). POS terminals, through communication with the computer, may authorize credit, calculate taxes, and give instructions to the operator by lighting the key that should be depressed, or by giving a message on a display panel.

In 1976 there were about 400,000 POS terminals, and by 1981 retailers expect to have 2.5 million. Montgomery Wards' chain alone expects to install several thousand POS terminals yearly for use in

FIGURE 10–35 Retail point-of-sale (POS) terminal.

stores having sales of $4 million or more per year. The growth of POS terminal usage has been somewhat slowed by consumers' apprehension of POS implementation where code numbers are shown on merchandise to the exclusion of prices.

The POS terminal can be connected either directly to a computer (see Figure 10–36a) or to a controller that has a microcomputer in it and that controls the magnetic tape recording process (Figure 10–36b). This tape is later read by computer for processing of sales. Input of sales data to the POS ter-

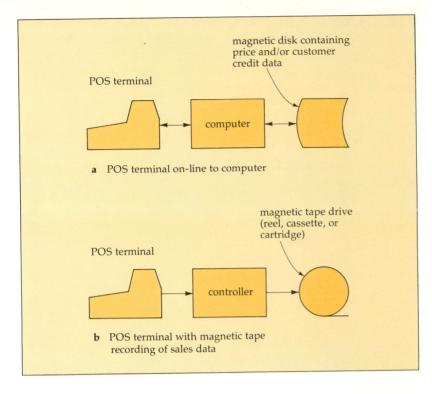

FIGURE 10-36 Flowchart of POS terminals.

minal may be through a keyboard or it may be optically read from the **Universal Product Code (UPC)** (see Figure 10-37) or some other machine-readable code. The UPC is used by the grocery industry and found on most items on the supermarket shelves. With the UPC, merchandise is passed over a reading platform (Figure 10-38) or read by a wand-

FIGURE 10-37 A Universal Product Code label.

FIGURE 10-38 A POS terminal with bar code slot scanner reading device.

CHAPTER 10: INPUT TO THE COMPUTER

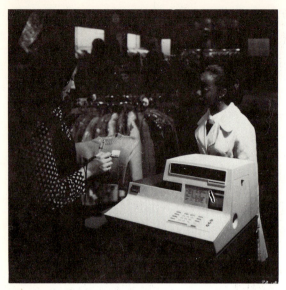

FIGURE 10–39 A POS terminal with a wand reader.

SAFEWAY STORE 275	
ROSEVILLE, CALIFORNIA	
10/13 17:03 6 151 53	
DELI	1.62*
ORANG MARMLD	1.05*
NONFAT MILK	.33*
TRIDENT	.19*
TRIDENT	.19*
1.59 LB @ 3/1.00	
BANANAS	.53*
STATIONERY	1.19 TX
SUBTOTAL	5.10
TAX DUE	.07
TOTAL DUE	5.17
ELIGIBLE	3.91
CASH DUE	1.26
THANK YOU	

FIGURE 10–40 Descriptive information on a POS terminal sales tag.

type device (Figure 10–39). Another code, the OCR-A, can also be read by wand-type devices.

The National Retail Merchants Association (NRMA) has adopted a Voluntary Universal Marking Program (VUVM) utilizing OCR-A code as its standard. The goal of the VUVM program is the use of the OCR-A price tag in retail stores. This price tag has the advantage of being readable by humans and machines. The management of big retailers such as Wards, Sears, Penneys, and Federated are strong advocates of VUVM, because of their stores' high sales volume.

With both UPC and OCR-A, the stock number represented by the code is transmitted to the computer, tape cassette, or magnetic tape. The sales ticket output of POS terminals that are on-line to a computer can be more complete than the traditional sales ticket, since the computer can send back to the POS terminal a descriptive caption of each item it lists on the sales tag (see Figure 10–40) as well as the price.

The advantages of POS terminals include a lower necessary skill level for the operators, faster checkout, better control over the issuance of credit, and more timely sales and inventory reports to management.

The major disadvantage of the POS system is that in an on-line system, the terminal depends on the continual operation of the central computer. If the computer fails, the whole POS system ceases to function. In high turnover stores like supermarkets, separate backup systems may be required. Other disadvantages include its relatively high equipment cost, highly constricted document format, the requirement of high-quality character images, and reject and error rates that are higher than for many other media. Finally, contrary to many consumers' preferences or best interest, to get maximum efficiency from a POS system, individual items of merchandise should not be price tagged. Consumer concern about using the Universal Product Code scanner at supermarket checkout stations and about elimination of item pricing has subsided from what it was several years ago. However, seven states and some cities in other states have passed laws that require item pricing; in these cities and states, the advantages of POS systems cannot be realized.

TRANSACTION PROCESSING: INPUT BY VOICE

The Monsanto Company sorts 25,000 pieces of mail each day semi-automatically by an electronic mail sorter. However, rather than have the sorting device optically read the name of the addressee, an operator wearing a microphone headset reads aloud the initial of the first name of the addressee and the first four letters of the surname. A **voice recognition system (VRS)** translates the spoken sounds into digital data and displays on a CRT the full name of the employee, or names several employees of like spelling. The operator then chooses the name that matches the addressee, and that name is transmitted so the person's mail can be physically sorted by the electronic sorting device. All the time, the operator's hands are free to handle the mail. Monsanto's mail processing speed has doubled by use of this system.

Other applications such as directing machine actions, collecting serial numbers or part numbers for inventory control (see Figure 10–41), and the programming of computers by persons who are severely physically handicapped, are currently in use.

Input for voice recognition can be in the form of words or short phrases; output goes to a computer memory, magnetic disk, or cassette in computer code. The VIP-100 pictured in Figure 10–41 stores a 32-word vocabulary of reference patterns in a minicomputer. These reference patterns can be stored in English or any other language. As a word is spoken into the microphone, it is translated into numeric code, and then the minicomputer matches it with the numeric codes of the prestored vocabulary. Once the match is made, the word or phrase is displayed on a CRT (see Figure 10–42) or other display device. First-time users are claimed to reach 97 percent accuracy, and with the CRT's visual display, the rate can be pushed to 100 percent. Some of the voice recognition systems operate in a time-sharing mode, allowing several persons using separate microphones and CRTs to input simultaneously.

The price of a VRS now ranges from $15,000 to $50,000, depending on its features, but this will decline as VRS popularity increases. Voice data entry will find its way into a wide variety of applications. Where voluminous amounts of numeric data are to be entered, keyboard or optical entry will still be preferable. However, when words and alphanumerics are entered, more and more users will find voice input cost-effective.

FIGURE 10–41   The VIP-100 voice recognition system.

ELECTRONIC FUNDS TRANSFER

The transfer of funds from your bank account takes place through electronic methods when you utilize either the ATM or the ATP systems. This movement of your money is called **electronic funds transfer (EFT).**

Also included in the EFT definition is the charging of merchandise to your 30-day, revolving, or other charge account via remote electronic devices. For example, if you purchase merchandise on account at a department store utilizing POS terminals that not only read bar codes, calculate amounts, and print sales tickets, but also add the charge purchase to your account, you are involved in an EFT.

A major hindrance to the rapid growth of EFT is lack of public acceptance. This has been caused by (1) consumer resistance to change; (2) the change

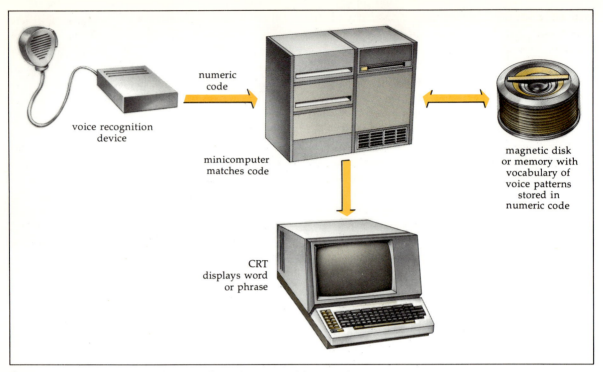

FIGURE 10-42 Functional parts of a voice recognition system.

from human-to-human contact to human-to-machine interface, and (3) the accessibility of an individual's financial records to unauthorized persons. The privacy of our personal and financial information is held far more valuable by many than 24-hour banking or other conveniences. This concern has triggered much debate at the state and federal levels. In fact, 24 states have already enacted legislation to regulate EFT. In 1978 Congress passed the **Electronic Funds Transfer Act (EFTA).** The act requires financial institutions to make available written documentation of each transfer of funds. Under EFTA, consumer liability for unauthorized transfers is limited to $50 per transfer and a maximum of $500 for more than one unauthorized transfer. Relating to privacy of information the EFTA directs financial institutions to notify a consumer if any of the consumer's information is released to a third party. The EFTA provides that a court may award treble damages to a consumer if a financial institution breaks the law.

Another reason that EFTs have not grown rapidly is their high cost to businesses that install them. Estimates of costs-per-transaction vary widely—from as high as $1.25 to as low as 6¢—depending on who is estimating and at what volume of transaction they are figuring. The higher the volume of transactions, the lower the cost is per transaction. Figure 10-43 shows the estimated EFT

FIGURE 10-43 Costs of processing transactions.

Type of Transaction	Annual Volume of Transactions	Handling Cost Per Transaction
Cash	200 billion	1.5¢
Check	28 billion	30.0¢
Credit card	5 billion	50.0¢
Electronic funds transfer	0.3 billion	6.0¢ to $1.25 (est)

cost along with the current cost of processing cash, check, and credit card transactions, according to a National Science Foundation study performed by Arthur D. Little, Inc.

In spite of the apprehension about EFT, banks and retailers are expending many millions of dollars annually on machines and programming for it. For example, a nationwide electronic payments network now links together 32 automated clearinghouses. These clearinghouses electronically exchange the value of checks and other financial documents between banks, government agencies, and corporations without transporting the actual documents. The impact of EFT on privacy will be discussed further in Chapter 20.

SUMMARY

In this chapter you have seen a variety of input systems. They range from inexpensive and simple (CRT terminals) to complex (point-of-sale systems). One system predates many of us (punched cards), while some are barely out of the experimental stage (voice recognition). Some devices are used in a wide variety of applications (intelligent terminals); others are much more limited in scope (automated teller machines). All of these devices have several things in common: They provide communication between people and computers; they are simply tools and depend on humans for proper use; their overall cost (purchase and operating) effectiveness depends on how well they fit into the overall information system. A device that is very economical for a small business might be terribly expensive when applied to large-volume information systems (for instance, keyboard entry of data versus optical character recognition).

Input devices are conceived, designed, tested, and marketed like many other products. Where their use provides significant advantages over alternative ways of handling data, they grow in popularity. As better devices are introduced (magnetic tape, for instance), the older devices decline (punched cards). By the time you complete your college education, some of the devices described here will have peaked in usage and be on the decline, as newer approaches to computer input and output are introduced. Others that we discussed are little known today, but will be in widespread use in a few years. Computer users must continually be alert to the changing offerings of input devices, and be ready to dispose of current procedures to take advantage of more efficient and economical ways of handling information.

Selection of an input device is based on a number of criteria, not all of which would apply in a given situation. The criteria include human readability, compatibility with other devices, speed of operation, reliability, and purchase and operating costs. This is not to say that hardware, software, and supply costs, since they are calculable, are the only costs that are relevant. There are social or "people" costs for which computer users are also responsible. For example, the employer who replaces a group of clerks with a special machine does have a responsibility to utilize those displaced employees, either through transfer or retraining. Another social cost is the infringement of privacy that can result from inadequate control of access to computerized data files. When made available to those who have no need or authority, these files can be damaging to the people whose data are in the file.

TERMS

The following words or terms have been presented in this chapter.

Input device	Mean time between
Batch processing	failures (MTBF)
On-line processing	Verifying
Transaction processing	Validation
Output device	80-column Hollerith
Medium	card
Compatibility	Rows
Protocols	Columns
RS232C standard	Field
Character per second	Keypunch machine
(CPS)	Punched card reader
Reliability	Cards per minute (CPM)

Unit record
Key-to-tape device
Key-to-flexible disk device
Key-to-cartridge device
Key-to-cassette device
Keystation
Disk pack
Interface
Communication controller
Media readers
Magnetic ink character recognition (MICR)
Magnetic ink encoder
Magnetic ink character reader
Optical character recognition (OCR)
OCR-A
OCR document reader/sorter
Light pen
Wand
Optical mark recognition (OMR)
Digitizer
Computer terminal
Cathode ray tube (CRT)
CRT terminal
On-line programming
Interactive programming
Printing terminal
Hard-copy terminal
Interactive terminal
Intelligent terminal
Automated teller machine (ATM)
Automatic telephone payments (ATP)
Point-of-sale (POS) terminals
Universal Product Code (UPC)
Voice recognition system (VRS)
Electronic funds transfer (EFT)
Electronic Funds Transfer Act (EFTA)

EXERCISES

The exercises that follow are grouped by level of difficulty. Problems in the A series are the easiest; B series problems are moderately hard; and C series problems are the most difficult.

A–1 What advantages does the punched card offer as an input medium that newer techniques such as key-to-tape, key-to-disk, or key-to-cartridge/cassette, do not offer?

A–2 What are the major advantages of using a magnetic medium for data preparation?

A–3 What is a keystation in contrast to a key-to-tape machine?

A–4 Describe a situation apart from computers where a medium and one or more machines that create or use the medium are involved.

A–5 Explain why input devices are so essential to the use of computers.

A–6 Explain why a bank that was ordering teller input devices that would be on-line to the bank's computers would be interested in the device's mean time between failures.

A–7 What does MICR represent?

A–8 Describe the major components of a POS system.

A–9 What are the major attributes of an intelligent terminal?

B–1 Data keyed into most types of key-to-magnetic media devices are displayed in what manner?

B–2 What are the advantages of a flexible disk as compared to magnetic tape?

B–3 What is the advantage of a multistation key-to-tape system over several individual key-to-tape units?

B–4 What function does a minicomputer serve in a multistation key-to-disk system?

B–5 What is the advantage of a key-to-cartridge over the key-to-tape (reel-type computer-compatible), and, conversely, the advantage of key-to-tape over key-to-cartridge?

B–6 Under what circumstances could you defend an on-line data entry system?

B–7 Who is the major user of MICR? Why has MICR not been applied to many other document-reading situations?

B–8 Why would some users choose OCR over MICR?

B–9 What printed characters can be read by OCR devices?

B–10 Why is the retail merchandise industry using OCR?

B–11 The voice recognition system utilizing a minicomputer has great potential for growth. Describe at least two appropriate applications.

B–12 Do you see any social risks to the widespread use of EFTs? Explain.

B–13 What benefits are derived for the public by the use of EFTs?

B–14 How would an automatic telephone payments system help you, if at all?

B–15 Describe what an interactive terminal is.

B–16 Which of the following applications would require the highest MTBF rating? Explain why.

  a. A computer that is adding purchase-on-account amounts to customers' balances.

  b. A computer that prints employee paychecks.

  c. A computer that is used in air traffic control for Kennedy International Airport.

C–1 How does a data preparation (or data entry) device relate in function to a conventional computer input device?

C–2 Both verification and validation are valuable steps in the processing of input data. Describe each of these operations and point out their differences.

C–3 Describe the advantages and disadvantages of MICR input.

C–4 Prepare a chart giving the various input media and their common uses, speeds, advantages, and disadvantages.

C–5 Differentiate between OCR and OMR.

C–6 What is the major limiting aspect of OMR?

C–7 Describe the major components of a voice recognition system and show how they relate to each other.

C–8 The digitizer can eliminate many slow, tedious, and error-fraught alternative methods of inputting data. Describe how the digitizer works.

C–9 What is the major attribute of POS terminals and automated teller machines that makes them different from most other computer input devices?

C–10 Do you believe the use of POS terminals should be encouraged? To what extent? Explain fully why you have answered each of these questions as you have.

C–11 Through the use of the Readers Guide to Periodical Literature or a similar publication in your library, locate an article dealing with POS or EFT, and write a brief summary of recent developments in one of these areas.

C–12 Describe the differences between an interactive terminal and an intelligent terminal.

C–13 How does an intelligent terminal relate to a data preparation device?

COMPUTER NEWS

MAGIC WAND COMES OF AGE WITH NEW USES

by Frederick W. Miller

One of the easiest and simplest ways to get data into a computer for processing is by scanning a bar code with a hand-held wand, or running the bar-coded package over a slot scanner.

It's a simple statement about a simple fact of life. But one may ask why more firms aren't using bar code scanning as a viable replacement for punched cards, or keyboard-to-disk data entry systems, or on-line CRT terminals.

The answer is that companies are using hand-held scanners and slot scanners in increasing numbers. The use is in areas that lend themselves to this type of data entry—areas in which a CRT terminal or badge reader or punched card device is not appropriate.

Technologies have been converging, of late, that make bar code printing easier, and therefore bar code reading easier; and new hand-held wands, or readers, have been introduced into the marketplace to provide alternate sources for such units.

There are two principal areas for the use of bar code scanning—in retail stores, such as supermarkets, general merchandise chains and discount stores; and in industrial or business enterprises, such as manufacturers, airlines, libraries, hospitals and clinics, and municipalities and government agencies.

Hand-held wand scanners can be and are used in all of these fields and additional application areas. To meet these various needs, several bar codes—all similar in general nature and purpose—have been developed. The two most widely used in the US are the Universal Product Code (UPC) in supermarkets, and the

> **After seeming to be asleep, bar codes and wand readers have found uses in retailing, hospitals, industries and libraries where data input needs to be quick and accurate but a keyboard device is not appropriate.**

"Code 3 of 9" and its variant, Code 39, in industrial applications.

The adoption of bar codes and their use for data entry/data collection applications involving computers has been somewhat of a "chicken-and-the-egg" problem. In short, which came first? Or, which will come first so that the other will work—the bar codes on the products, or the scanners in the stores and industrial plants to read the bar codes. That controversy has long since died out among firms that wish to sell their products through supermarkets, and there's the Uniform Product Code Council Inc. in Dayton, OH, to assign UPC bar codes to manufacturers.

Richard Mindlin, executive vice president of the council, told INFOSYSTEMS that this is a "case of economics," in that manufacturers "had to put the (bar code) symbol on the products first before it can be scanned."

The UPC bar coding program, he continued, was made final in about 1973 and there has been steady, but maybe slow, progress by companies to join the council and to be assigned the first five digits as the company's unique portion of the 10-digit UPC.

12,000 members

Mindlin, who is retired as assistant vice president of R&D at NCR Corp. and was long active in standardization work with UPC, said the council now has about 12,000 member companies and that others are joining the council at the rate of more than 200 per month. It's a minimum one-time fee, of $300, but the fee is based on a firm's annual sales volume.

"They join the council to symbolize their products (have a UPC code number assigned)," he said. "This is not just food products, but all goods sold in supermarkets and discount stores."

Installation of UPC scanners in supermarkets was slow for a time, but firms including NCR Corp., IBM Corp., Datachecker, Data Terminal Systems and Sweda have now installed "slot scanners" in more than 3,500 stores as of the end of the first quarter this year, according to Mindlin.

This number is more than double the 1,472 stores that had scanners at the end of 1979, and about 400 more than at the end of last year, Mindlin told INFOSYSTEMS.

According to figures published in the May 1981 issue of Scanning, Coding & Automation Newsletter, NCR Corp. equipment accounted for about 38 percent of the store locations, or 1,343 stores; IBM was second with 28 percent or 998 stores; Datachecker, a unit of National Semiconductor Corp., was third with 20 percent or 707 stores, and Data Terminal Systems and Sweda each had about 6 percent each or about 200 stores.

Similar applications

Use of the Universal Product Code in supermarkets, and similar retail outlets, is the same—for inventory control and product pricing at the point of sale. The UPC number represents an item in a retail store's computer system. Mindlin said it's up to the product manufacturer to assign the second five digits of the 10-digit code to a specific item.

Although supermarkets use slot scanners—ones that are built into the checkout line—other retailers have adopted hand-held scanners to read the bar codes on various nonfood products. More and more product manufacturers are adopting UPC and placing it on products, including periodicals (magazines); record albums and video tapes; liquor; and other beverages, Mindlin explained.

The Universal Product Code has one drawback, however. It can't be imprinted on corrugated cardboard boxes used for shipping products. The box material is too porous for the fine-line code. However, Mindlin said shippers can use Code 3 of 9, Code 39 or Code 2 of 5 on containers.

Bar codes, and thus bar code readers, also are being used in many other nonfood applications, particularly in industrial and business enterprises. Among these, according to Ance Thatcher, director of marketing at Ferranti-Identicon Inc., Franklin, MA, are:

• in the Atlanta, GA, airport by Delta Air Lines for sorting outbound baggage by flight destination;

• by the Delaware Port Authority for determining if a vehicle has a valid, paid-up sticker to cross one of the four bridges over the Delaware River;

- in automobile assembly plants for making sure the correct parts of a catalytic muffler are assembled, using bar-coded parts and a hand-held wand;
- in libraries for keeping track of books loaned and books returned by scanning bar codes in books, and on a borrower's card; and
- in sorting boxes, cartons or cases of merchandise as they move along a conveyor system.

The fastest-growing area for the use of bar codes and wand scanners is in factory data collection, Thatcher told INFOSYSTEMS. "One reason is the growing importance of computerized manufacturing systems—MSP, MRP, CRP and MRP II," he said. "These have made it essential to have fast and accurate feedback from the factory floor." Information is in these areas—work-in-process as it moves through the production process, where parts and assemblies are, and what has been completed, he explained.

Wand readers are used also in labor distribution reporting. Data is collected on how much time and at what rate a person has worked to build a product or assemble a subsystem at a work station; and for time and attendance reporting to indicate who is at work and what hours the person has worked, Thatcher continued.

Another manufacturing area in which bar codes and hand-held wands are used is inventory control, he added. And this includes component inventory, finished goods inventory and work-in-process inventory.

Thatcher predicts two major areas in which bar codes and wands will be used in the future. One is as a replacement for time clocks for worker check-in and check-out; and the other is as an attachment to a CRT terminal.

Using bar code readers attached to CRT terminals has stirred new interest among CRT manufacturers, Thatcher said, noting that Feranti-Identicon has developed a printed circuit board for CRTs for that purpose. One application would be by a supervisor or foreman to record exceptions to regular work, such as rework, late arriving parts, absenteeism, accidents and shortages of materials, he added.

One of the most recent applications is the use of the Norand Alpha-1 hand-held bar code scanners by Federal Express Corp. to expedite the sorting and handling of 90,000 bills of lading and associated packages daily. More than 450 scanners have been put in use at airline terminal points used in the Federal Express package delivery network that is based in Memphis, TN.

According to Robert L. Steele, president of Norand Corp., Cedar Rapids, IA, the scanners are used to read the bar code on each bill of lading that shows the account number, customer name, package weight and destination. This captured information then is transmitted by phone lines to a computer in Memphis that then sorts the in-bound package information into out-bound groups by destination. This is all done before the planes and packages arrive in Memphis and allows Federal Express to allocate outbound planes based on weight per destination.

Norand, which was a pioneer in developing a portable hand-held scanner for bar codes in 1971, has recently introduced a bar code reader that "takes a picture" of the bar code, according to Steele.

The firm's Model 20/20 uses a xenon flash tube to illuminate the bar code symbol and then captures that reflected image on a photo diode array and transmits it to a data storage device, such as the Norand Alpha 101, he continued.

"This offers a big breakthrough and should revolutionize scanning," Steele said, noting that the Model 20/20 would be "terrific for UPC" because it reads wrinkled wrappers and varied package shapes easily. This makes the new bar code reader applicable to both point-of-sale and backroom operations in supermarkets, as well as for other nonretail applications such as in manufacturing, and among smaller retailers, drug and convenience stores.

Another recently introduced handheld scanner is the HEDS 3000 digital bar code wand by Hewlett-Packard Co. The wand uses a light-and-lens system that focuses light on the bar code and an integrated photodetector chip to read the reflected light, the firm explained. A special version of the HP wand has been developed as an accessory to the HP-41C programmable calculator.

Other recently introduced products in this field are:

• The Datachecker POSitalker, a talking cash register that uses the National Semiconductor Co. speech synthesis chip to call out prices of items as they are scanned or entered manually into a keyboard.

• The Datachecker hand-held symbol reader that can be used to read the UPC symbol in remote locations, such as at a service desk.

"Shoppers have always liked to hear prices called out," said Johnny Humphreys, corporate vice president and general manager of National's Systems Division that markets the Datachecker point-of-sale laser scanning systems. "Today's technology has rapidly solved any lingering consumer doubts about the added value of scanning that the shopper may have had."

CHAPTER eleven

MEMORY AND DATA REPRESENTATION

Preview

Human and Computer Memories

Need for Primary and Secondary Storage

Need for Computer Memory

Memory Addresses

Decimal and Binary Systems
   Bridging the Decimal-Binary Gap
   Conversion Methods
   Hexadecimal Number Systems

Computer Data Notation Systems
   4-Bit BCD Notation
   Parity-Check Bit
   8-Bit Notation
   Fixed-Word Notation

Characteristics of Memory

History Capsule: Atanasoff and Berry's Special-Purpose Electronic Computer

History Capsule: Mauchly and Eckert's General-Purpose Electronic Computer

Memory Types
   Semiconductor Memories
   Charged-Coupled Devices
   Magnetic-Bubble Memories
   Techniques under Development

Summary
Computer News:
How Magnetic-Bubble Memories Work

PREVIEW

The two functional parts of the computer that store data and programs are primary storage (or memory) and secondary storage (or external storage). Primary storage can hold millions of characters of data and retrieve any one of the stored characters in a few billionths of a second. Secondary storage can hold much larger volumes of data—up to hundreds of billions of characters—and retrieves any one character of data in a few thousandths of a second. Most computers need to have both types of storage.

In this chapter we learn how primary storage relates to the other functional parts and, in turn, is served by them. We find that simplicity of design in computers dictates that they not use decimal numbers (0, 1, 2, 3, . . . 9) in their memory, but use only two digits (0 and 1). We explain methods of bridging the gap between decimal-oriented human beings and two-digit-oriented computers. You learn about the rapid changes and advances in computer memories that ultimately will cause personal computers to be just as popular as hand-held calculators are now.

HUMAN AND COMPUTER MEMORIES

The adult human brain may hold up to three billion pieces of information; it uses a small amount of energy; and it takes up only about 100 cubic inches of space. Signals are sent within the human nervous system at a speed of 350 feet per second.

In contrast to the marvelous human memory, a computer memory can store only about 16 million characters of information; many use enough energy to heat a home; and they may consume 10,000 cubic inches of space. However, a computer memory does have a few advantages over the human brain. Signals are sent within the computer at approximately 654,700,000 feet per second. Computer memories can be repaired or replaced, and some of them can withstand temperature and pressure variations far in excess of what the human brain can tolerate.

NEED FOR PRIMARY AND SECONDARY STORAGE

Before we examine how computer memories operate, let's reexamine our VISA accounts receivable billing system of Chapter 3. This system requires the computer to store the historical data about all customers in a master file and the data about purchases or payments of the current month in a transaction file.

Suppose that for each customer in our master file we stored the data shown in Figure 11–1. Also, let's hypothesize that for each charge or payment made we stored the data describing that transaction as shown in Figure 11–2. Figures 11–1 and 11–2 describe the formats of the records in our two files, customer and transaction. Each record is subdivided into individual items of data called **fields**. Some of the fields in Figure 11–1 are customer number, customer name, street, city, state, zip code, and overall balance. Some of the fields in the transaction record (Figure 11–2) are customer number, date sold, date posted, and amount of sale. Fields in a record can be of various types (numeric, alphabetic) and lengths as Figures 11–1 and 11–2 indicate.

If our VISA billing system has only a million customer master records, each having 133 characters, the customer master file would require 133 million characters of storage. Similarly, if each transaction record is 50 characters long and there are only five million of them, we still need 250 million characters of storage. In all, then, we need a total of 383 million characters of storage.

Computer programs that process data stored in a file access the desired records and manipulate the data of the various fields of each record. Our program for printing the customers' statements or bills could direct the computer to store all the data from both files in primary storage at once. This would require our computer to have at least 133 million bytes of primary storage. Computers with this amount of primary storage—memory—are not now being manufactured. Furthermore, with the price of memory in 1982 at $10,000 per million bytes, a com-

FIGURE 11-1 Customer master record description.

Field Name	Type of Data	Number of Characters
Customer number	Numeric	10
Customer name	Alphabetic	24
Street	Alphanumeric	16
City	Alphanumeric	16
State	Alphabetic	2
Zip code	Numeric	5
Finance charge	Numeric	10
Balance-over-30	Numeric	10
Balance-over-60	Numeric	10
Balance-over-90	Numeric	10
Balance-this-month	Numeric	10
Overall balance	Numeric	10
Total number of characters		133

FIGURE 11-2 Transaction record description.

Field Name	Type of Data	Number of Characters
Customer number	Numeric	10
Date sold	Numeric	6
Date posted	Numeric	6
Amount of sale	Numeric	10
Type (Charge/Payment)	Alphabetic	2
Description of sale	Alphanumeric	16
Total number of characters		50

puter with this amount of memory would cost at least $1,330,000, not including any input/output devices.

A second approach to printing the VISA statement would be to keep all the data for all customers in secondary storage. In this case, to print a statement for a customer we would transfer—read—the customer's data from external to internal storage, then print the statement. This approach would require an external storage device capable of holding 383 million characters and internal storage of only 383 characters (133 per master record + 50 each for 5 transactions per customer). An external storage device capable of holding 383 million characters costs $30,000, and with a million bytes of internal storage costing $10,000 in 1982 our total cost is $40,000. This second approach is the way VISA actually processes the data to print its statements.

Costs are a major consideration when using a computer system. By using external storage in conjunction with internal storage and taking advantage of the lower cost per character of external storage and the speed of internal processing we are able to have a VISA billing system at a low cost.

Internal and external storage use different kinds of physical devices to cause these cost and speed differences. In the remainder of this chapter we look at internal storage (or memory). In Chapter 12 we discuss external storage devices and how they store file-oriented data.

NEED FOR COMPUTER MEMORY

The computer has six major functional parts, one of which is memory—the place where data are stored or held. The portion of memory that receives data from an input device is called the **input buffer**. Memory holds intermediate results of calculations and decisions in an area called **working storage**. After processing, memory keeps data to be sent to an output device in its **output buffer**. In fulfilling these functions, memory is vital to every job the computer undertakes.

In addition to data, memory holds the programs that direct the computer's operations (see Figure

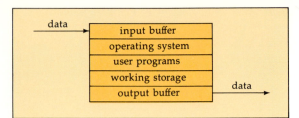

FIGURE 11–3 Contents of memory.

11–3). These include **user programs,** which tell the computer to perform specific jobs such as to calculate and print a paycheck, and **operating system programs,** which direct the various parts of the computer to operate in an orderly way.

MEMORY ADDRESSES

To help us see how memory works, we can view it as a series of storage locations for data, each with a unique numerical **address.** Any of the three types of data—alphabetic, numeric, and special characters—can be stored at any particular address within memory. You can, for convenience, think of the computer's memory as a series of bins in a warehouse, with only one item stored in each bin (see Figure 11–4). The bins are numbered starting with 1. The item in any bin can be taken out and a new item put in its place. So, the contents of the bin can change, but the address stays the same. To gain access to an item in a particular bin, you must know the address of that bin. To carry the analogy further, some warehouses organize their bins so that four items can be placed in each bin, others have bins that hold eight items, and still others have bins that accommodate variable numbers of items. The same is true of computers; that is, depending on the design of the machine, one or more items can be stored at each address.

A particular computer memory design can likewise be organized in different ways. Since only two possible states or conditions can exist in the basic component of the computer's memory, the appropriate number system to use in storing values is the number system that has only two unique digits.

This is the **binary number system,** with numerals zero (0) and one (1). A single binary character, either 0 or 1, is called a **binary digit** or, in shortened form, a **bit.**

Generally, data are stored as a group of bits in memory, as shown in Figure 11–5. The data are located when needed by an address number. We can say, then, that there are **addressable memory locations** at which data can be stored and/or from which data can be accessed by citing the particular address number.

Some computers use addressable locations that can store more than one alphanumeric character. The addressable location in this case is called a *word* and the computer is a **fixed-word** computer. The number of bits per word varies from 6 to 64 depending on the particular design. In a fixed-word computer, any decimal number (for example, 21 or 757 or 599,476) reserves a whole word of memory. If the small value 21 is stored in a 48-bit word, it reserves just as much space as the value 599,476; hence, there is a large amount of wasted space.

A memory location containing enough bits to store any alphanumeric character is commonly called a **byte.** In Figure 11–6 each byte consists of eight bits. Computers that store only one decimal digit, alphabetic character, or special character per memory address are called **variable-word computers.** For storing a three-digit decimal number, three consecutive bytes of memory would be used.

DECIMAL AND BINARY SYSTEMS

Many human systems of counting and measuring are based on groups of ten. For example, ten cents make a dime and ten dimes make a dollar in U.S. currency; the metric measuring system is built on tens, hundreds, and thousands. Counting systems based on ten are called "decimal systems." Such systems are not necessarily "natural," however. A more elemental way of looking at things recognizes only two values, such as yes/no or +/−. Such a number system, as we saw, is called **binary.** Computers are based on the binary system because computers operate using the principles of electricity

FIGURE 11-4 Storage of items in numbered bins.

and magnetic fields. Both of these have only two conditions—on or off in the case of electricity, and positive or negative attraction in the case of magnets. So computers represent data using various combinations of these two conditions, which are symbolized as 0 and 1. Electrical flow of magnetism in one direction can represent the numeric value 1, while the absence of electrical flow, or magnetism in the other direction can represent zero (0).

By now you may have anticipated the basic conflict between humans and their computers. Humans think in and work on the basis of decimal systems,

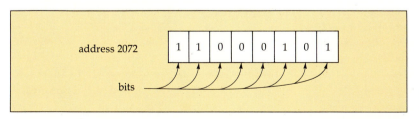

FIGURE 11-5 An addressable memory location.

CHAPTER 11: MEMORY AND DATA 255

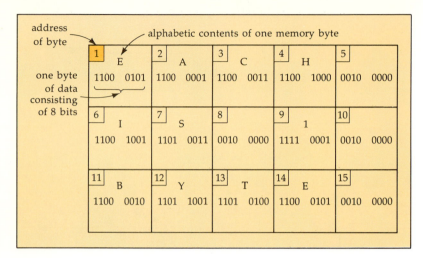

FIGURE 11-6 The phrase "each is 1 byte" stored in a variable-word computer memory.

while computers must operate using a binary system because of the physical laws governing their operation. But this conflict can—and has been—overcome.

Bridging the Decimal-Binary Gap

To represent alphabetic and special characters (A, B; #, ', and so on) in a binary machine requires the use of a coding system. In a coding system, a certain combination of binary digits is used to represent alphabetic and special characters. Similarly, decimal numbers are represented by combinations of 0s and 1s.

The decimal number system has a **base**, or **radix**, of 10 since it makes use of ten unique digits: 0, 1, 2, 3, 4, 5, 6, 7, 8, and 9. In writing a decimal value, the whole numbers go to the left of the **radix point** or **decimal point**. The fractional parts are written to the right. For example, with the number 2736.75 the 2736 is the whole number and 75 is a fraction. Each digit to the left or right of the radix point has a magnitude, called **place value** (sometimes referred to as **positional value**), which depends on how far to the left or right of the radix point the digit is. For example, in the value 7366, the right-hand 6 really means six ones, while the left-hand 6 represents six tens or 60. In the number 777, the right-hand 7 represents seven ones, the center 7 represents seven tens and the leftmost 7 stands for seven one hundreds. Thus, the value could be viewed as:

```
         hundreds
         │ tens
         │ │ ones
         │ │ │
         7 0 0
           7 0
       +     7
         ─────
         7 7 7
```

Notice the relationship between the place values of 100, 10, and 1. One hundred is equal to the base (10) times the place value to the right (10). The place value 10 is equal to the base (10) times the next value to the right (1). The place values could be described as powers of the base—for example:

	10^2	10^1	10^0
place values	100	10	1
a decimal number	7	7	7

where the base to the zero power (10^0) equals 1.

The value 6375 can be viewed as 6 thousands, 3 hundreds, 7 tens, and 5 ones.

	thousands	hundreds	tens	ones
				5
			7	0
		3	0	0
	6	0	0	0
	6	3	7	5

Another way of describing 6375 is:

place values in decimal number system	10^3	10^2	10^1	10^0
	1000	100	10	1
a decimal number	6	3	7	5

In the binary number system, just as in the decimal, there is a relationship between place values according to the base or radix. Since the radix of the binary number system is 2, each place value going from right to left is two times greater. For example:

place values	2^3	2^2	2^1	2^0
decimal equivalent of place value	8	4	2	1
a binary number	1	1	1	0

This grid shows the binary value 1110. It can be translated into its decimal equivalent by adding the individual place values:

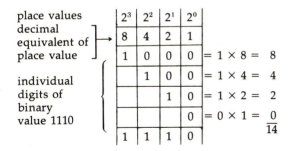

Conversion Methods

Almost every experienced programmer has faced a situation where the program causes the computer to yield erroneous results. After checking carefully to be certain that the input data are correct, that the program is logical, and the hardware is performing well, the programmer may find that what he or she thought was being performed by either the hardware or the software was not actually happening, but that something entirely different and illogical was taking place. This often happens when the programmer makes some false assumptions about how the hardware or software works. If the programmer knows how to translate binary to decimal or decimal to binary, however, he or she may be able to track down the problem.

Binary numbers are converted to decimal by this procedure:

binary number:

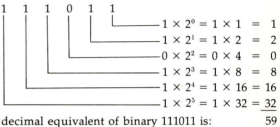

decimal equivalent of binary 111011 is: 59

You can convert a decimal number into its binary equivalent by this procedure:

divide

		remainders	place value
2 into	|59		
2	|29 (59 ÷ 2 = 29½)	1	1
2	|14 (29 ÷ 2 = 14½)	1	2
2	|7 (14 ÷ 2 = 7)	0	4
2	|3 (7 ÷ 2 = 3½)	1	8
2	|1 (3 ÷ 2 = 1½)	1	16
	0 (1 ÷ 2 = 0½)	1	32
	111011 ←		

Hexadecimal Number Systems

Large numeric values in binary notation contain many digits, and it is difficult for us to perceive their magnitude at a glance. Perhaps this is partially because we are so decimally oriented; but also, some of our difficulty comes from the large number of digits.

A shorthand form of binary notation is used by many computers manufactured since 1965. This

CHAPTER 11: MEMORY AND DATA

shorthand form of notation uses the **hexadecimal number system** (*hexa* meaning 6 and *decimal* meaning 10, or, 6 + 10 = 16), which has 16 unique digits or characters. The numbers 0 through 9 are the first 10 digits, while the characters A, B, C, D, E, and F were designated to be the symbols for the last six digits. In terms of decimal equivalents, the A = 10, B = 11, C = 12, D = 13, E = 14, and F = 15.

The advantage of a higher base system like the hexadecimal system is that the value of a many-digit binary number can be translated into hexadecimal by grouping the binary digits into groups of four. Hence, the binary number 100111101101011 becomes:

place values	8421	8421	8421	8421
binary number	100	1111	0110	1011
hexadecimal number	(4)	(8+4+2+1)	(4+2)	(8+2+1)
	4	F	6	B

Remember the decimal equivalent of B is 11 and the decimal equivalent of F is 15. Now let us look at the place value of hexadecimal numbers.

The place values of the hexadecimal number system follow the same pattern as the binary and decimal systems: moving from right to left, the base to the zero power (16^0), followed by the base to the first power (16^1), then the base to the second power (16^2), and so on. The hexadecimal place values, their decimal equivalents, and a sample hexadecimal number are:

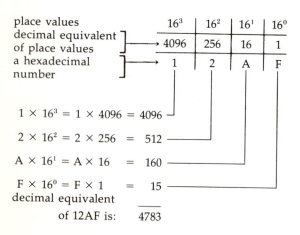

Key	
hexadecimal	decimal
A	= 10
B	= 11
C	= 12
D	= 13
E	= 14
F	= 15

The binary and hexadecimal number systems are related. This relationship exists because 16 (hexadecimal) is 2^4. A binary number can be translated easily to any number system with a base that is a power of 2 (such as 4, 8, 16, 32, 64). Unfortunately, since 10 is not equal to some power of 2, binary numbers cannot be broken directly into groups for determining decimal equivalents. However, many computers are designed to have each decimal digit represented by a 4-bit group.

COMPUTER DATA NOTATION SYSTEMS

A computer does not have to represent numbers in straight binary form in order to process them. In fact, because much of the computer's use is in processing business or financial data where digit-by-digit accuracy is essential, many computers maintain the integrity of each decimal digit by coding each decimal digit separately into binary notation. This type of notation is called **binary coded decimal (BCD)**.

In BCD notation, for instance, addition is performed decimal digit by decimal digit from right to left, just as you would perform addition in ordinary arithmetic. Carries that result when the sum of two decimal digits exceeds 9 are carried and added to the decimal digit immediately to the left.

4-Bit BCD Notation

Since decimal digits 0–9 may be represented in binary notation by using only four binary places,

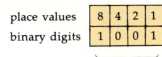

binary equivalent
of decimal value 9

binary coding of decimal numbers was originally limited to this 4-bit scheme. The decimal number 2,907 is represented by:

decimal number	2	9	0	7
4-bit BCD	0010	1001	0000	0111

In contrast, the pure binary equivalent of the decimal number 2,907 is:

place values	2048	1024	512	256	128	64	32	16	8	4	2	1
bits	1	0	1	1	0	1	0	1	1	0	1	1

Parity-Check Bit

To help detect and correct reading or writing errors within I/O devices or within the CPU, an extra bit position is set up besides those used to represent a decimal number or an alphabetic character. This extra bit is called a **parity bit.**

The computer's designers may decide that every decimal number, alphabetic character, and special symbol will be recorded with an even number of "one" or "on" bits and that any data that are received that do not have the even number of bits are invalid. But the value 4, for example, is recorded with just one bit.

place value	8	4	2	1	
binary digits	0	1	0	0	total number of "on" bits = 1

decimal value 4

Hence, an extra bit position is established to allow for recording of an additional one bit when the binary notation does not naturally contain an even number of bits.

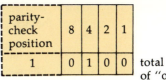

decimal value 4
with parity-check
bit set to 1

The decimal value 6 naturally has an even number of 1 bits, so the parity-check position is set to zero.

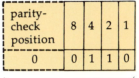

decimal value 6
with parity-check
bit set to 0

If an even-parity computer reads a character such as 4 or 6 or 3 and its parity-checking mechanism determines that an even number of bits including the parity-check bit does not exist, an "error" condition is signalled to the computer operator or to the operating system for corrective action.

If the computer operates on an odd-parity basis, the decimal value 4 would not need a parity-check bit of one since the bit pattern naturally contains an odd number of bits. In this case, all the 4-bit sets received would require an odd number of "on" bits.

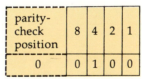

decimal value 4
with parity-check
bit set to 0

8-Bit Notation

Since the mid 1960s most computer memories have used eight adjacent bits to make a byte. In an 8-bit byte we can store at most one alphabetic character, one special character, or two decimal characters (in 4-bit BCD notation).

There are two commonly used 8-bit notations: EBCDIC and ASCII. IBM, among others, uses **EBCDIC** (*E*xtended *B*inary *C*oded *D*ecimal *I*nterchange *C*ode) in most of their computers that have been built since 1965.

The **ASCII-8** is another commonly used code. Its format is identical to IBM's EBCDIC. However, the bit patterns for the 256 possible individual characters are different. For a comparison of the bit code patterns of the many systems, see Figure 11–7.

Fixed-Word Notation

Word-oriented computer memories may be fixed-word or variable-word. Arithmetic calculations are simpler and faster to perform on fixed-word computers because all the digits of a number are the same length and all their digits are added at the same time in what is called **parallel arithmetic**. For example, all the binary digit positions for decimal numbers 183 and 12 are added simultaneously rather than digit by digit.

128	64	32	16	8	4	2	1	
1	0	1	1	0	1	1	1	= 183
+ 0	0	0	0	1	1	0	0	= 12
1	1	0	0	0	0	1	1	= 195

In contrast, in a variable-word computer, each number may be a different length and must be added digit by digit or serially, with what is called **serial arithmetic**. For example, the decimal numbers cited above (183 and 12) would be added as:

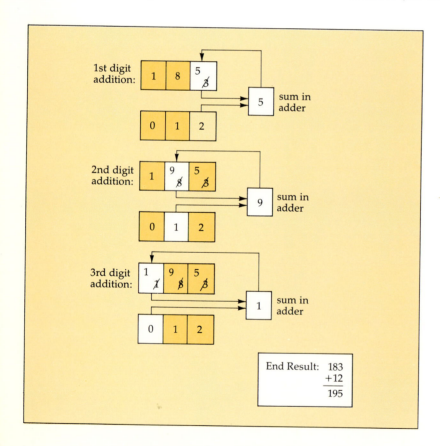

FIGURE 11–7 Standard notations for alphanumeric data exclusive of parity-check bits.

Characters	4-Bit BCD	EBCDIC	Hexadecimal Equivalent of EBCDIC	ASCII-8	Hexadecimal Equivalent of ASCII-8
(Place Values)	8421	84218421		84218421	
0	0000	11110000	F0	10110000	B0
1	0001	11110001	F1	10110001	B1
2	0010	11110010	F2	10110010	B2
3	0011	11110011	F3	10110011	B3
4	0100	11110100	F4	10110100	B4
5	0101	11110101	F5	10110101	B5
6	0110	11110110	F6	10110110	B6
7	0111	11110111	F7	10110111	B7
8	1000	11111000	F8	10111000	B8
9	1001	11111001	F9	10111001	B9
A		11000001	C1	11000001	C1
B		11000010	C2	11000010	C2
C		11000011	C3	11000011	C3
D		11000100	C4	11000100	C4
E		11000101	C5	11000101	C5
F		11000110	C6	11000110	C6
G		11000111	C7	11000111	C7
H		11001000	C8	11001000	C8
I		11001001	C9	11001001	C9
J		11010001	D1	11001010	CA
K		11010010	D2	11001011	CB
L		11010011	D3	11001100	CC
M		11010100	D4	11001101	CD
N		11010101	D5	11001110	CE
O		11010110	D6	11001111	CF
P		11010111	D7	11010000	D0
Q		11011000	D8	11010001	D1
R		11011001	D9	11010010	D2
S		11100010	E2	11010011	D3
T		11100011	E3	11010100	D4
U		11100100	E4	11010101	D5
V		11100101	E5	11010110	D6
W		11100110	E6	11010111	D7
X		11100111	E7	11011000	D8
Y		11101000	E8	11011001	D9
Z		11101001	E9	11011010	DA
+		01001110	4E	10101011	AB
−		01101101	6D	11011111	DF
,		01101011	6B	10101100	AC
.		01001011	4B	10101110	AE

Because it processes data more rapidly, fixed-word length with parallel arithmetic is common among scientific computers and minicomputers, while variable-word length computers are used for transaction and financial information processing.

CHARACTERISTICS OF MEMORY

The speed and efficiency of a computer can be no greater than the speed and efficiency of its primary memory. Early memory devices were neither fast nor reliable. Vacuum tubes similar to those used in older radios and television sets stored data in early computers. One vacuum tube was used to store one bit of data—thus, a single alphanumeric character required several vacuum tubes. IBM's first commercially available computer (IBM 701, 1953) used CRTs for primary memory. The average length of time between breakdowns, the MTBF, of the IBM 701 was about 30 minutes. Subsequent memory devices, used on the UNIVAC 1103 in 1953 and IBM's 704 in 1955, were much faster and more reliable, with an MTBF of about 40 hours for the 704.

Computer design, manufacturing technology, and economy of use have progressed by giant steps since those early computers. Computer memories are just as vital to computers today as they were in the 1950s. Memories still hold data (but in much greater volume), still store programs (but much larger ones), and still never seem quite large enough (but are measured in hundreds of thousands and millions of words or bytes, instead of thousands of words).

All primary computer memories have certain common characteristics. The major ones, in addition to size, are direct access ability, rapid access time, reliability, and reusability.

Direct access means that data stored at any memory address are directly and rapidly retrievable by citing the address; it is not necessary to examine other memory locations. This is especially important because with every loop through a program, data are retrieved from memory and stored in memory many times. Processing speed, another characteristic, therefore, depends greatly on rapid access to data. The time interval between the initiation and completion of the retrieval or storage process is known as **access time.** Access time for the IBM 704 memory (of the mid-1950s) was 12 microseconds (or 12/1,000,000 sec). Access times of 80 nanoseconds (80/1,000,000,000) are now available.

Memory must also be reliable, accurately storing data and yielding it when called for. Every time a character is stored in memory, it should be checked to see that all of the bits—and no extra ones—were stored. The parity-check bit we discussed earlier is used in this process. A memory also must be reusable. Over and over data are written into memory, then erased, and new data are written. Computer memory must be durable. And due to the electronic rather than electromechanical nature of primary memory, today's memory generally outlasts the other parts of the computer.

Also, data in a memory must remain stored until intentionally changed. Computer memories that retain data even if electrical power is lost are commonly referred to as having **nonvolatile storage.** Storage devices where data are rewritten (recharged) periodically and would not hold data through a power outage are dynamic or **volatile storage.**

"Sure it's depressing. This thing has a memory of 3 trillion bits, and I can't recall what I had for lunch."

262 MODULE THREE: HARDWARE

ATANASOFF AND BERRY'S SPECIAL-PURPOSE ELECTRONIC COMPUTER

Out of frustration over the tedium of using mechanical calculators to solve simultaneous equation systems, John V. Atanasoff began, during the 1930s, to develop a new calculator. Atanasoff, an associate professor of mathematics and physics at the Iowa State College, Ames, Iowa, examined various analog calculating devices that existed at the time. Gradually he turned away from analog devices because of their lack of accuracy and speed.

Atanasoff's idea for a digital computer came to him during a solitary drive to the Mississippi River hamlet of Moline, Illinois, one cold night during the winter of 1937–38. After arriving at an inn in Moline, Atanasoff rapidly sketched out the basics for a digital electronic circuit and a regenerative binary memory.

Having switched to a digital method, Atanasoff had to design logic circuitry, and he chose vacuum tubes. "Many people told me I was a fool to use vacuum tubes in a digital manner," says Atanasoff. But by December of 1939 Atanasoff and one of his graduate students, Clifford Berry,

had produced an operating model of a computing machine using vacuum tubes.

The computing machine was further developed, and by 1942 the ABC (for Atanasoff-Berry Computer) included two 1,500-bit drums for storing 50-bit words, 300 vacuum tubes, a spark printer and reader, and an electronic adder. The ABC's total cost was $5,000.

Although special-purpose by design, and thus not usable for general mathematical work, the ABC was unique and inventive in four respects: (1) Calculations were performed in serial fashion, (2) memory held data by continually regenerating its contents, (3) calculating logic was represented by circuitry, and (4) the machine operated digitally rather than analogwise, which was common in that day. In 1942, however, with the United States at war, Atanasoff left Iowa and the ABC's development to work at the Naval Ordinance Laboratory in Washington, D.C., and the ABC was not further developed.

MEMORY TYPES

Many new memory devices have been developed in laboratories over the past 40 years, but only a small portion have become commercially dominant. Capacitors (electronic devices for accumulating and holding a charge of electricity that consist of two conducting surfaces separated by a nonconductor) were used in the ABC, the first electronic digital computer, built in 1939. Cathode ray tubes (CRTs), magnetic drums, and vacuum tubes served as memory devices on the early commercially available computers. In a major breakthrough, first UNIVAC and then IBM introduced magnetic core memories in the 1950s; this type has dominated for the past 20 years. Today, however, semiconductor memories are the most commonly used memory device. In the following sections we examine semiconductor memories, as well as several that are still being developed, or are in only limited use.

Semiconductor Memories

A **semiconductor memory** is a primary storage device that uses circuits (that are turned on or off by

MAUCHLY AND ECKERT'S GENERAL-PURPOSE COMPUTER

During the 1930s a physicist named John Mauchly experimented and successfully built base-2 and base-5 counters while he was at Ursinus College near Philadelphia. Mauchly used these counters to build a digital device for encoding and decoding messages. Later, Mauchly was hired to teach at the Moore School of Engineering, University of Pennsylvania. In a letter dated 15 November 1940, Mauchly wrote a colleague: "In a week or two my academic work will not be quite so heavy, and I shall begin to give some thought to the construction of computing devices."

Mauchly gave more than thought, he began sketching his own ideas of how a general-purpose (as opposed to Atanasoff's special-purpose) electronic digital computer could be built. He circulated his ideas among the faculty and graduate students. A bright young graduate electronic engineering student named J. Presper Eckert, Jr., picked up on the idea, immersed himself in the meager literature available on counting circuits, and rapidly developed expertise in that field.

Meanwhile, Mauchly became acquainted with Herman H. Goldstine, the Army's representative at the Moore School. Goldstine and Mauchly had frequent conversations about computational matters during the fall of 1942. With the school director's blessing, Goldstine, Mauchly, and Eckert proposed the building of the first general-purpose electronic computer, the ENIAC (*Electronic Numerical Integrator And Computer*). This was a high-risk venture that would, if successful, push technology forward and be of great benefit to the war effort. The ENIAC was expected to be 45 times faster than the best operating computing device of that time, hence it would greatly speed up the computing of artillery-weapon aiming tables.

The proposed machine turned out to contain over 17,000 vacuum tubes of 16 different types and to operate at the rate of 100,000 pulses per second. Thus, in a single second, 1.7 billion tube operations took place—and 1.7 billion chances of failure. Eckert, in a memo to his team of engineers, estimated that the average vacuum tube life would be 2,500 hours. At that rate, one would fail every ten minutes or less.

Actually, during the first 1,000 hours of operation, the tube failure rate was only about one per day. The longest that ENIAC ran without failing was 120 hours. The venture was so risky and its accomplishment was so great because no one had ever before made an instrument capable of operating with this degree of reliability.

Work began on ENIAC May 31, 1943, and was completed on June 1, 1946. It operated until October 2, 1955, when it was disassembled and part of it sent to the Smithsonian Institute, Washington, D.C.

These events are an ancient part of computer history but a modern part of human history.

---

built-in solid-state switches) to represent bits of data. The semiconductor memory circuits are microminiaturized to the degree that up to 64,000 bits of data are stored in the circuits etched on separate layers of what will become a one-piece (monolithic) silicon square called a **chip** (see Figure 11–8). Because all parts of the circuits are within the chip, it is called "integrated," and because so many circuits are squeezed onto a chip, it is called a **large-scale integrated circuit (LSIC).**

The switchable on/off circuits store the two binary digits (0s and 1s). A circuit is set to an "on" or closed condition to represent 1, or to an "off" or open condition to represent 0. To read what has been stored, an electrical current is directed through the circuit. If the current flows, the switch has to be on, representing a 1; if the current does not flow, the switch has to be off, representing 0 (see Figure 11–9).

Semiconductor memories have the disadvantage of being a volatile memory device, meaning that if electrical power is lost, the stored data are lost also. However, their low cost and compact size outweigh their volatility in most uses.

a b

FIGURE 11–8 The making of semiconductor memory chips. (a) A complex of circuits goes into every memory chip. Here a draftsman begins by drawing a pattern about 500 times as large as the actual chip. Then separate drawings of each layer are photographically reduced. Hundreds of the resulting photo images are transferred to a circular silicon wafer. (b) A diamond-tipped stylus cuts finished chips from the wafer.

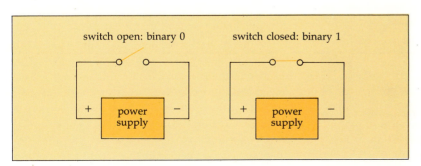

FIGURE 11–9 Semiconductor switchable on/off circuits.

CHAPTER 11: MEMORY AND DATA

The silicon chip is about ⅛ inch square and contains as many as 64,000 switches (see Figure 11–10). The chip can store 2K to 64K bits (K represents 1,000). Access times are measured in nanoseconds (billionths of a second). Access time for the chip is 80 to 200 nanoseconds (80 to 200 billionths of a second). Each chip is mounted on a frame, its contacts connected, and then it is encased in plastic. Each encased chip is about 1 inch by ¼ inch in size (Figure 11–11).

Charged-Coupled Devices

Another relatively slow but high storage capacity semiconductor device is being used for secondary data storage and may ultimately be used as primary memory in some computers. This is the **charged-coupled device (CCD)**. Currently, CCDs are being used as substitutes for magnetic disks and as re-

FIGURE 11–11 **Semiconductor memory chips.**

fresh memory for repeatedly displaying data on volatile display panels of terminal devices.

CCDs require fewer control circuits than do conventional semiconductor chips, hence ten times the number of data bits are squeezed onto the CCD. However, CCDs are only one-eighth as fast as conventional semiconductor chips because CCDs consist of groups of constantly circulating data. A group (or block) of data is directly accessed, but then the block must be read out serially. In spite of this slower access time, CCDs are 30 times faster than magnetic disk devices, and thus have a significant speed advantage over them. Cost per bit stored of CCDs is about 1/10 that of conventional semiconductor memory, but about five times that of magnetic disk storage.

Magnetic-Bubble Memories

In contrast to semiconductor memories, which consist of on/off circuits, **magnetic-bubble memories** have cylindrical areas (bubbles) on a chip of garnet crystal that are either magnetized to represent a binary one or not magnetized to represent zero. The bubbles (1/25,000 of an inch in diameter) can be moved about the chip and left at specified locations for later retrieval. Streams of these bubbles are directed down paths through gates and their values (0 or 1) "read out" as they pass a detector. (See the Computer News section at the end of this chapter

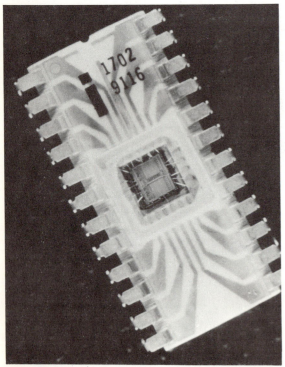

FIGURE 11–10 A semiconductor chip (top) and an encased chip (bottom) with case cut away for viewing.

for a detailed description of how bubble memories work.)

The discovery that magnetic bubbles could be moved about to represent data was made in 1966 by Andrew H. Bobeck and fellow workers at Bell Telephone Labs. Developing and refining the design and manufacturing the devices have been technically difficult and expensive. IBM alone has spent an estimated $100 million on its efforts. The potential rewards are sizeable, however. The advantages of bubble memory over semiconductor are: low power consumption; very high density (one million bits on a single chip; see Figure 11–12); and when power is turned off data are retained (nonvolatility). The disadvantages of bubbles as compared to semiconductors are that both access speed and data transfer speeds are much lower. For primary storage on high-speed computers, magnetic-bubble memory is too slow. However, on microcomputers and even minicomputers the high density may outweigh this slowness.

Bubble memories also have the potential of replacing some electromechanical magnetic disk secondary storage devices. The magnetic disk devices require high precision and fast moving parts that need careful use and regular maintenance, whereas bubble memories contain no mechanical moving parts. Magnetic-bubble memory, though more expensive per bit (1/10 cent) than magnetic disk (1/100 cent), is faster in access time (1/100 sec) than the disk (3/100 sec). Bubbles are also smaller in size and lower in weight than disks.

A bubble memory encased in a cassette has been introduced by Fujitsu, Japan's foremost computer maker. This bubble cassette is expected to compete with magnetic diskettes commonly used with personal computers.

Another storage consideration is volume. Magnetic-bubble memories may replace low-volume disk systems for microcomputers that need only limited storage. The first commercial application of the magnetic-bubble memory was in Texas Instrument's TI765 portable terminal, with its standard 20,000-byte capacity (expandable to 80,000 bytes), and a price range of $3,000 to $4,500. The bubble memory can replace magnetic flexible disk or magnetic tape cassette, while cutting down the total weight of the terminal and memory to 16 pounds.

Techniques under Development

With a faster access speed than CCDs and bubble memories, but a slower one than semiconductor chip memories, **electron beam accessed memory (EBAM)** is a variation of an old idea—storing data in a CRT. This technique uses the inner surface of a CRT-like tube to record spots (bits) as small as 1 micrometer (one-millionth of a meter or forty-millionths of an inch). At this rate a single tube can hold over 30 million bits of data. Research sponsored by both the federal government and industry is currently under way, and commercial uses may develop for EBAM.

Cryogenic memory, another new approach, makes use of the fact that supercold (−450 F) circuits become superconductive. This means resistance to current flow is eliminated and access can be instantaneous. The speed of cryogenic memory is 10 to 100 times that of today's semiconductor chips. Furthermore, since the supercold memory consumes less than 1/100 of the power of current memories, circuits can be packed more densely without creating problems arising from overheat-

FIGURE 11–12 The one million–bit magnetic-bubble memory chip.

ing. This density, in turn, cuts the distance between the memory elements and adds to the high speeds. Much research remains to be done, however, between current development and production readiness.

Photodigital memory uses an electron beam to record binary data permanently on small pieces of film. This approach, thus, is limited to use in archival memory, that is, storing and holding data indefinitely for future reference. The approach, however, is still too costly to compete with other memory devices. Another archival memory is **laser beam memory,** which records binary data by burning microscopic holes in a thin film of metal coated on a strip of polyester.

SUMMARY

Storage devices hold data, user programs, and the computer's operating system programs. Numeric or alphanumeric data, stored in memory, are actually represented as binary digits that, in turn, are represented by on/off switches. Groups of these binary digits form codes.

Memories are organized in a number of different ways. Scientific computers and minicomputers usually have fixed-word designs and perform fast parallel arithmetic. Business computers are usually variable-word (or a combination of fixed and variable) and perform slower, serial arithmetic.

Semiconductor memories are being used almost exclusively on new computers. Memories being developed offer the potential for great increases in volume and economy of storage.

TERMS

The following words or terms have been presented in this chapter.

Field
Input buffer
Working storage
Output buffer
User program
Operating system program
Address
Binary number system
Binary digit
Bit
Addressable memory locations
Fixed-word
Byte
Variable-word computers
Binary
Base
Radix
Radix point
Decimal point
Place value
Positional value
Hexadecimal number system
Binary coded decimal (BCD)
Parity bit
Parallel arithmetic
Serial arithmetic
EBCDIC
ASCII-8
Direct access
Access time
Nonvolatile storage
Volatile storage
Semiconductor memory
Chip
Large-scale integrated circuit (LSIC)
Charged-coupled device (CCD)
Magnetic-bubble memories
Electron beam accessed memory (EBAM)
Cryogenic memory
Photodigital memory
Laser beam memory

EXERCISES

The exercises that follow are grouped by level of difficulty. Problems in the A series are the easiest; B series problems are moderately hard; and C series problems are the most difficult.

A–1 Explain what primary memory is used for.

A–2 Describe the difference between alphabetic and alphanumeric data.

A–3 Describe what a binary number is. Why is the term *binary* used for the base-2 number system?

A–4 Explain the purpose of the parity-check bit.

A–5 What is the advantage of binary-coded hexadecimal notation over binary-coded decimal? Explain.

A–6 Which method of performing arithmetic within the computer is faster, parallel or serial? Why?

A–7 Explain what memory access time means. How important is memory access time in relation to the overall speed and efficiency of the computer?

A–8 What type of memory does the computer you use have? Is the coding system EBCDIC or ASCII-8?

B-1 What is the difference between a user program and an operating system program?

B-2 Give an analogy and graphic illustration to help describe the concept of an address.

B-3 List and describe, in order from smallest to largest units, the data that can be stored in a computer (that is, bits, bytes, and so on).

B-4 Explain why computers are designed around the binary number system rather than the decimal number system.

B-5 If the physical properties of electricity and magnetism were such that there were three natural conditions rather than two, what number systems would likely be common in computer design? Explain why.

C-1 Describe the difference between a word-oriented and a character-oriented computer. A graphic representation of your explanation should be included.

C-2 Which type of computer, a character (byte)-oriented or a word-oriented (32-bit fixed-word length) computer, would make more efficient use of memory space if the data were primarily large numeric, scientific values? Why?

C-3 Can you conceive of a number system that is either a modification of or radically different from the binary or decimal system described in this chapter? Describe how it would work. What would be its advantages and disadvantages?

C-4 Using current editions of periodicals, prepare a report giving the approximate proportions of various sizes of computers that utilize core, semiconductor, and other primary memory devices.

C-5 Using the periodicals mentioned in exercise C-4, prepare a tabular report giving the following data for each type of primary memory:
   a. access speed
   b. cost per bit
   c. current annual production volume in bits

COMPUTER NEWS

HOW MAGNETIC-BUBBLE MEMORIES WORK

Formation: Magnetic bubbles are tiny regions of magnetization in an ultrathin film, grown atop a nonmagnetic substrate. Bias magnets provide a stabilizing field (arrows, top) perpendicular to the film surface. As this field increases, snakelike magnetic regions shrink into bubbles. But a bubble generator, formed by a hair-pin-shape conductor atop the film, produces bubbles actually used. A current pulse in the loop produces magnetism opposing the bias field, allowing a bubble to form. **Propagation:** Bubble movement is achieved with various magnetic-alloy patterns—C's, T's, or chevron strips—atop the film layer. A rotating magnetic field, produced by current in two coils that sandwich the bubble chip, constantly alters the magnetic polarities of pattern elements. These changing polarities attract the bubbles just below, pulling them along. The propagation diagrams show a sequence of bubble movement as the magnetic field from the coils (arrows) rotates. **Replication:** A bubble can represent the binary one of computer language. The absence of a bubble indicates a binary zero. But before bubbles are "read out" or electronically detected, they are duplicated in the sequence above. Each bubble in a stream of data is stretched and split into two bubbles. One bubble stream goes back into storage so that the data won't be lost. The other stream is routed to the detector. **Detection:** Since bubbles are so tiny, they have little magnetic strength, and detecting their presence is impractical. But with long strips of chevron patterns, bubbles can be stretched to several hundred times their original diameter. As this bubble strip passes beneath the detector pattern (linked chevrons), an output pulse is generated. The detector has magnetoresistive properties: Its resistance to current drops as a stretched bubble moves beneath it.

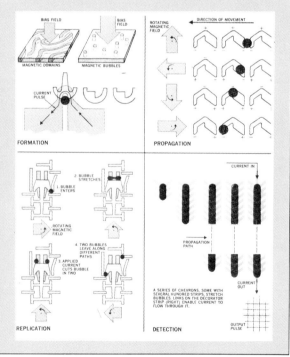

CHAPTER twelve

SECONDARY STORAGE/DATABASE MANAGEMENT SYSTEMS

Preview

Secondary Storage
    Magnetic Tape
    Magnetic Disk
    Drums and Cartridges

File Processing Methods
    Sequential
    Indexed Sequential
    Direct

History Capsule: Magnetic Tape and Disk

Database (DBMs)
    DBMS Techniques: Chains, Inverted Tables
    Types: Hierarchical, Network, Relational
    Comparing DBMSs

Summary

Computer News: IBM Drops the Other Shoe — and the Industry Relaxes

PREVIEW

In Chapter 11 you read about how a computer stores data in its memory. In the previous chapter the VISA accounts receivable system was analyzed and the amount of data that needs to be stored was calculated. If you have not read this material you should do so before going any further in this chapter.

Secondary storage devices allow a computer to store tremendous volumes (from millions to billions) of data, whereas internal storage holds smaller (a few million) amounts of data. Data stored on these devices must be accessed and processed using a program. In this chapter you will see the variety of ways these vast amounts of data are stored and processed. In a sense, all the previous chapters in this book have been leading to this chapter.

SECONDARY STORAGE

The primary storage or memory unit of the computer is capable of holding millions of characters or bytes of information. In our VISA problem, however, more data are collected than can be stored physically within memory. Also, there is a need to store the programs that process the data as well as the routines that aid in the running of the computer system itself.

Various types of secondary storage devices exist to hold this high volume of data. The two predominant external storage devices are magnetic **tape** and **disk** (sometimes spelled "disc"). Both devices are capable of holding anywhere from 100,000 to hundreds of millions of bytes of data. Other external storage devices include magnetic drum, cards, and cartridges, all with varying capacities.

Data that are stored on these units can be retrieved (accessed) by a computer program in a variety of ways. Some programs may need to process the data in some sequence, for instance alphabetically by last name. Another program may need to process only particular pieces of data, not disturbing the rest. Magnetic tape allows retrieval of data **sequentially** while disk allows retrieval sequentially or by the desired item of data directly.

These two differing retrieval requirements, sequential and direct, determine which kind of secondary storage device will be needed by a business. In our VISA system, statements are printed for each customer. Since each customer has a customer or account number, the statements could be printed in ascending order by customer number. Printing statements in this manner is ideally suited to tape devices. However, if statements are not printed in order by customer number but on some other basis—say, the state where the customer lives—a disk device may be a better choice for storing the data about each customer.

Magnetic Tape

Computer data on tape are stored sequentially; that is, records are stored one after the other (see Figure 12–1). The tape is wound onto a reel, which provides some protection for it. The amount of data that can be placed onto a reel of tape is related to the physical length of the tape and the number of characters of data that can be written per inch of tape—the tape's **density.** Tape comes in lengths from 600 to 3,600 feet, with the most common being

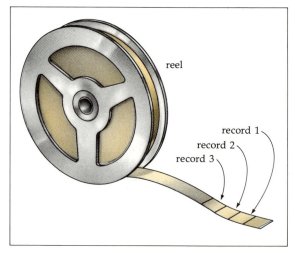

FIGURE 12–1 Sequential magnetic tape.

FIGURE 12−2   Tape handler or drive.

three full reels. In comparison, the same customer master file stored on 6,250 BPI density tape would take 21,280 inches (or 1,773 feet) of tape, not even a full reel. Since a 2,400-foot reel of tape costs less than $20, tape is a very inexpensive and compact medium of data storage.

To read the data stored on tape, a tape drive or handler is used (see Figure 12-2). The handler moves the tape across a device that can either read or write on the tape. On magnetic tape data are coded as tiny magnetic marks. The marks are coded across the tape in the various **tracks** to form a **frame** (see Figure 12-3).

The plastic base shown in Figure 12-3 gives strength to the tape, as well as providing a surface for the iron oxide coating that carries the coded data. The two primary codes for 9-track tape are ASCII and EBCDIC. Each of these codes uses a different spot pattern for data, but each allows the placement of either a single alphanumeric character (byte) or an 8-bit binary number in a frame. In addition to 9-track tape, older computers utilized magnetic tape that had only seven tracks.

2,400 feet. Densities also vary; they range from 200 to 6,250 characters per inch of tape. The most common density is 1,600 **bytes per inch (BPI).** Our VISA master file of one million records of 133 characters each would take 83,125 inches or 6,925 feet (133,000,0000 ÷ 1600 = 83,125) of tape, almost

To detect and prevent possible coding errors on the part of the handler, only eight of the nine tracks contain data. The ninth track, called the "parity track," has a mark placed on it to make the total number of marks in a frame odd or even. This **extra** mark is called the **parity mark** or parity bit. Some handlers use even parity, some odd parity, and

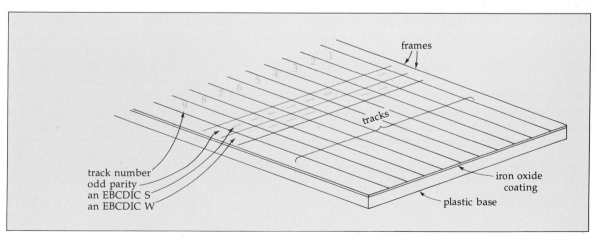

FIGURE 12−3   Magnetic tape characteristics.

CHAPTER 12: STORAGE/DATABASE SYSTEMS   273

some have a switch that will allow either parity. In addition to a parity check for each character, an extra parity mark may be placed at the end of each record. This parity mark is used to check each track. By combining the two parity checking schemes, the probability of detecting an error is maximized. When errors are encountered, some semiautomatic rereading is performed by the handler.

To protect the data coded on the tape, there is a 10- to 15-foot section of tape before the data begin. This **leader** gives the computer operator some tape to wind onto the take-up reel on the handler, and still leave the data portion on the reel untouched by human hands. A reflective strip on the tape marks the end of the leader and the beginning of the data portion (see Figure 12-4). The beginning-of-tape (BOT) **marker** (or "load point") denotes the first piece of data, while an end-of-tape (EOT) marker indicates to the tape drive that the last item of data has been processed.

The rate at which the computer can read or write data to and from the tape drive depends on density and tape speed. Drives can move tape at rates from 37.5 to 200 inches per second. Thus, a tape drive using tape with a density rating of 1,620 characters per inch and a speed of 100 inches per second is transferring data at 160,000 characters per second (1,600 × 100 = 160,000). Thus, for our 133,000,000-character VISA file, it will take 831.25 seconds to read the entire (133,000,000 ÷ 160,000 = 831.25) data file. This data **transfer rate** is an important factor in the selection of a tape drive for tape processing, since the higher this rate the less the cost will be per character processed.

Special tape labels are found at the beginning and end of each tape file. The first, the header label, provides the name of the file. The program process-ing a file checks the tape at the beginning of the program to verify that it is the correct one and to prevent other tapes from unauthorized or accidental use. The trailer label, at the end of the file, contains a tally of the number of records on the tape; this is tested by a program to make sure all records have been processed. If a file is too large to fit on a single reel of tape, a third type of label, the end-of-volume label, makes sure that the next tape processed is a continuation of the current tape.

Each time a read or a write is performed by the tape drive, a series of characters called a "block" is read or written. After the block has been read or written, the handler stops the magnetic tape. There is a blank space between blocks called the **interblock gap** (IBG), which is usually $^6/_{10}$ of an inch long. The handler needs this gap to accelerate the tape to read/write speed or to stop the tape after read/write has occurred. The VISA data file would appear on tape as shown in Figure 12–5. When the data and labels are blocked in this manner, the tape would have one million interblock gaps, each $^6/_{10}$ of an inch long, and one million records, each $^{133}/_{1600}$ of an inch long. When processing the file, the handler would have to start and stop one million times. Since a single start or stop may take over 0.005 second, the handler uses over 5,000 seconds of computer time starting and stopping the tape.

To speed the processing of a tape file, records may be grouped. If 20 records are grouped in blocks between IBGs, the file will appear as in Figure 12–6. If blocked as in Figure 12–6, only 50,000 interblock gaps will exist for the one million records; the handler will have to start and stop only 50,000 times, requiring 250 seconds. Blocking results in time savings, putting more data in less space on tape, and faster processing of the data by the computer. As a

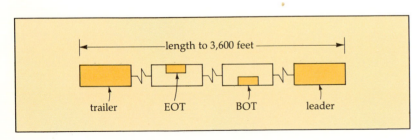

FIGURE 12–4 **Tape markers.**

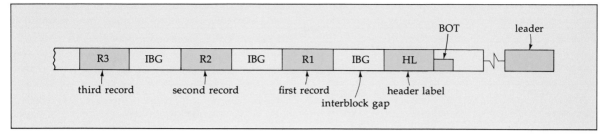

FIGURE 12–5 Single blocking.

result, most tape files are blocked and the number of records per block is referred to as the **blocking factor**. The blocking factor for Figure 12–6 is 20 records per block.

To protect a reel of tape from accidental destruction, a plastic ring is inserted on the back of the tape before any writing is done on that reel. This write-protect ring is a failsafe device that allows any reel of tape to be read at any time. However, tape can only be written when the ring is in place.

Regardless of blocking factor, transfer rate, density, or parity, all records on tape are stored sequentially—each record follows the previous one.

Magnetic Disk

To alleviate the major drawback of tapes—sequential data organization—most computing systems also have magnetic disks for secondary data storage. Disks resemble phonograph records in size and shape (Figure 12–7). Depending on the design, the disk pack may have from one to ten disks, sometimes called "platters." The disk drive spins the pack at speeds of 2,400 or 3,600 revolutions per minute. Each disk surface is coated with an iron oxide material similar to that on tape.

Data on disk are not written in a spiral pattern as are sounds on a phonograph record. Rather, the disk is divided into 200 or more circular paths, usually called **tracks,** each of which has the same center point (see Figure 12–8). Tracks are numbered from zero to 199, with track 0 usually being the outermost track and 199 the innermost.

Each track, in turn, is subdivided into a pie-shaped segment called a **sector.** Typically a disk will have 8, 10, 16, or 20 sectors to a track (depending on the manufacturer). Data are written on sectors of a track serially, as depicted in Figure 12–9. The amount of data that can be placed in a sector varies by manufacturer, but is usually about 500 bytes. The capacity of a disk can thus be calculated as follows:

(20 disks)(2 surfaces per disk)(200 tracks per surface)(20 sectors per track)(500 bytes per sector) = 80,000,000 bytes = 80MB (millions of bytes)

By varying the values of the factors, the actual capacity will change. A small disk pack might have only five million bytes (5 MB), while large ones may have over 800 MB per pack.

To place and retrieve the sector-stored data, a drive has a series of **read/write heads** on access arms

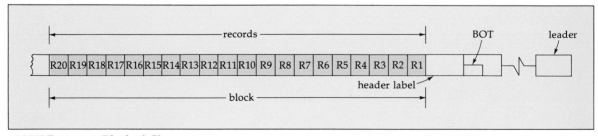

FIGURE 12–6 Blocked file.

FIGURE 12–7 Magnetic disks.

that are like the arm on a phonograph player. There is usually one read/write head for each disk surface. All the heads move together and are always over the same track of each disk surface (see Figure 12–10).

Some disk drives allow the packs to be removed. Thus, disk-stored data files can be made available to the computer only when necessary, and the disk drive can be used with another disk pack. Disk drives of this type are called **removable disks.** In contrast, some drives require that the disk pack be permanently attached; these are called **fixed disks.**

Programs that process data to and from a disk pack or data modules must tell the drive which disk track, which disk surface (read/write head), and then, which sector to read or write. The drive then moves the heads to that track (called "seeking"), activates the proper head, waits for that sector to spin past the head (called "latency"), and reads or writes the data as directed by the program. The total time it takes for these events to occur is called the "access time" of a disk. Typical access times range from 20 to 75 milliseconds ($1/1000$ sec).

Data from a disk can be retrieved without moving the read/write heads. This is done by placing the records in the same track on each of the disk surfaces. This means that the access time depends only on the time it takes the appropriate sector to

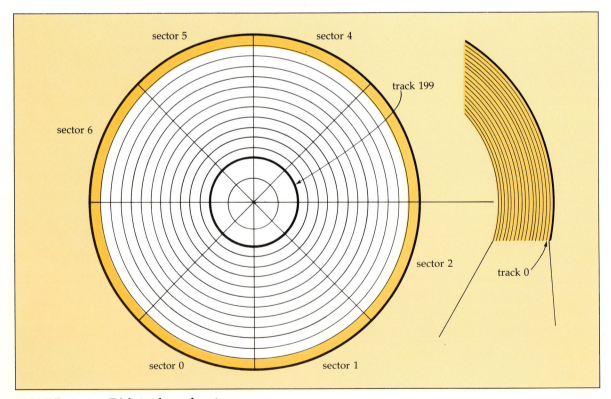

FIGURE 12–8 Disk tracks and sectors.

MODULE THREE: HARDWARE

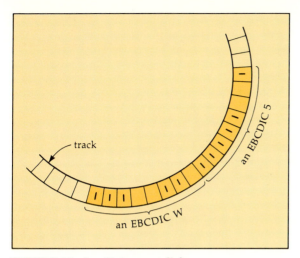

FIGURE 12–9   Data on a disk.

Another kind of disk, usually called a **floppy disk** or **diskette,** was introduced in the early 1970s to provide rapid input of software into the IBM 370 series of computers. Today we find diskettes still being used for software input to a computer (e.g., Hewlett Packard 3000/30). However, their use has now expanded to include also actual data storage on small business computers and home/hobby computers like the Apple II, and even storage of text material for word processing.

Physically, the diskette (Figure 12–12) is 7.8 inches in diameter, and is made of Mylar plastic packaged in an 8-inch square plasticized paper case called a "jacket," with openings for the drive hub, read/write head, and positioning sensors. Tracks are spaced 0.02083 inch apart for 48 tracks per inch. There are about 3,200 bits per inch along a track, and the disk revolves at 360 rpm with an access time of about 100 milliseconds. The storage capacity of a diskette ranges from 256,000 to 1,500,000 bytes.

There are IBM-compatible and non-IBM-compatible flexible disks. Most of the non-IBM-compatible flexible disks follow IBM's design for the disk, but merely organize the data in a different pattern.

In addition to the 8-inch diameter diskettes, there are 5¼-inch diameter "mini-floppys." This size disk has smaller data storage capacity, typi-

spin around to the read/write head. Data stored in track fashion are said to be stored in **cylinders** (Figure 12–11).

To speed the data from the disk to the computer (or vice versa), a few disk drives have many nonmoving read/write heads per surface or per track. With this capability, the access time for a disk is dramatically reduced. These **head-per-track disks** typically have access times of less than 10 milliseconds ($^{10}/_{1000}$ sec).

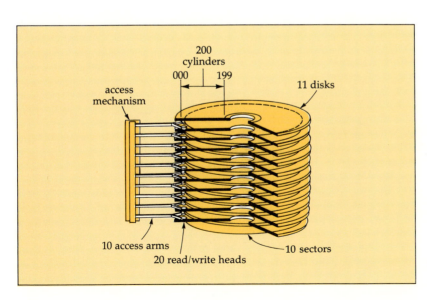

FIGURE 12–10   Disks and heads.

CHAPTER 12: STORAGE/DATABASE SYSTEMS

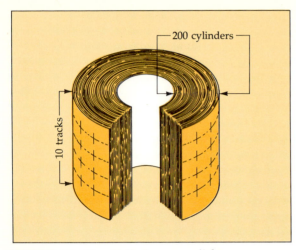

FIGURE 12–11   Cylinders on a disk.

cally 150,000 bytes, longer access times, usually one-quarter of a second, and operates on home/hobby computers.

Drums and Cartridges

Most computer installations have tape and/or disk as their secondary storage devices. Another magnetic device in use today is the **mass storage unit**. The actual number of these devices installed is small compared to the number of disks and tapes in use.

The mass storage unit is pictured in Figure 12–13. This unit offers even greater storage capacity than a disk. The total number of characters that can

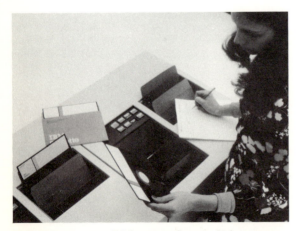

FIGURE 12–12   Diskette or floppy disk system.

FIGURE 12–13   Mass storage unit.

be held exceeds 400 billion bytes. Data are recorded on drumlike devices called "cartridges," which resemble cans 2¾ inches in diameter and 4 inches long. The cartridges are held in a honeycomb structure. To retrieve data, the proper cartridge is selected and the data it holds are transferred to a disk drive for actual processing. The time to locate a cartridge and transfer of data to the disk is 3 to 8 seconds.

FILE PROCESSING METHODS

There are four different ways we can process the VISA customer master and transaction files to gen-

MODULE THREE: HARDWARE

erate a statement. These are: sequential, indexed sequential, random, and database. Each uses different amounts of computer memory and secondary storage.

Sequential

To generate our VISA statement using the **sequential file** processing technique, all records in the customer master and transaction file must be sorted, by customer number, before the statement can be printed. Figure 12–14 shows you the order of events that must take place using sequential processing. During phase 1 the VISA receipts are read by an input device (an optical scanner) and written to a reel of tape. Also during phase 1, the various data items are validated to ensure their correctness (e.g., that dates are proper). During phase 2 a utility sort program takes the valid transaction records and reorders them by customer number and date. Dur-

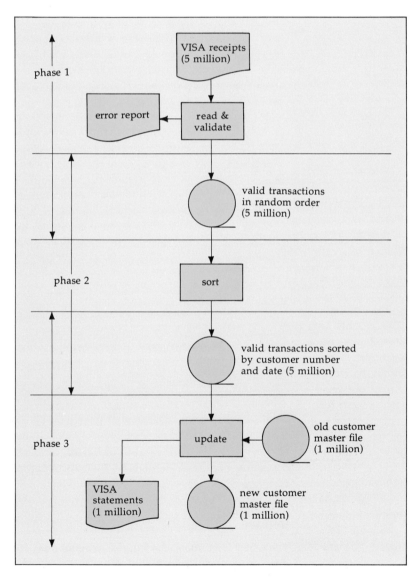

FIGURE 12–14 Sequential file processing.

"IT SAYS IT'S SICK OF DOING THINGS LIKE INVENTORIES AND PAYROLLS, AND IT WANTS TO MAKE SOME BREAKTHROUGHS IN ASTROPHYSICS."

ing phase 3 each transaction record is read and matched with a customer master record and the statement is printed. (See Chapter 5, 6, 7 for programs that validate, sort, and update files.)

Sequential file update programs are very complex. Records from old **master** and **transaction files** must be read and their customer numbers compared. If the customer numbers match, we can calculate the bill, add it to the old balance, print the bill, and write a record with these constant data and the new balance to the updated master file. However, some customers may make more than one purchase/payment a month; this requires our program to read more than one transaction record for each customer master record. Furthermore, there is a possibility that we do not have a customer master record for some transaction (an error was made in reading or recording the data).

The master file and the transaction file are usually saved after the update program has been run. This provides a **backup** in the event the updated master is lost, destroyed, or accidentally misused. For extra protection, two or more preceding master file and transaction files may be saved.

Next month the update program will be run again; the updated master file of the previous month becomes the old master file, the old master file becomes a backup, and the old master file of the month before that is usually reused by the update program or it can be made available to another tape file processing program. When a reel of tape is available for reuse, it is called a **scratch tape.**

Magnetic tape is an external storage medium that has backup and low cost, allows rapid input or output of data, compactness of data, and can be reused (unlike Hollerith punched cards). Tape does have some drawbacks, however: During the file updates, every master file record must be written on a "new" tape and the transaction file needs to be sorted prior to the update run. Master file updates can require up to three tape drives, which increases the overall cost of the computer system.

Sequential file processing requires that every record be read and processed. In phase 1 (Figure 12–14), five million records were read and five million were written to the tape file. In phase 2, the five million records were read, sorted, and written back to another tape file. In phase 3, the five million transaction records were read, as were the one million customer master records. Also, the program to update wrote a new customer master file of one million records and printed statements for one million customers.

	Phase 1	Phase 2	Phase 3
Records read:			
Transaction	5,000,000	5,000,000	5,000,000
Master (old)			1,000,000
Records written:			
Transaction	5,000,000	5,000,000	5,000,000
Master (new)			1,000,000
Total Records	10,000,000	10,000,000	12,000,000

The overall number of records processed to create the VISA bill using sequential file processing is therefore 32,000,000.

Indexed Sequential

There are four major drawbacks to sequential file processing. First, every record in the customer master must be read—it does not matter whether that customer had a charge or payment—the master record has to be processed. Second, data stored on a tape cannot be interrogated. That is, if we want to know what the current balance is of a particular customer, we must read the entire customer master file. We cannot read just the particular record we want. Third, the update program is logically complex. Fourth, we cannot post charges or payments to a customer as they occur; this drawback is somewhat related to the second. We must wait and batch the transactions together. This last drawback explains why a terminal on-line system cannot use sequential processing all of the time—such a system requires rapid access to a customer's record.

The **index sequential** method of processing data alleviates many of the problems associated with sequential file processing. Index sequential uses a directory (similar to a telephone directory) for holding the customer number and the location on the disk of that customer's data (Figure 12–15). To locate a specific customer's data, the update program searches the directory for a match; once it finds the customer's number in the directory, it randomly reads the disk at the location specified in the direc-

tory; updates the data read in; and writes the new data back on the disk in the same location where they were read. The directory is stored on disk as a file and is read into memory every time the update program is run (Figure 12–16).

For very large files whose directory would exceed available computer memory, a directory of directory is made (see Figure 12–17). The original directory then is stored on disk. To find the record we want,

FIGURE 12–15 Index sequential directory.	
Customer Number	Location on Disk (Sector Number)
1234561234	1
1472316821	2
1964321804	3
2034178140	4
2036134171	5
2036142641	6
3062780698	7
3066527074	8
4168780966	9
5047030698	10
5772330241	11
5947714687	12
6078854686	13
7024177201	14
9156525149	15

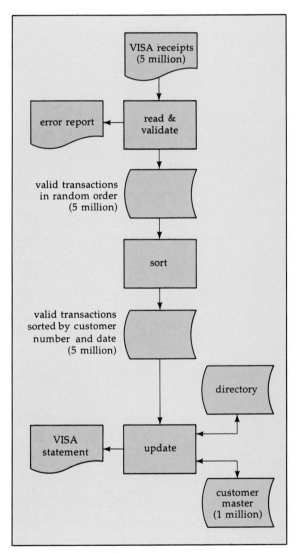

FIGURE 12–16 Indexed sequential file processing.

FIGURE 12–17 Directory of directory.

Directory of Customer Numbers	Customer Number	Location on Disk
1234561234	1234561234	1
	1472316821	2
	1964321804	3
	2034178140	4
2036134171	2036134171	5
	2036142641	6
	3062780698	7
	3066527074	8
4168780666	4168780966	9
	5047030698	10
	5772330241	11
	5947714687	12
6078854686	6078854686	13
	7024177201	14
	9156525149	15

the directory of the original directory is searched until we come close to the record desired. We then read from the disk a portion of the original directory, search it until we find a match, and then process the record in its normal manner. Files that have directories are sometimes called "ISAM" (Indexed Sequential Access Method) files or "KSAM" (Keyed Sequential Access Method). The number of records processed using the indexed sequential method to create our VISA statement is the same as that processed using the sequential method, 32 million.

Indexed sequential files provide both sequential and random modes of accessing the data. They do require a directory to find the desired record, but this mode of file processing is ideal for files that have no direct numeric keys but use names or addresses as the record identifier. In any event, the key must be unique—only one record can have that particular key.

Direct

Since data are stored in sectors and each sector has its own name or address, as in internal memory, a disk drive can read or write data in any sector, under program control, in any order. This capability causes disk drives to be referred to as direct access or random access devices. The programmer need only determine which sector is needed, access that sector, and process the data as usual.

Index sequential uses a directory to keep track of which sector a customer's data are found in. The directory must be built and changed frequently. The changes in the directory occur when new customers acquire their VISA card or when a customer decides to stop using the VISA card (or it is recalled by VISA). ISAM requires special programs to maintain the directory as well as process the data in the various files.

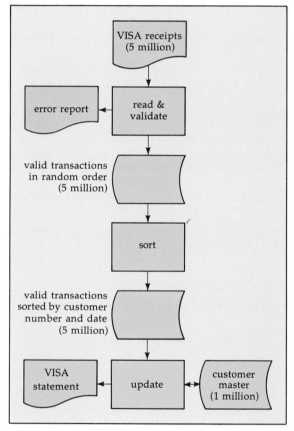

FIGURE 12–18 Direct file processing for VISA statements.

MAGNETIC TAPE AND DISK

Since the first commercial computer was installed in the early 1950s, there have been continuous attempts to find high-speed, low-cost secondary storage devices. Many devices were developed in the laboratory, but never worked successfully in the real world. Of all these devices, tape and disk were the most successful and are the most widely used.

Magnetic tape was invented by the Germans for audio use during World War II. Early versions, made on a steel base, were wound into reels 2 feet in diameter that weighed 200 pounds. Magnetic tape first appeared in the United States for computer use in the 1940s,[1] and used an aluminum base. Since the 1950s, plastic has become the dominant base material. The cost of tape has dropped in this same time period from $6 per million bytes to 10¢ per million bytes. At the same time, densities have gone from 100 to 6,250 bytes per inch.

Magnetic disk has undergone dramatic changes as well. The first disks appeared in the early 1960s and could hold 6 million bytes of data. The IBM 305 RAMAC, an early disk device, was about the size of a grand piano and looked like a stack of records on Goliath's changer.[2]

Today's disks can hold up to 800 million bytes of data in 1 to 3 cubic feet of space. To achieve these capacities, designers have had to place the tracks closer together and put more data onto each track.

Early disks had 50 tracks per inch, while today's models have more than 350. To read or write the data onto a track, the read/write heads are now only 35 microinches (35/10,000 of an inch) away from the disk, compared to the 1,000 microinches with early disks. This distance is approximately one-tenth the height of a fingerprint. Also, the amount of data per inch of track length has increased from 1,020 to 4,040.[3]

Computer people are still looking for faster and cheaper secondary storage media. Today's disks and tapes will carry us well into the 1980s. Then, perhaps a totally new approach will bubble up and shrink data storage again.

---

[1] Dan M. Gowers, "The Rough Road to Today's Technology," *Datamation*, September 1977, pp. 69–74.

[2] Donald Mattson, "Understanding Media," *Computer Decisions*, March 1976, pp. 44–46.

[3] Donald Mattson, "Understanding Media," *Computer Decisions*, March 1976, pp. 44–46.

Another technique to process data stored in disk files is the **direct method.** This method uses the record key, the customer number, to find the desired sector. We take a customer number—6078854686, for example—and divide it by the number of records in the file, 1 million, giving a quotient of 6078 and a remainder of 854686. So we can say that customer 6078854686 is in sector 854686. The problem with this method is that another customer number—for instance, 7072854686—will also give sector 854686 as its location. To overcome this problem, we could divide the customer number by 1,100,000. The remainder will be between 0 and 1099999, which will give us some empty record locations to use for those customer numbers that do coincide. When the calculated sector is a location that is already occupied, we sequentially search the next sectors until we find an empty sector.

The division and remainder method for locating a record's position on a disk is called a **hashing algorithm.** Many other hashing algorithms exist, some of which allow alphabetic record keys to calculate the record's location directly.

The printing of our VISA statements using the direct file processing technique is very similar to sequential and ISAM (see Figure 12–18). We still have to sort the transaction file and process 32 million records. The program is responsible for locating records in the customer master and for adding new customers and dropping existing ones.

DATABASE (DBMS)

In designing the VISA customer master file shown in Figure 11–1 it was necessary to determine every field in the file, the number of characters in each field, and the order of the records—a time-consuming job. In many instances, though, once a file has been designed and created there arises a need to add new fields of data to the file. For example, it may be desirable to have the date that our customer paid last month's bill. With this additional field, it would be possible to calculate any penalty or finance charges for late payments.

The traditional solution to the new field problem is to allow some extra space in each record for these fields to be added. This solution, however, is costly since extra tape or disk will be required for each record, it will not be used until some future date, and the computer will be made to read and write this field which has nothing in it. Another possible solution is to make another file with data extracted from the original file, plus data for the new field. This solution, however, creates a new file and wasted, duplicated data. If a change is made to a field of data in both files, a program must change both files, or if the original version of the file is no longer needed, a new program is still needed for accessing the new version of the file.

The ideal solution to both new fields and many access orders to a file is called **database management system (DBMS).** In DBMS, files are designed to allow many programs to share fields or to allow many different types of accesses: by customer number, by customer name, and so on. When a change is made in a field, that change is made only once, since a field only exists in one location. File systems that require the multiple access capabilities of DBMS are disk-oriented, since records must be randomly retrievable.

DBMS Techniques: Chains, Inverted Tables

A fundamental concept of database files is the **chain.** The chaining concept makes use of a **pointer,** which is a number showing the location of the next logical record in the sequence (it may not be the next physical record). As an example, let us assume that the customer number master file is built randomly, using the last six digits of the customer number (as in Figure 12–19). If we want to print a list by customer number, a pointer will be built that "points" to the next logical record in customer number or order (see Figure 12–19). The logical record retrieval sequence 561234(beginning), 316821, 321804, 178140, 134171, 142641, 780698, 030698, 330241, 714687, 854686, 177201, 525149, 00000(end), and the customer numbers retrieved would be 1234561234, 1472316821, 1964321804, 203478140, 2036134171, and so on, which is in ascending order by customer number.

Another program might require processing by customer name. A second chain would point through the file by customer name. When the records in Figure 12–19 are processed by customer name, the retrieval is 780966, 316821, 714687, 525149, 178140, 561234, 330241, 321804, 527074, 177201, 030698, 854686, 780698, 134171, 142641, 000000(end) and the records retrieved would be: Bissel, Mike; Broadwell, Lyman; Brophy, Pat; Burns, Cliff; Edwards, Jennifer, and so on— alphabetic by customer name.

Files in which pointers are used to connect the next logical record are called **chained** or **list files** (or sometimes called "hierarchical"). Some complex chained files allow backward as well as forward leading pointers; this allows the file to be accessed in either of two directions.

In many instances, it is necessary to be able to

FIGURE 12-19 Chains in a file.

Sector Number	Customer Number	Customer Number Chain	Customer Name	Customer Name Chain
030698	5047030698	330241	Ruhkala, Ruth	854686
134171	2036134171	142641	Stensaas, Kristen	142641
142641	2036142641	780698	Williams, Matthew	000000(E)
177201	7024177201	525149	Reid, Diane	030698
178140	2034178140	134171	Edwards, Jennifer	561234
316821	1472316821	321804	Broadwell, Lyman	714687
321804	1964321804	178140	Pisciotta, Frank	527074
330241	5772330241	714687	McCallum, Walter	321804
525149	9156525149	000000(E)	Burns, Cliff	178140
527074	3066527074	780966	Price, Susan	177201
561234	1234561234	316821(B)	Kleger, Samantha	330241
714687	5947714687	854686	Brophy, Pat	525149
780698	3062780698	527074	Skewis, Don	134171
780966	4168780966	030698	Bissel, Mike	316821(B)
854686	6078854686	177201	Sandven, Eddie	780698

retrieve all the records that have a given characteristic. Normally, each record would have to be accessed and tested for this characteristic. With the **inverted** (as opposed to chain) **file,** however, this is not the case. In this file, the records are stored randomly—in our case by the last six digits of the customer number. A directory is built giving the location of all the records with the same first three digits in their customer number (see Figure 12–20). To find all code 203 customers, for example, the directory is searched until the 203 match is made. The directory then gives the record locations: 178140, 134171, 142641.

Chains and inverted tables are not part of the update or validate programs. Instead they are kept and maintained by an extra "program" called the database management system (DBMS). A DBMS has the ability to maintain the customer master records in order by customer number and to keep the transaction records in order by transaction date (Figure 12–21). The arrows in this figure represent chains. Once customer number 2036142641 (at sector number 142641) is selected, a second chain through the transaction file is begun. If you follow this chain you can see that it retrieves records in order by date sold. Finally the end of the chain in the transaction file for customer 2036142641 is encountered. At this point we follow the chain in the customer master file to customer 5047030698. This customer also has a chain through the transaction file that gives the transactions in date-sold order.

FIGURE 12-20 Directory for inverted table.

Characteristic	Logical Record Number
123	561234
147	316821
196	321804
203	178140, 134171, 142641
306	780698, 527074
416	780966
504	030698
577	330241
594	714687
607	854686
702	177201
915	525149

FIGURE 12-21 A chained DBMS system.

Customer Master			Transaction File		
Sector Number	Customer Number	Customer Name	Customer Number	Date Sold	Amount
030698	5047030698	Ruhkala, Ruth	2036142641	020381	3.17
			7024177201	020481	44.02
			3062780698	020681	66.05
			6078854686	021481	74.95
134171	2036134171	Stensaas, Kristen	4168780966	022281	11.66
			2036142641	021681	105.92
			1964321804	020781	37.15
			2036142641	020981	88.12
142641	2036142641	Williams, Matthew	3066537074	021681	77.17
			7024177201	022081	50.05
			1472316821	020281	46.74
			6078854686	022281	92.22
177201	7024177201	Reid, Diane	5772330241	021781	41.18

Chains are a very important concept and give a database management system a lot of power in retrieving data in a logical manner. Not all database systems use chains, however. Inverted tables provide similar logical record relationships and powers.

Types: Hierarchical, Network, Relational

DBMSs are classified as belonging to one of three types: hierarchical, network, or relational. These classifications are really means of stating relationships between the records. In our VISA system we had a master record that held the customer's account number, address, balance fields, and so on; and we had the transaction records that had the customer account number, date sold, date posted, type of sale, and so on. (See Figures 11-1 and 11-2.)

In a **hierarchical** record relationship, sometimes called a **tree**, there are master or parent records and there are slave or children records. Each child (transaction) record belongs to (is owned by) one and only one parent record (Figure 12-22a). This diagram depicts a tree structure to two levels, but there could be additional levels in the hierarchical structure.

The second type of relationship is called **network**. In this structure each slave record can belong to more than one master record. Our VISA system does not lend itself to this structure unless we also want to keep track of what person sold each transaction. In this case, the transaction file would also have to keep track of the salesperson, and we would need another "file" to hold the data about each salesperson (name, sales number, gross sales, etc.). (See Figure 12-22b.)

The third type of DBMS is the **relational**. In this DBMS classification, records are not masters or slaves. Relationships are established between all of the "files" (Figure 12-22c). The data relationships that can be developed include: which customers bought from which salesperson; which salesperson sold to which customer; which salesperson sold which transaction; which customer bought which transaction, and so on. Of the three DBMS classifications the most complex is relational; the least complex is hierarchical.

Comparing DBMSs

The primary advantages of a database system are:

1. Reduces the programming effort for file updating
2. Encourages the use of standardized data naming
3. Provides data security and recoverability

4. Reduces operator intervention and associated production errors
5. Promotes use/support of data communication
6. Increases the accessibility and integrity of data
7. Provides multiple access paths and retrieval sequences
8. Reduces data redundancy, that is, duplication of data
9. Reduces the amount of time spent maintaining programs

When a database system is viewed in relationship to our VISA statement printing problem we would visualize the system as shown in Figure 11–23 In this diagram the read-validate program reads the VISA receipt, validates it, and passes the data to the DBMS. The DBMS then puts the data onto a disk file and alters all of the various chains or tables. When the update program is run it requests the data from the DBMS in the logical order desired. The DBMS retrieves the data and passes it to the update program. The update program prints the statement.

The program and the programmer in a database environment is not concerned with where the data are physically stored. Instead concern is focused on the logical relationship of printing the data. From a

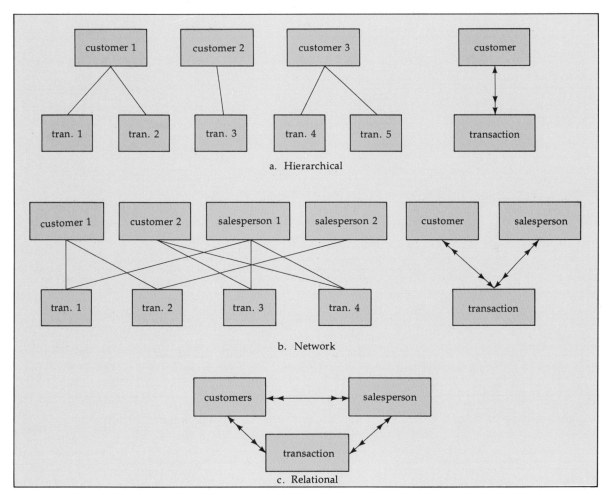

FIGURE 12–22 Types of DMBSs.

CHAPTER 12: STORAGE/DATABASE SYSTEMS 287

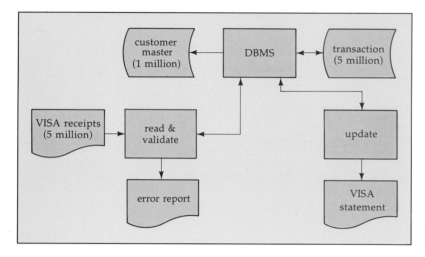

FIGURE 12–23 Database system for VISA statements.

logical perspective the programmer, when writing the programs for Figure 12–23, will process 16 million records (10 million in read/validate and 6 million in update).

In contrast, the sequential, indexed sequential, and direct file processing techniques had 32 million records processed. From the programmer's perspective, the computer processed half the number of records using the DBMS technique—apparently a substantial saving.

There are many DBMSs available. A chart comparing some of the more popular ones is shown in Figure 12–24. As the cost of programmers continues to rise and the cost of hardware falls, experts forecast that DBMS use is bound to increase in the future.

FIGURE 12–24 DBMS Comparison Chart.

Name	Supplier	Structures	Hardware	Price
IMS	IBM	Hierarchical	IBM	$1,145/mo
TOTAL	Cincom	Network	IBM, CDC, NCR, Prime	$1,350/mo $5,000/mo
DMS-II	Burroughs	Network and Hierarchical	Burroughs	$13,925 to $30,569
IMAGE	Hewlett Packard	Network	HP	$5,000
ADABASE	Software AG	Network	IBM, UNIVAC, DEC	$99,000 to $162,000
IDMS	Cullinane	Network and Hierarchical	IBM, UNIVAC DEC	$55,000
IDM-500	Britton-Lee	Relational	Any	$50,000

288   MODULE THREE: HARDWARE

SUMMARY

A file is a collection of records and is the fundamental unit in the processing of data. For processing purposes, a file may physically reside on a magnetic tape, disk, or other medium. The medium itself determines the kind of processing that can be done.

If a file is stored on tape, each record must be processed in sequence; this is called "sequential file processing." If a file resides on disk, only the records that have to be processed are processed, and the others are left alone. This type of processing is called "direct file processing." A database management system is a program(s) that manages the data while freeing the programmer from concern about the physical aspects of the file. The management aspect of data files is becoming more and more important and prevalent.

TERMS

The following words or terms have been presented in this chapter.

Tape	Head-per-track disks
Disk	Floppy disk
Density	Diskette
Sequentially	Mass storage unit
Density	Sequential file
Bytes per inch (BPI)	Master file
Tracks	Transaction file
Frame	Backup
Parity mark	Scratch tape
Leader	Index sequential
Marker	Direct method
Transfer rate	Hashing algorithm
Interblock gap	Database management systems (DBMS)
Blocking factor	
Tracks	Chain
Sectors	Pointer
Read/write heads	Chained file
Removable disks	List file
Fixed disks	Inverted file
Cylinder	Hierarchical
Tree	Relational
Network	

EXERCISE

The exercises that follow are grouped by level of difficulty. Problems in the A series are the easiest; B series problems are moderately hard; and C series problems are the most difficult.

A-1 What kinds of secondary storage devices does your computer system have?

A-2 Go to the computer center and gather the following statistics about the tape and disk drives being used:
  a. make and model number of tape handler
  b. tape speed
  c. transfer rate
  d. tape density
  e. even or odd parity
  f. data code in use: ASCII, EBCDIC, BCD
  g. make and model number of disk drive
  h. disk access time
  i. number of tracks
  j. number of disks per pack
  k. capacity of each pack

A-3 If your computer center has a data file stored on tape, find the name of the file, the number of records per block, and the length of each record, and sketch the file as shown in Figure 12-6.

A-4 Using Figures 12-14 and 12-16 for reference, determine how many tape handlers and disk drives are required for file updating.

A-5 Complete the following chart by answering yes or no for each provision.

Provision	Processing Method	
	Sequential	Random
Sequential processing		
Random processing		
Database		

B-1 Go to your computer center and find a write-protect ring. How big is it? How does it fit into the tape reel?

B–2 If a master file has 5,000 records and a transaction file has 250 records, how many records are read and written by a tape master file update program? How many records are read and written if the master file update is indexed sequentially? How many records if the file update uses the direct method of record access?

C–1 Redraw the chart of Figure 12–19 to have a forward pointer and a backward pointer by first name.

C–2 Magnetic disk files can be blocked as can tape files. If a disk file has three records in each sector, what does the directory contain?

C–3 The IBM 305 RAMAC has only one read/write head for all 50 or so of its disks. Do you suppose it has a fast access time? Describe.

C–4 From a periodical such as *Computerworld, Datamation,* or *Infosystems,* find the names of 2 other database management systems and add them to the chart of Figure 12–23.

COMPUTER NEWS

IBM DROPS THE OTHER SHOE—AND THE INDUSTRY RELAXES

With a dominant share of the worldwide computer market, International Business Machines Corp. sets both pricing and product standards for the entire industry. After keeping its competitors on tenterhooks for the past three years, IBM announced on Nov. 11, 1980 its new top-of-the-line computer—nicknamed the H series. But it turned out not to be a product that would force competitors to make wholesale changes in their market strategies.

In fact, the new 3081 processor will have nowhere near the impact of IBM's previous mainframe computer roll-out. Two years ago, IBM set the industry on its ear with its 4300 series at prices so low that competitors were hard put to match the price performance standards that the new computers set. The IBM 3081 "is like having a second baby in the family," says Stephen T. McClellan, a vice-president of Salomon Bros. in New York. "It's a major event, but nothing like the excitement of the first one."

Part of the reason for the lack of excitement was the more conservative pricing structure that IBM has indicated it will use for the new computer line. Unlike the 4300 series, which established a lower price umbrella for the computer industry, the 3081 will break no new ground. The reason is quite simple: While prices for the 4300 series devastated the makers of plug-compatible computers—copycat machines that run on IBM software and sell for less than comparable IBM models—they also had a boomerang effect and hurt IBM's earnings as well.

USER FEARS

When the 4300 series was announced, users of IBM's then top-of-the-line 303X series of mainframe computers anticipated that the company's impending H series would continue the aggressive pricing strategy of the 4300 machines. Expecting an H series announcement as early as a year ago, users began to lease rather than to purchase the 303X machines, because they feared that these computers would decline sharply in value as soon as the H series was rolled out. This sudden shift to leasing cost IBM purchase revenues and forced the company to finance a larger lease and rental base than it had planned for. As a result, IBM's earnings last year were down 3%—the first decline in more than 25 years.

This time around, IBM apprently is not taking any chances. Most experts say that the 3081—which offers twice as much power for the same price as the 3033, IBM's largest machine until now—is priced on the same curve as the 4300 line for the amount of processing power that it provides. If anything, say analysts, the

Business Week, December 1, 1980.

3081 is more expensive. "IBM made a mistake on the 4300 pricing, and now it's coming back into the fold," says George Elling, an analyst at Bear, Stearns & Co.

At the same time that IBM brought out the 3081, it slashed prices by up to 22% on its 303X series computers and dropped maintenance charges for them by 5% to 15%. The net effect of these moves will be to stimulate purchases of the 303X models. The first deliveries of the 3081 will not begin until late in 1981, so "users will be encouraged to go ahead and take delivery of the 303X," says Salomon's McClellan.

IMPACT ON PROFITS

The decision to go with a more conservative pricing strategy should have a positive effect on IBM earnings over the next three years. Indeed, McClellan already has raised his earnings estimates this year for IBM from $5.90 a share to $6 a share. This would mean an earnings gain of 16% over 1979. Strong sales of the 303X series should boost earnings by 18% in 1981, McClellan predicts. In 1982, when volume deliveries of the 3081 begin, earnings should increase by 25%, he estimates. And, if IBM comes out with additional models in the H series, as the industry expects, the growth in IBM's profits should continue at least through 1983.

Unlike the past, though, IBM's latest computer should do little to affect its competitors. For one thing, their anticipation of the announcement was clearly worse than the reality. "We expected their pricing to be a bit more aggressive," says Stephen G. Jerritts, head of the Information Systems Group at Honeywell Inc. As a result, he says, Honeywell will not reconsider its current pricing structure or plans for new product introductions. Similarly, H. Glen Haney, a vice-president at Sperry Corp.'s Univac Div., says that "we were ready for this."

IBM's plug-compatible competition—traditionally the most vulnerable to any new products from the computer giant—should fare equally well. In fact, Amdahl Corp. already has responded to the 3081. On Nov. 18 it introduced its 580 family of computers, which, the company claims, offers customers performance superior to that of the 3081 at comparable prices. And at Hitachi Ltd., Katsumi Fujiki, a director, says that his company "is fully capable of meeting the 3081 challenge."

CLEARING THE AIR

Several of IBM's plug-compatible competitors expect that the 3081 will stimulate their sales. For one thing, they believe that the long lead times on 3081 deliveries should encourage customers to look more closely at the plug-compatible alternatives. "Up to this point, customers have been hesitant," says David Martin, executive vice-president at National Semiconductor Corp.'s Advanced Systems subsidiary. "Announcements by IBM clear the air for customers to make decisions," he explains. Says Ulric Weil, a vice-president at Morgan Stanley & Co.: "Now everyone knows what the high end will look like for the next five years." And based on the first model in the H series line, the outlook seems favorable both for IBM and its competition.

CHAPTER *thirteen*

MICROS, MINIS, AND MAINFRAMES

Preview

**Microprocessors,
Microcomputers, and Microcomputer Systems**

- Microcomputer Functional Parts
- Microprocessor Functional Parts
- Bits Per Word
- Configurations
- Memory Capacity
- Processor Speed
- Software
- Space, Power, and Air Conditioning
- Costs
- Users and Uses
- Sources of Hardware and Software

History Capsule: Ted Hoff and the Microprocessor

Minicomputers and Minicomputer Systems

- Minicomputer Functional Parts
- Bits Per Word
- Configurations
- Memory Capacity
- Processor Speed
- Software
- Space, Power, and Air Conditioning
- Costs
- Users and Uses
- Sources of Hardware and Software

Mainframe Computers—Large, Medium, and Small

- Mainframe Computer Functional Parts
- Differentiating Features of Mainframes
- Mainframe Configurations
- Software
- Space, Power, and Air Conditioning
- Costs
- Users and Uses
- Sources of Hardware and Software

Summary

Computer News:

Computers—A Mainframe on Three Chips

PREVIEW

Would you like to buy a powerful computer for just $25? Does that sound ridiculous? At the moment, powerful computers cost much more—$100,000 to several millions of dollars. However, costs of manufacturing, and hence retail prices, have been steadily dropping since the first commercial computer was sold, about 30 years ago. More astoundingly, as the prices have dropped, the power of the computer has risen dramatically. For example, IBM's early computers, the 701s, manufactured between 1953 and 1956 and costing about $1 million, had less power than a single-board microcomputer that you can hold in your hand. The first general purpose computer, ENIAC, which was developed in the early 1940s, had the same computing power that is now etched into a silicon chip that can lay inside the capital letter O. This chapter examines the major types of computers that have resulted from such dramatic advances in electronics technology.

In Chapter 9 you learned how a program is called in statement by statement from memory, is decoded, and is executed by the processor. The processor is a major functional part of the computer. The decrease in physical size of the processor and memory portions of the computer account for much of this advancement in computing power per dollar cost.

Computers and their processors (arithmetic/logic and control units) are broken into three major categories: microcomputers, minicomputers, and mainframe computers. The differences among micro, mini, and mainframe computers are reflected in their processors and in their input and output devices. Other considerations in computer systems, such as programming, types of users, and sources of the hardware and software, are also discussed in this chapter.

You will also learn how blurred the boundaries are among the three categories—micro, mini, and mainframe. These boundaries are continuously moving; for example, a memory size that is typical of a mini now, may be more typical of a micro within a few years. Also, the speed of a mainframe of a few years ago equals the speed of today's minis. And the variety of instructions available on mainframes and minis will shortly be available on micros.

MICROPROCESSORS, MICROCOMPUTERS, AND MICROCOMPUTER SYSTEMS

In the mid-1960s dozens of electronic devices, called "transistors," and their connecting circuits were etched into a single piece (chip) of silicon; the result was called an **integrated circuit**. As hundreds of additional transistors were etched into the chip, the process became known as **large-scale integration (LSI)**. The most common sized memory chip now in production is the 16K. The largest capacity of chips presently being manufactured is 65,536 bits (called 64K[1]) (Figure 13–1). Producers of these chips find it uneconomical to redesign and retool for a new line of chips unless the density jump is by a factor of four—16K to 64K, for example. Following this logic, the next generation of chips will contain 256K transistors. However, in a Japanese government-sponsored joint effort, computer manufacturers in that country are working on a 1048K chip, which will be called **very large scale integration (VLSI)**.

Microcomputer Functional Parts

LSI chips are designed and built to function as memory, arithmetic, logic, or control units, or some combination of these. Commonly, the arithmetic, logic, and control functions are all placed on a single chip that is called a **microprocessor**. Before we examine the microprocessor in detail, however, let's examine the microcomputer of which the processor is a part.

The **microcomputer** in Figure 13–2 is an electronic machine that performs input, storage, arithmetic, logic (decision), and output operations following a set of instructions (program). It is ex-

---

[1] In the 64K the K represents roughly 1000, but actually it is 1,024 (binary 2 to the 10th power).

FIGURE 13–1   IBM's 64K-bit LSI chip.

tremely small in size and can be built with a few LSI chips or even one chip.

The memory of a microcomputer may be of two types: **random access memory (RAM),** where data, intermediate results, and temporarily needed programs are stored; and **read-only memory (ROM),** where permanently required programs such as language translators are stored. The connecting circuits or pathways over which data and instructions flow are called **buses** (Figure 13–3). Three types of buses may exist within the microcomputer. The **data bus** carries data between the various parts of the computer; the **address bus** transmits an address from the microprocessor to memory or to the input or output unit; and the **control bus** carries signals to maintain the timing of the various components.

A bus consists of multiple lines (you might think of them as thin wires) running in parallel from one device to another. The multiple parallel lines allow the separate bits of a character or word to be sent simultaneously down the bus (Figure 13–4). Thus on an 8-bit bus there are eight parallel lines, each carrying one bit of the byte.

In contrast to the parallel transmission of data bits on a bus, data output from the computer is often converted to **serial** format. In serial format only one bit is going into the cable at any particular moment (Figure 13–5).

With parallel transmission, many more data bits are transmitted within a particular time-frame than is the case with serial transmission. Similarly, if the bus were widened from 8 bits to 32 bits, four sets of 8 bits could be transmitted. Since the power of the computer depends partly on data transfer speed, bus width is an important consideration.

Microprocessor Functional Parts

The microprocessor contains the **control unit** that directs the activities of other main units in the microcomputer (memory, input, and output) and also directs the functions within the processor (see Chapter 2). Inside the microprocessor, in addition to the control unit, there are the address register, data register, accumulator, and arithmetic/logic unit (Figure 13–6).

The **address register** holds within memory the address of data that are to be accessed. The size of this register need only be as many bits as are needed to represent the number of memory locations. For example, a 16-bit address register will allow $2^{16} = 65,536$ words to be directly addressed.

FIGURE 13–2   Microcomputer.

FIGURE 13-3 Bus circuit.

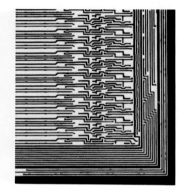

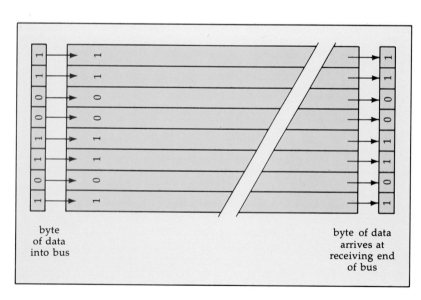

FIGURE 13-4 One byte of data being transmitted in parallel on a bus.

MODULE THREE: HARDWARE

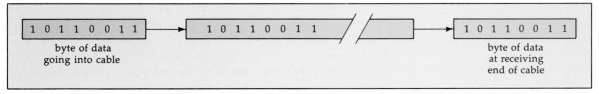

FIGURE 13–5 One byte of data being transmitted serially on a cable.

The **data register** receives and holds data received from memory or being sent to memory via the data bus. The size of the data register is determined by the number of bits in a data word. For example, if the data word is 1 byte in size, an 8-bit data register is needed.

The **accumulator** holds one of the numeric values that is input to the arithmetic/logic unit (ALU), and also holds the results of arithmetic and logic operations performed in the ALU (Figure 13–7). The size of the accumulator equals the size of the data word. Some microprocessors have two or more accumulators, making the processor more flexible and efficient.

You now have seen the functional parts of the microcomputer and of the microprocessor. Many of these functions also occur in mini and mainframe computers. What aspects of microcomputers differentiate them from minis and mainframes? There are several factors that allow a computer to be categorized as micro, mini, or mainframe.

Bits Per Word

The architecture of a computer includes the overall design of the hardware and software. The number of **bits per word** is one commonly used description of part of this architecture. For example, a computer designed around a 16-bit architecture will generally have 16 as the number of: bits per word of memory, parallel lines in the data bus; bit positions in various registers and accumulators; and bits that the arithmetic/logic unit can simultaneously operate on. Microcomputers have 4-, 8-, 12-, or 16-bit architecture, with 8-bit and 16-bit being the most popular. Intel Corporation, the developer of the first

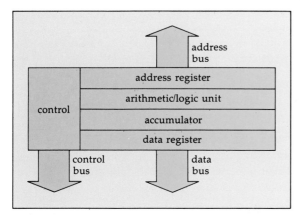

FIGURE 13–6 Diagram of microprocessor functional parts.

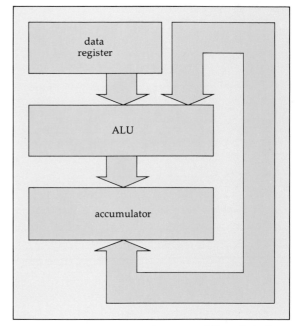

FIGURE 13–7 Accumulator providing data for the ALU and then receiving results of ALU operation.

computer-on-a-chip, recently introduced the first 32-bit microprocessor. The 32-bit processor has been available in some large minicomputers (1973–1981) but has been available on small minis only since 1978 or so.

Configurations

Microcomputers may be as small as a single encased chip. In this form they are quite limited in memory, number of instructions, and flexibility. These single chip microcomputers (Figure 13–8) are usually used for control purposes and are built into cameras, timers, microwave ovens, video games, and so on. Most microcomputers consist of many LSI chips on a circuit board, where a chip or several together serve as memory, processor, input, or output. Such **single-board microcomputers** are used as components in intelligent terminals, as controllers in disk drives, or as training tools by engineers, programmers, or hobbyists (see Figure 13–9). These single-board micros usually do not have the peripherals, such as keyboards, printers, or secondary storage devices, that are required by the user. When those items are added, together with operating systems programs and applications programs, the result is called a **microcomputer system** or **microsystem** (see Figure 13–10). A microsystem is usually desk size or smaller.

Peripheral devices (such as keyboard, CRT screen, magnetic disk, and printer) that are attached to microcomputers are generally quite different from those found on mini or mainframe computers. On the micro the keyboard and CRT screen are often separate devices and are smaller than those of larger systems. For example, on personal computers a 40-character-by-12-line CRT is more common than the 80-character-by-24 line configuration found on most CRTs. Magnetic disks are usually flexible; the 5¼ inch in diameter (called the **mini-floppy**) stores around 100,000 bytes, and the 8 inch stores up to 1.26 million bytes. The disk drives that read or write on the disks range in cost from $500 to $2,000.

Printers on microcomputer systems are either printer terminals (with keyboards) that usually print at 30 characters per second (CPS), or separate printers (no keyboard) that print from 30 to 180 CPS. The price for these printers ranges from $500 to $3,500.

On the least expensive personal computers magnetic tape cassette storage is most common and usually sells for under $100. Cassettes read and write data in the range of 30 to 200 CPS, in contrast to the mini-floppy disk rate of 750 to 19,500 CPS.

Memory Capacity

The computer-on-a-chip may have memory size of 4K to 64K bytes. In those micros that have memory expansion capability via the addition of a circuit board, the single-board memories range from 64K to 256K bytes. In microcomputer systems, separate memory boards can be added to bring memory up to 512K bytes.

FIGURE 13–8 Computer on a chip.

FIGURE 13–9 Single-board microcomputer.

Processor Speed

Computer operating speed can be measured in many ways including: access time of memory data; cycle time, for performing a single processor operation; or transfer rate of data along a bus. A more meaningful speed measurement is the time taken to perform one addition. The add time for microprocessors ranges from 8 microseconds down to 0.8 microsecond (0.8 microsec = 1.25 million additions per second).

Software

The extent of the software (operating system, language translators, applications programs, database management systems) found on a microcomputer is considerably less than what you would find in a minicomputer or a mainframe computer. In this section we discuss these software elements as they exist in micros.

An **operating system** is a set of programs that calls in programs stored on magnetic media, displays messages to the computer operator as needed, keeps records of hardware and/or software malfunctions, may log the amount of time spent on each user program or group of user programs, and performs similar tasks. A microcomputer may have a sophisticated operating system or none at all. The computer-on-a-chip that controls the lens opening on a camera has no need for an operating system since it is programmed to perform only one or two tasks that allow for no human intervention. How-

FIGURE 13–10 Microcomputer system.

CHAPTER 13: MINIS, MICROS, MAINFRAMES   299

ever, a microcomputer system that drives a graphic display terminal needs to give the users many instructions to direct their actions.

Another type of program included in operating systems is the **utility**. Some examples of utility programs are those that sort or rearrange data within files, copy files from one medium to another, and run tests on memory or I/O devices. Microcomputer systems have few of these, whereas minicomputers and mainframes generally offer extensive utilities.

Microcomputer systems generally offer at least one high-level language such as BASIC, Pascal, or FORTH, plus an assembly language. BASIC is by far the most common. Some systems even offer versions of FORTRAN or COBOL.

Because of the relative newness of microcomputers, applications programs are not as widely available as with minicomputers and mainframes. However, a microcomputer system is often purchased from a vendor called a **systems house**, which writes complete applications packages consisting of many programs. These are accompanied by operating manuals and program documentation for ease of use. Single programs may sell for $30 to $70, and complete packages such as accounts receivable, accounts payable, payroll, and general ledger accounting may be priced from several hundred dollars up to $10,000 to $15,000. Many free programs are available in books and popular computing magazines; however, many of them are amateurish and of low quality.

Only the more expensive microcomputer systems offer database management systems (DBMS). For example, the Hewlett-Packard Series 9800 System 45 offers a DBMS composed of a miniaturized version of its highly successful Image/Query system (Figure 13–11). In smaller micros, memory and secondary storage are not adequate to support DBMS. Many of the so-called DBMSs offered on microcomputers are actually file-management packages and do not perform the functions of true DBMSs.

Space, Power, and Air Conditioning

Because microcomputer systems, as the name implies, are based on microminiaturized electronic

FIGURE 13–11 **Hewlett-Packard microcomputer system with DBMS.**

components, they are usually no larger than an office desk. In addition, their power consumption is only about that of a television set, so they do not require special air conditioning or other environmental controls.

Costs

There are many costs involved in using computers. These include purchase price, maintenance, supplies, wages for operating personnel, rental or lease of space, electrical power and air conditioning, and—sometimes the greatest cost of all—programming. The purchase price for computers-on-a-chip may be as low as $10. Single-board microcomputers range in cost from $200 to $2,000. Personal microcomputer systems range from $250 to $8,000, and business microcomputer systems cost from $5,000 to $20,000. Even the $20,000 system, however, may be easily exceeded by the sum of the programming or operating costs.

Users and Uses

A wide variety of users exist for microcomputers, ranging from the home game player, to the serious home user who is running budgeting, stock market

TED HOFF AND THE MICROPROCESSOR

If "necessity is the mother of invention," then a Japanese calculator company's complex design of a family of high-performance, programmable calculators, was the mother of the microprocessor. In 1969 Busicom, the calculator company, asked semiconductor maker Intel Corp. to build a series of 12 chips for their planned calculators. Marcian Edward "Ted" Hoff, Jr., a young engineer from Stanford University, who had joined Intel a year earlier, was assigned the project because of his systems and applications work at Stanford. Hoff concluded that the Busicom design was too complex to be cost-effective.

Hoff had been working with a Digital Equipment Corporation PDP-8 earlier and was struck by that machine's lean architecture in contrast with Busicom's complex design. Intel, at the same time, was developing relatively dense semiconductor memories. Hoff reasoned that it would be cost-effective to simplify Busicom's logic design and make up for it by adding such a memory, one that could store a program that would direct the complex actions as a series of simpler steps. Hoff also realized that by minimizing the complexity of the calculator chip's logic circuits the resultant processor would be more generally usable. In the calculator, a stored program in an expanded memory could utilize sequences of more general instructions. With this flexibility, Hoff realized, the processor might find uses in other applications—and hence be a general-purpose processor.

For a long time Hoff had wanted to build his own computer and had never had a chance. Now he proposed the processor development and found strong backers in Intel's top executives: President Gordon E. Moore and Chairman Robert N. Noyce, the coinventor of the integrated circuit. While others visualized the processor as something far in the future, Noyce and Moore sensed the potential of Hoff's idea and were enthusiastic.

Other Intel engineers headed by Frederico Faggin took over the detailed design work, and Hoff's invention was built with 2,250 microminiaturized transistors on a chip about one-sixth by one-eighth of an inch. The microprocessor was called the 4004, and the whole microcomputer was called the MCS-4 (microcomputer system 4). The power of the MCS-4 was about equal to the original ENIAC computer built in the early 1940s. The microprocessor, introduced in 1971, was just what the electronics and computer industry needed, for the semiconductor makers had been involved in a costly search for ways of automating the design and building of custom circuits. Now the programs directed the general-purpose processor to perform the "custom" actions. Somewhat like a rocket that seems to hesitate before it takes off, the microprocessor faced some initial resistance, but soon its potential was recognized. By 1979, 75 million microprocessors of various types were being manufactured each year.

---

analyzing, or loan payment scheduling programs, to the business owner who is keeping accounting records or printing customer bills. With the limited memory, secondary storage, and operating speed of the microprocessor, only small businesses or small departments in larger businesses will find the micro adequate. This should not discourage their serious use, and apparently it hasn't since over two-thirds of the 500,000 "personal" computers sold were sold to organizations—not individuals. And usage is growing; in the five years from 1978 to 1983 the number of desk-top microcomputer systems alone is expected to grow from about 180,000 to 1,200,000 units in use. Other kinds of microcomputers usually found in consumer products will raise that figure to over 2.5 million.

Sources of Hardware and Software

There are more than 30 manufacturers of microprocessors or microcomputers. A large portion of micro sales are to **original equipment manufacturers (OEMs),** companies that package the micro with input, output, and secondary storage devices and software (operating system and/or applications programs). An OEM that does not include applications programs may sell the microcomputer system to a systems house that writes the applications programs and sells the whole as a single package. Personal computers such as Apple, Commodore, Tandy, and so on are prepackaged and sold in retail stores. Big name companies such as Hewlett-Packard and Texas Instruments sell their microcomputer systems either directly to users or through systems houses. Still other companies do not deal in hardware at all, but write and sell software directly to users or through computer stores.

"Yes, it computed the answer in a billionth of a second and printed it instantly, but until I find my glasses..."

MINICOMPUTERS AND MINICOMPUTER SYSTEMS

The small size and low costs of microcomputers were brought about by large-scale integration (LSI) of circuits. But about ten years before micros were developed, less dense LSI circuits, called simply "integrated circuits," were the driving force in developing **minicomputers.** In 1965 Digital Equipment Corporation, currently the largest maker of minis, introduced its first minicomputer, the PDP-2.

Minicomputers are general-purpose computers (as are micros and mainframes) that can be programmed to do a variety of tasks. They are generally designed to operate interactively; that is, the user enters transaction data under the control of the program, the data are processed, and the program calls for the next transaction data. As we saw, this method of processing data is sometimes called "transaction processing."

In the early days of minicomputers, their major use was in controlling ongoing scientific or industrial processes. Sensing devices collected data regarding the process (for example, the pressure inside a chemical refining tank) and transmitted the data to the minicomputer; the data were then processed, and a resulting action was triggered by the computer—to alter the ongoing process if the computer determined that it was necessary to do so.

The early minicomputers had very limited software (operating systems and applications programs, just as is the case with the microcomputers of today). Minicomputers originally contained memories of 2K or 4K as compared to small mainframe computers of that time, which usually offered 12K to 32K memories. They were small in size; weren't designed to handle common business-oriented peripheral devices; and were sold at a relatively low price. In addition, peripheral devices necessary to business uses, such as high-speed printers, card readers, and magnetic disk and tape devices, could not be attached to early minicomputers.

As the low cost and flexibility of minicomputers were recognized by other types of users, minicomputers were used in a wide variety of applications. As more manufacturers began making minicomputers, competitive forces caused them to develop sophisticated software, to attach many peripheral devices, to expand memory, and generally become competitive with mainframe manufacturers such as IBM, Burroughs, Univac, and so on. So what was once easily recognized as a minicomputer—and not a mainframe—is no longer. Some minis are more powerful than smaller mainframes, and even some large microcomputers are more powerful than small minis.

Minicomputer Functional Parts

Minicomputers consist of the same basic functional parts as micros, but there are some differences that relate to size and numbers. For example, the arithmetic/logic and control units (processor) of the micro are generally on a single LSI chip or, at most, on several chips. In minicomputers, however, the arithmetic/logic unit may consist of multiple chips, as may the control unit. Minicomputers also have the capability of performing floating point (decimal) arithmetic within hardware, whereas microcomputers generally perform this function with software.

A number of minicomputers expand their hardware instruction set by using microprograms. Microprograms are stored on a separate read-only memory (ROM) chip(s) that is programmed by the manufacturer and usually cannot be altered by the user.

Minicomputers are less likely than micros to use common buses. For example, micros have a single data bus that serves traffic in both directions (but not simultaneously) between memory, processor, input, and output. Minicomputers are more likely to have a separate bus linking one part (i.e., memory) with another (i.e., output), while another bus joins two other parts (i.e., input and processor). With multiple buses, vital functions are not delayed while waiting for the bus to complete its transfer of data for another part of the mini.

This architecture increases the complexity, number of parts, speed, and flexibility of the minicomputer compared to a micro.

Bits Per Word

Most minicomputers installed in the 1970s have 16-bit architecture. In the past few years, however, several manufacturers have introduced 32-bit word minis. With 32 bit positions in the memory address register, the size of memory that can be directly accessed reaches $2^{32} = 4.294$ billion characters in contrast to the $2^{16} = 65,536$ in 16-bit architecture. The jump from 16 to 32 bits allows more memory to be addressed. Some examples of 32-bit minicomputers are the Digital Equipment Corp.'s VAX-11/780, the Honeywell DPS 6/92, Hewlett-Packard HP 3000, and the Prime 400.

Configurations

A minicomputer, in its simplest form, usually consists of a processor circuit board, one or more memory boards, slots for inserting circuit boards (called **interfaces**) for attaching peripheral devices, and a power supply. These are all enclosed in a cabinet about a cubic foot in size (Figure 13–12). Minis are

FIGURE 13–12 Two minicomputers without peripheral devices.

usually mounted in a cabinet that also accommodates magnetic disk units, and paper or magnetic tape. Peripherals such as CRT terminals, high-speed line printers, and other disks (Figure 13–13) can be attached to minicomputers.

Small minicomputers generally use 8-inch floppy disks rather than the more expensive hard disks. The 8-inch floppy-disk drive sells for around $2,000 and holds about 500,000 bytes of data. Hard disks hold from 12 to 250 million bytes of storage, cost from $5,000 to $27,000, and can also be attached to minicomputers.

Line printers found on minicomputer systems print from 300 lines per minute (lpm) up to 3,000 lpm, and are priced from $4,500 to $66,000.

A minicomputer may be built into a CRT terminal, thus making it an **intelligent terminal** (Figure 13–14). Other minicomputers are designed into multistation data entry systems (Figure 13–15). Minicomputer systems for transaction processing may have up to 128 interactive terminals.

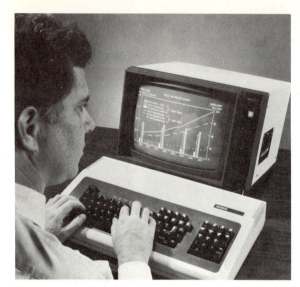

FIGURE 13–14   Intelligent terminal with built-in minicomputer.

Memory Capacity

Minicomputer memories have grown dramatically over the years and now average 300,000 bytes—equal to the large mainframes of the early 1970s. Some large minis have memories of 1 to 4 million bytes.

Processor Speed

Processor speed is measured as the time needed to perform one addition. The minicomputers' add time ranges from 4.5 microseconds to only 0.30 microsecond—3.3 million additions per second, or about twice the speed of microcomputers.

FIGURE 13–13   Minicomputer with peripherals.

FIGURE 13–15   Minicomputer controlled data entry system.

Software

Minicomputers use software consisting of operating systems, language translators, applications programs, and in many cases database management systems.

Minicomputers generally have more sophisticated operating systems than microcomputers. Some of the most advanced operating systems designed for mainframe computers in the 1960s are now being offered on minicomputers. Minicomputer operating systems may link separate jobs together in a series and thus allow nonstop program execution. Furthermore, minicomputer operating systems usually support **multiprogramming,** the running of two or more programs at a time. In multiprogramming, the operating system directs the computer to execute a portion of one program that might, for example, need to use the printer while another program is executing some calculations, and a third program is calling data from magnetic disk.

A larger number of utility programs are generally available with minicomputers than with micros. These utilities may maintain program and data libraries on disk, print reports on demand, sort files, copy files, condense files, and run tests.

Minicomputer systems usually offer assemblers and a wider variety of language compilers than do micros. Smaller minis usually offer a subset of COBOL and FORTRAN along with BASIC, Pascal, RPG, or APL. Larger minis offer complete versions of COBOL and FORTRAN.

In the early years of minicomputers, their manufacturers offered almost no applications programs. Over the years, however, some mini manufacturers, Hewlett-Packard Company for example, have developed extensive business and engineering applications programs. Other manufacturers leave programming to original equipment manufacturers (OEMs), who package the hardware along with OEM-written programs. Others assume that the user has the expertise or will seek out a software company to write programs.

As with applications programs, some minicomputer vendors offer powerful database management systems (DBMS). In fact, one of the most highly rated DBMSs, Hewlett-Packard's IMAGE, operates on a minicomputer.

Space, Power, and Air Conditioning

The minicomputer's environment is more likely to warrant concern than is that of a micro. Small minis generally use no more space than a couple of office desks. Large minicomputers with disk drives, line printers, and other peripherals consume considerable space, 200–400 square feet. The power requirements of many minicomputers can be served by the 110 volt wall outlet, but large systems require special electrical arrangements at higher voltages. Heat dissipation on minis is relatively small, but in cramped or non-air conditioned quarters, air conditioning may be required.

Costs

The purchase price of minicomputer systems ranges from about $20,000 to $300,000, depending on size of memory, word size, peripherals, and extent of software included. Because of its greater complexity, a mini is generally more expensive to maintain. Service contracts for hardware maintenance range from 1 to 2 percent of purchase price. For example, one particular mini costing $40,000 is maintained by its manufacturer for $450 per month.

The cost of supplies varies almost directly with the volume of processing. Operator wages, likewise, will vary with the volume of processing, but may be greater for minis than for micros because of the higher skill level required to operate its more complex operating system.

Programming the mini to its fullest potential requires a more skilled programmer than is required by micros programmed in the same language. However, some minis have data management software that may simplify and speed up the programming process, thus moderating costs. Also, sophisticated prewritten program systems in accounts receivable, accounts payable, payroll, inventory control, and others are more widely available for minicomputers and cost significantly less than custom-written programs.

Users and Uses

As large-scale integration of circuits has progressively brought us more computing power per dollar, many business, education, and government organizations have found that they can now afford to acquire and use a computer. At the same time, rising labor costs have made manual information processing more and more expensive. Thus, there has been a double incentive to computerize. Often this first computer is a mini.

The uses of minicomputers fall into five categories (Figure 13–16).

The largest group of minicomputer users, the "traditional minicomputer" users, consists of scientific instrument data processing, industrial automation, and data communication control. These process control computers account for about 60 percent of current expenditures for minis. As the U.S. economy faces stiff competition in the world market, minicomputers that control industrial processes and even direct the assembly of goods have become vital tools to our economic well-being.

The second largest group of minicomputers, small business systems, consists of those designed and packaged with printers, magnetic disks, and data entry keyboards and screens, and business or accounting program systems. These very popular systems are often called **small business computers** and are used in small businesses and professions for doing accounts receivable and payables, general ledger, payroll, and other accounting functions (Figure 13–17). Minis configured for small business systems account for 23 percent of the market.

Data entry systems account for the third largest use of minicomputers. Such systems usually have 4 to 20 or more data entry stations all tied into the minicomputer. The mini, using validating and formatting programs, records the key-entered data onto magnetic media for subsequent processing by another computer (Figure 13–15).

Another use of minicomputers is to provide the "intelligence" in intelligent terminals. The minicomputer enables the terminal to do far more than simply input data to a central computer. The mini-controlled intelligent terminal preprocesses the entered data. For example, the data may be validated, summarized, and reformatted prior to being transmitted to the central computer. Intelligent terminals account for 4.5 percent of minicomputer sales. This spreading of computing power out to the terminal is called **distributed data processing** and is discussed further in Chapter 15.

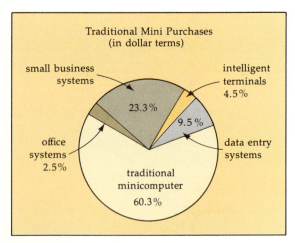

FIGURE 13–16   Minicomputer systems expenditure by use.

FIGURE 13–17   Minicomputer-based small business computer.

Finally, a small but growing number of minis are being designed into office systems that electronically transmit mail, record voice messages for later communication, and perform word processing (recording, editing, and reformatting of text).

Sources of Hardware and Software

There are more than two dozen manufacturers of minicomputers. Until a few years ago none of the major computer manufacturers such as IBM, Burroughs, Honeywell, and others attempted to penetrate the mini market. It was left to the traditional mini makers—Digital Equipment Corporation, Data General Corporation, Hewlett-Packard Company, Wang Laboratories, and others. Within the past several years, however, IBM, Burroughs, Honeywell, Sperry-Univac and Control Data—all manufacturers of mainframe computers—have introduced minicomputers. IBM introduced its Series 1 minicomputer in the mid-1970s, but this system was handicapped by its very limited software. Perhaps more significantly, in 1978 IBM's large-computer division announced its first minicomputer, the IBM 8100, which is designed to operate on-line to its large computers. With this announcement, IBM in effect legitimized the concept of distributed data processing, which it had long ignored. Currently, if you add IBM's minicomputer and small mainframe computer sales together, then IBM is the second largest supplier of mini/small computers (Figure 13–18); Digital Equipment Corporation is the largest supplier.

As with micros, a large portion of minicomputer sales are made to OEMs, who in turn write operating systems and applications software and then market the mini/software as a package. These OEMs often aim at particular market segments; for example, some sell medical accounting packages that include a mini, operating system, and applications programs for patient billing, accounting, and insurance claim preparation. Such a hardware-software-applications programming system is called a **turnkey system.** Minicomputer users can also choose from local contract programmers, or regional or nationwide systems houses such as Computer Sciences Corporation, Cullinane Corp., University Computing Co., and Boeing Corporation for their hardware/software solution.

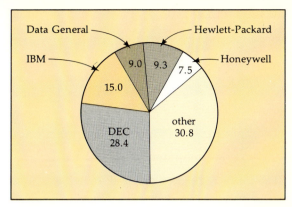

FIGURE 13–18 Minicomputer sales by vendor.

MAINFRAME COMPUTERS—
LARGE, MEDIUM, AND SMALL

During the first twenty years of their history (1945–1965), computers were neatly classified as large, medium, and small, and there was general agreement about which computers fell into each category. Even then, though, computing speed and data storage capacity were continually improving, causing periodic revisions of these roughly drawn categories. Then along came minicomputers. The minis were genuinely mini in size to begin with and were substantially smaller (memory of 2K to 4K) than the "small" computers (memory of 12K to 32K) of the mid-1960s. Also, the minicomputer was usually simply the CPU. It did not include peripheral devices such as printers and card readers, and it did not have much in the way of software. Further, minis were manufactured by firms that weren't traditional computer makers (like IBM, Burroughs, Honeywell, Sperry-UNIVAC, NCR, and Control Data). However, as minis began to grow in capacity and configuration to the point of overlapping small computers, the term **mainframe** was applied to the small, medium, and large computers to differentiate them from minis. Now there are almost no practical ways of differentiating between mini and small computers—especially since traditional manufacturers now build minis, and several traditional minicomputer makers now build medium-size computers. The small computer and the minicomputer, for all practical purposes, have become a single category.

Mainframe Computer Functional Parts

Mainframe computers have the same basic functional parts (input, memory, arithmetic/logic, control, secondary storage, and output) that mini- and microcomputers have. However, there are major differences compared to minis and micros within the mainframe parts and with the data flow among those parts.

Differentiating Features of Mainframes

There are a number of hardware features that differentiate mainframes from minis and micros. The data paths or buses that connect the parts of mainframe computers are likely to be 32, 48, or 64 bits in width. That is, 32, 48, or 64 bits of data flow simultaneously down as many parallel lanes. This size allows more data and/or instructions to be accessed per period of time than would narrower 8-bit or 16-bit buses. Micros, and sometimes minis, use a common bus that connects their major functional parts (Figure 13-3). On mainframe computers the functional parts are connected point to point, with separate buses. In other words, the functional parts don't have to share buses.

Mainframes are likely to have separate modules of memory, each with its own address register. For example, a four-module memory allows simultaneous access to each module so that within a certain time-frame four times as many words are transferred from memory to the processor as would be possible with a single module. This concurrent transfer from separate memory modules is called **memory interleaving** (Figure 13-19). A data item being acted upon is often found in close proximity to the subsequent data item to be processed. Memory interleaving increases processing speed since several instructions are provided almost simultaneously.

Mainframe computers generally have large **buffers** for holding data temporarily as they come in from an input device prior to being sent on to main memory or to the processor. Likewise, data headed for an output device that operates more slowly than memory transmits the data will be held in an output buffer until the device is able to use them. The output devices attached to mainframe computers are no faster than those used on micro or mini computers, but the internal operating speed of the mainframe may be 100 or even 1000 times faster than the smaller computers. Thus, mainframes require sizable buffers in order to cope with the difference between internal and external speed.

Another differentiating characteristic of mainframes is register size. Just as data paths of mainframes transmit larger data words, the data registers and others hold those larger words. The address register of the mainframe, for example, must be large enough to store the highest numbered memory address. A micro of 65K words uses a 16-bit register to record the address 65,535 and lower addresses (Figure 13-20). In contrast, a large-scale computer with 5,000K memory would have its highest number memory address recorded as 5,120,000 and stored in 23 bits. Since word size is usually increased by powers of 2, the jump from 16 bits would be to 32 bits—not 23 (Figure 13-21).

Moving up the size scale in computers also brings increased speed of instruction execution. The speed of the processor is sometimes measured in **millions of instructions per second (MIPS)** or **thousands of operations per second (KOPS)**. The MIPS measures processor speed based on the average of instruction cycle times, but much happens within the computer's complex operating system and hardware that may consume MIPS that don't directly produce resulting data. For example, if a parity error is detected in memory, it may be essential to note the error condition in a log in order for subsequent trouble shooting by a repair technician to be possible; however, the data are not directly involved. The more involved measure, KOPS, is calculated based on a "typical" group of programs being executed, including sorts, compiles, and ap-

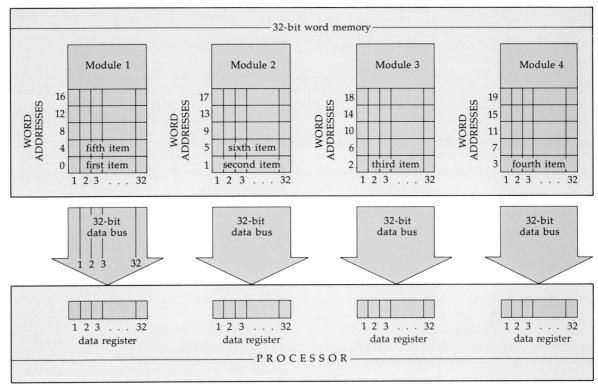

FIGURE 13-19 Memory interleaving with multiple memory modules, data processor, and data registers.

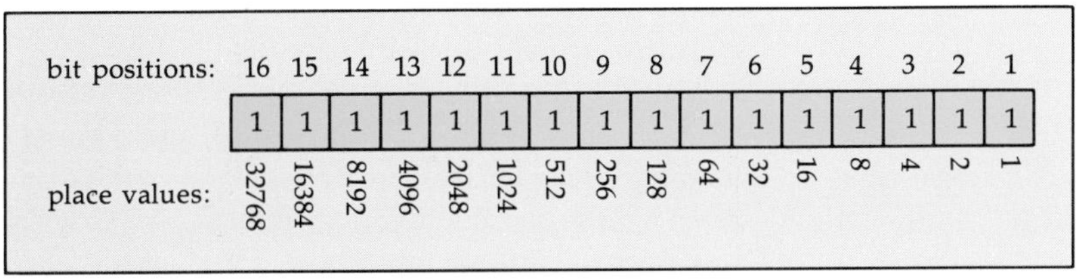

FIGURE 13-20 An address register storing memory location number 65,535.

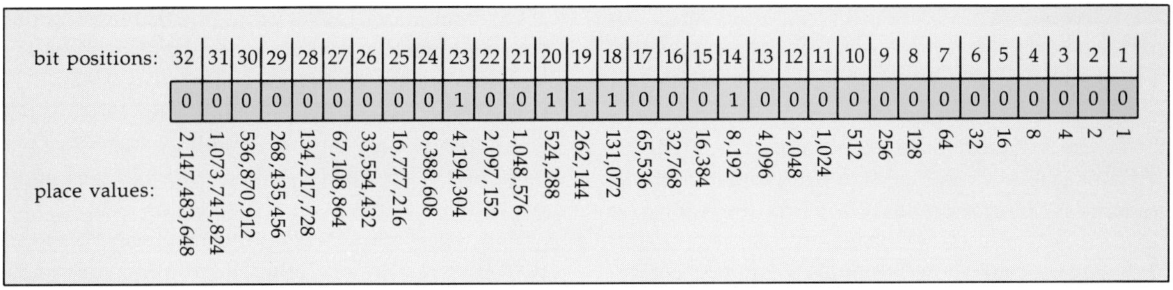

FIGURE 13-21 An address register storing memory location number 5,120,000.

CHAPTER 13: MINIS, MICROS, MAINFRAMES

plication programs. Even the KOPS measurement, however, is subject to 10% to 30% error due to variations in the way particular computers function on certain kinds of jobs.

In spite of the frailties of MIPS and KOPS, we will use KOPS to illustrate variations in computer speed. Even within the mainframe category there is a vast range of speeds. For example, IBM System 32 is rated at 20 KOPS, the IBM System 34 at 110, the IBM 4331 at 213, the IBM 3032 at 2,500 and the IBM 3033U at 5,900. A survey by *Datamation* magazine shows the KOPS for the top three computers: Control Data Corporation's (CDC) CDC 7600 at 10,000 KOPS, and both the "supermainframes," CDC Cyber 205 and the Cray 1-S, at 800,000 KOPS. As you see, there is a far greater speed difference between the mainframe and these two supermainframes than there is between minis and smaller mainframes.

Mainframe computers generally have memory ranging from 500,000 bytes to 16 megabytes (16 million bytes). This is roughly 10 to 100 times that of minicomputers. However, some large minis have more memory than small mainframes—a situation typical of the blurred boundaries between computer categories. Mainframes may have secondary storage of as low as 50 megabytes to as high as 4,000 megabytes.

Mainframe Configurations

A mainframe computer, in its simplest form, may have a single input device such as a CRT terminal or magnetic tape drive and operate strictly on a single-user **batch** basis—that is, process as a group an accumulation of transactions that are input to the computer. The computer processes one batch of transactions at a time—and nothing else. When the last transaction in the group is completed, the computer can then go on to a second batch of transactions using the same or a different program.

In another configuration, a mainframe might divide its resources and execute two programs simultaneously. Operating in this mode the computer could batch process accumulated transactions and at the same time allow terminals to query the computer's files. Such a system might be used by a small savings bank, enabling the bank to serve customers promptly while they wait, while at the same time the computer prints the monthly statements.

In a more complex configuration, the mainframe may be connected to minicomputers that collect and summarize data that are then transmitted to the mainframe. Such an arrangement might be used by a firm that has branch offices where data are collected, local reports generated for use within the branch, and the summary data passed on to the computer at the firm's headquarters.

Some mainframe computers are even connected to another mainframe. In this configuration, one mainframe coordinates incoming data from multiple terminals and then directs it to the other mainframe. The coordinating computer is called the **front-end computer.** Often this front-end computer is a minicomputer. As you can see, configurations are infinite in number, each being designed to meet the unique needs of the user.

Software

An enormous variety of software is available to a mainframe computer. Vendors of the hardware often provide a very sophisticated operating system as part of the total system, and its cost is included in the system price. The operating system provides for: computer-to-operator communications; operator-to-computer communications; program loading; scheduling of input/output operations; error monitoring and logging; internal job scheduling; job accounting; and recovery from hardware or software failure.

Available as part of the vendor's total system package, or purchased from software companies, are system management programs that log and prepare summary reports on tape and disk file usage, schedule jobs, and keep account of usage and bill uses. The management programs may also measure computer performance and aid in balancing the computer's workload between various types of applications programs.

Very powerful database management systems (DBMS) are also available and common on mainframe computers. The DBMS may be acquired from the hardware vendor or from a software company. DBMS software prices range from several thousands to several hundreds of thousands of dollars.

Many applications packages are also sold by hardware vendors and software companies. These range from accounting programs such as payroll, to inventory control, to market simulation and budgeting, to industrial process control such as directing the operation of an automated warehouse. Applications packages range in price from several hundreds to several hundreds of thousands of dollars.

Finally, mainframe computers generally offer a variety of high-level programming languages such as COBOL, FORTRAN, PL/1, BASIC, RPG, and Pascal. Still other languages, such as APL and ALGOL, are usable on many mainframes. The purchase price of language compilers for mainframe computers begin at several thousands of dollars and may have a maintenance fee of $50 to over $200 per month.

Space, Power, and Air Conditioning

Today's mainframe computers are much smaller than those produced ten or even five years ago. Together with their related peripheral devices they usually consume a space of several hundred square feet. The CPU has shrunk to the point it is often one of the smaller components of the mainframe.

Electrical power required for mainframe systems is usually far greater than the 110 volts supplied by the wall outlet. In fact, special transformers costing tens of thousands of dollars may be necessary; this expense should be anticipated and included in cost analysis and acquisition decisions.

With large-scale integration of computer circuitry, the volume of heat dissipated per bit of memory has dropped dramatically. But, as pointed out, the CPU has become a small portion of the total hardware. Printers, disk drives, tape drives, CRTs, and power transformers still generate considerable heat. Thus, provision should be made for handling heat given off by the hardware. This is not only for the comfort of the operator, but also for the reliability of the processing since transistors and other components change their behavior with temperature fluctuations, and unpredictable and erroneous data may result.

Costs

The cost of using mainframe computers, as with micros and minis, includes purchase price or monthly rental, maintenance, supplies, operation and programming, personnel wages, space rental, and electrical power and air conditioning costs. Carefully collected, realistic cost figures need to go into any computer acquisition.

Mainframe hardware costs range from $150,000 for an IBM 4331 to $5.9 million for a Cray-1 supercomputer. As with micros and minis the cost of applications programming can exceed by far the purchase price of the hardware and operating system.

Users and Uses

The diversity of uses for mainframe computers is mind boggling. The main use areas are accounting, scientific research, engineering design, process control, inventory management, economic modeling, telecommunication control, resource exploration, and archival storage. Users range from small businesses to huge corporations, from local government to the IRS and the FBI, from elementary schools to research groups at large universities, from churches to casinos, and from taxi companies to airlines.

Sources of Hardware and Software

Mainframe manufacturers account for most hardware sales. These include the major firms: Burroughs, Control Data Corp., Digital Equipment Corp., Honeywell, IBM, NCR, and Sperry-Univac. Others include the supercomputer maker Cray and the manufacturers of IBM "look alikes," Amdahl and Magnuson, whose hardware runs IBM software and drives IBM peripherals.

In contrast to minis and micros, about half of the mainframe computers in use are leased or rented from the manufacturer. Mainframe computers can also be leased from banks and leasing companies. Companies selling used computers and companies outgrowing their own equipment offer sizable savings for the informed buyer who doesn't need a brand new computer.

Software sources for mainframes are similar to those described for minis. However, the variety of packages is much greater, as is the number of suppliers. Practically any software a user would ever need is available from some software vendor.

SUMMARY

Computers are classified as micro, mini, and mainframe. Figure 13–22 compares these types of computers. Mainframe computers are the type most people think of when they think of computers. They are often relatively expensive and are large in size and capacity compared to the other kinds of computers. Minicomputers have existed since the mid-1960s. Originally they were small in physical size, capacity, and cost. A more recent phenomenon is the microcomputer; this can be held in the hand, has a relatively small capacity, and is very inexpensive when compared to a mainframe.

Differentiating between micros and minis and between minis and mainframes is not easy. Characteristics that traditionally were associated with mainframe computers (large instruction sets, large word size, large memory size) are now found in some minicomputers. Likewise, attributes of the mini (16- and 32-bit words, 100K to 500K byte memory, and diverse peripheral devices) are shifting down to the micro.

With this very fluid structure of computer classes, perhaps the major feature that differentiates mainframes from their upstart younger siblings in the computer family is that mainframes have separate data paths connecting each functional part with the others. These point-to-point data paths offer fast data transfer. Minis and micros still often use a common bus (shared data paths) connecting memory and other functional parts.

Just as hardware advances have brought increased computing power to mainframes, minis, and micros, software developments have pushed sophisticated operating systems, DBMS, and applications programs from mainframes down to minis. And uses for minis of five to ten years ago are being seen on today's micros.

FIGURE 13–22	Comparisons of micro, mini, and mainframe computers.		
Comparison Category	Microcomputer	Minicomputer	Mainframe Computer
Architecture	Bus	Bus	Point to point
Bits/word	4, 8, 12, or 16	16, 32	32, 48, 64
Memory Capacity	4K–64K	64K–4000K	500K–16000K
Processor Speed			
(MIPS)	.25–.60	N/A	.20 to 24
(KOPS)	N/A	N/A	20 to 10,000
Space	1–10 sq ft	20–200 sq ft	100–5000 sq ft
Power	12v–110v	110–220v	220v and higher
Air Conditioning	Not usually	Sometimes	Almost always
Costs	$200–$20,000	$20,000–$250,000	$100,000–$10M
Software			
a. Operating Systems	Low level	Midlevel	High level
b. Languages	BASIC, Pascal	BASIC, Pascal, FORTRAN COBOL, RPG	All languages
c. DBMS	Not usually	Sometimes	Almost always
d. Utilities	Sometimes	Usually	Always

The benefactor of these shifting boundaries is the user. Computing power that previously cost millions of dollars now costs only hundreds of thousands, and capacity that formerly cost hundreds of thousands of dollars now costs tens of thousands or less.

TERMS

The following words or terms have been presented in this chapter.

- Integrated circuit
- Large-scale integration (LSI)
- Very large scale integration (VLSI)
- Microprocessor
- Microcomputer
- Random access memory (RAM)
- Read-only memory (ROM)
- Buses
- Data bus
- Address bus
- Control bus
- Serial
- Control unit
- Address register
- Data register
- Accumulator
- Bits per word
- Single-board microcomputers
- Microcomputer system
- Microsystem
- Mini-floppy
- Operating system
- Utility
- Systems house
- Original equipment manufacturers (OEMs)
- Minicomputer
- Interface
- Intelligent terminal
- Multiprogramming
- Small business computer
- Distributed data processing
- Turnkey system
- Mainframe
- Memory interleaving
- Buffer
- Millions of instructions per second (MIPS)
- Thousands of operations per second (KOPS)
- Batch
- Front-end computer

EXERCISES

The exercises that follow are grouped by level of difficulty. Exercises in the A series are the easiest; B series problems are moderately hard; and C series problems are the most difficult.

A-1 Describe the microprocessor and its various parts.

A-2 Differentiate between a microcomputer and a microcomputer system.

A-3 What is the function of an address register?

A-4 Describe several commonly used peripheral devices of microcomputers.

A-5 What languages are generally available on microcomputers? Minicomputers? Mainframe computers?

A-6 Cite several applications for microcomputers. For minicomputers. For mainframe computers.

A-7 Describe sources of mini, micro, and mainframe computers.

A-8 Describe sources of software for micro, mini, and mainframe computers.

A-9 Describe how minicomputers provide the intelligence to intelligent terminals.

B-1 Differentiate between a microprocessor and a microcomputer.

B-2 Explain how integrated circuits are related to microprocessors.

B-3 Describe a microprocessor bus and its function.

B-4 Why is a 32-bit data bus faster than an 8-bit data bus?

B-5 Describe some functions of computer operating systems.

B-6 Name several ways in which processor speed is measured.

B-7 Describe the physical environment required for operating a microcomputer. A minicomputer. A mainframe computer.

B-8 Describe the similarities and differences between microcomputers and minicomputers.

B-9 Contrast the availability of applications software for micros, minis, and mainframes.

B-10 Describe what memory interleaving is and what its advantages are.

C-1 Why are data buses, address buses, and control buses all needed in a microprocessor instead of just a single multipurpose bus?

C-2 Explain the difference between serial and parallel transmission of data.

C-3 What relationship do address register, address bus, and memory size have to each other?

C-4 Prepare a table showing the major attributes of mini, micro, and mainframe computers. Include purchase price ranges, memory size, external storage capacity, word size, bus structure, and speed.

C-5 For micros, minis, and mainframes contrast the cost of applications programs to hardware and the cost of operating systems.

C-6 Describe what KOPS and MIPS are and explain their limitations.

COMPUTER NEWS

COMPUTERS—A MAINFRAME ON THREE CHIPS

Although it is not yet 10 years old, the microprocessor—or computer on a chip—has added computing power to a vast range of products from autos to appliances and has even created entirely new industries such as electronic games and intelligent computer terminals. An incredible 150 million of the fingernail-size semiconductor devices were shipped worldwide last year. The market for just the chips alone, virtually nonexistent in 1973, rocketed past $750 million in 1980.

Now semiconductor makers are readying a new generation of microprocessors that promises to be the most significant advance in integrated circuits since the invention of the microprocessor itself. Leading the way is Intel Corp., the company that pioneered the computer on a chip.

A NEW GENERATION

On Feb. 17 the Santa Clara (Calif.) company announced the first of this new generation, a product that packs the power of a large mainframe computer on just three semiconductor chips. "With these chips, you can put the capabilities of a mainframe on a desktop," says Leslie L. Vadasz, senior vice-president at Intel. "That's an enormous amount of intelligence at the fingertips of the user."

The new chip set, called the micromainframe, was five years in development and will open up applications for which earlier microprocessors lacked sufficient power and conventional computers were too costly. Like traditional mainframe computers, the micromainframe handles 32 bits of data information—twice as much as today's most powerful microprocessor. As a result, the Intel product can handle more complex tasks than previous microprocessors.

Indeed, Intel executives say that the new 32-bit microprocessor is so powerful that it could become the "brains" for such currently unavailable products as office workstations that can understand human speech, and industrial robots that "recognize" the parts on an assembly line. Adds Vadasz: "At least half of the applications that will exist in 5 or 10 years, we can't even imagine today."

Most of these future smart products, however, will require tremendous amounts of software, the instructions that tell the computer what to do. Writing software is a labor-intensive effort for which costs are moving upward at a fast clip. To hold down these soaring costs, Intel has built more of the instructions into the 32-bit chips than they have ever had before.

Programmer productivity increased as much as fivefold in preliminary tests with the micromainframe, Intel claims. "In the past, programming microprocessors was a superhuman effort," says William A. Wulf, a computer science professor at Carnegie Mellon University who has experimented with the new Intel product. "That will change now," he says.

The telecommunications and office-automation markets are likely to be the first to employ the new generation of 32-bit chips. American Telephone & Telegraph Co. sees such a huge potential for these powerful microprocessors that its Bell Laboratories is developing its own 32-bit chip. AT&T could design this chip into a telephone and program it, for example, to refuse incoming calls from certain telephones. "To put a small minicomputer into the telephone today, you need a box the size of a small refrigerator," says Solomon J. Buchsbaum, executive vice-president for customer systems at Bell Labs. With the new chip, however, the telephone would not look much different than it does today, he adds.

WORKSTATIONS

Other companies are now talking seriously about building computer-based workstations for the office around these chips. Such terminals would handle data processing, word processing, electronic mail, and electronic filing—all at the same time. "Everyone has talked about doing that—now we'll really be able to do it," says Neil Gorchow, vice-president for product strategy at Sperry Corp.'s Univac Div., which plans to evaluate the new Intel chip for use in Univac products.

The power of the new microprocessors will also enable manufacturers to make office equipment easier to use. "Building a system that is friendly to the user requires a lot of processing power," points out James Kasson, vice-president of engineering at Rolm Corp. Kasson figures that the micromainframe will enable manufacturers to build an advanced office workstation that will be so easy to use that operators will require no training.

Another equipment maker that has big ideas on how to use the new chip computer is Hewlett-Packard Co. The micromainframe could help the company build more reliable machines that can be more easily expanded to include more features, predicts E. David Crockett, manager of computer strategy. He notes, for example, that the new Intel device has "redundancy built right in" to reduce breakdowns.

Unlike previous chips, the micromainframes can also be easily hooked together to obtain still higher performance levels as a user's needs grow. "It's as if Ford Motor [Co.] could build everything from Lynx to Lincoln with the same set of tooling," says David P. Best, Intel's marketing manager for the product.

NEW END PRODUCTS

The micromainframe and other microprocessors in its class are expected to do more than spawn new applications. Industry watchers say that these integrated circuits are so powerful that new companies, and even new industries, will spring up to build new end products using these superchips.

In the next five years, Intel's Best predicts, "dozens of companies" will be formed to build products around the micromainframe. In all, the market for the micromainframe and other 32-bit chips now on the drawing boards at other semiconductor makers could top $200 million by 1985, forecasts Creative Strategies International, a San Jose (Calif.) market researcher.

Intel has yet to set a price for its latest microprocessor. But Daniel L. Klesken, an industry analyst at Dataquest Inc., figures that systems built around the 32-bit microprocessor could sell for as little as 20% of the cost of a minicomputer today—or about $6,000. "This will put computing power into applications where minis are too expensive," he says. Klesken predicts, for example, that the micromainframe will have a "tremendous impact" in signal-processing applications for the military and for companies engaged in oil exploration. At the same time, Intel's Best expects that medical imaging systems—now a high-cost item for hospitals—could become cheap enough for every doctor to afford.

EDUCATING USERS

To turn these predictions into a reality, Intel is mounting an aggressive marketing effort to explain the potential of the new chips to customers. For more than a year now, top company officials have been holding briefing sessions for Intel customers, and, in March, the company will begin shipping "evaluation systems" to give customers hands-on experience with the new chips. By 1983, Intel figures it will be able to turn out the micromainframe in large volume.

In the meantime, other semiconductor makers are working feverishly on similar products.

"Right now," says Subhash Bal, product manager for National Semiconductor Corp., "the Intel micromainframe is too expensive for the needs of microprocessor applications." He maintains that National's new microprocessors being introduced later this year can easily grow into full 32-bit devices when the market is ready.

But many industry analysts believe that the new generation of chips, like those before it, will create its own market as it becomes available. And they believe that Intel's competition will need at least a year to match the micromainframe. "Timing continues to be Intel's forte," says Dataquest's Klesken. "By getting to the market early, Intel should be able to reap good margins before the entry of lots of competition."

CHAPTER fourteen
DATA OUTPUT DEVICES

Preview

Introduction to Output

Visual Display Devices
 Alphanumeric Terminals
 Graphic Displays
 Flat Panel Displays

Printer Output
 Print Media
 Impact Printers
 Nonimpact Printers
 Advantages and
 Disadvantages of Various Types of Printers

Other Output Devices
 Computer Output on Microfilm
 Plotters
 Audio Response Devices

Summary

**Computer News: Peripherals:
Amoco's Credit-Card Billing Coup**

PREVIEW

In previous chapters we have discussed data input (Chapter 10), storage (Chapters 11 and 12), and processing and computer systems (Chapter 13). Let's now examine ways of outputting data from the computer and consider the advantages and disadvantages of various procedures and devices commonly used. Some newly developed methods of output that are not widely used will also be described.

INTRODUCTION TO OUTPUT

In Chapter 10 you saw how data are input to the computer via an input device reading from an input medium. Once processing of data is completed, output from the computer usually follows. An **output device** is the mechanism by which the computer communicates to us or to another machine. The output device may transmit its data via a particular **medium:** the printed page, a television tube, magnetic spots on plastic tape, punched holes in card, or on other media.

Without the ability to transmit information the computer would be worthless. Thus, understanding computers and their use depends, in part, on understanding output devices and their media.

As with input devices, the selection of an output device and the medium with which it functions depends on five factors: human readability, compatibility, speed, reliability, and cost. These factors together govern the choice of the actual device required for the computer system.

The first factor, **human readability,** refers to the need to see and read the data the computer has produced as output. For example, a billing notice for a charge account holder must be in a form that can be transmitted to and read by the customer, that is, it must be a printed document. However, a response to an inquiry from a retailer as to whether a customer's current balance and credit limit justify an additional extension of credit generally does not require a printed document response. An audio response is usually all that is desired. The human readability of output, then, is determined by each particular application of the computer and is of paramount importance when considering output devices and media.

VISUAL DISPLAY DEVICES

Visual display devices of two major types, both using a television-like screen, have become common. The first is an **alphanumeric terminal** that displays alphabetic and numeric characters. The second is a **graphics terminal** that displays two- or three-dimensional images rapidly and economically.

Alphanumeric Terminals

The vast majority of the more than two million visual display devices in use are alphanumeric CRT terminals. These are used in a variety of applications that fall into four major categories. The first is inquiry, in which computer-stored data are accessed by entering instructions through the keyboard. The data are displayed on the CRT terminal as directed by the computer's program.

Another use of alphanumeric terminals is in **word processing (WP).** In WP, text material such as correspondence, reports, and legal documents that have previously been entered into the computer's storage is displayed on a screen. The user then edits (corrects, alters, deletes) to get a revised document.

A third use of an alphanumeric terminal is in **interactive programming.** Here the programmer enters program instructions, tests them, and then may alter them by making additions, deletions, or changes, much like in WP.

Finally, alphanumeric terminals are used for data input to magnetic media as described in Chapter 10.

The alphanumeric CRT consists of four major functional parts: the CRT display monitor, CRT control unit, keyboard, and a controller. Some CRTs have output jacks for printers, communication interface, and other devices (see Figure 14–1).

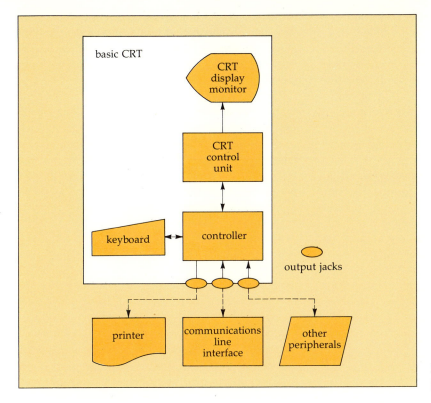

FIGURE 14–1 Functional parts of a CRT.

The **display unit monitor** is basically a high-quality television without a tuning mechanism. The common CRT display consists of a horizontal array of lines (typically 525) that cover the screen from top to bottom. A beam of electrons strikes the screen, which is coated with a substance called "phosphor," resulting in a bright spot. The beam is deflected from left to right along each of the horizontal scan lines progressively down the screen. When the bottom of the screen is reached, the process starts again at the top and continues downward. By aiming the beam at selected spots, characters can be formed and information displayed.

The CRT **control unit** creates the character pattern and stores the image for repeated use by the display unit. It also displays a pointer, or **cursor,** that shows the position where the next character entered will be displayed.

The **controller** is the "brain" of the CRT terminal and may itself be a microcomputer. It coordinates the flow of data within the terminal.

CRTs are relatively low in cost and are the most reliable method for combining input and output for computers. With diverse uses in mind, manufacturers have produced a wide variety of CRT designs, with screen sizes varying from 6 inches to 21 inches diagonally. The number of data lines displayed on the screen varies from 6 to 36 and line lengths vary from 32 to 132 characters. The physical size of the screen does not indicate the number of characters that can be projected since some small screens are simply miniatures of larger ones, displaying the same number of characters. Most CRTs are designed so that telephone lines may be used to connect the CRT to the computer. These CRTs operate in the range of telephone data transmission speeds of 10 to 960 CPS. Other terminals are directly cabled to the computer and can operate at speeds as high as 55,000 CPS. CRTs may project light characters on a dark background or dark characters on a light background. The number of displayable symbols ranges from a standard 64 up to 224.

More expensive CRTs may offer special features, including color, flashing characters, variable intensity, display of "preprinted" forms on the screen, and **scrolling,** the ability to go back to a prior point to delete or correct characters. This last feature requires the CRT device to have a built-in memory that allows the user to "roll back" or redisplay lines that have "rolled off" the top of the screen. This feature is especially helpful when entering the programs through the CRT.

The advantages of CRT alphanumeric terminals include high-speed output, ease of corrections, and relatively low cost. Perhaps the primary disadvantages of CRTs are their lack of hard copy of the data and the fact that screen size limits the volume of data displayed to less than 25 percent that of a page of output from a line printer. Furthermore, the less expensive CRTs lose the data that "roll off" the top of the screen. Finally, the lack of sharpness resulting from the dot matrix display of many screens is undesirable in some applications.

Graphic Displays

Images in color and/or in two or three dimensions may be output by a computer on a graphics terminal. Such displays communicate large amounts of data rapidly. A study by Hewlett-Packard Company indicates that humans can read words and numbers at a maximum rate of 1,200 words per minute. However, humans can view numeric data displayed in graphic form at a rate equivalent to 40 million words per minute (see Figure 14–2). Even if this were exaggerating the value of graphic display by a thousand times, graphic display would still be 33 times more rapid than reading numeric characters. With such an advantage, the graphics industry's growth rate of 28 percent per year is understandable.

The traditional users of graphic display are engineers, scientists, and statisticians. As costs have dropped drastically with the widespread use of microprocessors, however, other users such as architects, business people, and educators have found graphics display a cost-efficient tool.

Graphic display devices draw on three levels of complexity: (1) simple two-dimensional charts such as pie charts and line graphs (see Figure 14–3), (2) two-dimensional angled forms such as topographic maps (see Figure 14–4), and (3) three-dimensional hidden surface images such as population maps (see Figure 14–2).

Graphic display terminals may be attached to a wide range of computers. For example, the Apple II personal computer has graphics capability. Other desk-top computer graphics units include the Hewlett-Packard System 45, which may cost over $40,000 (see Figure 14–5). And still other high priced graphics systems for engineering design graphics systems may be supported by computers costing several million dollars.

Computer graphics systems include a variety of features. Some graphics terminals use a **light pen** that allows parts of the displayed object to be deleted, changed, or relocated. The light pen sends input data back to the computer, which can then change the mathematical description of the object to conform to the new drawing. This type of interaction requires complex programs and a powerful CPU.

Graphics terminals are offered with a variety of concepts and features. Screen sizes vary from 6-×-8 inches up to 15-×-19 inches. Line lengths range from 42 to 160 characters and the number of lines varies from 25 to 64. Most graphic displays utilize the dot matrix method of displaying objects; however, some have continuous lines. Hard copy output devices as optional attachments are common. Variable intensities or incremental intensities of display are available with as many as 32 increments. Up to 15 different colors can be displayed simultaneously by some graphics terminals.

Computer graphics is a young application area with a relatively high cost for hardware and software. However, as economies of scale are effected, prices of hardware and software should decline.

Flat Panel Displays

With the development of desk-top and briefcase computers, a need has arisen for more compact alphanumeric and graphic display. More than a dozen manufacturers are now working on **flat panel**

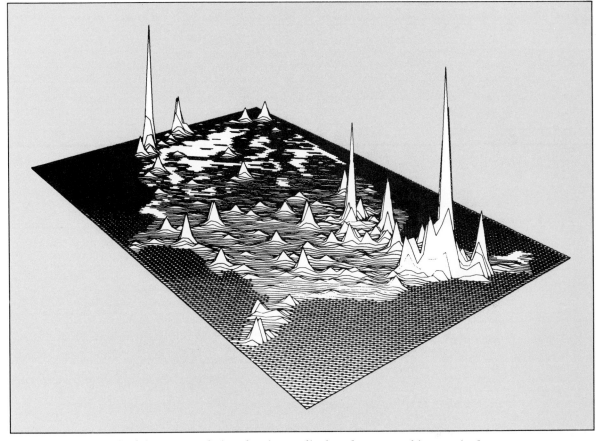

FIGURE 14–2 United States population density as displayed on a graphics terminal.

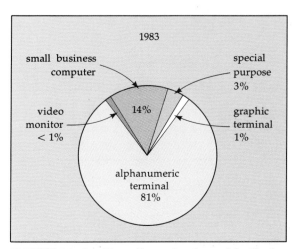

FIGURE 14–3 Two-dimensional graphic display of CRT terminal applications projected for 1983.

displays, thin glass-panel displays containing gases, liquid-crystal display (LCD), or electroluminescent (EL) substances that glow when electrically stimulated (Figure 14–6).

One flat panel display using a glowing gas is called the **plasma screen.** The plasma screen terminal was developed at the University of Illinois for use as a computer-directed teaching device. Its first use was in Programmed Learning and Teaching Operation **(PLATO)** at the university. Under this system, the student is offered drill-and-practice, tutorial, inquiry, dialogue, simulation, computer games, and problem solving. Control Data Corporation (CDC) supplied computer hardware to the University of Illinois PLATO system in the late 1950s. Magnovox Corporation and Owens Illinois Glass Company manufacture the terminal itself.

FIGURE 14-4 Two-dimensional topographic map displayed on a graphics terminal.

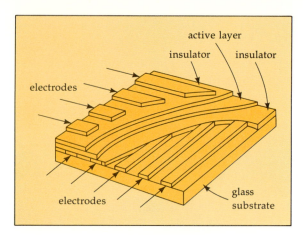

FIGURE 14-6 Hycom's display consists of glass substrates on which a solid-state EL structure is fabricated.

The PLATO terminal's plasma screen is a translucent plastic-covered glass panel that provides an 8.5-×-8.5-inch viewing screen. (See Figure 14-7.) Within the screen is a grid of 512 horizontal and 512 vertical fine wire electrodes. These electrodes are embedded in two glass plates separated by a space containing neon gas. Each section in the grid can be individually ionized, causing it to glow as a small orange dot. By ionizing a group of sections, patterns representing characters, symbols, or lines can be displayed. In one horizontal line, 63 standard characters can be displayed. There are 126 individual fixed characters in memory.

Burroughs Corporation and EXXON Corporation in the United States, and several Japanese manufacturers, are also developing flat panel displays that

FIGURE 14-5 Hewlett-Packard System 45 graphics computer.

FIGURE 14-7 Plasma display terminal.

324   MODULE THREE: HARDWARE

may become price competitive with CRTs within a few years.

The advantages of flat panel display, in addition to its slimness, are low power consumption, high daylight visibility, shock resistance, and a longer life expectancy than CRTs.

PRINTER OUTPUT

Since we are a society oriented to the printed word, printing devices for computer output are vital to most computer systems. In many cases, simply having data available for viewing on a television screen or sharing a single printed output with others is not acceptable from an efficiency standpoint, for emotional reasons, or for legal requirements. Many output users "need" their own paper copy, commonly referred to as **hard copy.**

Printer output devices have increased in speed and reliability over the past decade. Traditional printers operate like a typewriter in that the type strikes the inked ribbon, which in turn strikes the paper to transfer an image. These are called **impact printers.** More recent innovations have brought about the computer printing of characters by heat, ink spray, lasers, and photography. These printers, as a group, are called **nonimpact printers.**

Printers can also be classified by the sequence in which printing takes place. Like the typewriter, many of the slower and less expensive computer printers begin printing at the left-hand margin and print character by character across the page to the right-hand margin. This method is called **character-at-a-time** or **serial printing.** The other technique used is called **line-at-a-time printing;** with this, printing takes place randomly along the print line. There are several approaches to line-at-a-time printing.

As the automated office has been developing, still another class of printers has been introduced. They are called **letter quality printers** and are typified by sharp, clear characters. These are used on word-processing computers and produce correspondence of print quality, matching that of an electric typewriter.

Print Media

Paper used for computer printing devices ranges from inexpensive newsprint to special heat sensitive paper. Widths vary from just a few inches up to 16 inches or more. Preprinted forms with company logo, address, and so on, as well as with lines and boxes for clarifying output data, are available and common but expensive when compared to the simple lined or shaded-band paper usually referred to as **stock tab** (see Figure 14–8). The shaded-band paper is commonly called **gray-bar paper.** High-speed printers usually require the paper to have sprocket holes; these holes allow the paper to be sprocket fed, thus ensuring proper alignment and fast movement without slippage.

FIGURE 14–8 Gray-bar stock tabulating computer paper.

Impact Printers

Impact printers generally use inked ribbon, type, and paper. To transfer the image, some printers use hammers while others have the type itself create the impact. This latter, the typewriter technique, has the character or type strike the ribbon, which in turn presses against the paper. The hammer method places the **type device,** which contains all characters to be printed, behind the ribbon with the paper in front. A hammer behind the paper forces it to press against the ribbon, which in turn presses against the type, thus transferring the image (see Figure

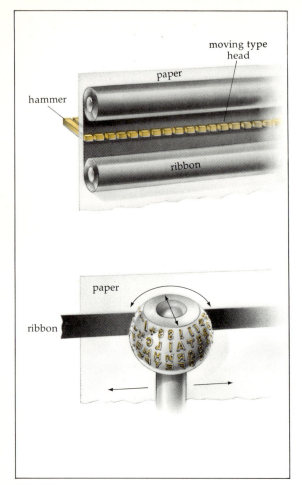

FIGURE 14-9   Image transfer methods.

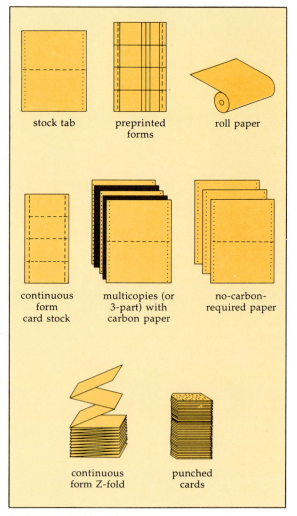

FIGURE 14-10   Common printer media.

If multiple copies of an output are required, preinserted one-time-use carbon paper or **no-carbon-required (NCR) paper** can be used. NCR paper is imprinted by the impact of the print mechanism on pressure sensitive paper.

Extensive use of punch cards as turnaround documents in billing applications has resulted in card-stock being used often as print "paper." Card-stock may be in continuous form, which has to be cut or torn apart **(burst),** or a special printer can be used that will print on individual punched cards. Such a printer is more expensive, but it eliminates the bursting operation.

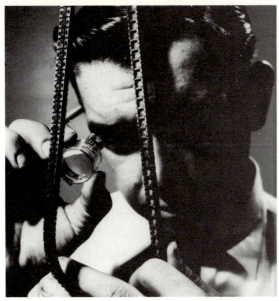

a

c

b

FIGURE 14–11 (a) An IBM 1403 printer chain. (b) A print train section (on the scale) and print train in track. (c) A print band from an NCR 8000 printer.

14–9). Impact printers use any of the media shown in Figure 14–10.

Impact-type devices vary widely in design. Generally, they are categorized as chain/train/-band, drum, matrix, and daisy wheel/ball/thimble printers.

Chain, train, and **band printers** utilize several complete sets of type, which move by the print line in a type carrier. The type carrier revolves horizontally, separated from the paper by an inked ribbon (see Figure 14–11). With the chain printer, the type carrier is literally a chain whose type is permanently connected like links of a bicycle chain. The train printer functions identically, except that the type is not permanently part of a carrier but instead rides freely around a track and, hence, can be replaced individually. The band (sometimes called "belt") printer has a flexible metal band with the type spread around the outer surface.

Depending on the printing mechanism design, chain/train/band printers may be line-at-a-time printers or character-at-a-time printers. Chain/train/band printers that print line-at-a-time range in speed from as low as 200 lines per minute (LPM) up to 2,000 LPM. In contrast, chain/train/band printers of the character-at-a-time design (usually of band type), have speeds ranging from 30 to 120 characters per second (CPS). Translated into CPS,[1]

---

[1] If the printer prints the common line length of 132 characters, multiply the LPM by 2.2 to yield the CPS. Conversely, divide the CPS by 2.2 to yield the LPM.

CHAPTER 14: DATA OUTPUT DEVICES

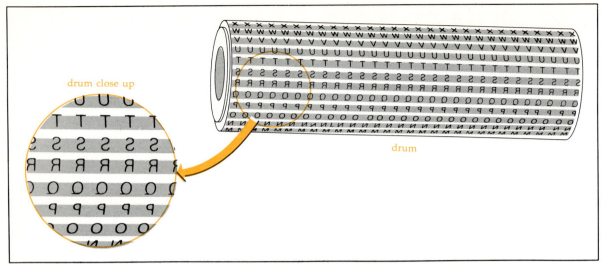

FIGURE 14–12   Drum printer.

line printers of chain/train/band-type print at speeds ranging from 440 to 6,600 CPS—notably faster than the character-at-a-time range of 30 to 900 CPS.

The **drum printer** has complete character sets wrapped around the circumference of the drum at each print position. If the print line is 132 positions wide, there are 132 sets of type wrapped around the drum. Drum printers are line-at-a-time printers, as each revolution of the drum brings any character in the set to each print position on the print line (see Figure 14–12). In one revolution of the drum a complete line is printed; in 300 revolutions 300 complete lines can be printed.

The printed image is transferred to the paper when a hammer strikes the paper, pressing it against the inked ribbon, which, in turn, is pressed against the type on the drum. If the print line is 132 positions in length, there must be 132 print hammers. The range of speeds for drum printers is 125 to 3,000 LPM or 275 to 6,600 CPS.

The **matrix printer**, or dot matrix printer as it is sometimes called, prints a pattern of dots in the shape of an alphabetic character, a number, or a special symbol (see Figure 14–13). A simple matrix printer has a seven-position, vertically arranged set of wires that strike the inked ribbon, which in turn strikes the paper, as shown in Figure 14–14. As the left-hand fifth of the letter is printed, the print head moves to the right and the second fifth of the letter is printed. After five strikes, one in each fifth of the print position, the character is completed. The print head skips to the next print position. The frequency of the strikes required per line results in a limited speed. The range of speed for the matrix impact character printer is 30 to 900 CPS (13.6 to 400 LPM).

The matrix print method is generally used on character-at-a-time printers although there are a few line-at-a-time matrix printers. One matrix line

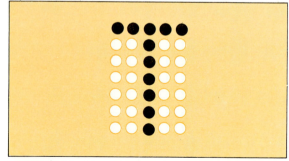

FIGURE 14–13   Matrix print pattern showing the letter T.

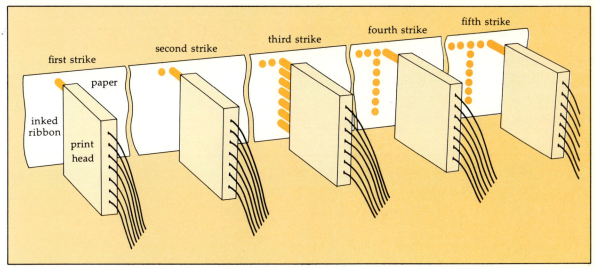

FIGURE 14–14 Matrix print mechanism printing a letter *T*.

printer utilizes a 132-wire print head and attains a print speed of 200 LPM.

Other groups of character-at-a-time impact printers are the **daisy wheel,** the **ball,** and the **thimble printers.** These printers use a moving, rotating, or pivoting head. The print device moves serially across the print line, from left to right in most cases. It generally uses a typewriter arrangement to move the paper over a platen. The ribbon moves in front of the paper, and the print head strikes the front of the ribbon to transfer the ink to the paper. Most of these printers are bidirectional; that is, they print left to right and then on the next line print right to left, to eliminate the time lost in returning the print head to the left-hand margin. Most letter quality printers are daisy wheel, ball, or thimble type.

The daisy wheel printer consists of a daisy-shaped plastic wheel whose spokes or petals have character types at the outer ends. As a character is selected for printing, the daisy wheel revolves until the desired spoke is aligned with a hammer. The hammer then strikes the spoke, pressing the type against the ribbon, which in turn presses against the paper (see Figure 14–15).

The ball printer has the printing characters on

FIGURE 14-15 Daisy wheel printer.

the face of a ball-like replaceable element; this printer was first seen in the IBM Selectric typewriter (see Figure 14-16).

The thimble printer is similar to a daisy wheel printer. With the thimble, however, the spokes are angled up at 90 degrees from the hub. The revolving-hammer-striking-and-ink-transfer sequence is identical to that of the daisy wheel printer (see Figure 14-17).

A summary of printers of various designs, giving speed ranges, cost ranges, character mode (full versus dot), and paper requirements is given in Figure 14-18.

FIGURE 14-17 Thimble printer.

FIGURE 14-16 IBM Selectric type ball printer.

FIGURE 14–18 Printer characteristics.

	Line-at-a-Time				Character-at-a-Time (Serial)			
	Speed	Price Range	Full character Dot character	Special Paper	Speed	Price Range	Full character Dot character	Special Paper
Impact								
Chain/train band	200–2,000 LPM	$3,600 to $71,000	Full	No	30–46 CPS	$2,000 to $4,550	Full	No
Drum	125–3,000 LPM	$9,000 to $49,000	Full	No				
Ball					10–100 CPS	$800 to $9,000	Full	No
Thimble					55 CPS	$2,300 to $3,200	Full	No
Daisy wheel					30–55 CPS	$1,825 to $3,600	Full	No
Matrix	125–500 LPM	$3,700 to $20,000	Dot	No	30–400 CPS	$1,000 to $6,450	Dot and overlapped dot	No
Nonimpact								
Electrostatic	275–3,600 LPM	$4,300 to $14,200	Dot and overlapped dot	Yes	160–225 CPS	$500 to $1,600	Dot	Yes
Ink jet	3,000 LPM	$110,000	Dot overlapped	No	300 CPS		Dot	No
Laser-Electrophotographic	13,000 LPM	$310,000	Full	Yes				
Magnetic	90–180 LPM	$3,100 to $4,100	Dot	No				
Thermal					10–140 CPS	$1,200 to $3,500	Dot	Yes
Xerographic	2,800–4,000 LPM	$66,300	Full	No				
Laser-xerographic	8,000–18,000 LPM	$295,000	Full	No				

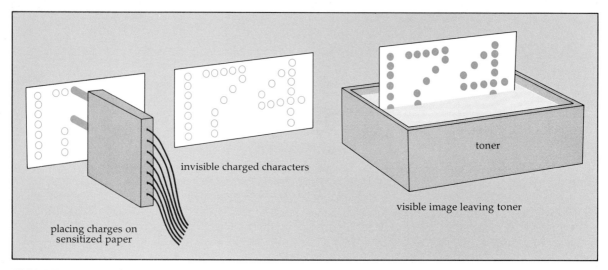

FIGURE 14–19 Electrostatic printing.

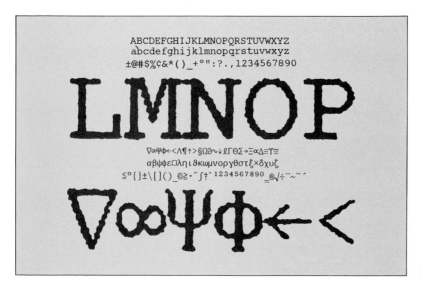

FIGURE 14–20 Ink jet printed characters.

Nonimpact Printers

To increase speed or to reduce the noise or the cost of manufacture, computer printers have been developed that do not depend on one part striking against another. These devices are called "nonimpact printers." Extremely diverse approaches to nonimpact printing have developed. The technology of the photocopying industry has been borrowed for some. A heat process has provided the least expensive mechanism. Laser technology has brought the fastest printer to date. Some of these printers can print graphics such as pie charts, line or bar charts, and more. Although nonimpact printers represent only a small part of the printers in use, the low-speed type, such as thermal printing, may increase in popularity where silence is desired and volume is low. High-speed nonimpact printers, such as IBM's 3800 laser printer may also expand usage where very high volume is required. See Figure 14–18 for characteristics of nonimpact printers.

The **electrostatic printer** places an electrostatic pattern of the desired character on sensitized paper by means of a matrix of electrodes or charged pins. The paper then passes through a toner or solution containing ink particles of the opposite charge. The particles adhere to the charged spots on the paper, yielding the image (see Figure 14–19). Some electrostatic printers imprint overlapping spots or dots and, as a result, print a solid though irregular line. Electrostatic printers operate at speeds of 275 to 3,600 LPM. Graphical output can also be printed on the electrostatic printer since the dots can be combined to form pictures. Due to the few moving parts in this type of printer, it is very reliable. However, the sensitized paper costs several times more than regular paper—partially offsetting the savings of faster printout.

The **ink jet printer** shoots tiny droplets of ink to the target paper at the rate (on the IBM 6640 printer) of 117,000 droplets per second. A microprocessor aims the droplets and causes them to overlap. The resulting printed characters (see Figure 14–20) are about equal in quality to the print of a cloth ribbon typewriter.

A color printer that uses three ink supplies—yellow, cyan, and magenta—and that can print any of seven colors by overlaying the ink was recently announced (see Figure 14–21). This color ink jet printer is designed to receive images from a color graphics CRT. Ink jet printer usage, through relatively small, is the fastest growing area of computer printing.

The **magnetic printer** has charged particles written by a dot matrix device (similar to the electrostatic printer), but the dots are placed on a belt rather than directly on the paper. The belt then passes through a toner containing black ink particles in suspension. The ink particles adhere to the belt where the magnetic dots were recorded. The belt is then pressed against regular paper that is heated, causing the characters to fuse to the paper (see Figure 14–22). Magnetic printers operate at the low end of the line printer speed range: 90 to 180 LPM. They have the advantage, however, of using regular paper rather than the higher cost special paper.

The **xerographic printer** outputs printed pages in single or multiple copies using a combination of computer and Xerox office copier techniques. Introduced in 1973 by Xerox Corporation, the xerographic printer (Figure 14–23) gives sharp character images on letter-sized (8½-×-11-inch) paper rather than on the traditional 11-×-14⅞-inch computer printout sheet, thus reducing paper consumption by up to 40 percent and providing a convenient document size for handling (Figure 14–24).

Operating off-line from a computer-generated magnetic tape, or on-line connected to a medium-

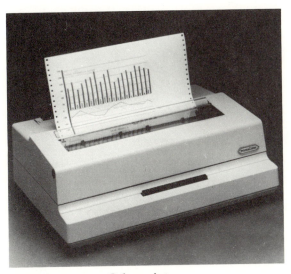

FIGURE 14–21 Color printer.

sized computer, the Xerox printer runs at 4,000 LPM, giving single or multicopies of reports. Operating under the direction of a built-in minicomputer, the Xerox printer can collate multi-page reports in page number orders as it prints. By using a forms overlay, column and row lines (Figure 14–25) are superimposed on the printout (Figure 14–26). Overlays also can contain company name and logo. In large-volume operations (100,000 sheets or more per month), printing costs are about 3¢ per sheet, and at still higher volume, can drop to only 1¢ per sheet. Atlantic Richfield Corporation's Western Data Processing Center uses xerographic printers to print 1.8 million pages a month, and the smaller paper size per page has cut paper cost by over $4,000 per month.

The concepts used in designing the xerographic printer are quite straightforward. First, images of print characters are created by an optical character generator drum (analogous to the engraved drum of impact printers) that has negative character images (like a stencil) arranged around the drum's circumference. Inside the drum a light source flashes on and off as the drum rotates. Light energy in the

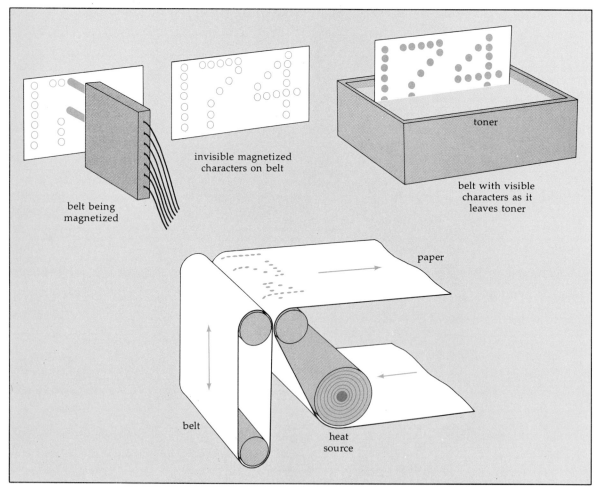

FIGURE 14–22 Magnetic printing.

MODULE THREE: HARDWARE

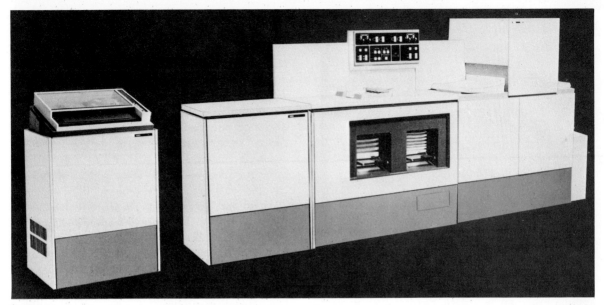

FIGURE 14–23 Xerox on-line/off-line printer.

shape of computer output characters is projected from the stencil-like openings, through a lens system, and onto a metal drum coated with a light-sensitive material. The computer output data are now on the drum's surface in exactly the same order in which they will finally appear on paper.

The drum is electrically charged and dusted with a toner (dry ink). The toner on the drum surface, in the shapes of print characters, is now transferred to the paper and fixed by a combination of pressure and heat as the drum rolls against the paper.

In 1975 IBM announced its 13,360 LPM **laser electrophotographic printer** (a laser is a unique source of pinpoint accurate light). The laser beam forms character images on a rotating drum by scanning the drum 144 times to the vertical inch to transform dot patterns to character images. As the drum turns, a powder toner that adheres only to the images is

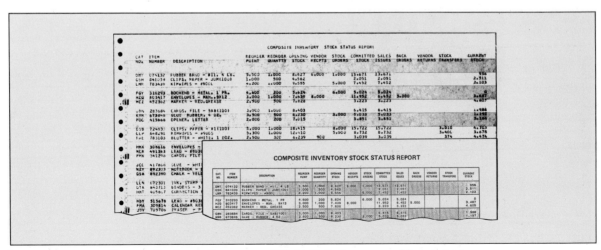

FIGURE 14–24 Conventional printing versus 8½-×-11-inch xerographic printout.

CHAPTER 14: DATA OUTPUT DEVICES   335

FIGURE 14-25 Forms overlay on xerographic printer.

applied to the drum surface. Paper is then pressed against the drum to transfer the images to it. A final step fuses the ink to the paper.

With this printer, text and forms can be printed simultaneously on plain paper to eliminate the need for preprinted forms. A variety of character styles and sizes is available. Character sets can even be intermixed on the same page. This printer is costly to purchase and would be restricted to very large volume users.

In 1977 Xerox Corporation announced its laser light Model 9700 printing system that prints from 8,000 to 18,000 LPM, uses regular paper, and prints forms, text, and other images vertically or horizontally on the sheet. Using a magnetic tape drive, built-in magnetic disk, and minicomputer for providing input, buffering, and information processing respectively, the printer can operate either on-line or off-line. The printing process differs from the earlier xerographic printer in that it generates character patterns on a belt by use of the minicomputer-controlled laser light. Electrically charged toner particles are attracted to the light patterns on the belt; the images are then transferred from the belt to the paper and fused to the paper (see Figure 14-27).

Thermal printers utilize print heads that convert electricity to heat. The image is created on special heat-sensitive paper by the heated wires in the print head, a method similar to the matrix impact printer (see Figure 14-14). The thermal printer does not require an inked ribbon, however, since the images are created by heat.

Thermal printers are generally used where volume of output is small, as the heat-sensitive paper is relatively expensive. Speed is low since the heated wires of the printhead must cool before moving to the next position. Speeds range from 10 to 140 CPS.

Advantages and Disadvantages of Various Types of Printers

Choosing one printer over another involves a tradeoff of features. A decision to attach an impact printer to a computer means that multiple copies are easily attained, but noise is almost a certainty. On the other hand, if the decision is to install a nonimpact printer, quiet is enjoyed but simultaneous multiple copies are usually not possible. If both quiet operation and low initial cost are required, a thermal printer may be the answer, but its heat-sensitive paper is relatively expensive. If an inexpensive impact printer is chosen, hidden costs of lowered efficiency due to noise fatigue may occur.

The selection of a printing device should give consideration to:

FIGURE 14-26 Printed report with form superimposed on computer output.

1. Costs. Purchase, lease, or rental costs must be

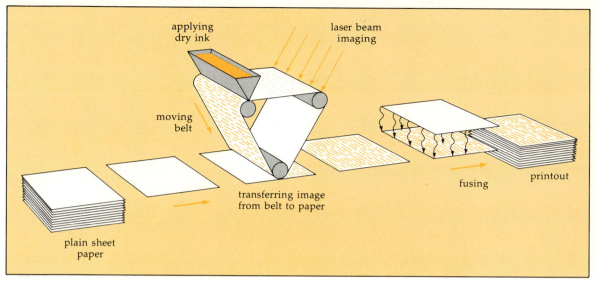

FIGURE 14-27 Laser electrophotographic printer.

considered, as well as costs of supplies such as paper, inked ribbons, toner, and so on.

2. Speed. Requirements for speed will vary greatly and depend on speeds of input and of the computer's CPU.

3. Multiple copy capability.

4. Character sets and line width. Some printing devices have a very limited range, while others offer various type sizes. The normal range of line lengths is 72 to 132 characters. Special purpose printers may print a line as short as 20 or as long as 160 characters.

5. Print quality. Sharp high contrast characters printed with good alignment and clarity to the last carbon copy are desirable.

6. Interface requirements. With the growing number of remote terminal operations, a diversity of printer uses develops. The compatibility of a main computer that communicates to the remote terminal is essential. If special interface devices are required to enable the CPU, communication devices, and printer to function, their cost and availability should be known.

7. Reliability. Although not usually cited in sales literature, except in vague terms, reliability is measurable. Mean time between failure (MTBF) figures are generally available on request. For example, the manufacturer of one serial printer cited an MTBF rating of 130 million characters printed (200 hours) before failure.

OTHER OUTPUT DEVICES

We now explore some of the less common output devices—devices that are extremely valuable, even essential, to certain computer uses. We discuss output devices that create microfilm, draw illustrations and charts, and speak in English.

The use of the first output device we discuss, computer output microfilm, has been expected to increase dramatically for several years, but so far this has not happened. The second device, plotters, has seen a steady moderate growth, and the last, audio response devices, has great potential but is still quite crude.

Computer Output on Microfilm

The adaptation of microfilm to the computer as an output medium was introduced in the mid-1960s and has become known as **computer output mi-**

crofilm (COM). Many business and government agencies have implemented COM, and are experiencing sizable savings over printing voluminous paper reports. For example, Master Card's western group, which processes over a half-million transactions daily and makes reports totaling hundreds of thousands of pages per month, was using four line printers and had a fifth on order when it switched to COM. With COM, in spite of a rapidly growing volume of transactions, Master Card was able to cancel its order for the fifth printer and remove its fourth.

Microfilm media for data storage are available in several forms: 105 mm card, called **microfiche** (Figure 14–28a); 16 mm roll (Figure 14–28b); 16 mm cartridge film (Figure 14–28c); 35 mm **aperture card** (a section of film is inserted in the cutout portion of standard punched cards) (Figure 14–28d); and 35 mm strips that are inserted into see-through cards called **jackets** (Figure 14–28e). Based on recent surveys, 74 percent of microfilm users choose the microfiche as opposed to microfilm rolls or other forms. The word *microfiche* is a combination of the prefix "micro," meaning very small, and the French word "fiche," meaning file index card. Microfiche, then, is a card of microfilm with many small images in a grid pattern.

Microfiche is replacing other forms of microfilm storage because, as a card, it is easily stored in a drawer, and because it provides random access to any of up to 3,000 pages **(frames)** that are recorded on a single 4-×-6-inch card. This random access capability offers improved efficiency in looking up data. For example, the Grange Mutual Insurance Company, Columbus, Ohio, which operates in six states and had approximately 650,000 policies on file when it switched to COM, can now locate information about a particular policy five times faster than before. The format of microfiche consists of the grid of frames and a large print title band across the top for easy reading. The frame in the lower right-hand corner at position M-16 is reserved for the index, which describes the content and location of each document recorded on microfiche (see Figure 14–29). If the index shows that the document is at C-3, the frame is located by going to row C and across to column 3. When the microfiche is placed in a reader, an index pointer moves across a facsimile of the grid and, at the same time, a lens moves over the microfiche. When the frame is located on the facsimile, the lens is over the respective microfiche frame and the image is displayed on the screen for reading (Figure 14–30).

The compactness of images on microfilm saves up to 99 percent of the space required for printed documents (Figure 14–31). A 210-page report printed

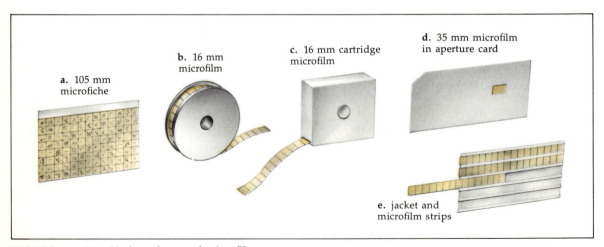

FIGURE 14–28 Various forms of microfilm.

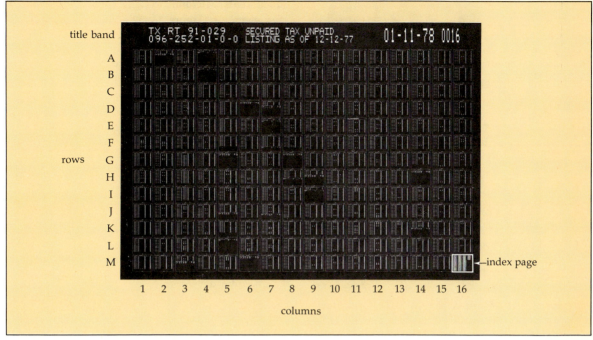

FIGURE 14-29 Format of microfiche arranged for 208 frames of images of 11-×-14-inch original size.

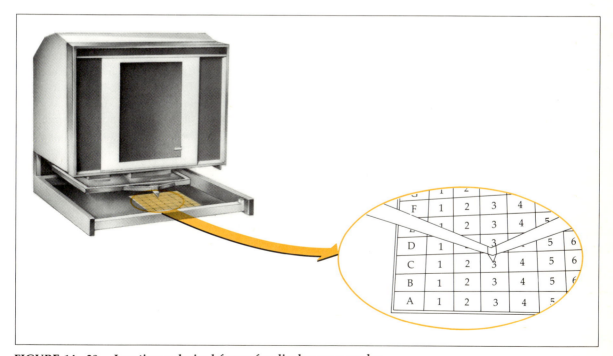

FIGURE 14-30 Locating a desired frame for display on a reader.

CHAPTER 14: DATA OUTPUT DEVICES   **339**

FIGURE 14–31 Printed data and the same data on microfiche. The handful of microfiche cards contains as much information as the stack of 12,000 sheets of computer printout.

on typical computer paper, size 11-×-14 inches, will weigh about 3 pounds and cost $3.01 to $4.56 to mail first class within the continental United States. One microfiche card containing the full 210-page report could be mailed at the present time for 20¢.

Although printers are essential for many uses, there are situations where hard copy is not needed or even desirable. Alternatives to hard copy output where the data must still be visible are available. Until recently, only alphanumeric output was recorded on microfilm, but now COM devices can project and record graphic output. For example, business charts and graphs and engineering drawings are displayed on a graphics CRT and recorded on film.

When a printed document is needed, it can be reproduced relatively inexpensively from the microfiche frame as a single copy or in multicopies by a printing device attached to the reader. COM systems vary widely, depending on the volume of documents, the number of microfiche duplicates needed, the frequency of reference to the microfiche file, and the need for hard copies of the microfiched documents. Microfilm systems consist of the following elements (Figure 14-32 shows the overall system; Figure 14-33, the recorder only):

1. The computer that produces the documents or document images to be filmed.
2. Magnetic tape output device on the computer that stores the images for later filming.
3. Magnetic tape input device for reading taped data.
4. Recording machine consisting of:
   a. front-end minicomputer (on 80 percent of the new recorders) that titles the frames and prepares the index page
   b. device that projects data images onto film
   c. device that projects forms image on film
   d. microfilm camera
   e. film developer
5. Microfilm reader for human viewing of documents.
6. Hard copy printer for making single or multiple copies of documents.
7. Duplicator for making multiple copies of microfilm.
8. File cabinets for storage of microfilm.

A COM system has a number of advantages. Its speed is 10 to 20 times faster than high-speed line printers. It has a compact storage capability. Further, the cost of developing microfilm is approximately 20 percent of the cost of paper printout. Distribution costs are also greatly reduced as a result of the small size and low weight of microfilm as compared to paper. Other advantages of microfilm are rapid retrieval of data, ability to make graphic recordings such as charts and drawings, and no need to separate pages such as is necessary with continuous form computer printout.

COM does have some drawbacks though. Microfilm requires special viewing equipment. Second, if a printed copy of the microfilmed report is needed, a special reader/printer is required. Third, with microfiche, if a single frame needs to be changed, a whole fiche must be redone beginning back with the computer. Finally, microfilm is generally economical only when a high volume of docu-

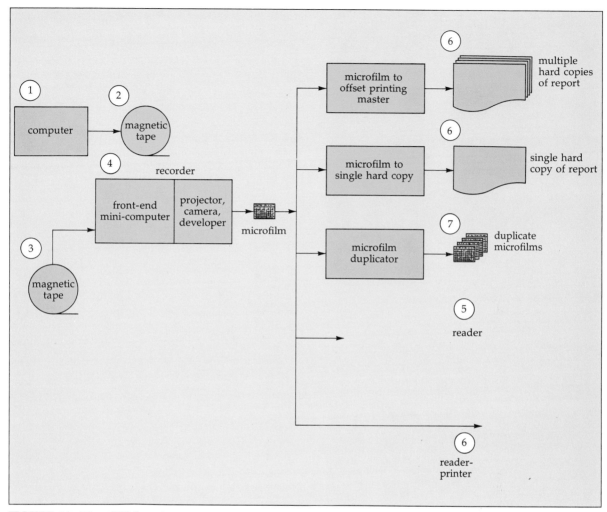

FIGURE 14–32 COM system.

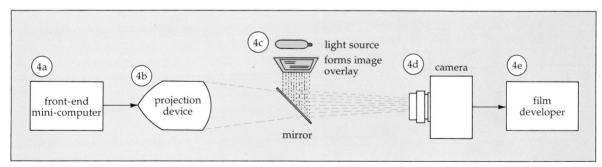

FIGURE 14–33 COM recorder using CRT projection.

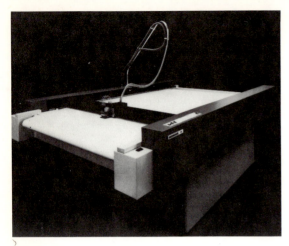

FIGURE 14–34   Flatbed plotter.

ments is regularly output, or where large files of data must be retained.

Plotters

A device that outputs line drawings on paper is called a **plotter**. Actually, plotters are special-purpose printers that can output bar charts, line graphs, engineering drawings, maps, and many other two- or even three-dimensional illustrations.

Plotters utilize sheet paper, fanfold continuous form paper, or roll paper. The paper is usually conventional paper, although some plotters use photosensitive paper that is drawn on by a ray of light, or electrographic paper that attracts ink powder in the electrostatic process. The paper may be preprinted with a grid of scaling lines, or it may be plain.

Hard copy plotting devices are of two types: the **flatbed** (or table) design that has nonmoving paper and a writing pen that moves across and/or up and down the paper (see Figure 14–34); and the **drum** design that moves the paper back and forth as the pen moves across the paper (Figure 14–35).

Large flatbed plotters can draw illustrations up to 6 feet square; some small plotters are limited to drawings of less than 1 foot square. Many plotters can draw with up to four different colors, each color being under the control of the computer. Pen movement ranges from 1 inch to 40 inches per second after overcoming starting inertia, and may take several thousand increments within that second. The movements taken by the pen are illustrated in Figure 14–36.

The major limitation of plotters has been the lack of prewritten programs or software that direct the plotter to perform tasks such as drawing arcs, letters, numbers, and arrows—tasks that are common to many applications. These programs are time-consuming, tedious, and complex to write. Most plotter manufacturers, however, now offer such software, and some specialized firms package plotters, minicomputers, and software and sell them as a graphics system.

Audio Response Devices

Audio response (also called "voice response") is an output of spoken English, such as telling the status of a checking account or giving instructions to a terminal user. Inquiry to the computer is through a push-button telephone (Figure 14–37) or a special voice response terminal. The result is computer-directed transmissions of voice messages to the inquirer's telephone. Audio response systems are

FIGURE 14–35   Drum plotter.

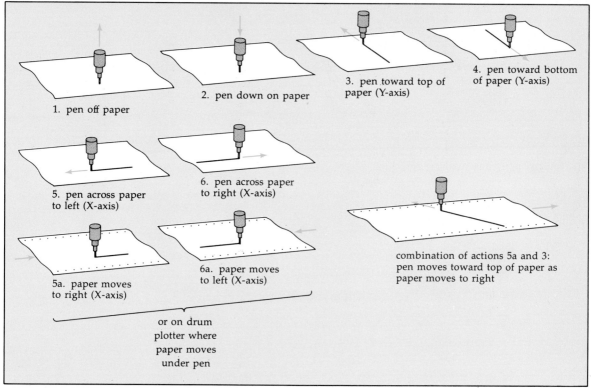

FIGURE 14–36   Pen movements of a plotter.

used by banks for quoting checking account data to retailers trying to determine the quality of a check being passed. They are also used by charge card companies for giving information regarding the validity of credit cards and whether or not a cardholder should be extended additional credit.

The **audio response** or **voice response terminal** is a special I/O device with a keyboard for inputting the account number and amount of transaction, a coupler for connecting the telephone handpiece, and a speaker for announcing the computer's response. It is used when the push-button telephone is not available.

The other half of an audio response system is the **audio** or **voice responder.** One type of responder receives a digital output from the computer that is associated with a word or phrase. Each word or phrase is prerecorded photographically or magnetically on a series of sound tracks. The computer gives a series of digits, which causes the audio responder to play the series of words and/or phrases that make up the appropriate response to the inquiry. This response is transmitted over the telephone circuit to the inquiring person. Audio responders can simultaneously serve 8 to 60 inquirers and choose the wording of the response from 50 to 2,000 words.

In contrast to the audio responders, which play back prerecorded sound tracks, Texas Instruments has developed a **voice synthesizer (VS)** that digitally synthesizes human speech. The VS utilizes a computer chip that electronically models the human voice tract. The chip's output is then converted to an analog signal for use by the speaker unit.

There has been some effort to use audio responders in educational applications to provide the student with human voice responses rather than written words on a screen or on paper. As a concise, fast (response time in milliseconds) way of responding to high-volume inquiries, audio response systems are effective and inexpensive.

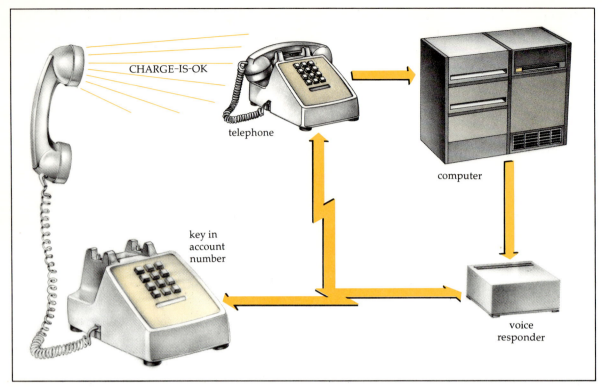

FIGURE 14–37 Touch-tone phone inquiry with voice response.

SUMMARY

Output devices are vital links to the computer. They enable computers to communicate with people, as well as allowing them to communicate with other computers or machines. Fundamental to their operation is the medium or information carrier. The printed page is the most highly used and visible medium. The use of visual display devices is growing because of their low cost and because of the computer's growing use for data inquiry.

The selection of an output device is based on a number of criteria, not all of which would apply in a given situation. The criteria include human readability, compatibility with other devices, speed of operation, reliability, and purchase and operating costs.

Other output such as microfilm is steadily growing in use primarily because of economies in materials, handling, and storage. Plotters provide hard copy graphic output for business, scientific, and engineering users and provide revised versions of drawings rapidly. Audio response and voice synthesizer are offering computer voice output, opening new uses to the computer.

TERMS

The following words or terms have been presented in this chapter.

Output device	**Interactive**
Medium	**programming**
Human readability	**Display unit monitor**
Alphanumeric terminal	**Control unit**
Graphics terminal	**Cursor**
Word processing (WP)	**Controller**

Scrolling
Light pen
Flat panel display
Plasma screen
Hard copy
PLATO
Impact printers
Nonimpact printers
Character-at-a-time
   printing
Serial printing
Line-at-a-time printing
Letter quality printer
Stock tab
Gray-bar paper
No-carbon-required
   (NCR) paper
Burst
Type device
Chain printer
Train printer
Band printer
Drum printer
Matrix printer
Daisy wheel
Ball printer

Thimble printer
Electrostatic printer
Ink jet printer
Magnetic printer
Xerographic printer
Laser
   electrophotographic
   printer
Thermal printer
Computer output
   microfilm (COM)
Microfiche
Aperture card
Jackets
Frame
Plotter
Flatbed plotter
Drum plotter
Audio response
   terminal
Voice response
   terminal
Audio responder
Voice responder
Voice synthesizer (VS)

EXERCISES

The exercises that follow are grouped by level of difficulty. Problems in the A series are the easiest; B series problems are moderately hard; C series problems are the most difficult.

A–1 Explain why output devices are so vital in the use of computers.

A–2 Explain the difference between character printing and line printing.

A–3 Under what circumstances are visual display devices appropriate for computer output, as opposed to printed copies? Give several examples of users who need printed copies.

A–4 The human body has many input and output mechanisms. List them as either "input" or "output or "combination."

A–5 Under what circumstances would COM be appropriate?

A–6 Under what circumstances would COM not be an appropriate output medium?

A–7 If a microfiche has 12 rows and 30 columns, how many frames can the fiche hold?

A–8 What percentage of storage space can be saved by switching from paper output to microfilm?

A–9 What are the six movements taken by plotter pens?

A–10 What function does the voice responder have in an audio response system?

A–11 Describe at least two uses of an audio response system.

A–12 Many libraries use microfiche for storing old issues of newspapers and magazines. Using your college or local library, find the headline on page 1 of the New York Times (or a local newspaper) for the day you were born.

B–1 If you were the manager of a computer center and you determined that your Brand X computer needed a faster output device, but manufacturer X's price was more than you could justify paying, what would you do? Explain why.

B–2 Describe a computer application in which a printed document as an output is necessary. Explain why it is necessary.

B–3 Describe a computer application in which a printed document is *not* required as an output. Explain why it is not necessary.

B–4 Why has microfiche's popularity grown much faster than reel-type microfilm?

B–5 What are the major functional parts of a COM recorder?

B–6 A plotter is used as a computer output device for what kinds of applications?

B–7 What has been the single most limiting factor in plotter usage?

B–8 Explain the difference between voice response and voice recognition of Chapter 10.

C–1 If you were asked to specify the output medium for a computer being used to monitor the progress of surgical patients during and after surgery, which of the devices described in this chapter would you recommend? Why?

C–2 If you were employed by an oil company and were asked to recommend an output device to be utilized in printing credit card customer billings, what printing device would you recommend? The following conditions prevail: billings per hour to be output: 10,000; number of lines per bill: 15; number of customers: 1.5 million; carbon copies are not needed.

C-3 Contact the manager of a computer installation in your locale and ask him or her what direct, indirect, and intangible costs are incurred annually. Describe those costs. Also describe any costs being incurred that the manager omitted.

C-4 Describe the relationship between CPS and LPM and write formulas translating CPS to LPM and LPM to CPS, assuming a line length of 120 characters.

C-5 Locate in your college library or borrow from your instructor a periodical that gives a summary of printer characteristics. Compare the new data with those given in Figure 14–18. In the time since this book was written, what aspects of computer printers have changed? Which one has changed the greatest?

C-6 In reference to the exercise C-5, are any completely new types of printers now available that were not described in Figure 14–18? Describe them.

C-7 Contrast the situation where a plotter is operated on-line directly cabled to the computer with at least one alternative arrangement for computer output on a plotter.

C-8 To what extent do you think that audio response devices and other computer system components will displace the classroom teacher in the next ten years? Why do you anticipate that extent of impact?

C-9 Prepare a chart giving the various output media and their common uses, speeds, advantages, and disadvantages.

COMPUTER NEWS

PERIPHERALS: AMOCO'S CREDIT-CARD BILLING COUP

Six years after setting out to beat the avalanche of paperwork threatening to bury its credit-card billing operation, Amoco Oil Co. figures that it has the problem licked. Now the subsidiary of Standard Oil Co. (Indiana) is gearing up for nationwide installation of what it calls Signature Verified Billing (SVB), which might also help banks process checks more efficiently.

The highly automated system uses computers and new image-processing technology to streamline billing procedures dramatically. It eliminates the costly practice of collecting data from carbon copies of individual sales slips and returning the slips to customers along with the monthly statement. Many retailers and bank-card companies now have stopped mailing the separate charge slips to customers and simply send a statement listing the month's transactions by date, location, amount, and, in some cases, the nature of the purchases. With SVB, the customer gets similar information. But each transaction is documented by an exact reproduction of the signature and other handwritten notations on each charge slip.

Amoco felt that it had to give its customers more than the usual descriptive-billing information, explains William E. Bauer, coordinator of credit card projects, "because our customers are making so many repetitive purchases of gasoline. At the end of the month, it can be difficult to distinguish one transaction from another without the more complete [SVB] record."

650,000 SLIPS

The SVB system begins at the service station. When a customer gets the charge slip for signing, it will be presented not on the familiar little aluminum clipboard but on a notebook-size device called a "transaction recorder" (developed by Amoco and Dymo Industries Inc.). The customer signs the slip in a 1-in. × 3-in. area, outlined in a heavy blue border, that also provides space for such additional notations as the car's odometer reading or license-plate number—crucial bookkeeping information for Amoco's commercial customers. The customer and the station each get the usual sales-slip record.

For Amoco's home office, however, the new device generates a new type of sales record. The carbon-copy impressions of every transaction are recorded in a 1-in.-deep line on special log sheets inside the recorder. The log sheet rolls forward for each sale and thus compiles 12 transactions on a single, stationery-size sheet. When the sheets are scanned by the Amoco computer, the handwritten data inside the blue box are digitized and later reproduced on the SVB statement. The facsimile image is generated by an ink-jet printer—Mead Corp.'s Dijit printer—that "paints" the signature and notations exactly as they were written.

With the old system, Amoco had been receiving a staggering 650,000 separate sales slips every day, and each of them was being handled about 14 times. By comparison, the SVB system will reduce the incoming paper load by 90% and eliminate all but one handling. "Until now we've had computers capable of gobbling up the information," says Erdman O. Spradlin, a systems analyst at Amoco who conceived SVB, "but we didn't have a way to feed it in fast enough and efficiently enough."

OTHER SYSTEMS

Amoco's feat of creating facsimile reproductions of signatures prompts speculation that the SVB approach might be adopted by banks to eliminate the need to return canceled checks. That would save money not only by trimming back the paper handling that is now done but also by lowering postage costs and reducing the "float" of funds in transit. U.S. banks will handle an estimated 33 billion checks this year, according to the Bank Administration Institute, at a cost of 40¢ to $2 each.

Despite skepticism in some banking quarters, there apparently is growing interest in systems that get rid of at least some of the paper handling. Indeed, Recognition Equipment Inc. (REI), a pioneer in automated check-processing, plans to unveil one later this month at a meeting of the American Bankers Assn. (ABA). The REI process will streamline the processing of checks by processing digital images in a computer rather than the physical paper.

Burroughs Corp. announced last month that it will be testing a similar scheme in cooperation with Britain's Midland Bank. "The ultimate objective," says Michael A. Brewer, senior manager for document management systems at Burroughs, "is to put the check into a machine, have it scanned by an image scanner and digitized, and thereafter use the digitized data for all purposes." Brewer is convinced that the market for such image-processing equipment could reach hundreds of millions of dollars a year. While Burroughs has not set a date for a commercial entry, Brewer acknowledges that "this kind of test is always geared to a product."

LEGAL HANGUP

REI has been working on its version of an image-processing system for years, says Group Vice-President Patrick A. Beeby, but it had been holding off introducing the equipment pending some positive indication that the banks were ready to buy. "Now we've bitten the bullet," he notes, and decided "to do it anyhow." That decision seems to have been spurred in part by Amoco's and Burrough's moves, because the REI system has been designed to work with oil-company charge slips as well as checks. REI now supplies the high-speed sorting equipment used "by all the oil companies and American Express," claims Beeby. "Now what we're talking about is adding to that [system] the ability to capture the image at the same time you capture the data. Then you sort the images" by account number and use a laser printer to generate a statement with slightly reduced facsimiles on it "rather than the actual checks or credit card stubs."

There are some legal questions that need resolving. For example, will the Internal Revenue Service accept a facsimile check as proof of payment? An ABA committee reportedly does not see this as a big stumbling block.

Of more immediate concern are the economics of image processing. None of the three potential suppliers has put a price tag on the systems yet, but the printer that reproduces signatures can cost up to $1 million. And that could be just for starters because, as Beeby points out, "to capture all of the [check] images for a whole month at a large bank would take a very, very sizable data-storage requirement. Some day," he adds, "the cost of storage will get down far enough that you can do it, but it's going to be a while." Meantime, REI proposes that its image-processing system be used in banks only to prepare monthly statements for mailing.

MODULE *four*
MANAGEMENT

a

Not only is computer hardware getting smaller by the minute, so is the business world, thanks to the rapidly expanding field of data communications.

The desk-top computer in Photo A is used for data and word processing for small businesses, as well as for remote-terminal or stand-alone decision support for departments of large corporations. A growing trend in communicating between central computer and remote sites is the use of fiber optics; to improve the quality of transmission and squeeze a larger number of messages into a cable of the same size, messages are communicated by light pulses through cables of glass fibers (Photo B). Fiberoptics are generally *intra*city systems, connecting with microwave stations like the one on top of the building in Photo C. This is the initial transmission in a series of ground relay stations that eventually terminate in a ground relay receiving station such as the tower on the right side of Photo D. Ground communications often then transfer to outer-space communications via the dishes in a domestic satellite system station, like the AT&T station at Three Peaks, California, shown in Photo D. Photo E simulates the view of the earth with the moon in the distance from the vantage point of the Telstar satellite orbiting through outer space.

Scientific data processing, like business data processing, also uses microwave communication by satellite; data are collected from deep space through receiving stations such as the one in Photo F, located near Madrid. The other stations in this network, which is used in support of all the planetary and interplanetary NASA missions, are at Goldstone, California, and Canberra, Australia. Computer technology is bringing the stars closer to our everyday world.

d

CHAPTER *fifteen*

SYSTEMS: ANALYSIS, DESIGN, AND IMPLEMENTATION

Preview

What Are Accounts Receivable?

The Systems Process

Analysis
  Investigation of Current System
  Alternatives
  Cost Factors
  Proposal

Design
  Output Requirements
  Data Collection
  File Design and Processing

Implementation
  Programming
  Testing
  Training
  Conversion
  Auditing, Evaluating, and Documentation

Summary

Computer News: Systems Houses: An Option for Success

PREVIEW

In Chapter 3 we examined the BANKAMERICARD VISA system from an overall point of view. In Chapter 4–8 we wrote the various programs that are required to collect the data; validate it; sort it into order; access the customer's name and address from a master file; and print the statement that is sent out to customers. We did not examine the reasons why we did all that processing, but in this chapter we will. This chapter also focuses on how you decide what you are going to have the computer do; what the order of events should be; what data we should have the computer store for later use; how we get the billing system into actual operation; and what the costs are and what savings may be realized.

Instead of examining a hypothetical system, we are going to use an actual system that is in use now. You will see how a real system is analyzed, designed, and implemented.

WHAT ARE ACCOUNTS RECEIVABLE?

The accounting term **accounts receivable (AR)** describes an arrangement where a customer buys goods or services from a business but does not pay for the goods and services at that time. Instead, the customer "pays" for the goods and services at a later date. At the time the goods and services are bought the customer charges the transaction and the seller bills the customer, usually monthly, for the charged goods and services. The customer then sends the seller a check (or pays in some manner) for the items that were purchased. Accounts receivable systems are used by many businesses in the United States, since almost 80 percent of all purchases are done on a charge or credit basis.

There are three distinct types of accounts receivable systems: balance only, balance forward, and open item. In a **balance only** AR system the seller keeps track of how much the customer owes. No effort is made to inform the customer as to what the charges represent, and interest is usually charged for unpaid or past-due amounts.

A **balance forward** AR system tells the customer what each charge represents, how much is past due, and how old the past-due amounts are—for example, over 30 days, over 60 days, or over 90 days. For each charge or payment a customer makes, a separate line is printed on the bill that shows the date of the charge or payment, the dollar amount involved, a description of what this charge represents, and an invoice or reference number.

The third type of AR system is the **open item**. Here customers are provided with exact information about each unpaid charge and customers make payments for these specific charges.

Of these three types of AR systems the most complex is open item and the least complex is balance only. If you reexamine the sample VISA statement in Chapter 3 you will see that it is a combination of balance only and balance forward. The VISA statement has a separate line for each charge or payment but does not tell you how old the past-due amounts are.

THE SYSTEMS PROCESS

You probably see or hear the word *system* daily. In the early part of this chapter, *system* is used more than a dozen times. There are payroll systems, accounts payable systems, inventory systems, personnel systems, and many others. In this context, the word **system** refers to people, equipment, procedures, or programs that are interrelated and that work together to perform some specific task, job, or function.

When the word *system* is related to computers or information processing, it may become part of the terms *systems analysis, systems design,* or *systems implementation*. Here the word *system* has a different meaning. **Systems analysis** is the study of a task, job, or function for the purpose of improving or better understanding the task, job, or function. **Systems design** extends analysis past the point of studying into actually developing a new set of procedures to replace the older ways that a task, job, or function was performed. **Systems implementation** extends design into actually converting older ways into the newer and into monitoring the new ways to ensure their success.

Together, systems analysis, design, and implementation comprise the systems process or systems study. The person who makes this study is called a **systems analyst.**

ANALYSIS

The first step in the systems study is analysis. Here we investigate the current system, make a list of alternatives, examine preliminary cost factors, and prepare a report showing the findings of the study.

Investigation of Current System

The first step in systems analysis is fact finding. Here the analyst uses interviews or questionnaires to gain an understanding of the system under study. The analyst also collects copies of the various forms and operating manuals that are in use. Frequently he or she will chart the way the current process works using flowcharts, decision tables, or other techniques.

Let's analyze an existing accounts receivable system in use in a small community. A local florist, "Flowers by Footes," does business on a cash or credit basis. Cash customers pay for their purchases when they are made; credit customers are billed at the end of each month. The florist has almost 5,000 customers that can purchase on a credit basis, but only 500 or so make a purhase in any given month. Purchases vary from bouquets of real or silk flowers to arrangements for funerals, weddings, or parties. Some orders are received by telephone, others are taken over the counter by the shop staff, and others are wire service orders.

At the present time credit transactions are recorded on an order form (Figure 15–1) and then posted to a ledger card like the one shown in Figure 15–2. At the end of the month, the ledger card is photocopied, and the copy is sent to the customer. Customers then send checks (or pay cash) to the shop, and the amounts are recorded on the ledger card.

The owner of the shop is unhappy with the ledger card system because (1) it is taking too long to post charges and payments; (2) there is no easily available information about past-due accounts; (3) photocopies of the ledger card are not attractive and make the shop appear unprofessional; (4) the time and expense of photocopying ledger cards is becoming excessive; and (5) a new florist has come to town and is increasing competition.

Alternatives

The second step in systems analysis is for the systems analyst to examine the various alternatives—although being under analysis does not necessarily mean the system will or should be replaced.

For the florist shop we can list the following alternatives:

1. Do nothing: Leave the system as it currently exists.

2. Modify the existing system with the purchase of a faster, higher quality photocopy machine.

3. Develop a new system using a computer to assist in collecting data, printing statements, and tracking past-due accounts. The new computer system could be:

   a. an in-shop micro or minicomputer bought for this purpose

   b. computer time rented from a service organization, usually called a "service bureau", that specializes in this kind of work

Cost Factors

The third step in the analysis is to determine, on a preliminary basis, the cost of each alternative. The various cost components include those associated with equipment, labor, supplies, and software. Some of the costs are one-time (purchase of equipment); some are variable or recurring (maintenance, postage); some are indirect (heat, light, power); and some are direct (paper for statements). Costs such as losses on uncollectible accounts receivable, which result because data on past-due accounts are not compiled, are hard to categorize and quantify.

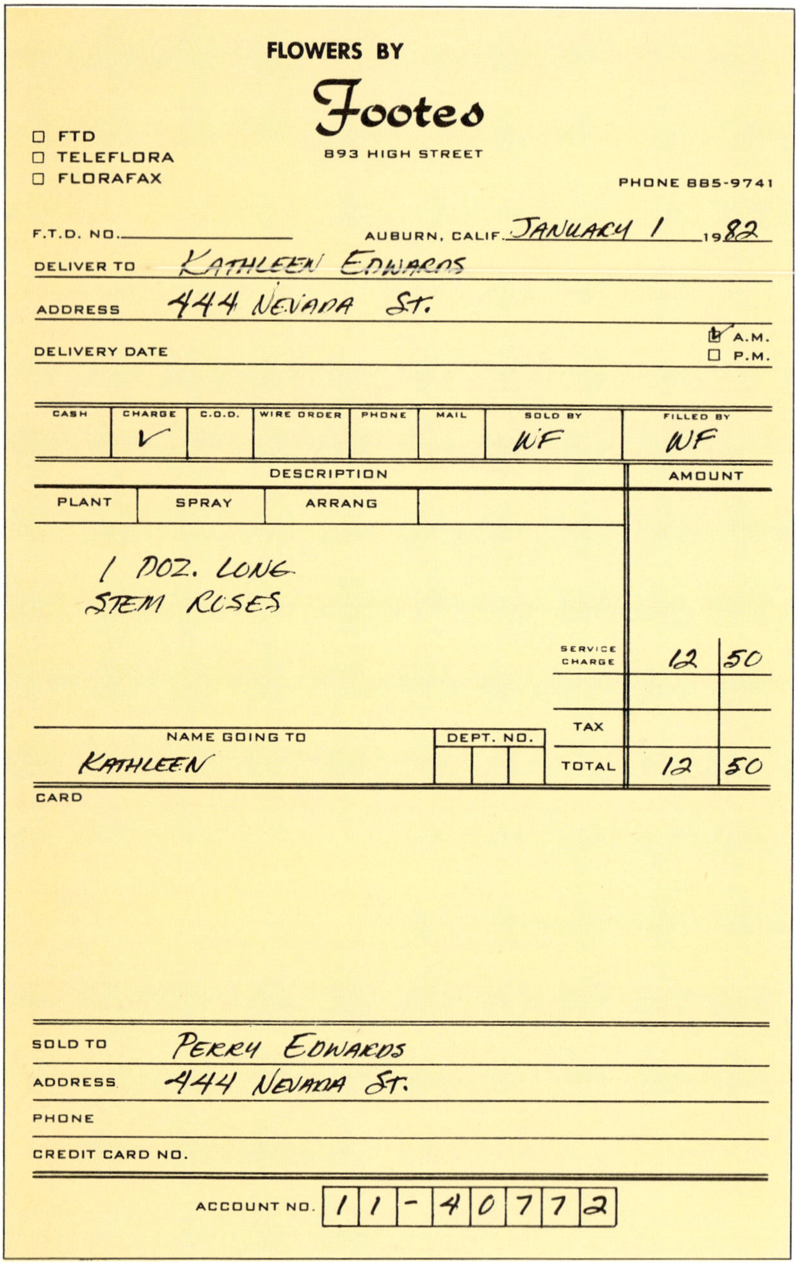

FLOWERS BY

Footes

893 HIGH STREET

PHONE 885-9741

☐ FTD
☐ TELEFLORA
☐ FLORAFAX

F.T.D. NO. ______ AUBURN, CALIF. JANUARY 1 1982

DELIVER TO KATHLEEN EDWARDS

ADDRESS 444 NEVADA ST.

DELIVERY DATE ☑ A.M. ☐ P.M.

CASH	CHARGE	C.O.D.	WIRE ORDER	PHONE	MAIL	SOLD BY	FILLED BY
	✓					WF	WF

DESCRIPTION				AMOUNT
PLANT	SPRAY	ARRANG		
1 DOZ. LONG STEM ROSES			SERVICE CHARGE	12 50
			TAX	
NAME GOING TO: KATHLEEN		DEPT. NO.	TOTAL	12 50

CARD

SOLD TO PERRY EDWARDS

ADDRESS 444 NEVADA ST.

PHONE

CREDIT CARD NO.

ACCOUNT NO. 11-40772

FIGURE 15–1 Order form.

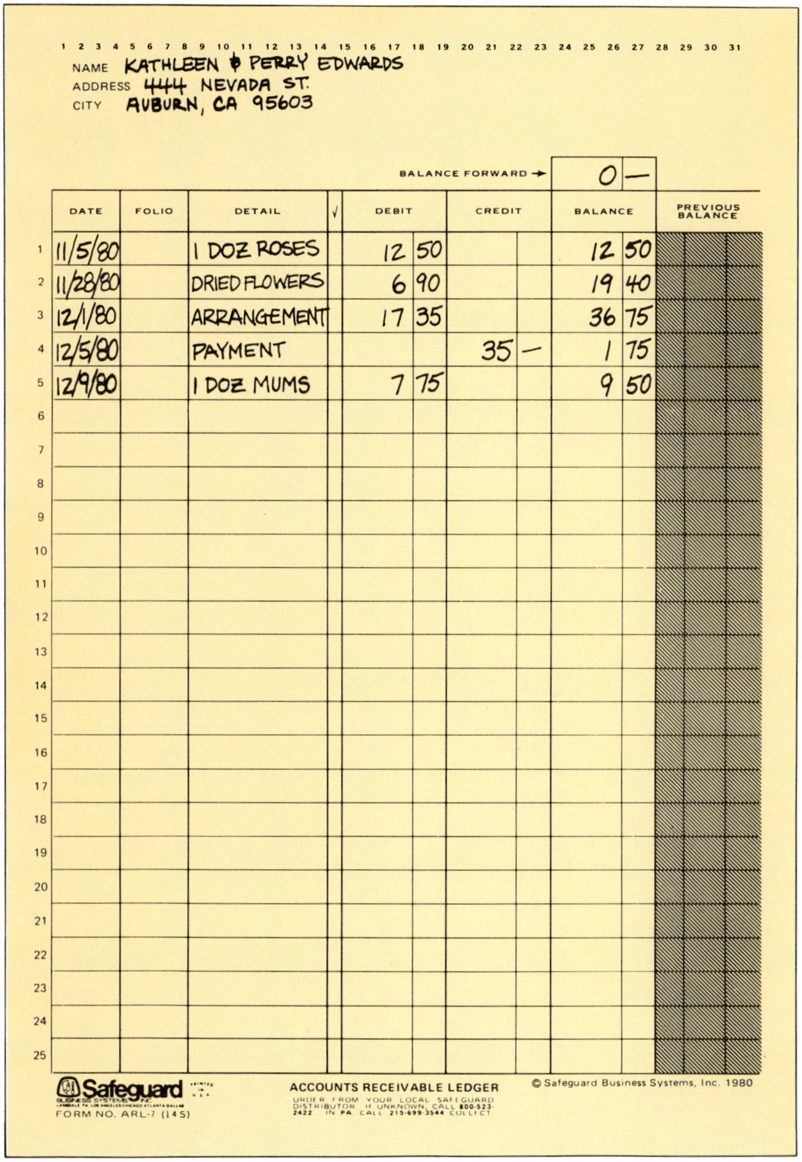

1 2 3 4 5 6 7 8 9 10 11 12 13 14 15 16 17 18 19 20 21 22 23 24 25 26 27 28 29 30 31

NAME KATHLEEN & PERRY EDWARDS
ADDRESS 444 NEVADA ST.
CITY AUBURN, CA 95603

BALANCE FORWARD → 0—

	DATE	FOLIO	DETAIL	√	DEBIT	CREDIT	BALANCE	PREVIOUS BALANCE
1	11/5/80		1 DOZ ROSES		12 50		12 50	
2	11/28/80		DRIED FLOWERS		6 90		19 40	
3	12/1/80		ARRANGEMENT		17 35		36 75	
4	12/5/80		PAYMENT			35 —	1 75	
5	12/9/80		1 DOZ MUMS		7 75		9 50	
6								
7								
8								
9								
10								
11								
12								
13								
14								
15								
16								
17								
18								
19								
20								
21								
22								
23								
24								
25								

Safeguard BUSINESS SYSTEMS INC.
FORM NO. ARL-7 (14S)

ACCOUNTS RECEIVABLE LEDGER
ORDER FROM YOUR LOCAL SAFEGUARD DISTRIBUTOR. IF UNKNOWN, CALL 800-523-2422. IN PA. CALL 215-699-3544 COLLECT

© Safeguard Business Systems, Inc. 1980

FIGURE 15–2 Ledger card.

FIGURE 15-3 Cost analysis.

Cost Factor	Cost Type	Alternative			
		Do Nothing	Buy Photocopy Machine	Buy Computer	Service Bureau
1. Equipment:					
a. Computer	One Time	0	0	2000.00	0
b. Disk	One Time	0	0	1,800.00	0
c. Printer	One Time	0	0	2,500.00	0
d. Terminal/CRT	One Time	0	0	250.00	1,700.00
e. Misc.	One Time	0	0	300.00	265.00
2. Software	One Time	0	0	650.00	1,000.00
3. Maintenance ($/mo)	Recurring	0	50.00	50.00	15.00
4. Photocopying 500 @ $.80	Recurring	400.00	0	0	0
5. Photocopy Machine	One Time	0	3,995.00	0	0
6. Computer Time	Recurring	0	0	0	190.00
7. Postage 500 @ $.15	Recurring	75.00	75.00	75.00	75.00
8. Posting of Charges/ Pay @ $5.00/hr	Recurring	100.00	100.00	80.00	80.00
9. Paper for Statements 500 @ $.02	Recurring	0	10.00	10.00	10.00
10. Past-due data Available		No	No	Yes	Yes
11. Statement has professional appearance		No	No	Yes	Yes
12. Meets Competition		No	No	Yes	Yes
13. Sum of One Time		$0	$3,995.00	$7,500.00	$2,965.00
14. Sum of Recurring		$575/mo	$235/mo	$215/mo	$360/mo

For the florist shop, the costs of each alternative are listed in Figure 15-3. Note that the sum of the one-time costs and the sum of the recurring or monthly costs differ greatly for each alternative. Some have high one-time costs (buying a computer); others have high monthly costs (service bureau); and some meet the perceived needs of the shop's owner (service bureau or buying a computer), while others solve none of the owner's perceived problems (do nothing).

Proposal

The fourth and final step in a systems analysis is a **proposal,** which reports the findings of the systems analyst. The proposal is a formal written document that presents all of the details and costs, and recommends a course of action. The proposal is reviewed by the management and user departments, and a final decision is made by the appropriate vice-president or president of the organization.

For the floral shop, the proposal would include copies of Figures 15-1, 15-2, and 15-3; the list of reasons why a change is wanted; some background information about this business; and a recommendation to rent computer time. Renting time is the best of the four alternatives since it meets all the perceived needs and has the lowest one-time cost and a monthly cost almost $200 less than the current cost. The monthly cost of renting time, $360, is larger than the monthly cost of buying a computer, $215; however, the difference, $145, is not enough to offset the difference in the sums of the one-time costs ($7,500 − $2,965 = $4,535).

DESIGN

The second step in the systems process is the designing of the new system. This second step starts only after the systems analysis approval and the approval of the recommendation made by the systems analyst. Systems design includes three phases: output forms design, data collection procedures, and file processing design.

Output Requirements

The first phase of systems design is to lay out the various reports that will be printed by the system. The format of the printed reports is depicted on a printer spacing chart that shows what data are to be printed and where on the page they are to be placed (Figure 15–4).

For our accounts receivable system there are two main reports—the statement to be sent to each customer (Figure 15–5), and the accounts receivable aging schedule (Figure 15–6). These printer spacing charts will later be used by the programmer when the programs are written. The charts also ensure that what was designed is produced exactly.

Figure 15–5 shows the design of the statement. Once the program is written to generate statements, the data themselves will be printed on a preprinted form (Figure 15–7). The statement must be readable, show all the pertinent charges, payments, and amounts. In an accounts receivable system, the statement is usually designed to tear into two parts. One part is kept by the customer and the other part, the remittance stub, is returned with the payment. Remittance stubs are less expensive than carbon copies, contain the customer account number, and are easy to handle and stuff into envelopes.

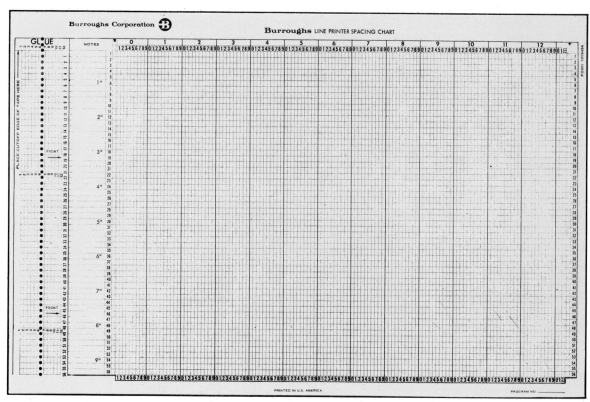

FIGURE 15–4   Printer spacing chart.

CHAPTER 15: SYSTEMS ANALYSIS

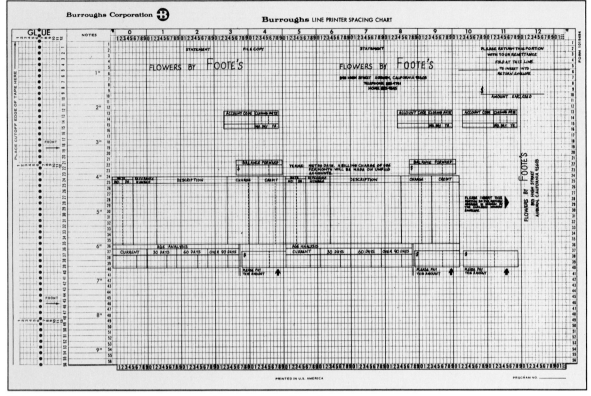

FIGURE 15-5 Customer statement drawn on a coding form.

The report shown in Figure 15-6 is the aging schedule, which used to be called the "aged trial balance." Its main purpose is to recap what various customers owe and indicate how old these debts are. The aging schedule can assist in collecting money from customers who are not paying their bills promptly.

Data Collection

The second phase of systems design is to determine what data need to be collected to give the two required reports and how these data are going to be collected.

In the florist shop, the analysis pointed to a CRT terminal located in the shop that would be used for data input purposes. The terminal's screen must be formatted to allow the user to:

1. Collect all the data about a new customer.
2. Post charges.
3. Post payments.
4. Change the data that are stored about a customer (for instance, if they move, a new address will be needed).

Figure 15-8 is an example of a screen format designed to collect the data about a charge. The screen has places reserved (represented by X's or 9's) to allow for the entry of the account number, date of purchase, a code number for kind of purchase, and the amount of the purchase. The form used for screen designs is similar to a printer spacing chart except that it has only 80 horizontal positions and 24 vertical lines. The screen design depends on the brand and model of CRT terminal that is used since terminals have different capabilities.

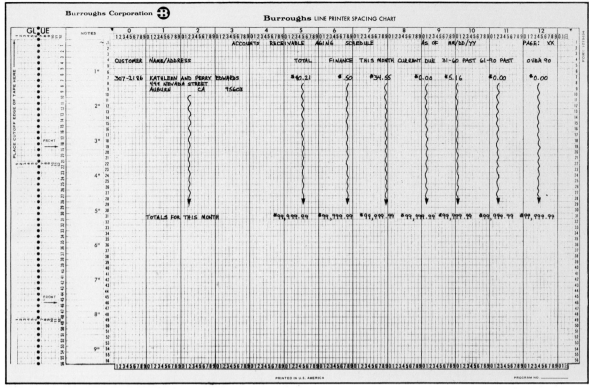

FIGURE 15-6   Accounts receivable aging schedule.

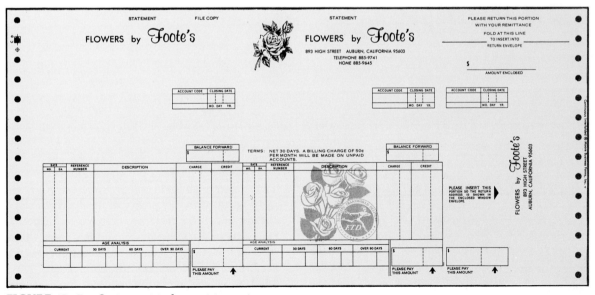

FIGURE 15-7   Statement to be sent to customers.

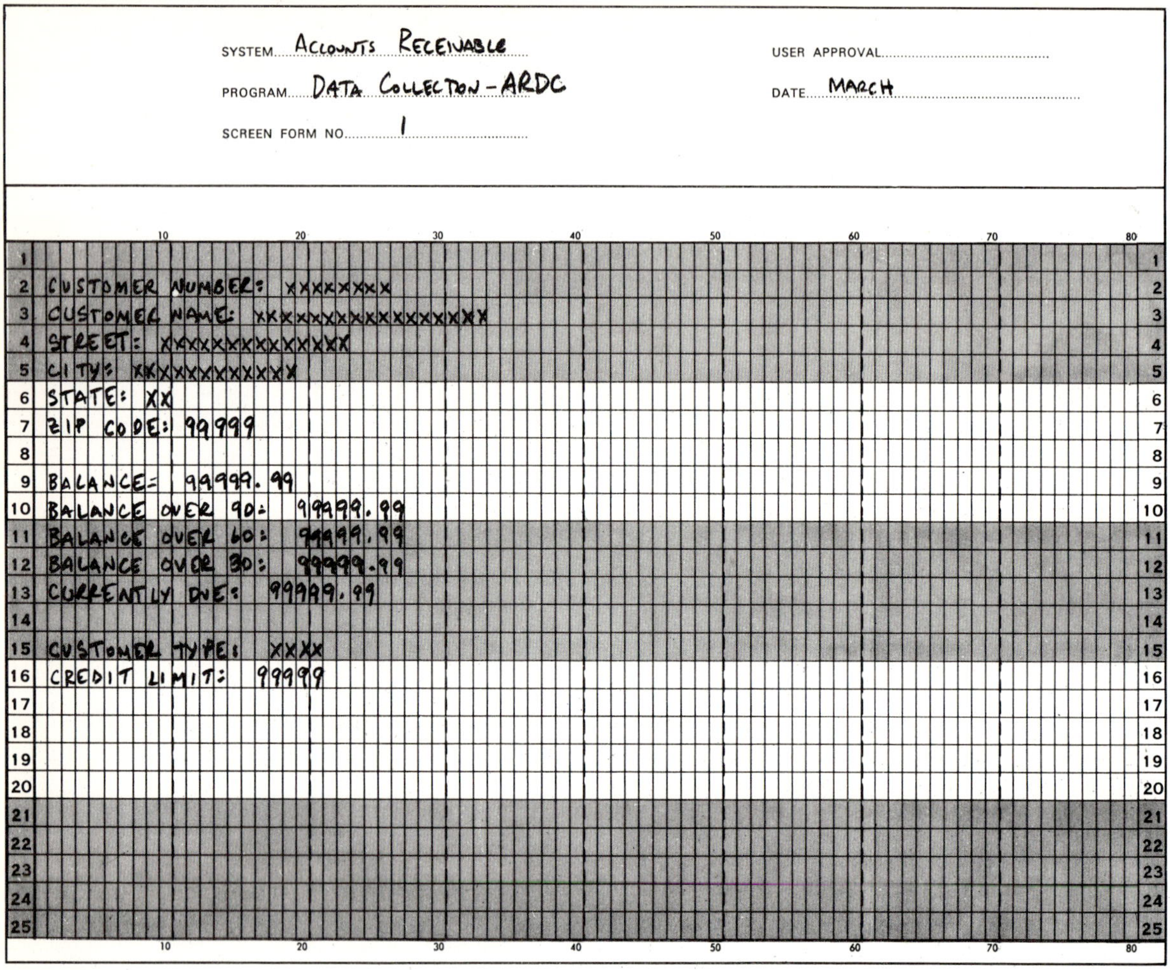

FIGURE 15–8 Screen lay-out to collect data.

Other factors considered in the data collection phase of systems design are the editing (or validating) requirements for the data being collected, the volume of data collected, and the frequency of data collection. For example, when the date of the purchase is entered, it must have a month number from 1 to 12, day number from 1 to 31, and a year number that is either the current year or the preceding one. Also, the account number must be checked to make sure it is for a customer that already exists. Dollar amounts should have two decimal places, and the code numbers for types of purchases should be within an acceptable set. Thus, for each charge or payment we have to enter and validate four quantities.

The analysis phase of the systems process should have determined some of the processing volume and suggested the frequency of data collection. We already know, for instance, that we can expect to have data on 5,000 customers and that there will be 500 purchases each month. In addition, we will need to collect the data on the 500 payments (hopefully) from the previous month. These volume figures indicate that 1,000 or so charges/payments will need to be entered each month, in addition to the data on any new customers and changes in the data on existing customers.

Thus, about 250 transactions per week can be expected, each transaction taking about 15 seconds (four quantities at 3 seconds each plus 3 seconds to prepare to enter the next transaction). Data entry, then, will require 3,750 seconds per week—a little over an hour.

File Design and Processing

The third and final phase in systems design concerns storing the data in a computer file and how the data will be processed. The analysis portion of the systems process indicated only that data will be stored. It did not show on what kind of a device, disk or tape, it would be stored. It also did not show the logical flow of events necessary to generate the desired reports, statements, and aging schedule.

The input design revealed that we need to store data about customers and their charges/payments. For each customer in our balance forward accounts receivable system we need to store the customer's account number, name, address, and various balances (Figure 15–9a). For each charge or payment, we need to store the customer's account number, date of purchase, code number, and amount (Figure 15–9b).

FIGURE 15–9 Data storage requirements for each customer.

Field Name	Field Type	Length	Number of Decimal Places
Customer last name	Alphabetic	15	0
Customer first name	Alphabetic	12	0
Customer middle initial	Alphabetic	2	0
Customer number	Numeric	8	0
Street address	Alphabetic	26	0
City	Alphabetic	14	0
State	Alphabetic	2	0
ZIP code	Numeric	5–9	0
Over 90 days	Numeric	8	2
Over 60 days	Numeric	8	2
Over 30 days	Numeric	8	2
Current charges	Numeric	8	2
Finance charges	Numeric	8	2
Balance of account	Numeric	8	2

a. master customer data set

Field Name	Field Type	Length	Number of Decimal Places
Customer number	Numeric	8	0
Date	Numeric	6	0
Amount	Numeric	6	2
Type of transaction	Alphabetic	1	0
Invoice number	Numeric	6	0

b. detail charge payment data set

The two data files together represent a **database**. In a large organization a special person may assist the systems analyst in designing files. This individual who specializes in file design is called a **database administrator (DBA)**. The database administrator may also recommend the use of a **database management system (DBMS)** to help control access to the data and keep the data relationships correct—linking the customer name-address-balance data with the charges/payments made by that customer. In a smaller business where there is no DBA, the systems analyst may function in this capacity. Today's computer systems are using DBMSs and DBAs more and more frequently, and the number of DBAs will increase even more in the future. DBMSs are found on large computer systems like the IBM 3081, Amdahl V8; medium-sized ones like Honeywell 66, Burroughs B6900; and mini-computers like HP 3000, PDP VAX 780.

The method of processing data depends on the file system used. Let's assume that our customer master file and charge/payment transaction (or detail) file are going to be managed by the IMAGE DBMS used on Hewlett-Packard computers (Figure 15–9). We need three programs in our accounts receivable system. The first program accepts data from the CRT terminal input device, validates them and updates the customer or charge/payment file. The second prints statements, and the third prints the aging schedule. Additional programs that print a list of customers in order by customer name or by account number can be written at some future date.

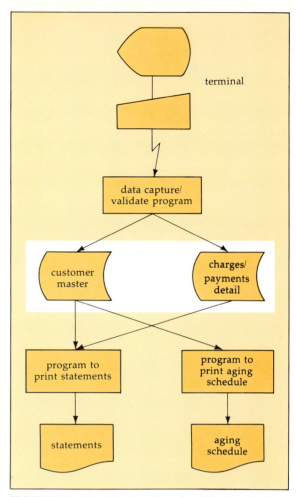

FIGURE 15–10   System flowchart for floral shop.

IMPLEMENTATION

The third and final step in the systems process is systems implementation. In this step programmers are assigned to write the needed programs; programs are tested to ensure their correctness; the staff that will be using the system is trained; any existing data are taken from the old system and converted to the new system; and, lastly, the new system is audited and evaluated. All of these activities are scheduled by the systems analyst, and this schedule of events is usually depicted with a Gantt chart (Figure 15–11).

Programming

The first phase in implementation is writing the required programs. The systems analyst develops a written set of specifications for each program that outlines exactly what that program is going to do. The program specifications usually include copies of the screen or printed report layouts, the format of the data files (base) that are to be read or written, and a copy of the system flowchart (Figure 15–10).

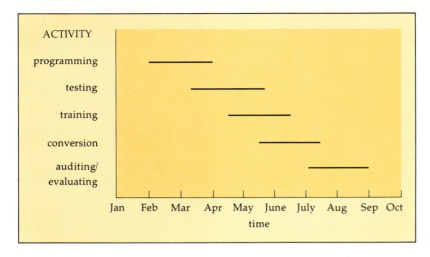

FIGURE 15-11   Gantt chart.

The programmer takes these specifications and writes the necessary programs. For most large organizations the programs will be written in COBOL. For smaller organizations the programs may be in BASIC, RPG, FORTRAN, or Pascal.

Testing

The **testing** phase of implementation takes old data that are now obsolete and processes them with the new programs. If no data exist, the programmer makes up false data and tests the programs with them. In either case, when the data appear to give the proper results the new system is ready for use.

Training

The third phase of implementation is training the staff in how to use the new system. The computer center operations staff must be shown what data files the system is going to use, and they need blank statement forms to put into the printer. They must be instructed when and how to run the programs that print the statements and aging schedule, and they have to be told what to do with these statements and aging schedule after they are finished.

The people who are going to use the CRT terminals to input data must also be trained. These people have to be shown how to use the terminal, how to key the data, what to do if the validation routine rejects their entry, and how to handle other problems that may occur.

The management of the business must be trained, too. The data now being provided are valuable and can help managers run the business more efficiently. Management should be shown that the accounts receivable aging schedule can help them prod their customers into paying their bills sooner. Quicker payments will help the business by providing needed cash for operating expenses.

Training is often overlooked in implementation, but the success or failure of the system can hinge on it (and on the resulting goodwill) just as much as on

"SURE YOU CAN BECOME A SYSTEMS ANALYST IF YOU WANT TO — BUT TELL DADDY, WHAT IS A SYSTEMS ANALYST?"

the skill of programmers, analysts, or database administrators.

Conversion

The changeover from the old system to the new is known as conversion. There are two approaches to conversion: parallel and direct. In a **parallel conversion**, the old system and the new one are in simultaneous operation for a short period. The results of the new system—the computer printed statements—are checked with those of the old—hand-posted ledger cards. If the results are the same, the old system is discarded and the new one takes its place. The advantage of parallel conversion is that a last test can be made of the new system. The primary disadvantage is that both systems must be operated concurrently, and this may be expensive.

Direct conversion means discarding the old system and using the new one immediately. Any errors that remain in the new system will be discovered during its operation on real data. Direct conversion is risky and is usually used on very small systems or on systems that are brand new.

Auditing, Evaluating, and Documentation

Once the new system is converted and in use, it should be examined to see if it is doing what it is supposed to do. This evaluation step is intended to see if the new system is actually meeting the needs that were originally expressed. Evaluation allows us to check the costs incurred relative to those estimated and to analyze any differences.

At this point, spot checks may be made to audit the data and ensure that they have not changed from entry time.

During the systems analysis, design, and implementation, a lot of paperwork has been generated. This paperwork is now formally put together into a **documentation report.** Included in the documentation are copies of the programs that were written, training materials that were developed for the operations and data entry staffs, the systems analysis report, system flowcharts, and so on. The system documentation is filed for future reference by other analysts and company personnel.

SUMMARY

There are three types of accounts receivable: balance only, balance forward, and open item. Each type differs in the kind of data that must be kept.

The systems process involves three steps: analysis, design, and implementation. Systems analysis involves investigating a business activity with a view toward finding a better way of performing it. Analysis also includes recommending a particular alternative as the best course of action.

Systems design involves building a new system. In this step the systems analyst specifies new reports, files, procedures, or programs that need to be developed or written.

The last step of the systems process is implementation. At this point the system is actually built. Programmers write the needed programs and, when these are completed, the new system is put into operation.

In many respects the systems process is like constructing a building. The owner of the property tells an architect (systems analyst) his or her wants or needs. The architect designs the building. Finally, the building is built and turned over to the owner.

TERMS

The following words or terms have been presented in this chapter.

Accounts receivable (AR)
Balance only
Balance forward
Open item
System
Systems analysis
Systems design
Systems implementation
Systems analyst

Proposal
Database
Database administrator (DBA)
Database management system (DBMS)
Testing
Parallel conversion
Direct conversion
Documentation report

EXERCISES

The exercises that follow are grouped by level of difficulty. Problems in the A series are the easiest; B series problems are moderately hard; and C series problems are the most difficult.

A-1 Why is the remittance stub attached to the statement?

A-2 Why is the customer's account number printed on both halves of Figure 15-7?

A-3 Which type of accounts receivable system does Sears Roebuck use? J. C. Penneys?

A-4 Make a list of at least four other uses of the word *system*.

B-1 Make a diagram like that in Figure 15-9 that depicts the customer master file for a balance only accounts receivable system.

B-2 Go to your computer center and find out if a DBMS is being used. Find out its name.

B-3 Design a screen similar to that in Figure 15-8 for use in collecting data on new customers.

C-1 Look through a recent issue of *Computerworld* and find the names of some other DBMS systems.

C-2 In Supplement A there is a series of programs describing a payroll system. Design a data collection screen for this system.

C-3 In Supplement A there is a series of programs describing an inventory system. Design a data collection screen for this system.

COMPUTER NEWS

SYSTEMS HOUSES: AN OPTION FOR SUCCESS

Suppose you're big, possibly the biggest, in a field whose companies typically are rather small. You have some unique problems. In an effort to solve them, you buy your own computer and enlist a data processing staff. That isn't enough. You buy a larger computer; then you struggle to find workable programs for it. No software package meets all your needs. You buy bits of software, devise more in-house, and improvise on the whole. Finally, you have to face up to the fact that you've created a very expensive junior-grade monster. It's too much, yet not enough. What to do?

Anthony Abraham Chevrolet, as you might suspect, is a Chevrolet dealership. Signs displayed on its sprawling property call it the world's largest Chevrolet dealership in retail sales. Perhaps it is—Chevrolet doesn't confirm or deny that claim. But there is no question that Abraham is big.

The dealership employs more than 350 people—not including those concerned with car leasing and rentals. In 1980, a recession year, the company sold roughly 12,000 new vehicles, delivering more than 30 each day. It sold more than 4,000 used cars. Add to that a thriving parts, service, and body business, and you have an operation generating sales of $120 million a year, roughly 15 percent of which is attributed to exports.

Abraham found in 1977 that its DEC (Digital Equipment Corp.) PDP-8, fitted with Sci-Data software, just wasn't enough. It replaced the machine with a DEC PDP-11/70, a unit capable of accommodating 40 to 50 terminals, with the idea of assigning all accounting, billing, and inventory control chores to it. The company then bought some programs and set its small data processing staff to work developing others. "You might say," says Abraham's vice president, Ronald A. Feldner, "we were going about it piecemeal."

The dealership's systems ran the gamut—parts inventory, parts invoicing, vehicle inventory, vehicle invoicing, payroll, merchandising programs, and, of course, a general ledger and accounting system. But early in 1979 the staff concluded that about the only thing living up to expectations was a vehicle billing system developed by Roxy Elliott, director of data processing.

"At that point," says Feldner, "we sat down and said, 'It's decision time. What're we going to do?'" Basic to the whole operation, he knew, was a general ledger accounting system. Should they spend the time and money necessary to develop it in-house, perhaps even changing computers again? Or should they try to buy a software package that would run on the hardware they already owned? Obviously the latter course would be more economical. But an extensive search for a suitable package revealed that the few software houses that provided automotive programs didn't come close to meeting the needs of an operation the size of Anthony Abraham.

There was, however, an interesting prospect in Business Data, a division of Wallace Business Forms, Inc. The Chicago-based systems house had made the computer needs of auto dealership a specialty, and it had developed an accounting system with which it serviced—on a timesharing basis—some 50 dealerships in the Chicago area. Furthermore, the system was designed to work on all DEC hardware in the PDP-11 series, so it could be run immediately on Abraham's PDP-11/70.

There was, of course, a hitch: the system, while considered excellent as an accounting device, wasn't geared to an operation of Abraham's size. It would have to be modified and expanded.

Abraham's Feldner and Elliott huddled with Business Data's general manager, Ernest Freudman, to think through some priorities. The accounting system was central to their objectives, they knew. Expanding was no problem, said Freudman. But what about Elliott's vehicle billing system, which the Abraham people considered the best they'd seen? Or the payroll and inventory systems already being developed by Abraham's in-house staff? Could they be salvaged? Freudman assured the Miamians they could be.

So what amounted to a turnkey package was worked out: Abraham would use its PDP-11/70 computer; the general ledger accounting system would undergo minor modifications so that it could handle the varied needs of the Abraham operation; the in-house systems for vehicle billing, parts inventory, parts invoicing, and payroll would be integrated completely with the accounting program; and a schedule would be worked out for adding other capabilities, to be devised jointly by Business Data and Abraham's five-man data processing team—all to be integrated with the central accounting program. "What we had," says Feldner, "was a lot of little satellites. What we needed was the hub—Business Data's general ledger system."

After running a dual system—the Business Data program along with the old Sci-Data program—for several months, Abraham switched over completely to the Business Data software on January 1, 1980.

Tying the package neatly together was a maintenance contract under which Business Data would service the Miami computer program from Chicago, using a dial-up port. "That sounds a little like Buck Rogers to the uninitiated," says Business Data's Freudman. "But it's very commonplace these days."

Simply put, Business Data maintains a Chicago terminal that's linked by telephone to a port (an input connection to the computer) at Abraham. If something goes wrong with the Miami system or if programming alterations are needed, members of Business Data's staff place a long-distance telephone call to the Miami port's number; they then feed in repair instructions or new data just as if they were on-site.

According to Ron Feldner, the most important thing Abraham bought was flexibility. Because all of Business Data's software has been developed to run on DEC's PDP-11 series, the Miami dealership can add standard software packages, modifying them when necessary to put them more in tune with its business volume. So before 1981 runs much more of its course, Abraham expects to incorporate considerably more Business Data software into its overall data processing system.

"We don't hesitate to have them modify their material," says Feldner. "That gives us tailor-made systems, even though Business Data isn't in the customizing business.

"Most software dealers can't, or won't, permit modifications. But, having our own data processing staff, we know what we want, and we can say to them, 'Let's change this to accomplish such and such.' We will have thought it through already and worked out any problems, so they don't have to analyze and test. Usually their answer is, 'We see what you need and, sure, we can change that.'

"A lot of companies get carried away with computers; they buy a system and hire data processing people, and then they tinker with it, trying to see what they can come up with. We don't play around. We start at Square 1: What is our objective and how do we achieve it?"

PROCESSING MODES AND DATA COMMUNICATIONS

Preview

Symbol Definition

Processing Modes

    Batch Processing: Single User,
    Remote Job Entry, Stacked Jobs
    Time-Sharing: Partition and Swapping Methods
    Multiprogramming: Fixed and Variable Partitioning
    Multiprocessing
    Virtual Memory

Data Communications

    Data Communications Terminals
    Modems
    Acoustic Coupler
    Interfaces
    Carriers, Lines, and Channels

History Capsule: People in Communications

    Transmission Modes
    Multiplexing
    Line Configurations
    Communications Protocols
    Data Communications Alternatives
    Computer Networks
    Distributed Processing

Off-Line, On-Line, and Real-Time Processing

Summary

Computer News: Electronic "Copy Boy" Hired by Texas Daily

PREVIEW

If you want to travel from one place to another, you have many alternate means of transportation. You can use a car or take a taxi, bus, train, or airplane. The car could be rented or bought. If you choose to drive your own car, but do not own one, you have to decide what particular type or brand you should buy. Is it to be a subcompact, a compact, intermediate, or full-sized? Is it to have many or few options? Is it to be a foreign-made or a domestic model? Is it to be sedan, station wagon, or van? The alternatives to consider and the decisions to be made are almost endless.

So it is in information processing. There are many alternate approaches to processing data. In this chapter we examine a wide variety of computerized information processing approaches and consider their strengths, weaknesses, similarities, and differences. The discussion should provide you with a frame of reference for viewing a computer system.

Usually no single need can dictate the choice of computer system and the total needs of a user do not always dictate the use of a computer; some process-

---

FIGURE 16–1 Term/figure definition.

Term	Symbol	Definition
arithmetic/logic unit	ALU	The portion of the computer that performs arithmetic and makes decisions.
control unit	control	The portion of the computer that decodes program instructions, sets up the appropriate circuitry to execute the particular instruction, and transfers data to and from the desired locations within the computer.
memory	memory	The portion of the computer that receives, temporarily stores, and then transmits data during an information processing job.
central processing unit	CPU	The major internal processing portion of the computer. Consists of the ALU, CONTROL, and MEMORY.
operating system	OS	The instructions (programs usually provided by the manufacturer of the computer) that supervise the computer during processing of user's program.
user program(s)	Prog or Program A / Program B / Program C	The program(s) the computer uses to process particular user data according to specific desired procedures and sequences.

ing is best accomplished by hand or, at most, by devices that are less sophisticated than computers. The needs of a potential user of data processing can be analyzed in terms of frequency, volume, and type of processing, physical location of the processor, and by many other criteria.

As an example of a match between user need and processing system, imagine a small savings association of 1,000 savers. The cost of owning or renting a computer for the association's exclusive use is likely to be prohibitively high. However, the part-time use of an existing computer system that was designed to handle processing for another savings association's customers' accounts might be economical. In this case, a small-scale business computer could process depositors' transactions for one savings association during part of the day, and the other association's transactions during the remaining time.

A second example is an engineering firm that occasionally (maybe five times a day) needs 1 to 10 minutes of computer time to process surveying data. At that low usage rate it would be uneconomical to own a computer. However, a terminal could connect the engineer-user to a computer by telephone connection. The computer would process the

FIGURE 16–1   Term/figure definition (continued).

Term	Symbol	Definition
data file		A group of transactions or records being input to or output from the computer.
input/output device	I/O	A general description that can represent an input or output, or a combination input/output, device.
punch card input device		A device that reads data from a punched card and transmits them to a central processing unit.
on-line storage device		A magnetic data storage device that is electronically connected to the CPU. Generally stores user data, user programs, and/or operating system.
data flow line		Shows flow or movement of data within the computer system.
rotary switch		An electronic rotary switching of data to two or more input/output devices. The solid flowline indicates flow of data to the I/O device presently being serviced. The broken flowline represents flow of data in the past or future.
modem		An electronic device that converts business machine data codes to sound that can be transmitted by phone. Conversely, a modem converts sound back to business machine data codes.

survey data, send back results to be printed on the terminal, and then be disconnected. The firm is charged only for the value of the computer time actually used.

As we examine the many approaches to computerized information processing, we will find it helpful to describe them in diagrams as well as in words.

SYMBOL DEFINITION

For purposes of clarity and simplicity, we need to define some terms and describe the symbols we will be using to explain the various processing approaches graphically (Figure 16–1).

PROCESSING MODES

We will explore a wide variety of information processing systems. The systems range from small computers that process one job at a time to large ones that simultaneously process a number of jobs. We examine a system that effectively expands memory to many times its actual capacity. And we discuss tying computers into distant computers and/or terminals. Finally, we examine processing systems in terms of their responsiveness: from systems that require considerable human involvement and, hence, are slow to respond to information need, to those that require no human interaction and respond immediately.

Batch Processing: Single User, Remote Job Entry, Stacked Jobs

When transaction data are collected and held until we have a large group of transactions that are then processed as a group, we are **batch processing** (see Chapter 10). Assume a business accumulates sales slips throughout the business day, and at the end of the day inputs all the sales slips to the computer for processing (see Figure 16–2). The batch processing method is appropriate when results are not required immediately after a transaction.

Small-scale business computers generally can execute only one program at a time. Thus, if several batches of transaction data are being processed, the batches are handled sequentially (Figure 16–3).

In the batch processing illustration (Figure 16–3), the symbol

indicates the inflow of data to the computer. The symbol

indicates that program A is being used to process A data. Finally, the symbol

shows that the end product of the processing is flowing from the computer to an output device such as magnetic tape drive, printer, or CRT. This process is repeated until all of A's data are input, processed, and output. Once program A is completed, program B can be started. No parts of any two programs are performed simultaneously.

The series of batches of data, such as those shown in Figure 16–3 (A data file, B data file, and C data file) can be processed without operator intervention. With proper instructions to the operating system, program A is executed; upon its completion, program B is automatically begun. When program B is completed, the next program is executed. This process is controlled by instructions in what is sometimes referred to as **job control language (JCL)**.

The input or output devices in batch processing may be at the same physical location as the CPU or many miles away, with data being transmitted by telephone lines. Most often the I/O devices are located at the same site as the CPU. When I/O devices are located apart from the CPU, the procedure is called **remote job entry (RJE)**. Under this arrangement the I/O devices are not permanently connected

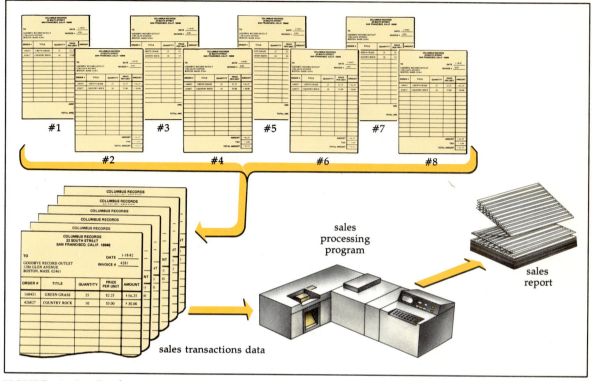

FIGURE 16–2 Batch processing of sales data.

to the CPU. Generally, the physical connection between them is made through telephone lines (Figure 16–4). As a batch of data is accumulated, the remote I/O devices (or **remote job entry station**) are connected to the distant CPU. The CPU then receives and processes the data and transmits the results to the output portion of the RJE station.

Look at Figure 16–4, and note that a single RJE station (see Figure 16–5) may consist of input devices such as:

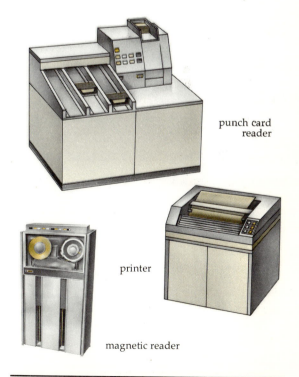

CHAPTER 16: PROCESSING MODES

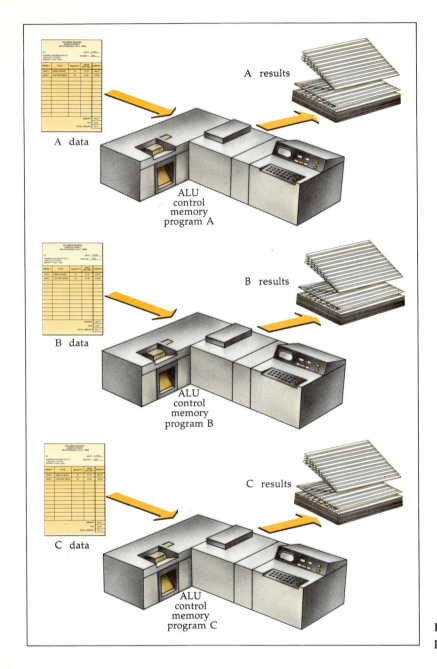

FIGURE 16-3 Batch processing in series.

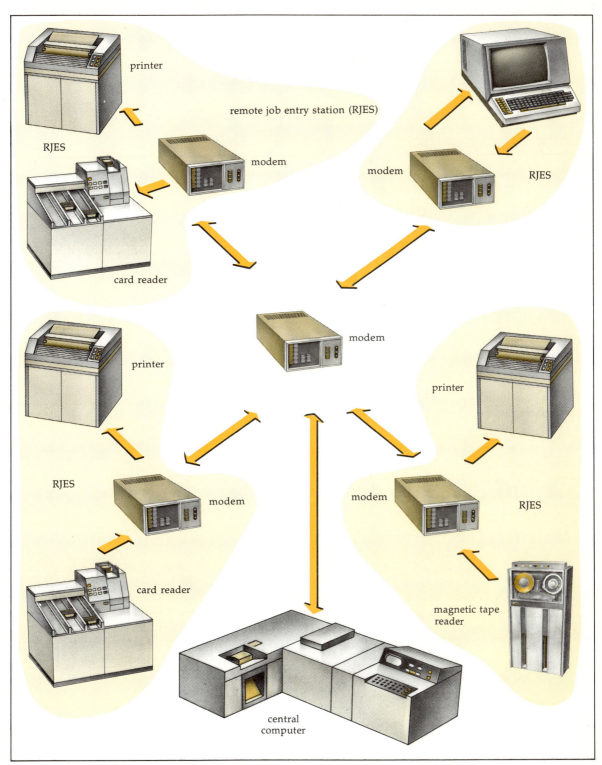

FIGURE 16-4 Remote job entry diagram.

FIGURE 16-5 A remote job entry station.

The I/O devices are connected to the computer through a connecting device called a **modem,** symbolized as:

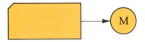

Within an RJE station, data are read by an input device and sent to the modem:

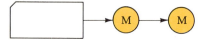

The modem then changes the digital machine codes into sound signals that are transmitted over the telephone lines to the central computer's modem:

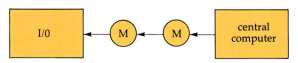

The modem attached to the central computer then changes the sound back into digital machine codes and sends these codes to the central computer's input device:

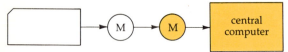

When the computer has processed the data, the results are sent back to the RJE station's output device via the telephone connection, using the opposite procedure.

If the central computer is truly a batch computer, only one RJE station can be handled at a time. However, in some RJE systems, the central computer is more complex and can process more than one RJE station or program at a time.

Time-Sharing: Partition and Swapping Methods

When two or more users utilize a single CPU almost simultaneously and have equal use of the CPU's resources, it is called **time-sharing** (Figure 16–6). Time-sharing is accomplished in such a way that a user is unaware that any other users are on the system. To do this, an electronic switch sequentially connects the CPU in a rotary pattern to one user, then another, and another, and so on. The time during which a particular user is connected to and being serviced by the CPU is called a **time slice.** This predetermined time slice may be as short as 0.005 sec.

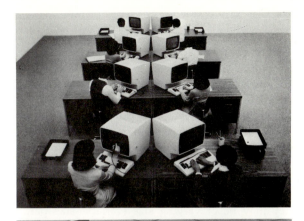

FIGURE 16–6 A time-sharing system.

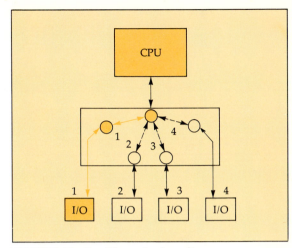

FIGURE 16–7 Time-sharing diagram.

In Figure 16–7, flowline number 1 shows that the data flow is currently between the CPU and I/O device 1. After the current time slice, the switch will disconnect flowline 1 and connect flowline 2, and data will flow between the CPU and I/O device 2. This pattern will continue until I/O device 4 has been serviced; the switch will then connect I/O device 1 for another time slice. The speed with which each I/O device receives its turn at the CPU is so great that an I/O device is rarely delayed. This is because of the relatively high operating speed of the CPU and the relatively low operating speed of I/O devices.

There is one other major aspect of a time-sharing computer. The CPU must be able to store each user's program, data, and partial results during the interruption and must resume processing each user's program at the point where it was interrupted. Two major approaches are available to process each program completely and with continuity, in spite of such frequent interruptions.

By dividing memory into as many sections as there are users, the CPU is able to process a particular user's program, data, and partial results as needed. Time-sharing by **partitioning** of memory is illustrated in Figure 16–8.

The solid flowline in the rotary switch within the control unit shows how I/O device 1 is connected with partition 1 in memory. Program 1 can then use the arithmetic/logic and control units. When I/O device 1's time slice is over, the solid flowline will be set so that I/O device 2 is connected with memory space 2. This pattern is repeated on through 3 and 4, and then user 1 is serviced again.

The partitioning of memory can be altered to give certain users larger or smaller spaces in memory as their needs dictate. Called **dynamic partitioning,** this method is generally used on large systems.

Time-sharing systems usually use a direct access storage device such as a magnetic disk to hold the programs, data, and intermediate results of each user during the time he or she is not receiving a time slice. This process frees memory space, thus allowing user programs to be much larger. When

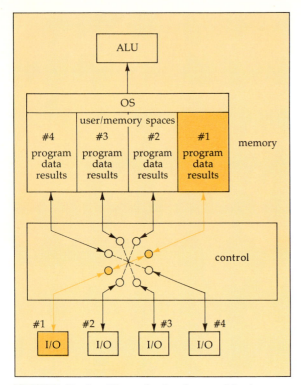

FIGURE 16–8 Time-sharing by partitioning.

Multiprogramming: Fixed and Variable Partitioning

With time-sharing systems, each user is serviced on a schedule, each taking a turn, and each user has equal use of the CPU's resources. Other computer systems are designed to process programs on a more flexible schedule. These computer systems are called **multiprogramming** and **multiprocessing systems.** In a multiprogramming system, memory may be subdivided in much the same way as the partitioning illustrated in Figure 16–8. The divisions may be all the same size (fixed-size partitions) or they may be of varying size (variable-size partitions). However, the similarity ends here.

In most multiprogramming systems, the user assigns a higher priority to the processing of one program than to all others. That high priority program then has freedom to make use of the arithmetic/logic unit and I/O devices at any time. In a procedure called an **interrupt,** the program with higher priority can usurp the use of any needed input or output device or the arithmetic/logic unit that a lesser priority program is using. The highest priority program is stored in the portion of memory called the **foreground memory** or partition, and the lesser priority program(s) is stored in the **background memory** or partition(s). Since the decision as to which program is to be processed at any given time must be made repeatedly, the operating system's decision-making or control program must also reside in memory. Memory for fixed-size partition systems is illustrated in Figure 16–10.

Actually, not all of the operating system is in memory at any one time. A direct access device such as a magnetic disk is used to store the complete operating system. Portions of the operating system, called **segments** or **overlays,** that contain the currently needed instructions are brought to memory, replacing the previous segment.

When the foreground program (which has priority) needs an input or output device, the operating system receives an interrupt signal. The foreground program then uses the I/O device it needs. When the foreground program no longer needs that device, the operating system directs the interrupted pro-

user 1's time slice comes, for instance, the program, data, and intermediate results are pulled into the user memory space from user 1's space on magnetic disk (see Figure 16–9). When user 1's time slice is over, the program, data, and intermediate results are stored back on magnetic disk, and user 2's respective information is brought into memory. Time-sharing in this manner is called **swapping.** It allows each user the total memory space not required by the operating system. However, in order to use the swapping system, an on-line mass storage device must be included in the computer system. A side benefit of having such a mass storage device is that programs and data files not currently in use can be stored on the device for later use. A disadvantage of the swapping system is that the operating system becomes more complex, and a mechanical device (the disk drive) adds to maintenance and purchase costs.

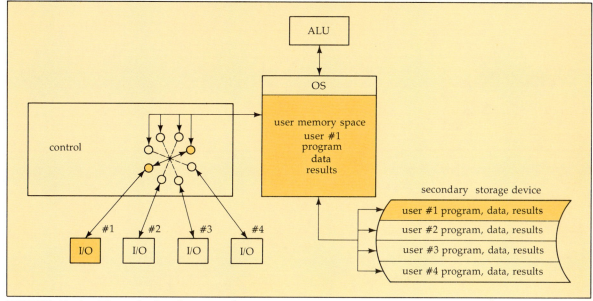

FIGURE 16–9   Time-sharing by swapping.

gram to its next logical instruction. Processing of the interrupted program then resumes.

As an illustration, suppose that a multiprogramming computer system is set up as shown in Figure 16–11. The speed of each I/O device is noted next to it. Suppose the computer is to execute two programs. The first is a payroll program that reads cards containing hours worked and rate of pay, calculates the gross pay, and prints a paycheck. This is shown diagramatically in Figure 16–12. The compu-

tations required would be a few multiplications and some subtractions, which take 0.2 sec.

The second program is a data validation routine. Data have been prepared on a key-tape device and will be checked by the computer before they are actually processed. If the individual items of data are correct, they will be written onto magnetic disk. Incorrect data items will be displayed to the computer operator. Figure 16–13 illustrates this program.

Figure 16–14 shows the computer system executing the two programs in a multiprogramming mode. The illustration shows a time span over which both programs alternately use the CPU. During time frame 0 to 0.1 sec the payroll program initiates a card read. During this same period, an interrupt signal detected by the operating system allows the background program to be read from tape, and it begins to validate data. At time 0.1 sec, the foreground program card input is completed and the interrupt delays the background program and starts calculating the payroll information. From time 0.1 to 0.3, the foreground routine has full use of the CPU. During time frame 0.3 to 0.4 sec,

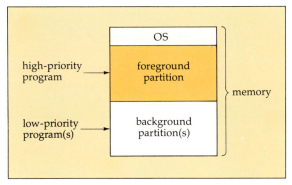

FIGURE 16–10   Multiprogramming diagram.

CHAPTER 16: PROCESSING MODES   381

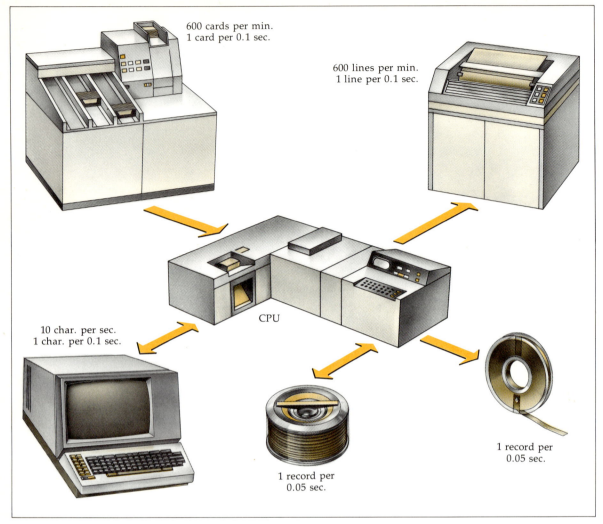

FIGURE 16–11   Multiprogramming CPU and its I/O devices.

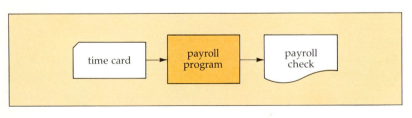

FIGURE 16–12   Payroll program.

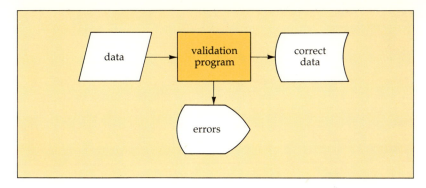

FIGURE 16–13 Validation program.

foreground outputs a payroll check. This output allows work to resume on the background program and output on its results to be recorded on the disk. At time 0.4 sec the cycle is completed. Both programs have read and processed one record or transaction. The computer, coupled with its operating system, has run two jobs in what appears to be the same time span. Note that during time frame 0 to 0.05 sec, both routines were using the I/O devices simultaneously. With more memory and an additional interrupt, a third program could have been processed by the CPU.

A multiprogramming environment allows programs to be processed at a lower cost per program, but problems arise if both programs require the same I/O device (for example, a printer) simultaneously. To alleviate this, the operating system diverts the output of the background program to disk. The data that would be printed are temporarily stored there until the foreground program is completed. At this point, the operating system has the disk-stored data printed. The temporary diversion and recalling of data output is called **spooling**. Spooling is a prime requirement in a multiprogramming computer system like that in Figure 16–15.

Multiprocessing

In contrast to multiprogramming systems that use a common CPU (arithmetic/logic, control, and memory), a multiprocessing system has separate arithmetic/logic and control units called **processors**. All processors share the memory and operating system. On some of the larger multiprocessing sys-

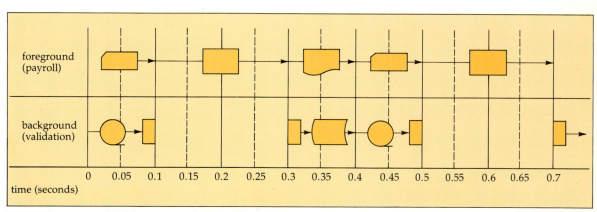

FIGURE 16–14 Multiprogramming and interrupts.

FIGURE 16-15   A multiprogramming computer system.

tems, a separate processor may direct the activities of the other processors (see Figure 16-16). In multiprocessing systems, as many separate instructions can be executed as there are individual processors. Thus, a four-processor system can execute four separate instructions simultaneously. Multiprocessor systems can also do multiprogramming. For example, the two jobs (payroll and validation) illustrated in the discussion on multiprogramming could be processed along with two additional jobs on a multiprocessing system without interrupting the CPUs.

Virtual Memory

With the advent of faster hardware and special operating systems, the user can now view the internal storage or memory as being virtually unlimited in size. These special operating and related hardware systems are called **virtual memory systems** or **virtual storage systems.** To accomplish the appearance of unlimited memory, the operating system divides a user's program into sections called **pages.** Pages are stored on a direct access storage device such as magnetic disk and are called into memory by the operating system as needed. After the page is used, it is written back on the magnetic disk and another page is called in from disk and stored in memory where the prior page was located. The total space required for all the pages that make up a program may be much larger than the physical internal memory, but this presents no problem since only a portion of the program will be in memory at a time. More efficient use of memory is possible with virtual memory since the pages of a program need not be stored in sequential order, which is the way they were written in the program. They are simply inserted by the operating system wherever they will fit. Parts of the program that are used over and over again are repeatedly called in from a direct access device, so it is vital that the direct access device operate at a very high speed.

Figure 16-17 depicts a computing system that operates in a virtual memory mode. Note that page 13 is being written out to disk (time span 1), page 14 is being read into memory (time span 2), and page 32 is being written out to disk (time span 3). This shuttling of pages between primary memory and direct access storage is called "paging." The pages in the figure are numbered 1 to 42, but the pages are from several separate programs. Virtual storage provides for a more efficient multiprogramming computer system since pages from a number of programs may reside in memory and be executed concurrently. When programmers write programs, they need not concern themselves with the limited size of primary memory or with how they might break the program into sections—the virtual memory operating system automatically divides the program into pages and then brings into memory only as many pages of the program as are needed at one time. A program might consume several hundred thousand bytes of disk space, but at no time use more than 20,000 bytes of primary memory.

DATA COMMUNICATIONS

In remote batch processing a tie is made between the computer and a remote site where data have

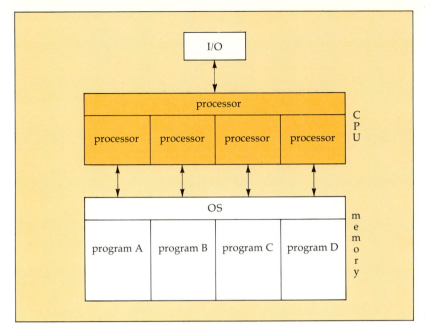

FIGURE 16–16 Multiprocessing diagram.

been collected. The data are transmitted to the computer and processed, and the resulting information sent by the computer back to the remote site. This process of transmission, processing, and distribution of information using computers and telecommunication facilities is called **data communications.**

Let's explore data communications in greater detail. We will examine the components of a data communications system and consider the implications of rapid worldwide expansion of these systems.

Data Communications Terminals

Any device that transmits or receives computer data via telecommunications is considered a **data communications terminal.** The terminal may be a CRT or hard-copy device or even another computer. Other devices that serve as terminals in a data communications system are point-of-sale terminals, remote job entry stations, process control sensors, and plotters. Data communications terminals have four functions that are not obvious to the user:

input control, output control, error checking, and synchronization.

Input control receives a signal from the computer indicating that a message is to follow. Input control then receives the message, stores it in a buffer (a temporary holding space), and then transfers the message to the terminal's output mechanism at whatever speed the mechanism can handle.

Output control accepts information from the terminal's input mechanism (such as a keyboard) and stores it in a buffer. Upon a signal from the computer, output control transmits the information in a rapid burst as a sequential stream of data bits.

Error checking involves checking the number of bits in each character as it arrives, or checking the whole message to determine that all the bits that were transmitted have arrived.

Just as musicians in an orchestra must "keep in time" with each other, the transmitter and receiver (the computer and the terminal or vice versa) must "keep in time" or be **synchronized.** This synchronization must be maintained for the duration of the message. Synchronization can be accomplished by

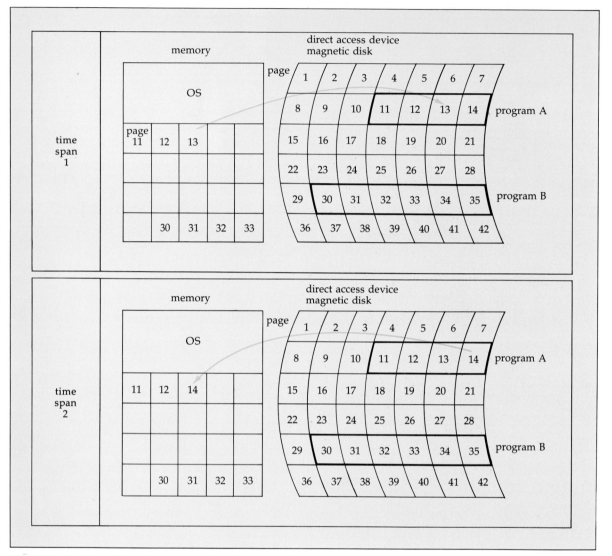

FIGURE 16-17 Virtual storage and paging.

clock circuitry or by timing data inserted into the message.

A data communications terminal may be used in close proximity to the computer by connecting a cable directly from the computer to the terminal. This direct connection is called **hardwired.** Or the terminal may be a mile or thousands of miles away—too great a distance for hardwiring. In this case a telecommunications line is used to connect the computer to the remote terminal.

Modems

Computer terminals and computers themselves transfer information in digital format, sending and/or receiving a series of electrical pulses along a wire. Each pulse may be one of two voltages, one voltage representing a binary zero and the other representing a binary one (see Figure 16-18). In contrast, telephone lines carry information in an analog format, continuously varying in voltage and frequency (see Figure 16-19). Thus, it is necessary

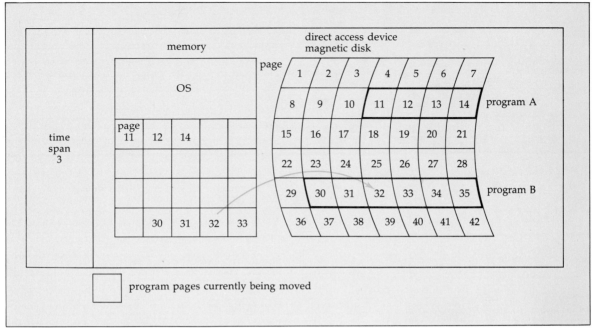

FIGURE 16–17   *Continued*

to convert digital data into analog format for transmission over telephone lines. This conversion is performed by a device called a **modem** (see Figure 16–20). The word *modem* is a contraction of the two functions it performs: **modulation** and **demodulation**. Modulation indicates that the digital pulses are being placed onto (modulating) an electromagnetic carrier wave (see Figure 16–21). As the information in modulated form leaves the telephone line, it must be demodulated—that is, converted back to the digital format of the terminal or computer (see Figure 16–22).

Earlier in this chapter we indicated that terminals must be synchronized with the receiving computer for the duration of each message. Actually, modems may operate in two ways: *synchronous* or *asynchronous*.

A synchronous modem transmits characters (such as C × 4 B u 0 3 ? #. E) in continuous stream, with no intervals between each character. Each character is sent at a precisely timed moment. The synchronous receiving modem expects a continuous stream of characters (see Figure 16–23) from the sending modem.

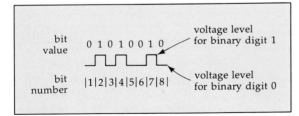

FIGURE 16–18   Two-level voltage pattern for representing an 8-bit character.

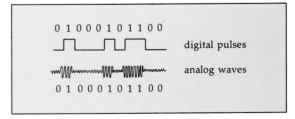

FIGURE 16–19   Comparison of digital and analog transmission of 11 bits.

FIGURE 16–20 Modem.

Asynchronous modems operate at random speeds, depending on the speed of the stream of digital pulses coming from the terminal. For example, with a keyboard terminal the flow of data will coincide with the striking of the keys—and that striking is far from perfectly timed. With this somewhat random speed of characters flowing from the terminals, the beginning and ending of the character must be identified by some method other than timing. A **start bit** signifies the beginning of character and a **stop bit** indicates the ending of the character (see Figure 16–24). Notice the random time intervals between each of the three 8-bit characters.

Asynchronous modems usually operate with nonbuffered keyboard terminals. By "nonbuffered" we mean there is no memory to hold the keyed-in data, so each character must be transmitted immediately after being keyed. Speeds of asynchronous modems are typically 2,400 bits per second (bps) or less. Synchronous modems can handle speeds up to 9,600 bps.

Acoustic Coupler

In many situations where a terminal is used there is no modem connected directly to the telephone line. In these cases a standard telephone can be used if a combination device containing a modem and telephone adapter called an **acoustic coupler** is available (see Figure 16–25). When a terminal transmits to a remote computer via the sending modem, acoustic coupler, telephone lines, and destination modem, the following steps are involved (see Figure 16–26):

1. The terminal outputs digital pulses to the sending modem.

2. The sending modem modulates the digital pulses to an analog carrier wave.

3. Carrier waves are received by the acoustic coupler, which converts the waves to audio tones.

4. Audio tones enter the mouthpiece of the telephone handset and are converted back to analog carrier waves for transmission over telephone lines.

5. At the destination computer center, a telephone line feeds analog carrier waves into the modem for demodulation.

6. The modem sends digital pulses into the computer.

Using an acoustic coupler and modem, a terminal simply needs your home telephone in order to gain access to computers anywhere around the world.

Interfaces

Whether a terminal is hardwired or connected via modems, acoustic couplers, and telephones, the various devices must be physically connected. Furthermore, so that modems can be interchanged, it is

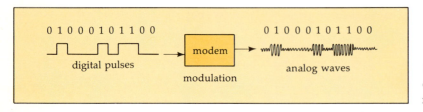

FIGURE 16–21 A modem converts digital data into analog format.

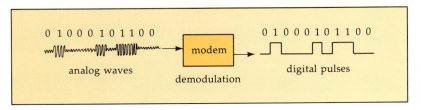

FIGURE 16–22 A modem converts analog data into digital format.

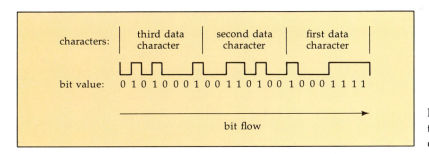

FIGURE 16–23 Synchronous transmission of three 8-bit characters.

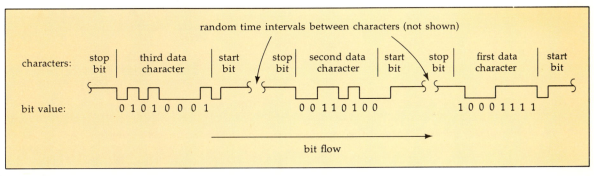

FIGURE 16–24 Asynchronous transmission of three 8-bit characters.

FIGURE 16–25 Acoustic coupler.

vital that a standard interconnection be used. The connecting plugs and outlets, together with their predetermined wiring arrangement, are called **interfaces**. A standard interface for North America that was adopted by the Electronics Industries Association (EIA) and that is closely followed is the **EIA RS232C Standard** (see Figure 16–27). This standard specifies a 25-pin connector with lettered pins for ground, data, control, and timing circuits. The RS232C also specifies mechanical and electrical requirements of the interface.

CHAPTER 16: PROCESSING MODES

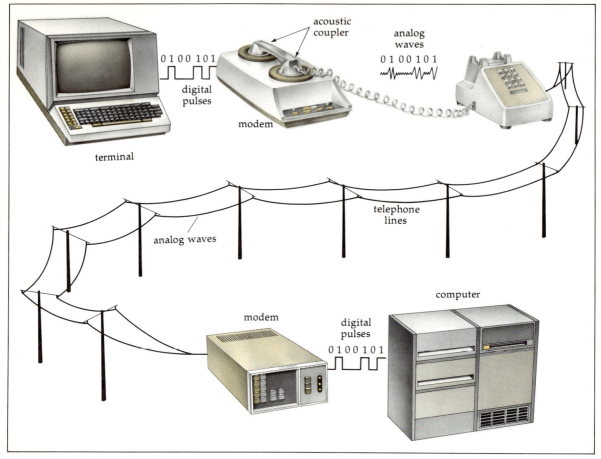

FIGURE 16–26 Data communication from remote terminal that uses an acoustic coupler.

FIGURE 16–27 EIA RS232C standard interface 25-pin outlet and plug.

In Europe the International Telegraph Telephone Consultative Committee (CCITT) standard interface is used. It is called the **CCITT V24 standard** and closely resembles the EIA RS232C.

The term *interface* is also used to describe the electronic circuits that are used to adapt two devices whose timing and/or coding procedures differ. Such interfacing may exist between parts within the computer—for example, between the memory unit and the data bus; or an interface board may be required between a computer and a peripheral device such as a printer or magnetic disk.

Carriers, Lines, and Channels

A communication **carrier** is a provider of transmission services. American Telephone and Telegraph is the largest voice and data communications carrier. However, there are many other carriers that are less well known and offer less extensive services.

Lines and channels in data communications are somewhat analogous to highways and lanes. Just as a highway may carry traffic in two directions, so may data communication lines. And, similar to highways that may have several traffic lanes in each direction, a data communication line can handle several or many parallel channels of data flow. A **line** is the physical equipment used in telecommunications. Carrying the highway analogy further, a highway may cover roads, bridges, tunnels, and even ferries over water. So it is with telecommunication lines; they may consist of wires, cables, microwave relays, and other media. The wire, cable, and microwave relay, all linked together in series, form the line. A **channel** is a path within a line through which information flows.

Making up a large portion of our existing telecommunications network are the standard telephone wires called **twisted wire pairs** that run from your telephone to the telephone exchange (or switching center). Most computer-to-remote-terminal communications use wire pairs at some point along the line.

Most long-distance voice and data communications travel on **coaxial cable.** A coaxial cable consists of up to 20 tubes that are bundled inside each other, all having the same center. (See Figure 16–28.) A coaxial cable can transmit data at a much higher speed than standard wire pairs. Underground and underocean cable are generally coaxial.

Coaxial cables are often tied to **microwave relay** systems that transmit data in analog format. The systems consist of antennas on towers spaced about 30 miles apart in a grid that spreads across the country. Each tower contains amplifying equipment to strengthen the received signals and pass them on to the next tower. (See Figure 16–29.) Because microwaves do not bend with the curvature of the earth, each tower must be in line-of-sight of the next. In the United States, MCI Communications

FIGURE 16–28 Coaxial cable.

Corp., SP Communications Company, and ITT all offer microwave relay communications on a fee basis.

A variation of the microwave relay tower system is a **communications satellite** that orbits 23,000

FIGURE 16–29 Microwave relay station.

CHAPTER 16: PROCESSING MODES 391

PEOPLE IN COMMUNICATIONS

Many scientists believe that more than 65 million years ago our ancestors were communicating by gesture and sound. But it wasn't until about 5,000 years ago that humans began communicating by written symbols. Mass communication began with the Gutenberg press circa 1450. In the 530 years since Gutenberg, communication between people has grown tremendously; communication between people and machines has developed; and now machine-to-machine communication is common. Several men are recognized for their contributions to this tidal wave of communication that has swept us up.

"I see no reason why intelligence may not be transmitted instantaneously," stated Samuel Morse in 1832. Just 12 years later, on May 24, 1844, Morse achieved that feat as he tapped out the first telegraph message; it traveled from the United States Supreme Court Chambers in Washington, D.C., to the Baltimore and Ohio Railroad station in Baltimore, Maryland, 40 miles away. His message, traveling over iron wire, read, "What hath God wrought?" This electrical exchange of information set the stage for another development.

Electrical communications between people by voice began in 1876 when Alexander Graham Bell spoke into the first telephone the words "Mr. Watson, come here, I want you."

And developments did not cease. In 1894 at age 20, Italian inventor Guglielmo Marconi heard of a method of transmitting and receiving an electromagnetic wave through the air. He determined to put these waves to practical use by devising a method of using them to transmit messages. Not able to get support for his efforts from the Italian government, Marconi moved to England where he obtained his first radio patent in 1896 and transmitted a signal over nine miles. With funding from the British government and businesses, Marconi developed a radio used in ship navigation. In 1901 he transmitted a radio signal across the Atlantic Ocean.

Exchange of information between a calculating device and a distant teletype machine via standard telegraph lines was accomplished by Dr. George Stibitz in 1940. This exchange of information occurred between Dartmouth College, in Hanover, New Hampshire, and the Bell Telephone Laboratories calculator in New York City, and initiated data communications as we know it today.

---

miles above the earth. A message is sent from a ground station to the satellite, which in turn amplifies and sends the message on to another ground station that can be almost halfway around the earth from the sending station (see Figure 16–30). Users who send large volumes of data more than 500 ground miles may experience cost savings by using satellites. In the United States three companies, apart from the telephone companies—American Satellite Corp., RCA-Americom, and Western Union—offer satellite communications. For overseas information transmission ITT Worldcom, RCA-Globecom, TRT Telecommunications, and Western Union International offer satellite communications service.

As a potential replacement for coaxial cable, fiber optics (sometimes called "waveguide") is being developed and tested by telephone companies. These glass fibers transmit light to represent sound or digital data at high transmission speeds and compactness, enabling telecommunications systems to carry a greater volume of messages at a lower cost (see Figure 16–31). Still further ahead are lasers, which may be the future light source and greatly increase transmission capacity, while at the same time lowering costs.

Transmission Modes

Data communications channels vary widely in design and operating mode. One mode is called **full duplex** because it allows simultaneous transmission

FIGURE 16-30 Satellite communications.

of data on a channel in both directions. For example, a terminal on one end of a full-duplex channel can be sending data out of the channel, while a computer at the other end is sending data back to the terminal (see Figure 16-32). Analogous to this is a two-lane highway with two-way traffic.

Another transmission mode, **half duplex,** allows two-way flow, but never simultaneously. In other words, data can flow from terminal to computer, but a return flow of data (computer to terminal) cannot begin until the first flow is completed. (See Figure 16-33.) This is analogous to a section of highway in a construction area, where you have to wait while oncoming traffic is guided through and then accumulated traffic traveling in your direction is guided through.

Full duplex offers greater transmission volume since there is no waiting for the reverse flow to be completed, and the cost is only about 10 percent greater than half duplex. However, not all terminals are designed to take advantage of full duplex.

Multiplexing

In a computer system with many remote terminals, the cost of telephone lines and modems may exceed that of the computer and terminals. There are several ways of connecting more than one terminal to a single modem and telephone line. One method of connecting multiple terminals is called **multiplexing.** Multiplexing requires an electronic device called a **multiplexor** at each end of the telecommunications line (see Figure 16-34). The function of the multiplexor is to consolidate multiple flows of data into a single flow, thus requiring only a single line. Let's examine two methods of multiplexing.

The first method, **time division multiplexing (TDM),** involves rapid switching from line to line to line, picking up just one character from each line. These characters are sent across a single communication line to a receiving multiplexor that routes the sequence of incoming bits back to their respective individual lines (see Figure 16-35). Four parallel inputs from terminals to multiplexor A become a serial stream for transmission, then are switched back to their original parallel positions at multiplexor B.

A second multiplexing method, called **frequency division multiplexing (FDM),** allows data to maintain their identity as a separate serial stream and not merge with other data to form a composite character, as with TDM. The design of FDM is analogous to a radio receiver. Many stations simultaneously

"IT'S ANALYZED OUR SITUATION THOROUGHLY, AND HAS CONCLUDED THAT OUR BUSINESS DOESN'T NEED A COMPUTER."

CHAPTER 16: PROCESSING MODES

CHANNEL		CHANNEL BANDWIDTH (HERTZ)	ESTIMATED CHANNEL CAPACITY (BITS PER SECOND)
TELEPHONE WIRE (SPEECH)		3,000	60,000
AM RADIO		10,000	80,000
FM RADIO		200,000	250,000
HIGH-FIDELITY PHONOGRAPH OR TAPE		15,000	250,000
COMMERCIAL TELEVISION		6 MILLION	90 MILLION
MICROWAVE RELAY SYSTEM (1,200 TELEPHONE CHANNELS)		20 MILLION	72 MILLION
L-5 COAXIAL-CABLE SYSTEM (10,800 TELEPHONE CHANNELS)		57 MILLION	648 MILLION
PROPOSED MILLIMETER-WAVEGUIDE SYSTEM (250,000 TELEPHONE CHANNELS)		70 BILLION	15 BILLION
HYPOTHETICAL LASER SYSTEM		10 TRILLION	100 BILLION

FIGURE 16–31 Estimated capacity of various communication media.

broadcast on different frequencies, but you the listener select the particular station you want. In FDM each incoming line is modulated to a unique frequency of analog wave. The several analog wave frequencies are transmitted simultaneously over a single communications line. The receiving multiplexor contains demodulators, each looking for a particular frequency. Each analog wave frequency is then demodulated (converted to digital pulses) and sent down its respective communications line (see Figure 16–36).

Line Configurations

There are two basic approaches in configuring data communications lines between computers and terminals. The two line configurations are point-to-point and multipoint.

A direct connection between two points in a data communications system is called **point-to-point**. The two points being connected can be terminal-terminal, terminal-computer, or computer-computer. The two devices are interconnected either on

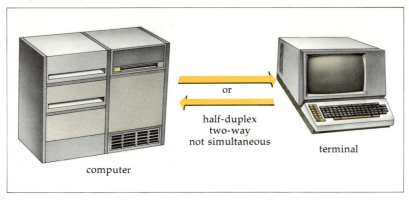

FIGURE 16–32 Half-duplex transmission mode.

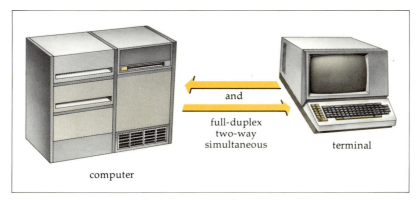

FIGURE 16–33 Full-duplex transmission mode.

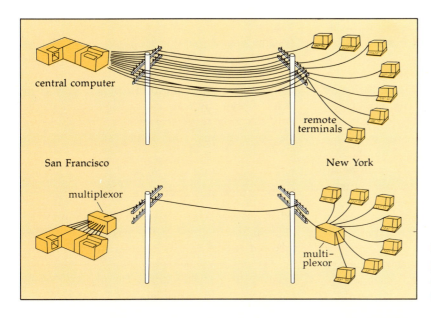

FIGURE 16–34 Using multiplexors to consolidate data communications to a single telephone line.

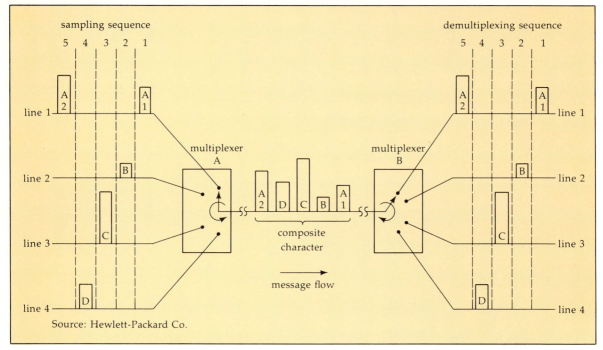

FIGURE 16-35   Line division multiplexing by character.

a hardwired (see Figure 16–37) or a data communication basis.

Since each data flow in a point-to-point system requires a separate line, communications costs are high, but this cost may be justified when the line is used almost continuously and sharing would not be workable.

The second line configuration is analogous to the telephone multiparty line used in rural areas or in heavily loaded urban telephone systems. On a party line, two or more customers share a single line between their neighborhood and the central switching center. The party line allows only one of the sharing customers to use the line at a time. In **multipoint** (sometimes called "multidrop") data communications lines, a single line is shared (see Figure 16–38). In multipoint lines the computer continuously polls, terminal by terminal, to see if the terminal has anything to transmit. Each terminal has a unique address so that if a particular terminal needs more frequent polling than others, its address can appear in the polling list more than once.

Terminals used on a multipoint line are required to be more intelligent than those on point-to-point lines. Therefore, smart or intelligent terminals are used rather than dumb ones.

Multipoint lines are commonly used in inquiry systems where multiple terminals exist but each terminal uses the line for only short periods of time. Another use is for programmers doing interactive programming. Since much of a programmer's time is spent keying in data that is then held in a buffer until the program statement is completely keyed, the communication line is needed only momentarily.

Communications Protocols

When data are transferred from one location to another in a computer system, a set of rules must be followed governing how the information is to flow. These rules are called **protocols.** They define the order of the message parts, including: (1) the ultimate destination of the data, (2) control characters

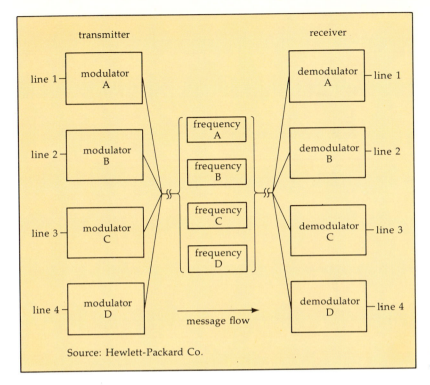

FIGURE 16–36 Frequency division multiplexing.

to mark the beginning and end, (3) the data themselves, and (4) a check character that enables the receiving terminal to test the incoming message for errors. A protocol also defines how a terminal acknowledges a message or, if it detects an error, how it requests retransmission. Finally, a protocol specifies how to cope with two simultaneous requests for access to the communication line.

Because a protocol adds information to the data that is not related to the data themselves, a major consideration of protocol design is how to hold those additional data to a minimum.

Most protocols in use are based on IBM's binary synchronous communication (bisynch) protocol. IBM's newest protocol is called **Synchronous Data Link Control (SDLC)**. An international effort by the Consultative Committee on International Telephone and Telegraph (CCITT) has developed a standard protocol known as **X.25/HDLC (High-Level Data Link Control)**. The major inpact of the X.25 protocol will be in developing new data communication networks. Using the X.25 protocol, these networks will make the interconnection of remote computers far less expensive and more reliable than current methods can. An important contributing factor in lowering costs to data communications networks is that equipment manufacturers must follow the

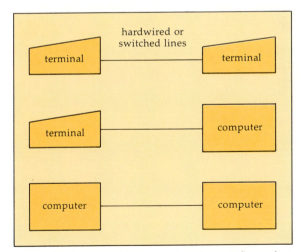

FIGURE 16–37 Point-to-point line configuration.

CHAPTER 16: PROCESSING MODES 397

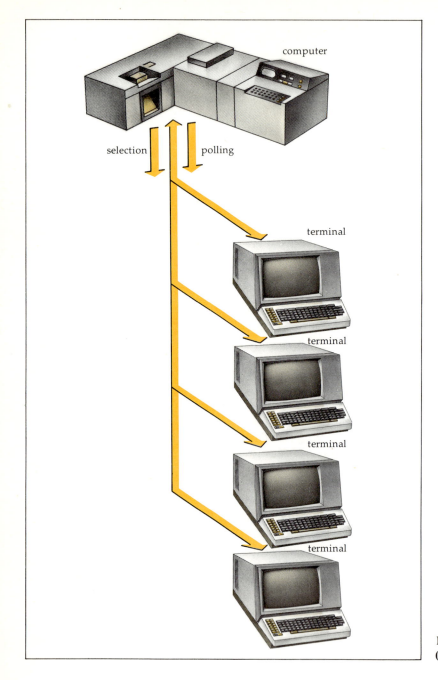

FIGURE 16-38 Multipoint (multidrop) line configuration.

standard if their equipment is to be connected to the networks. This differs from the current situation in which a given vendor can "lock in" a user to their equipment by basing all communications on protocols that are unique to their products.

Data Communications Alternatives

The alternative approaches to setting up a data communications system are almost endless. In this section we have examined a variety of transmission modes, line configurations, and methods of carrying data. When the data communications system does not include any switching as a result of "dialing" a certain telephone number, the system is **nonswitched.** Figure 16–39 shows nine nonswitched alternatives. When the connection between computer and terminal requires dialing, the system is **switched;** several switched alternatives are shown in Figure 16–40. These diagrams show only computer-to-terminal connections; however, data communications may be from computer to computer or even terminal to terminal.

Computer Networks

A series of interconnected terminals and communication lines is said to be a **network.** A single CPU with a number of interactive terminals or RJEs is sometimes also called a network. The so-called computer utility of the future that is conceived as providing a computer terminal for every home, similar to today's gas, water, and electricity utilities, is really a network.

Computer networks may be viewed as comprising (1) one or more computers, (2) the **nodes** or the connecting points of the communication channels, and (3) the communication channels (see Figure 16–41).

Computers in a network may all be identical, they may be different brands, or they may be different models of the same computer. Although there can be a wide variety of terminals in a network, the more they have in common, the simpler the communication links. Terminals can range from simple teletypewriters to keyboard/CRT displays, to RJEs, to electronic cash registers, to coded card readers.

The nodes in a network control outgoing data flow on some or all of the channels connected to it through a **channel allocating mechanism.** This mechanism may be part of a computer or a **multiplexor** that allows messages from many low-speed terminals to be combined and sent simultaneously over a single communication circuit. Sending many messages over a single high-speed line is less costly than sending many messages over many separate low-speed lines.

The single-computer network, such as a time-sharing network, is perhaps the simplest type (see Figures 16–6 and 16–8).

Another type of network has one central computer with multiple channels (nodes), each of which services a series of terminals (see Figure 16–42).

A distributed network uses a number of computers (see Figure 16–43). Generally, each computer specializes in the type of processing it does. For instance, one of the computer systems may consist of a large databank of medical research information, another might be especially powerful as a computational tool, and still another might have a large library of programs available for users. Any terminal anywhere on the network can use any of the individual computer systems.

The most ambitious network development to date is the experimental ARPA network (Department of Defense Advanced Research Project Agency). The ARPA network connects 40 computers at locations spread across the nation (see Figure 16–44). It uses satellite radio communication links. A few of the organizations tied into the network are Carnegie Technological Institute, Harvard University, University of Southern California, Stanford University, Ames Research Center, and the Rand Corporation.

Commercially, TYMSHARE, Inc., offers the TYMNET network, which includes a "central store" of data. Branches of user companies can feed their data into the central store, and the data are then available for the user's home office (Figure 16–45). Another commercial network is General Electric Corporation's G.E. Time Share network, which covers 600 cities in such places as Mexico, Canada, Europe, and Japan, and includes more than 100 computers.

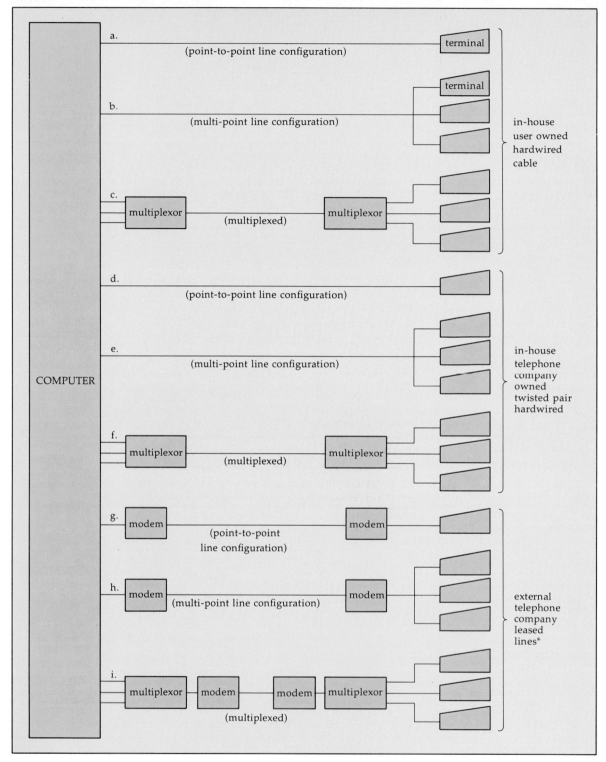

FIGURE 16-39 Nonswitched data communications alternatives.

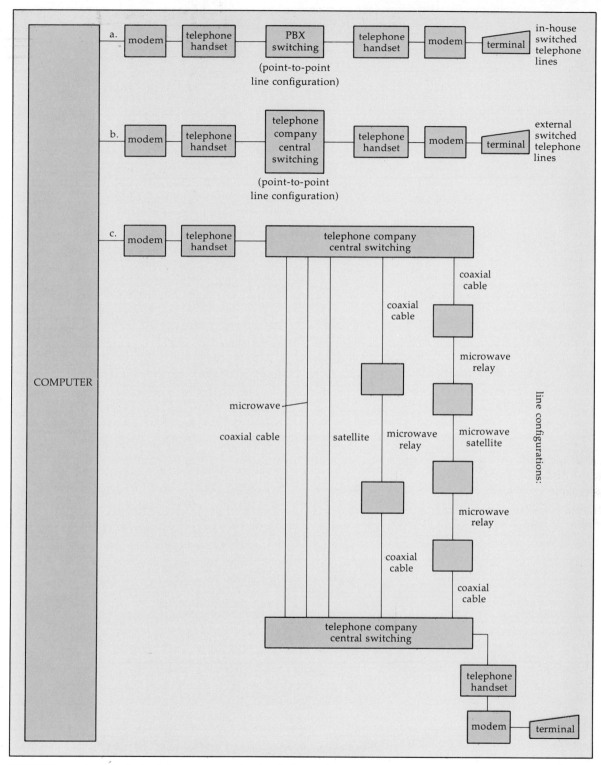

FIGURE 16–40 Switched data communications alternatives.

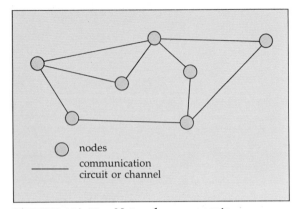

FIGURE 16-41 Network components.

In 1965 the state of California authorized and in 1970 made operational CLETS (California Law Enforcement Telecommunication System). This network consists of computers in Sacramento and in Los Angeles. The system serves approximately 1,300 users (police and sheriffs). CLETS has 40 million on-line records, handles 17,000 messages per hour, and took 20 man-years to program. CLETS can tie in with the NCIC (National Crime Information Center) in Washington, D.C., on a two-minute response-time basis. It also has ties with crime information systems in Arizona, Nevada, and Oregon.

The advantages of networks include shared resources for lower unit cost to users, access to powerful computers and to databanks that are otherwise not available, and rapid access to data that are a long distance away. Disadvantages include the relatively high cost of the communication links and the complexity of tying many unrelated users and dissimilar pieces of equipment together. Networks also have inherent social implications—that is, since data can be available to any user at any time, some users' privacy may be jeopardized.

As the cost of minicomputers continues to drop, especially with the introduction of microcomputers such as the TRS-80 and the Apple II, many prospective network users may find that their needs can be met on a local basis. If this trend continues, network growth may be slowed.

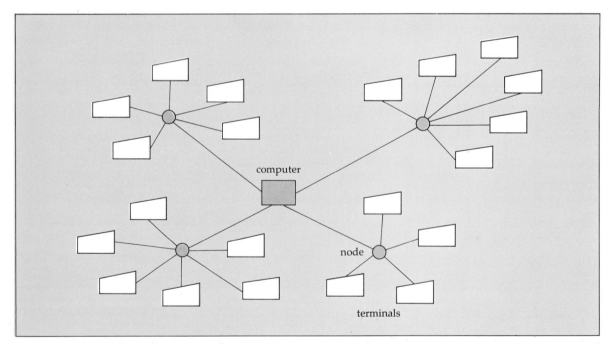

FIGURE 16-42 Centralized network.

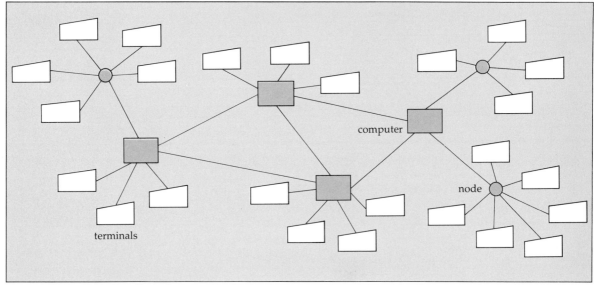

FIGURE 16–43 Distributed network.

Distributed Processing

Many decisions should be made at the lowest level of an organization, either by the employees who are intimately involved in the actual operations of the business or by the local computer. Recognizing this, an approach called **distributed processing** has been developed. In a distributed processing system some sophisticated equipment, such as a minicomputer, is situated at remote locations. The minicomputer accepts data at the remote site, processes them, per-

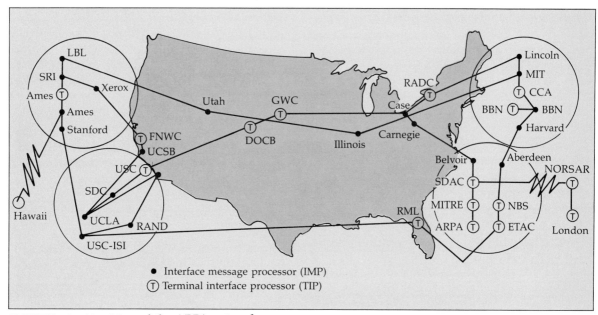

FIGURE 16–44 Map of the ARPA network.

CHAPTER 16: PROCESSING MODES **403**

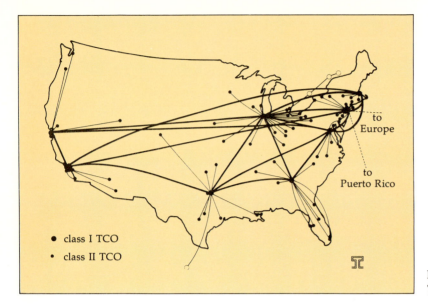

FIGURE 16–45 The TYMSHARE network.

haps referring to data files stored on attached direct access devices, and produces reports or summary information that are forwarded over a data communications channel to the central computer. The central computer uses the summary information, along with similar information received from other remote sites, to update its central files.

An example of distributed processing is a large grocery store chain that has five warehouses at widely dispersed locations. Each warehouse has a minicomputer system that receives grocery orders via terminals located at each store in that warehouse's distribution area. Orders are processed by the warehouse's minicomputer, which updates its own inventory records, prints shipping orders, and prints purchase orders for its own restocking. Several times a day the minicomputer ties into the central computer at corporate headquarters to transmit summary data regarding both the warehouse's activity and individual stores' activities. Figure 16–46 shows a typical distributed computing system.

A distributed processing system, then, is actually a specialized computer network that performs a certain task or group of tasks. The networks we discussed previously were less specialized in function and less likely to have preprocessing such as validation, calculation, and editing at the remote sites.

Distributed processing is growing in popularity; by some industry estimates, 10 percent of the computer systems currently installed are distributed systems. Some of the reasons for the growth of distributed processing are dramatically lowered equipment cost (mini and microcomputers), decline in data communications costs, difficulty in scheduling and coordinating remote site activities from the central computer, and increased overall efficiency at remote sites. However, the complex software required for communication between sites in a distributed system and the reluctance of managers of centralized computers to give up some control are reasons why distributed processing is growing at only a moderate rate.

OFF-LINE, ON-LINE, AND REAL-TIME PROCESSING

Data input into or output from the computing system can be accomplished by one of many kinds of devices. This data flow through an input or an out-

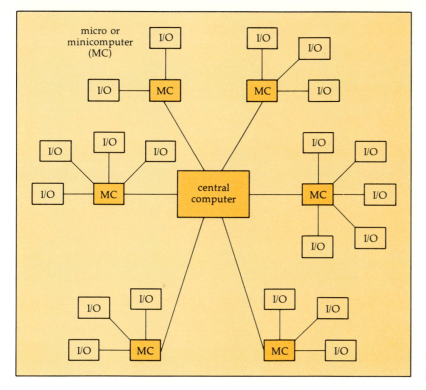

FIGURE 16–46 Distributed processing system.

put device can be said to be on an off-line, on-line, or real-time basis. And these data flow systems may apply to a single, a multiprogramming, or a multiprocessing system; to mini or supercomputers; or to a network of computers.

A device that functions independently of the CPU is called an "off-line" device. The operations that call for **off-line processing** include conversion, collection, storage, and output of data. The conversion of data from an invoice form to a machine-readable document via a keypunch machine (Figure 16–47) is an example of off-line processing. The conversion of invoice data to magnetic disk data by use of a key-to-disk system (Figure 16–48) is another example of off-line processing.

Other off-line processing devices include MICR (magnetic ink character recognition) to tape or disk; OCR (optical character recognition) to tape or disk; and cash register key input to magnetic tape or disk. Data are thus stored temporarily until the device is connected to a computer. The data are then transferred to the computer. In some cases, a special purpose computer actually controls the transfer of the data to the magnetic disk (Figure 16–49). However,

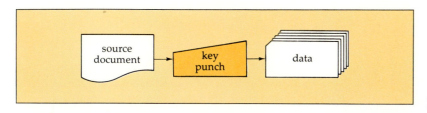

FIGURE 16–47 Off-line data preparation via keypunch.

until the disk device is connected to the main computer, processing is off-line.

Another example of off-line processing is the use of a special-purpose computer to drive a printer. In this case, the main computer sends print-line images to a magnetic tape, which can receive the data at a much higher rate of speed than a printer can operate; thus, the main computer is not slowed down by the slower printer. When the tape is filled with the data, the tape device can be switched off-line to the special-purpose computer with printer (see Figure 16–50). Another tape device is switched to the main computer, so it can continue its rapid outputting of print-line images. The special-

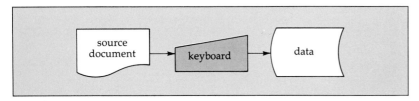

FIGURE 16–48 Off-line data preparation via key-to-disk.

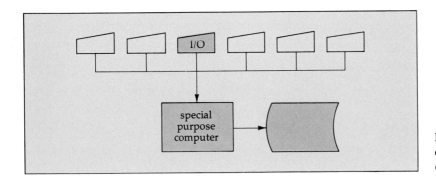

FIGURE 16–49 Off-line data entry using special-purpose computer.

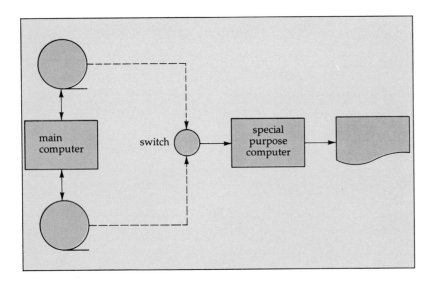

FIGURE 16–50 Off-line data output using main and special-purpose computers.

purpose computer then reads print-line images from tape and sends them to the printer.

On-line processing is a term that in a narrow sense indicates that an I/O device is under the computer's direct and absolute control. More broadly defined, on-line pertains to a user's ability to interact at any time with a computer. An I/O device that is inputting or outputting data to or from the computer is on-line. An example of an on-line computer is an inquiry system where an order clerk uses a terminal for answering questions about the current number of items on hand of a particular stock. The computer responds immediately with no human intervention (Figure 16–51). Another example is a law enforcement agency's ability to inquire into the NCIC (National Crime Information Center) to determine the status of a suspect and get an immediate response.

An on-line device can be physically adjacent to the CPU or thousands of miles away. The tie can be simply a few feet of cable, a transcontinental telephone line, or a satellite signal.

The ultimate in on-line processing is **on-line real-time processing.** With **real-time processing,** there is an automatic update of the data file without human intervention. For instance, the order clerk in the previous example probably had entered the number of items in the current order. In a real-time system, the "balance on hand" value would be decreased to reflect the sale and, hence, the decrease in inventory. The computer's response to the next interrogation of the inventory file would reflect this newly decreased inventory volume (see Figure 16–52). Other examples of real-time processing systems are systems for airline reservations, missile control, rapid transit train control, and gasoline manufacturing process control.

In the extreme, an on-line system called a **process control system** uses computer-connected devices that physically control an ongoing process. If a

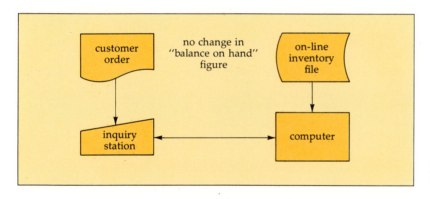

FIGURE 16–51 On-line inquiry.

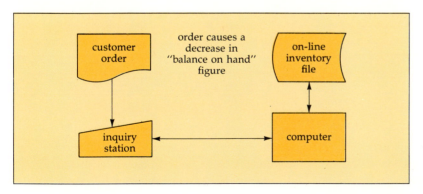

FIGURE 16–52 On-line real-time processing of transaction.

warehouse were automated, the inventory balance would be decreased on the basis of how many items were pulled from stock by a computer-controlled, robotlike carrying device.

SUMMARY

In this chapter we examined a variety of processing methods ranging from the simple batch processing where only one job is performed at a time, to the complex networks of large computers spread across the nation. Between these two extremes are multiprogramming, multiprocessing, distributed processing, time-sharing, and virtual memory computers.

Data communications systems that tie one computer to another computer or to terminals were described. Communications channel components such as interfaces, acoustic couplers, modems, multiplexors, and media were discussed. Media were examined, ranging from simple telephone wires to microwave relays to powerful satellite systems.

We discussed data flow systems, beginning with off-line processing such as printing from data stored on a magnetic tape where the data go directly from tape to printer—not through the computer. On-line processing was described as a system that offers immediate computer action—there is no waiting for a series of transactions to accumulate. Real-time processing and process control systems were also discussed.

There is no "best" approach to computerized processing; rather, computer users should analyze their needs and find a computer or combination of computers that best matches those needs.

TERMS

The following words or terms have been presented in this chapter.

Batch processing
Job control language (JCL)
Remote job entry (RJE)
Remote job entry station
Modem
Time-sharing
Time slice
Partitioning
Dynamic partitioning
Swapping
Multiprogramming system
Multiprocessing system
Interrupt
Foreground memory
Background memory
Segment
Overlays
Spooling
Processors
Virtual memory systems
Virtual storage systems
Pages
Data communications
Data communications terminals
Synchronized
Hardwired
Modulation
Demodulation
Synchronous
Asynchronous
Start bit
Stop bit
Acoustic coupler
Interfaces
EIA RS232C standard
CCITT V24 standard
Carrier
Line
Channel
Twisted wire pairs
Coaxial cable
Microwave relay
Communications satellite
Full Duplex
Half Duplex
Multiplexing
Multiplexor
Time division multiplexing (TDM)
Frequency division multiplexing (FDM)
Point-to-point
Multipoint
Protocol
Synchronous Data Link Control (SDLC)
X.25 HDLC (High-Level Data Link Control)
Nonswitched
Switched
Network
Nodes
Channel allocating mechanisms
Distributed processing
Off-line processing
On-line processing
On-line real-time processing
Real-time processing
Process control system

EXERCISES

The exercises that follow are grouped by level of difficulty. Problems in the A series are the easiest; B series problems are moderately hard; and C series problems are the most difficult.

A–1 Describe the chief difference between a conventional batch computer and a computer with remote job entry stations.

A–2 What difference is there, if any, between a printer output device that is used on a conventional batch computer, and a printer used on an RJE station?

A–3 What kinds of input and output devices can be used on an RJE station?

A–4 Describe a computer network other than those cited in this chapter.

A–5 Trace the components that might exist in a computer network, starting with a terminal and ending at the central computer.

A–6 Is a terminal in a data communications system simply a CRT or teleprinter, or more? Explain.

A–7 Why are acoustic couplers necessary in some terminal uses?

A–8 What organizations and what standards have influenced data communications interfaces?

B–1 Since batch processing allows for processing of only one job at a time, why would a computer user use a batch processing system?

B–2 If a batch computer user needs to run more jobs within a time span than the batch computer can execute, what are some possible remedies to the situation?

B–3 Explain what modems are, and why they are necessary in some computer systems.

B–4 In multiprogramming systems, one program is considered the foreground program and any others are considered background programs. Explain what background programs and foreground programs are.

B–5 Describe what a modem is and indicate if modems must always be used between computer and data communications terminals.

B–6 Explain the difference between digital and analog data transmission.

B–7 Contrast synchronous and asynchronous data transmission and explain why the sending modem and the receiving modem must both use the same mode.

B–8 Explain which transmission mode (synchronous or asynchronous) a nonbuffered terminal uses and why.

B–9 Differentiate among carriers, lines, and channels.

B–10 Explain the similarities and differences of half-duplex and full-duplex transmission.

B–11 Some kinds of terminals can share a single communication channel. Describe what kind can and under what arrangement.

B–12 What are communications protocols, what standards exist, and who has developed these standards?

C–1 Using your college library, determine in greater depth than this text does, how a modem enables data to be transmitted over voice-grade telephone lines. Draw an illustration to explain the modem's functioning graphically.

C–2 Discuss the advantages and disadvantages of time-sharing by partitioning memory versus time-sharing by swapping.

C–3 Explain the major differences between multiprocessing and multiprogramming.

C–4 If you were employed as a manager of a computer center and were requesting that the owners replace the current computer system with one that operated on a virtual storage basis, what justifications would you give to support your request? Explain each one fully.

C–5 Differentiate between an on-line system and a real-time system. Give examples.

C–6 Describe three data communications media and explain under what circumstances each would be appropriate.

C–7 Fiber optics and laser transmission media are not widely used yet. Using the *Reader's Guide to Periodical Literature* in your college library, locate, study, and summarize an article describing either medium.

C–8 Describe what multiplexing is, name two types, and explain when it is used.

C–9 On the basis of your personal knowledge, the knowledge of someone more familiar with computers, or on the basis of research in your college library, describe by words and illustrations an actual distributed processing system.

COMPUTER NEWS

ELECTRONIC "COPY BOY" HIRED BY TEXAS DAILY

Space-age cartoon character George Jetson goes to work every day, leaving behind wife Jane, daughter Judy, son Elroy and Astro the dog. So even in the 21st Century there is room for the drudgery of commuting (albeit by rocket) and a continuation of the nine-to-five grind. And, significantly, women are still at home, at least in this fictional scenario.

Today social change is the slowest in coming. Working at home still implies self-employment. But technology is changing that. True, there aren't any sleek home workstations that harmonize with home decor but working from a residence and elsewhere is more than feasible; it's a fact.

Portable terminals are playing a role in this home-as-office transformation of the workplace. And in the newspaper business—where timeliness is business—deadlines are being met with the help of portable terminals. Columnists, reporters and others at the Houston Chronicle, Houston, TX, use a 17-lb. portable terminal, the Silent 700 Model 765 portable memory terminal from Texas Instruments (TI) to get fast-breaking news into print faster.

ADVANTAGES OF PORTABLE

"We had more trouble introducing the electric typewriter," said Don Pickels, managing editor. "At that time, the wailing and gnashing of teeth were tremendous." Pickels calls the new system "really very expeditious," noting that it avoids rekeyboarding and unnecessary trips to the office.

"A lot of our best people have them. Many staff members really don't need to come into the office every day." Syndicated columnists, the TV critic, reporters in outlying bureaus and others make use of the TI terminals.

"The TV editor sends stories in at night or comes in at night." Pickels also mentioned that previously the paper used FAX for such needs.

Robert Goff, director of information systems at the paper, calls it a "proven technology. There are many newspapers going this way." There has been a positive reaction from reporters, too.

"They love the system when it's working right," said Goff. But as every DPer knows there is always a snag somewhere.

"Reporters are not very patient when there's a hardware problem or if we scramble a story because of telephone lines," said Goff. He mentioned one instance when a sports reporter "lost" a fast-breaking story at a major sports arena. Arena management turned the lights down momentarily to indicate to the audience that the game was over. And that's electronic hari-kari.

Three members of Goff's DP support staff of 55 are responsible for handling technical problems with the portable terminals.

The TI 700 Model 765 incorporates built-in modem, coupler and standard 20,000 characters of bubble memory. In addition, there's full or half duplex operation, self-test diagnostics and 30 cps thermal printing.

AVOIDS REKEYBOARDING

Reporters at the *Chronicle* can type and edit at the terminals and input is transferred directly to an editor's queue. Goff says the newspaper has a cluster of terminals on Telstar equipment that can receive TI input. Edited stories are then transferred electronically to a Merganthaler typesetting system.

Mary Moody, the *Chronicle's* metropolitan editor explained that using the terminals increases the speed and accuracy at which reporters can send stories.

Was introducing the terminals a problem?

Moody said that when reporters found out they had to use the terminals, "there was a little apprehension." But training has not been a problem. Moody did note, however, that the terminals are not that easy to edit on. "Once you get to the end of a story it's essentially written," she said.

OFFICE OF THE FUTURE? It's probably not intentionally ironic, but Glenn Smith, *Chronicle* bureau staff member, set up his portable terminal on an antique rolltop desk at his home. Smith works out of the Huntsville, TX, bureau—a good 70 miles from the *Chronicle's* home base in Houston.

> **Introducing the terminals was relatively easy—easier in fact than introducing electric typewriters.**

Portability from Moody's viewpoint also is a key factor.

According to the metro editor, "On a court case a reporter can cover a story on-site. So when a reporter finds a major story to cover I know where he or she is." The terminals also save the paper from having to hire extra personnel.

AREA BUREAUS BENEFIT

More than a year ago the paper established area bureaus in several counties around Houston. And the system has worked out well there, too.

Moody explained that each of the nine bureaus has a portable unit assigned to him or her—usually located in an office in the reporter's home.

"They're small enough to carry to meetings and there have been no major problems with them as long as the telephone lines and computer systems are up." Other beats inside Houston are covered using the 700. Reporters at City Hall, the police station or at the Federal Court, for example, can now easily key in a story while action is still happening.

Washington Bureau Chief Norman Baxter also uses the 700. "We keep one in the Senate Press Gallery," Baxter explained. News is transmitted to the downtown office on Pennsylvania Avenue and edited there. Finished news is then transmitted directly to Houston.

Covering a campaign also is easier with a portable. "When reporters are out on the road with candidates (news is) transmitted to Washington, edited there and sent to Houston," Baxter said.

Like Moody, Baxter also mentioned "less convenient" editing capabilities as the single drawback to the TI terminal.

When the paper covers international news the TI terminals are equally handy. Reporters covering international news have successfully used the terminals over international telephone lines. And that kind of reliability means a lot.

A FUNCTIONAL, PORTABLE TOOL

Richard Harris, marketing manager of the terminal and peripheral div. of Texas Instruments, explains. "In terms of portability, the terminals mean being able to take a functional tool and move it from location to location." For reporters, said Harris, "It's a timeliness factor."

TI sources also report that other newspapers including the *Dallas Morning News*, the *Des Moines Register and Tribune* and a Swedish newspaper, *Dagens Nyheter*, have 700s "on staff."

What do portables mean for the future? Harris noted that potential personal uses for the terminals are "mind boggling." Trends to on-line data services such as news services are available to individuals as well as businessmen. Online stock information is just one example.

But the future—and increased productivity are already here—at least for the *Chronicle*. And the portables help provide fresher, more timely information that is being translated into news—faster and more accurately. That's increased productivity. And according to TI's Harris, "Productivity is the major calling card in our industry."

CHAPTER seventeen

TRENDS AND FUTURE DEVELOPMENTS

Preview

Computer Maid, Cook, Timer, and Tutor

Hardware Developments and Trends
 Computer Logic and Storage
 Secondary Storage
 I/O Devices
 Terminals

Firmware Developments and Trends

Software Developments and Trends
 Operating Systems
 Systems Management Software
 Database Management Systems (DBMs)
 Report Generators
 Languages and Programming Techniques
 Software Costs

Personal Computers

Data Communications Developments and Trends
 Fiber Optics

Summary

**Computer News: Applications:
Voice Mail Arrives in the Office**

PREVIEW

In the early 1950s, at an installation ceremony of an early computer, one of the speakers predicted that 50 computers would satisfy the nation's computational needs for the rest of this century. Now, a little over halfway through the end of the century, the federal government alone uses nearly 10,000 computers, and private industry and state and local governments use hundreds of thousands more. An explosion in home computers is inhibited only by design, manufacturing, and marketing lead time. In fairness to that unfortunate speaker, no one but a clairvoyant could have predicted the wildfire spread of computers into every facet of life in developed countries.

Now the computer population and information are exploding around us. How are we utilizing this flood of information? Computer consultant John Diebold warns, "Few corporations will prosper in the next decade without developing an overall strategy for acquiring, utilizing, and managing information."

This chapter examines what some experts and researchers are predicting will happen in computer hardware, firmware, software, and communications during the next three to ten years.

Though this look into the future is based on well-established facts and trends, we cannot guarantee that it will be any more correct than the 50-computer prediction of 1950. The computer field changes on an almost daily basis.

HARDWARE DEVELOPMENTS AND TRENDS

Computer hardware has evolved rapidly since its birth in the 1940s—so rapidly, in fact, that *evolution* seems the wrong word for it. The stored program

---

COMPUTER MAID, COOK, TIMER, AND TUTOR

It is 6:30 A.M. as Alex and Fredda Addison are gently brought to consciousness by the soft strings of their favorite concerto generated by their stereo music synthesizer. Their central computer has already directed the furnace to raise the room temperature to a snug 72 degrees; gently turned the rheostat-controlled lights from OFF to barely a glow, to low, and finally to bright, in place of the pokey winter sunrise; and switched off their electric blankets. In anticipation of the Addisons' morning showers, the hot water heaters were activated an hour ago from their overnight low setting. The aroma of freshly brewed coffee signals that the computer-directed kitchen is operating on schedule. Then, morning communications begin with a preselected newscast programmed to screen out murders, rapes, auto accidents, and deaths unless they involved someone on the Addisons' recorded list of friends, relatives, or professional associates, or was a newsworthy event that took place within a 1-mile radius of the Addisons' house. After the television news the facsimile machine spews out correspondence accumulated since its last programmed communiqués were released last evening. As the facsimile machine displays its last word from the computer network, a chime announces that Alex and Fredda's individually controlled showers are on and have reached their prescribed temperatures.

By this time, similar scenes are under way in son Felix's and daughter Sally's rooms. But rather than morning news, a review of Sally's frosh English-composition assignment is stepping through its program, while Felix is receiving some last-minute tutoring on complementary colors for his Art 20 class.

As the breakfast chimes signal 7:30, the Addisons descend to the kitchen, finding individually selected menus translated into breakfast plates, cooked and held to their choice temperatures—except for Sally, for she did not respond to the kitchen computer's selection request. By default, Sally has cold cereal, orange juice, and a high-protein pattie.

was first used on the EDSAC built at Cambridge University in 1949. Magnetic core memory used on a limited scale in the UNIVAC I in 1953 became available in up to 32K words on IBM's 704 computer in 1955. Transistors replaced vacuum tubes with the advent of second-generation computers around 1960; integrated circuits appeared on third-generation computers in 1965; and large-scale integration (LSI), sometimes called computer-on-a-chip, appeared in the early 1970s. Since 1975, semiconductor memories have been widespread. In 1981 a $1,500 three-chip, 32-bit microcomputer was introduced that has the processing power of the $400,000 medium-scale mainframe (IBM 370/148) of five years ago. No one sees any slackening of this pace for at least the next ten years.

What has happened to the cost and performance of computers during this 35-year growth period? To get an idea, let us compare IBM's 704 (1955) to current technology. The 704 had a memory of 32K words, a memory access time of 12,000 nanoseconds, and a magnetic drum storage device that held only 16K words. It probably weighed more than a ton and it cost $3,000,000 (in 1980 dollars).

A model of IBM's Series/1 computer has 128 bytes of memory (approximately equal to 32K words on the IBM 704) and magnetic disk storage of 20 million bytes (equal to about 5 million words). The Series/1 weighs only several hundred pounds and costs less than $40,000—only 13 percent of the "ancestor" IBM 704.

Furthermore, hardware is now much more reliable. The IBM 704 had an MTBF (mean time between failures) of several days, whereas by 1960, computer hardware MTBF had reached 600 hours and by 1980 reached 100,000 hours.

With such advances in economy, capability, and reliability, future improvements may be difficult to imagine.

Computer Logic and Storage

Like the computer, the familiar hand-held calculator has been changing. The logic circuit ("brain" or calculating mechanism) may be identical in the $4 model and in the more capable $20 model. The less expensive unit simply lacks some keyboard characters and connecting wires that would allow it to take advantage of its logic circuit's ability to do more complex calculations. It is cheaper for the manufacturer, however, to design and build a single type of circuit and to use only parts of it on certain calculator models than it would be to design and manufacture several kinds. Thus, it is economical to waste some of the circuit's abilities in some cases. Like these calculators, computers consist of standardized integrated circuits used in different ways to perform various functions within the many parts of a computer. When a particular circuit is used for a certain function, that function may use only part of the circuit's capacity.

Since memory is essential for supplying the program to the processor, one or more chips containing memory are tied to it. The microprocessor chip (ALU function and CU function) and the memory chip together comprise a **microcomputer** (Figure 17–1). With these compact, inexpensive microprocessors, the way is open for all kinds of new developments.

Recent studies foresee the extension of multiple processor use to the point that computers will consist of a complex of component processors at three levels of power. Rather than designing a series of computers (such as mini, small, and medium), each having its component parts custom designed, each computer in the series will be made of building blocks that are standardized, inexpensive microprocessors. The programming for each microprocessor will provide it with its particular function.

Another new approach to computer logic and storage places multiple processors within the memory. As memory databases become massive, the time it takes to move the data from memory to the processor for operating on becomes unacceptably long. If each memory module has its own processor, the data access time will be greatly reduced, thus improving overall computing speed.

Another area of potential computer logic improvement involves the speed of calculating and moving information within the CPU. Based on Britisher Brian Josephson's theory that electrical switching becomes much faster near absolute zero ($-459.69°F$), future CPUs may be refrigerated inside tanks of liquid helium and operate 100 times faster

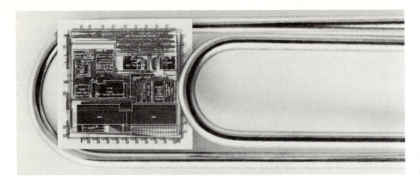

FIGURE 17-1   The one-chip computer.

than today's CPUs. By applying Josephson's theory, CPUs with nanosecond access time are predicted by IBM scientists by the late 1980s (Figure 17-2).

Economies enjoyed in mass producing the processors will cause their prices and the computer's prices to drop so drastically that computers will become as commonplace by 1990 as today's stereo tape decks. Processors will be integrated into even such common home appliances as mixers, toasters, and hair dryers.

Also changing are computer memories. Every three to five years the density of data storage in semiconductor memory quadruples. However, each quadrupling becomes more difficult than the previous. The revolution in computer memories, if it comes, may result from a breakthrough in miniaturizing semiconductors. The performance of semiconductors depends largely on how fine a line can be drawn by electron beams making the mask from which semiconductors are then photore-

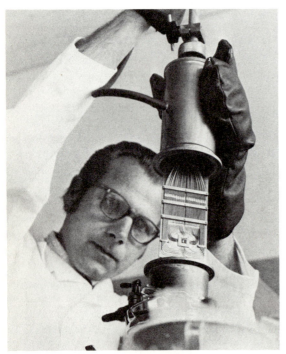
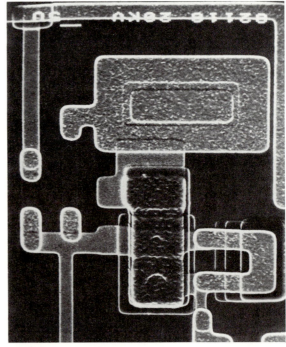

FIGURE 17-2   Josephson junctions being used in experimental memories.

416   MODULE FOUR: MANAGEMENT MODULE

produced. Circuits operating at the molecular level (lines only one molecule wide) conceivably could be created through a chemical action, resulting in extremely compact, fast, and inexpensive processors and memories.

The number of bits of data per chip has steadily increased from 1,024 to 4,096 to 16,384 to 65,536 bits within just a few years. Manufacturers are now developing 256K memories that store 262,144 bits of data on a chip and calling them very large scale integrated circuits (VLSIC). The incentive to develop greater density chips (more bits per inch) is lower cost per bit and increased access speed. The cost per bit is expected to drop to half its current cost as the move is made from the 64K bit chip to the 256K bit chip. As the physical size of a chip is lessened, the distance between bits is likewise cut, and the shorter distance means less time to transfer data in or out. However, there appears to be hazards in this miniaturization. IBM researchers have found that alpha particles that constantly bombard us from outer space may actually destroy a bit if the transistor holding the bit is tiny enough.

Secondary Storage

The future should also bring new types of secondary storage devices. Electron beam accessed memory (EBAM) is currently being developed by General Electric Corp., Amdahl, and Control Data Corp. EBAM utilizes an electron beam that writes on chips within a CRT. Theoretically, a million bits could be stored within a CRT, but much research and development is needed to produce EBAM competitively. Optical disk storage (ODS) systems are being developed by North American Phillips and others but are not yet on the market. Optical disk systems record data in concentric patterns of dots on 12-inch disks. These laser-based devices store over 1 billion bytes per side. The recorded dots are not erasable, hence ODS is a read-only medium after the initial recording of data. ODS would be appropriate for archival storage.

Most of the improvement in disk-tape devices will be in the form of increased density of recording: more tracks per inch laterally across the magnetic disk face, and more bits per inch longitudinally on disk and tape. A fortyfold increase in density, which will result in much lower cost per bit, appears possible.

In 1975 a semiconductor secondary storage medium, called a "charged-coupled device" (CCD), was introduced, but because of improvements in magnetic disk CCD usage has been limited. However, CCDs, together with another semiconductor variation called "magnetic bubbles," will likely be in widespread use by 1985 as secondary storage devices. As of 1981 1-million-bit, 1-inch square bubble memories were in production. By 1990 the CCD or magnetic bubble devices will improve retrieval speeds for secondary storage by 200 times over currently used disks. Each bubble memory chip can hold 150 pages of this book. IBM scientists are experimenting with bubble memories that could store 100 million bits per square inch (equal to all the print in 30 books the size of this one). A comparison of storage media by cost and access times projected up to 1990 is given in Figure 17–3.

I/O Devices

Most input and output devices are electromechanical in nature, and speeding them up without increasing their cost will be difficult. Hence, experts expect relatively little improvement in their cost/performance ratio. However, most I/O devices will have built-in intelligence from on-board microprocessors. This will allow more of the control functions to be handled by the I/O devices, thus relieving the main computer of using its CPU for those functions and saving both time and memory space.

In the area of optical character recognition (OCR), designers are developing smaller, more sophisticated, and cheaper devices for reading letters and other input characters. These improvements, together with increased speed of circuits and new electro-optics technologies (such as the laser beam), are resulting in small, lighter weight, less expensive, faster, and more accurate scanning elements. One of the obvious goals here is an OCR device that can read script and less constrained handprinting. The need is for software that gives the processor powerful heuristic (learning) capabilities. Such an OCR seems far in the future. The most

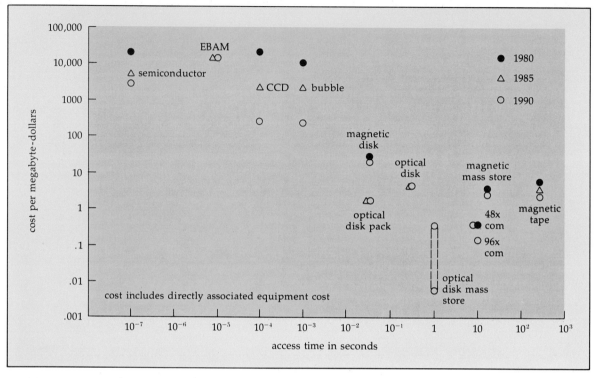

FIGURE 17-3 Storage media costs and access times projected to 1990.

likely improvements are in costs only, with cost/performance ratios improved two to four times by 1990. These improvements in OCR will eventually be followed by the widespread use of still more capable OCR devices that can read almost any business document—eliminating the need for key entry of data.

Also changing is computer output microfilm (COM). Because new circuits and electro-optical devices cost less and manufacturing volume of COM devices is rising, a COM should cost 10 percent less by 1990. At the same time, output to microfilm should increase in speed by about 50 percent and density of data is predicted to double.

In spite of the rapid growth in visual display device use, printed output continues to grow about 10 percent yearly. Nonimpact printing (laser, ink jet, thermal, and so on) will grow at 20 percent annually through 1988, while impact printing will increase considerably less. By 1988 nonimpact printers will account for 40 percent of printers sold compared to only 7 percent in 1979.

Color printing has been limited and expensive, but in 1980 IBM introduced a four-color, less expensive (only about double the cost of comparable black, in printers) dot matrix plain-paper printer. Rapidly growing use of color printers is expected, especially in graphics output.

Terminals

Computer terminals are the fastest growing (28 percent annually) type of computer hardware, with 6 million terminals installed as of 1981. Four million of these are printers and 2.7 million are CRTs. As a result of this growing volume and improvements in electronics technology (microprocessors, for example) manufacturing costs are dropping about 10 percent yearly. Terminals such as teletypewriters are expected to be 25 percent cheaper and CRT terminals 50 percent cheaper by 1988.

By 1988 the dumb terminal will disappear and the smart terminal will take its place at the low end of the line because of competitive forces and the low cost of microprocessors and memory.

Flat panel displays will begin to make inroads into the CRT market by 1985, and by 1990 half the nonprinting terminals are likely to be flat panel displays. High cost is the limiting factor at present.

Other terminals, such as printers without keyboards and credit card and badge readers, are expected to decline in price by about 20 percent. Finally, voice-input and voice-response units, benefiting from the declining cost of microprocessors and memories, will cost one-third to one-half less. The days of unemployment and dependency for physically handicapped persons are undoubtedly numbered as computer-controlled voice-input and voice-response units substitute for human functions. Some telephone operators are already being assisted by voice-input devices.

In spite of lower terminal costs, the trend is for terminals to represent a growing percentage of the total cost of computer systems. Indeed, some industry experts foresee computer systems in which peripheral devices including terminals account for 85 percent of the total systems cost.

"WHEN YOU COME OVER, BRING YOUR COMPUTER. WE'LL SIT AROUND AND SWAP DATA."

FIRMWARE DEVELOPMENTS AND TRENDS

The term **firmware** or **microcode** describes something that is between hardware and software. Hardware generally consists of physical, hard, rigid devices. Software, on the other hand, is the term applied to programs that, among other things, provide communication between user and computer; do such maintenance tasks as sorting, copying, logging of malfunctions; and compile or interpret programs in languages such as COBOL, FORTRAN, or BASIC.

Firmware or microcode permits the functions of the processor to vary according to its preprogrammed task. In other words, a series of identical microprocessors are individually microcoded to perform particular tasks; these allow the computer system to function as if it has many unique circuits, each performing a programmed task. The overall cost savings resulting from the use of standardized microprocessor circuits is substantial, and the speed of operation is several times faster than with software—but less than one-quarter as fast as hardwired circuits.

Some computer scientists believe that in the future most large, general-purpose computers will be a collection of individual microprocessors, each with a memory containing microcode for doing a particular function.

SOFTWARE DEVELOPMENTS AND TRENDS

The term **software** generally encompasses a set of computer programs and procedures concerned with the operation of computer systems. Examples of these are user programs; language compilers, assemblers, and interpreters; operating systems programs; and systems management programs, including programs that log operating and hardware errors, and programs that provide file protection. Other items that can be included in software are database management systems (DBMS), data communication control systems, program development aids such as test-data generators, and utility routines including sorters and file copiers.

The trend over the past 30 years has been to provide software that reduces both the time consumed and the level of sophistication required to program and to operate a computer system. This trend, which makes computers available to a broader, less experienced group of users, will continue into the future. Sophisticated software will also offset some of the rising nonhardware costs associated with computer usage—primarily the costs of people involved in programming—and will provide more timely, accurate, and complete information to users.

Operating Systems

An **operating system,** the set of routines that direct the computer, provides for: computer-to-operator communications; operator-to-computer communications; program loading; scheduling of input/output operations; error monitoring and logging; internal job scheduling; job accounting; interrupt handling; and recovery from hardware or software failure. Many of the functions now performed by the operating system are likely to be performed by computer microcode by 1985. If so, the functions that will remain will be those such as internal job scheduling, error monitoring, and recovery.

Before 1990 it is likely that some operating system will have DBMS functions as integral parts in contrast to the current situation in which DBMS is now, in effect, add-on software.

Systems Management Software

Some of the systems management activities carried out by software by 1985 will be the automatic logging and reporting of data needed to control such external activities as tape and disk library operations, job scheduling, and user accounting and billing. These capabilities become more desirable in the face of growing misuse of computerized data and will become more widespread.

Software that measures the performance of the computer system, which is already available, will become more popular. This software enables the user to observe the performance of programs and the balancing of computer system resources for more efficient operation. By 1985, system software will enable users to predict how their system will behave after a specified change.

Database Management Systems (DBMS)

In 1970 there were about 100 users of DBMS in the United States. By 1980 major DBMS packages were installed in about 12,000 computer systems, and the trend is toward increasing use with an expected increase of 600 percent between 1980 and 1989.

The organization of DBMS is evolving toward the structure shown in Figure 17–4 according to an Arthur D. Little, Inc. (a management consulting and accounting firm) study.

IBM and several software firms have introduced a **relational** (as opposed to the chained and inverted types discussed in Chapter 12) database management system that theoretically allows the user to recombine all of the elements in the database to form different relationships as required for a specific application. This enables the user to utilize the data without knowing how they are physically structured. For widespread and efficient use of large relational DBMSs, computer memory improvements must be developed. These hardware advances aren't expected before 1985.

Languages and Programming Techniques

Computer languages have evolved over the past 30 years from all-numeric codes or machine language to the more easily programmed assembly language (which is now on the decline), and finally to the more English-like or algebralike high-level languages such as COBOL, RPG-II, FORTRAN, BASIC, PL/1, and APL. The functional capabilities of COBOL, FORTRAN, BASIC, APL, and the others will not improve dramatically, but will evolve into dialects that accommodate new programming tech-

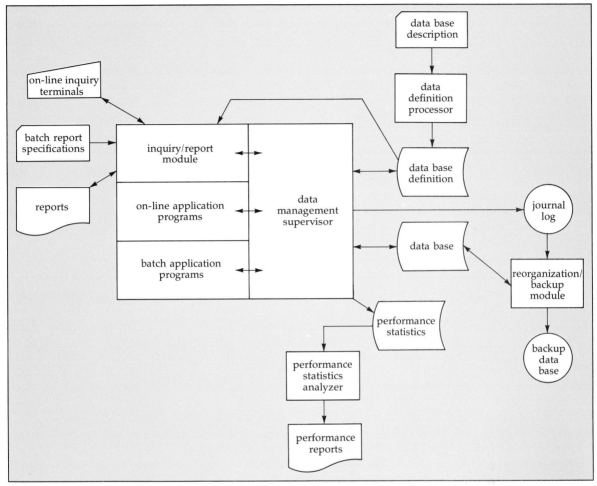

FIGURE 17–4 The Arthur D. Little, Inc., forecast of future DBMS structure.

niques such as structured programming. For small computers, and even microcomputers, limited versions of the languages will be widely used.

A new programming language called **ADA** is being developed by the U.S. Department of Defense (DOD). The DOD's objective is to have a single language that meets all of its programming needs. It is structured as is Pascal, has strong file processing capability like COBOL, and can handle high computational demands. These same capabilities exist in PL/1, but ADA is more streamlined.

The development of "very high level" languages, commonly described as "problem-oriented" languages, will continue, but such languages will likely be less efficient than procedure-oriented languages and, hence, will not displace them.

The current programming trend involves a technique called **structured programming** (see Chapter 8). Notice the absence of GO TO's in the structured program of Figure 8–4. The result of this and other procedures is a more linear program.

Another technique now receiving widespread attention is **top-down programming.** As the name suggests, you start at the highest level of information in a hierarchy and end at the bottom with the programs that input the raw data. As you finish and test the topmost programs, you design and write the programs that yield the data to be input into the topmost programs. As these second-level (or next-to-top) programs are completed and tested, you design and write the third-level programs, and so forth until you reach the raw data entry program. Growth in the use of structured and top-down programming should continue through 1990.

Software Costs

Costs of software are expected to rise faster than inflation during the next few years. This is due in part to greater use of database systems and systems management software.

At the same time software costs are rising, hardware costs are declining in relation to computing power. However, this decline in hardware cost will only partially offset the rising software cost. The net result is an increase in total costs (Figure 17–5).

Report Generators

Rather than write a complete program from scratch every time a simple report is needed, many computer users are taking advantage of automatic program writers called **report generators**. A report generator generally runs in a batch processing mode, accesses a file or database, and prints the report based on the data. DBMS is one factor encouraging use of report generators. A DBMS does not in and of itself provide reports. However, DBMS systems may use query languages to provide limited-format reports. But when greater format control is required query languages give way to report generators. Not yet available, but likely by 1985, is an interactive report generator. Ultimately a question-and-answer dialogue between computer and user will result in a generated report.

PERSONAL COMPUTERS

In 1977 there were 20,000 general-purpose computers in American homes; by 1980 there were 300,000; and the figure may reach 1.2 million by 1983 (one home out of 100) or, according to others, 5 million by 1985! Some market researchers are predicting that annual sales of personal computers will reach 3.7 million units by 1985. A growing number of personal computers are being equipped with telephone modems to enable the user to tie into time-sharing computers. Personal computers are programmed in machine, assembly, or BASIC languages or, more recently, in Pascal.

Nearly two-thirds of today's personal computer users are programmers, technicians, or engineers by trade, and nearly three-quarters of the home users also use computers on their jobs.

Personal computer prices are roughly related to the cost of the peripheral devices connected to the computer. The microprocessor and memory often sell for under $300. Peripherals, including a small CRT, keyboard, and cassette tape recorder, raise the price to $500 or $600. More capable peripherals such as floppy disk and dot matrix printer can easily raise the price of the personal computer to $2,500 or more, but that is less than half the price of those devices in 1975. Once the mass merchandisers can find economies of scale, the price of personal computers will probably drop to around $200, exclusive of applications software.

Applications programs that display menus, maintain the family budget, and so on are likely to be sold separately and at prices ranging from $5 to $100, depending on their complexity and on the market size. Just as in large business systems, it will

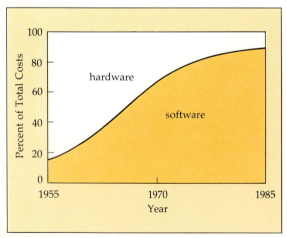

FIGURE 17–5 Changing mix of software and hardware costs.

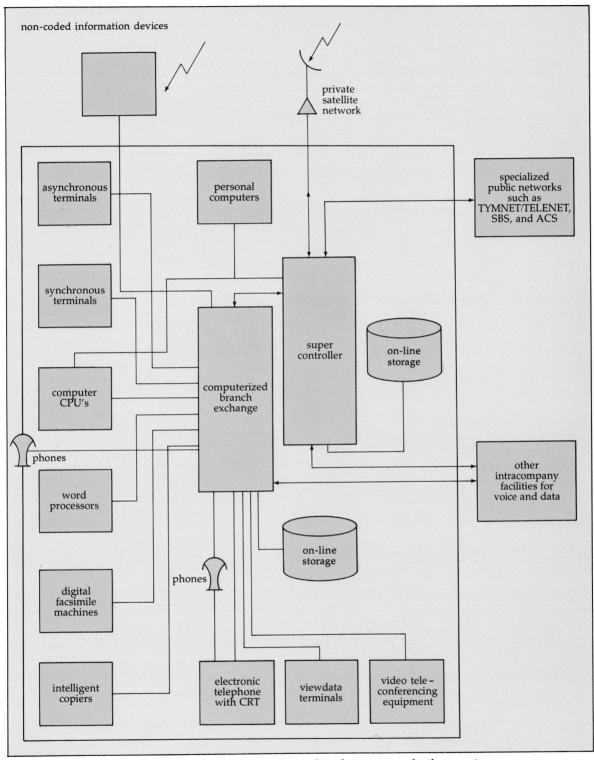

FIGURE 17-6 A growing variety of devices connected to data communications systems.

be possible to spend more on software than on hardware. A major new publishing field is developing, centered around applications programs and computer hobby magazines.

A new and rapidly developing use of personal computers is as a terminal tied via telephone to database services. Two services (The Source, owned by *Reader's Digest*, and CompuServe) enable tens of thousand of subscribers to access news, financial data, weather data, airline schedules, and other data. Responding to this exploding market, Radio Shack offered its TRS80 Videotex terminal for less than $400. Using the home television set, keyboard, modem, and adapter, the database service transmits from its computer over telephone lines to the home TV set-terminal. By 1992 electronic information services could reach 10 percent of all U.S. homes, according to Arthur D. Little, Inc.

Within the business community Dow Jones News Service and The New York Times Co. have been selling information to remote customers for several years. Dow Jones had 9,000 terminals connected in 1980, almost double their 1979 figure. By 1992 electronic information services are likely to reach 50 percent of all businesses.

DATA COMMUNICATIONS DEVELOPMENTS AND TRENDS

Currently, over half of all computer systems use telecommunications for input and/or output. Some industry experts predict that by 1985, 100 percent of computer systems will have connections to telephone, microwave, satellite, or laser beam communication devices. This universal access should be possible in part because of advances in computer hardware, but also because of falling communication line fees. In 1980 computers in the United States transmitted and received an estimated 250 billion data transmissions over telecommunication lines. It is predicted that data traffic in the United States will continue to grow by 35 percent a year through 1985. The increasing volume of data communications can be seen in the increasing use of computer terminals—from 50,000 in 1965 to 586,000 in 1972, over 2,000,000 in 1977, and 6,000,000 in 1981.

A growing variety of devices will be connected to data communications systems, including viewdata terminals, word processors, personal computers, and intelligent copiers (see Figure 17–6).

The telephone lines, microwaves, and satellite links we now use will be supplemented by laser beam transmission/receiving devices and by glass fiber carriers, fiber optics.

Fiber Optics

Perhaps the most dramatic change in telecommunications since the dial telephone bypassed the local operator, will be the use of glass wire to carry messages. This transmission and reception of light through glass fibers is called **fiber optics**.

Breakthroughs have produced glass fibers so clear that more light can travel through a 500-foot strand than can travel through ordinary glass the

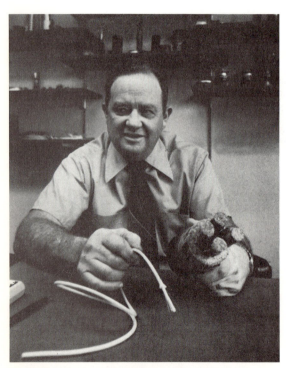

FIGURE 17–7 Fiber-optic cable (left) with capacity equal to copper cable (right).

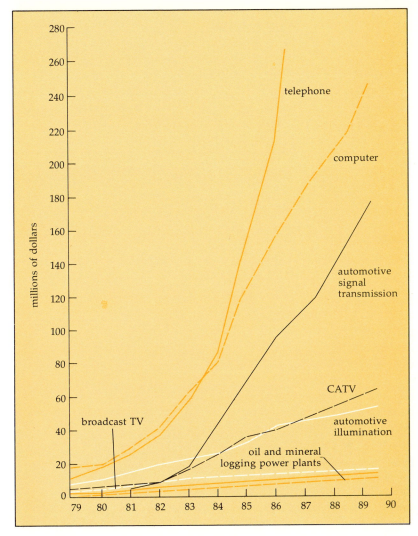

FIGURE 17-8 Projected growth of fiber-optic communications.

thickness of a window pane. By using a cable of strands to transmit laser beams, signals can be sent without interference over long distances.

AT&T's research arm, Bell Telephone Laboratories, is testing a 144-fiber cable that can transmit 50,000 telephone calls at once. Current AT&T copper cables are about seven times thicker and weigh over 100 times as much as fiber cable (see Figure 17–7).

Unlike copper, which is in short supply, the raw material for fiber-optic cables is purified silicone oxide, derived from sand. One thimbleful of the oxide can produce a mile-long strand. The use of fiber optic (or lightwave) communication may soon affect television, automobile components, and many other electronic devices.

Fiber optics communications are also being used to connect terminals to computers. The city of Houston, Texas, uses fiber-optic cables to link CRT terminals in its library to its computer 4,900 feet away. Another use is intracomputer connections, such as CPU to magnetic disk. (The anticipated growth of fiber optics is shown in Figure 17–8.)

SUMMARY

Looking from the past, through the present, and into the future, we have seen striking and even awesome changes in computing. We have moved from a point where the computer was a huge, expensive, and hard-to-use device to where it is compact, inexpensive per calculation, and, through high-level languages, easier to program. Methods, media, and machines that were central to older computers (machine language programming, paper tape and punched cards, vacuum tubes, and core memory) have become obsolete or nearly so.

Computer design and manufacturing have become so efficient and sophisticated that we now have microprocessors programmed to do a wide range of tasks that in the past required complex wired circuits. We can afford to underuse circuits when they are assigned an easy task because they are so inexpensive; or we can use an identical circuit to function as a processor in a microcomputer.

The use of standardized microprocessors, which depend on microcode for their unique functions, has resulted in economies of mass production that, in turn, have lowered microprocessor costs. Operating systems are becoming more complex and comprehensive, providing the user with communications, scheduling, logging, accounting, and other capabilities. Database management systems are becoming available to more users as memory and processor costs drop.

Computer languages will become simpler to use. Perhaps the biggest change in languages over the next ten years will be the growing use of problem-oriented languages tailored to a specific industry or profession. Programming techniques will become more refined, based on experience and sophisticated logic. Continued growth in top-down and structured programming is foreseen. With anticipated inflation in salaries, software costs are expected to rise. Use of report generators will become more common and interactive ones will be available in a few years.

Personal computers are and will continue to be the most dynamic aspect of the computer industry. Many brands will come on the market, but many will not be competitive in quality of hardware or software or will be poorly marketed and, hence, will go out of production.

TERMS

The following words or terms have been presented in this chapter.

Microcomputer	ADA
Firmware	Structured programming
Microcode	Top-down programming
Software	Report generator
Operating system	Protocol
Relational	Fiber optics

EXERCISES

The exercises that follow are grouped by level of difficulty. Problems in the A series are the easiest; B series problems are moderately hard; and C series problems are the most difficult.

A–1 Describe the difference between a CPU and a processor.

A–2 Will I/O devices or CPUs improve more in cost/performance in the next five years? Explain.

A–3 What are two probable replacements for disks for secondary storage that will appear within the next five years?

A–4 What are the functional parts of a database management system?

A–5 Describe "top-down" programming.

A–6 What is the trend in the portion of computer systems using telecommunications?

A–7 What is "telephone tag" and how can the 3M Company's voice mail system eliminate it?

B–1 Explain why "it is economical to waste logic circuits' abilities."

B-2 What is gained by making computer components smaller?

B-3 Why should COM devices cost less by 1985?

B-4 What is the current trend in cost of terminals in relation to total cost of computer systems? Why do you think this trend has developed?

B-5 What major changes will take place in computer languages in the next few years?

B-6 What are the price relationships between hardware and software (now and for the foreseeable future)?

B-7 By what method does 3M Company's voice mail system store messages?

C-1 How small might semiconductor memories ultimately become? What technological hurdles must be overcome before reaching that ultimate size?

C-2 How has microcode enabled computer manufacturers to offer an improved price/performance ratio?

C-3 What do you see as the primary factors that enable less sophisticated users to do more sophisticated tasks with computers?

C-4 What are some of the advantages of fiber optics (in telecommunications) over copper cables?

C-5 How should 3M Company's voice mail system lower costs?

COMPUTER NEWS

APPLICATIONS: VOICE MAIL ARRIVES IN THE OFFICE

"Telephone tag" is the merry-go-round of futility that has become one of the most frustrating games that businessmen play. For example: Mr. Jensen calls Mr. Burkhardt, who is away, so someone takes a callback message. When Burkhardt returns the call, Jensen is on another line, so Burkhardt leaves a message. Jensen calls again, but now Burkhardt is in a meeting. The game can go on and on, sometimes for days.

But James R. Jensen, G. William Burkhardt, and 1,000 other executives and office workers at 3M Co. are getting ready to celebrate the end of telephone tag. In May the St. Paul company installed the world's first commercial system that turns spoken words into digital "mail." Now, when Jensen, 3M's director of office administration, needs to tell Burkhardt, manager of market development services, something that is not urgent, he simply dials a special number to get on the voice-mail system and dictates his message into the phone. The system attempts to deliver the message immediately, but if Burkhardt is not in, it files it in memory. Later, when Burkhardt dials his voice "mailbox," the system tells him that a message is waiting, then it reconstitutes the digital data back into Jensen's voice and delivers the message. "We play telephone tag at incredible rates around here," says Jensen, "especially Burkhardt and I. It will be just great to eliminate that—and all the wasted time that goes with it."

While 3M was busy installing its voice-mail system, Bell Telephone Co. of Pennsylvania, a subsidiary of American Telephone & Telegraph Co., announced in Philadelphia that it plans to put similar technology to work in its switching offices. The computerized equipment will provide simple storage and delivery services for voice mail, at a cost of about $15 per month. The Bell System company figures that the new service will appeal especially to residential users and small businessmen who cannot afford the $300,000 to $500,000 cost of a full-blown system such as the one that 3M has.

'MISSING LINK'

Communications experts unanimously applaud the new technology—particularly the 3M version, which was developed with 3M's help by Electronic Communication Systems Inc. (ECS). The two-year-old Dallas company has jumped off to a big head start over Rolm, Northern Telecom, Datapoint, and International Business Machines—all of which are reported to be working on voice mail systems. The ECS equipment, dubbed Voice Message System, or VMS, has the functions of an information processing system plus electronic-mail capability (drawing). A. Terrence Easton, a San Francisco-based telecommunications consultant, terms such voice mail networks "the missing link to the office of the future."

Most automated-office developments are currently aimed at improving the productivity of secretaries and typists, not the executive. The typical manager is getting almost no new tools. He spends 75% of his day talking to people, according to a study by SRI International, and is reluctant to learn to use word processing equipment.

Voice-mail systems could save managers' time, because once the caller's voice has been converted into digital data—much like that stored on voice-synthesis memory chips—the message can be handled just as if the information had been generated on a word processing terminal. The same voice message can be sent to groups of people, for example, or it can be transmitted during the night to someone at a distant office with another voice mail system for next-day delivery.

3¢ A MESSAGE

Voice mail "offers an opportunity for enormous gains in productivity," declares Howard Anderson, president of Yankee Group, a market research firm that tracks automated-office technologies. A recent study by his Cambridge (Mass.) firm found that nearly three out of four phone calls do not get through to the right person, and half the calls that are completed are inconsequential—requests for a printed document or notifications of a meeting, for example. Studies by SRI and the National Aeronautics & Space Administration confirm that the telephone can be a dreary drain on executive time.

3M's Jensen notes that "VMS will not replace normal voice communications," because urgent calls will still have to be dialed direct, and a lot of calls require a dialogue, but it should go a long way toward alleviating the disruptions caused by trivial calls. Based on a study of how 3M headquarters personnel handle internal communications, Jensen estimates that each person on the VMS network will use voice mail to send 15 messages per day. "We think that, to some extent, it will replace memo-writing because of its quickness," he adds, "and because it is actually less expensive to pick up a phone and dictate a call than it is to spend time writing a memo."

If Jensen's estimate of 15 messages per day is accurate, voice mail clearly is a communications bargain. 3M intends to charge each user $10 per month for VMS services. That comes to a mere 3¢ per message. Yet Jensen says that $10 per month times 1,000 users will recover the system's capital and operating costs in 36 months. "Since I've been testing it these past few days," he says, "I think [usage] should easily be that, and maybe more."

And if 3M can ultimately serve 1,500 to 1,800 users without adding any hardware, as Jensen projects, voice mail will be an even bigger bargain. If the productivity gains are factored in, VMS "can offer a payback in less than a year," says Neill H. Brownstein, a partner in the venture-capital arm of Bessemer Securities Corp., one of the principal investors in ECS.

It is no wonder, then, that Gordon H. Matthews, founder and chairman of ECS, reports that "the response [to VMS] so far has been simply phenomenal." In fact, his company is sold out for the balance of this year. A second voice-mail system will soon be shipped to Hercules Inc.'s headquarters in Wilmington, Del.

Yankee Group's Anderson is so bullish about voice mail that he forecasts a $500 million market for such equipment in 1985. But by then, he predicts, AT&T will have taken the lead, with 40% of the market, followed by Northern Telecom with 25%, ECS with 15%, and IBM and Rolm with 10% each.

SECRET SYSTEMS

Bell's leadership will not stem from the services now being tested in Philadelphia, however, some observers conclude. Yankee Group's Anderson figures that many businessmen would simply buy automatic answering machines rather than subscribe to the new Bell service.

But Bell has a secret weapon or two back in the laboratory. The telephone giant is working on a super-PBX (private branch exchange), code-named Antelope, that will provide full voice-mail services. Several sources report that Datapoint Corp., a Dallas maker of distributed processing systems, has a similar project going under the cover name of Evergreen. None of the potential voice-mail contenders, however, will admit that they have voice-mail systems under development. Anderson of Yankee Group says that the main goal of all the future vendors is a "super switch" that will serve as the nerve center of the automated office and handle all forms of digital communications—voice and data.

Even though 3M is just now getting its system into operation, Jensen expects that rapid advances in the technology will obsolete it. The company intends to recover its costs in no more than 36 months, he explains, because "we think that in three years something's going to happen—the VMS system is going to be expanded, enhanced, changed, or whatever."

And with other new systems around the corner, Jensen does not want to be locked into VMS when IBM and AT&T introduce their equipment. "You know that they have the technical capabilities; what you don't know is how they'll choose to tariff it."

Matthews of ECS also is well aware of the competition in the offing and, as a result, refuses to discuss the details of his company's VMS product. "I won't even talk to customers about our technology," he explains, "because we have a lot of trade secrets." Perhaps chief among those secrets is how VMS converts human speech into digital data and back again without injecting a "Donald Duck" sound.

Ordinarily this requires enormous amounts of computer memory—12 to 300 times more than if the same message had been generated on a keyboard. But such companies as Compression Labs Inc., in Cupertino, Calif., are working on esoteric computer algorithms that will allow more data to be squeezed into less memory. "Data reductions far below anything we have now," says Vice-President Cloyd Marvin, "are just around the corner."

Daniel A. Hosage, manager of Datapoint's Office Systems Group, believes that voice mail "will absolutely be part and parcel of the way we communicate in the future." Consultant Easton muses that, while suppliers of word processing systems have spent hundreds of millions of dollars in efforts to develop electronic mail systems that can be used with word processors, "all the time the most efficient and most natural form of communications was right in front of them—human speech."

CHAPTER eighteen
COMPUTER INDUSTRY

Preview

The Computer Industry in the United States
   Mainframe Computer Manufacturers
   Peripheral Devices Manufacturers
   Minicomputer Manufacturers

History Capsule:
Thomas Watson: The "Old Man" of IBM
   Microcomputer Manufacturers
   Semiconductor Manufacturers
   Software Services
   Computing Services
   Facilities Management
   Computer Stores

International Computer Industry

Summary

Computer News: Small-Computer Shootout

PREVIEW

The objective of this chapter is to provide you with an overall world view of the computer industry. We look first at the American industry, examining major companies and minor companies, and manufacturers of general-purpose computers, peripheral devices, and mini and microcomputers, software vendors, and computing services. Finally, we look at the international computer industry and examine its relationship to our own.

In the 35 years since the first electronic computer was built, the computer industry has progressed from vacuum tubes to microminiaturized devices centered around large-scale integrated (LSI) circuits and very large-scale integrated (VLSI) circuits. The industry has evolved through several generations of computer design. It has seen companies enter and leave the computer field, and markets developed from nothing. The field is still new—in fact, 29 of the top 50 U.S. companies in the data processing field did not exist before 1950.

Computers are used by and have an impact on all major industries. In the transportation industry, computers help design and manufacture automobiles, are an integral part of automotive electrical and fuel systems, control the movement of mass transit vehicles, control space probe vehicles, handle reservations, and analyze weather. In the financial field, computers maintain records of checking and savings accounts, bill for charge account purchases, and even provide cash at remote automated teller stations. In the medical field computers monitor the body's functions during surgery, maintain patient charts, and prepare billings. In government, computers keep records of our income, payroll taxes, tax reports, and tax payments. The list of computerized activities grows daily and is limited only by our imaginations.

THE COMPUTER INDUSTRY IN THE UNITED STATES

The U.S. computer industry, since its birth 34 years ago, has enjoyed a steady growth aided by both increased paperwork within government and private industry, and a rapidly improving cost/performance ratio for hardware and software. By 1985 we should see about 500,000 computers costing over $50,000 and another 500,000 computers costing between $5,000 and $50,000 in the United States, with the computer industry accounting for 2.2 percent of the gross national product.

The combined annual revenue worldwide of the 100 largest U.S. companies in the data processing industry is about $55 billion, with IBM earning about 38 percent of that. The industry's revenues grew about 10 percent per year from 1970 to 1975 and 9 percent from 1975 to 1979, and this rate is expected to continue up to 1986 (see Figure 18–1). General-purpose computer revenues are expected to grow even faster—about 15 percent annually over the next five years. The computer industry is also healthy in terms of international sales, showing a sizable excess of exports over imports; 1978 imports were $2 billion, while exports were $4.6 billion.

The computer industry in the United States is often equated with IBM and with machines that have blinking lights, whirling disks, and spinning tape reels. As you now know, however, computers involve a lot more than IBM hardware and blinking lights. The industry involves machines, organiza-

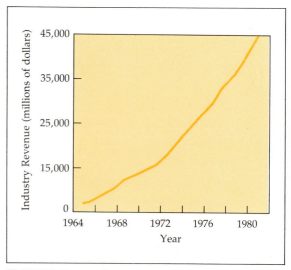

FIGURE 18–1 Growth of U.S. computer industry revenues.

"I'VE GOT A HOME COMPUTER IN MY DEN AND A DESKTOP COMPUTER IN MY OFFICE. HERE, I FEEL LOST."

tions, people, programs, and supplies. In the following discussion, we look at the trends within the industry's subdivisions: general-purpose computers (or mainframes); peripheral devices; minicomputers; microcomputers; semiconductors; software; computing services; and facilities management.

Mainframe Computer Manufacturers

Mainframe computers are designed, built, and marketed in a variety of types and sizes. These computer systems have traditionally been rented or leased rather than sold because a short-term agreement enables the user to switch to a different model or different brand as computing needs change. However, in recent years more and more vendors are pricing their systems to encourage purchases as opposed to renting. Almost half of all mainframes are now purchased.

Although mainframe manufacturers build mainframes primarily, most of them have entered the minicomputer market, and several, including IBM, now offer microcomputers.

IBM dominates the mainframe computer market and is almost certain to continue to do so in the foreseeable future. The industry's revenue leader as well, IBM currently accounts for about 38 percent of the total data processing revenue in the United States. Among mainframe manufacturers, IBM accounts for 62.2 percent of the market, far above the roughly 8 percent of the next two companies (see Figure 18–2). IBM and the other eight U.S. mainframe computer manufacturers (Amdahl, Burroughs, Control Data, Cray, Honeywell, NAS, NCR, and Sperry-Univac) collectively account for 60 percent of all U.S. computer industry revenues.

Within the last decade three mainframe manufacturers (RCA, General Electric, and Xerox) have closed their computer divisions because of lack of profits. Despite this, potential profits in the field have attracted others. Cray Research, Inc. delivered its first computer, the Cray-1 in 1976, and is now producing about a dozen computers a year. Patterned after the large CDC 7600 computer, the Cray-1 is designed to run four to five times faster than the CDC but sell for the same price, $7.5 million. The market for these very large computers is limited, and therefore not critical to IBM.

However, several developments, if not critical to IBM, are certainly getting its attention, as reflected

FIGURE 18–2 Sales and market shares of mainframe computer manufacturers.

	1980 Revenues (Millions of dollars)	Share of Group Market (Percent)	Share of Top-100 Market (Percent)
IBM	$21,367	62.2	38.4
NCR	2,840	8.3	5.1
Control Data	2,791	8.1	5.0
Sperry-Univac	2,552	7.4	4.6
Burroughs	2,478	7.2	4.5
Honeywell	1,634	4.8	2.9
Amdahl	394	1.1	0.7
National Advanced Syst.	245	0.7	0.4
Cray Research	61	0.2	0.1
Total	34,362	100.0	61.8

Data: *Datamation*.

CHAPTER 18: COMPUTER INDUSTRY

in substantial price cuts by IBM. CDC has introduced its Omega 480 CPU which offers improved price/performance ratios, to replace IBM's System 370's and 4300's.

Amdahl Corporation, Control Data Corporation, Magnuson Corporation, and several others have designed IBM-look-alike computers. That is, their computers function in a manner similar to some of IBM's and can operate on IBM software. Furthermore, these look-alikes can utilize IBM peripheral devices such as disk and tape drives. The IBM central processor can be removed and replaced by plugging in the look-alike and the programs "don't know the difference." Therefore, the look-alikes are called **plug-compatible machines (PCMs).** Amdahl's 470/v and 580 computers are compatible with IBM's 3033 and 3081. The Amdahls, however, provide greater computing power than the IBMs of comparable costs. As of December 1980, over 400 of the $2 to $4.25 million Amdahls had been shipped to customers.

National Semiconductor, the second largest manufacturer of computer chips, entered the PCM mainframe business first simply as a manufacturer. Now, through a subsidiary, National Advanced Systems (NAS), National is building, selling, and servicing mainframes. The NAS's AS/8 offers 35 percent greater performance than the IBM 3033 it competes with.

Several other companies have entered the PCM business as manufacturers and/or marketers. They are Two Pi, a corporate relative of Holland's Philips; NCSS, a large time-sharing service bureau; Magnuson, whose M-80 system was designed in part by Carl Amdahl, son of Gene Amdahl who started the whole PCM mainframe effort; and Nanodata, which aims at distributed processing systems.

Peripheral Devices Manufacturers

Input/output, mass storage devices, and other support devices are generally available with the CPU as a total system. However, many independent companies are manufacturing and marketing peripheral devices that compete directly with mainframe manufacturers' own peripheral devices.

The widespread acceptance of these independently manufactured peripheral devices is the result of a number of factors. Generally these devices are plug-compatible. This allows mainframe-manufactured disks, printers, tape, microfilm devices, terminals, optical scanners, auxiliary main memory, and many other peripherals to be interchanged with peripherals manufactured by the independent companies. These **independent computer peripheral equipment manufacturers (ICPEMs)** generally sell their devices at up to 40 percent less than the mainframe manufacturers. On leased equipment, the discount is generally up to 20 percent. The cost savings to the user is frequently even greater since ICPEM devices are often better than the equipment they replace. This price and performance advantage has become especially important as computer systems costs have shifted to where over 50 percent is attributable to the peripherals. As use of large-scale integration and microprocessors, and competition in the CPU market increase, the cost of CPUs will decline in relation to performance. Thus, the proportion of total cost spent on peripherals will increase. The annual growth of sales revenue in peripheral devices is around 20 percent, while growth of sales revenue in general-purpose computing systems is less than 10 percent.

Many of the ICPEMs, such as Storage Technology, Dataproducts, Centronics, Memorex, Telex, and Computer Machinery, were established to produce and market a particular peripheral device or a line of devices. Companies like General Electric, Tektronics, 3M, Ampex, AT&T, Xerox, and Eastman Kodak manufacture many non-computer-related devices in addition to their computer peripherals.

As with mainframe manufacturing, many firms have entered the peripheral manufacturing field but have not survived because of the intense price competition, the large amount of capital required to get established, or the lack of management, marketing, or technical expertise. This "washing out" of the less able firms will continue and may even intensify in the next few years.

Minicomputer Manufacturers

The fluidity of the computer industry is well illustrated by the minicomputer. In fact, most manufac-

THOMAS WATSON: THE "OLD MAN" OF IBM

Born in a farmhouse in upstate New York, Thomas Watson showed no early signs of greatness. At age 18, Watson gave up a bookkeeping job to sell pianos, organs, sewing machines, and caskets with a friend, George Cornwell. Learning from Cornwell's easy manner, he developed skill in selling. This ability to observe others, focus on the good traits, and weave them into his own approach to people was to play a major role in his success.

At age 21, selling shares of corporate stock door to door for a lively person named C. B. Barron, Watson took on another technique. Barron believed that first impressions (preferably prosperous first impressions) were vital. "Sell yourself and you sell your product," he told Watson. Barron had some good ideas but some poor scruples; he skipped town with the funds and Watson had to find a new employer.

Still 21 years old, Watson took a selling job with National Cash Register (NCR), whose powerful president, John Patterson, was to also be a strong influence on Watson. Patterson's approach was the carrot-and-stick method, with great rewards for success and a strong tongue-lashing for failure. Patterson called this approach "character building." Under Patterson's sales manager John Range, Watson learned to handle customers gently, giving them confidence in their own ability to manage—better, of course, with an NCR cash register. Watson learned quickly and in 1899, at age 25, he was asked to manage the Rochester, N.Y., office of NCR on a 25 percent commission. Watson's sales efforts were sometimes fierce, and he eliminated a number of local competitors, which pleased Patterson.

In 1903 Watson was put in charge of NCR's national campaign, which used the tactic of setting up cutrate cash register outlets, ostensibly independent ones, to buy up or drive out competitors. In later years it was understood that Watson never approved of NCR's knockout technique, but his involvement in these sales efforts was to cause him grief.

In Ohio in 1912, an antitrust lawsuit was filed naming Watson and other NCR officers. In 1913 they were convicted and sentenced to a $5,000 fine and a year in jail. While appeals were under way, Dayton,

Ohio, NCR's headquarters city, had a severe flood. Never failing to seize an opportunity, Patterson returned to Dayton, leaving Watson in New York City. The hilltop NCR plant had escaped the flood ravages, giving Patterson the opportunity to set up a relief center at the plant's canteen, recreation building, and medical facilities. Meanwhile, using NCR's telegraph line, the only one that survived the flood, Patterson in Dayton and Watson in New York were the only sources of news of the flood tragedy. Watson launched a nationwide appeal for help, coordinated relief supplies, began a drive to rebuild the city, and to build a proper flood control system.

Soon after the flood, as a result of a growing conflict between the powerful Patterson and the strong Watson, Watson was fired. Now married, with his wife Jeannette expecting a child, in the midst of an economic depression and still under threat of a year in jail, 40-year-old Watson had reached a low point in his life. But all was not lost.

CHAPTER 18: COMPUTER INDUSTRY

Watson had had 15 years of valuable experience with Patterson and Jeannette stuck by him. Drawing as he always had on the desirable traits he saw in others, he adopted Jeannette's deep belief in the Golden Rule as a guide in dealing with employees. Watson's experience and past performance brought him a job in 1914 with a company called Computing-Tabulating-Recording (C-T-R), which had been created in 1911 by combining 13 separate companies, including Herman Hollerith's Tabulating Machine Company established in 1896. For this job, Watson was paid $25,000 per year plus 5 percent of "any profits he could wring out" of the faltering company. (This 5 percent eventually made Watson the highest paid executive in the United States.)

Watson carried on a running battle with Hollerith, who was still involved in the company, feeling that Hollerith's technical genius was not matched by business genius. For the rest of his life, Watson favored sales people over technical people.

In March 1915, Watson's earlier conviction was set aside and a new trial called but never pursued in light of Patterson's and Watson's having "saved the city" as some news stories told.

Now Watson was general manager of C-T-R, and he continued in that office until 1924 when, after the death of C-T-R's president, he became the chief executive at age 50. In that year Watson changed C-T-R's name to International Business Machines (IBM).

Building on Hollerith's licensing and marketing arrangements throughout Britain and Europe, Watson's IBM, through secret negotiations, gained control of one (Swiss Bull) of its two tabulating machine competitors (the other being Remington Rand).

With the rising conflict throughout Europe that led to World War II, IBM's European companies were restricted from sending cash profits back to the U.S. Meanwhile, the United States was in the depths of its worst depression, and IBM sales plummeted. In spite of falling sales revenue, however, Watson refused to lay off his employees and continued manufacturing machines, storing them in warehouses. Then, in 1935, the U.S. Congress passed legislation setting up the Social Security program. This program required a massive accounting and disbursing system to provide payments to millions of citizens. IBM won the contract to provide the machines because it could deliver them immediately (from its overflowing warehouses). Although saved from financial disaster, IBM soon faced the uncertainties of wartime.

With the United States drawn into World War II, many IBM employees, domestic and foreign, were drawn into military service. Watson, with many IBM offices located in enemy or occupied territory, was able to collect intelligence information regularly for the U.S. State Department. Much of this was done at considerable risk by the IBM employees. For instance, Oskar Hoerrmann, head of IBM France during the German occupation, hid inventor Jean Ghertman although at one point he was told that if he did not produce Ghertman within 24 hours, he himself would be sent to a concentration camp.

IBM employees and Watson aided the victory effort in other ways, too. IBM, at Watson's direction, set up tabulating centers, which were run by the Red Cross, for keeping track of prisoners of war. Some of IBM's foreign profits were used to smuggle downed pilots out of enemy territory. Tom Watson's concern for loyal employees was typified in his treatment of Ed Corwin, an IBM salesman in Poland who spent most of the war in concentration camp and who, when released, was paid back salary for the war years.

During the war, Watson made a decision that was to prove embarrassing later. With the military in dire need of improved calculating devices for computing firing tables for artillery weapons, IBM financed the efforts of Howard Aiken at Harvard University to build a huge mechanical computing device, but turned down a request from the University of Pennsylvania, which wanted to build an electronic computer device. The U.S. Army, however, did support Penn's effort, which resulted in ENIAC, the first electronic computer. IBM's MARK I made 6 calculations per second, while ENIAC made 5,000.

Still not convinced that electronic computers had any business value, Watson ignored his sons, Tom, Jr. and Dick, who were now officers in the company, and who wanted IBM to manufacture electronic computers. Meanwhile, ENIAC's prime builders, John Mauchly and J. Presper Eckert, had set up their own computer business, which was soon bought out by Remington Rand. Remington Rand's first commercial computer, the UNIVAC, finally convinced the elder Watson that there might be a market for commercial computing machines. Although a late entry into the computer field, Watson was not too late. With the help of his sons, his wife Jeannette, and of course many talented and dedicated employees, the Old Man, as he had become known, entered the computer business and within a short time became its dominant force.

Watson held tight control over IBM's management until just a few months before his death at age 82 in 1956.

---

turers and users cannot even agree on a definition of the term. When minicomputers first hit the market in the late 1960s, a minicomputer was generally defined as CPU with a parallel, 16-bit fixed-word-length computer with 4K to 32K memory, which, in its minimal configuration, sold for around $20,000.

Now, however, minicomputers have evolved beyond this definition. For example, the Hewlett-Packard 3000-III has models that sell for over $200,000, and Digital Equipment Corporation's DEC-System 20 sells for $750,000. At the other extreme, some desktype minicomputers are selling for under $10,000. The trend is toward a wider range in memory sizes, languages, peripherals, and applications. The major minicomputer manufacturers even offer database management systems.

As of 1979 there were 310,000 American-made minicomputers installed within the United States, up from only 190,000 in 1976. The total market for minicomputers is expected to grow 27 percent per year through 1985, reaching $25 billion (Figure 18–3). Such rapid growth occurred probably because the minicomputer manufacturers adhered strictly to a sell rather than rent policy, and received a steady, rapid return on their investment.

Digital Equipment Corporation (DEC), the leading manufacturer of minicomputers, accounts for 29 percent of the minicomputer market, with Hewlett-Packard (17 percent) and Data General (9 percent) following (Figure 18–4). In the past few years mainframe manufacturers IBM (System 1), Control Data (Cyber 18), Sperry Univac (UNIVAC V77), Burroughs, Honeywell (DPS 6), and NCR (8300), have entered the minicomputer market.

In contrast to mainframe manufacturers who sell primarily to end users, minicomputer manufacturers sell over half their output to other manufacturers or to companies that combine the minicomputer with their own software and then sell the package as a system for accounting, monitoring building security, controlling a manufacturing process, or doing other specific activities. These manufacturers or packagers are often called **original equipment manufacturers (OEMs)**.

Minicomputers have not only established themselves in the industry as competitive in price, but have proved to have an attractive price/performance ratio, which contradicts an earlier theory that the larger the computer, the more economical. In fact, it

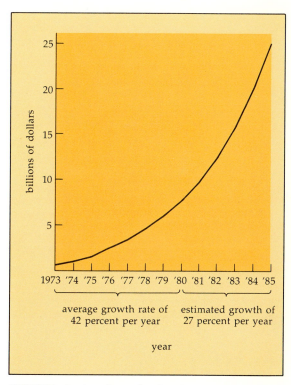

FIGURE 18–3 Growth of U.S. minicomputer sales.

CHAPTER 18: COMPUTER INDUSTRY 437

FIGURE 18-4 Estimated sales and market share of minicomputers.

	1980 Sales (millions of dollars)	Share of Market (Percent)
Digital Equipment	$2,235	29
Hewlett-Packard	1300	17
Data General	662	9
Honeywell	340	4
IBM (series 1 only)	320	4
Datapoint	319	4
Wang Labs	316	4
Prime	235	3
Perkin-Elmer	215	3
Management Asst.	208	3
Four Phase	200	3
Texas Instruments	155	2

is estimated that by 1983, 91 percent of all computers in use will be mini or microcomputers.

Microcomputer Manufacturers

The microcomputer industry is maturing rapidly from just a few manufacturers putting out low-speed microprocessors with limited instruction sets to over 65 manufacturers offering systems that include faster, more reliable processors, single-chip memories, more extensive instruction sets, and training in program writing. One of the major limitations of microcomputers has been the difficulty of connecting peripheral devices, but peripheral interface adapters are now becoming available, greatly reducing the cost of attaching peripherals such as floppy disks, keyboards, and CRTs. Dozens of companies give seminars and offer training courses and consulting services. As the industry continues to mature in the next few years, only the more innovative and better managed companies will survive. Microcomputer manufacturers that aim at the commercial market include Motorola, RCA, Texas Instruments, Burroughs, Fairchild, Intel, Mostek, National Semiconductor, and others. Microcomputer makers that market personal computers are Apple, Atari, Commodore, Cromemco, IBM, Hewlett-Packard, North Star, Tandy, Vector Graphics, Xerox, and others.

Microcomputers are being used extensively in cash register terminals, microwave ovens, and computer peripheral equipment. They are now being sold as personal computers in retail outlets or "computer stores" in assembled and kit form. There are now over 500,000 microcomputers in the hands of users. Prices for kits start below $200, while assembled models sell for as low as $250. Most microcomputers must be equipped with I/O devices at additional cost. Micros bought today at computer stores are apparently mainly used for running game programs or are related to hobbies, but a tremendous potential market is the business executive, private investor, or other professional who needs the computer's power to improve job productivity. An estimated one-third of all personal computers sold have found their way into private offices or are used at home in work-related uses.

Another large, but harder to tap market exists for more practical household functions such as heating and air conditioning control, fire and entry detection, menu generation, and recordkeeping.

The trend toward greater microcomputer use means a continuation in the 50 percent per year drop in the cost of circuitry. The Intel 8080 microprocessor, for example, was introduced in 1974 at a price of over $300, and within two years dropped to $21. Some experts predict that prices will continue to decline for the next ten years as sales climb. From virtually no sales base several years ago, sales of microcomputers reached $500 million by 1978 and are predicted to jump to $2.4 billion in 1982 and $4.9 billion by 1985.

Semiconductor Manufacturers

The driving force behind the computer industry's phenomenal growth is the silicon chip. Built into these chips are memory, logic circuits, and even whole processors. These semiconductor chips become integral parts of micro, mini, and mainframe computers, and components of many other products. For example, seven million 4-bit microcomputers were installed in "Simon" games. The U.S. automobile industry purchased $100 million worth of microprocessors in 1980 for ignition, carburetion, and other systems.

Roughly 20 semiconductor manufacturers produce in the United States and account for 65 percent of the world's semiconductor production. (See Figure 18–5 for the top six.) U.S. sales reached $11 billion in 1979, $13 billion in 1980, and are projected to $100 billion by 1990. This dollar increase, in spite of a 20 to 30 percent drop in prices per year, is possible because the volume of bits shipped has doubled each year since 1974 and is expected to continue doubling through 1984.

The future for semiconductor builders is clouded by intense foreign competition. A volume equal to 30 percent of domestic chip production was imported from Japan in 1979. Furthermore, in the drive to build very large scale integrated circuits (VLSIC), Japanese manufacturers enjoy government financial support. U.S. manufacturers are facing shortages of trained engineers; only token, if any, government support; and heavy demands for capital in the face of slimmer profit margins. A production line for building chips cost $1 million in 1965, but now costs $50 million.

Software Services

The cost of software as a percentage of total computer system cost has increased dramatically in the past few years. For example, in the late 1950s the U.S. Defense Department was spending about 15 percent of its system cost on software and the remainder on hardware. Currently, about 70 percent is being spent on software, and the department predicts that software spending in 1985 will account for 90 percent of their computer systems budget.

What has brought about this shift in spending? One major reason has been the 10 to 20 percent per year decrease in computer hardware cost enjoyed by the industry since its birth. Other major reasons relate to software itself. Another major reason for increased software costs is the increased level of sophistication of computer applications. More complex applications are being computerized than before. Another reason is the rising cost of programming labor at the same time computer costs per calculation have dropped dramatically. Also, in the early 1970s IBM began to charge its customers for certain software that had previously been hidden in the hardware price. Other manufacturers followed the pattern gradually. This separating of the price of hardware and software is called **unbundling**. Once a software item was tagged with a price,

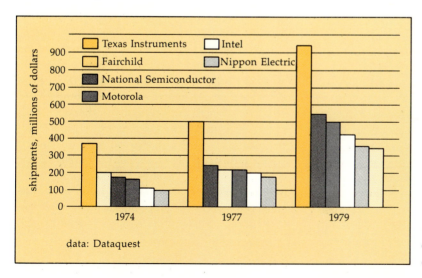

FIGURE 18–5 Semiconductor company sales of integrated circuits.

however, users began to look for alternatives such as in-house writing of software or purchasing programs from independent software suppliers.

This shift to the independent market built up a demand for software that, in turn, attracted hundreds and then thousands of writers and sellers of software. This software can be divided into two categories. **Proprietary software packages** are programs developed by a software writer to be sold or leased to many users. Examples of these programs are payroll, inventory control, accounts receivable, data entry, general ledger, and database management systems. By selling the package to several users, the writer is able to spread the development cost and, thus, offer the package at a lower price while still making a profit. Since their income depends completely on satisfied customers, proprietary software companies usually turn out more efficient and more quickly implemented programs than those provided by computer manufacturers. Some of the major firms in the software industry are Informatics, Management Sciences America, Cincom Systems, and University Computing.

The other category of software service is **contract programming,** where a software firm writes a custom program for the user on a pay-per-hour or pay-per-program basis. The user may have a one-time staffing need, a complex program requiring outside expertise, or assistance in installing a package. Many small, even one-person, companies have developed in the field of contract programming. Currently, one-half of the software industry's sales are in contract programs, and half are in packages. Figure 18–6 shows the revenues for ten large software firms and the mix of software packages and other software sales.

The annual growth rate of the software industry has averaged about 25 percent in recent years (Figure 18–7). During the past ten years the software industry has grown ninefold. About one-third of package sales have been for operating systems software, two-thirds for applications software (Figure 18–8), and the trend is toward the increasing use of application packages. Sales of applications software packages are growing at about 30 percent a year as users recognize more and more the cost effectiveness of packages. Application packages fall into the major areas of manufacturing, payroll/personnel, accounting, insurance, and banking (Figure 18–9).

Computing Services

Computing services provided by outside organizations range from comprehensive—including data entry, processing, mailing of output, systems planning and programming, and hardware acquisition, operation, and management—to limited—including only one activity. Currently, over 20 percent of all data processing-related expenditures by end users are for computing services by outside vendors. In 1980 this reached an annual sales total of $14 billion, and, with a projected 20 percent annual growth rate, computing services revenue will reach $35 billion by 1985.

Service bureaus supply computer processing services to others for a fee. By servicing many users, the service bureau is able to provide computing on larger, more capable equipment than any one of its users could afford on its own. Service bureau processing has proved beneficial to many small to medium-sized firms over the past 15 years, as evidenced by the large number of service bureaus that have developed. Traditionally, service bureaus have concentrated on batch processing services; however, in recent years many service bureaus have added remote on-line data entry and inquiry capabilities. The batch services provided have grown from $500 million in 1967, to $8.6 billion in 1980 and are projected to increase to $10.2 billion in 1985. Total revenues from batch and remote services are expected to reach $18.8 billion in 1984 (Figure 18–10), for an average annual increase of about 17 percent. The underlying strength of the over 1,600 service bureaus nationwide has been familiarity with local markets and specialization within a specific industry or within application areas such as payroll, accounts receivable, or data preparation. The six largest service bureaus, including Automated Data Processing and Tymeshare, Inc. with revenues of over $130 million each (Figure 18–11) follow this pattern of market specialization.

The growth of service bureaus has been significantly less than the growth of other computing ser-

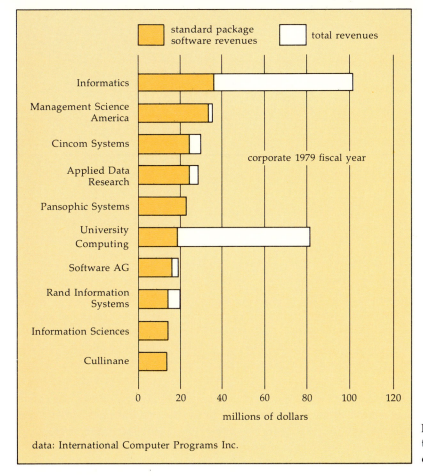

FIGURE 18–6 Revenues of the top ten computer software companies.

vices (such as network information services at 22 percent annually) because of the increasing availability of cost-effective small and minicomputers.

Network information services (NIS) offer remote time-sharing and remote batch services regionally and internationally over communications networks (see Chapter 16). Often called **computer utilities,** they offer low-cost access to powerful computers. Network systems are changing their service emphasis from almost exclusively interactive time-sharing to remote batch processing, which accounted for about 40 percent of the NIS market for 1978.

Until recently, many computer watchers anticipated a vast growth in computer utilities, to the point where even individual consumers would subscribe to the service, much as they do for electricity or telephone service. Although there are economies of scale in sharing computing resources in NIS, several factors have restrained their growth. These include the complexities of large networks, new cost-effective small and minicomputers that can perform tasks that had been delegated to time-sharing systems, cost of communication links, and the desire for internal control of processing. As more and more management decision-making data are computer-generated, the need for security makes in-house processing more appealing—all other factors being equal.

In spite of these forces, however, NIS market has grown from $45 million in 1967, to $430 million in 1971, and is expected to reach $6,200 million in

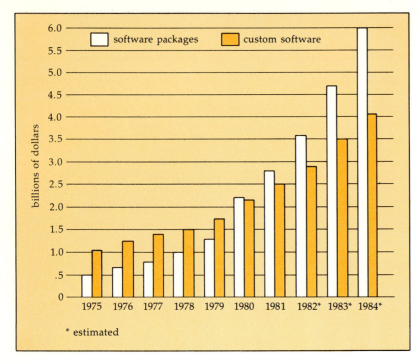

FIGURE 18–7 Sales of software packages and custom software.

1982. This 27 percent annual growth rate is expected to continue through 1985 and should encourage large vendors such as General Electric, Tymshare, McDonnell Douglas, Computer Sciences, Boeing Computer Services, and National CSS to remain in the market and other vendors to enter it.

In a recent development several computer time-sharing companies have joined with information providers to offer home or business information services. For example, National CSS, Inc., was acquired by Dun & Bradstreet, Inc., a publisher of financial and credit information. In another arrangement Mead Data Corp. provides the Associated Press, *The Washington Post, Newsweek,* and *Duns Review* with continuously updated information via computer network. The Dow Jones News Service, publisher of the *Wall Street Journal,* has offered since 1978 an information network, the Dow Jones Data Bank, that serves over 9,000 terminals. This relatively new information providing section of the computer industry is called **information retrieval service.**

An information retrieval company aiming at residential customers is Telecomputing Corp. of America, owned by *Reader's Digest*. It uses United Press International (UPI) and the *New York Times* for its data and calls its information service "The Source."

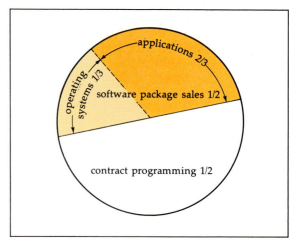

FIGURE 18–8 The sales mix in the software industry in 1980.

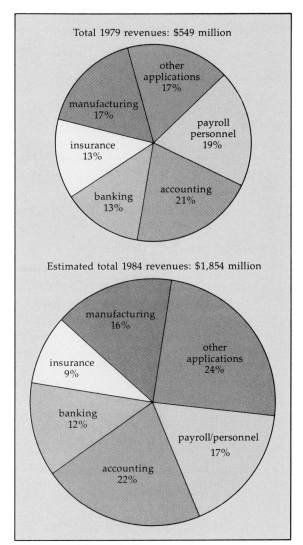

FIGURE 18–9 Application software packages by type.

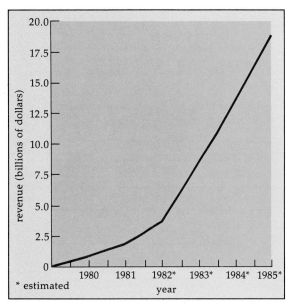

FIGURE 18–10 Computer processing service sales.

Facilities Management

An arrangement whereby an outside vendor operates and manages a client's computer installation is called **facilities management (FM)**. FM means that data processing services are handled by specialists at a predictable or firm cost.

FM companies often specialize in a particular industry such as medical insurance, finance, or banking and, hence, build expertise that enables them to operate efficiently. Operating in a particular industry also allows software developed for one client to be applied to others, thereby spreading the development costs over several customers. Further, an FM firm may stay with a certain brand and model computer and become very proficient in using it. Contracts for FM services have a high renewal rate, thus cutting the FM's marketing costs. Finally, FM companies can justify hiring highly trained systems people and spreading their cost over several installations. These advantages benefit both the user and the provider of the services.

The Environmental Protection Agency and the Federal Energy Agency are using FM firms to implement large-scale database management systems with remote data entry and inquiry from hundreds of terminals all over the United Sates. The FM approach has enabled those systems to become operational quickly and efficiently without having to hire sophisticated personnel.

FM has grown from $110 million annually in 1967, to $645 million in 1971, and is expected to reach $7,000 million by 1982. This 25 percent annual growth rate should continue into the mid 1980s.

FIGURE 18–11 U.S. computer processing services: estimated revenues of 21 largest companies in 1979.

	Estimated 1979 Revenue (in millions)	Estimated Market Share
Control Data Corp.	$420	7%
Automatic Data Processing, Inc.	409	7%
General Electric Information Systems	290	5%
Tymshare, Inc.	160	5%
United Information Systems, Inc.	138	3%
McDonnell Douglas Automation Co.	135	2%
Computer Sciences Corp.	129	2%
NCR Corp.	93	2%
Bradford National Corp.	89	2%
National CSS, Inc.	77	1% or less
Bank of America	70	1% or less
Comshare, Inc.	67	1% or less
Mead Data Corp.	65	1% or less
Boeing Computer Services Co.	62	1% or less
TRW Information Systems	55	1% or less
University Computing Co.	60	1% or less
Xerox Computer Services	60	1% or less
National Data Corp.	54	1% or less
Trans Union Systems Corp.	50	1% or less
First Data Resources	50	1% or less
Bunker Ramo Corp.	50	1% or less

Computer Stores

Sales of personal computers, the bulk of which are made in retail stores, are expected to reach $2.4 billion by the end of 1982. Sales of computers in the $500 to $10,000 range are increasing by about 25 percent yearly. By 1985 yearly sales of personal computers alone will reach $4.9 billion with another $1 billion in software sales. Let us look at the retail computer store in terms of who is in the business, how they operate, and their likelihood of success.

The largest number of outlets are Tandy Corporation's Radio Shack stores, numbering over 8,000. Three other regional or nationwide groups of stores are the Computer Store, Computerland, and Byte Shop. Computerland stores are franchises in which the owner gets support services from Computerland, Inc., and pays a one-time $20,000 franchise fee and 8 percent royalty (or commission) on sales. Establishing a retail computer store requires an investment of about $100,000. The average successful stores generate annual sales of less than $1 million and need a gross markup of 35 percent of sales to cover costs and earn a reasonable return on investment. By one industry estimate the average gross markup is currently only 28 percent and 10 to 12 percent net profit before taxes.

As with most businesses, customer satisfaction is vital to the success of the computer store. A common customer complaint against computer stores is that the dealer lacks knowledge of hardware and software. The key to a successful computer store seems to be to have skilled electronic technicians for repair and knowledgeable programmers to help buyers use their computers. Some owners are trying to hire salespeople with accounting backgrounds. Many stores offer free seminars to purchasers in an effort to build customer utilization and satisfaction.

Until recently, computer stores were owned and operated exclusively by small businesspeople. However, names such as IBM, Xerox, Control Data (CDC), and Digital Equipment (DEC) are now appearing on store fronts. IBM has began retailing through its Business Computer Centers, and DEC has opened over 20 retail stores nationwide. Xerox is establishing stores to carry Apple, Hewlett-Packard, and their own personal computers along with typewriters, programmable calculators, dictating machines, and their own word processors. Control Data expects to have 200 stores in operation by the end of 1982 selling Ohio Scientific microcomputers and others.

INTERNATIONAL COMPUTER INDUSTRY

The international computer industry consists of four major geographical areas: Japan, Western Europe, the United States, and all others. Of the estimated, total value of computers installed worldwide, U.S. manufacturers account for 52 percent; Western European manufacturers, 31 percent; Japanese manufacturers 12 percent; and others, 5 percent. The "other" category includes Eastern bloc nations and any other nation that produces computers (see Figure 18–12).

The U.S. manufacturers' 52 percent share does not include the products of foreign subsidiaries of U.S. manufacturers. Computers built by U.S. companies and their subsidiaries are estimated to have a dominant 84 percent of the world market (Figure 18–13).

U.S. manufacturers have a major advantage in that the domestic market is so large (over two-thirds of the world market). Thus, U.S. manufacturers enjoy an economy of scale that non-U.S. manufacturers do not have—this should help ensure a continued strong overseas market for U.S. manufacturers. Nevertheless, competition from non-U.S. manufacturers is strong. In fact, the revenues of the top ten foreign manufacturers now exceed those of the top ten U.S. manufacturers. The ten foreign companies are: Hitachi, Toshiba, Fujitsu, and Nippon Electric (NEC) of Japan; CII-HB of France; Siemens AG and Nixdorf AG of Germany; ICL of

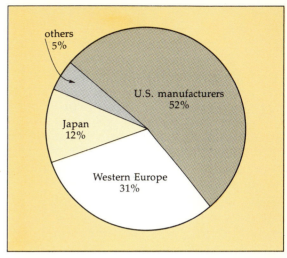

FIGURE 18–12 Estimated values of computers installed worldwide by U.S., Western European, and Japanese manufacturers.

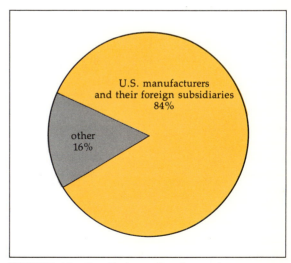

FIGURE 18–13 Estimated values of computers worldwide by U.S. manufacturers and subsidiaries.

Great Britain; Olivetti of Italy; and Phillips N.V. of the Netherlands.

On the Western European scene, one study shows that although U.S. manufacturers' sales increased by 71 percent from 1975 to 1980, the United States' share of the market dropped from 68.2 percent to 66.3 percent. This decline will result from improvements in the sophistication of Western Europe's hardware and software, as well as from the "buy-at-home" desire of Europeans.

Just as the U.S. computer industry has seen the demise of several major computer brands (General Electric, RCA, and Xerox) and the combining of efforts (NCR and CDC, and Honeywell and CDC) to manufacture peripherals, the Japanese and Western European computer industries have also seen the withdrawal of and consolidation of competitors. In Japan, Fujitsu, Hitachi, and Mitsubishi Electric established an organization to manufacture large-scale integrated circuits. Fujitsu and Hitachi carlier had formed a subsidiary called Nippon Peripherals Ltd. to manufacture disk drives. Fujitsu and Hitachi also cooperated in the design and development of the "M-Series," which make up part of their present product lines. Hitachi's M280H is designed to compete with IBM's large 3081 model.

In Western Europe, Germany's Telefunken Computer and Siemens joined in 1974 and France's Compagnie and General Electric joined in 1964 to become Bull-GE. But with General Electric's dropping out of the computer mainframe business, Bull-GE and Honeywell established Compagnie Honeywell-Bull (HB), which later set up with Compagnie Internationale pour l'Informatique (CII), a firm named CII-HB. CII and Control Data set up Magnetic Peripherals in 1976. Does all this sound more confusing than your own family tree? It probably is.

We have looked at the market penetration of U.S. firms in overseas markets, and the ties of U.S. and non-U.S. companies in joint ventures overseas. Have non-U.S. companies penetrated the U.S. market or joined with the U.S. firms to establish joint ventures aimed at our domestic market? The answer is a qualified yes. Hitachi Limited, Japan's fifth largest industrial company and its second-place computer maker, has installed over 100 mainframe computers in the United States, carrying the Itel or National Advanced System (both U.S. companies) label. In 1981 an estimated $165 million worth of Hitachi-built mainframe computers were installed in the United States under National's AS/7000 and AS/9000 nameplates. Fujitsu, Japan's first-place computer builder, has joined U.S.'s TRW Inc. in marketing Fujitsu's V830 computers to compete with IBM's System 38 and Hewlett-Packard's 3000 Series, and the Fujitsu M series to compete with IBM's 3030 and 4300 series. Earlier Fujitsu provided financing for the United States' Amdahl Corp. and holds a 26 percent interest in it. Germany's Nixdorf is marketing a series of computers including general business (Figure 18–14), distributed processing, and integrated office systems.

Outside the United States, international competition and trade is growing. Fujitsu is now supplying Germany's Siemens with large computers, and Hitachi is selling computers to Italy's Olivetti. France's CII-HB earns 47 percent of its revenues from outside customers, and Britain's ICL computer maker sold a similar 47 percent outside the United Kingdom.

Eastern bloc countries are not far behind the United States in technology, especially CPU technology. In peripheral devices, however, they are only at the stage of our second-generation devices. Although some computers are totally manufactured within a particular country, such as the USSR's BESM-6, the most powerful of Soviet computers, others, such as the Ryad computer series was developed and is produced as a joint venture by seven socialist countries (see Figure 18–15). The Ryad series is approximately equal to the IBM 360 and 370 line. The Ryad ES1040, built by East Germany's Robotron organization, contains parts manufactured by other socialist countries such as Bulgaria, which builds the disk drives. The central processor uses integrated circuits and microprogram control. Memory has a core design and is relatively slow, but is to be replaced with integrated circuits. A Ryad ES1040 was acquired by Control Data Corporation and underwent tests in Washington, D.C., giving U.S. engineers their first in-depth look at a Soviet computer.

Like hardware, programming languages in the

FIGURE 18–14   Nixdorf 8870 computer.

Eastern bloc are not far behind that of the West. Commonly used languages are FORTRAN, ALGOL, and a "Russianesque" COBOL. An ANSI version of COBOL is now being introduced. Russian and English versions of BASIC are also common on their several dozen time-sharing systems.

With the freer exchange in recent years of engineering and scientific information between East and West, the gap between our respective technologies should lessen during the next decade. The Soviets, for instance, are planning a nationwide computer utility including 10,000 terminals. The Ryad 3 series, the Soviets' third-generation computers, are now being developed. They are seven times as cost-effective as the current Ryad 2 and are expected to be five times as reliable. The Ryad 3 will contain LSI circuits, use microprogramming, feature memory of two to five million bytes, and have disk storage of up to 200 million bytes per disk.

The level of computer production in the USSR, the bloc's major producer, has grown from a value of 50 million rubles in 1960, to 710 million rubles in 1970, to 2,200 million rubles in 1974 (one ruble equals $1.56). With increased production throughout the bloc, combined with a shortage of hard currency, and the West's trade embargo that resulted from USSR's invasion of Afghanistan, the percentage of purchase from Western nations has declined.

Computer use and computer manufacturing capability have become high priority items to most nations, including the developing nations. Saudi Arabia, for instance, is interested in sophisticated information systems utilizing satellite-based communications; national education networks; and online systems with closed-circuit TV to track the progress of their development projects in real-time.

Spain has an international electronic funds transfer (EFT) system operating between department stores and branch banks. France and Switzerland have 25-, 50-, and 100-lane supermarkets (called "hypermarkets") using POS terminals; Sweden has a highly computerized hospital system; Sao Paulo, Brazil, is installing the world's second computerized subway system, allowing on-line command entry and status displays of four functional systems: passenger traffic, auxiliary systems, electrification, and train control.

The United States has been in the forefront in computer technology, but many other nations are adopting the state-of-the-art technology more rapidly than we are. The U.S. computer industry will continue to lose a percentage of the international market in countries that have strong computer industries, such as Japan and France. However, U.S.

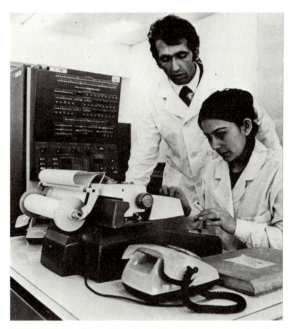

FIGURE 18–15   The first Ryad computer in the United States.

vendors' dollar value of sales will continue to grow into the mid-1980s.

SUMMARY

The computer industry has spread worldwide, and in the United States has become a major industry. Growth of telecommunications-based computers has brought sophisticated computing power to remote areas and caused telephone companies to become information processing companies. In spite of the rapid growth in computer demand and sales, the industry has remained very competitive. In fact, competition has driven several otherwise very successful firms (such as General Electric, RCA, Singer, Xerox) out of the computer CPU business. Internationally, the United States has dominated many national markets, but is now experiencing strong competition. This will cause the U.S. share of the market to decline slowly, although, since demands are so strong, U.S. computer sales will continue to grow into the mid-1980s. Non-U.S. computer manufacturers are beginning to venture into foreign markets, including our own. However, stiff competition from foreign vendors is not anticipated in the foreseeable future.

TERMS

The following words or terms have been presented in this chapter.

Plug-compatible machines (PCMs)
Independent computer peripheral equipment manufacturers (OEMs)
Original equipment manufacturers (ICPEMs)
Unbundling
Proprietary software packages
Contract programming
Service bureaus
Network information services (NIS)
Computer utilities
Information retrieval services
Facilities management (FM)

EXERCISES

The exercises that follow are grouped by level of difficulty. Problems in the A series are the easiest; B series problems are moderately hard; and C series problems are the most difficult.

A-1 What change is taking place in the computer industry relative to the sale, lease, or rental of computers by their manufacturers? Why do you think minicomputer manufacturers almost always sell rather than rent their products?

A-2 What has taken place in the microprocessor area in the past few years relative to price, quantity produced, and uses?

A-3 What is the trend in the overseas sales of U.S.-built computers? In dollars? As a percentage?

A-4 Describe the Eastern bloc countries' computer industry in relation to that of the West.

A-5 Name several companies, and their computers, that manufacture plug-compatible machines.

B-1 What is the trend relative to the number of manufacturers in the computer mainframe business?

B-2 What uses of microprocessors do you foresee in the next five years?

B-3 Differentiate between proprietary software and user-written software.

B-4 Why is the status of the semiconductor industry so important to the computer industry generally?

B-5 What do you perceive as the future of information retrieval services?

C-1 Upon what assumptions do Amdahl and Cray base their entry into the computer market?

C-2 What impact have minicomputers had on the attitude that the bigger the computer, the more cost-effective it will be?

C-3 What impact has the growth of micro and minicomputer use had on traditional mainframe manufacturers such as IBM, Burroughs, Honeywell, and NCR?

C-4 What has been the impact of unbundling on hardware and software costs?

C-5 Explain how the fact that IBM is the de facto standard for the industry encouraged the development of plug-compatible machines.

COMPUTER NEWS

SMALL-COMPUTER SHOOTOUT

The Japanese and IBM are poised to jump into a fast-growing new market

After the tragic MGM Grand Hotel fire in Las Vegas last November, rescue workers were faced with a daunting task: how to keep track of the 4,500 guests and employees at the disaster scene. Nervous relatives and friends quickly overwhelmed the police department with calls seeking information about missing people. Executives of Commodore International Ltd., who were attending a convention in the city, moved seven of their small PET machines into disaster headquarters at the Las Vegas Convention Center. Commodore personnel programmed the computers to list names and rooms of the people staying at the hotel and drew up injury and death lists, helping police to end the confusion.

Introduced in 1974, personal computers, which look like portable TV sets with keyboards, have advanced from being toys for electronic tinkerers to important tools in small businesses, schools and an increasing number of homes. Sales are growing so rapidly that personal computers are the leading product in the explosive field of electronic calculating and information equipment. Says Benjamin Rosen, the editor of a computer industry newsletter: "The under $10,000 sector of the market is going to be one of the great growth industries of the 1980s."

Sales of small computers are increasing at a rate of 50% to 60% a year. More than 1 million have already been bought, at prices ranging from $500 to $10,000. By 1985 small computers are expected to be a $9 billion-a-year business, according to California-based Vantage Research Inc.

Users of small computers have found that the machines can perform nearly all the functions of their bigger brothers, the refrigerator-size minicomputers and the main-frame models that occupy whole rooms. In San Francisco, President Fritz Maytag of Anchor Brewing Co. uses the Apple II machine on his desk to plot his company's financial future. The United American Bank of Knoxville, Tenn., has sold Tandy computers to 115 customers, who pay bills and check statements and balances at home on the machines. Bruce Kemp, an executive with Merrill Lynch in New York City, does stock analysis on his Apple II in his den. When he is not at the keyboard, his son Michael, 10, and daughter Nell, 6, use the machine to play computer games like Space Invaders.

Experts have long predicted that personal computers would be a great new market, but sales were hindered because the equipment was too complicated for most people. Now manufacturers have started marketing products that are both cheaper and less technically complex. In the jargon of the business, computers have become "user friendly."

Although computer buffs dream of the day when home computers will print movie tickets or order the groceries, such applications are still uncommon. The vast majority of personal computers are being bought by small businessmen, doctors and lawyers, who use them for prosaic things like record keeping, billing and checking inventories.

In 1981 about 75% of the personal computer industry's estimated $1 billion in sales will be controlled by just three companies. They are:

TANDY

The Fort Worth–based Tandy Corp. has the broadest reach of any computer manufacturer through its 8,012 Radio Shack stores. The firm introduced its first small computer, the TRS-80, in 1977. A newer version of the TRS-80 (popular models now cost $999) has become the largest-selling computer of all time, and Tandy now commands 40% of the small-computer market. Tandy recently introduced the first pocket computer, which shows only one line of information and sells for $249.

APPLE

The story of Apple Computer has by now become part of American folklore. The business was officially founded in 1977 by Steven Jobs and Stephen Wozniak, two college dropouts who scraped together $1,300 from the sale of a Volkswagen to build their first prototype. In 1977 Apple's revenues topped $184 million and the public offering of its stock in December was one of the biggest and most successful stock launchings in the history of Wall Street. The company is now aiming its sales effort primarily at the educational market, under the assumption that children who are raised on Apples are likely to buy Apples for themselves when they get older. A basic version of its hot-selling Apple II costs about $1,435. The firm recently introduced the larger Apple III model, which is expected to help push sales this year to $250 million.

COMMODORE

The PET computer (cost: $995), which is manufactured by Commodore International, based in Norristown, Pa., is the bestselling personal computer in Europe. The company has not been a major factor in the U.S. market, but Commodore President James Finke says: "We've got 60% of the market in Europe, and we're now ready to compete head on with anyone." This month it started running full-page ads in leading U.S. newspapers that read: COMMODORE ATE THE APPLE. This spring the company will introduce the VIC 20 computer, aimed at the home market and selling for $299.95. Commodore sales this year are expected to grow by 40% to $185 million.

Beneath computerdom's Big Three, a host of other companies, including Hewlett-Packard, Texas Instruments, Zenith and Atari, are scrambling for a share of the growing market. Such large, well-established computer firms as Digital Equipment, Data General and Xerox are reportedly about to introduce home-size machines.

Moreover, the industry is anxiously awaiting the entry of International Business Machines. Thus far, the Armonk, N.Y., behemoth (1980 sales: $26 billion) has shunned the personal computer market (Editor's note: In August 1981 IBM introduced a personal computer.); its smallest model costs about $10,000. But sales of big main-frame computers are not growing as fast as those of the small machines, and experts believe that IBM will not ignore the potential profits in the new market. Says William D. Barton, president of the Datel computer store in Manhattan: "IBM's entry into the field is imminent." IBM has not yet announced any plans to market small machines, but late last year it opened its first retail stores in Baltimore and Philadelphia. These may be the beginning of a network that will eventually provide outlets for the new smaller models.

The pioneers of the small computer business will also soon face stiff competition from the Japanese, who will begin landing their first machines in the U.S. this spring. Commodore Founder Jack Tramiel warned a group of executives recently: "Gentlemen, the Japanese are coming." Representatives of Hitachi, Toshiba, Mitsubishi and NEC (Nippon Electric) have all paid calls on U.S. retailers to find out what products Americans want and how much they are prepared to pay. The Japanese are expected to enter the market with state-of-the-art machines that will be cheaper than competing American products. The first arrival is likely to be NEC, one of the world's largest telecommunications and electronics firms. Shortly thereafter Matsushita is expected to start selling a handheld computer under its brand names Quasar and Panasonic. An informal poll of American computer executives revealed that they expect the Japanese to capture a third of the market by 1985. Says Radio Shack Vice President Jon Shirley: "The Japanese are bound to be competitive, and I worry about the Japanese much more than IBM."

The rush of new firms into this flourishing market will result in a tumultuous battle for profits, and possibly some company failures. Says William Neal, group vice president of Automatic Data Processing Inc. in Clifton, N.J.: "There is going to be a tremendous shakedown and consolidation in this industry."

Growing as fast as the microcomputer manufacturers are the companies that design the programs that go into them. An Apple or a Tandy computer is a winking mute until detailed instructions or computer programs are fed into it. Producing these programs, which are recorded on cassettes or disks, is already a $265 million-a-year business that is expected to rise to $1 billion in sales by 1985.

Another expanding computer service field is data banks that provide information for personal computers. After an initial hookup fee of $100, for example, a home computer can be connected through telephone lines to a machine in Alexandria, Va., that houses an immense information service called The Source. Customers can tap into 2,000 sources of data, ranging from a nationwide listing of job openings and up-to-the-minute financial news to world airline schedules and the entire catalogue for the wine library of Les Amis du Vin. During evening hours and weekends, the cost of bringing this information into the home is $2.75 an hour.

Industry watchers predict that by the end of the decade a family's three largest investments will be its home, car and computer. With costs for the machines dropping quickly, some visionaries even foresee three computers in every home; one in the den for financial use, one in the living room for education and entertainment, and one in the kitchen for information. The current shootout in the industry will determine whether brand names like Panasonic and IBM will soon become as common on small computers as Radio Shack and Apple. —*By Alexander Taylor. Reported by Michael Moritz/Los Angeles.*

MODULE *five*
SOCIAL ISSUES

Artoo-Detoo, taking a message for help from Princess Leia to Ben Konobi, may seem a far cry from the problems facing our society. To most of us, robots are nothing more than an appealing fantasy—who hasn't toyed with the idea of swinging on a hammock in the backyard while Artoo-Detoo or his earthly counterpart washed the dishes or fixed the garden fence?

But, increasingly, robots are becoming a reality. Ben Skora of Palos Heights, Illinois, programmed "Arok" (Photo C) not only to walk the dog but also to take out the garbage and do other household chores. And the 16 mechanical robots in Photo B deliver messages for a promotional firm in Florida. People are fascinated by robots—fascinated by their almost human appearance and by their ability to relieve us of those mundane tasks that take up so much time.

But robots in the workplace don't have the same endearing, humanoid appeal. In Chrysler Corporation's completely retooled Jefferson Assembly Plant in Detroit (Photo D), a computer-controlled robot welding line is programmed to apply nearly 3,000 welds to each body throughout the system. And CYRO, the arc-welding robot in Photo E, by working together with the welder as a team, can advance the welder's productivity four to eight times.

Robots in the workplace don't get sick (they break down only 2 percent of the time), don't get to work late, and in some cases can even work 24 hours a day. Because of these great economic advantages to the employer, industrial robots are replacing women and men in many skilled and unskilled work areas. How will our society adjust in the next decade to more robots in the factory and more people at home without jobs?

CHAPTER *nineteen*

AUTOMATION AND ROBOTICS

Preview

The Doom and Gloom Prophecies

What Is Automation?

Employment Areas Impacted by Automation
　Robotics and the Manufacturing Industry
　The Office of the Future

Economic Impact
　Short-Term Impact on Employment
　Long-Term Impact on Employment
　Automation and Productivity

Sociopsychological Impact
　Work Ethic
　Workers' Attitudes
　Workers' Experience
　Life-styles

Responsibilities for Coping with Automation
　Government
　Business
　Education
　Labor

Summary

Computer News: The Latest Robot Who's Who

PREVIEW

Experts have predicted that automation will have grave consequences on our society. Automation will change our working conditions and life-styles, and increase the time available for outside hobbies and activities. This chapter examines automation beginning with early predictions about it; then it looks at automation and mechanization as it is today. We will discuss two major employment areas that are being severely affected by automation: manufacturing (with its rapid implementation of robots) and offices (with word processing, micrographics, and teleconferencing). Lastly, we consider how we should cope with an automated society and examine who has responsibility for the transitionary period of automation.

THE DOOM AND GLOOM PROPHECIES

As early as 1954 Norbert Wiener, a mathematician and computer theoretician, said in *The Human Use of Human Beings*: "It is perfectly clear that (automation) will produce an unemployment situation in comparison with which the present recession and even the depression of the thirties will seem like a pleasant joke."

In 1962 sociologist Donald N. Michael wrote in his book *Cybernation: The Silent Conquest* that: "Once the computers are in operation, the need for additional professional people may be only moderate, and those who are needed will have to be of very high caliber indeed. Probably only a small percentage of the population will have the natural endowments to meet such high requirements."

Dr. Bruce Gilchrist summed up the feelings of many people when he said: "Historically, the free enterprise response (to automation) has been, 'You got in the wrong job—too bad.' The weakest go to the wall."

Wiener, Michael, and Gilchrist were expressing what many feared. Have these fears come true? Not entirely. We have not had another Great Depression, and we have not become a nation in which only the mental elite can find work. But our unemployment rate is high, and jobs for highly skilled and educated people seem to be increasing faster than those for the unskilled.

Dr. Gilchrist also said: "There is no evidence that computerization over the last 20 years has lessened the total number of jobs. There are a lot more people employed now than in the 1950s, at the start of the computer age. New jobs have been created. There are some exceptions of course. We have increased telephone use, but there are fewer operators employed."

WHAT IS AUTOMATION?

Automation, coined by D. S. Harder of the Ford Motor Company and, at about the same time, by computer expert John Diebold, refers to a system for making a machine or a group of machines perform a process automatically—that is, without human intervention. Usually the machines are directed by a computer.

In manufacturing, automation is a two-phase process of: (1) instructions and (2) feedback. **Instructions** are electronic signals, generated by the computer as a result of a program, that guide the operation of the machines. **Feedback** is signals generated by sensing devices that flow back to the computer from the machines. For example, in a Levi Strauss & Co. automated warehouse, as cartons of goods come in from the Levi's factory, a machine-readable label is scanned by a photoelectronic reader connected to a computer, and the carton's weight is relayed from an in-motion scale to the computer. The computer compares the predetermined weight of that particular carton (which is already stored on a secondary storage device) with the weight data from the scales. If the weights agree, the computerized inventory record for that stock number is updated, showing that new merchandise has been added to the balance on hand. If they do not, the computer calls for human followup.

Automation should not be confused with **mechanization,** in which a machine or group of machines carries out processes under the direction of a human operator. If the Levi Strauss warehouse had been only mechanized, a human operator would have had to read a label giving the stock number and number of items enclosed, referred to a chart showing the weight for so many items of that stock number, compared that precalculated weight with the scale's reading and, had they not agreed, pressed a button to direct the carton off the main line for further human action. Most of the production, processing, and handling of products in the United States is mechanized in some way, and much is automated as well.

EMPLOYMENT AREAS IMPACTED BY AUTOMATION

During the 1980s experts are predicting that automation will impact:

1. Industries involved in manufacturing; these industries will change significantly due to the widespread use of robots.
2. The office worker who has traditionally used electric typewriters to develop correspondence, filing cabinets to store historical data, and photocopy machines to duplicate materials. These workers will find a new way of doing these tasks using a new breed of "office machines."

Robotics and the Manufacturing Industry

The Robot Institute of America defines a robot as a "reprogrammable multifunctional manipulator designed to move materials, parts, tools, or specialized devices through variable programmed motions for the performance of a variety of tasks." A **robot** is essentially a machine that is capable of performing a task. The task may be gently transporting parts for color television tubes from coating machine to conveyor (Figure 19–1); operating a gun attachment in applying a powder coating to an appliance liner (Figure 19–2); or assembling Texas Instrument hand-held calculators (Figure 19–3).

Industries around the world are rushing to buy computer-run robots so fast that one manufacturer,

FIGURE 19–1 An industrial robot at RCA's color television assembly plant in Scranton, Pa.

ASEA, Inc., of White Plains, New York, sold its entire 1980 production in March of 1979. The primary reason for this rush is the following: A robot costs from $7,500 to $150,000 (average $40,000); a factory worker earns $15–20 per hour (including fringe benefits) or from $20,000 to $25,000 per year. A robot works from 16 to 24 hours per day (7 days a week) and is only broken for 2 to 3 percent of that time; a factory worker works 8 hours per day and is absent as much as 9 percent of the time. Based on these statistics one user of robots, General Dynamics, calculated a cost savings of $93,000 in the first year it used its Cincinnati Milacron's T-3 robot to drill holes (to tolerances of 0.005 in.). The T-3 could produce 24–30 parts per shift with zero rejections, while

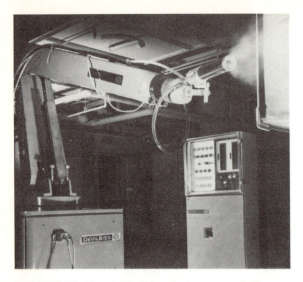

FIGURE 19-2   A Trallfa robot spray painting.

a person doing the same task could produce only 6 parts per shift with a 10 percent rejection rate.

So far the major manufacturers of computers (IBM, Texas Instruments, and Digital Equipment) have not yet begun producing robots. The major manufacturers of robots and their robot sales are shown in Figure 19-4. The major computer manufacturers, as well as others, are expected to begin making robots in the near future.

The first country to use robots to a great extent has been Japan (Figure 19-5). The bulk of the robots are found in their automotive and television industries. In the United States, GM expects to spend more than $200 million by mid-1983 for about 800 robots. These machines can save 70 percent, GM estimates, of the cost of stamping, welding, and assembling car bodies. By 1990 GM plans to use almost 14,000 robots.

FIGURE 19-3   A robot assembling calculators.

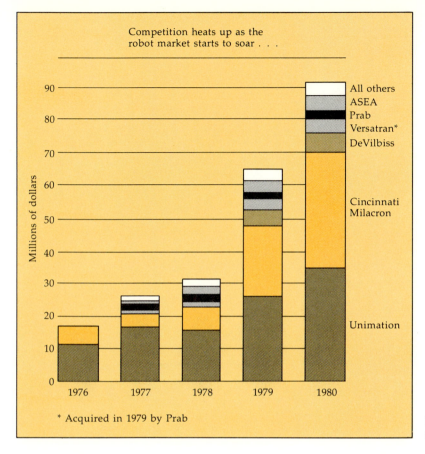

FIGURE 19-4 Robot sales by manufacturers (*Business Week*).

Productivity International, Inc., surveyed the 23 top robotics vendors. They found that the average price for a robot ranged from $20,000 to $100,000 and cost its owner $300–$400 per day to operate. The heaviest robot weighed 4 tons while the lightest weighed only 20 kilograms (44 pounds). The most powerful robot could lift a ton while the weakest only 1.65 pounds. Memory capacities for robots varied from 1K bytes to 128K bytes, with most robots having 2 to 23K bytes.

The Office of the Future

The second area that will experience an unusually high rate of automation during the 1980s is the office. The primary reason for the push toward automation in the office is that more than 75 percent of all office costs are labor-related. In 1979 U.S. businesses spent $800 billion on office operations. Of this amount $600 billion were spent on wages and fringe benefits. The remainder was spent on supplies, space, and equipment. In a recent study by Booz, Allen, and Hamilton, Inc., a prediction was made that by 1990 the cost of office operation could be expected to be $1.5 trillion unless some new technological steps are taken. In another study, this same firm shows that the $800 billion represented only 27 percent of total office costs. The remainder of the costs were caused by managers, professionals, and other associated workers.

Economists have shown that increases in productivity are directly related to the capital investment made by a company in machines or other equipment to support the worker. In the late 1970s

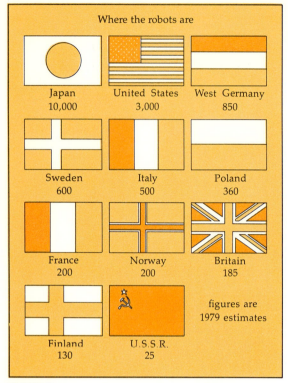

FIGURE 19-5 Countries that use robots.

and early into 1980 studies showed that the capital investment for the average farm worker is almost $70,000, for the factory worker almost $35,000, but for the office worker capital investment is a paltry $2,000. The conclusion to be drawn is that increasing the productivity of office workers will require capital investment in office machines/technology. Mr. Thomas J. Murrin, president of Westinghouse Public Systems Company, states, "As part of our near-term productivity improvement effort we plan on applying technology in the office to help improve white-collar productivity."

In the 1960s and 1970s computers were used to process business data for payroll, billing, accounts payable, general ledger, and other similar purposes. In the 1980s computers will be applied for word processing, micrographics, and teleconferencing.

Word processing involves the use of a computer to prepare text, letters, or reports. Once entered, the text can be easily modified and printed at the location where it was entered or at another location. The concept and application of word processing has led to increased productivity of secretarial personnel.

Micrographics is the use of microfilm to replace paper as a storage medium. A savings of almost 90 percent can be achieved by the use of microfilm. A 4-×-6 microfiche card can hold 270 standard size pages. Retrieval of data stored on a microfiche has been considerably enhanced by computerized software systems that use identities to locate the desired information. When they are found, the data can be taken off microfilm using CIM (Computer Input from Microfilm) equipment and sent to the appropriate individual.

Teleconferencing can also be helped by computers. Here, individuals communicate with each other through their terminals and can carry on a dialogue from remote distances—without the parties having to travel to one location.

All three of these applications of computer-based technology are aimed at stemming the rising costs of office operations by increasing productivity. In addition, the new generation of office machines should decrease the dependence on paper, increase the speed of information flow, and allow managers to be more responsive to customer wants and needs.

ECONOMIC IMPACT

The impact of automation on the economy and the people is both short term and long term. The lathe operator who is laid off may suffer until gaining new employment, but through retraining he or she may acquire a new job that is even more rewarding. By automating and, hence, staying competitive, a manufacturer may continue to contribute to the economy's strength by being an employer, a profit maker for owners, a taxpayer, a researcher, and a developer of new and better products.

Short-Term Impact on Employment

In the 1950s and early 1960s many recognized experts warned that automation would cause massive unemployment. They expected unskilled and semiskilled workers to be displaced rapidly and in larger numbers. Has this actually happened?

Unemployment has been running about 7 percent. How many of these people are out of work because of automation? This question is hard to answer.

Automation may lead to firings or layoffs, or it may eliminate jobs before they are taken. That is, some companies that automate may simply not replace employees who retire or quit. This method of cutting the payroll is called **attrition.** Although not as traumatic as firings or layoffs, the effect of attrition is the same—there are fewer jobs available.

Consider a lathe operator whose employer automates. After January 1, all lathes will be controlled by a computer program, and the operator's 15 years on the job, superb hand–eye coordination, and grade school education will at once be obsolete. The worker has three choices: step down to a less skilled job supervising the new machines, learn to be a programmer of the new automated lathe, or look elsewhere for work. If this person does not have what it takes to retrain, he or she is said to be **structurally unemployed.** In other words, there is a job, but this particular worker cannot fill it. The makeup or structure of the job market has shifted, leaving many highly skilled and technical jobs unfilled while unemployment is running from 7 to 14 percent.

Economists expect shifts in the job market, with displacement of workers (Figure 19–6). For instance, General Motors predicts that by the year 2000 50 percent of employees will be skilled tradespersons, up from only 16 percent now. This growth in skill level will take place as the number of unskilled assembly line workers drops drastically.

The Bureau of Labor Statistics predicts that by 1985 we will have nearly 40 percent fewer farmworkers than we had in 1974 (with only a 9 percent increase in the kind of work displaced farmworkers would be likely to move into); and only 13 percent more blue-collar workers, compared to a 20 percent overall increase in the labor force.

What is the outlook for displaced workers? Can they be retrained for the clerical or service jobs that are increasing faster than the total labor force? Perhaps—if they have enough education, or can ac-

"ALL THAT? THEY JUST USED A TINY BOX TO REPLACE ME."

quire it. But they will be competing with a generally more highly educated group of job applicants.

In recent years there has been a general increase in the education level of people in the job market. Over the past ten years the proportion of workers who are high school graduates has increased by 10 percent or more. Also, the proportion of blue-collar workers with one year or more of college has doubled (from 5 to 10 percent) over the past decade. Educational requirements vary with job category, with professionals generally needing more education than, for example, service workers. Major occupational categories and the educational level of workers in those categories are illustrated in Figure 19–7.

What happens to the lathe operator who, because of age, lack of ability, or lack of motivation is not retrained to be an automated lathe programmer? Chances are that the operator is unemployed or employed in jobs below his or her skill level (called **underemployed**). Some of these unemployed and underemployed persons could be fully employed if they were willing to move to another city or state, but the economic and personal cost of moving may outweigh the potential gain of employment. Others can be retrained to perform higher level jobs, or retrained for horizontal movement to different jobs of similar skill level.

Even as technological advances cause unemployment through layoffs or shifts in demand, several factors tend to absorb some of the impact. For example, employment has increased in service occupations and in retail and wholesale trades. Amer-

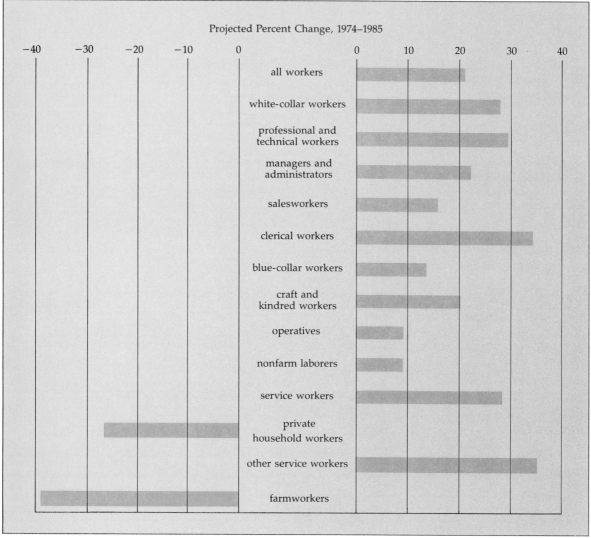

FIGURE 19-6 Employment projections through 1985.

ican citizens are demanding more government services and medical care, and more recreational and entertainment activities. Another factor that helps offset layoffs caused by automation is **occupational mobility,** that is, moving from one job to an entirely different kind of job. Studies of the 1970 Census of Population show that nearly one-third of those working in 1965 had transferred to a different occupation by 1970—only five years later. Fortunately, most automation-caused layoffs fall in the lower job categories, where job mobility is the greatest.

Long-Term Impact on Employment

Before computers brought automation into the American economy, output of goods and services was related to the size of the work force. At that time, employment was society's way of distributing

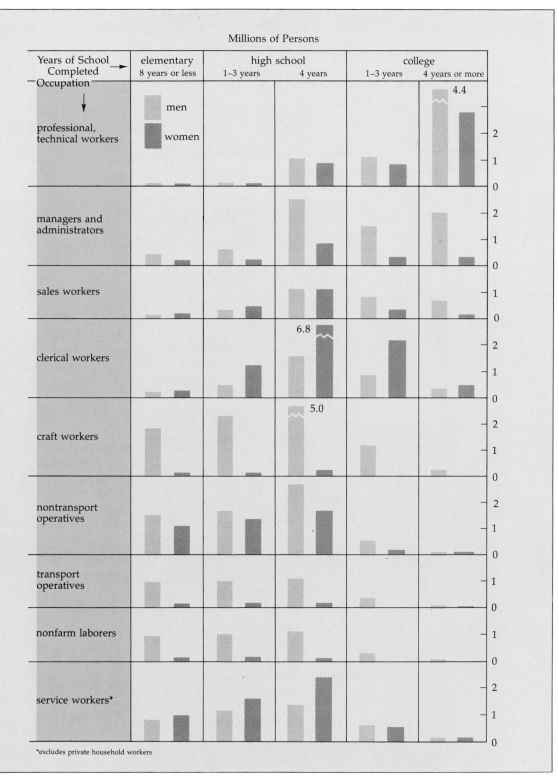

FIGURE 19-7 Educational attainment of employed persons in nonagricultural occupations.

economic resources. However, with automation, fewer workers can produce more—and the trend seems to be toward still fewer workers producing still more. In an economy like this, where only a few workers can find jobs, jobs alone can no longer be a means of distributing resources. Nevertheless, as the Ad Hoc Committee on the Triple Revolution pointed out in its report to President Johnson in 1964, we have not yet adjusted to this change—we are clinging to an outdated system. Those who cannot be employed receive unemployment compensation, old-age assistance, or welfare grants—none of which are really adequate for people's needs.

When masses of people are unemployed—as the Committee predicted would eventually happen—and are receiving inadequate incomes, they might give up peaceful methods of changing their situation and opt for revolutionary methods. The Committee, therefore, advocated recognizing that the traditional link between jobs and incomes was already being broken, and further advocated committing our society "to provide every individual and every family with an adequate income as a matter of right." It also advocated massive public works projects supported by expanded educational programs, low-cost housing, rapid transit systems, and public power systems. It recommended restructuring taxes to equalize income and, although not against automation, the Committee suggested using the licensing power of government to regulate its speed and direction. The Committee, in fact, saw a new economy built on the encouragment and expansion of automation.

Some experts feel that change can come gradually and will prove beneficial in the end, largely because they see automation as increasing our national productivity. What is productivity? Productivity can be defined as output per a given amount of effort or time. For example, a bookkeeper may be able to complete two times as much work per day using an adding machine as when adding in his or her head. If so, the bookkeeper's productivity has increased by 100 percent. Our national productivity is the composite of all individual productive efforts.

In the long term, will automation increase national productivity and do so in a manner that is not disruptive to particular trades or vocations? Or do we face a long period of automation characterized by high unemployment and resulting social chaos?

Automation and Productivity

Not all predictions for the effects of automation are as grim as Wiener's and Michael's. James S. Albus, a government scientist, focuses his prediction on automation's original purpose: increasing productivity. Automation was, and is, intended to raise output per hour worked, and Albus predicts that if we double our investment in automation, productivity will grow at a rate of 10 percent per year instead of at the 5.9 percent rate that prevailed in the early 1970s.

If this happens, our gross national product will be ten times larger by the year 2000—and only one-tenth as many workers will be needed to produce all these goods and services. Thus, Albus does not deny that heavy automation will displace most workers; however, he points out that instead of one-tenth of the workers working all of the time, all of the workers might work one-tenth of the time. Moreover, the government would receive so much more money from taxes that it could afford to provide a minimum income for the displaced workers.

Albus has a plan. He visualizes a hybrid economic system where everyone gets a basic minimum income from profits from automated industries, but people who want to work can supplement that basic income through wages. Profits from the automated industries will be distributed through a semiprivate investment corporation, the National Mutual Fund (NMF).

Albus suggests that the NMF start as a pilot study, borrowing $10 million the first year and, if it develops satisfactorily, borrowing three times as much every year for another 13 years. Within 25 years, he predicts, the dividend payments to each citizen will reach $6,000 to $12,000 a year in 1970 dollars.

Such a program raises many pleasant possibilities. You would have more control over your own life-style. If you chose to live off the land in a rural or wilderness area, your income would be enough. If you chose to live in a more traditional way, you could do so while working less than full time.

Before you start counting your acres in Oregon or West Virginia, however, notice that the plan also raises some very tough questions. Can we afford the high consumption of natural resources implied by a GNP of $16 trillion? Would we not simply shorten the life of our high living standard, and as natural resources dwindled, fall into rapid decline in both GNP and living standard? Or would our technological advances and high productivity enable us to develop alternative sources of raw materials and more efficient use of existing ones? Certainly it would be shortsighted to speed up consumption of scarce resources without the assurance that the speedup was short-term or that alternative resources were available.

Assuming we could solve the scarcity-of-resources dilemma, if GNP should increase tenfold and the work force decrease tenfold, how are business, labor, consumers, and government going to cope with the changes? Will people who have been taught to measure their worth by work be able to adjust to leisure? Or will we become even more of a nation of pill-poppers than we are now? If no one has to work, can anyone be found to collect garbage, mine coal, change bedpans, sweep streets, clean house, or do any other dirty or dangerous job society may still need to have done? There are no simple answers to these questions, but they must be faced. Albus offers an innovative if controversial proposal for dealing with the problem of distributing economic resources. What about the sociopsychological problem?

SOCIOPSYCHOLOGICAL IMPACT

President Kennedy's Advisory Committee on Labor-Management Policy stated in 1962 that "automation and technological progress are essential to the general welfare, the economic strength, and the defense of the nation," but that "this progress can and must be achieved without the sacrifice of human values." Most would agree that it must, but can it? In the remainder of this chapter, we examine how humane automation has been and how the computer affects our social-political system.

Work Ethic

"Work is what gives life meaning in our society," says Jerry M. Rosenberg in his book *Automation, Manpower, and Education.* Before you jump up and shout "That's the Puritan work ethic" or "That's archaic," notice that Rosenberg qualified his statement by adding "in our society"—meaning: as it has been, and partly still is, influenced by its agricultural and early industrial roots when survival of the family or community depended on the toil of every member. We are now moving into an era that will not need everyone's toil. Already we seem to get along without some 14 percent of our workers, especially the unskilled ones. Unfortunately, the work ethic may survive most strongly among these very workers who are least employable and thus, to their many problems, they add the mental problem of feeling immoral and unworthy in the eyes of those around them.

Workers' Attitudes

A Gallup poll early in the 1960s named automation as the American public's second greatest fear, after the Soviet Union. A study conducted in 1962 among members of two major unions in the New York metropolitan area brought out more specific fears. Workers were particularly concerned about job satisfaction after automation. They felt that automation would threaten their sense of identification with their jobs and their opportunity to exercise their own initiative. They believed they would have little say in deciding how to do a job, less chance for advancement, and worse relations with their employer. On the positive side, the union workers in the study believed that automation would make the work physically easier and thereby reduce accidents. The workers, then, seemed most concerned with the intangible sociopsychological factors, whereas they thought their union would protect their interest in wages, working conditions, transfers, and layoffs.

What causes these attitudes? The higher the educational level, the more positive the attitude toward automation. Workers who had seen coworkers displaced because of automation tended to have poorer attitudes toward it. Surprisingly, age, years with the company or union, salary, and marital status did not predictably influence attitudes toward automation.

Workers' Experience

Automation has been implemented with varying degrees of preplanning, human awareness, and computer control versus human control; and applied to a wide range of industries and processes. Georges Friedman, a French industrial sociologist, found that workers who are paced by a machine get tense, tired, and bored. Others have found that in transferring to an automated environment from a mechanized environment, some employees have found more flexibility in performing their duties and fewer situations where they had to submit to the machine's rhythm. An advocate of automation, Hugh D. Luke, writes: "From the standpoint of the workman, automation eliminates the undesirable characteristics of mechanization in which the operator functions as an integral mechanical part of the production cycle. Instead, it makes the operator a skilled director of an integrated production sequence; it requires greater knowledge of the product; it calls for increased responsibility; and returns in large measure, pride in knowledge and workmanship." On the other hand, Ida Hoos's study in firms using computers found that "work is more routine, monotonous, pressured, and confining for the clerical workers involved."

A study by Shooshana Zuboff shows that managers who have volumes of rigorously defined computer-generated information lose "free space" for actions that feel inspired; that is, their creative abilities have a narrower latitude within which to function. According to Zuboff, this free space is fundamental to the psychology of professional work—it is the reason most people would prefer to be professionals than assembly-line workers.

Pierre Naville found that "the great defect of automated systems is that they more or less destroy curiosity. And curiosity, involving anticipation and imagination, is the mainspring of concentration." Any threat to concentration is counterproductive, for in many automated environments there are periods of time that require great concentration.

Robert Blauner found auto workers more subject to alienation than other industrial workers because they work on a much smaller part of the total product than workers in craft, continuous-process, and even most machine industries. These workers do not lack a sense of purpose or a knowledge of how their function fits into the whole assembly scheme—the problem is they need not know anything more than their jobs in order to perform efficiently.

In contrast to the study of the automobile industry, a study of automated power plant employees conducted by F. C. Mann and L. P. Hoffman found:

> The results of transferring men from more specialized jobs in the older plants to the enlarged jobs in the new plants were for the most part positive. Expression of increased job interest and job satisfaction were found in a large proportion of these transferred operators. The combination of job enlargement and job rotation increased for many of these men—at least temporarily—the intrinsic satisfactions which could be derived from the work itself.

However, on the negative side, workers experienced increased tension, which was traced in part to insufficient on-the-job training.

A study by Jon M. Shepard revealed that office workers, too, felt much more involved in their work than did assemblers and, hence, less alienated—probably because their jobs are less specialized. However, the degree of alienation varied from one group of office employees to another. Keypunch operators were more alienated than computer operators; computer operators more alienated than programmers. Alienation felt by workers, then, seems to depend more on the particular job environment than on the industry or general category of work (blue collar or white collar). Alienation results from feelings of powerlessness and meaninglessness, advancement divorced from achievement, work rewarded only by money, and a tendency to evaluate oneself according to one's job.

In short, the experiences of workers in automated environments are diverse. Some workers move to more skilled and more rewarding jobs when a firm automates; others are downgraded to less skilled, less rewarding tasks, and are faced with monotony, loneliness, and a sense of meaninglessness.

Life-styles

What workers experience on the job affects their attitudes, personality, and life-style away from the job. Few of us can leave all aspects of our jobs behind us when we go home at the end of the workday. Instead, our conscious and subconscious minds mull over our successes and our failures, our challenges and our monotony, and our interpersonal experiences. We often share these events with our families and friends, and our dreams release some of our frustrations. We are molded by our experiences, including our work experiences, throughout life.

What happens to the personalities of the workers and their families when automation brings a high level of tension, anxiety, and loneliness? Such stress probably damages the physical health of the worker, puts an emotional strain on all family members, and in turn diminishes their ability to be positive, constructive forces in their community. Of course, some automations have relieved workers of a monotonous task, provided them with more varied activities, and hence, provided a healthier work experience.

Many of the patterns in our life-styles relate to work. The "up at 6:30, off at 7:30, work at 8:00" routine is very much a part of our lives. With mechanization, and now with automation, however, the need to make full use of costly machines and systems has forced many people into less traditional work schedules. Such schedules often lessen the workers' contact with their families. And where both parents work, but are on different work schedules, the security of a common pattern, the communication that can come during regular contact, and the frequency of family activities are sacrificed.

The shorter workweek is slow in coming, but automation has already brought it about in some fields. This increased leisure obviously affects the life-styles of workers. However, it is distributed very unevenly. In some computer-automated fields, for example, supervisors and managers may work more hours per week than previously, with in-service education on their own time, preparing reports at home, and business trips away from home.

As the need for workers decreases faster than the available work force, the workday and/or workweek will undoubtedly be cut, and early retirement encouraged. Instead of working until 60 or 65 as is now common, people will be able to retire or shift to part-time work at 50 or 55. How are we going to spend these extra leisure hours? Some see this period as a release from the bondage of work, providing us with the freedom for creative, helpful, and fulfilling experiences in the arts, crafts, travel, politics, athletics, and volunteer service areas. At the other extreme are those who feel threatened by this increased leisure, who still see idleness as immoral. These people foresee aggressive action by the under- or unemployed and a degeneration of spirit because people will not feel needed. The attitude of most people toward this leisure time, however, will probably fall somewhere between these two extremes and will depend to a large degree on how well the newly leisured are educated for their new role, and how deeply involved they become in meaningful nonwork activities.

RESPONSIBILITIES FOR COPING WITH AUTOMATION

Various sectors of society may respond to automation in conflicting ways. For example, labor may respond by asking that portions of the increased profits resulting from the automation of a process be shared with the workers. Business, on the other hand, may respond by investing the increased profits in research and development to create better and more competitive products. The consumer is likely to respond by demanding lower prices. Naturally, no sector will see all its demands met. Negotiations, compromises, and tolerance of others will be required to bring about a smooth transition to a highly automated society.

Government

Liberal and conservative economists disagree about the government's responsibilities in the transition to a highly automated society, and individual experts have seen government's role as everything from pervasive to nonexistent.

Some responsibilities of government as seen by automation experts are: (1) retraining programs for workers displaced by automation; (2) encouraging transferability of pension benefits from job to job; (3) paying relocation costs when a worker must move to keep a job; (4) encouraging all employers to take positive steps to humanize jobs that would otherwise become drudgery; (5) to operate employment services that would include a nationwide databank of employment opportunities and available workers; (6) to become the "employer of last resort," hiring hard-core unemployed for useful community enterprises.

Business

Automated businesses have responsibilities to workers, consumers, and others. Some of these are: (1) to provide an equal or better product at an equal or lower cost; (2) not to use the computer or other automatic device as a scapegoat for human error; (3) to minimize any negative impact caused by technological change by providing (a) open communications with employees, (b) adequate lead time before layoffs or transfers, (c) cooperation with employee representatives in meeting problems, (d) adequate leadtime so changes will have minimum negative impact, and (e) on-the-job retraining to minimize layoffs; (4) to humanize the work environment by adapting work to human needs; and (5) to recognize *all* costs—economic, social, environmental, and psychological—when studying the feasibility of further automation.

Education

The responsibilities of education in meeting technological change begin in the elementary school and continue through graduate school. Elementary students need to become aware of the changing nature of the world of work. As they plan their careers in junior and senior high school, students must think about alternative careers, must learn to accept and adapt to change, and must build skills in planning. High schools, adult schools, and colleges must recognize and keep in tune with changing employment fields by establishing and updating vocational education. Retraining programs should be flexible and responsive to the needs of those moving from one vocation to another. Educational institutions also need to help students explore a wide range of leisure activities.

Labor

Labor unions and worker and professional associations can be valuable in easing the transition to a highly automated society. They can keep workers informed of industrywide and local trends that will affect their jobs, provide a clearinghouse for employment opportunities, and cooperate with local educators in developing retraining and upgrading programs.

In times of change, labor organizations provide a unified voice to which management can listen and, in turn, can carry plans and proposals back to the workers. Cooperative plans for coping with dramatic changes in production systems can and have been drawn up by unions and businesses.

Professor Calvin C. Gotleib (University of Toronto) contends that computers are "job killers." Furthermore, the responses of trade unions to the introduction of computers are hardening and will continue to do so, he predicts. In the UK, for example, the Trade Union Congress has adopted two principal points for future action:

1. No technology that has major effects on the work force should be introduced unilaterally—full agreement on the range of negotiation issues must be a precondition to the change along with full job security for the existing work force.

2. Technological change should be linked to a reduction of the work week and working lifetime—or job sharing.

In the United States the United Auto Workers (UAW) has taken a similar approach. In 1955 a production worker produced 12.8 vehicles, while in 1978 it was 18. During this same time period the number of auto workers remained stable at 700,000. In return for rising productivity a UAW worker earns $14.50/hour, has 20 holidays (not counting vacation or sick leave), and has one of the best benefit packages in U.S. industry.

SUMMARY

Automation is the process whereby a machine or group of machines performs under the direction of a computer. Two major employment areas are heavily impacted by automation. These are manufacturing, where computer-driven robots are replacing human workers; and the office, where word processors, micrographics, and teleconferencing are being used to improve efficiency. The overall short-term effect of automation has, fortunately, not been as disruptive to the economy as some experts had predicted. The long-term effects of automation remain in doubt.

Automation has brought some workers more interesting, less strenuous jobs, while it has given others repetitive, uninteresting, and stifling routines. If technological advance means simply mechanizing a process so humans must interface with and be paced by a machine, then humanity has lost. If, however, it means bringing a series of processes under the direct control of a computer and under the supervision of a person, then humanity has gained.

An expanding economy, increased government hiring, the demand for services, and the occupational mobility of workers have partially offset the layoffs and attrition cutbacks in firms that have automated. The impact of automation can be harsh. Unskilled workers are easily displaced by machines and are difficult to retrain for new jobs because of age, immobility, or lack of innate ability.

Responsibility for coping with the impact of automation must be shared by several groups. Government responsibility in an automating society involves softening the impact of unemployment through retraining programs, unemployment compensation, job-finding services, and so on.

Employers must plan ahead to minimize the trauma of layoffs and to implement automation responsibility. They must recognize that the computer or other automated devices are simply reflections of the humans who direct them. Automation should be undertaken not only to lower costs, but to provide better products for consumers.

Educational institutions are responsible for helping with retraining, studying the impact of an automated environment on human beings, and exposing students and workers to positive, rewarding leisure activities.

Labor organizations and individual workers must be alert to developing trends, take positive steps to meet the trends, and work cooperatively with business to bring about smooth transitions.

TERMS

The following words or terms have been presented in this chapter.

Automation	Micrographics
Instructions	Teleconferencing
Feedback	Attrition
Mechanization	Structural unemployment
Robot	Underemployed
Word processing	Occupational mobility

EXERCISES

The exercises that follow are grouped by level of difficulty. Problems in the A series are the easiest; B series problems are moderately hard; and C series problems are the most difficult.

A-1 Explain what "feedback" is and give an example other than that described in this chapter.

A-2 Differentiate between automation and mechanization.

A-3 Explain how the process of attrition contributes to unemployment.

A–4 From a worker's standpoint, what are some disadvantages of working in an automated environment?

A–5 Describe some of the tasks best suited to robots.

B–1 Do you think the "momentous changes automation is effecting in our lives," as predicted by John Diebold, have materialized and simply have not been recognized by the general public, or have such changes simply not occurred? Explain.

B–2 What events or conditions, if any, did Donald N. Michael predict that have materialized?

B–3 Was Norbert Wiener incorrect or simply exaggerating in his conception of the impact of automation on society?

B–4 Should labor unions support or fight the installation of robots? Give some support for your answer.

C–1 James S. Albus has presented a plan that would encourage automation and provide a radically different approach to distributing profits from automation. Using your college library as a source, locate and write a summary of the description of the other proposals for (1) improving productivity, and (2) distributing the benefits of high productivity.

C–2 Describe what sociological and psychological effects automation has had on you or on someone you know.

C–3 Has automation's impact nationwide resulted in a net decrease in employment? Explain.

C–4 Describe how structural unemployment differs from the general unemployment that results from economic recession.

C–5 Using your college library as a source describe how at least one generally recognized economist would increase our nation's productivity.

C–6 Census data for 1970 show that about one-third of those employed had changed occupations since 1965. Economically, socially, and psychologically, is this a healthy sign? Explain.

C–7 Is there a relationship between productivity (output per man hour) and gross national product (GNP)? Explain.

C–8 Does employment level enter into the relationship of productivity and GNP? Explain.

C–9 How do the "work ethic" and the higher productivity impact of automation conflict? How do you think this conflict should be resolved?

C–10 What are the motivations behind manufacturers' drive to install robots?

COMPUTER NEWS

THE LATEST ROBOT WHO'S WHO

Industrial robots look nothing like the androids of *Star Wars* fame—a distinct letdown for many aficionados—but they have grown increasingly smarter and more versatile in recent years. And in the past two years, the pace of robot evolution has quickened markedly, as the following genealogy indicates.

INDUSTRIAL ROBOTS all have armlike projections and grippers that perform factory work customarily done by humans. The term is usually reserved for machines with some form of built-in control system and capable of stand-alone operation. But in Japan, it also includes manipulators operated by humans, either directly or remotely.

A PICK-AND-PLACE ROBOT is the simplest version, accounting for about one-third of all U.S. installations. The name comes from its usual application in materials handling: picking something from one spot and placing it at another. Freedom of movement is usually limited to two or three directions—in and out, left and right, and up and down. The control system is electromechanical. Prices range from $5,000 to $30,000.

A SERVO ROBOT is the most common industrial robot because it can include all robots described below. The name stems from one or more servomechanisms that enable the arm and gripper to alter direction in midair, without having to trip a mechanical switch. Five to seven directional movements are common, depending on the number of "joints," or articulations, in the robot's arm.

A PROGRAMMABLE ROBOT is a servo robot directed by a programmable controller that memorizes a sequence of arm-and-gripper movements; this routine can then be repeated perpetually. The robot is reprogrammed by leading its gripper through the new task. The price range is $25,000 to $90,000.

A COMPUTERIZED ROBOT is a servo model run by a computer. The computer controller does not have to be taught by leading the arm-gripper through a routine; new instructions can be transmitted electronically. The programming for such "smart" robots may include the ability to optimize, or improve, its work-routine instructions. Prices start at about $35,000.

A SENSORY ROBOT is a computerized robot with one or more artificial senses, usually sight or touch. Prices for early models start at about $75,000.

AN ASSEMBLY ROBOT is a computerized robot, probably a sensory model, designed specifically for assembly-line jobs. For light, batch-manufacturing applications, the arm's design may be fairly anthropomorphic.

Business Week, June 9, 1980.

CHAPTER twenty
PRIVACY

Preview

Introduction

What Is Privacy?

How Is Privacy Threatened?

The Information Revolution: Databanks

The Computer's Godlike Image

Examples of Computer Threats to Privacy
- Credit Bureaus
- Arrest Records
- Universal Identifiers

How Do We Meet Threats to Privacy?
- Laws and Government Action
- Business Self-Regulation
- Privacy Publications
- In-Service Education
- The Courts
- Other Organizations

Summary

Computer News: Computer Codes Get Censors Edgy

PREVIEW

In this chapter we examine computerized information systems as they relate to personal information privacy. We discuss past and present threats of invasion into personal data, as well as the actual misuse of data by both government and business that results in invasion of privacy. We examine several federal laws that affect privacy, look at some possible modifications to existing privacy laws, and survey nongovernment efforts to protect information privacy.

INTRODUCTION

Jerry Smith, a 17-year-old living in a metropolitan area, was walking home from a movie late one summer evening when police looking for a burglar roared up in a patrol car. The car stopped, an officer jumped out and asked Jerry where he was headed, where he had been, and what his name was. Jerry had never been in trouble, had not broken any law more serious than playing hooky from school several times and running away from a foster home. He certainly had never been arrested. Yet, within 30 seconds after Jerry had given his name, a mobile computer terminal in the police car printed out a summary of Jerry's vital statistics and past activities, including the truancy and the succession of foster homes.

Where did such information on Jerry come from and how was it collected? The answer is that Jerry was lucky—or unlucky—enough to have played soccer, shot pool, and participated in several other activities at a city youth recreation center funded by a grant from the Federal Law Enforcement Assistance Administration (LEAA). Under this program, the city kept computerized records on youths' home situations, attitudes, leisure activities, and so on. If they moved to another city and that city's officials requested their records, a copy was sent. Truly, then, Jerry has a "record," although he has never committed a crime or been arrested.

Would the police officer who stopped Jerry be prejudiced by Jerry's background? Had Jerry's privacy been infringed on? Who besides the officer had access to Jerry's record? (In at least one state the county must send personal identification information about youths in such programs to the state's bureau of criminal statistics.)

Susan, a bookkeeper for a manufacturing firm, receives a letter from a bank offering her a VISA card. "Because of your outstanding credit record," says the letter, "we invite you to accept . . ." Since she sometimes has trouble getting credit because of her low salary, she is at first elated by the invitation and immediately sends off her application form. Later she wonders who told the bank her credit record was so good—or, for that matter, anything at all about her credit record. No one notified her the records were being sent anywhere.

WHAT IS PRIVACY?

"Privacy" can be defined in many ways. Privacy in your financial affairs, for example, is very different from spiritual or physical privacy. Since we are interested here in privacy of personal information, we define privacy in two related ways.

On the **individual** level, **privacy** is the right to decide what personal information you want to share with others. On the **social** level, **privacy** is a voluntary withholding of information, reinforced by the willing indifference of others. **Loss of privacy** is the unauthorized collection or examination of personal data, or the intrusion of public scrutiny, without your permission, into certain areas of your personal life. Such intrusions are called **invasion of privacy**. These definitions imply that privacy is absolute; that is, that individuals can decide to give no information to anyone, including—or perhaps especially—the government.

What would absolute privacy imply? Strictly speaking, **absolute privacy** is possible only in a nation of hermits. Any contact with others brings some loss of privacy. Many of the social benefits we now take for granted have privacy tradeoffs. For example, when you were first registered in primary school, your parents were asked to fill out a health history form that asked if your birth was complicated in any manner, what illnesses you had had, and what, if any, medical problem(s) you currently had. Furthermore, for financial reasons, the school probably asked if your parents were employed by the federal government. Now, you would be asked if you are one-sixteenth or more Native American.

In an advanced and often overcrowded society like ours, what would absolute privacy mean? For one thing, most of our government programs would collapse. If people and corporations chose not to report their incomes and, thus, to pay no income tax, the money to support most government programs would simply not be collected. If people refused to talk to census takers, the information that government departments need to plan all their programs would be missing. If people refused to report the births of their children and insisted on educating them at home, or not at all, our system of universal education would be no more. And, of course, the entire credit system that underlies much of this country's economy today would also collapse, as most businesses would be unwilling to extend credit without some means of checking the risks involved.

With a little thought, you could probably think of just as many examples. Obviously, since we do pay income taxes, give personal information to census takers, send our children to public schools, and buy on credit, we have moved away from absolute privacy. We settle for less.

As a society, we have agreed that some invasions of privacy are acceptable or necessary. As former President Ford said in a speech at Stanford University, government has acquired "a legitimate reason to inquire . . . into the private lives of students seeking scholarships, professors seeking research grants, businessmen wanting government loans or requiring government licenses, and professional persons doing business with the government or participating in subsidy programs. The list is endless."

The list, of course, is not really endless, but there are reasons to fear that it might become so. In other words, even our **relative privacy** now seems to be threatened. When we look at the narrower field of **information privacy,** which is the one that concerns us here, we look at one of the foremost reasons for this fear—the computer.

Information as we use it refers to data that have been collected and organized into a meaningful form. For example, the computer-stored data:

5555544440NEILL/JOE/W416125805000404821112782001

is fairly unintelligible. Following a program's instructions, however, a computer prints the otherwise unintelligible data with captions and inserts or deletes characters (such as -/.:), and inserts spaces, making the data meaningful to anyone.

SSN:	555-55-4444
NAME:	
Last:	ONEILL
First:	JOE
Initial:	W
OCCUPATION:	Student
BIRTHDATE:	
Day/Month/Year:	16/12/58
CREDIT LIMIT:	500
CARD ISSUANCE DATE:	04/04/82
LATEST DATE OF PAYMENT:	11/12/82
TOTAL NO. OF LATE PAYMENTS:	1
AVERAGE NO. OF LATE PAYMENTS:	.10

HOW IS PRIVACY THREATENED?

Threats to information privacy are not new. They have existed as long as information has been collected. Five thousand years ago, Egypt had a well-developed secret service, and in ancient Rome, spies were as plentiful as they are today in Moscow or Washington. Citizens of totalitarian countries take it for granted that their letters will be opened, and many public figures, from senators to leaders in the women's movement, have had a phone tapped at one time or another.

So why all the fuss? For one thing, people are becoming more aware of protecting their civil rights as the increasing complexity of daily life undermines those rights. More to the point, the threat of some kind of intrusion has suddenly mushroomed,

CHAPTER 20: PRIVACY   475

mostly because of computers. With computers, literally mind-boggling amounts of information can, for the first time, be stored, processed, and flashed to would-be users all over the country in seconds. And this information is not just about kings or other public figures, or about military secrets, but about you and me and our unpaid bills and how we get along with our families. This is a threat of another color.

Let us take a close look at this new type of threat.

THE INFORMATION REVOLUTION: DATABANKS

Existence of information tempts people to use it, just as existence of the atomic bomb tempts military leaders to plan to use it. Even though the bomb—like the databanks—is amoral, its irresponsible use can be devastating to the victims. So it is with databanks. Properly used, their data are vital to the economic and timely operation of business, government, education, and labor. But if knowledge is power, information can be control. Then, do we want vast amounts of information collected and held in computerized databanks? No matter, we have it anyway! As examples of computerized data files, the IRS has income tax information on 140 million individuals and businesses, the Social Security Administration also has personal data on millions of persons, and FBI files contain records on over 8 million persons. Furthermore, these systems are growing.

In 1977 the Internal Revenue Service proposed a new computer system, one that was to have 8,300 terminals in IRS offices throughout the country and be tied to ten regional computer centers. Through the terminals, the computer would have displayed, in a few seconds, your tax returns for the past several years. The system would have been accessible to 48,000 IRS employees. Because of cost and potential privacy invasions, the system has not been okayed.

Could this rapid access by many people to all tax returns invade the privacy of individuals? An employee might access his landlord's return to determine how much profit is being earned on the house he or she is leasing and, thus, be in a stronger position to negotiate a lease renewal; an employee with personal knowledge of someone's gambling winnings might threaten the winner with blackmail after learning via the IRS terminal that he or she had not reported the winnings as income; or an employee might sell information relating to a business to one of its competitors. The opportunity to access such data under the present IRS system is much, much less. Under the proposed system the three attributes that encourage misuse are: (1) widespread accessibility (48,000 employees), (2) rapid access (a few seconds), and (3) access to practically an unlimited number of tax returns.

The Carter administration blocked the development of the IRS system because of the "threat to civil liberties, privacy, and due process of taxpayers." The IRS, however, is only one of the many government (Figure 20–1) and business institutions updating and expanding their computerized data systems as necessitated by a growing population and economy. The federal government alone holds almost 4 billion records on individuals, most of it stored in computers.

In 1981 the General Accounting Office (GOA) (the federal government's financial watchdog) recommended a shared federal data telecommunications network. The GOA estimated $20 million could be saved annually by establishing a federal network. This is the third proposal by federal agencies over the past 15 years that would centralize data access and/or data files. Former administrations, along with the Congress, have scuttled those proposals on grounds that privacy risks outweigh the benefits. The $20 million savings amounts to 8¢ per citizen.

In addition to the federal government, each of the 50 states maintains computerized files on wage earners, taxpayers, aid recipients, and automobile owners and drivers. Most county and city governments maintain computerized records of property owners, law offenders, and others. In addition, schools, charitable organizations, businesses, and labor groups maintain computerized files on individual citizens.

With so much information genuinely needed by

FIGURE 20–1	Federal data files.
Where Filed	Type of File
Internal Revenue Service	Tax (1040)
Social Security Administration	Regular account
Veterans Administration	Military service record
Bureau of Alcohol, Tobacco & Firearms	Gun collections
Clerk of Congress or Federal Election Commission	Political contributions over $100
Coast Guard	Boat registrations
Defense-Intelligence Agency	Executives in companies with military contracts
Federal Aviation Administration	Applicants for and holders of private plane licenses
Federal Communications Commission	Ham operators, boat radio licensees
Federal Trade Commission	Many top executives, multipurpose files
Dept. of Education	Parents of students seeking student loans
Justice Dept.	Families of juveniles facing drug or similar charges in a court
Securities & Exchange Commission	Corporate insiders
Small Business Administration	Loan applicants
State Dept.	Passports
Treasury Dept.	Banking transactions over $10,000
White House	Advisory commission appointees, candidates for federal jobs

Data: Privacy Protection Study Commission (Courtesy of Business Week)

many institutions, doesn't having files computerized add an unnecessary risk? It does add a risk, but a necessary one in most cases. Why? The cost-per-record-processed is generally significantly lower with computer processing of data than with manual processing if the volume of transactions is large. The computer's processing speed is usually 10, 100, or even 1,000 times faster than manual processing. This lower cost and higher speed of computer processing dictates the switch to computers when data volume is high. And you might greatly appreciate the high data access speeds if you were a victim of a robbery. Having an automobile license number, MO (method of operation), and fingerprint analysis processed by computer rather than by hand speeds up and enhances the chance of tracking down lawbreakers. Computer files and processing work in your favor also as the IRS responds quickly and accurately to your federal income tax return's (Form 1040) request for a refund. With manual processing, the 4- to 6-week wait would likely stretch out to 8- to 16-weeks and consume more labor in the process.

If we recognize and accept the potential value of computerized databanks, we must accept also some risk of misuse. How can misuses take place without notice? We examine one major reason next.

THE COMPUTER'S GODLIKE IMAGE

In manual systems we expect human errors that result in incorrect data. With the computer, however, we expect fail-safe security and valid data. Is the computer fail-safe? Can it protect data from unauthorized intrusion or inaccurate input?

Recall from our discussion of computer languages that computers operate through programs, and programs are only sets of human-written directions. Since a human-written program directs the computer, a computerized information processing system operates under human direction much as a manual system does. Why, then, does the computer's godlike, fail-safe image exist? Perhaps it is because some computer systems have been successfully programmed to run independently of human operators and to give a high (but not absolute) degree of data security.

Seeing this independence and security in some systems, people tend to associate data security with physical hardware. They fail to realize, though, that such security is primarily the result of programming; the programming (access codes, passwords, access logging, and validity checks such as check digits) that can bring about tight data security is transparent to the layperson. Further contributing to the computer's godlike image is its extremely high speed of calculating and its very accurate recall from memory in comparison to us mortals. The mind-set of many uninformed users, thus, becomes one of blind faith in the infallibility of the computer and its data. This mind-set can be deadly. For instance, an Orange County (Florida) sheriff's deputy ordered an innocent woman from her car at gunpoint after a check of her license tag indicated that her car was listed as stolen. She had reported her car stolen several months earlier, but the car had been recovered within several hours. Apparently the recovery information was never included in the computerized Florida Crime Information Center's (FCIC) stolen vehicles data file.

In a similar case less than a year earlier, an innocent driver ordered from his car was shot and killed when the officer thought the driver was reaching for a gun. Certainly the officer expected more from the computer than it was programmed to give. Would the officer have concluded that he was dealing with a dangerous (rather than an innocent) driver if his source of information had not been given the aura of infallibility by the computer?

EXAMPLES OF COMPUTER THREATS TO PRIVACY

Credit Bureaus

Almost every adult has a credit record maintained by a **credit rating bureau** (a company that collects from its member businesses and from public records information relating to the buying and bill paying habits of millions of consumers). The Fair Credit Reporting Act of 1970 regulates the reporting from and access to credit bureau data files. The case of Eric Fenley illustrates how computerized credit reporting can affect consumers.

"TRUE, WE DON'T GIVE OUT PERSONAL INFORMATION, BUT EVERY ONCE IN A WHILE THE COMPUTER TAKES IT UPON ITSELF TO SPILL THE BEANS."

Eric Fenley moved into town with his wife and three children, settling into a small but comfortable rented house. He paid the usual first and last month's rent as well as a cleaning deposit, leaving $150 in his bank account to supply his family with groceries for the week and a half before getting his first paycheck from his new job. Eric had already filed an application, been interviewed by the manager and the machine shop foreman of the Southwest Manufacturing Co. and had been told he had a job as machinist, but to call in on the tenth of the month to find out which shift he would be assigned to. Southwest was the only industrial firm in town, but it was expanding and had advertised in the nearest metropolitan newspaper, some 100 miles away.

The move for Eric and his family was difficult since both he and Louise, his wife, had been born and raised in a small town a couple of hundred miles away and, except for short periods of time, had always lived there. They would miss their friends and relatives, but the work was here or in the metropolitan area—and that was not appealing to Eric or to Louise.

With most of the unloading and unpacking behind them, Eric drove the several blocks to the nearest pay phone to call Southwest Manufacturing to check on which shift he had been assigned. An hour later Louise heard their car pull up in front of the house and rushed out to see which shift Eric would work. Eric slowly climbed out of the car, his face ashen, his eyes staring into space as if in shock. Eric had been shocked, in fact, when he was told by the foreman, "There has been a change in plans; the machinist job has been canceled." "But, did you talk to the manager?" Louise asked. Eric replied, "Yes, I went to talk face to face with him. He told me the same thing—job canceled."

Dejected, puzzled, and shocked, Eric walked down a block to his landlord's home. He woefully explained the turn in events to her. She tried to be optimistic and suggested that there were other employers in town who might need workers.

There were and, in fact, Eric did locate a job as a service station attendant, allowing him and his family to get by, but barely. As time passed, Eric's reputation as a responsible, hard-working employee led to a succession of progressively better jobs until after a year he was earning almost as much in a maintenance job at the regional power company as he would have as a machinist.

During that year the Fenleys made friends with many people within the community. The husband of one of Louise's PTA friends was a bowling partner of a foreman of Southwest Manufacturing's shipping and receiving department. Through this friend-of-a-friend-of-a-friend communication link, Eric and Louise finally learned why he was, in effect, fired before his first day on the machinist job. It was not a matter of the job having been canceled. In fact, it was filled the next week. Contrary to the federal Fair Credit Reporting Act of 1970, a credit bureau had responded to Southwest Manufacturing's consumer credit check with a computer printout, but had failed to send a notice to Eric, as required, that they had issued a report that might have an adverse effect on his ability to gain employment. The credit check disclosed that Eric and Louise had filed bankruptcy because of losses suffered in the machine shop Eric had operated for the three years prior to their move. The manager of Southwest said "Fenley should have disclosed the bankruptcy on his employment application; not doing so was dishonest. I won't hire a dishonest person."

Should Fenley have disclosed the bankruptcy on his application form? Would Fenley have disclosed his bankruptcy if he had known that the consumer credit bureau was disclosing it? Was there a computer error involved? If the credit bureau had not been computerized, would the same mistake have been made? In what way was Fenley hurt by his failure to receive the notice of disclosure of his bankruptcy?

The nation's 2,000 credit bureaus conduct about 150 million credit checks each year for member businesses. The biggest credit bureau is TRW Information Services. Fully computerized, it has over 70 million records and is still growing. If you have ever borrowed money or bought anything on time, you probably have a file, and a rating, at TRW or a similar company.

Regardless of which credit bureau has data on you, the accuracy or inaccuracy of those data affects you. And errors do creep into credit files in many ways. Some credit bureaus check official records of notices of arrest, law suits, judgments, marriages, divorces, births, and deaths of or pertaining to people in their files. The possibility of mistaken identity is substantial, especially in large cities where there are many people with identical names. Furthermore, the final outcome of an arrest, lawsuit, or lien may not appear in the record and, thus, never get into the file. Some credit bureaus even collect data from newspapers. Equifax, which does over 60 percent of all insurance investigations, was ordered by the Federal Trade Commission in 1981 to stop several illegal practices. The alleged violations are the imposition of production quotas on field investigators, resulting in rewards for the amount of adverse information gathered; failure to disclose computerized information to consumers; failure to promptly reinvestigate disputed matters; and misrepresenting the identity of its investigators. The vice-president of one major consumer credit rating bureau admitted that *about a third of his company's credit reports contained errors.* What protection do we have against use of erroneous data?

The Fair Credit Reporting Act of 1970 protects consumers by giving them the right to inspect their own files and protest wrong or obsolete information. But the damage may already have been done by the time an error gets corrected. For example, a person who refuses to pay for faulty or misrepresented merchandise may later be refused a loan or a credit card simply because the merchant reported the person's account overdue. If the case is settled in the customer's favor, the bad report may still, by error, not be removed from the file, and the person's credit rating would drop.

Even if credit bureaus were 100 percent accurate, they would still be encroaching on your privacy, since businesses can meet your demand for credit only if they are able to judge your credit worthiness, and because in order to obtain credit you authorize the sharing of your financial data. Credit rating bureaus, then, can supply ratings of your credit worthiness only if you will accept less than absolute privacy and allow the bureau to collect and report data about you. But do credit bureaus represent a risk to your privacy of unwarranted invasion? It is safe to say yes—and the risk is growing.

The risk of unwarranted invasion of your privacy by credit bureaus becomes greater as (1) more credit bureau employees and member businesses have access to your credit data; (2) credit bureaus become more centralized, with larger files that contain many similar, if not identical, names; (3) computerization provides rapid, easy access to more and more data; and (4) computerization gives the air of infallibility to credit bureau reports.

Arrest Records

Do you have an arrest record? The federal government estimates that 50 percent of all males have arrest records and that 60 percent of nonurban males and 90 percent of all urban males will have arrest records in their lifetimes! Are these records computerized and, hence, accessible to all who can access the "crime file" via a terminal? The FBI's **National Crime Information Center (NCIC)** alone has over 6,600 remote terminals that can access the crime file.

Does arrest mean guilt? In many cases, no. But in many cases the arrest record stays on the books and the dropping of the charge or the judicial finding of "not guilty" fails to enter your record. Such a record, showing arrest but no finding, leaves a cloud of suspicion over you. But does it really matter, since the record is stuck in a file cabinet along with thousands or millions of others, like a needle in a haystack? Yes, since that record may be far from hidden. In fact, since the vast majority of arrests are reported to computerized files at the state level and many even to the FBI's Computerized Criminal History file, it may be very accessible.

In Massachusetts, a state that has demonstrated an exceptionally strong awareness of privacy rights, several state police were arrested for allegedly selling criminal history material to credit rating bureaus. The Massachusetts criminal history files, including arrests, are computerized and available to state police.

In the Massachusetts system, each inquiry into the criminal history file is automatically logged. The log revealed an unusually large number of inquiries by the police who were subsequently arrested. Without such a log and a periodic review of the log, the Massachusetts computerized criminal history data would probably still be subject to abuse by police.

Out of computerized files may come an old marijuana charge or a reckless driving record dating back to your college days, uncovered by a background investigation years later when you apply for a job or are considered for promotion. Such background investigations often are performed by credit rating bureaus. In many states it is illegal to steal such data, but *legal* to *buy* it, as was the case in Massachusetts. A 35-year-old Cincinnati sales supervisor's job and promotion were threatened when a background investigation using illicitly obtained data revealed an arrest when in college for disturbing the peace after a football game.

Invasion of privacy through arrest records is becoming more likely with (1) the increased number both of computer terminals and law enforcement employees nationwide that have access to NCIC files; (2) the FBI's planning to serve as a central switching center connecting the computers of law enforcement agencies in the various states; and (3) increased use of computerized crime files at state and local levels. However, with the increased awareness of privacy invasions or risks of invasions, many states are acting to limit access to arrest files, and other files as well.

Universal Identifiers

If you store valuables in a safe deposit box, you gain access to the box through a lock key that is numbered to correspond with the number of the box. For ease of access computerized data are also often organized on the basis of a number called an **identifier**.

In a small group, an identifier can be your name. Your first name alone can serve as an identifier in your immediate family. In an extended family that includes close relatives, there are often identical first names or even identical first and last names. Hence, some variation is adopted to maintain uniqueness, such as calling the senior John and the junior Johnnie. However, this method is inadequate in large groups.

When dealing with thousands or even millions of persons, some method of uniquely identifying each individual is essential. In many cases your Social Security number is used with your name as the unique identifier.

Ideal for ease and accuracy of computer processing would be an identifier unique to you and always used by any computer in processing data related to you—in other words, a **standard universal identifier (SUI)**. Each SUI must meet all the following criteria:

- **Uniqueness:** It must be unique for each person.
- **Permanence:** It must not change during the life of an individual and should not be reused after his or her death until all records concerning the person have been retired.
- **Ubiquity:** Labels must be issued to the entire population for which unique identification is required.
- **Availability:** It must be readily obtainable or verifiable by anyone who needs it, and quickly and conveniently regainable in case it is lost or forgotten.

- **Indispensability:** It must be supported by incentives or penalties so that each person will remember his SUI and report it correctly.
- **Arbitrariness:** It must not contain any information, for example, state of issuance.
- **Brevity:** It must be as short as possible for efficiency in recognition, retrieval, and processing by hand or machine.
- **Reliability:** It must be constructed with a feature that detects errors of transcription or communication.

Some people favor SUIs and think the Social Security number is the logical identifier, but others fear any such idea. Discussing such fears, the U.S. Department of Health, Education, and Welfare (HEW), in a report entitled *Records, Computers, and the Rights of Citizens,* said:

> *Fear of a standard universal identifier is justified. Although we are not opposed to the concept of an SUI in the abstract, we believe that, in practice, the dangers inherent in establishing an SUI—without legal and social safeguards against the abuse of automated personal data systems—far outweigh any of its practical benefits. Therefore, we take the position that a standard universal identifier should not be established in the United States now or in the foreseeable future.*

This abuse of automated personal data systems that HEW had in mind might be called Big Brother or a "police state," and involves a large-scale computer network that can tie financial, educational, social service, tax, and law enforcement agencies together for the sharing of data. *The key to sharing would be a standard universal identifier* that would pinpoint your data. In the extreme, each agency would lose control of how its own data were used by other agencies. For example, the information you agree to share with your college registrar you may not want to share with the IRS or the FBI. Or data you give on your tax return to the IRS, you probably would not choose to share with your neighborhood police. But sharing is *not* the worst that can be done.

By collecting data relating to you from diverse files and concentrating them into a single record, officials could learn a great deal about a citizen's spending patterns, whereabouts, health, political affiliations, and associates. Such sharing and concentrating of data is unnecessary and, more important, dangerous. For example, how much easier the FBI's surveillance of civil rights leader Dr. Martin Luther King would have been if, using a computer network and an SUI, they had simply concentrated data from his bank account activity, charge account activity, gasoline credit card charges, local law enforcement contacts, and other events into a daily summary.

Similar savings of effort could have been enjoyed by the FBI in their investigation of leaders of the Women's Liberation Movement. Instead of using informants, they could have used their computer. Tying into databanks, gasoline charge accounting systems, American Express, Master Card, Diner's Club, retail stores, and airline reservation systems, the concentrated data could have yielded profiles of the women's daily activities. In this case, though, the computerized surveillance might have fallen short of the investigation's aim since the FBI director had also instructed his agents to collect data on the political and sexual attitudes of women activists.

The "Daily Surveillance Sheet" in Figure 20-2 comes from *The Compleat Computer* by Dennie Van Tassel. In it, he shows the sort of report on an individual that could be compiled if a proposed "National Data Bank" is established. As Van Tassel says "Hopefully, it will help illustrate that *everyone* should be concerned."

Privacy invasions are possible because of lack of foresight, lack of vigilance, overzealousness, carelessness, and personal gain (in a few cases). Being aware of privacy invasions does not mean they will not occur again. Definite steps to minimize them are in order.

HOW DO WE MEET THREATS TO PRIVACY?

Efforts to protect privacy are as old as walls and fences, huts and houses. Efforts to protect the kind of privacy that interests us here—the privacy of personal data—are at least as old as the classical culture of the Greeks and Romans. But the threat to privacy took on a whole new dimension when computers came into being and began being used to collect information on people. Thus, the effort to protect privacy must enter a new dimension as well. Unfortunately, this effort always lags behind the ever faster pace of the threat. We are in one of these lag periods right now, and must run hard to catch up.

Laws and Government Action

Once aware of the threats to information privacy, Congress can become one of our main weapons against them. It can hold committee hearings that make people aware of the danger. The responsible committee can make recommendations to change the regulations and operations of government agencies or can propose new laws. In fact, the House Committee on Government Operations held an extensive investigation into telephone wiretapping and the use of lie detectors by federal agencies. The committee report resulted in 1964 in the creation of a special subcommittee on Invasion of Privacy. The subcommittee held hearings into a proposed national databank, federal investigative activities, computerized personal data files, private credit rating bureaus, and other privacy matters in 1965 and 1968.

These hearings, together with a growing public awareness and concern over privacy invasion, resulted in the **Fair Credit Reporting Act (FCRA)** of 1970. Passed to regulate credit rating bureaus, FCRA's stated purpose is: (1) to require that consumer reporting agencies adopt reasonable procedures for meeting the needs of commerce for consumer credit, personnel, insurance, and other information, and (2) to do so in a manner that is fair and equitable to the consumer with regard to confidentiality, accuracy, relevancy, and proper utilization of such information.

Provisions of FCRA allow consumer credit reports to be issued in response to a court order or in response to a written request from the consumer. Such reports may be issued to a person who is (1) having a credit transaction with the consumer; (2)

```
                NATIONAL DATA BANK
                DAILY SURVEILLANCE SHEET
                    CONFIDENTIAL
                    JULY 9, 1987
SUBJECT:
    DENNIE VAN TASSEL
    UNIVERSITY OF CALIFORNIA
    SANTA CRUZ, CALIF.
    MALE
    AGE 38
    MARRIED
    PROGRAMMER
PURCHASES:
    WALL STREET JOURNAL              .25
    BREAKFAST                       2.50
    GASOLINE                        6.00
    PHONE (328-1826)                 .15
    PHONE (308-7928)                 .15
    PHONE (421-1931)                 .15
    BANK (CASH WITHDRAWAL)      (120.00)
    LUNCH                           3.50
    COCKTAIL                        1.50
    LINGERIE                       26.95
    PHONE (369-2436)                 .35
    BOURBON                        11.40
    NEWSPAPER                        .25

            ****COMPUTER ANALYSIS****
```

OWN STOCK (90 PERCENT PROBABILITY).

HEAVY STARCH BREAKFAST, PROBABLY OVERWEIGHT.

BOUGHT 6.00 DOLLARS GASOLINE. OWNS VW. SO FAR THIS WEEK HAS BOUGHT 14.00 DOLLARS WORTH OF GASOLINE. OBVIOUSLY DOING SOMETHING BESIDES JUST DRIVING 9 MILES TO WORK.

BOUGHT GASOLINE AT 7:57. SAFE TO ASSUME HE WAS LATE TO WORK.

PHONE NO. 328-1826 BELONGS TO SHADY LANE—SHADY WAS ARRESTED FOR BOOKMAKING IN 1975.

PHONE NO. 308-7928. EXPENSIVE MEN'S BARBER—SPECIALIZES IN BALD MEN OR HAIR STYLING.

PHONE NO. 421-1931. RESERVATIONS FOR LAS VEGAS (WITHOUT WIFE). THIRD TRIP THIS YEAR TO LAS VEGAS (WITHOUT WIFE). WILL SCAN FILE TO SEE IF ANYONE ELSE HAS GONE TO LAS VEGAS AT THE SAME TIME AND COMPARE TO HIS PHONE NUMBERS.

WITHDREW 120.00 DOLLARS CASH. VERY UNUSUAL SINCE ALL LEGAL PURCHASES CAN BE MADE USING THE NATIONAL SOCIAL SECURITY CREDIT CARD. CASH USUALLY ONLY USED FOR ILLEGAL PURCHASES. IT WAS PREVIOUSLY RECOMMENDED THAT ALL CASH BE OUTLAWED AS SOON AS IT BECOMES POLITICALLY POSSIBLE.

DRINKS DURING HIS LUNCH.

BOUGHT VERY EXPENSIVE LINGERIE. NOT HIS WIFE'S SIZE.

PHONE NO. 369-2436. MISS SWEET LOCKS.

PURCHASED EXPENSIVE BOTTLE OF BOURBON. HE HAS PURCHASED 5 BOTTLES OF BOURBON IN THE LAST 30 DAYS. EITHER HEAVY DRINKER OR MUCH ENTERTAINING.

****OVERALL ANALYSIS****

LEFT WORK EARLY AT 4:00, SINCE HE PURCHASED BOURBON 1 MILE FROM HIS JOB AT 4:10. (OPPOSITE DIRECTION FROM HIS HOME).

BOUGHT NEWSPAPER AT 6:30 NEAR HIS HOUSE. UNACCOUNTABLE 2½ HOURS. MADE 3 PURCHASES TODAY FROM YOUNG BLONDES. (STATISTICAL 1 CHANCE IN 78.) THEREFORE PROBABLY HAS WEAKNESS FOR YOUNG BLONDES.

FIGURE 20-2 National Data Bank daily surveillance sheet.

considering employing the consumer; (3) considering issuing an insurance policy to the consumer; (4) reviewing the consumer's eligibility for a license or franchise; or (5) otherwise having a legitimate business transaction with the consumer.

Since old information may falsely describe your current financial responsibility, FCRA provides that no consumer reporting agency may report (1) bankruptcies that are more than 14 years old; (2) suits and judgments that are older than 7 years unless the governing statute of limitations is longer; or (3) paid tax liens more than 7 years before. FCRA further provides that no report be issued for (1) accounts placed for collection more than 7 years prior; (2) records of arrest, indictment, or conviction of crime and related release that occurred more than 7 years before; or (3) any other adverse information from more than 7 years earlier unless the transaction amount was $50,000 or more.

Disclosing false information about you can be damaging; so can disclosure of information to unauthorized persons. The FCRA provides some protection against these acts by requiring that users of consumer information state their identity, certify the purpose for which the data are sought, and certify that they will be used for no other purpose. FCRA also provides that the reporting agency follow reasonable procedures to assure maximum accuracy of data. Disclosure of data to the subject consumer is required of all data except medical information. Furthermore, in most cases sources of information must be disclosed to the consumer. Finally, the names of recipients of credit reports must be provided the consumer if the report was for employment purposes no more than two years prior, or for any other purpose no more than six months prior.

If you are not satisfied that your credit data are being properly handled, or if you are denied access to or correction of data collected by credit rating bureaus, FCRA provides you with recourse through the courts.

The U.S. Department of Health, Education and Welfare named an Advisory Committee on Automated Personal Data Systems to study the impact of computer databanks on individual privacy. The committee's 1973 report recommended federal legislation for a code of fair information practices embodying five basic principles:

1. There must be no personal data record-keeping systems whose very existence is secret.

2. Individuals must be able to find out what information about them is in a record and how it is used.

3. Individuals must be able to keep information obtained for one purpose from being used or made available for other purposes without their consent.

4. Individuals must be able to correct a record.

5. Organizations creating, maintaining, using, or disseminating records of identifiable personal data must assure the reliability of the data and must take precautions to prevent misuse of them.

As a result of this report and other stimuli from government and the citizenry, Congress considered over 100 privacy bills before passing the Privacy Act of 1974 (PA74).

In the **Privacy Act of 1974 (PA74),** Congress found that:

1. Privacy of an individual is directly affected by collection, maintenance, use, and dissemination of personal information.

2. Increasing use of computers has greatly magnified the harm to individual privacy that can occur.

3. Opportunities for employment, insurance, and credit, and right to due process are endangered by misuse of information systems.

4. Privacy is a personal and fundamental right protected by the Constitution.

5. It is necessary for Congress to regulate collection, maintenance, use, and dissemination of personal information by federal agencies.

In view of these findings, Congress described the purpose of PA74 as safeguarding individuals against invasion of personal privacy by requiring federal agencies to:

1. Let individuals determine what records pertaining to them are collected, maintained, used, or disseminated by such agencies.

2. Let individuals keep their records, collected for one particular purpose, from being used for another purpose without their consent.

3. Let individuals have a copy made of all records pertaining to them and be able to correct such records.

4. Handle personal records only for necessary and lawful purposes, ensure that such records are current and accurate, and safeguard them to prevent misuse.

5. Permit exceptions only by law.

6. Be subject to civil suit for damages that result from willful or intentional violation of an individual's rights under the PA74.

The law also provides that all agencies except the Central Intelligence Agency (CIA) and law enforcement agencies annually publish the "Federal Personal Data Systems," a list of all record systems and the number and names of each one. PA74 also regulates the transfer of data between agencies and prohibits the sale of an individual's name and address for use in mailing lists. Further, it seeks to limit the use of the Social Security number as a universal identifier by forbidding any federal, state, or local government to require individuals to disclose their Social Security number for use in record systems established on or after January 1, 1975. Finally, no government agency shall deny an individual any right, benefit, or privilege because of refusal to disclose his or her Social Security number for use in record systems established on or after January 1, 1975.

PA74 established the Privacy Protection Study Commission to study the effectiveness of PA74 and to recommend revisions. In its 1977 report, the commission declared that PA74 is a "good start," but needs "considerable improvement." One obvious major loophole is the exceptions for the CIA and law enforcement agencies. Some of the commission's other recommended improvements are:

1. See that privacy standards for the private sector are voluntarily adopted by business or, in the absence of voluntary standards, are legislated for them.

2. Eliminate overlap between the Privacy Act and the Freedom of Information Act (FOIA) by making the Privacy Act the sole vehicle for individuals seeking access to their own information.

3. Give individuals the right to see records derived from the original record.

4. Notify sources and prior recipients of information of errors found.

5. Close the loophole that allows data to be transferred between agencies without notice to the person involved.

6. Discard all unverified information on individuals in the law enforcement area.

These and other recommendations were submitted to Congress and will likely result in a stronger, more comprehensive privacy act.

The **Tax Reform Act of 1976 (TRA76)** contains several provisions limiting the IRS, one of the largest users of computers, in its access to personal information. For example, the IRS now needs a court order to gain access to bank records and limits the IRS's disclosure of personal files to other government agencies.

The **Right to Financial Privacy Act of 1978 (RFPA78)** gives individuals the option to review personal financial data within the records of banks, credit unions, and credit extending businesses. RFPA78 also provides for correcting inaccuracies in financial records. Prior to RFPA78, the U.S. Supreme Court had held in 1976 in *Miller* v. *The United States* that financial data about the customer were strictly bank property. The customer had no right of access or correction.

The **Electronic Funds Transfer Act of 1978 (EFTA78)** as implemented by the Federal Reserve Board's Regulation E describes the responsibilities of both the customer and the financial institution in electronic funds transfer. In regards to privacy concerns, EFTA78's Regulation E requires financial institutions to notify consumers of any release of customer information to a third party (see Chapter 10).

As Congress, government agencies, business, and citizens grapple with efforts to develop further privacy protection, we face the question of the best balance between the needs of the individual and the collective needs of the people and their government. By gathering and concentrating too much information of too broad a scope and making it too easily available, we have created comprehensive dossiers that are ready and waiting for Big Brother. At the opposite extreme, however, too severe a limitation in the scope of data collected and filed, and in the exchange of data between agencies, could hamper vital government functions such as research, planning, providing of social services, and law enforcement. Today's privacy laws and those still being debated in legislatures are far from perfect, but as time passes, both laws and the need for laws will change and adapt. Are laws and government regulation the only limiting factors of privacy invasion? Fortunately, no.

Business Self-Regulation

The self-regulation of collection, access, and disclosure of personal information by business was advocated by the Privacy Protection Study Commission as a desirable alternative to laws and government regulation. Recognizing the desirability of such an action, some businesses have already tightened their internal policies on personal data files. For example, IBM no longer asks job applicants for name of spouse, or for data about treatment by psychiatrists or arrest records. J. C. Penney Co. has implemented many of the privacy commission's recommendations by eliminating much of the health information and criminal conviction information (unless the job applied for involves a position of trust) from job applications, and allowing employees access to their personnel file and the privilege of correcting errors. Some companies now refuse to give outsiders such as credit agencies private information without prior approval of the employee.

The American Management Association (AMA) has held seminars on privacy regulation and its implications to help businesspeople in implementing self-regulation. If the AMA and individual business efforts bring about widespread self-regulation, further federal legislation is unlikely.

Privacy Publications

Playing a vital role by stimulating public interest in privacy protection have been numerous books, journals, reports, and newsletters. Some of the books are: *Privacy and Freedom* by Alan Westin, *Information Technology,* also by Westin, *Databanks in a Free Society* by Westin and Michael A. Baker, and *Data Banks and Privacy and Society* by Willis H. Ware. Some fiction writers who dramatized privacy invasions are Vance Packard with *The Naked Society,* Arthur R. Miller with *Assault on Privacy,* and Arthur Koestler with *Darkness at Noon*.

The monthly *Privacy Journal* and the American Civil Liberties Union's *Privacy Reporter* provide summaries of current developments in privacy protection.

One of the major governmental reports to influence information privacy protection was HEW's *Records, Computers, and the Rights of Citizens.*

Periodicals of general interest such as *Saturday Review, Atlantic Monthly,* and the *Christian Science Monitor* also have stimulated public interest in privacy. Within the business community, the *Wall Street Journal, Fortune,* and *Business Week* have brought attention to privacy and the computer. Finally, within the computer field itself, the weekly *Computerworld* frequently reports on privacy. Computer professionals also read of privacy in the monthly magazines *Datamation, Infosystems, Computer Decisions,* and others.

In-Service Education

Data processing and computer professional associations regularly sponsor conferences, addresses, and discussions of privacy needs, methods, and costs. Some of these organizations are the Data Processing Management Association (DPMA), the Association for Computing Machinery (ACM), and the American Federation of Information Processing Societies (AFIPS). Several private consulting firms also offer seminars and workshops that deal with information privacy. Many computer users also offer in-house training relating to privacy issues.

The Courts

Court cases in the United States relating to privacy date back to 1868, when a Michigan state court declared that privacy was a constitutional right. In

1890 the U.S. Supreme Court ruled an individual had the right to be "left alone." This right of privacy was upheld in 1965 in a Connecticut court that stated that privacy was protected under the First, Third, Fourth, and Ninth Amendments. But in 1976 the U.S. Supreme Court examined privacy from an information perspective and declared an individual has neither a legitimate expectation of privacy nor a "protectable interest" in his bank of records. In other words, you could not control who has access to your bank records. This decision recognizing that privacy is not absolute reflected the balancing approach of the courts. The court balanced the benefits for you with the benefits for society by making your bank records somewhat accessible to third parties and unaccessible to you. However, RFPA78 partially voided the Supreme Court's decision and gives individuals the rights to review bank records relating to themselves and to correct inaccuracies.

Many more information privacy cases are in the courts or will ultimately reach them. Where the Constitution is vague and Congress has not specified in law—or at least not specified clearly—the courts must decide.

Other Organizations

Among other organizations that have expressed interest in the impact of EDP on privacy and individual liberties is the American Civil Liberties Union, which has frequently opposed the expansion of large, centralized databanks. Several political groups of both the right and the left have also occasionally opposed what they view as governmental efforts to "keep tabs" on their activities or memberships.

SUMMARY

The invasion of information privacy is the unwarranted collection or examination of personal data or the unjustified intrusion of public scrutiny into inappropriate areas. Government, business, and individuals have all been guilty of such invasions that public awareness has brought about corrective action by both government and business through tighter policies and procedures, education of personnel, and, recently, federal and state laws. Many oppportunites still exist for invading privacy, and more federal and state legislation will need to be enacted to help minimize opportunities for abuse. Aiding in the protection of privacy are writers, publishers, and computer users through self-regulation, professional societies, the American Civil Liberties Union, and the courts. Eternal vigilance is the price of liberty—it is also an essential part of maintaining privacy.

TERMS

The following words or terms have been presented in this chapter.

Individual privacy
Social privacy
Loss of privacy
Invasion of privacy
Absolute privacy
Relative privacy
Information privacy
Information
Credit rating bureau
National Crime Information Center (NCIC)
Identifier
Standard universal identifier (SUI)

Fair Credit Reporting Act (FCRA)
Privacy Act of 1974 (PA74)
Tax Reform Act of 1976 (TRA76)
Right to Financial Privacy Act of 1978 (RFPA78)
Electronic Funds Transfer Act of 1978 (EFTA78)

EXERCISES

The exercises that follow are grouped by level of difficulty. Problems in the A series are the easiest; B series problems are moderately hard; and C series problems are the most difficult.

A–1 Define "privacy" in your own words.

A–2 Figure 20–1 lists and briefly describes 17 federal files that may contain information about you. How many of those files do you think do contain personal information on you?

A-3 Explain what a universal identifier is.

A-4 List several advantages of widespread use of universal identifiers.

A-5 Describe some of the costs incurred by government and business in providing more privacy of information.

A-6 What provision of the Electronic Funds Transfer Act of 1978 implementation in Regulation E concerns privacy?

B-1 Differentiate between the right of privacy and the right of personal data privacy.

B-2 Do you believe that privacy is an absolute right? Explain.

B-3 In addition to the files cited in Figure 20-1, many state and local government agencies, educational institutions, medical offices, and commercial establishments contain data on individuals. Name at least five such files and tell what type of data are likely to be included in the particular file.

B-4 Why would applicants for credit or employment authorize a personal and financial investigation of themselves? Do you feel such an authorization should be a requirement? Explain.

B-5 Besides Social Security numbers, what other keys are or could be used as universal identifiers?

C-1 What basis is there for the right of privacy according to the United States Constitution?

C-2 Do you agree with former President Ford that government has "a legitimate reason to inquire . . ." into your private life? Explain.

C-3 What values or social goods may conflict with an absolute right of privacy?

C-4 Has your privacy been invaded by government or business? In what way?

C-5 Are you aware of any invasion-of-privacy incident not described in this chapter? If so, describe. If not, do some research in a library to locate a report of an invasion and write a summary of the incident.

C-6 Do you agree with the U.S. Supreme Court's decision that allowed bank account records to be disclosed to third parties? Explain your stand.

C-7 The federal Freedom of Information Act of 1966 regulates federal agencies primarily. The act requires federal agencies to make known to the public the kinds of files they maintain, and the agencies' structures, purpose, policies, and so on. Further, it provides recourse through the courts for individuals seeking information from agencies that do not comply. Determine a particular piece of information you would like to collect, request that information of the appropriate agency, and see how responsive the agency is. (If you have ever been arrested, check the FBI's computerized criminal history file. If you have ever signed an antiwar petition, or been active in the women's rights movement, you might try the FBI's Security Index File.) Look up the agency's address in the *United States Government Manual* in the reference section of your college library.

COMPUTER NEWS

COMPUTER CODES GET CENSORS EDGY

By Evans Witt
Associated Press

WASHINGTON—Working quietly, a university researcher develops a brilliant abstract theory that might result in a virtually unbreakable computer code.

Such a code would mean vastly improved protection of privacy for millions of Americans whose records are stored in computers and whose everyday transactions are handled by computer.

But an American intelligence agency steps in, arguing that publication of the theory could threaten national security.

Should the government prevent publication? Does it have the right?

These aren't hypothetical questions. They are the crux of a growing conflict between the supersecret National Security Agency and academic researchers invoking freedom of research and the First Amendment.

The implications are vast. There may not be a "supercode" yet, but researchers are working on theories that could lead to such protection of information stored in computers and the messages transmitted from computer to computer.

This conflict has already produced an unusual result: the agreement by a group of researchers to a system of voluntary censorship of their research in an esoteric field called cryptography, the study of codes and code breaking.

The researchers have agreed to give the National Security Agency a peek at research papers in cryptography before they are published, with the NSA reserving the right to ask for censorship.

The deal has sent shivers through the academic community.

"It smacks of prior restraint," says Philip Handler, outgoing president of the National Academy of Sciences.

The system is voluntary, based on self-restraint, but some worry that it is a step toward broader government control over research.

"You start out with submission of the papers voluntarily," says Steven Unger, professor of computer science at Columbia University. "Then, you'll be required to submit them and the third step is you're required to do what they say. At that point, you've got pre-publication censorship. It's a disaster."

But officials of the intelligence community—when they'll say anything for the record—are equally emphatic in arguing that research in this area could hurt national security.

"There is a very real and critical danger that unrestrained public discussion of cryptologic matters will seriously damage the ability of this government to conduct signals intelligence and the ability of this government to carry out its mission of protecting national security information from hostile exploitation," said Adm. B. R. Inman, then director of the NSA, in an unprecedented public speech in March 1979.

The dispute has been going on ever since. For the NSA, it goes to the heart of its function. Its job is to protect U.S. government communications from eavesdroppers—while trying to eavesdrop on other governments.

The debate over non-governmental cryptography, now largely confined to the academic and intelligence communities, is likely to widen.

More and more personal information about Americans is stored in computers. And much of it is being shuttled back and forth between computers through telephone lines, microwave links or satellite channels.

Bank accounts, money transfers, credit card charges, mental and physical health records—to mention a few—are now routinely stored on computers and are thus vulnerable to tampering, illegal disclosure and misuse.

Cryptography holds one key to protecting the data. By scrambling or "encoding" the information, the would-be eavesdropper is prevented from reading it.

George Davida, a professor at Georgia Institute of Technology, was the only member of the academic study group to vote against the voluntary censorship system. He argued it would hamstring efforts to develop codes to protect personal and financial information without significant benefit to national security.

Says David Kahn, author of "The Codebreakers," a history of cryptography: "The advantage of having good codes is so great that you have to weigh it against the small potential for harm."

This fight over public cryptography is just the latest in a series of clashes between the NSA and researchers over the past four years. On several occasions, NSA moved to prevent individual researchers or inventors from putting their cryptographic ideas to work in public. Davida was one researcher hit by NSA's effort.

Meantime, private companies working in cryptography are trying to agree on similar limits on their commercial research.

At issue is whether the government can or should prevent scientific information privately developed from being published. The First Amendment, guaranteeing freedom of press and speech, is invoked here.

Prior restraint of publication was vetoed by the Supreme Court in the Pentagon Papers case, whereas in the instance of the Progressive magazine, which wanted to run an article on making H bombs, a federal court held that the Atomic Energy Act permitted government restrictions on such information, whether privately developed or not. But the magazine eventually published the article anyway.

The NSA argues that some research can hurt national security in two ways:

First, it could inadvertently expose a weakness in a code system now used by the U.S. government. A foreign power could use the finding to read secret U.S. messages.

Second, the research could give a foreign government a better coding system than it is now using, making it harder, perhaps impossible, for NSA to decipher that government's codes.

Some find these arguments less than persuasive.

"If somebody can think of something like this, isn't it better for it to be out than to have a false sense of security about it?" asks Mary Cheh, professor at the National Law Center of George Washington University.

Some researchers say the second argument is simply an attempt by the NSA to make its own job easier.

After a period of debate, the American Council on Education agreed to establish a committee, the Public Cryptography Study Group, to work things out.

The committee is made up of educators, and Daniel Schwartz, NSA general counsel, decided that:

• The NSA will notify the researchers of its interest in reviewing papers dealing with cryptography, defining as precisely as possible what kinds of papers it wants to see.

• When papers are submitted, the NSA will review them promptly and notify the author of any changes the NSA would like.

• If the author disagrees with the proposed changes, the matter would be referred to a board consisting of two members from the NSA and three from outside the NSA. They would hear NSA's arguments and recommend action to the author and the NSA director.

• The authors' submissions of papers and agreements to changes would be voluntary.

"Today, there is the reality that there are genuine requirements for national security," says Handler, of the National Academy of Sciences. "We should see to it that we do minimal injury to scientific freedom."

"This agreement is the only thing possible," says Dr. Robert Gluckstern, chancellor of the University of Maryland. "A voluntary system is the only one the academic community would find acceptable."

The system's success or failure may depend in large part on how well the NSA deals with authors.

"If the NSA isn't acting sensibly, this isn't going to work. It will if their behavior is reasonable," says Ira Michael Heyman, co-chairman of the committee and chancellor of the University of California at Berkeley.

Whether voluntary compliance with NSA requirements will work is questionable.

In favor of the plan is an attitude expressed by David Kahn. "No one wants to hurt the

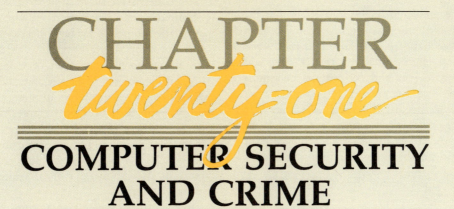

CHAPTER twenty-one
COMPUTER SECURITY AND CRIME

Preview

Introduction

Lack of Security Leads to Abuse
    Fraud
    Theft
    Sabotage
    Espionage
    Accident

Improving Computer Systems Security
    Physical Security
    Internal Security Mechanisms
    Operational and Procedural Security
    Auditing Procedures
    Ethical Controls
    Legal Deterrents

Summary

**Computer News:
Accused Embezzler Had Record of DP Crime**

PREVIEW

Ada Lovelace predicted in the mid-1800s that the computer would one day compose music. But neither she nor Babbage ever dreamed that when the "analytical engine" became reality it would hand society's thieves and con artists their most powerful tool since the revolver. In this chapter we define computer security, discuss what happens when it is lacking, and outline some steps for achieving it. We also examine several actual cases of theft and fraud, and include a computing news article on computer fraud.

INTRODUCTION

23 December 1945 3:00 P.M.: Steam pipe going thru window ventilator broken. Capt. Ryan and Brainerd notified.

25 December 1945 9:30 P.M.: Heavy rain and melting snow leaking into 2nd floor.

26 December 1945 3:00 A.M.: About five men still working mopping up water and emptying buckets which catch drip.

These entries are from the service log at the birthplace of the first general-purpose electronic computer, ENIAC. Perhaps it was fitting that ENIAC came to "life" in the face of hazards, for computer users ever since have risked fire, flood, terrorist bombs, thieves' program modifications, and many other hazards. Security from these and other hazards will always be a burden and a challenge to computer users and abusers. As one computer expert said, "Whatever safeguard one human mind can devise, another human mind can devise a way around or through it." If this is true, it leaves the computer owner with an awesome challenge in attaining computer system security.

Computer systems security involves (1) protecting processed and raw data from unauthorized intentional or accidental disclosure; (2) protecting both buildings and equipment from intrusion for unauthorized use of the computer or for harm; and (3) protecting the computer operating system and user programs from unauthorized use, modification, or destruction.

The concern for security of data is not unique to computerized information systems. Protecting handwritten journals, ledgers, messages, and other sources of information from unauthorized eyes has been a concern for thousands of years. However, with computers and especially with telecommunications, data have become both more plentiful and more vulnerable than ever. In precomputer days, anyone who wanted to steal or change your records had to sneak into your house or shop and physically do so. Now the thief may be able to work from thousands of miles away, merely typing codes on a terminal keyboard.

An added concern is that as computing equipment gets cheaper, facilities are often decentralized. This development requires that security efforts be coordinated nationwide and even worldwide. At the same time, intrusions have become more likely because (1) the information stored in many databanks is valuable; (2) more and more people have sophisticated enough training to penetrate se-

"IT SEEMS THAT THEIR DATABANK HAS ALL THE INFORMATION THAT'S IN OUR DATABANK, PLUS INFORMATION THAT'S NOT IN OUR DATABANK, PLUS INFORMATION ABOUT OUR DATABANK."

curity systems; and (3) with rapidly falling costs of computers and the availability of inexpensive home computers, a skyrocketing number of people have remote access through their own computer terminal.

Systems are seldom well protected against intrusions. According to the federal government's General Accounting Office (GAO), 10,000 computers are ill protected against sabotage, fire, flood, theft, and misuse. Fewer than half of the 28 federal computer centers spot-checked had plans for continuing operations after a loss of data files or equipment.

One glaring proof that computer information and systems are not secure enough is the amount of computer-assisted fraud (CAF) that is reported: $100 million yearly and growing rapidly. Ten years ago CAF was only $5 million. Furthermore, the reported crime ($100 million) is less than 5 percent of the estimated CAF actually committed (over $2,000 million).

Cenco stock was thus inflated in value, misleading potential purchasers.

Perhaps the prize of all known computer frauds was the case of Equity Funding Life Insurance Company. Officers and employees of the firm set up over 60,000 bogus insurance policies within a three-year period and then sold the worthless policies to other insurance companies. The computer, programmed by an employee, created and kept track of these phony policies. This fraud was carried on to cover up its otherwise poor profits. With inflated income figures, Equity's stock appeared attractive and was bought by many investors. The top officers involved thus were able to maintain their high salaries and posh offices. The total loss to the unsuspecting purchasers of these bogus policies and inflated stock was $27 million.

The vast majority of these crimes are being committed by white-collar workers. Also, the known cases are just the tip of the iceberg since computer crime often leaves no trail.

LACK OF SECURITY LEADS TO ABUSE

Data security can be penetrated for purposes of fraud, theft, sabotage, or espionage, or simply by accident.

Fraud

Deceit, trickery, or breach of confidence for the purpose of gaining unfair or dishonest advantage is called **fraud**. Computer fraud differs from ordinary fraud only in the unusual dollar value per incident. The national average for bank frauds is $23,000, but for computer-assisted fraud it is over $430,000. Two common frauds are inflating on-paper profits in an effort to sell a company or its stock at a higher price and overstating assets in an effort to secure a loan that the firm could not otherwise qualify for. Nineteen employees of Cenco, Inc. (a manufacturer and distributor of health-care products and services) were recently accused of using Cenco's computer system to inflate its revenues by placing almost $28 million in nonexistent inventory on its computerized records and by duplicating some of its sales.

Theft

The **theft** of money by computer manipulation is much less likely to be discovered than thefts of physical property such as stereo equipment or clothing. Computer money-thieves can leave so little trace that if their crimes are discovered at all, it is likely to be by accident. While the average bank robbery nets $3,000, the average computer-assisted theft nets $100,000—and nobody knows about it until it is too late.

In the largest known bank theft to date, an operations officer at Wells Fargo Bank allegedly produced bogus deposits in an account at one branch belonging to a boxing promotion outfit. He did this by using the bank's computerized interbranch account settlement process to withdraw funds from a different branch. To keep the computer from flagging the imbalance, he created new fraudulent credits to cover the withdrawal. The process was allegedly repeated many times over a period in 1979 and 1980 and resulted in a take of $21.3 million.

In spite of the greater difficulty, merchandise can be stolen using a computer. Mr. D was indicted on being responsible for the loss of $1 million in prescription drugs belonging to E. R. Squibb & Sons, Inc. Mr. D masterminded the scheme while employed as a computer operator in Squibb's Burlington, Massachusetts, distribution center, according to prosecuting attorneys. Mr. D took goods weekly and kept track of product numbers and quantities.

In order to cover up the thefts, Mr. D billed two Squibb house accounts normally used to cover inventory disbursements that did not result in billing of customers, such as samples and exchanges. Mr. D is subject to $3,000 fine and 15 years in prison.

Cash and merchandise are not the only items likely to be stolen. Mr. C, former programmer for Applied Systems, Inc., of Mobile, Alabama, has been convicted and fined $50,000, for copying his former employer's programs. Mr. C, the jury determined, copied Applied's programs, started his own service bureau shortly afterward, and offered Applied's customers lower rates if they would switch to his firm. Eight customers did switch.

Sabotage

The Department of Defense (DOD) has a special concern with computer systems security. In wartime, its own computers, along with those at every military base in the country and at key industries, would be prime targets for **sabotage**. In 1972 the DOD published a manual outlining security standards, but six years later no computer manufacturer had fully certified its operating system as meeting that standard. In fact, not until 1979 did the Air Force start testing a prototype of the "secure" Honeywell Multics computer. Meanwhile, we can only hope that external measures such as security clearance, passwords, and physical access restrictions will provide adequate protection at the DOD.

Computer centers have already been sabotaged in efforts to bring attention to certain causes such as the antiwar (Vietnam) feelings of the 1960s and early 1970s. Computer centers are also vulnerable to sabotage that results from labor unrest, civil disturbances, political unrest, and others. The most likely risk of peacetime sabotage is from a disgruntled employee or former employee. For example, a programmer who was fired wrote a program to scramble the data within a file. Pretending he had to work late to complete a program, he ran his scrambling program and made most of the company's major data files useless.

Espionage

Spying on others—**espionage**—is likely to affect computer centers. As more valuable kinds of information are stored or processed by the computer, the risk of espionage is greater, and many businesses need to consider the risk of being spied upon. An oil company lost an undeterminable amount of money because of espionage. Data relating to oil lease bids were stolen from the oil company during transmission from its computer in Texas to its terminal in Alaska. The victimized company became suspicious when it was narrowly outbid at many oil lease sales. Upon investigation it found a wiretap a few miles down the road from its Alaska terminal. Some areas that may be vulnerable to business espionage are:

- sales and service information, market analyses, bid prices
- corporate finance, stock discussions, stockholder information
- legal negotiations, plans, policy changes
- expansion plans, mergers, acquisitions
- production figures, goals, problems
- proprietary product developments, tests, processes, formulas
- personnel changes, payroll data, general administrative matters

Accident

Not all breaches of computer facilities or data are intentional. Losses have resulted from flood, fire, hurricane, faulty operation of sprinkler systems, and human error in processing. Let us look at a few actual accidents involving computer systems.

A chemical company on the East Coast thought it had provided adequately for data security by storing backup copies in files several blocks away from its computer center, but when the company's refinery was destroyed by fire, so were its computer center and the backup files, even though located some distance away.

Accidental operation of a fire sprinkler in August, 1979, at the U.S. Census Bureau caused damage to four UNIVAC computers in a room containing $40 million worth of equipment. Two CPUs were completely destroyed and two others damaged. The replacement cost of one CPU was about $7 million. This catastrophe happened as the Census Bureau was gearing up to tally the 1980 Census. Processing was shifted to other government computer centers for several months pending installation of replacement CPUs.

The sprinkling accident was traced back to a mistake in the type of sprinkler heads that were installed a couple of years earlier. Nontoxic Halon gas fire-suppression systems are available that cause no damage and allow immediate resumption of operation.

The Arizona State Finance Center in Phoenix once discovered that one of its tape files had disappeared. When its personnel went to retrieve the backup punched card file, it found that 2,000 of the cards had been folded, gilded, and used for Christmas decorations. And in August 1975, a programming error in Maryland resulted in $10 million in overpayments to about 15,000 people covered by Supplemental Security Income.

IMPROVING COMPUTER SYSTEMS SECURITY

As we have seen, there are many approaches to computer abuse, from intricate changes made in computer programs, to changes in input or output data, to physical destruction of data, programs, or equipment. No wonder so many computer experts and information users are deeply concerned with improving computer security.

How good can such security get? That is, no matter what measures are taken by human beings, won't there always be another human being who can figure out a way to penetrate them? Most computer experts would answer yes to this question. Absolute security is impossible. The question then becomes how much security is necessary or feasible? A general answer can be found in Parker's **prudent person theory:** "If a data processing center were to suffer a loss and a prudent person would conclude that there was adequate protection against that loss, then enough security has been provided."

Another basis for deciding how much security is feasible is to compare the costs of a possible loss with the costs of providing security. For example, if a high degree of security for a computer center would cost $100,000 per year, but the costs of not being secure (such as fraud, theft, destruction of data files, and so on) would be appreciably greater than $100,000 per year, then the center should buy more security.

Security efforts are often divided into the following six categories:

1. Physical security to control access to the computer room and to data storage facilities

2. Internal computer security mechanisms that are built into computer equipment, software, and data communication circuits

3. Operational and procedural security measures that put limits on people and computer use—for example, allowing only operators, not programmers, to operate the computer and, conversely, prohibiting operators from making program changes

4. Auditing procedures and testing by persons independent of the computer department, or independent of the firm

5. Ethical controls that every person involved in the collection, processing, storage, and communication of data offer because of their own ethical standards

6. Legal deterrents such as state and federal laws and enforcement of those laws

We examine each of these six as possible ways to make computer systems more secure.

Physical Security

The geographic location of a computer facility should be chosen carefully. It should be far from any risk of natural disaster such as flood, fire, and earthquake. It should be in a low crime area, with secure telephone and power service, and should have a protected, fail-safe air-conditioning system.

Access to the computer, data preparation areas, and data storage areas should be controlled. Smoke and fire detection and alarm systems, as well as fire-suppression equipment, should be installed and tested regularly. Also, readily available equipment covers and adequate room drains can protect computers and data files against damage from the water used to put out a fire.

Physical security measures are the most obvious, often the least expensive, and perhaps the least valuable. Theft, fraud, espionage, and sabotage may happen in spite of physical safeguards. Nevertheless, they are necessary and must not be ignored.

Internal Security Mechanisms

Security mechanisms can be built into computer hardware, software, and data communications equipment. Hardware controls include parity checks to assure that machine failure is caught and does not allow incorrect or invalid internal codes to be treated as good data. Some of the latest hardware is designed to test the circuitry as it is being used and to bypass any weak or malfunctioning circuit from that time on. When enough defective circuits develop, the whole circuit board is replaced.

Software controls include those designed into the computer's operating system, data communications software, and application programs. The operating system, the group of programs that directs and controls much of the internal processing and I/O activity, can offer a large degree of internal security. For instance, it may require an authorization test (account number and password) before allowing a user to operate the computer or a remote terminal. Or the operating system may allow access only to a certain preestablished list of programs or data files. It may limit a user's time on the system, and log in the time consumed, the names of programs executed, and the names of files accessed. Further, it may make a special note if the user tries to get programs or files he or she is not authorized to use. Such a log of activities and special notices is worthless, however, unless a responsible person (such as manager, supervisor, or auditor) regularly checks it.

Other operating systems controls could limit users' access to files of a certain date, or keep old files from being destroyed until they reach a certain age. This feature protects against intentional or accidental attempts to write over good data.

Security in data communications is complicated by the fact that data are passing out of the physical control of the computer owner and into the hands of a communication company, usually a telephone company. Even though computer data being transmitted over telephone lines sound like just a series of audio tones, they can easily be converted back to digital and then English-language format. Security-conscious computer users in the area of data communication are looking to **codes** for help. Datotek Corporation, specializing in communications security, manufactures a Datacoder that, it says, provides complete data security over ASCII circuits. An example of coding is shown in Figure 21–1. Considering the Datacoder's relatively low cost ($8,000 for both sending and receiving site units), it or something like it could be a good buy for some users.

Once written into a program, security checks and controls work automatically. An often used security check is one for upper and lower limit. For instance, a payroll record contains a number of hours an employee worked during the pay period. Common sense should tell us that no employee would be likely to work 1,000 hours in one week, or 500 hours, or even 150 hours. In many departments, in fact, even 60 hours would be out of line. A payroll program could be written to test the "hours" data for each employee, and if any were greater than 60, to generate an exception notice for the department's supervisor. The supervisor would then determine whether the excessive hours had been entered accidentally or intentionally and, if intentionally, why. Many other kinds of limit checks can be written.

Another internal security mechanism is checking the validity of code numbers. This checking involves performing a specific sequence of arithmetic operations on the digits of the code number to yield an additional digit, called a **check digit**. At various

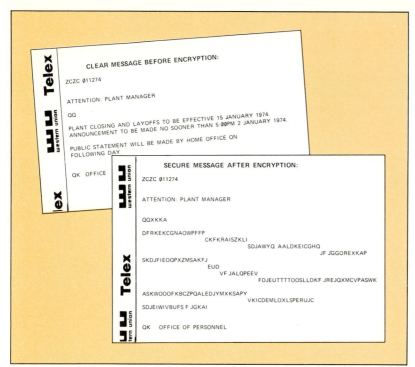

FIGURE 21–1 Message before and after encoding.

points in the subsequent processing of the record containing the check-digited number, the special sequence of calculations is repeated. If the resultant check digit is the same as the one previously attached to the code number proper, validity is assumed. Check digits are used extensively to validate account and stock numbers.

Sequence checks in a special program can check the order or sequence of files as they are processed. This check ensures that transaction data are not applied to the wrong account.

Other programs can tally each transaction processed and compare the total against a predetermined total. These and many other program checks can work efficiently, unobtrusively, and consistently to guard against computer-related abuse.

Finally, all application programs should be described by narrative, systems flowchart, detail flowchart (or hierarchical chart and pseudocode), and operating instructions called "documentation." Furthermore, any changes in the documentation should be noted, along with the reasons, dates, and authorizers of the changes.

Operational and Procedural Security

Separation of responsibility is one of the main operational safeguards against computer abuse. For instance, one person should transcribe data from source document to magnetic media, and another person should verify the accuracy of the data on magnetic media. Computer operators should not have access to data files, except for those required for scheduled jobs, and programmers and systems analysts should not have access to data files or to the computer.

Copies of files should be stored in remote locations along with operating instructions for their use in recovering from a loss. Operational logs should account for all users, programs, and times used. Finally, strict procedures should be set up *before* abuse starts.

Auditing Procedures

The purpose of **auditing** is to determine by testing, inquiring, and observing that recorded and processed data accurately reflect actual transactions and the financial condition of the organization. Auditors also examine established policy and compare it with operating procedures to determine that policies are being followed, and determine whether there is enough separation of duties to allow checks and balances to work.

Auditors are especially concerned that financial transactions can be traced from their inception (such as a cash sale at a cash register) through each processing step, and ultimately to the output of financial reports, such as a balance sheet showing a cash amount. This path of processing steps should have "trail markers" at each step, directing the auditor back to the prior step. For example, amounts entered in a customer's account should have a notation of the invoice's number from which the amounts were taken. A series of such markers make up an **audit trail**.

With on-line computerized processing, special steps have to be taken to ensure that the audit trail is not broken somewhere along the path. For example, in an on-line banking system, an automated teller machine (ATM) (see Chapter 10) feeds cash deposit and withdrawal data to the computer's central processing unit (CPU). A program then calls the customer's record in from on-line storage, alters the cash balance figure, and places the customer record back on the on-line storage device. Meanwhile, another ATM has sent transaction data to the CPU for processing, replacing data from the prior transaction. To make sure that the location, terminal, operator's name, time of day, day of month, and so on can be traced if the customer later disputes the bank's transaction data, all transactions are recorded on a magnetic tape file (Figure 21–2). As a by-product, when the transaction file is listed or microfilmed (Figure 21–3), it provides auditors with a vital link in the audit trail from transaction to financial report.

In addition to building audit trails into application programs, auditing firms often use special

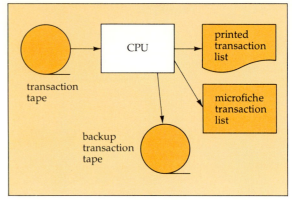

FIGURE 21–2 Processing transactions and accumulating the transaction file.

programs that feed test data through the computer system to determine the capability of the user's system to function accurately and to spot invalid transactions.

Ethical Controls

This safeguard, **ethical control,** is probably the hardest to establish and certainly the hardest to mea-

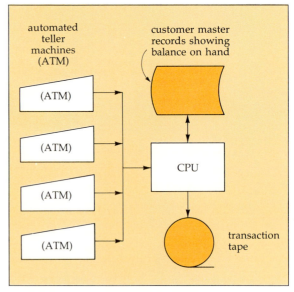

FIGURE 21–3 Sorting and listing or microfilming of transactions.

sure. The very prevalence of computer abuse, though, seems to show that many people feel little, if any, ethical concern in the computer area. In the Equity Funding case, several top executives and many subordinates, including one programmer, were apparently willing to ruin dozens of investors in order to fill their own pockets. How can managers be sure their employers are ethical?

Is there a lack of ethics? Or is it more a lack of experience in using computers for a long enough period of time—that is, we have not learned fully yet the areas of potential abuse and ways to limit them? In double-entry accounting, for example, experience dates back 400 years, providing many generations of accountants opportunities to develop checks and balances and auditing procedures. The computer is only 40 years old—little over one generation.

Perhaps another reason for the seeming lack of ethics is the tremendous potential for abuse being concentrated in the hands of so few. For example, accounting work traditionally was shared by dozens of people, each in a sense serving as a check on the others. With a computer, however, all the work may be concentrated in the computer, the program, and, thus, the programmer. In other words, the stakes offered for being unethical may be far greater for the programmer than they were for the manual record-keeper. Although this explanation does not justify the lack of ethical behavior, it helps clarify why it exists.

Perhaps the starting point is the hiring process. Employers should check the data on application forms. When integrity is the question, a face-to-face meeting with people given as references is much more revealing than a telephone conversation. Experience and education, of course, can be checked by telephone or even by mail. The important thing is to check. One survey indicates that the chances of an applicant's references being checked are only 1 in 4; the work they say they did, 1 in 5; and the college degrees they list, less than 1 in 5. This may be sidestepping the issue, however. Should we instead ask how we can raise our level of ethical awareness?

Some experts have recommended college courses in ethics for computer students. Others say ethics should be integrated into existing courses. Still others are of the opinion that computer students and employees should not be singled out, but that we should give ethics more attention in all levels of education. Some would legislate ethics; the U.S. Senate is considering federal legislation that would sharply define computer crime.

Employers too can have a valuable role in building ethical behavior. Employee group discussions can help raise the ethical consciousness of computer personnel; and the standards of the group may serve as the ethical standards for the computer center.

Finally, managers have a responsibility to learn how trustworthy employees are and not assign them to positions of trust that exceed their temptation limit. A good system of internal controls, though, can come to the rescue when managers make a mistake.

Perhaps the key to computer systems security is to recognize that since there are loopholes in every system, we need to test a system periodically to see if it can be intruded or compromised. A computer center must set up multiple lines of defense and not assume that one massive, expensive procedure eliminates all risk.

Legal Deterrents

Laws are passed based on ethical standards and serve as a basis for enforcing the collective ethics of our society. These laws do not ensure that the collective ethics of our citizens are fully adhered to; however, laws generally raise the level of adherence. Relating to computer crime, only 11 of the 50 states have laws aimed specifically at computer-related crime.[1] Nine other states have laws under consideration in their legislatures. There is not, at this writing, a federal law that deals directly with computer crime, although Senators Abraham Ribicoff (D-

---

[1] Arizona, California, Colorado, Florida, Illinois, Michigan, New Mexico, North Carolina, Rhode Island, Utah, and Virginia.

Conn.) and Charles H. Percy (R-Ill.) proposed laws in 1977 and 1979. The proposals have received lengthy debate in Congress and in the legal and computer professions, but have not been enacted into law.

Without a specific law, courts and law enforcement agencies have to "shoe horn" prosecution efforts into existing remotely related laws. In many cases the "fit" is very poor, and an ineffective prosecution results.

The primary objectives of Ribicoff-Percy's **Federal Computer Systems Protection Act (FCSPA)** are:

1. To facilitate the preparation of evidence and prosecution of computer crimes

2. To remove the gaps and inconsistencies in existing laws and cases so as to simplify court action

3. To improve the likelihood of more appropriate punishment

4. To dramatize the damaging nature of computer crime and be viewed as a significant deterrent

SUMMARY

As more and more computer devices become accessible to people, and more and more computer technicians are trained, risks to the security of data, equipment, and software in both government and business, and hence the risk to the private citizens, steadily grows. The burden, then, is on computer-using agencies and businesses to secure their computers.

Security steps involve tightening access to the computer facility and setting up internal procedures that discourage misuse of computers and data. Programs and operating systems should contain procedures that can screen out unauthorized use; independent outside auditors should examine computer systems periodically to assure integrity of processing; and greater attention should be given to the ethical soundness of employees.

Continued alertness, awareness, and aggressive action by computer professionals, managers, legislators, and citizens are the only insurance against computer abuse.

TERMS

The following words or terms have been presented in this chapter.

Computer systems security	**Check digits**
	Sequence checks
Fraud	**Auditing**
Theft	**Audit trail**
Sabotage	**Ethical control**
Espionage	**Federal Computer Systems Protection Act (FCSPA)**
Prudent person theory	
Codes	

EXERCISES

The exercises that follow are grouped by level of difficulty. Problems in the A series are the easiest; B series problems are moderately hard; and C series problems are the most difficult.

A–1 How might a computer be used to steal?

A–2 What is the relative size of a computer-assisted bank theft versus an old-fashioned bank robbery assisted only by a gun?

A–3 Explain the "prudent person theory."

A–4 Do you think the University of Maryland Hospital was unusually lax when they hired Barry E. Wyche. Why?

B–1 Define computer systems security.

B–2 How can a computer be used for fraud?

B–3 Are any computers secure against intrusion? Explain.

B–4 Describe some physical security measures that might protect a computer center.

B–5 What precautions do you suggest should be taken before a computer operator or programmer is hired?

C-1 Describe some internal security procedures you might take to protect data and software.

C-2 What operational and procedural steps can be taken to make a computer more secure?

C-3 How do ethical controls and internal controls relate? Are they both necessary? Desirable? Explain.

C-4 Do you think Barry E. Wyche's probation officer had a responsibility to notify the University of Wyche's prior conviction? Why?

COMPUTER NEWS

ACCUSED EMBEZZLER HAD RECORD OF DP CRIME

BALTIMORE—A hospital data center here, already embarrassed that lax security aided a computer operator in embezzling almost $40,000, was further chagrined recently to learn that, when hired, the culprit was on probation for a similar computer crime in New York City.

The defendant, Barry E. Wyche, 31, was hired by the University of Maryland Hospital data center last September. He was charged in January with reprogramming an accounts-payable tape to divert two checks totaling $39,322 to his address in nearby Owings Mills, Md. [CW, Feb. 2].

In sentencing Wyche to five years in jail, Judge Frank E. Cicone of the Baltimore County Circuit Court said last week the jail term was deserved because the offense was the second of the same nature.

Wyche had been sentenced to five years probation by a New York court in 1979 for using a computer to divert a $5,576 check from his employer, the city's Financial Information Services Agency.

According to sources close to the Maryland investigation, Wyche was also under investigation for allegedly trying to cash payroll checks stolen from his previous employer, Blue Cross-Blue Shield of Maryland.

GUILTY PLEA

Wyche pleaded guilty to one of the hospital-related charges in exchange for the five-year term and an agreement from prosecutors not to seek an indictment in the Blue Cross-Blue Shield matter.

According to Assistant Maryland Attorney General Bruce C. Spizler, all but approximately $7,000 was recovered from the hospital embezzlement. The stolen money was regained after Wyche's bank froze his account early in the investigation. Although Wyche had already withdrawn about $12,000, some of that was also recovered when the bank attached a car Wyche had bought with the stolen funds, Spizler said.

Officials at the university hospital center conceded lax security procedures were a recognized problem when Wyche was hired. He was employed after he falsified an employment application, stating he has never been arrested. No formal security check was made of his background.

Robert Ginn, Hospital director of finance and systems, said the DP center was not contacted by Wyche's probation officer about his criminal record even though the officer presumably realized Wyche was being employed in a position similar to that he held in New York when he was convicted there of embezzlement.

The probation officer would not discuss the handling of the Wyche case, citing administrative guidelines that preclude her from discussing the matter. Wyche will be returned to New York to face charges of violating his probation there, prosecutor Spizler said.

Computerworld, April 13, 1981.

MODULE six
SUPPLEMENTS

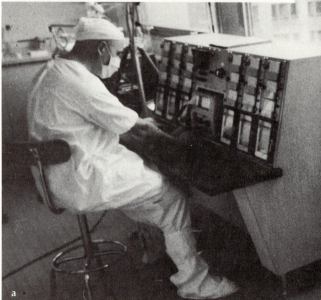

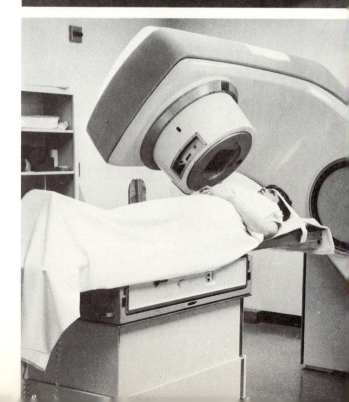

Computers are taking over the human role in medicine, as in other fields, because they do what people do better—more accurately, more efficiently, more quickly—but they are also contributing to the development of entirely new techniques and methods.

Computers in medicine offer a round-the-clock vigilance that is hard to match in medical personnel. At the Neonatal Biological Research Center of the Hospital of Port Royal in Paris (Photo A), a computer is used to monitor premature babies. The machine continuously records the baby's respiration, temperature, and pulse, as well as sounding an alarm in an emergency. At another French hospital (Photo F), a computer-controlled graphoscrope helps the anesthesiologist monitor a patient's progress during open-heart surgery. Computers are also used for more accurate and convenient storage and updating of medical records (Photo D).

A new technique developed at the Radiation Control Center of the University of Louisville Medical Center (Photo E), uses a linear accelerator, rotating on a central axis, to give an X-ray scan to a cancer patient during treatment. The myo-electric arm in Photo B, designed by Dr. Jacobsen at the University of Utah, picks up signals from the brain and translates them into kinaesthetic movement. And the digital X-ray in Photo C is a new technique used primarily in the exploration of veins and arteries. In traditional X-ray techniques a contrast material is injected into the bloodstream at the site the doctor wants to examine, which can be extremely painful. But in digital X-rays a picture is taken before injection (called background); the contrast material is injected into the arm and another picture taken; and the computer then separates out the background to show a "subtracted" image. The advantages are less trauma to the patient, shorter hospital stays, and a better diagnostic image.

Machines may be short on bedside manner, but computers are leading to more and more breakthroughs in sophisticated diagnosis and treatment.

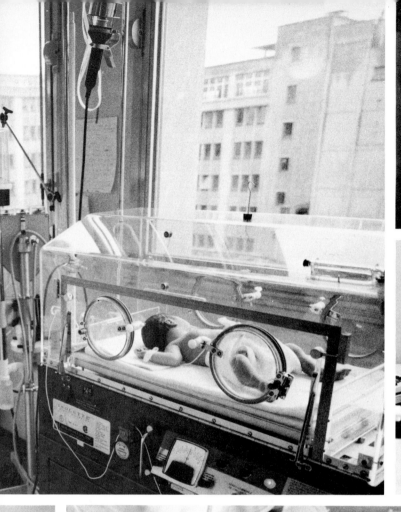
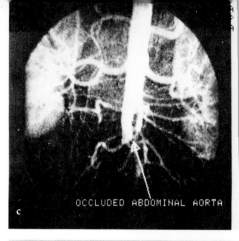

OCCLUDED ABDOMINAL AORTA

c

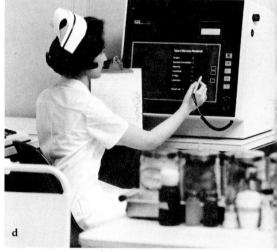

d

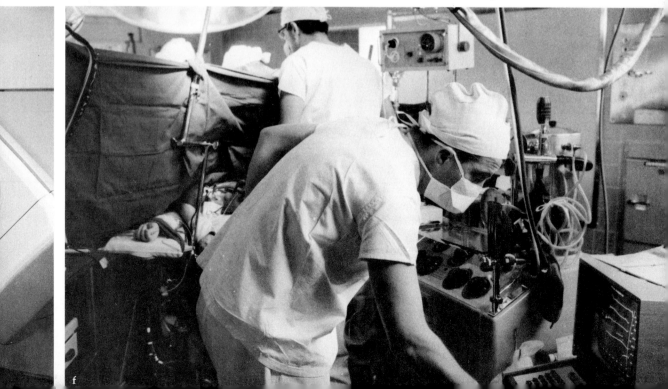

f

SUPPLEMENT a

THE CHALLENGE OF PROGRAMMING

Preview

Problems to Solve

Payroll System

Inventory System

PREVIEW

One of the best ways for you to fully understand programming and, thus, how a computer solves problems, is to write some programs yourself. In so doing, you will become more familiar with the computational powers and decisional capabilities of a computer. In addition, you can gain insight as to what a programmer actually does to cause the computer to process data into meaningful information.

PROBLEMS TO SOLVE

The problems in this section have been grouped into nine categories: (1) language familiarization, (2) simple looping structures, (3) computational routines, (4) complex looping structures, (5) simulations, (6) file processing, (7) single and double numeric arrays, (8) alphanumeric and string processes, and (9) logical situations.

Problems in category 1 are designed to introduce you to keypunching or entering a program into the computer for compiling and executing.

The looping problems, categories 2 and 4, are used to illustrate this important capability of computers. These looping problems are a mixture of simple, nested, and multiple loops; some of the routines will cause hundreds of cycles, others only a few.

The computational routines in category 3 emphasize the ability of a computer to evaluate complex mathematical formulas rapidly and to yield accurate results. The problems in this series involve a range of subjects from interest rates to statistics.

In the simulation category, category 5, is a series of problems that ask you to create programs that cause the computer to play games or otherwise imitate real life phenomena. Simple games like coin matching and craps are relatively easy to program.

Problems in category 6 on file processing are typical data processing uses of computers. Most business uses of computers involve the manipulation of data kept in files. Problems in this category require you to write programs to create and update files. Most of the problems are concerned with sequential files, but can be easily modified for randomly processed files.

In many programs, the use of an array can dramatically shorten the program length and, hence, the programming effort required. The problems in category 7 illustrate the variety of ways that programmers use arrays. The problems in this group are quite varied: some use single arrays, others double arrays; some arrays contain data for reference purposes, others are used for counting purposes. The array (mathematicians call them "matrices") is one of the most powerful programming techniques.

Many of the data that businesses use are not numerical, but alphanumeric. The problems in category 8 involve programming routines to process these types of data. They require you to write programs that deal with box scores, analyze the reading difficulty of textual material, figure inventories, and calculate days of the week and telephone bills.

The last group of problems deals with "logical situations." These problems require careful analysis because the solution is not a simple series of: Do this, then this, then that. Instead, the solutions require that you do something only under certain circumstances; under different circumstances, you must do something else.

Figure A–1 lists the titles of the various problems, the numbers of the categories from which they are drawn, some commentary about the problem, and a difficulty rating factor for each (A: easiest, B: more difficult, C: most difficult). Problems that cross category boundaries are listed as belonging to more than a single category.

A–1 Pounds and Kilograms Enter the following BASIC program on the terminal. Execute the program by typing "RUN."

```
1      PRINT "POUNDS", "KILOGRAMS"
10     LET P = 200
20     LET K = P/2.205
30     PRINT P,K
40     LET P = P − 10
50     IF P = 0 THEN 999
60     GO TO 20
999    END
```

FIGURE A-1 Program categories.

Problem Number	Title	Difficulty	Category Number(s)	Commentary
A-1	Pounds and Kilograms	A	1	BASIC-2 column captions
A-2	Metric Heights	A	1	BASIC-3 column captions
A-3	Powers of Two	A	1	BASIC-overflow, E notation
A-4	Oakes Pancake Breakfast	B	2	E notation
A-5	Manhattan Island for $24	B	2,3	Compound interest
A-6	Effective Rate of Interest	A	2	Precedence order
A-7	Number of Digits	B	2	Division by 10, INT
A-8	Monthly Payment	B	3	Precedence order
A-9	Squares of Numbers	B	2	Totaling and squaring
A-10	Number Pyramid	C	2	Difference in pairs
A-11	Calculating π	B	2	Sums of terms
A-12	Retirement Plans	C	3,4	Backward loop counter
A-13	Angular/Decimal Conversion	A	2	Functions
A-14	Fractions and Accuracy	C	3,4	Number presentation
A-15	Half Life of Kr-85	A	2	
A-16	Perfect Numbers	C	2,9	
A-17	Palindrome	C	2,9	
A-18	Water Consumption	B	2,3	Conservation
A-19	Number Rounding	B	2	
A-20	Birthday Probabilities	B	3	Real numbers
A-21	Monthly Payment	B	3	Exponents
A-22	Depreciation: Sum-of-the-Years Digits	C	4	Nested loops
A-23	Sunrise/Sunset	B	5	Functions
A-24	Waiting Time Costs	B	7	
A-25	Random Numbers by Squaring	A	5	INT
A-26	Loan Repayment Schedule	C	4,9	Short-term notes
A-27	Want Ads	B	4,9	Billing routine
A-28	Water Billing Routine	A	9	Rate schedule
A-29	Golden Mean	A	5	Fibonacci numbers
A-30	Gymnastics Statistics	C	7,8	Searching
A-31	Doctor Hudson's Secret Journal	C	8	Data encryption
A-32	Rule of 78's	A	3	Loan pay-off
A-33	Travel and Waiting Costs	B	4,7	Multiple arrays
A-34	Division by Subtraction	C	4,9	How the computer divides
A-35	Golf Handicap	B	7,9	Sorting of data
A-36	Soundex Codes	B	8	
A-37	Roman to Decimal Numerals	B	8	

FIGURE A–1 continued

A–38	Decimal to Roman Numerals	C	8	
A–39	Basketball Statistics	C	4,7,8	Box score
A–40	Numbers into Words	B	8	
A–41	Words into Numbers	B	8	
A–42	Discount Code	B	9	Pricing
A–43	Page Headings	A	3,7	Totals
A–44	Paschal Full Moon	A	7,8	Remainders in division
A–45	Units of Production Depreciation	A	3	
A–46	Fleisch Readability	C	8	
A–47	Line Balancing	B	8	Testing for spaces
A–48	Height and Weight Standards	A	9	Grouping by category
A–49	Inventory Statement	A	8	Totaling
A–50	Electrical Billing Routine	B	9	
A–51	Statement of Account	B	3	Totaling
A–52	Solar Heat	A	9	Functions
A–53	Marginal Propensity	B	3	Economics
A–54	Days of Week	B	3	Trivia

A–2 Metric Heights Enter the following BASIC program on the terminal. Execute the program by typing "RUN."

```
10   PRINT "YOUR NAME"
20   PRINT "HEIGHT", "HEIGHT", "HEIGHT"
30   PRINT "INCHES", "CENTIMETERS", "METERS"
40   LET H = 60
50   LET C = H*2.54
60   LET M = C/100
70   PRINT H, C, M
80   LET H = H + 1
90   IF H = 79 THEN 110
100  GO TO 50
110  END
```

A–3 Powers of Two Enter the following BASIC program. Execute the program by typing "RUN." Note the results. What happened? How do you interpret this?

```
10   PRINT "N", "2 ↑ N", "(1/2) ↑ N"
20   FOR N = 0 TO 35 STEP 1
30   LET A = N − 1
40   LET B = 2 ↑ N
50   LET C = 1/2 ↑ N
60   PRINT N,B,C
70   NEXT N
999  END
```

A–4 Oakes Pancake Breakfast Every Saturday morning since 1950, the Oakes family of Loomis, California, has had a special sour dough batter pancake breakfast. The original starter consisted of approximately 1,000 grams (about 35 ounces) of batter. The pancake recipe requires that $1/3$ (0.33) of the starter be combined with an equal amount of flour and water and saved for the next time. The remainder is used for this breakfast. Print a report that shows how much of the original recipe remains after 20 weeks. Your report should look as follows:

Week	Mixture
1	1000
2	333.333
.	.
.	.
.	.
20	8.60392E−07

A–5 Manhattan Island for $24 In 1626 Peter Minuit bought Manhattan Island from the Indians for $24. If that money had been deposited in a savings account paying 7 percent compounded annually, what would its value have been in 1676, 1726, 1776, 1826, 1876, 1926, 1976? What would it be in 2026? In other words, what would $24 invested at 7 percent interest compounded annually have increased to by 1676? By 1726? And so on.

Compound interest can be calculated using the following expression:

$$S = P(1 + I)^N$$

Where P is the value of the original investment (that is, 24); I is the interest rate (7 percent = 0.07); N is the number of years that the money has been invested; and S is the value of the investment at the end of the specified (N) period of time.

Print the results in the following format:

1676	50	XXX.XX
1726	100	XXXX.XX
.	.	.
.	.	.
.	.	.
2026	400	XXXX.XX

A–6 Effective Rate of Interest The following formula calculates the true per annum interest rate R for a loan of P dollars with N monthly payments of M dollars each:

$$R = \frac{24(MN - P)}{P(N + 1)}$$

Monthly Payment, M	Number of Payments, N	Loan, P
129	36	4000
201	300	28000
55	10	450

Calculate and print the effective rate of interest for each of the three sets of data.

A–7 Number of Digits It is often necessary to know the number of digits in a number. With this knowledge it is possible to design format statements with commas and dollar signs in the proper place, so a number like 50731285 (with 8 digits) can be printed: $50,731,285. Design a program that will read eight numbers and will print the number and the number of digits in the number. Your program should also print a caption causing the next entry to be written.

Original Number	Number of Digits
40731285	8
237	3
1645	4
29	2
5	1
167748	6
5677829	7
0	1

A–8 Monthly Payment The formula to compute the monthly payment on a loan is:

$$M = \frac{P \times \frac{I}{12}}{1 - \left(\frac{1}{1 + \frac{I}{12}}\right)^{T \times 12}}$$

Where I is the interest rate, P is the principal, and T is the duration of the loan in years. Write a program to calculate varying M's when $P = \$80,000$; I varies from 9.25% to 16%, in ¼% increments; and $T = 30$. Your program must output M's values and the corresponding values of I and T, with proper captions.

A–9 Squares of Numbers The square of any positive integer N can be found by adding N number of consecutive odd integers starting with 1. For example:

$$5^2 = 1 + 3 + 5 + 7 + 9 = 25$$
$$9^2 = 1 + 3 + 5 + 7 + 9 + 11 + 13 + 15 + 17 = 81$$

Input a list of 8 integers and output a list of squares.

A–10 Number Pyramid In Robert Moses's book *Having Fun With Mathematics* (New York: W. W. Norton, 1968), the number series

0	1	3	6	10	15	21	28
1	2	3	4	5	6	7	

is described as the "number pyramid." Notice that each new number in the series is formed by adding a number to the previous pyramid number. Write a program to print the first 25 numbers in the pyramid.

A–11 Calculating π The number represented by the mathematical symbol π, 3.14159 . . . , is really a ratio of a circle's circumference to its diameter. It can also be calculated by evaluating the sequence

$$\pi = \frac{4}{1} - \frac{4}{3} + \frac{4}{5} - \frac{4}{7} + \frac{4}{9} - \frac{4}{11} + \ldots$$

Write a program that will calculate the value of π for N terms. The value of N should be read into the program. Print the value of π for each computation (loop cycle).

A–12 Retirement Plans If an amount of money A is placed in a bank that pays interest rate R, and that money stays in the bank for N years, the value V of the money in the future is given by the formula:

$$V = A(1 + R)^N$$

If next year the amount of money increases by 5% (that is, $A = A + 0.05A$), while N goes down by one year, the same formula holds for this next value of V. Write a program that prints for N varying from 40 to 1 the value V of an arbitrary amount A and interest rate R (read in by your program). Also, find the total amount of money in the bank account (that is, the sum of the V's).

A–13 Angular/Decimal Conversion Most angles are measured in degrees, minutes, and seconds. For computation, they must be in decimal form. For example, the angle 37 degrees, 20 minutes, 38 seconds (written 37°20'38") is converted as: 37 + 20/60 + 38/3600. Write a routine that converts the following angles to their decimal equivalents:

45°0'0"	97°13'16"
37°20'38"	360°0'0"
91°27'47"	359°59'59"
0°0'0"	30°30'0"
0°1'0"	30°30'30"
0°0'1"	12°27'14"
15°0'0"	36°24'36"

A–14 Fractions and Accuracy Most computers approximate real numbers. To check the accuracy of these approximations, write a program that will sum fractions as shown:

$1 = \frac{1}{2} + \frac{1}{2}$
$1 = \frac{1}{3} + \frac{1}{3} + \frac{1}{3}$
$1 = \frac{1}{4} + \frac{1}{4} + \frac{1}{4} + \frac{1}{4}$
$1 = \frac{1}{5} + \frac{1}{5} + \frac{1}{5} + \frac{1}{5} + \frac{1}{5}$
.
.
.
$1 = \frac{1}{20} + \frac{1}{20} + \frac{1}{20} + \frac{1}{20} + \frac{1}{20} + \ldots \frac{1}{20}$

Your program should print the sum of the fractions and the difference between this sum and 1.0.

A–15 Half Life of Kr-85 The radioactive isotope krypton-85 has a half life of 11 years. This isotope is a direct by-product of a fission nuclear reactor. If 10,000 grams of this isotope are available now, draw a flowchart that prints a table like the following and that continues until $\frac{1}{20}$ of the isotope remains.

Year	Amount of Kr-85
1979	10000
1990	5000
2001	2500
⋮	⋮
	500

A–16 Perfect Numbers The factors of 6, other than 6 itself, are 1, 2, and 3. Their sum, as it happens, is 6. Any number with this interesting property is called a "perfect number." There are two more perfect numbers between 6 and 500. Find them, and then find the perfect numbers between 500 and 1500.

A–17 Palindrome A number that reads the same forward as backward is a palindrome. Examples are: 1, 606, 1221, 343, 7007. Find all the palindromes from 1 to 9999.

A–18 Water Consumption A water district needs a program to monitor the water consumption of customers to see if water usage has decreased by 25 percent or more from the same period last year. A list of customers who have *not* decreased usage by at least 25 percent should be printed. Your program should use the following as input:

- N: customer account number
- C1: consumption during billing period this year
- C2: consumption during same period last year

It should print a report similar to the one that follows. Use the data listed after the formula.

LIST OF USERS NOT MEETING
25 PERCENT CUTBACK

Account Number	Last Year	Current Year	Percent Decrease
101	2000	1800	10
112	3000	2460	12
115	1500	1200	20

Formula:

$$\frac{\%\ \text{decrease}}{(\text{or increase})} = \frac{\text{last year's consumption} - \text{this year's consumption}}{\text{last year's consumption}}$$

Account Number	Last Year	Current Year
101	2000	1800
102	1550	1000
103	2530	1810
104	2610	1350
105	1470	1021
106	1221	831
110	4392	2107
111	3569	2139
112	3000	2640
113	2975	2201
115	1500	1200
116	600	505

A-19 Number Rounding In many business transactions, the result of a computation needs to be rounded to two decimal places for output purposes. Use the following numbers as data: 47.382, 0.045, 571386.4913, 89.5, 12.973, 12.977. Write a routine that rounds them.

A-20 Birthday Probabilities Ignoring leap years, the probability that two people in a room of M people do not have the same birthdays is 364/365. The probability that a third person's birth will differ from the first two is 363/365, a fourth's is 362/365, and so on. For ten people, we multiply the nine fractions together to obtain the probability that all ten birthdays are different. Write a program for 30 people, listing the individual probabilities for 2, 3, 4, 5, 6, . . . , 27, 28, 29, 30, as they are calculated.

A-21 Monthly Payment The following formula calculates the amount of the monthly payment required to pay off a loan:

$$P = IA \left\{ \frac{(1 + I)^N}{(1 + I)^N - 1} \right\}$$

Where I is the monthly interest rate as a decimal (for example, 6% per annum = 0.06 = 0.005 per month); A is the total number of monthly payments, and N is the number of payments.

Enter the following values for I, A, and N:

Monthly Interest Rate, I	Number of Payments, N	Loan, A
0.005	36	4000
0.006	300	38000
0.015	10	450
0.020	36	2000

Calculate and print the monthly payment P for each of the three sets of data.

A-22 Depreciation: Sum-of-the-Years Digits A method of calculating depreciation is known as the sum-of-the-years digits (SYD). This method depreciates an asset faster in the early part of its life than in the latter part. The method requires that you first calculate the SYD factor. This can be done as shown in the following example:

* Item: 1 Initial cost: $1,000 Scrap value: $100
* Expected life: 4 years
* SYD factor's devisor = 4 + 3 + 2 + 1 = 10 = $\frac{(\text{Life})(\text{Life} + 1)}{2} = \frac{(4)(5)}{2}$

Write a program that will print a table for each of the following:

Item	Initial Cost	Scrap Value	Expected Life
1	1000	100	4
2	2800	50	10
3	700	75	15

The depreciation schedule for item 1, for example, is as follows:

Item	Initial Cost	Scrap Value	Expected Life
1	1000	100	4

Year	SYD Factor	Total Depreciation	Yearly Depreciation
1	4/10	900	360
2	3/10	900	270
3	2/10	900	180
4	1/10	900	90

Note: The SYD factor consists of the calculated divisor divided by the years of life remaining.

What Copy Travel and Waiting Time Costs					
This chart shows the cost of an employee's time to travel to and from copiers or copy centers. This information inspired Reliable investors to place their convenience copiers closer to the user.					
Pay per 40-hour week	Approx. pay for 10-min trip	3 trips/day approx. extra cost	Approx. extra cost per 5-day week	Approx. extra cost per 4-week month	Approx. extra cost per 50-week year
$128	.53	$1.59	$ 7.95	$31.80	$397.50
143	.60	1.80	9.00	36.00	450.00
161	.67	2.01	10.05	40.20	500.50
181	.76	2.28	11.40	45.60	570.00
202	.84	2.52	12.60	50.40	630.00
225	.94	2.82	14.10	56.40	705.00

Source: U.S. Government Civil Service Commission figures interpreted by The Rath Organization.

A-23 **Sunrise/Sunset** The computational procedure to find the exact time of the sun's rise or set is quite complex, involves spherical geometry, and depends on a host of miscellaneous factors (such as mountains or hills close to the location of the point being computed). A rough approximation of the time can be found from the following formulas:

Hour-angle = (90 − Sin^{-1} [Tan(−Dec)*Tan(Lat)])/15
Time-of-sunrise = 12 − (Hour-angle)/15
Time-of-sunset = Hour-angle from noon to sunset point

In the formulas:

1. Dec is the declination and is found from the following relationship

Dec = 360 [(t − 80)4365.23]

where t is the Julian day whose sunrise/sunset is to be found.

2. Lat is the latitude in radians of the desired point (for Chicago, 42°; Houston, 30°; Philadelphia, 40°; Miami, 26°; and Seattle, 48°).

3. Sin^{-1} is the arc sine and can be accessed in using the ARSIN function.

Write a program to calculate the sunrise and sunset for March through April of 1982. Your program must have captions.

A-24 **Waiting Time Costs** The above chart is reprinted from the March 1979, issue of *Modern Office Procedures*. Write a program to create and print the chart with column captions like those shown. The formula for $143 for a 4-week month is:

($143/wk)(1 wk/40 hrs)(1 hr/60 min)(10 min/trip)
(3 trips/day)(5 days/wk)(4 wks/mo)

Use a one-dimensional array to store the pay per 40-hour-week quantities.

A-25 **Random Numbers by Squaring** A random number is a number whose probability of occurrence is equal to that of any other number. One method of finding random numbers is to take any 4-digit number and square it. The middle four digits of this number is a random number. To get the next random number, square the newly generated number. Generate 100 random numbers by this process.

A-26 **Loan Repayment Schedule** Money is borrowed from a lending institution, and interest on the loan is computed on the unpaid balance at the end of each month. If a known amount of money is borrowed at a known rate of interest and at a given monthly payment, compute for each month the amount paid on the principal and to interest, plus the amount of the loan balance. Also determine the total amount paid to interest and principal during the life of the loan. For $1,000 at 12% per year and payments of $256 per month, the repayment schedule would appear as:

PAYMENT NUMBER	INTEREST CHARGED	DECREASE IN PRIN- CIPAL	LOAN BAL- ANCE
1	10	246	754
2	7.54	248.46	505.54
3	5.05	250.95	254.59
4	2.54	253.46	1.13
5	.01	1.13	0

TOTAL INTEREST: 25.14
TOTAL PAID ON PRINCIPAL: 1000

Select your own interest rate, amount borrowed, and monthly payment. The formula for computing interest charged is:

Interest = (Principal)*(Rate of interest)*
 (Time in years)

Hint: Construct your program so that the final payment will cause the balance to be zero. Before running the program with your own data, test it with the loan data given in this problem.

A–27 Want Ads The commercial want ad rates for a newspaper are:

1 or 2 times	$3.75
3 times	2.96
4 to 6 times	2.33
7 to 9 times	1.68
10 to 13 times	1.54
14 to 29 times	1.49
30 times	1.43

These rates apply for *each line* (two-line minimum) for each time the ad is placed in the paper. Write a program to calculate the charge to be made for a want ad. Use the following data:

Number of Lines	Times Ad to Be Run
4	3
1	2
12	3
16	1
30	3
45	6
9	2
5	8

Thus, a five-line ad that appears eight times is charged: (5)(1.68)(8) = $67.20.

A–28 Water Billing Routine A certain water company bills customers according to the amount of water used. If a customer uses less than 1,500 cubic feet in a month, the bill is $2 plus 1-½¢ ($0.015) for each cubic foot used. If the customer uses at least 1,500 cubic feet but less than 2,000 cubic feet, the bill is $1 plus 1¢ ($0.01) per cubic foot (with no $2 fee). If a customer uses 2,000 or more cubic feet, the bill is ¾¢ ($0.0075) for each cubic foot used (with no $2 fee). Calculate the monthly bills for the following customers of the company:

Cubic Feet Used	Cubic Feet Used
500	3000
1500	1999
1501	2000
2	2001

A–29 The Golden Mean The number pattern 0, 1, 1, 2, 3, 5, 8, 13, 21, and so on is called the Fibonacci sequence. After looking at the sequence, you should see that each number is the sum of the preceding two numbers. Write a program to list the first 30 Fibonacci numbers. Also in your program divide each number in the sequence by the next highest number and print this quotient. What do you find happens after the fourteenth number in the sequence? For some interesting reading, look at William Hoffer's article in *Smithsonian* (February 1976).

A–30 Gymnastics Statistics You have been commissioned to write a computer program to score a gymnastics meet. For each event, each team can enter up to six contestants. The number of events is either four or six, as a women's meet has four events and a men's meet has six events. The score for each individual per event is as follows:

1. Four judges give a score between 0.0 (low) and 10.0 (high).

2. The lowests and highest scores are discarded.

3. The remaining two scores are averaged, with the resulting score for the event between 0.0 and 10.0.

In addition to the single events, there is an extra event called the "all-around," which is the sum of all single events for an individual.

TEAM—SC					
NAME	FLOOR EXERCISE	VAULTING	UNEVEN BAR	BEAM	ALL-AROUND
PARKER	9.25	8.70	7.50	9.10	34.55
SOUTHWICK	9.10	8.80	8.20	8.20	34.30
JONES	0.00	0.00	8.50	8.80	17.30
SMITH	6.25	5.80	0.00	0.00	12.00
TOTAL	48.00	47.50	46.25	48.50	190.25

TEAM—ARC					
NAME	FLOOR EXERCISE	VAULTING	UNEVEN BAR	BEAM	ALL-AROUND
JONES	9.10	9.20	9.30	6.10	33.70

As the data are arranged by event (all competitors from both teams completing a single event before the next event), print out each competitor's name, team, and score with appropriate headings. As you move from competitor to competitor, it will be necessary to accumulate the single event score so that you can determine the team score.

The team score is determined by adding the individual scores per event. This should be printed at the bottom of each event, along with the name of the individual with the highest score.

Competitors do not compete in the same order from event to event (they are usually arranged from worst to best but not necessarily alternating between teams). Print a summary table like the one above.

As you move from competitor to competitor and event to event and team to team, it will be necessary to store the names and scores earned by an individual (use a two-dimensional array). Totals are found by adding horizontally and vertically.

A–31 Doctor Hudson's Secret Journal For centuries data have been encoded so that others cannot easily read them. Today encoding is being discussed as a method of transmitting computer data so corporate data remain unknown to competitors.

In a novel written by Lloyd C. Douglas,[1] the main character, Doctor Hudson, keeps a journal that relates the secret of his success in the field of brain surgery. The entries in the journal are written in a secret code that has no apparent key. Early in the novel Doctor Hudson drowns, and his journal is discovered by his protégé, Bob Merrick. In trying to decipher the journal, Merrick notes that each entry ends with a ? (actually the Greek letter omega, ω in the novel), and occasionally there is an exclamation point ! in the middle of each entry (actually the Greek letter mu, μ in the novel). The first sentence in Doctor Hudson's secret journal is

RAE OSDRYUM RED!EDRICNIE O YFIN!

During the deciphering process, Merrick breaks the phrase into two parts after the !, and places the right part under the left part.

RAE   OSDRYUM RED
EDRICNIE O YFIN

"Moved by sheer caprice, he wrote the two lines again, the second division lacking one space of meeting the left margin."

RAE   OSDRYUM RED
EDRICNIE O YFIN

"His pencil shook rapidly as he rewrote the letters, mortising the lines:"

READER I CONSIDER YOU MY FRIEND

"I have it!"[2]

Write a program to encode ten messages in Doctor Hudson's secret code. Print both the encoded and decoded versions of each message.

A–32 Rule of 78's When you decide to pay off a loan before the end of its original life, the "Rule of

---

[1] Lloyd C. Douglas, *Magnificent Obsession* (New York: Houghton Mifflin, 1928).

[2] Douglas, page 102.

78's" is used to determine the payoff amount. The "Rule of 78's" is:

1. Calculate the Total interest due on the loan.

   Total interest = (Number of payments)
   × (Monthly payment)
   − (Amount borrowed)

2. Compute the Rebate by following:
   Rebate = (Total interest)
   $$\times \left(\frac{(N - K + 1)(N - K)}{N^2 + N} \right)$$
   where N = number of payments in original loan
   K = number of payments made

3. Find Payoff amount by:
   Payoff amount = $(N - K)$
   × (Monthly payment)
   − (Rebate)

Write a program that inputs the required data and outputs, with captions, the data input and the payoff amount. Use the following data:

N	Monthly Payment	Amount Borrowed	K
360	202.50	28,500	120
60	1302.70	62,000	15
36	129.00	4,000	30
36	129.00	4,000	1

A−33 Travel and Waiting Costs The following chart is reprinted from the March 1979, issue of *Modern Office Procedures*. Write a program to create and print the chart with column captions exactly the same as those shown. The formula for $5/hr. and 5 employees is:

($5.00/hr)(5 employees)(2 overhead/hr)

$$(255 \text{ days/yr})\left(\frac{1}{12}\right) = 1062.49$$

(*Hint:* You'll need two one-dimensional arrays.)

Once you have "run" this program, use the second program you developed in problem A−30 to print the report again.

A−34 Division by Subtraction Division is equivalent to repeated subtraction of the divisor from the dividend until the quantity left is smaller in magnitude than the divisor. The number of subtractions is the quotient, and the quantity left is the remainder. This process, if done straightforwardly, is very time-consuming. It is substantially speeded if the most significant digits of the divisor and the dividend are aligned before the first subtraction and the divisor then shifted to the right one position whenever the partial remainder becomes smaller than the divisor before shifting. If the initial alignment makes the divisor larger than the dividend, one shift may be necessary before any subtraction. This procedure is as follows:

```
    012
 9)112
   −9
   ‾‾
    22
   −9    two subtractions before
   ‾‾    shifting
    13
    −9
    ‾‾
     4
```

What "Only Five Minutes" Lost-Time Each Day Costs*						
Hourly Rate	5 Employees	10 Employees	25 Employees	50 Employees	100 Employees	500 Employees
2.90	616.35	1,232.67	3,081.68	6,163.35	12,326.70	61,633.50
3.35	711.96	1,423.92	3,559.80	7,119.60	14,239.20	71,196.20
4.25	903.12	1,806.24	4,515.62	9,031.24	18,062.49	90,312.49
5.00	1,062.49	2,124.99	5,312.49	10,624.49	21,249.99	106,249.99
6.00	1,275.00	2,550.00	6,375.00	12,750.00	25,500.00	127,500.00
7.00	1,487.49	2,974.99	7,437.49	14,874.99	29,749.99	148,749.99
8.50	1,806.24	3,612.50	9,031.24	18,062.49	36,124.90	180,624.50
10.00	2,124.99	4,249.98	10,624.75	21,249.50	42,499.00	212,495.00

* Based on 8-hour day, 5-day week, 255 working days per year, overhead cost taken equal to hourly rate.

Write a program that reads two numbers (*I* and *J*) and calculates:

$$K = I/J$$

Output *K* and the remainder. Calculate 15 different *K*'s for 15 different sets of *I* and *J*.

A-35 Golf Handicap A handicap is a number that indicates how good a golfer is supposed to be. One method of calculating a handicap is to take the golfer's ten most recent scores, find their average, subtract 72 from this, and multiply by 80 percent. The resulting number is called the "handicap." Let us suppose that the North Placer Country Club records on cards the 15 most recent scores for each of its 27 members in the form shown in Figure A–2.

The five-digit date and score fields are coded, with the date as the left three digits (using the Julian calendar) and the score as the right two digits. Print a report that lists the various members and their handicaps. Your report must contain captions (headings) across the top of the page.

A-36 Soundex Codes The National Archives in Washington, D.C., stores census records that are indexed according to an elaborate coding system called "Soundex." This system uses the first letter of a name for alphabetical filing, and converts all the other letters into numbers as follows:

- 1 is assigned to b, f, p, v
- 2 is assigned to c, g, j, k, q, s, x, z
- 3 is assigned to d, t
- 4 is assigned to l
- 5 is assigned to m, n
- 6 is assigned to r

No value is assigned to a, e, h, i, o, u, w, y.

Complications sometimes arise because only one of any two consecutive equivalents is recorded. The final result must be adjusted to consist of the first letter and a 3-digit number. Extra digits are discarded and absent ones are recorded as zeros. Some examples are:

Name	Converted	Soundex Code
EDWARDS	E3632	E363
LEE	L	L000
CONWAY	C5	C500
DOUGLAS	D242	D242
PHILLIPS	P4412	P412
KLEGER	K426	K426

For further information on Soundex codes, see the March 1980 issue of *Microcomputing,* page 138.

A-37 Roman to Decimal Numerals The Roman numeral system was in use until the eighteenth century, when the introduction of the printing press saw a rapid change to decimal numbers. Unlike the decimal system, Roman numerals do not have place values, that is, the position of a symbol does not represent a quantity. The Roman symbols used are:

Roman Numeral	Decimal Equivalent
M	1000
D	500
C	100
L	50
X	10
V	5
I	1

member number	date & score #1	date & score #2	date & score #3	etc. ...	date & score #15
1–5	6–10	11–15	16–20		76–80

FIGURE A–2   Data card for problem A–35.

Thus, 29 decimal is XXVIIII (using the unsophisticated version of Roman notation rather than XXIX). Write a program that inputs at least 15 Roman numerals and outputs their decimal equivalents. You must convert the following—DCCCCLXXXXVIIII, I, C, XXVI, XXV, XXIIII—in your group of 15.

A–38 Decimal to Roman Numerals   In problem A–37 the Roman and decimal numeral systems are discussed. Write a program that inputs at least 15 decimal numbers and outputs their Roman equivalent. Include the following in your input: 500, 25, 24, 26, 1979, 1776.

A–39 Basketball Statistics   You have become the statistician for the Portland Trailblazers. A file with information for each game about each player is stored in the computer as BLAZER. As the previous statistician quit several weeks ago, you must generate box scores (a printout for one game at a time) and the composite or summary table for all players and their respective statistics. The Trailblazers have only 11 active players at any one time, but they can have more players play for them during the season. (You can assume there will not be more than 25 for the season.) Produce a box score for each game in the file along with the totals for the Trailblazers and the opponents. You should not break a box score between pages, so be as concise as possible (frugal in use of paper). After the last box score, the summary of the team should be printed, along with: free throw average, field goal average, rebounds per game, average points per game, steals per game, assists per game, and turnovers per game. (Per game refers to games played by individuals.) This should be followed by totals for the team and totals for opponents also.

Input: (A record for a game)

Position	Description
1–10	name
11–12	minutes played
13–15	field goals made
16–18	field goals attempted
20–21	free throws made
22–23	free throws attempted
24–25	rebounds
26–27	assists
28–29	personal fouls
30–31	steals
32–33	turnovers
34–36	total points

Output: See a newspaper for the format of "box scores," which is the team and players' statistics. For the summary table, see a newspaper or use your imagination. The averages should appear in a column adjacent to the date.

A–40 Numbers into Words   Write a program that will read 25 two-digit numbers and print them in words. For example, the number 47 would be output as: 47 is FORTY SEVEN.

A–41 Words into Numbers   Write a program that accepts a number as it would be written in words, for example, "THIRTY NINE," and calculates its numeric equivalent. For example: THIRTY NINE is 39. Process at least 15 words into numbers.

A–42 Discount Code   Discounts are often given to certain types of business customers. The amount of the discount depends on many factors. Use the following data:

Quantity	Stock Number	Unit List Price	Discount Code
8760	477536	3.56	A
7690	987123	.02	B
7690	442338	.05	B
0015	753158	35.76	C
0575	128664	.15	D
1512	23587	.13	E
6543	753108	102.34	B

Print a report with the following captions and values:

QUANTITY	STOCK NUMBER	UNIT LIST PRICE	UNIT TRADE PRICE	AMOUNT
8760	477536	3.56	2.848	24948.48

Use the following table to determine the discount rate.

Discount Code	Discount Percentages
A	20
B	20, 10
C	20, 10, 5
D	20, 10, 5, 2

Another way of stating the procedure for computing unit trade prices is based on the percentage

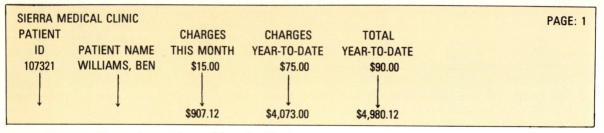

FIGURE A–3 Report layout for problem A–43.

to be paid after the discount percentage is deducted from 100 percent; for example, 80% = 100% − 20%. The 80 percent is then changed to the decimal fraction 0.80 for use as a multiplier.

    IF Discount Code = "A", THEN Unit Trade Price = Unit List Price*.80.

or

    IF DC="A", THEN UTP = ULP*.80
    IF DC="B", THEN UTP = ULP*.80*.90
    IF DC="C", THEN UTP = ULP*.80*.90*.95
    IF DC="D", THEN UTP = ULP*.80*.90*.95*.98

A–43 Page Headings Data have been collected from a local doctor that concern each patient. The following information is available:

Positions	Content
1–8	Patient ID number
10–40	Patient Name
51–60	Charges this month
61–70	Charges this year-to-date

    The data have been sorted into ascending order by patient ID number. A report is to be printed (see Figure A–3) that lists patients by ID number and calculates their new year-to-date charge. The report should total (1) charges this month, (2) charges year-to-date, and (3) new year-to-date charges for each of the four providers. In addition, your report should print captions across the various columns (see the following example). Finally, the report should print new page headings if there are more patients for a provider than will fit on a single page. (Remember that a page has a maximum of 66 lines.)

A–44 Paschal Full Moon The holiday of Easter falls on the first Sunday *following* the arbitrary Paschal Full Moon. The date of the Paschal Full Moon (not necessarily a real or astronomical full moon) is calculated by adding 1 to the remainder obtained by dividing any year by 19 and applying the following table:

1–Apr. 14	6–Apr. 18	11–Mar. 25	16–Mar. 30
2–Apr. 3	7–Apr. 8	12–Apr. 13	17–Apr. 17
3–Mar. 23	8–Mar. 28	13–Apr. 2	18–Apr. 7
4–Apr. 11	9–Apr. 16	14–Mar. 22	19–Mar. 27
5–Mar. 31	10–Apr. 5	15–Apr. 10	

Thus, for 1977 the key (remainder plus 1) is 2. The following Sunday (Easter) occurs on April 10. Write a program that reads in 15 years and prints the dates of the Paschal Full Moon for those years.

A–45 Units of Production Depreciation There are many ways for a business to depreciate an asset. One method, called units of production, calculates the depreciation for any year using the following relationship:

$$D_j = (C - S) \frac{U_j}{U_n}$$

Where D_j is the depreciation in year j, C is the original cost of the asset, S is the salvage value, U_j is the number of units made in year j, and U_n is the number of units the asset will produce during its life.

    Write a program to read C, S, U_j, and U_n and calculate D_j. Print all five values with headings.

A–46 Fleisch Readability The Fleisch Readability procedure is a method of examining printed material to determine the grade level of that material. The procedure is described as follows:

How to Test Readability
Rudolph Fleisch
(New York: Harper, 1951)

I. Count each individual word to read 100. Figure the average number of words per sentence in the sample you are testing, by dividing the number of words (100) by the number of sentences. Count incomplete sentences as one sentence.

II. Count all syllables in the sample.

III. Apply formula as follows:

- Multiply average number of words per sentence by 1.015
- Multiply number of syllables by .846
- Add top two figures
- Subtract this sum from 206.835
- Your reading ease is

Grade levels are assigned according to reading ease by the following chart:

Ease

- 90–100 = 5th grade: very easy (comics)
- 80–90 = 6th grade: easy (pulp fiction)
- 70–80 = 7th grade: standard (*Reader's Digest, Time,* mass nonfiction)
- 60–70 = 8th and 9th grades: fairly difficult (*Harpers, Atlantic*)
- 50–60 = 10th to 12th grades: difficult (academic, scholarly papers)
- 30–50 = 13th to 16th grades: very difficult (scientific, professional papers)
- 0–30 = college graduate level: practically unreadable

Each word in the 100-word sample is separated by a space. Each syllable will have a '/' between the two letters. Thus, the word "letter" would appear as LE/TTER. Each sentence ends with a period. No words are hyphenated. Write a program to calculate and output the reading ease. Also output the number of words, syllables, and sentences.

A–47 Line Balancing Words printed in the newspaper or in most books are "balanced." This term means that the words printed on the line always end on the right boundary and begin on the left boundary. Read 25 lines, each containing 70 characters, and print the 25 balanced lines. The spaces on the right of an original line should be distributed evenly among the other words on the balanced line. (This process is also called "justifying.")

Original unbalanced line:

Four score and seven years ago our fathers brought

Balanced line:

Four   score   and   seven   years   ago . . .
⟵——————— 70 character line ———————⟶

A–48 Height and Weight Standards Until a recent court decision, many organizations used standards of minimum weight and height for hiring new employees. Some also used a weight per inch minimum standard. If a prospective employee was less than 140 pounds in weight *or* less than 69 inches (5'9") in height, he or she could not qualify. Also, if the weight per inch of height was less than or equal to 2, the person could not qualify for employment. (Weight per inch is calculated by dividing height in inches into weight in pounds.)

Use the computer to determine the acceptability of prospective employees on the basis of these requirements. The printed report should look like this:

Applicant Number	Weight	Height	Weight per Inch	Status
1234	173	72	2.40	
4062	165	70	2.35	
0731	128	64	2.00	reject
.	.	.	.	.
.	.	.	.	.

The input data might be these:

Applicant Number	Weight	Height
1234	173	72
4062	165	70
0731	128	64
9738	197	75
6432	186	78
4263	155	71
1243	125	68
2157	140	69

A–49 Inventory Statement Prepare a program to print the following invoice:

```
              SIERRA MERCHANDISING COMPANY
   Sold to:  C. J. Goldielocks
             1117 Bruin Lane
             Little Bear, California 99000

   ITEMS         STOCK NO.         UNIT PRICE         AMOUNT

     10            2743              15.00            150.00
      5            7449               1.00              5.00
     20            8130              10.00            200.00

   Subtotal                                           355.00
   6% sales tax                                        21.30

   TOTAL                                              376.30
```

Data for computer input are:

ITEM	STOCK NO.	UNIT PRICE	
10	2743	15	
5	7449	1	
20	8130	10	
9999	9999	9999	(end-of-data sentinals)

Analyze this problem in terms of before-the-loop one-time activities, within-the-loop repetitive activities, and after-the-loop one-time activities.

A–50   Electrical Billing Routine   Write a program to compute the electrical charges for the following customers and their kilowatt hour usage.

Account No.	KWH
15251	40
1472	250
1689	3
18510	2
19401	1
2031	101

Set up appropriate headings to identify the customer account number, the KWH consumed, and monthly bill. The following rates were established for the sale of electric energy by the city. The residential rate on monthly billings is: consumer charge, per meter, per month, $1; energy charge to be added to consumer charge:

- 1st 40 KWH @ 3.5¢ per KWH
- Next 60 KWH @ 3.7¢ per KWH
- Next 100 KWH @ 4.0¢ per KWH
- Next 200 KWH @ 6.0¢ per KWH
- Over 400 KWH @ 8.9¢ per KWH

Thus, for 47 KWH the bill would be:

$$\text{BILL} = \underbrace{(40)(.035) + (7)(.037)}_{\text{energy charge}} + \underbrace{1}_{\text{consumer charge}}$$

A–51   Statement of Account   Every month you probably receive a statement from some merchant or company (e.g., Exxon, Sears, VISA, Penneys) that shows the charges and payments you made the previous month.

Prepare a program to print the following:

STATEMENT OF ACCOUNT			3/81
TO: J. Jones 111 49th St. Los Angeles, CA 90024			
REFERENCE #	DATE	PAYMENT	CHARGE
10732	022480		37.00
00008	022580	16.50	
10799	022980		12.00
10802	030180	14.27	14.25
00000	030280		
	TOTAL	30.77	63.25

MODULE SIX: SUPPLEMENTS

Assume the data for the statement are:

Reference Number	Date	Account
10732	022482	37.00
00000	022582	16.50
10790	022982	12.00
10807	030182	14.25
00000	030282	14.27

Note that a reference number of zero means a payment, while a nonzero one means a charge.

A−52 Solar Heat In the July 1979, issue of *Popular Mechanics* (page 48) is outlined the procedure for calculating the amount of overhang needed to allow a window to block the summer sun. The formula is:

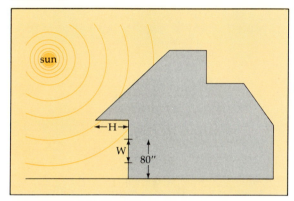

H = (Window height) (tangent of your latitude)

The formula is based on the top of the window being set at 80 inches (6'8") from the floor. Write a program to find H for window heights (W) of 12; 15, 18, 21, 24 . . . 60 inches. Print a chart, with appropriate captions, of the given values of window heights and overhang lengths, H.

A−53 Marginal Propensity In economics, the term *marginal propensity to save* is the amount of money saved for each extra dollar earned. If the marginal propensity to save is 10 percent, an extra $100 of income will result in $10 saved and $90 spent. The money spent results in a $90 income to another individual who, in turn, saves $9 and spends $81. The process goes on until the additional income is $1. The total spent by individuals is the sum of $90 + $81 + $72.90 + $65.61 + . . . + $1.

In July, August, and September of 1976, the federal government underspent $11 billion. If this $11 billion had been spent, $11 billion in additional income would have been earned by wage earners, suppliers, contractors, and others. Write a program that inputs this extra income and prints the sum of the individual terms that the marginal propensity yields.

A−54 Days of Week To find the day of the week of any date, do the following (use September 4, 1752, as an example):

Take the last two digits of the year	52	
Add a quarter of this number (neglect the remainder)	13	
Add the date of the month	4	
Add according to the month:		
January:	1	
February:	4	
March:	4	
April:	0	
May:	2	
June:	5	
July:	0	
August:	3	
September:	6	6
October:	1	
November:	4	
December:	6	
Add for the century:		
18th:	4	4
19th:	2	
20th:	0	
21st:	6	
		79
Divide the total by 7 (79 ÷ 7 = 11, remainder 2)		11

The remainder gives the day of week:

Sunday:	1
Monday:	2
Tuesday:	3
Wednesday:	4
Thursday:	5
Friday:	6
Saturday:	0

Thus, September 4, 1752, was a Monday.

Read ten dates and output the day of the week.

PAYROLL SYSTEM

Of all the various uses of computers, the one that comes to mind most frequently is payroll. This is probably due to the fact that major savings can be made in the area of clerical labor. Furthermore, the creating of payroll checks is a necessity. They must be printed on time and they must be accurate—otherwise employees' morale is adversely affected. As a side benefit, a payroll system provides management with accounting information such as data for general ledger entries, job costing, and labor distribution (who worked on what, for how long, and how much did it cost), and federal quarterly and year-end tax reports. The problems in this section involve programming a payroll system.

Like the accounts receivable system presented in Chapters 3–8 and 14, a payroll system consists of a master file and a transaction file. The master file contains all the permanent data about an employee: Social Security number; employee name; number of tax exemptions; marital status; payrate; employee number; year-to-date gross pay; and many more. The transaction file contains data about one pay period: employee number; regular hours; overtime hours; sick time; vacation time; special deductions; and the payroll time period. The data for the transaction file are usually collected from time cards, while the master file data are collected on some type of "new employee" form specifically designed for this purpose when the employees begin their employment. The spiral of programs that follow build a transaction and master file and conclude by printing the payroll check.

P–1 *Enter the following BASIC program and RUN it.* List your program to see if it matches those shown. If they do not, you did not enter your program correctly and you will need to correct it.

```
10     PRINT "EMPLOYEE", "HOURS", "PAYROLL"
20     PRINT "NUMBER", "WORKED", "DATE"
30     READ E,H,D
40     DATA 345,40,820206
50     DATA 999,50,820207
60     DATA 7890,42,820270
70     DATA 0,0,0
80     IF E = 0 THEN 110
90     PRINT E,H,D
100    GO TO 30
110    END
```

P–2 *Inserting an Additional Column* Modify your P–1 program to print a fourth column that shows the overtime hours worked. Your printed output should look like the following:

EMPLOYEE NUMBER	REGULAR HOURS	OVERTIME HOURS	PAYROLL DATE
345	40		820206
999	40	10	820207

P–3 *Validating Input* In the preceding programs you have developed a routine that reads data about hours worked by employees. We have not dealt with whether the data are correct or not. Now modify the P–2 program to use the following validation criteria:

EMPLOYEE NO.: Within the range of 100 through 999
HOURS: 0 through 80
DATE: A six-digit number with the left two digits representing the year, middle two the month number, and right two the day number.
    YEAR: this year
    MONTH: 1 through 12
    DAY: 1 through 31

P–4 *Documenting with REMark Statements* Professional programmers usually place comments in their programs explaining the hows, whys, and whats about the programs. Now modify your P–3 program using REM statements to do the following:

a. Explain the purpose, author, and date of the program.
b. State each variable and its purpose.
c. Separate each functional module within the body of the program.
d. Explain the various logic portions of each module.

P–5 *Error Messages* The program of problem P–3 is called a "validation program." It tests the data read and allows only the correct data to be printed. Now modify the program to print an error message whenever invalid data are encountered, reflecting how the data are wrong. Your error messages might be:

INVALID EMPLOYEE NO.
INVALID YEAR
INVALID MONTH-MUST BE 1-12
INVALID DAY-MUST BE 1-31
INVALID HOURS-CAN'T WORK MORE THAN 80

P–6 *Key Entry of Data During Program RUN/ Writing to a File* The READ statement in BASIC always uses the same data every time the program is RUN. In a business environment this would not be realistic or acceptable. Modify program P–5 to use the INPUT statement that allows for inputting new data with each RUN. Use a PRINT statement before each INPUT to tell you what is to be keyed. Validate each entry as it is input, and if it is incorrect, print an error message. Those items that are correct should be written to a data file.

P–7 *Sorting a File* Most computer systems have a utility program to sort a data file. Use your utility sort to sort by employee number the data file created by P–6. If the utility sort allows sorting on more than one field, have it also sort on date. You have now developed a data collection system that builds a transaction file.

P–8 *Creating a Master File* We now have the first half of our payroll system. The second half represents the processing of our sorted transaction file to update a master file. Before we can write this program we need to create a master file. Use the data in Figure A–4 to create the master file.

P–9 *Updating the Master File* You are now ready to write the master file update program. Using the data in the sorted transaction file, write a program to update the year-to-date gross and net fields, and insert the gross and net pay into the master file for this pay period. The system flowchart for the update program is:

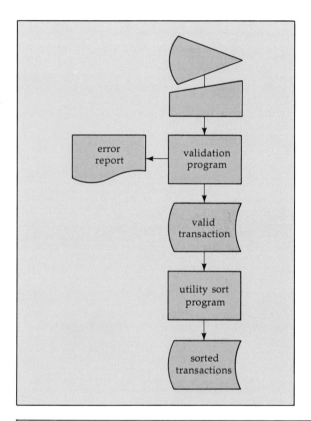

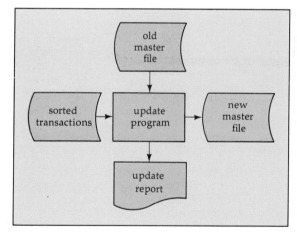

EMPLOYEE NO.	117	345	999
NAME	WILLIAMS, CARRIE	EDWARDS, BEN	KLEGER, HILLARY
NO. OF TAX EXEMPTIONS	2	3	1
MARITAL STATUS	S	M	D
PAY RATE	1120	6.25	6.79
EMPLOYEE-TYPE	SALARIED	HOURLY	HOURLY
YEAR-TO-DATE GROSS	11000.00	7222.56	8470.67
SEX	F	M	F
JOB TITLE	SUPERVISOR	PROGRAMMER	ANALYST
GROSS PAY THIS PERIOD	0	0	0
NET PAY THIS PERIOD	0	0	0

FIGURE A–4 Data for P–8.

Payroll Register				Quarter Ending June 30, 19XX	
EMPLOYEE NO.	MARITAL STATUS	NO. EXEM	Y-T-D GROSS		GROSS PAY
EMPLOYEE NAME	JOB TITLE	SEX	Y-T-D NET		NET PAY
117	S	2	11000.00		1120.00
WILLIAMS, CARRIE	SUPERVISOR	F	8947.16		417.26

FIGURE A-5   Report for P-11.

To calculate the net pay, multiply hours worked by payrate if the employee is hourly, then subtract the deductions. Deductions are figured by subtracting 6.6 percent of the gross for Social Security and 0.6 percent for state disability insurance.

P-10   *Printing a Payroll Check*   The new master file can now be used to print a payroll check. Using the master file as the data source, print a paycheck for each employee like the following:

```
DATE: January 27, 1982              Check No. 18107

Pay to the order of ___Carrie Williams___  $ 417.26

Four hundred and seventeen and 26/100 ----- Dollars
_____

Payrate      1120.00
Y-T-D Gross 12120.00
Y-T-D Net    9364.42
```

P-11   *Printing a Payroll Register*   A frequently produced report in a payroll system is the payroll register. The register is an entire listing of everything stored in the master file. Print a payroll register similar to the one shown in Figure A-5.

INVENTORY SYSTEM

Managing a company's inventory is a necessary task since the inventory serves as a buffer between production and distribution to buyers. A firm needs to have enough items on hand to meet anticipated demand, but not so many extra items that excessive costs are incurred for manufacturing and storing them. The problems in this section all concern inventory control.

The inventory system is similar to the accounts receivable system that is developed in Chapters 3 through 8 and Chapter 14. The problems start with a BASIC program listing that grows in a spiral fashion to become, finally, a complete inventory system.

I-1   *Enter the following BASIC program and RUN it.* Check to see if the results match those shown. If they do not, you did not enter your program correctly and you will need to find the error and correct it.

```
10   DIM T$(2)
20   PRINT "PART#","DATE","QUANTITY","SALE"
30   FOR I=1 TO 2
40   READ N,D,Q,T$
50   DATA 103,820112.,5,"SA"
60   DATA 567,820222.,100,"SA"
70   PRINT N,D,Q,T$
80   NEXT I
90   END
```

PART#	DATE	QUANTITY	SALE
103	820112.	5	SA
567	820222.	100	SA

I-2   *Modifying the Program*   Modify the program from problem I-1 to have seven sets of data. Use the following items:

PART NO.	DATE	QUANTITY	SALE
4093	820234	16	SA
3962	820607	22	SA
103	820204	4	SA
567	820330	37	SA
103	820328	18	SA

I-3   *Inserting an Additional Column*   Modify the program of problem I-2 to print in a fifth column numbers that represent quantities purchased. Use the following purchase data along with the sales data of the earlier program.

PART#	DATE	QUANTITY	PURCHASE
4093	820609	72	PH
567	820717	43	PH
103	827015	29	PH
3962	820742	106	SA

I–4 *Validating Input* The preceding program prints a list of parts that have been purchased or sold from inventory. We have not yet determined, however, whether the data are correct or not. Now modify the program of problem I–3 to print only those items that meet the following criteria:

PART NO: 4093, 103 or 3962
DATE: A six-digit number with the left two representing the year, middle two the month number, and right two the day number.
          YEAR: this year
          MONTH: 1 through 12
          DAY: 1 through 31
TYPE: PH for purchase; SA for sale

I–5 *Documenting with REMark Statements* Professional programmers usually place comments in their programs explaining the hows, whys, and whats about the programs. Now modify your program using the REM statement to do the following:

a. Explain the purpose, author, and date of the program.
b. State each variable and its purpose.
c. Separate each functional module within the body of the program.
d. Explain the various logic portions of each module.

I–6 *Error Messages* The program of problem I–5 is called a "validation program." It tests the data read and allows only the correct data to be printed. Now modify the program of I–4 to print an error message whenever invalid data are encountered. Reflecting how the data are wrong, your error messages might be:

INVALID PART NO.
INVALID YEAR
INVALID MONTH MUST BE 1-12
INVALID DAY MUST BE 1-31
INVALID TYPE MUST BE PH OR SA

I–7 *Key Entry of Data During Program RUN/ Writing to a File/End of Data Sentinel* The READ statement in BASIC always uses the same data every time the program is run. In a business environment this would not be realistic or acceptable. Modify program I–6 to use the INPUT statement that allows for inputting new data with each run. Use a PRINT before each INPUT to tell you what is to be keyed. Validate each entry as it is input and, if it is incorrect, print an error message. Those items that are correct should be written to a data file. Do not use a FOR/NEXT statement to cause the looping. Instead, use an end-of-data sentinel. Your program should stop when a zero is entered for the part number.

I–8 *Sorting a File* Most computer systems have a utility program to sort a data file. Find the name of your sort program and have it sort your data file by part number. If it will allow working on more than one field, have it also sort by date. You have now developed a data collection system that builds a transaction file. The system flowchart for our inventory system is shown in the diagram:

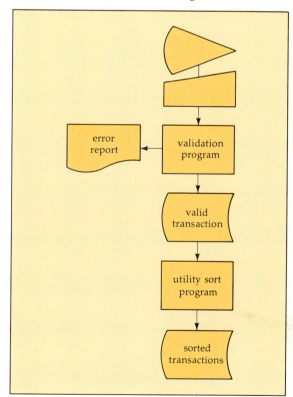

PART #	103	3962	4093
DESCRIPTION	TERMINAL	CABLE	CONNECTORS
UNIT PRICE	695.00	47.75	.87
UNIT COST	550.00	32.62	.63
UNIT OF MEASURE	EA	FT	PR
QUANTITY ON HAND	14	575	16
QUANTITY ON BACKORDER	0	0	0

FIGURE A–6 Data for I–9.

I–9 *Creating a Master File* We now have the first half of our inventory system. The second half represents the processing of our sorted transaction file to update a master file. Before we can write this program, however, we need to create the master file. Use the data in Figure A–6.

I–10 *Updating the Master File* You are now ready to write the master file update program. Using the data in the sorted transaction file, write your program to alter the quantity on hand and backorder as the transaction file dictates. Remember that a sale (SA) decreases inventory, while a purchase (PH) increases inventory. The system flowchart for the update routine is:

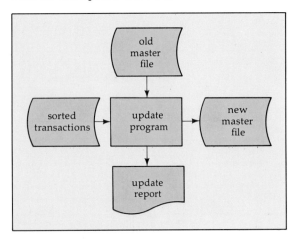

The update report is a listing of changes made to the records in the master file. Your update program should print a line for each transaction record, showing the transaction data and the master file data as they were before and after the updating.

I–11 *Printing an Inventory Report* The new master file reflects the current state of our inventory. Write a program using either the TAB function or IMAGE statement that will print a report similar to Figure A–7.

I–12 *Using an Array* In the program you wrote for problem I–4 you had to validate the year, month, and day. As you are aware, not every month has the same number of days. Modify your I–4 program to validate the day field according to the month. The chart below lists the days in each month.

Month Number	Number of Days	Month Number	Number of Days
1	31	7	31
2	28	8	31
3	31	9	30
4	30	10	31
5	31	11	30
6	30	12	31

Use an array to hold the number of days in each month. Ignore leap years.

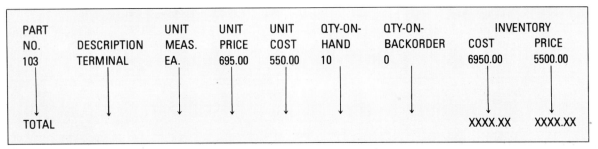

FIGURE A–7 Report for I–11.

SUPPLEMENT B

DECISION TABLES

Preview

Function and Structure of Tables
- Header
- Condition Stub
- Action Stub
- Condition Entry
- Action Entry

Some Sample Tables
- Testing Two Numbers
- Accounts Receivable—Validation Routine

Complex Tables
- Compressing the Table
- Types of Tables

Advantages and Disadvantages of Decision Tables

Payroll-Merging Decision Tables

Summary

Computer News: Social Security's Decrepit Computers

PREVIEW

Suppose you were required to write a computer program to calculate the charge that should be made for a long distance telephone call. Your program would have to take into account the time the call was placed, the time it was concluded, and whether it was day-evening or holiday rate; operator assisted, direct-dial, collect, or credit card; interstate or intrastate. Since the list of items that would have to be considered is quite lengthy, the flowchart you would have to draw could be four or five or more pages long. And how would you be sure that you did not miss or forget something? For complex problems like this, a flowchart alone is not appropriate. A supplement to, or an alternative to, a flowchart is a **decision table.** A decision table provides data processing people with a means of organizing solutions to complex problems. This supplement describes how the logic of complex problems is analyzed by use of a decision table.

FUNCTION AND STRUCTURE OF TABLES

If a computer is going to process data into meaningful information, the conditions and actions to be taken on the data must be precisely stated. In most instances these conditions and actions are so elementary and so few that a flowchart can depict them easily. For example, if a worker earns $75 in a given week and the minimum earnings required before income taxes are calculated is $100 a week, that worker will not pay income taxes. Workers whose income exceeds the $100 per week will be required to pay income taxes.

In other instances, conditions and the resulting actions required on the data are lengthy and complex. A flowchart of the various conditions would itself become involved, with decision points leading to a variety of possible actions. As an example, consider an income tax calculation that takes into account a minimum income, the number of dependents being claimed, Social Security tax withholdings, tax-sheltered income, and so on. Many interrelated conditions and subsequent actions need to be performed on the data for this tax calculation.

The purpose of a decision table is to help you more effectively visualize and understand complex interrelated conditions and actions. A decision table is compact, and thus is easy for both programmers and nonprogrammers to read and understand. Decision tables are used daily by people in almost every walk of life. Examples of decision tables that we often use are railroad, bus, and airplane timetables; mathematical lists of numbers (logarithms, tangents); and the too familiar income tax table (Figure B–1). Generally, a decision table has five sections (Figure B–2).

Header

The first section of a decision table is the **table header.** This portion gives the title of the table, the author, and the date the table was made, and it allows space for any remarks to be made about the table. The remarks may include definitions of terms, abbreviations, explanations, or formulas the author used.

Condition Stub

The **condition stub** of a decision table (located in the upper left-hand portion) lists the various tests that need to be made on the data. The tests are usually written in the form of questions answerable by a YES or NO; these are similar to the decision block in a flowchart.

Action Stub

In the lower left-hand corner of a decision table is the **action stub.** This part of the table lists all the possible actions that could be taken as a result of the questions asked in the condition stub. If the action is some specific computation, the actual formula to be used can be written here. If the action is not a calculation, then it is described in normal terms, such as "tax is zero."

FIGURE B–1 1980 income tax short form 1040A.

Condition Entry

The third section of a decision table is the **condition entry**. Arranged in vertical columns called **rules** are the responses for each condition stub question. Each rule is numbered so that it is easily identifiable. The number of rules in a decision table is re-

SUPPLEMENT B: DECISION TABLES

lated to the number of tests found in the condition stub. If there are three tests, there are $2^3 = 8$ rules. In general, the number of rules is stated by the formula:

number of rules = 2^N

where N represents the number of tests. The following chart shows the number of rules with various values of N.

N	1	2	3	4	5	6
No. of Rules	2	4	8	16	32	64

The responses in the condition entry are usually written Y for YES and N for NO, to answer the tests in the condition stub. In order to determine all the possible combinations of conditions, the Y's and N's in the condition entry are placed in a **bifurcated** arrangement. If a decision table has three conditions, eight rules, the bifurcated arrangement calls for placing four Y's in succession and four N's in succession in the first row: YYYYNNNN. In the second row, you place Y's and N's in alternating pairs: YYNNYYNN. In the third row, the Y's and N's alternate: YNYNYNYN. Arranging the Y's and N's in bifurcated form ensures that every possible combination has been included with no duplicates.

Action Entry

The last section of a decision table is the **action entry.** Located in the lower right-hand portion of the table, the action entry has an X or a dot (·) placed at the intersection of each rule and its appropriate action stub line. The X indicates that this action is to be taken as a consequence of the responses in the condition section. A dot is entered for actions that are not used. All intersections of rules and action lines have either an X or a dot. A blank indicates that this action has been overlooked.

SOME SAMPLE TABLES

Testing Two Numbers

As an example of a decision table, let us suppose that we have recorded the dates on which two transactions took place, and we need to determine which transaction is the oldest. There is a possibility, of course, that the two transactions took place on the same date. If we let T represent the date of the first transaction, and S the date of the second transaction, we need to know if T is less than S (in which case T is the older transaction), if S equals T (in which case both took place on the same date), or if T is greater than S (in which case S is the older transaction). Since decision tables use YES/NO tests (like flowcharts), we have only two tests to write in the condition stub: does $T = S$? or is $T < S$? The negative of the first and the second implies $T > S$. With two tests, the condition stub will have four rules, numbered 1, 2, 3, and 4. Each condition and action in a decision table is assigned a name. Condition and action names are usually sequential letters of the alphabet: A, B, C, D, and so on. The decision table for this problem is shown in Figure B–3; the corresponding flowchart is shown in Figure B–4.

After examining the decision table, you should notice that there are four actions possible, not three. The decision table forces you to think of all the pos-

FIGURE B–3 Decision table to determine the oldest date.					
Determining the Oldest Date				
		1	2	3	4
A. $T=S$ B. $T<S$		Y Y	Y N	N Y	N N
C. Same dates D. T is oldest E. S is oldest F. Error		· · · X	X · · ·	· X · ·	· · X ·

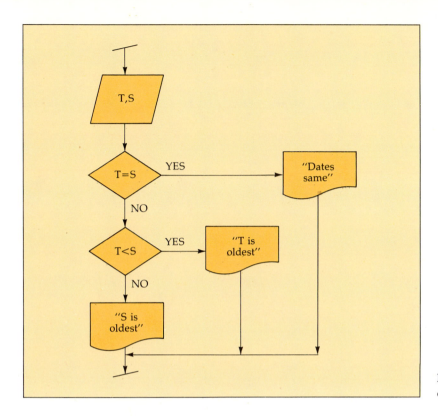

FIGURE B-4 Flowchart to determine the oldest date.

sible events. You must decide what should be done if $T = S$ and $T < S$. Since T cannot be both equal to S and less than S at the same time, you may choose to ignore this error condition. Decision tables force data processing people to examine all the possible situations and decide what should be done in all cases. The flowchart of Figure B-4 does not show the $T = S$, $T < S$, to be self-evident. As an example of what importance might be associated with this error condition, let us imagine that the dates were supposed to be in numeric form (for example, February 17 would be 217). The person entering the date could mistakenly enter "Feb. 17". The decision table would detect this mistake while the flowchart would not, unless special steps were taken.

As an aid to the individual who actually writes a decision table, a special form is available (see Figure B-5). The form has places for the header, condition stub, action stub, rule numbers, and condition/ action names. Boxes are provided for the Y, N, X, and the dot (·).

Accounts Receivable—Validation Routine

As a second example of a decision table and as an illustration of the decision table form of Figure B-5, let us write the decision table for the validation routine in our accounts receivable routine. As a review, remember that the routine accepts five quantities: an account number; a reference number; a date; an amount of money; and an indicator to represent whether this is a charge or payment. We consider the transaction to be valid IF:

1. all five quantities are entered
2. the indicator is the letter C or P

3. the date field is of the form YYMMDD where
   YY is the year number and must be 81, 82
   MM is the month number and must be 1-12
   DD is the day number and must be 1-31

Valid transactions are written to a file. Transactions with errors are not written to a file but have error messages printed that tell what is wrong with the transaction. The three conditions and four actions required for the validation routine are shown in the decision table in Figure B–6.

Decision tables are best used on problems of great complexity with many conditions and actions. The primary advantage of a decision table over a flowchart is that these complex problems can be studied easily. In addition, every possible condition is considered and covered by a separate rule in a decision table. This advantage leads to more accurate computer programs.

COMPLEX TABLES

The two decision tables that you have seen have depicted relatively simple processes with very few conditions and actions. The more conditions and actions that are present in a process, the more advantageous it becomes to use decision tables over flowcharts. Decision table experts generally agree that the point at which a decision table is better than a flowchart is where there are more than three conditions in a problem.

As an illustration of a complex problem, suppose a company has two warehouses. One warehouse is located on the East Coast and the other on the West Coast. A potential customer can place an order by calling a toll free, area code 800 telephone number, and the item will be shipped from the nearest warehouse. If the nearest warehouse has an insuffi-

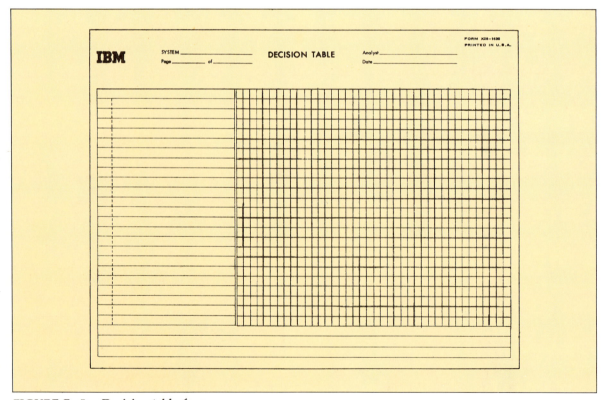

FIGURE B–5   Decision table form.

536   MODULE SIX: SUPPLEMENTS

FIGURE B-6 Decision table for validation routine.

Validating								
	1	2	3	4	5	6	7	8
A. Were five items entered?	Y	Y	Y	Y	N	N	N	N
B. Is indicator a C or P?	Y	Y	N	N	Y	Y	N	N
C. Is date field correct?	Y	N	Y	N	Y	N	Y	N
D. Print not enough data	.	.	.	.	X	X	X	X
E. Print indicator field wrong	.	.	X	X	.	.	X	X
F. Print date field wrong	.	X	.	X	X	.	X	.
G. Transaction correct—write to file	X	.	.	.	.	.	.	.

cient supply of the item, the other warehouse will ship it. If neither warehouse has a sufficient supply, the item will be backordered. Two types of customers exist: wholesale and retail; each type is charged a different price on the items. Obviously, many conditions and actions exist. In fact, there are four conditions and five actions. The decision table with its 16 potential rules is shown in Figure B–7.

Compressing the Table

The decision table of Figure B–7 lists every possible action for the 16 required rules. After careful analysis of the rules and actions, you can see that rules 7, 8, 15, and 16 all cause a backorder. The conditions for all four of these rules are an insufficient quantity on hand at both warehouses. It does not matter what kind of customer is making the call, or where the call originated from—there are not enough items to fill the order. These four rules can thus be combined into one. The combining of two or more rules into one is called **eliminating redundancy.** To indicate redundancy, a dash (−) is placed in the condition entry to show that this condition stub is irrelevant and can be ignored. By the redundancy rule, the decision table of Figure B–7 can now be rewritten as shown in Figure B–8.

Further examination of Figure B–7 or B–8 reveals

FIGURE B-7 Decision table for ordering procedure.

Ordering Procedure																
	1	2	3	4	5	6	7	8	9	10	11	12	13	14	15	16
A. Customer wholesale?	Y	Y	Y	Y	Y	Y	Y	Y	N	N	N	N	N	N	N	N
B. Qty. sufficient at East Coast?	Y	Y	Y	Y	N	N	N	N	Y	Y	Y	Y	N	N	N	N
C. Qty. sufficient at West Coast?	Y	Y	N	N	Y	Y	N	N	Y	Y	N	N	Y	Y	N	N
D. Call from East Coast?	Y	N	Y	N	Y	N	Y	N	Y	N	Y	N	Y	N	Y	N
E. Ship from West Coast	.	X	.	.	X	X	.	.	.	X	.	.	X	X	.	.
F. Ship from East Coast	X	.	X	X	.	.	.	.	X	.	X	X	.	.	.	.
G. Bill at wholesale price	X	X	X	X	X	X	.	.	.	.	.	.	.	.	.	.
H. Bill at retail price	.	.	.	.	.	.	.	.	X	X	X	X	X	X	.	.
I. Backorder	.	.	.	.	.	.	X	X	.	.	.	.	.	.	X	X

FIGURE B-8 Decision table with one redundancy.

Ordering Procedure

	1	2	3	4	5	6	7	9	10	11	12	13	14
A. Customer wholesale?	Y	Y	Y	Y	Y	Y	—	N	N	N	N	N	N
B. Qty. sufficient at East Coast?	Y	Y	Y	Y	N	N	N	Y	Y	Y	Y	N	N
C. Qty. sufficient at West Coast?	Y	Y	N	N	Y	Y	N	Y	Y	N	N	Y	Y
D. Call from East Coast?	Y	N	Y	N	Y	N	—	Y	N	Y	N	Y	N
E. Ship from West Coast	.	X	.	.	X	X	.	.	X	.	.	X	X
F. Ship from East Coast	X	.	X	X	.	.	.	X	.	X	X	.	.
G. Bill at wholesale price	X	X	X	X	X	X	.	.	.	.	.	.	.
H. Bill at retail price	.	.	.	.	.	.	.	X	X	X	X	X	X
I. Backorder	.	.	.	.	.	.	X	.	.	.	.	.	.

more redundancy rules. These new redundancies are: rules 1 and 3; 2 and 6; 9 and 11; 10 and 14. By combining these rules we get the decision table of Figure B–9. Removing the redundant rules compresses decision tables and makes them easier to program.

Types of Tables

The bifurcated decision table of Figure B–7 and the compressed tables of Figures B–8 and B–9 are usually called **limited-entry** decision tables. The other three types of decision tables in use are extended-entry, mixed-entry, and open-ended.

An **extended-entry** table has the item to be tested listed in the condition stub and the possible values of the item being tested listed in the condition entry. Thus, for Figure B–9, condition A (Customer wholesale?), the extended-entry would phrase the question as "Customer type" and the condition entry would have the words *wholesale* or *retail* placed for the various rules. The extended-entry version of Figure B–9 is shown in Figure B–10. Notice that the action stub entries can also be simplified in this type of table. Extended-entry tables reduce the number of conditions and actions while still showing the same information.

A **mixed-entry** table is a combination limited-

FIGURE B-9 Decision table with four redundancies.

Ordering Procedure

	1	2	4	5	7	9	10	12	13
A. Customer wholesale?	Y	Y	Y	Y	—	N	N	N	N
B. Qty. sufficient at East Coast?	Y	—	Y	N	N	X	—	Y	N
C. Qty. sufficient at West Coast?	—	Y	N	Y	N	—	Y	N	Y
D. Call from East Coast?	Y	N	N	Y	—	Y	N	N	Y
E. Ship from West Coast	.	X	.	X	.	.	X	.	X
F. Ship from East Coast	X	.	X	.	.	X	.	X	.
G. Bill at wholesale price	X	X	X	X	.	.	.	.	.
H. Bill at retail price	.	.	.	.	.	X	X	X	X
I. Backorder	.	.	.	.	X	.	.	.	.

FIGURE B–10 Extended-entry ordering procedure decision table.

Ordering Procedure									
	1	2	4	5	7	9	10	12	13
A. Customer type	wh.	wh.	wh.	wh.	—	ret.	ret.	ret.	ret.
B. East Coast quantity	>	—	>	<	<	>	—	>	<
C. West Coast quantity	—	>	<	>	<	—	>	<	>
D. Location of call	east	west	west	east	—	east	west	west	east
E. Ship from	east	west	east	west	back	east	west	east	west
F. Billing routine	wh.	wh.	wh.	wh.		ret.	ret.	ret.	ret.

and extended-entry table. The basic characteristic of this type of table is that any condition stub row must be either all extended-entry or all limited-entry. The rule columns are a mixture of limited and extended. The decision table of Figure B–11 shows the ordering procedure in mixed-entry form.

The last type of decision table is the **open-ended.** An open-ended table allows access to another decision table. To show this access, a GO TO or EXIT is written. As an example of an open-ended table, suppose that wholesale customers are classified as type 1, type 2, or type 3. A business may give some customers different prices on an item depending on the number of items ordered because they do a large volume of business with the company, or because they pick up the merchandise at the warehouse, thus saving the cost of shipping. A type 1 customer will receive a 10 percent price discount, type 2, 12 percent, and type 3, 13 percent. The two decision tables for our modified ordering problem are shown in Figure B–12.

The open-ended type of decision table allows very complex problems to be analyzed as a series of smaller problems. Exits are not restricted to one decision table but can be made to several tables with additional EXITs as action stubs.

As you gain skill and knowledge in problem analysis and decision table construction, you may want to make use of the **ELSE** rule. This rule uses no particular pattern of Y's or N's in the condition entry, but is designed to cover all those Y/N patterns not specified. An example of the ELSE rule is shown in Figure B–13 for the wholesale bill table. The word ELSE is written vertically as a rule, and the action for it is to be followed when all the other rules fail. The use of ELSE should be minimized, however,

FIGURE B–11 Mixed-entry ordering procedure decision table.

Ordering Procedure									
	1	2	4	5	7	9	10	12	13
A. Customer type	wh.	wh.	wh.	wh.	—	ret.	ret.	ret.	ret.
B. Qty. sufficient on East Coast	Y	—	Y	N	N	Y	—	Y	N
C. Qty. sufficient on West Coast	—	Y	N	Y	N	—	Y	N	Y
D. Location of call	east	west	west	east	—	east	west	west	east
E. Ship from	east	west	east	west	bck	east	west	east	west
F. Billing routine	wh.	wh.	wh.	wh.		ret.	ret.	ret.	ret.

SUPPLEMENT B: DECISION TABLES

FIGURE B-12 Open-ended decision tables.

Ordering Procedure	1	2	4	5	7	9	10	12	13
A. Customer type	wh.	wh.	wh.	wh.	—	ret.	ret.	ret.	ret.
B. Qty. sufficient on East Coast	Y	—	Y	N	N	Y	—	Y	N
C. Qty. sufficient on West Coast	—	Y	N	Y	N	—	Y	N	Y
D. Location of call	east	west	west	east	—	east	west	west	east
E. Ship from	east	west	east	west	back	east	west	east	west
F. Billing routine	wh.	wh.	wh.	wh.	·	ret.	ret.	ret.	ret.
G. Exit to wholesale bill	X	X	X	X	·	·	·	·	·

Wholesale Bill	1	2	3	4	5	6	7	8
A. Customer type 1	Y	Y	Y	Y	N	N	N	N
B. Customer type 2	Y	Y	N	N	Y	Y	N	N
C. Customer type 3	Y	N	Y	N	Y	N	Y	N
D. 10% discount	·	·	·	X	·	·	·	·
E. 12% discount	·	·	·	·	·	X	·	·
F. 13% discount	·	·	·	·	·	·	X	·
G. Error	X	X	X	·	X	·	·	X

FIGURE B-13 ELSE in a decision table.

Wholesale Bill	1	2	3	4
A. Customer type 1	Y	N	N	ELSE
B. Customer type 2	N	Y	N	ELSE
C. Customer type 3	N	N	Y	ELSE
D. 10% discount	X	·	·	·
E. 12% discount	·	X	·	·
F. 13% discount	·	·	X	·
G. Error	·	·	·	X

since it could hide conditions and actions that might not be readily evident.

ADVANTAGES AND DISADVANTAGES OF DECISION TABLES

For a person trained in using a flowchart to represent the conditions and actions required to process data into useful information, a decision table may seem like extra effort and work. However, there are definite advantages to decision tables. These include:

1. Increased productivity for programmers and for those who analyze problems

2. Fewer error-prone solutions to problems since all possibilities have been examined

3. Computer programs that convert decision tables directly into computer programs

4. Easy readability by noncomputer personnel and computer programmers

5. Easy changeability when it becomes necessary to perform new conditions or action on the data

6. Better documentation of what is wanted in a concise and simple form

Decision tables also have some drawbacks. These include:

1. Tables being unwieldy in size when there are many conditions and actions

2. The need to retrain traditional flowchart-oriented programmers into decision table users

3. Long programs that execute slowly, resulting from translators

PAYROLL-MERGING DECISION TABLES

As another example of a decision table, consider a company that pays its employees on a piece-rate basis. At the end of each workday, each employee writes down on a card his or her employee number and the number of items produced. At the end of every month the cards are sorted into numerical order by employee number. To pay each worker, the company maintains another set of cards with the employee's number and name. This set of cards is also in numerical order by employee number. We want to develop a decision table that brings the two sets of cards together into a single group, with each name card followed by all the production cards of the respective employee. This process is called **merging** and is diagrammed in Figure B–14. The procedure for merging the two sets of cards together is to read a name card and then a production card. If the employee numbers match, the name card is grouped with the production card; then another production card is read. If the employee numbers

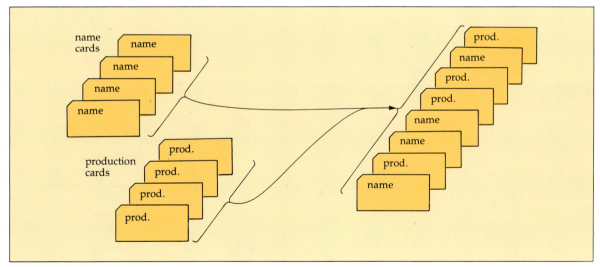

FIGURE B–14   Merging.

FIGURE B-15 Decision table for payroll merging.																
Payroll-Merging																
	1	2	3	4	5	6	7	8	9	10	11	12	13	14	15	16
A. Does employee number on name card = employee number on production card?	Y	Y	Y	Y	Y	Y	Y	Y	N	N	N	N	N	N	N	N
B. Is employee number on production card > employee number on name card?	Y	Y	Y	Y	N	N	N	N	Y	Y	Y	Y	N	N	N	N
C. Have all cards been read from name set?	Y	Y	N	N	Y	Y	N	N	Y	Y	N	N	Y	Y	N	N
D. Have all cards been read from production set?	Y	N	Y	N	Y	N	Y	N	Y	N	Y	N	Y	N	Y	N
E. Read another name card.	·	·	X	·	·	·	X	·	·	·	X	·	·	·	X	·
F. Read another production card.	·	X	·	X	·	X	·	X	·	X	·	·	·	X	·	X
G. All cards have been read—end of job.	X	·	·	·	X	·	·	·	X	·	·	·	X	·	·	·
H. Error: no name card for this employee.	X	X	X	X	·	·	·	·	X	X	·	X	·	X	·	·

do not match, then a new name card is read. This procedure is depicted in the decision table of Figure B-15.

SUMMARY

A decision table shows the conditions and actions that must be performed on data to provide useful information. In this sense it is an alternative to flowcharting.

TERMS

The following words or terms have been presented in this supplement.

Decision table	Eliminating redundancy
Table header	Limited-entry
Condition stub	Extended-entry
Action stub	Mixed-entry
Condition entry	Open-ended
Rule	ELSE
Bifurcated	Merging
Action entry	

EXERCISES

The exercises that follow are grouped by level of difficulty. Problems in the A series are the easiest; B series problems are moderately difficult; and C series problems are the most difficult.

A-1   How many rules exist using the formula: number of rules = 2^N, for an N of 7, 8, 9, 10, 11? What does this imply?

A-2   Redraw the limited-entry decision table of Figure B-7 as an extended-entry decision table.

A-3   Are any of the rules in Figure B-3 redundant? If so, list the redundant ones. If not, explain why there are no redundancies.

A-4   Why are there eight rules in the wholesale bill decision table of Figure B-12?

B-1   Obtain a bus, train, rapid transit, or airplane time schedule. Identify the header, condition stub, condition entry, action stub, and action entry.

B-2   Redraw the limited-entry decision table of Figure B-3 as an extended-entry table.

B-3   Redraw the decision table of Figure B-10, making the customer type a mixed-entry.

B-4   Redraw the open-ended wholesale bill decision table of Figure B-12 to include a fourth type of customer who receives a 20 percent discount.

B–5 Convert the wholesale bill decision table of Figure B–12 into an extended-entry table.

B–6 Which of the rules in Figure B–15 are redundant?

C–1 From Figure B–7, why are rules 1 and 3; 2 and 6; 9 and 11; and 10 and 14 selected rather than 1, 3 and 4; 2, 5 and 6; 9, 11 and 12; and 10, 13 and 14?

C–2 Using Figure B–3 as a reference, draw a decision table that compares three dates (call them S, T, and U) and finds the oldest. Assume that S, T, and U are not equal in any combinations.

C–3 Redraw the open-ended wholesale bill decision table of Figure B–12 with all the redundancies removed.

C–4 Redraw Figure B–15, removing all redundancies.

C–5 Would it be possible to write condition stubs A and B in Figure B-15 in an extended- or mixed-entry form?

COMPUTER NEWS

SOCIAL SECURITY'S DECREPIT COMPUTERS

WASHINGTON

Still reeling from President Reagan's proposed Social Security cuts, Congress was told yesterday that the agency's computers are "one of the largest collections of antiques in existence."

Commissioner John A. Svahn told two House Ways and Means subcommittees he wants to redesign Social Security's computers from scratch, but the task will take more than $500 million and five years to complete.

Meanwhile, the agency is trying to move its "archaic" equipment from an old firetrap of a building at its headquarters outside Baltimore to an adjacent, new building, he said.

Svahn, who warned before taking office this spring that the system could break down in the move, said the agency is using emergency "survival" measures to make sure it pays benefits each month to 36 million Americans.

"We are walking a couple of thousand tapes a day back and forth between two buildings," Svahn said in an interview after the hearing. "That is data that goes into computing benefits. You always run a risk . . . just taking them out and walking them across the road that you can lose a wheelbarrow full."

Despite the "severe" problems, he added, "I think for sure the checks will go out on the third of the month. The No. 1 priority is getting checks out. Everything else takes a back seat to that."

Svahn said past administrations have "swept underneath the rug" Social Security's computer troubles and "patched and repatched" the system, he said.

The agency is not even able to document all of its software, he said. "In the systems jargon, that means that no one can figure out how they work," he said.

"I don't understand how the nation that leads the free world can get fouled up in just a check-paying system," said Charles Rangel, D-N.Y., chairman of the Ways and Means oversight subcommittee.

Svahn said Social Security does more than pay checks. It keeps wage records on 200 million Americans and even handles such tasks as draft registration, he said.

He said Social Security's main hardware consists of 18 large computers, none of which is manufactured today. The agency cannibalizes two of them for spare parts to keep the rest running, he said.

Svahn said it takes new programmers "up to two years to get up to speed to be able to work with Social Security software." It is hard to keep the programmers, and in fact, the agency has lost 20 percent of them—more than 100—to private industry in the past year, he said.

SUMMARY OF ANSI MINIMAL BASIC

Preview

ANSI Minimal BASIC
   Characters and Strings
   Programs
   Constants
   Variables
   Expressions
   Functions
   Statements

PREVIEW

BASIC language is available with a wide range of capabilities. Some versions are minimal and are aimed at microcomputers where only limited resources are to be expended for the language. In other systems, more capable versions, often called Extended BASIC, are available. These enable the user to perform sophisticated file processing, matrix functions, and print formatting with relative ease.

A limited BASIC, called Minimal BASIC, is being standardized, but no standard version of Extended BASIC exists. In extended BASIC, therefore, there are and will continue to be diverse ways of writing statements and functions. In any one particular version of BASIC, however, you must adhere strictly to the writing rules.

Below we summarize the May 1977 proposed American National Standard Minimal BASIC (numbered X3,60D) developed by the American National Standards Institute's Committee X3J2, established in 1974. This summary describes Minimal BASIC's required characters and strings, program structure, constants, variables, expressions, functions, and statements.

Computers that use BASIC also have instructions called *systems commands* that direct the computer's operating system to perform certain actions. For example, the HELLO command generally means that someone at a terminal wants to be connected to the computer. LIST generally directs the operating system to print (or on a CRT, to display) all the program lines. Currently there is no formal effort under way to standardize systems commands, and the versions used by various computer models vary widely. Therefore, systems commands are not included in this summary.

ANSI MINIMAL BASIC[1]

Characters and Strings

The BASIC character set includes letters, digits, and other symbols. The letters are:

ABC . . . Z

The digits are:

012 . . . 9

A string is a sequence of letters or digits or other characters from the list below:

Character	Graphic
space	
exclamation-point	!
quote	"
number-sign	#
dollar	$
percent	%
ampersand	&
apostrophe	'
open	(
close	)
asterisk	*
plus	+
comma	,
minus	−
period	.
slant	/
colon	:
semicolon	;
less-than	<
equals	=
greater-than	>
question-mark	?
circumflex	∧
underline	—

A keyword is a word that represents the action of the statement; it is similar to the verb in English. Minimal BASIC contains the following keywords:

BASE/DATA/DEF/DIM/END/FOR/GO/GOSUB/
GOTO/IF/INPUT/LET/NEXT/ON/OPTION/
PRINT/RANDOMIZE/READ/REM/RESTORE/
RETURN/STEP/STOP/SUB/THEN/TO

Programs

BASIC is a line-oriented language. A program is a sequence of statement lines, the last of which contains an end statement and each of which is identified by a keyword. Each line contains a unique

---

[1] Portions of this summary are excerpted from American National Standards Institute's publication X3Js/77-26, dated 77-05-04, and titled "Proposed American National Standard for Minimal BASIC, May 1977."

line number, which serves as a label for the statement contained in that line.

Lines in a program can contain up to 72 characters; the end-of-line indicator is not included within this 72-character limit.

Constants

A numeric constant is a decimal numeric value written into a BASIC statement. Examples are:

```
1      500     −21.    .255
5E−1   .4E+1   1E10
```

A string-constant is a character string enclosed in quotation marks. Examples are:

```
"XYZ"   "X−3B2"   "1E10"
```

Variables

Variables are associated with either numeric or string values and, in the case of numeric variables, can be either simple variables or references to elements of one- or two-dimensional arrays; such references are called subscripted variables.

Simple numeric variables consist of a letter followed by an optional digit. Examples are:

```
X    A5
```

Subscripted numeric variables consist of a single letter denoting an array followed by one or two numeric expressions enclosed within parentheses. Examples are:

```
V(3)    A(C)    B(C,D+4)
```

String variables consist of a letter followed by a dollar sign. Examples are:

```
S$    C$
```

Expressions

Expressions can be either numeric expressions or string expressions. Numeric expressions can be constructed from variables, constants, and function references using the operations of addition, subtraction, multiplication, division, and involution (raising to a power). String expressions are composed of either a string variable or a string constant. Examples are:

```
3*X−Y^2    A(1)+A(2)+A(3)    2^(−X)
−X/Y       SQR(X^2+Y^2)
```

The formation and evaluation of numeric expressions follows the normal algebraic rules. The symbols circumflex (^), asterisk (*), slant (/), plus (+), and minus (−) represent the operations of involution, multiplication, division, addition, and subtraction, respectively. Unless parentheses dictate otherwise, involutions are performed first, then multiplications and divisions, and finally additions and subtractions. In particular, -2^B is interpreted as $-(2^B)$. In the absence of parentheses, operations of the same precedence are associated to the left; that is, A−B−C is interpreted as (A−B)−C, A/B/C as (A/B)/C, and A^B^C as (A^B)^C.

Functions

A function is a predefined algorithm that is performed and yields a result for use in a statement or a numeric expression within a statement. In the descriptions below, X stands for a numeric expression.

Function	Function Value
ABS(X)	The absolute value of X.
ATN(X)	The arctangent of X in radians; that is, the angle whose tangent is X. The range of the function is $-(\text{pi}/2) < \text{ATN}(X) < (\text{pi}/2)$ where pi is the ratio of the circumference of a circle to its diameter.
COS(X)	The cosine of X, where X is in radians.
EXP(X)	The exponential of X; that is, the value of the base of natural logarithms (e=2.71828 . . .) raised to the power X; if EXP(X) is less than machine infinitesimal, then its value shall be replaced by zero.
INT(X)	The largest integer not greater than X; that is, INT(1.3)=1 and INT(−1.3)=−2.
LOG(X)	The natural logarithm of X; X must be greater than zero.

RND   The next pseudorandom number in an implementation-supplied sequence of pseudorandom numbers uniformly distributed in the range $0<=\text{RND}<1$.

SGN(X)   The algebraic "sign" of X: -1 if $X<0$, 0 if $X=0$, and $+1$ if $X>0$.

SIN(X)   The sine of X, where X is in radians.

SQR(X)   The nonnegative square root of X; X must be nonnegative.

TAN(X)   The tangent of X, where X is in radians.

Statements

A BASIC statement is a single line of the program and consists of several parts: a line number of one to four digits; a keyword such as LET, READ, or GOTO; and it may also contain a variable, the line number of the next statement to be executed, an equals sign, and/or an expression.

Each of the 17 statements is described briefly below.

The let statement: A let statement provides for the assignment of the value of an expression to a variable. The general syntactic form of the let statement is:

LET variable = expression

The expression is evaluated and its value is assigned to the variable to the left of the equals sign. Examples are:

LET P=3.14159   LET A$="ABC"
LET A(X,3)=SIN(X)*Y+1   LET A$=B$

Control statements: Control statements allow for the interruption of the normal sequence of execution of statements by causing execution to continue at a specified line, rather than at the line with the next higher line number. The goto statement:

GOTO line-number

allows for an unconditional transfer. Examples are:

GOTO 120   GOTO 999

The if-then statement, which has the form:

IF exp1 rel exp2 THEN line-number

where exp1 and exp2 are expressions and rel is a relational operator, allows for a conditional transfer. Examples are:

IF X>Y+83 THEN 200   IF A$<>B$ THEN 550

The gosub and return statements, which have the forms:

GOSUB line-number
RETURN

allow for subroutine calls. Examples are:

GOSUB 500   RETURN

The on-goto statement, which has the form:

ON expression GOTO line-number, . . . , line-number

allows control to be transferred to a selected line. An example is:

ON L+1 GOTO 300, 400, 500

The stop statement allows for program termination. For example:

STOP

The end statement both marks the physical end of a program and terminates the execution of the program when encountered. For example:

END

For and next statements: The for statement and next statement provide for the construction of loops. The general forms of the for statement and next statement are:

FOR v=initial-value TO limit STEP increment
NEXT v

where v is a simple numeric variable and "initial-value," "limit," and "increment" are numeric expressions; the clause "STEP increment" is optional. Some examples are:

FOR I=1 TO 10   FOR I=A TO B STEP -1
NEXT I   NEXT I

The for statement and the next statement are defined in conjunction with each other. The physical sequence of statements beginning with a for statement and continuing up to and including the first next statement with the same control variable is termed a "for-block."

In the absence of a STEP clause in a for statement, the increment is assumed to be +1.

The print statement: The print statement is designed for simple generation of labeled and unlabeled output or of output in a consistent tabular format. The general syntactic form of the print statement is:

PRINT item 1 item 2 . . . item n.

Some examples are:

PRINT X
PRINT X; (Y+Z)/2
PRINT
PRINT TAB(10); A$; "IS DONE."

PRINT "X EQUALS",10
PRINT X,Y
PRINT , , , X

The input statement: An input statement provides for interaction with a running program by allowing variables to be assigned values that are supplied from a source external to the program. The input statement enables the entry of mixed string and numeric data, with data items being separated by commas. The general syntactic form of the input statement is:

INPUT variable, . . . , variable

Examples of input statements and their related input data are:

INPUT X	INPUT X, A$, Y(2)	INPUT A,B,C
3.14159	2, SMITH, −3	2.5,0,4.66

The data, read, and restore statements: The data statement provides for the creation of a sequence of data items for use by the read statement. The general syntactic form of the data statement is

DATA datum, . . . , datum

where each datum is either a numeric constant, a string constant, or an unquoted string.

The read statement provides for the assignment of values to variables from a sequence of data created from data statements. The general syntactic form of the read statement is:

READ variable, . . . , variable

Examples of data statements and their related read statements are:

DATA 3,4.1,−6E10	DATA 2,BASIC,","
READ X,Y,Z	READ X(1),A$,B$

The read statement causes variables in the variable list to be assigned values, in order, from the data sequence. A conceptual pointer is associated with the data sequence. When the execution of a program is initiated, this pointer points to the first datum in the data sequence. Each time a read statement is executed, each variable in the variable list in sequence is assigned the value of the datum indicated by the pointer, and the pointer is advanced to point beyond that datum.

The restore statement allows the data in the program to be reread. The general syntactic form of the restore statement is:

RESTORE

The restore statement resets the pointer for the data sequence to the beginning of the sequence, so that the next read statement executed will read data from the beginning of the sequence once again. For example:

RESTORE

Array declarations: The dimension statement is used to reserve space for arrays. Unless declared otherwise, all array subscripts have a lower bound of 0 and an upper bound of 10. Thus, the default space allocation reserves space for 11 elements in one-dimensional arrays and 121 elements in two-dimensional arrays. By use of a dimension statement, the subscript(s) of an array may be declared to have an upper bound other than 10. The general form of the dimension statement is:

DIM declaration, . . . , declaration

where each declaration has the form:

letter (integer)

or

letter (integer,integer)

Examples are:

DIM A(6), B(10,10)

By use of an option statement, the subscripts of all arrays may be declared to have a lower bound of one (1). The general form of the option statement is:

OPTION BASE n

where n is either 0 or 1.

An example is:

OPTION BASE 1

User-defined functions: Besides the implementation-supplied functions provided for the convenience of the programmer, BASIC allows the programmer to define new functions within a program. The general form of statements for defining functions is:

DEF FNx = expression
DEF FNx(parameter) = expression

where x is a single letter and a parameter is a simple numeric variable. Some examples are:

DEF FNF(X)=X/4−1   DEF FNP=3.14159
DEF FNA(X)=A*X+B

The randomize statement: The randomize statement overrides the implementation-predefined sequence of pseudorandom numbers as values for the RND function, allowing different (and unpredictable) sequences each time a given program is executed. For example:

RANDOMIZE

The remark statement: The remark statement allows program annotation. If the execution of a program reaches a line containing a remark statement, it proceeds to the next line with no other effect. An example is:

REM CHECK FOR NEGATIVE DISCRIMINANT

CAREERS WITH COMPUTERS

Preview

Role of the Computer in a Business

Management of the Computing Resource

Jobs Involved with Computing
  Manager of Computing Services Department
  Systems Analyst
  Database Administrator
  Systems Programmer
  Applications Programmer
  Computer Operator
  Data Entry Operator

Career Ladder

Summary

Computer News: A Company That Works at Home

PREVIEW

Our examination of computers thus far has centered around the computing equipment (hardware), programs of various types to make the computer do what we want it to do (software), and the social implications of computerization. This supplement examines the people involved with managing, operating, and programming the computer. Here we look at the various jobs that directly relate to the computer—what the requirements and pay rates are for those jobs—and how the computer is integrated into a business.

ROLE OF THE COMPUTER IN A BUSINESS

Right now most large and medium-sized businesses have their own computer. Furthermore, it is predicted that in the near future (3–7 years) most small businesses (3–30 employees) will also have a computer to help them operate more efficiently.

The selection of the right computer for any business requires that the organization study its needs, examine the potential benefits to be derived from computerization, estimate costs, and hire people to manage the computer system. The right computer for one business may not be the right computer for another. The sizes of businesses (dollar sales, number of employees) vary; their products and services (banking, manufacturing, retailing) are different; and their uses of the computer (payroll, inventory control, accounts receivable) may not be the same. One factor affecting the decision about which computer to acquire is the question of where, within the business organization, to place a computing services department. There are two possibilities for this placement—*centralized* and *decentralized*.

In a **centralized** placement, the computing system is viewed as being on the same level as other departments within the organization (Figure D–1). Figure D–1 is called an **organization chart**; it shows the responsibilities and relationships of one department with another hierarchically. Charts like these are read top-down (like a structure chart) and identify levels of authority, reporting channels, and titles (and status) of the individuals involved. In this case, the stockholders elect a board of directors who, in turn, hires a president, who reports to the board of directors. The president, in turn, hires vice-presidents for each of the departments. Vice-presidents have their departments subdivided with managers responsible for each area within the department. (In the finance department of Figure D–1 these include accounting, budgeting, auditing.)

In a **decentralized** or distributed placement, the computing resource/responsibilities are a part of each department (see Figure D–2). With this approach, there may be a single computer shared by all departments or there may be a computer(s) in each department. The various computers may be tied together to share data and form a network.

Each of these placement modes has distinct advantages and disadvantages (see Figure D–3). In the past, most medium/large businesses used the centralized approach. With the advent of lower cost minicomputers over the past decade we are starting to see more decentralized operation. In the future we are likely to see a combination of the two modes—local computing services for particular needs using smaller computers, and a centralization of summary data at the corporate home office. Just what the organization chart for this placement mode will look like is not yet known.

MANAGEMENT OF THE COMPUTING RESOURCE

Regardless of which placement mode a business uses, people are necessary to program and operate the computer. Centralization will have all the people in one group, whereas decentralization has the people in each department.

Figures D–1 and D–2 show organization charts for a business as a whole. Organization charts can be drawn for each department as well. For the centralized mode of operation you may find the computer services department structured as shown in

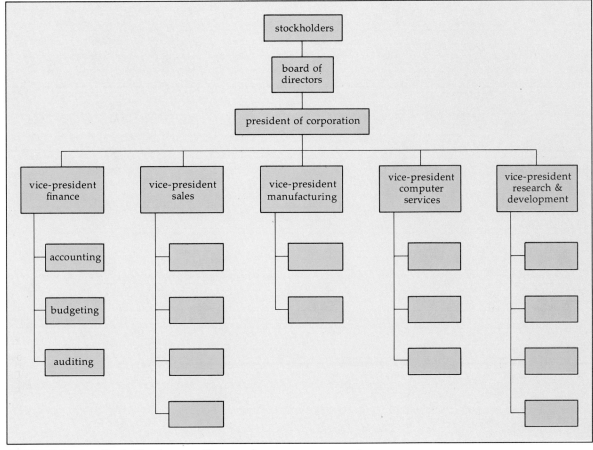

FIGURE D-1 **Centralized computing services.**

Figure D-4. Here we see a highly divided organization with each manager responsible for a particular portion of the computing services department. The numbers to the sides of the rectangles indicate the number of individuals in that area, and the S shows secretarial positions.

Decentralization of the computing resource can lead to a completely different structure (see Figure D-5). In this organization chart we find the division of duties less structured. Computer operators, for instance, are responsible not only for operating the computer but also keeping track of which disk or tape is required for a particular program. Like operators, programmers in a decentralized organization may be assigned tasks that are not strictly programming.

There are other organizational structures for the computing services department. In the pool structure, for example, the programmers and the analysts may be viewed as being available to aid other departments. The manager assigns the various individuals to special tasks as the need arises. In the project structure, analysts and programmers are permanently assigned to a specific application, say, accounts payable.

JOBS INVOLVED WITH COMPUTING

As you can see from the organization charts in Figures D-4 and D-5, there are many different jobs in a

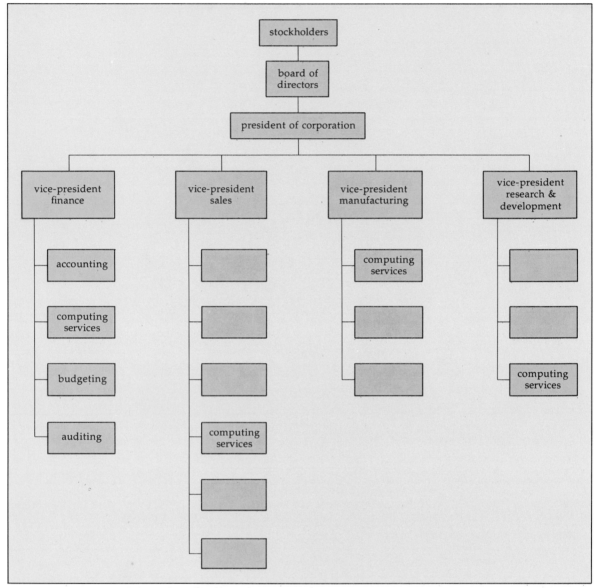

FIGURE D-2 Decentralized or distributed computing services.

computer services department. Along with each of these jobs there are certain educational requirements, prior levels of experience, and differing rates of pay and responsibility. There are jobs that are managerial in nature, those that require technical training, and some that are clerical positions.

Many businesses have a **job description** that outlines the position: its duties, responsibilities, and requirements. To give you a better idea of all these factors, the next seven figures are job descriptions for the positions of vice-president or manager of a computing services department, systems analyst,

FIGURE D-3	Comparison of centralization and decentralization.	
	Centralized Placement	Decentralized Placement
Advantages	1. Economies of scale by large system 2. Overall responsibility for computing services established 3. Can have large software packages like database management systems 4. Promotes standardization of procedures	1. Direct control by the department 2. Equipment specific to the department 3. Higher reliability since not all machines likely to fail at once
Disadvantages	1. Increased communication costs required to link departments 2. Larger users may get higher priority than smaller ones 3. Tendency to form a bureaucracy and lose responsiveness	1. Higher cost 2. Additional personnel 3. Sharing of data may be difficult

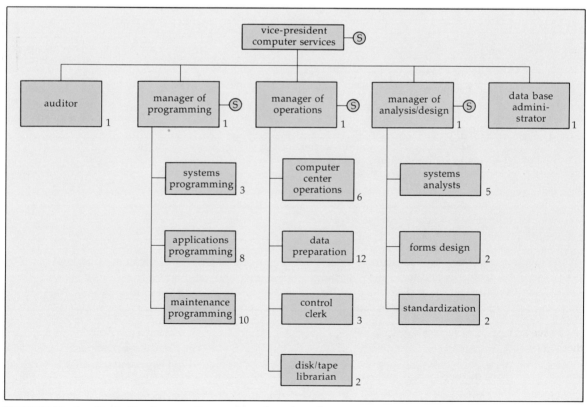

FIGURE D-4 Centralized computer services department.

SUPPLEMENT D: CAREERS WITH COMPUTERS 555

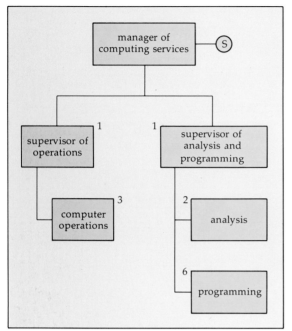

FIGURE D–5 Decentralized computing services.

database administrator, systems programmer, applications programmer, computer operator, and data entry operator. Within each of these positions there may be five levels. For instance, in the area of applications programming, you can find the following jobs: programmer trainee, programmer, senior programmer, lead programmer, and manager of programming. Similar job progressions appear in operations and in analysis.

CAREER LADDER

Are you wondering—with all these jobs where do I start? How do I progress? What are my long-term salary expectations?

In the computer field the beginning, or entry level, job for most people is in operations, programming, or data entry. As a trainee, with no previous experience, you are assigned tasks that will help you become familiar with the operations involved and build your skill level (see Figure D–13).

Title: Manager of Computing Services Department
Reports to: President of Company
Duties and Responsibilities:
  1. Provides overall direction and management of the computing services department.
  2. Implements the needs established by various users.
  3. Responsible for acquisition and maintenance of all hardware and software.
  4. Prepares and submits budget for the department.
  5. Establishes guidelines, standards, and procedures for the department.
  6. Provides direction and guidance in the development of new systems and programs.
  7. Confers, consults, advises, and coordinates with other department managers for proper integration of computing services.

Prior Experience and Education: Knowledge of management techniques, systems analysis, programming, planning, budgeting, scheduling, and operations. Must be able to express ideas clearly both verbally and in writing. Bachelors degree (masters preferred) in computer science, business mathematics, or closely related field. Five years experience in data processing of which two years must have been in managerial or supervisory position.

Pay Range: $39,710–50,945*

* Pay range varies considerably from one industry to another, between small and large companies, and based on supply and demand within a particular geographic area.

FIGURE D–6   Job description—manager of computing services department.

MODULE SIX: SUPPLEMENTS

Title: Systems Analyst
Reports to: Manager of Analysis or DP Director
Duties and Responsibilities:
1. Participates in systems analysis, feasibility studies, and designs new systems for computer applications.
2. Prepares logic diagrams and flowcharts to essential operations from initial stages to job completion.
3. Performs all programming functions from logic diagramming through coding, debugging, test data preparation, and documentation.
4. May be called upon to operate equipment and train personnel.
5. Keeps abreast of new computer technologies.
6. Contributes to the successful operations of the EDP department in other capacities.
7. May act as project leader.
8. Performs related work as required.

Prior Experience and Education:
   1. College degree with computer science major or, completion of the requirements for an associate of arts or higher degree, including sixteen units of data processing and accounting, plus 3 to 4 years of progressively responsible experience in computer programming and some systems analysis.
   2. Proven ability to analyze data and draw sound conclusions; analyze situations accurately and take effective action; speak and write effectively; prepare clear, concise reports; work well with others and gain their respect and confidence; demonstrate the ability to accept work requiring a high degree of mental concentration; and conduct themselves generally in a professional manner.

Pay Range: $20,812–28,300

FIGURE D–7   Job description—systems analyst.

Title: Database Administrator
Reports to: Manager of Computing Services Department
Duties and Responsibilities:
1. Directs, plans, and designs corporate database(s).
2. Develops written proposals.
3. Establishes and administers rules pertaining to the database and its security.
4. Advises analysts and systems programmers on the best ways to access the database.

Prior Experience and Education: 3–7 years programming using database, data communication, and query software. Minimum BS or BA degree in business, mathematics, or computer science.

Pay Range: $22,375–29,724

FIGURE D–8   Job description—database administrator.

Title: Systems Programmer
Reports to: DP Manager or Database Administrator
Duties and Responsibilities:
1. Evaluates, selects, installs, and maintains operating system software and utilities.
2. Participates in projecting hardware and software requirements.
3. Designs and programs specialized utilities such as cost allocation algorithms.
4. Installs changes and enhancements to the operating system.
5. Monitors and suggests changes to optimize system performance.

Prior Experience and Education: Minimum of 3 years experience in programming or analysis. A minimum of a BS or BA degree in computer science or equivalent.

Pay Range: $21,878–26,058

FIGURE D-9 Job description—systems programmer.

Title: Applications Programmer
Reports to: DP Manager or Systems Analyst
Duties and Responsibilities:
1. Makes block diagrams, codes, debugs, tests, and documents programs.
2. Revises existing programs and procedures.
3. Carefully follows programming and operating standards.
4. Operates terminal and other EDP-related equipment.
5. Assists on-the-job training of less experienced programmers.
6. Involved in the control, operations, programming, and user staffs.
7. Assists in other ways as requested by the data processing manager.

Prior Experience and Education: Must have completed the requirements for an associate of arts or higher degree, including approximately 16 to 20 units of data processing and accounting, with a minimum of one semester of COBOL.

—or—

Successfully completed a programming curriculum at a resident school covering approximately 200 hours, including COBOL.

Special Abilities: Must have the ability to follow verbal and written instructions; to speak cooperatively with others; to generally have a professional attitude towards work.

Special Personal Characteristics: Must be willing and able to accept increasing responsibility and to perform work requiring a high degree of mental concentration.

Pay Range: $16,856–22,631

FIGURE D-10 Job description—applications programmer.

Title: Computer Operator
Reports to: Manager of Operations
Duties and Responsibilities:
1. Operates the computer and peripheral equipment.
2. Schedules production.
3. Maintains tape and disk libraries.
4. Helps train new operators.
5. Maintains backup and off-site storage of programs and files.
6. Maintains operating records, such as machine performance and production reports.
7. Confers with technical personnel in the event of errors.
8. Performs other duties as directed by the operations manager.

Prior Experience and Education: Must have a minimum of ten units in EDP and accounting at the college level. Additional experience may be substituted for education.

Pay Range: $12,601–15,515

FIGURE D–11 Job description—computer operator.

Title: Data Entry Operator
Reports to: Manager of Operations
Duties and Responsibilities:
1. Enters data and programs for computer processing on a keyboard device.
2. Distributes work load to other data entry operators.
3. Maintains flow of data input required for computer processing.
4. Performs a variety of related clerical activities such as filing, typing, answering telephones.
5. Operates peripheral equipment such as sorters, bursters, decollators.
6. Does other related work as required.

Prior Experience and Education: High school graduate, or equivalent, and typing experience.

Pay Range: $11,577–13,271

FIGURE D–12 Job description—data entry operator.

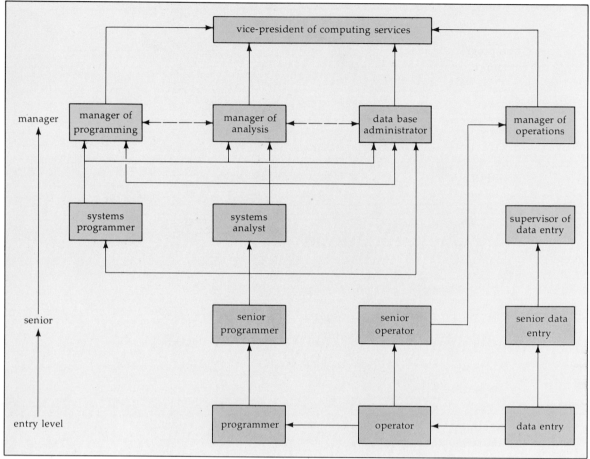

FIGURE D-13 Career ladder.

As your skills develop, you progress to the senior level. Here you are qualified to work on all phases of your area. You can work without direct supervision most of the time, and you may give direction to trainees.

After achieving senior classification, the next step in programming is to database administrator, systems analyst, or systems programmer. Operations/data entry people move into a managerial classification or can transfer to the programming area.

After this senior programmer level, the lines of progression begin crossing (see Figure D-13). If you like more technical jobs, then systems programmer and database administrator are for you. If you are more interested in working with individuals in the business who are outside of computing services, then systems analysis is your goal.

As a manager you supervise all the activities and tasks of the department. You are in charge of all personnel and set policy for your staff and department. You have to demonstrate leadership and be able to communicate with your staff and with those above you both verbally and in writing. At this point in your career, technical expertise is not as important as skills in managing, organizing, budgeting, and interpersonal relationships.

SUMMARY

It is people who program, operate, and manage the computing system. It is people who will determine if the system is successful or not. The people involved must have technical skills in order to program and operate the computer efficiently. They must be supported by a data entry staff that accurately and quickly prepares the data for processing. Systems analysts are the go-between that link the technical staff with the users of the computing system. Data processing is a team effort. All the individuals must work together to make the computer the valuable resource it is and will continue to be.

TERMS

The following words or terms have been presented in this supplement.

Centralized
Organization chart
Decentralized
Job description
Manager of computing services department
Systems analyst
Database administrator
Systems programmer
Applications programmer
Computer operator
Data entry clerk

EXERCISES

The exercises that follow are grouped by level of difficulty. Problems in the A series are the easiest; B series problems are moderately hard; and C series problems are the most difficult.

A–1 Match each of the following.

a.	Manager of computing services department	1.	Uses COBOL or other language
b.	Systems analyst	2.	Designs new processes
c.	Applications programmer	3.	May use a key-to-disk device
d.	Database administrator	4.	Sets policy
e.	Data entry operator	5.	Responsible for data security

A–2 What are the differences between applications, maintenance, and systems programmers?

A–3 Find a recent issue of *Computerworld* newspaper. In the back of the issue you will find a section called "Position Announcements." List three job titles not cited in A–1.

B–1 Draw an organization chart of the pool structure of organization.

B–2 Draw an organization chart of the project structure of organization.

B–3 Why is a data entry operator the lowest paid of all computer-related jobs?

B–4 From a recent issue of *Computerworld* count the number of job announcements there are for each of the jobs defined in Figures D–6 through D–12.

C–1 There are a number of professional societies associated with computing. What are the names of three of them?

C–2 Why are the EDP auditors so important in a business now when they were not in the past?

C–3 Does your college or university use the centralized or decentralized structure of organization?

C–4 In the early 1960s and to a lesser extent even today, the computing services department was a department under the vice-president of finance. Why do you suppose that was the case?

C–5 The job of EDP auditor was not defined in this supplement. Make a job description for this position.

COMPUTER NEWS

A COMPANY THAT WORKS AT HOME

For a company with 600 employees, the home office of F International Ltd. is modest, to say the least. It houses a computer, but little else. The British computer software company has no need of long rows of offices, because it is perhaps the leading corporate example of telecommuting, a growing trend by which employees communicate directly with the office computer from their homes. . . . Almost all of F International's personnel work at home, and about half use computer terminals.

The British company's business lends itself to this novel work arrangement. F International offers services for computer users, ranging from writing computer programs to designing complete data processing systems. This work is usually done directly on computer terminals in any case, making the location of these units irrelevant. The company was founded in 1962 by Vera S. Shirley, now chairman, after she quit her programming job to raise a family. She had assumed that many women left jobs for the same reason but still wanted to work. Such women continue to account for 95% of the company's staff.

A SUITABLE ARRANGEMENT

The company grew from a handful of employees to 200 staffers by 1970, with those working at home using pencil and paper for their programming chores. The shift in recent years has been to home terminals, which are linked via phone lines either to the client's computer or to F International's own computer center. "This suits me perfectly," says Jeannette E. Scott, a marketing executive who began work on a terminal as a home-based computer programmer. "It lets me combine a demanding career with my other interests. I don't want to dump the children at 8 a.m. and pick them up at 6 p.m."

Working on the terminal at home "saves time, effort, and it's easier," adds Elizabeth Hull, 37-year-old mother of two who has worked three years for F International. In addition to saving commuting time, Hull can work at night, when it is most convenient. "You have complete choice [of time of day] to try out your computer coding," she says.

By careful staff selection and the right kind of management, the home workers can be more productive than office-based workers, maintains Suzette M. Harold, F International's managing director. Office-based professionals, she says, tend to whittle away at an 8-hour work day with coffee breaks and lunch hours. "We're working five useful hours on the average," Harold says, "so we're producing a week's work in less time." Most home workers are paid by the hour.

DISCIPLINE

Working at home is not without its problems, however. It requires a new set of disciplines for the worker, says Mary M. Smith, one of F

International's production managers for home work. "It's difficult to go into the study and shut the neighbors out," she says.

F International also has had to develop the right kind of management for home workers. "People you don't see need as much management, attention, and support as those you do see," says Harold, so her project managers often call the homes of employees. And only people with at least four years' experience—the average is 10 years—are hired, to ensure their ability to adhere to deadlines.

QUALITY SPURS GROWTH

F International has prospered with' its team of home workers. The company "is on a 20% real growth path," according to Harold. While she will not provide numbers, industry observers estimate that the privately held company's annual sales in Britain run about $5 million, a fair size for a computer software services company. F International has opened subsidiaries in Denmark and the Netherlands, and it has begun marketing its services in Thailand and Australia. Heights Information Technology Service Inc. in White Plains, N.Y., has licensed F International's management approach to use with its programmers working at home.

The company has been able to sustain this growth rate because its customers have overcome their initial skepticism of home workers. This acceptance has been helped by the unusually tight job market: "The computer industry is very, very short-staffed," says Harold.

Lloyds Bank International Ltd. (London) was initially wary about doing business with F International because of concern about "extremely confidential documents being shipped around the country" to workers' homes, according to a bank official. But now, he says, "we have a good opinion of them. If anything, they did higher quality work than other firms." These days, boasts F International's Scott, "people treat us as an ordinary computer software firm—and that's how we prefer it."

A LAYPERSON'S GLOSSARY

The terms defined in this list are not exhaustive of the jargon you are likely to encounter in reading about computers. But they should give you a start toward establishing a common vocabulary. The terms are not arranged alphabetically because you are unlikely to use this as a glossary; instead, they are grouped according to their meanings. Subordination is indicated by indentation, so that the relationships between the terms will be clearer. To begin, we can classify everything as related to either hardware or software.

HARDWARE   The term *hardware* refers to all the physical computer machinery, from the tiny silicon chips with all that circuitry printed on them, to the huge metal frames the largest computers are stored in, and everything in between.

Central processing unit   The CPU is the heart of the computer, and it consists of the three elements below.

Control unit   They named it right. It controls the exchanges between the other elements of the entire computer system.

Memory unit   The memory is the part of the computer where data are stored for later use.

Byte   A byte is a unit of measurement of memory. If a computer is said to have 256K bytes of memory (sometimes people abbreviate and say just "256K"), that generally means that it can store the equivalent of 256,000 letters or numbers in its memory. This very sentence would use up 63 bytes of a computer's memory.

Bit   There are eight bits in a byte, on most computers. A bit is the smallest thing a computer recognizes, and every piece of data must be converted into its own unique sequence of bits before it can be processed.

Arithmetic/logic unit   The ALU is the part of the CPU where the numerical computations are performed.

Peripherals   Generally speaking, any hardware other than the CPU is a peripheral, but the term is usually reserved for only the less essential items, like plotters, phone hook-up equipment (modems), etc.

Input/output unit   Its friends call it I/O for short. Any piece of equipment that a person uses to give data to or take data from a computer is an I/O unit.

Terminal   The terminal is the thing with the keyboard and the TV screen that all those students sit at to do their assignments.

Cathode ray tube   We never call it that; we always say CRT instead. It's the TV screen part of the terminal, and often people will just say CRT to indicate the whole terminal. Why? Probably because people like letters better than words.

Printer   The machine that prints the computer's "output" in "hard copy" form, like on those wide sheets of endlessly folding computer paper with the holes down the sides.

Unit record equipment Machines that punch holes in those computer cards that we're not supposed to fold, spindle, or mutilate. Also, machines that read such cards. Unit record equipment is gradually being phased out for better, faster methods of I/O, like the terminal.

External storage Any kind of memory device added to a computer system to expand its data storage capability.

   Tape Magnetic tape just like the reels or cassettes you use on your stereo can be used for external storage of data. Popular on home computers.

   Disk Faster and more accessible than tape. Looks like a phonograph record.

   Floppy disk A cheaper enhancement for low-budget uses, like word processing systems, etc. There are also minifloppies.

(*Computer Types*)

Mainframe When the only computers were the big computers, the term *mainframe* was synonymous with CPU. But it now simply means bigger than a minicomputer. Most computers made by IBM, Control Data Corporation (CDC), Burroughs, etc., are mainframe computers.

Minicomputer There's no rigid distinction between a minicomputer and a mainframe or a microcomputer. In terms of speed, cost, and storage capacity it's simply midway between the other two. Digital Equipment Corporation (DEC) is the leading seller of minicomputers, and you'll see their PDP-11 minis all over the place, as well as their newer VAX machine.

Microcomputer Generally synonymous with personal computer or home computer—Apple, TRS-80, Pet, Atari, etc. IBM makes one also.

   Microprocessor A complete CPU, less memory, on a single silicon chip, smaller than a fingernail. The invention of the microprocessor made possible the hand-held calculator and the microcomputer.

SOFTWARE Usually this term is synonymous with program, but it really means anything that tells the computer what to do or how to do it. Hardware is the brawn; software is the brains.

Operating system Software that comes with the hardware from the manufacturer and is essential to its use is called its operating system (OS).

   Batch When a programmer punches each instruction of the program on an IBM card, the resulting batch of cards will be processed by the computer in the batch mode.

   Interactive The opposite of batch. The programmer sits at a terminal, where the program is entered and processed in the interactive mode.

   Time-sharing Terminals that are hooked up to the same CPU operate in a time-sharing environment—like a chess master playing twenty simultaneous games with a bunch of amateurs.

Compiler A compiler is a massive program that translates programs in a specific language into the machine's terms. Therefore, you always hear of a compiler referred to for a specific machine and a specific programming language; e.g., a COBOL 74 compiler for the IBM 4341 computer.

Programming Programming is the practice of writing detailed instructions for the computer to follow so that it can perform given tasks. Actually, it isn't at all that simple, which is why we wrote this textbook.

Pre-programming Before any instructions are actually written, a programmer must plan ahead; this is the pre-programming stage.

   Algorithm An algorithm is a list of steps in a problem-solving process. If you were to write a list of ordered steps for mailing a letter, washing your hands, or any other activity, that list would be an algorithm.

   Flowchart A graphic representation of an algorithm is a flowchart. Arrows show the order and repetition of steps, and the steps themselves are contained in boxes of various shapes, depending on the kind of steps they are.

     Structured flowchart This kind of flowchart doesn't use arrows, but instead uses boxes within boxes and other conventions to indicate the same things that arrows do.

Pseudocode An alternative to flowcharting as a pre-programming technique. No boxes or arrows, just words written with indentations to show subordination. A page of pseudocode is very much like an actual program (that's how it got its name). The page you are reading is much like pseudocode.

Top-down Remember when you wrote essays for your English class and you had to do outlines? First you wrote down your thesis statement, then you listed the main points, then the subpoints under each of the main points, and so on until you had a complete outline. That process is to essay writing as top-down design is to program writing. Programmers just re-named it, that's all.

Structured programming This means different things to people, so be careful. To some, it can mean merely avoiding GOTO statements in programs (so the instructions don't jump all around and make the logic hard to follow); to others it can mean a whole discipline of specific techniques for standardizing the program writing process. The whole point of structured programming, however, has to do with style: writing a program so that it is readable and understandable by someone other than the one who wrote it.

  Data The raw facts (like salaries, temperatures, etc.) that are fed into the computer so there will be something for the program to act on. Note: it is fashionable to say that data go in, but information comes out.

  Integer data Whole numbers, like 39, −46, 28.

  Real data Numbers with decimal places in them, like 4.79, −16.22.

  Character data Letters and words, sometimes called strings.

LANGUAGES Just as English, French, Spanish, and Portuguese are all ways of communicating verbally, programming languages are all unique ways of writing programs. Each was invented by someone, usually for a specific purpose, and each contains its own vocabulary, grammar, syntax, etc.

High-level languages High-level doesn't mean more difficult in this case; it means more refined or sophisticated. High-level languages are those that are closer to English than they are to the off-on language of the computer's circuitry.

  BASIC Stands for Beginner's All-purpose Symbolic Interaction Code. Its main characteristics are that it's easy to learn, not as powerful as other popular languages, and nearly always used interactively.

  FORTRAN Stands for FORmula TRANslation. It's the first high-level language ever developed, and its main use is for number-crunching, as in scientific areas like engineering.

  COBOL COmmon Business Oriented Language. Designed specifically with an eye to satisfying business data processing needs.

  Pascal Named after the French mathematician Blaise Pascal. It's the first naturally structured language and is designed to be an all-purpose teaching language.

Low-level languages Closer to the machine's logic than to English. Require a lot more programmer time to use, but the computer runs much more efficiently.

ANSI The American National Standards Institute is a body that recommends common standards for things like programming languages. So you'll see things like "ANS COBOL." Like a Parent's Magazine seal of approval.

Machine specific This means it will work only on a particular computer system. For example, the ANSI standard for BASIC is very minimal, so the version of BASIC that runs on an Apple Computer will have some machine-specific differences from the version for a TRS-80.

GLOSSARY

Some of the terms in this glossary are defined twice. The first definition is taken from either the *1977 September X3 Technical Report, American National Dictionary for Information Processing*[1] or the *IBM Data Processing Dictionary*[2] (marked with an asterisk*). The second definition is written in a less technical, more easily read manner. Sometimes these "layman" definitions are further expanded by use of an analogy, a reference to a section in this book, or an example.

Access time The time interval between the instant at which an instruction control unit initiates a call for data and the instant at which delivery of the data is completed. Also the time interval between the instant at which data are requested to be stored and the instant at which storage is started.

Accounts receivable The collection of data about goods or services owed by a person, organization, or corporation. The three types are balance only, balance forward, and open item.

Accumulator A storage area within the computer that holds one of the numeric values to be input into the arithmetic/logic unit (ALU). Also holds the results of ALU operations.

---

[1] Published by the Computer and Business Equipment Manufacturers Assn., 1828 L St. NW, Washington, D.C. 20036.
[2] Published by IBM Corporation, Department D58, P.O. Box 390, Poughkeepsie, New York 12602. IBM Order No. GN200360.

Acoustic coupler A data communication device that permits use of a telephone handset as the connection to the telephone network.

Address A character or group of characters that identifies a register, a particular part of storage, some other data source or destination, or the name of a particular memory location. Usually memory locations are given consecutive names such as 0, 1, 2, 3, 4 . . . . Thus, a computer with 16,384 memory locations would have addresses of 0, 1, 2, 3, . . . 16383.

Algorithm A finite set of well-defined rules for the solution of a problem in a finite number of steps. For example, to find the average of a group of numbers the steps are: (1) add together all the numbers; (2) divide this sum by the number of numbers in the group.

Alphabetic character set A character set that contains letters and may contain control characters, special characters, and the space character, but not digits.

Alphanumeric Pertaining to a character set that contains letters, digits, and usually other characters such as punctuation marks. The following characters are a few examples: A, B, C, a, b, c, !, :, ;, 0, 1, 2, #, +, *.

Argument An independent variable; any value of an independent variable.

Arithmetic/logic unit (ALU) A part of a computer that performs arithmetic operations, logic operations, and related operations. One of the six major parts of a computer. Often, the ALU is considered a part of the central processing unit of a computer.

*Arithmetic operator An operator that can be used in an absolute or relocatable expression, or in an arithmetic expression to indicate the actions to be performed on the terms in the expression. The arithmetic operators allowed are: +, −, *, /.

Array An arrangement of elements in one or more dimensions.

ASCII *A*merican *N*ational *S*tandard *C*ode for *I*nformation *I*nterchange. The standard code, using a coded character set consisting of 8-bit coded characters (9 bits including parity check), used for information interchange among data processing systems, data communication systems, and associated equipment. The ASCII set consists of control characters and graphic characters.

Assembler A computer program used to assemble. Synonymous with assembly program.

Assembly language A computer programming language whose statements may be instructions or declarations. The instructions usually have a one-to-one correspondence with machine instructions. Synonymous with computer-dependent language, computer-oriented language.

Asynchronous transmission Data flow between two or more devices at random speeds.

Automation The implementation of processes by automatic means; the conversion of a procedure, a process, or equipment to automatic operation. A self-regulating device (a computer, for instance) which replaces the human control of a machine.

Background processing The execution of lower priority computer programs when higher priority programs are not using the system resources.

*Backup copy A copy of a file or data set that is kept for reference in case the original file or data set is destroyed.

BASIC *B*eginners *A*llpurpose *S*ymbolic *I*nstruction *C*ode. An algebra-like language used for problem solving by engineers, scientists, and others who may not be professional programmers. A programming language originally intended for time-sharing student use, BASIC is now used by businesses in their data processing and is considered one of the easiest programming languages to learn.

Batch processing The technique of executing a set of computer programs such that each is completed before the next program of the set is started; the original method of taking data from its source and processing it into more useful information. All of the data are grouped together before being processed by the computer.

Binary-coded decimal notation (BCD) A binary-coded notation in which each of the decimal digits is represented by a binary numeral; for example, in binary-coded decimal notation that uses the weights 8-4-2-1, the number "twenty-three" is represented by 0010 0011 (compare its representation 10111 in the pure binary numeration system).

Binary digit (bit) In binary notation, either of the characters 0 or 1. A single character (usually denoted by a 0 or 1) that is used to represent the ON-OFF, YES-NO states of computer memory, disk, or tape devices; groups of binary digits, called bits, are grouped together to code data and instructions. For instance, the bit group 1100 0001 is the pattern for the letter A in the EBCDIC notation.

Binary notation Any notation that uses two different characters, usually the binary digits 0 and 1; for example, the gray code. The gray code is a binary notation, but not a pure binary numeration system.

Bit An abbreviation for binary digit.

Block A collection of contiguous records recorded as a unit. Blocks are separated by interblock gaps and each block may contain one or more records.

Block diagram A diagram of a system, instrument, or computer in which the principal parts are represented by suitably annotated geometrical figures to show both the basic functions of the parts and the functional relationships between them.

*BPI *B*its *p*er *i*nch.

Buffer A routine or storage used to compensate for a difference in a rate of flow of data, or time or occurrence of events, when transferring data from one device to another.

Bug A mistake or malfunction.

Bulk storage See *mass storage*.

Burst To separate continuous-form paper into discrete sheets.

Bus Connecting circuit or pathway over which data and/or instructions flow within a computer.

Byte A binary character string operated upon as a unit and usually shorter than a computer word. Usually a group of eight bits. For instance, the 8 bits for the letter A are 1100 0001 in EBCDIC.

Calculator A device for carrying out logic and arithmetical digital operations of any kind.

Card column A line of punch positions parallel to the shorter edge of a punch card.

Card deck A group of related punched cards.

Card punch A device that punches holes in a card to represent data. See also *keypunch*.

Cathode ray tube (CRT) A device that presents data in visual form by means of controlled electron beams. Usually found in the form of a TV-type terminal with a keyboard.

Central processing unit (CPU) A unit of a computer that includes circuits controlling the interpretation and execution of instructions; consists of the control unit, arithmetic/logic unit, and memory. It is analogous to the brain, central nervous system, and cardiovascular system in the human body. Synonymous with central processor, main frame.

Central processor See *central processing unit*.

Chained list A list in which each item contains an identifier for locating the next item.

Channel A path along which signals can be sent, for example, data channel, output channel; the portion of a storage medium that is accessible to a given reading or writing station, for example, track, band.

Character A letter, digit, or other symbol that is used as part of the organization, control, or representation of data.

Character-at-a-time-printer A device that prints a single character at a time, for example, a typewriter.

Checkout See *debug*.

Chip A minute piece of semiconductive material used in the manufacture of electronic components. An integrated circuit on a piece of semiconductive material.

COBOL *Co*mmon *B*usiness *O*riented *L*anguage. A programming language designed for business data processing. The instructions are written in sentence form. Sentences are combined to make paragraphs, and paragraphs are combined into divisions. The four divisions are Identification, Environment, Data, and Procedure.

Command A control signal; an instruction; a mathematical or logic operator.

Comparison The process of examining two or more items for identity, similarity, equality, relative magnitude, or order in a sequence.

Compile To translate a computer program expressed in a problem-oriented language into a computer-oriented language. FORTRAN, COBOL, RPG-II, Pascal, and BASIC require translation.

Compiler A computer program used to compile. The program is usually provided by the manufacturer of the computer. It treats a program written in a high-level language as data, and it translates the data into an equivalent machine language program.

Computer A data processor that can perform substantial computation, including numerous arithmetic operations or logic operations, without intervention by a human operator during a run. It always operates under the direct control of a program while performing its tasks.

Computer instruction An instruction that can be recognized by the central processing unit of the computer for which it is designed. Synonymous with machine instruction.

Computer output microfilm Microfilm that contains data received directly from computer-generated signals.

Connector A flowchart symbol that represents a break in a flowline, the same flowline being continued elsewhere.

Console A part of a computer used for communication between the operator or maintenance engineer and the computer.

Control break A type of program that causes a

specific and different action to take place (for instance the printing of totals) when a change occurs on a particular field.

Controller   A functional unit in an automatic data processing system that controls one or more units of peripheral equipment. Synonymous with I/O controller, peripheral control unit.

Control structure   The manner in which programs are built. The three types are simple sequence, repetition, and selection.

Control unit   In a central processing unit, the part that receives instructions in proper sequence, interprets each instruction, and applies the proper signals to the arithmetic and logic unit and other parts in accordance with this interpretation. It oversees the retrieval and execution of each instruction in a program.

Conversion   The change-over from one kind of system to another; for instance, from batch processing to transaction processing.

Core   A magnetic storage in which the data medium consists of magnetic cores. Each core is shaped like a miniature doughnut as small as 18/1000 of an inch in diameter (about the size of a grain of salt). The cores can be polarized in a binary manner, ON-OFF. Most computers made since 1975 use semiconductor chips as the memory medium instead.

Counter   A device whose state represents a number and that, on receipt of an appropriate signal, causes the number represented to be increased by unity or by an arbitrary constant; the device is usually capable of bringing the number represented to a specified value, such as zero.

CRT display   Cathode ray tube display.

Cryogenic storage   A storage device that uses the superconductive and magnetic properties of certain materials at very low temperatures.

Cycle time   The minimum time interval between the starts of successive read/write cycles of storage.

Daisy wheel   A removable unit used on letter-quality printers. Consists of a plastic wheel of which the spokes or petals have character types at the outer ends.

Data   A representation of facts, concepts, or instructions in a formalized manner suitable for communication, interpretation, or processing by humans or by automatic means. The collection of facts is historical in nature and has not yet been processed or grouped. Some examples are temperatures, amounts of money owed or received as payments, or names of individuals, corporations, or partnerships.

Database   A set of data which is a part or the whole of another set of data, and consisting of at least one file, that is sufficient for a given purpose or for a given data processing system. As an example, the data collected for each individual belonging to VISA or Master Card credit card charging systems.

Data code   A structured set of characters used to represent data items; for example, the codes 01, 02, . . . , 12 may be used to represent the months of January, February, . . . , December of the data element months of the year; in data communication, a set of rules and conventions according to which the signals representing data should be formed, transmitted, received, and processed.

Data communication   Transmission, processing, and distribution of information using computer and telecommunication facilities.

Data management   The function of controlling the acquisition, analysis, storage, retrieval, and distribution of data; in an operating system, the computer programs that provide access to data, perform or monitor storage of data, and control input/output devices. A series of programs which ease the access to the database by divorcing the physical order of the data from the logical order. Also referred to as a DBMS (*D*ata*b*ase *M*anagement *S*ystem).

Data name   A character or group of characters used to identify an item of data.

Data processing   The execution of a systematic sequence of operations performed upon data, for example, handling, merging, sorting, computing. Synonymous with information processing.

DBMS   *D*ata*b*ase *M*anagement *S*ystem. See *data management*.

Debug   To detect, trace, and eliminate mistakes in

computer programs or in other software. Synonymous with checkout.

Decision table   A table of all contingencies that are to be considered in the description of a problem, together with the actions to be taken.

Default option   An implicit option that is assumed when no option is explicitly stated.

Density   The number of useful storage cells per unit of dimension, for example, the number of bits per inch stored on a magnetic tape track.

Destructive read   A reading that also erases the data in the source location.

Detail file   See *transaction file*.

Digit punch   A punch in rows 1, 2, . . . , 9 on a punched card.

Direct access storage   A storage device in which the access time is in effect independent of the location of the data.

Disk   A magnetic storage in which data are stored by selective polarization of portions of magnetic material in use. Allows random retrieval of data since many surfaces, called platters, can be stacked together, each with its own reading and writing device.

Documentation   The management of documents, which may include the actions of identifying, acquiring, processing, storing, and disseminating them. The documents describe a system, the programs that are a part of it, the data input and its format, the information that is output, changes made to it, authorship, and other pertinent facts.

Dot matrix printer   A printer in which each character is represented by a pattern of dots.

Drum   A magnetic storage in which data are stored by the selective polarization of portions of magnetic material of the curved surface of a cylinder that rotates in use.

Drum printer   A line printer in which the type is mounted on a rotating drum that contains a full character set for each printing position.

EBCDIC code   A coded character set consisting of 8-bit coded characters. 256 possible characters.

Edit   To prepare data for a later operation. Editing may include the rearrangement or the addition of data, the deletion of unwanted data, format control, code conversion, and the application of standard processes such as zero suppression.

Execution   The process of carrying out the instructions of a computer program by a computer.

External storage   In a hierarchy of storage devices of a data processing system, any storage device that is not internal storage. Usually these devices are magnetic tapes or disks. The devices have large capacities but slow access times in comparison with memory.

Field   In a record, a specified area used for a particular category of data, for example, a group of card columns in which a wage rate is recorded.

File   A set of related records treated as a unit. For instance, in stock control, a file could consist of a set of invoices. The records are kept in some order by invoice number, customer name, or vendor number. The types are master, transaction, indexed, sequential, hierarchical, and inverted.

Floating point   A representation of a real number in a floating-point representation system; for example, a floating-point representation of the number 0.0001234 is 0.1234×10^{-3}, where 0.1234 is the fixed-point part and -3 is the exponent. The numerals are expressed in the variable-point decimal numeration system.

Flowchart   A graphical representation of the definition, analysis, or method of solution of a problem, in which symbols are used to represent operations, data, flow, equipment, and so on. A system flowchart shows the interrelationship of various files and programs. A program flowchart depicts the logic or sequence of steps that need to be written in a program.

Flow line   On a flowchart, a line representing a connecting path between flowchart symbols, for example, a line to indicate a transfer of data or control.

Format   The arrangement or layout of data in or on a data medium.

FORTRAN   *For*mula *Tran*slator. A programming language primarily used to express computer programs by arithmetic formulas. The formulas are written using familiar symbols (called operators): "+" for addition, "−" for subtraction, "*" for multiplication, and "/" for division. The FORTRAN statement to multiply quantity by price and add 6% for sales tax, would be: TOTAL = PRICE * QUANTITY * (1+.06).

Frame That portion of a tape, on a line perpendicular to the reference edge, on which binary characters may be written or read simultaneously.

Functional diagram A diagram that represents the working relationships among the parts of a system.

Hardware Physical equipment used in data processing, as opposed to computer programs, procedures, rules, and associated documentation. Some of these pieces of equipment are terminals, line printers, card readers, disks, tapes, and so on. Compare *software*.

Hash total The result obtained by applying an algorithm to a set of data for checking purposes, for example, a summation obtained by treating data items as numbers.

Head A device that reads, writes, or erases data on a storage medium, for example, a small electromagnet used to read, write, or erase data on a magnetic drum or magnetic tape, or the set of perforating, reading, or marking devices used for punching, reading, or printing on perforated tape.

Hexadecimal Pertaining to a selection, choice, or condition that has sixteen possible different values or states.

High-level language A programming language that does not reflect the structure of any one given computer or that of any given class of computers. Some examples are FORTRAN, BASIC, COBOL, RPG-II, APL, PL/1, and Pascal.

Hollerith card A punch card characterized by 80 columns and 12 rows of punch positions.

Identifier A character or group of characters used to identify or name an item of data and possibly to indicate certain properties of those data.

Impact printer A printer in which printing is the result of mechanical impacts.

Index In programming, a subscript, or integer value, that identifies the position of an item of data with respect to some other item of data; a symbol or a numeral used to identify a particular quantity in an array of similar quantities. For example, the terms of an array represented by $X(1)$, $X(2)$, . . . , $X(100)$ have the indexes 1, 2, . . . , 100 respectively.

Index register A register whose contents may be used to modify an operand address during the execution of computer instructions, so as to operate as a clock or counter. An index register may be used to control the execution of a loop, to control the use of an array, as a switch, for table lookup, as a pointer, and so on.

Indicator An item of data that may be interrogated to determine whether a particular condition has been satisfied in the execution of a computer program; for example, a switch indicator, an overflow indicator.

Information The meaning that a human assigns to data by means of the known conventions used in their representation. The results of data that have been processed. As an example, consider a retail shoe store. Every time a shoe is sold the size, type, and price are recorded. These facts are data. When these data have been applied to "number of shoes in inventory" and "gross sales," we have information.

Information processing See *data processing*.

Initialize To set counters, switches, addresses, or contents of storage to zero or other starting values at the beginning of or at prescribed points in the operation of a computer routine.

Input Data being received or to be received into a device or into a computer program.

Input device A device in a data processing system by which data may be entered into the system. Examples are card readers, terminals, key-to-disk devices, key-to-tape devices, optical character readers, and magnetic ink character readers. Compare *output device*.

Instruction In a programming language, a meaningful expression that specifies one operation and identifies its operands, if any. The expression gives the memory locations to be used and what the computer is supposed to do with the data contained in those memory locations.

Instruction execute To perform the execution of an instruction or of a computer program.

Instruction fetch To locate and load a quantity of data from storage.

Instruction set The set of instructions for a computer, a programming language, or the programming languages in a programming system.

Integer One of the numbers 0, +1, −1, +2, −2 . . . . Synonymous with integral number.

Interblock gap A space between blocks on magnetic tape; an area on a data medium used to indicate the end of a block or physical record.

Interface A shared boundary. An interface might be a hardware component to link two devices or it might be a portion of storage or registers accessed by two or more computer programs.

Internal storage A storage device directly controlled by the central processing unit of a digital computer.

Interpret To translate and execute each source language statement of a computer program before translating and executing the next statement.

Inverted In information retrieval, a method of organizing a cross-index file in which a keyword identifies a record; the items, numbers, or documents pertinent to that keyword are indicated.

I/O(input/output) The sending or receiving of a group of related characters, a record, by a device. Every time a line is printed, that device receives the group of characters for the line and has them printed.

*ISAM Indexed Sequential Access Method.

JCL *Job Control Language*. A group of commands to the computer's operating system that tells it what to do with a program or to various files that may need some modification, or allocates computer time or memory. As an example, in the Burroughs Job Control Language (called WFL, *Work Flow Language*), to cause the system to compile and execute a program, you write: "BEGIN JOB TRIAL; COMPILE TRIAL FORTRAN; RUN."

Job description A list of duties, responsibilities, educational requirements, prior experience, and usually rate of pay associated with an occupational position or job.

K When referring to storage capacity, two to the tenth power, 1024 in decimal notation. Thus, a computer that is described as having 16K of memory has 16 groups of 1024 memory locations, a total of 16,384 memory locations.

Key One or more characters within a set of data, that contain information about the set, including its identification.

Keypunch A keyboard-actuated device that punches holes in a punch card. The most widely used varieties are the IBM 026, 029, and 129 devices.

KOPS Thousands of operations per second.

Latency The time interval between the instant at which an instruction control unit initiates a call for data and the instant at which the actual transfer of the data is started. Synonymous with waiting time.

Leader The blank section of tape at the beginning of a reel.

Line-at-a-time printer See *line printer*.

Line printer A device that prints a line of characters as a unit. Synonymous with line-at-a-time printer.

Linkage editor A utility routine that creates a loadable computer program by combining independently translated computer program modules and by resolving cross references among the modules.

Literal In a source program, an explicit representation of the value of an item, which value must be unaltered during any translation of the source program, for example, the word FAIL in the instruction IF X=0 THEN PRINT "FAIL".

Load In computer programming, to enter data into storage or working registers.

Load-and-go An operating technique in which there are no stops between the loading and execution phases of a computer program, and which may include assembling or compiling.

Location Any place in which data may be stored.

Logical record A record independent of its physical environment. Portions of the same logical record may be located in different physical records, or several logical records or parts of logical records may be located in one physical record.

Logic unit A part of a computer that performs logic operations and related operations. A part of the CPU, this unit takes two quantities and tests them to determine which is larger, smaller, or if they are the same.

Loop A set of instructions that may be executed repeatedly while a certain condition prevails. In some implementations, no test is made to discover whether the condition prevails until the loop has been executed once.

Machine instruction See *computer instruction*.

Machine language A language that is used directly by a machine. The language is in a binary form (although it may be written on paper in octal or hexadecimal form for convenience), and is directly understandable by a computer. As an example, the instruction 1A63 (written in hexadecimal) tells an IBM 360/370 computer to add registers 6 and 3 and put their sum in 6. See also *computer instruction*.

Macroinstruction An assembly language instruction composed of many machine language instructions.

Macroprogramming Computer programming with macroinstructions.

Magnetic core See *core*.

Magnetic disk See *disk*.

Magnetic drum See *drum*.

Magnetic ink character recognition (MICR) Recognition of characters printed with ink that contains particles of a magnetic material.

Magnetic tape A tape with a magnetic surface layer. Data occur on the ½ inch wide tape in a very compact manner. Each item of data follows the previous one and, thus, data on tape are in sequence. To retrieve data, each item of data must be read and processed in order.

Main frame See *central processing unit*.

Mainframe computer A computer having the same basic functional parts (input, memory, arithmetic/logic, control, secondary storage, and output) that mini- and microcomputers have, but having major differences within those parts. Also differs from minis and micros in respect to data flow between functional parts.

Main storage See *memory*.

Mass storage An auxiliary storage with very large capacity used to store data to which infrequent reference need be made. Synonymous with bulk storage.

Master file A file that is used as an authority in a given job and that is relatively permanent, even though its contents may change.

Matrix printer See *dot matrix printer*.

Mean-time-between-failures For a period in the life of a functional unit, the mean value of the lengths of time between consecutive failures under stated conditions.

Media reader A device that reads data directly from a source document eliminating human transcribing.

Medium The material in or on which a specific physical variable may represent data.

Memory Often referred to as "core" (even though the physical devices for storing of data may be chips and not cores), this functional part stores data and instructions. It can retrieve the items rapidly (in billionths of a second) but is more expensive than other storage devices of equivalent capacities. Synonymous with main storage.

*MFT Multiprogramming with a Fixed number of Tasks.

MICR See *magnetic ink character recognition*.

Microcomputer An extremely small computer consisting of a few LSI chips or even a single chip.

Microfiche A sheet of microfilm capable of containing microimages in a grid pattern, usually containing a title that can be read without magnification.

Microprocessor A single LSI chip containing arithmetic, logic, and control units.

Microprogram A sequence of elementary instructions that correspond to a computer operation, that is maintained in special storage, and whose execution is initiated by the introduction of a computer instruction into an instruction register of a computer.

MIPS Millions of Instructions Per Second.

Mnemonic A symbol chosen to assist the human memory, for example, an abbreviation such as "mpy" for "multiply."

Modem (MOdulator-DEModulator) A device that modulates and demodulates signals transmitted over communication facilities.

Module (1) A program unit that is discrete or identifiable. The modules may be written and tested separately and then put together to form the complete program; this is called "modular programming." (2) An interchangeable plug-in unit containing electronic components.

Monitor Software or hardware that observes, supervises, controls, or verifies the operations of a system.

Move In computer programming, to copy from locations in internal storage into locations in the same internal storage.

Multiplexing Interleaving or simultaneous transmission of two or more messages on a single data path.

Multiprocessor A computer employing two or more central processing units under integrated control.

Multiprogramming A mode of operation that provides for the interleaved execution of two or more computer programs by a single central processing unit.

*MVT Multiprogramming with a Variable number of Tasks.

Nest To incorporate a structure or structures of some kind into a structure of the same kind. For example, to nest one loop (the nested loop) within another loop (the nesting loop); to nest one subroutine (the nested subroutine) within another subroutine (the nesting subroutine). To imbed subroutines or data in other subroutines or data at a different hierarchical level such that the different levels of routines or data can be executed or accessed by each other, that is, recursively.

Network A complex consisting of two or more interconnected computers.

Nondestructive read A read process that does not erase the data in the source. Synonymous with nondestructive readout.

Non-volatile storage A storage whose content is not lost when the power is removed.

Normalize To make an adjustment to the fixed-point part and the corresponding adjustment to the exponent in a floating-point representation to ensure that the fixed-point part lies within some prescribed range, the real number represented remaining unchanged.

Object program A fully compiled or assembled program that is ready to be loaded into the computer.

OCR Optical Character Recognition.

Octal Pertaining to a fixed-radix numeration system having a radix of eight.

Odd-even check See *party check*.

Off-line Pertaining to equipment or devices not under control of a central processing unit. Compare *on-line*.

On-line Pertaining to equipment or devices under direct control of a central processing unit. A terminal that is used to enter a program or data into the computer is an example of this. The equipment could be located at a remote distance from the computer and be linked by a telephone line. Compare *off-line*.

Operating system Software that controls the execution of computer programs and that may provide scheduling, debugging, input/output control, accounting, compilation, storage assignment, data management, and related services. Some examples of these are IBM's DOS (*d*isk *o*perating *s*ystem), VOS (*v*irtual *o*perating *s*ystem), and OS (*o*perating *s*ystem); Burroughs' MCP (*m*aster *c*ontrol *p*rogram); NCR's VRX (*v*irtual *r*esource *ex*ecutive); and Hewlett-Packard's MPE (*M*ultiprogramming *E*xecutive).

Operation code A code used to represent the operations of a computer.

Operator (1) A symbol that represents the action to be performed in a mathematical operation. (2) A person who runs a computing system.

Output Pertaining to a device, process, or channel involved in an output process, or to the data or states involved in an output process. Once the data have been collected and processed, the resulting information presented to the user is said to be output.

Output device A device in a data processing system by which data may be received from the system. Examples are line printers, computer output on microfilm, and plotters. Compare *input device*.

Parallel addition Addition that is performed concurrently on digits in all the digit places of the operands.

Parity A check bit appended to an array of binary digits to make the sum of all the binary digits, including the check bit, always odd or always even.

Parity check A check that tests whether the number of 1s (or 0s) in an array of binary digits is odd or even. Synonymous with odd-even check.

Partition Deprecated term for *segment*.

Peripheral control unit See *controller*.

PL/1 *Programming Language 1*. A programming language designed for use in a wide range of commercial and scientific computer applications.

Plotter An output unit that presents data in the form of a two-dimensional graphical representation.

*Pointer An address or other indication of location.

Positional representation system Any numeration system in which a real number is represented by an ordered set of characters in such a way that the value contributed by a character depends upon its position as well as its value.

Precedence The relative order of events. The arithmetic operators in BASIC (in their high-to-low order) are ↑, */, +−.

Printer A device that writes output data from a system on paper or other medium. Some types are chain, train, band, drum, thermal, matrix, and daisy wheel.

Problem-oriented Pertaining to a program language that is especially suitable for a given class of problems. Procedure-oriented languages such as FORTRAN, ALGOL; simulation languages such as GPSS, SIMSCRIPT; list processing languages such as LISP, IPL-V; information retrieval languages.

Procedure The course of action taken for the solution of a problem.

Process control Automatic control of a process, in which a computer is used to regulate usually continuous operations or processes.

Processor In software, a computer program that performs functions such as compiling, assembling, and translating for a specific programming language. In hardware, a data processor, the CPU.

Program The set of instructions to solve a problem. The instructions are usually written in one of the high-level languages, such as FORTRAN, COBOL, or BASIC.

Program flowchart A flowchart representing the sequence of operations in a computer program.

Programmer A person who designs, writes, and tests computer programs. The person usually has some college training, a background in accounting, and will work alone or as part of a small team. This job is one of the first ones available to a person interested in working with computers. The two types are systems and applications.

Pseudocode A code that requires translation prior to execution. A concise English-language description of the step-by-step instructions within a computer program.

Punched card reader A device that reads or senses the holes in a punched card, transforming the data from hole patterns to electrical signals.

Radix Of a digit place in a radix numeration system, the positive integer by which the weight of the digit place is multiplied to obtain the weight of the digit place with the next higher weight. For example, in the decimal system the radix of each digit place is 10 and in binary the radix of each digit place is 2.

Random access An access mode in which specific logical records are obtained from or placed into a mass storage file in a nonsequential manner. The placing and retrieval of the next record has little relationship with that of the current one. This technique is mandatory for on-line processing of data and database files.

Random access memory (RAM) The computer's primary storage where the data, intermediate results, and program being executed are stored.

Random number A number selected from a known set of numbers in such a manner that the probability of occurrence of each number is predetermined.

Read To acquire or to interpret data from a storage device, from a data medium, or from another source.

Read only memory (ROM) Memory whose values cannot be changed.

Read/write head See *head*.

Real number A number that may be represented by a finite or infinite numeral in a fixed-radix numeration system.

Record A collection of related data or words treated as a unit. For example, in stock control each invoice could constitute one record. Compare *file*.

Reentrant program A computer program that may be entered repeatedly and may be entered before prior executions of the same computer program have been completed, subject to the requirement that neither its external program parameters nor any instructions are modified during its execution. A reentrant program may be used by more than one computer program simultaneously.

Register In a computer, a storage device usually intended for some special purpose, capable of storing a specified amount of data such as a bit or a word. Each device usually has a unique address, and the data stored there can be changed.

Relative address An address expressed as a difference with respect to a base address.

Remote batch processing Batch processing in which input/output units have access to a computer through a data link.

Report generator A special program that produces highly formatted reports as directed by specific parameters imbedded in the program for each report.

RJE (Remote Job Entry). Submission of jobs through an input unit that has access to a computer through a data link.

Robot A device equipped to detect input signals, with a calculating mechanism to make decisions, and a guidance mechanism to provide control.

Robotics The study and application of robots to our society.

ROM See *read only memory*.

Row A horizontal arrangement of characters or other expressions. Compare *card column*.

RPG-II *Report Program Generator*. A high-level programming language that is especially powerful in the production of printed reports. The language is generally used on small computers like the IBM System 32, 34, and 38.

RUN A single performance of one or more jobs; a single, continuous performance of a computer program or routine.

Sector A part of a track or band on a magnetic drum, a magnetic disk, or a disk pack.

Seek To position selectively the access mechanism of a direct access device.

Segment A self-contained portion of a computer program that may be executed without the entire computer program necessarily being maintained in internal storage at any one time.

Semiconductor A solid with an electrical conductivity between that of metals and insulators such as silicon or germanium. These solids are fabricated to form chips that can perform various tasks.

Sequential Pertaining to the occurrence of events in time sequence, with no simultaneity or overlap of events.

Serial addition Addition that is performed by adding, digit place after digit place, the corresponding digits of the operands.

Sign bit A bit or a binary element that occupies a sign position and indicates the algebraic sign of the number represented by the numeral with which it is associated.

Software The collection of programs and routines associated with a computer. The routines include the operating system, language compilers, and utility routines. Compare *hardware*.

Sort To arrange a set of items according to keys that are used as a basis for determining the sequence of the items; for example, to arrange the records of a personnel file into alphabetical sequence by using the employee names as sort keys.

Source program A computer program written in a high-level language.

Spooling The reading of output from and the writing of input onto auxiliary storage concurrently with job execution in a form suitable for later processing or output operations.

Statement In a programming language, a meaningful expression that may describe or specify operations and is complete in the context of its programming language.

Stop instruction An exit that specifies the termination of the execution of a computer program.

Storage The action of placing data into a storage device and retaining them for subsequent use; the retention of data in a storage device. The device may be main memory, disks, tapes, or a drum. The data stored may be immediately changed or stay unaltered for a long period of time.

Storage capacity The number of bits, characters, bytes, words, or other units of data that a particular storage device can contain.

Structure chart A diagram like a flowchart that shows the hierarchy of program modules.

Structured program A technique for designing and writing programs that constructs a program in independent modules with a hierarchical structure. Modules are written to minimize the number of GO TO instructions; they have a single entry and exit point and read top down. This technique improves the organization, readability, documentation, and reliability of a program.

Synchronous transmission Data flow between two or more devices where all devices operate on the same timing.

System A collection of people, machines, programs, and methods organized to accomplish a set of specific functions.

Table An array of data each item of which may be unambiguously identified by means of one or more arguments. A collection of data in which each item is uniquely identified by a label, by its position relative to the other items, or by some other means.

Tape drive A mechanism for controlling the movement of magnetic tape. This mechanism is commonly used to move magnetic tape past a read or write head, or to allow automatic rewinding.

Task The basic unit of work from the standpoint of a control program.

Telecommunication The transmission of signals over long distances, such as by telegraph, radio, or television.

*Terminal A device, usually equipped with a keyboard and some kind of display, capable of sending and receiving information over a communication channel. The device may be "intelligent" (have some memory and logic capability), have the ability to print information, or allow pictures to be drawn on it.

Time-sharing A mode of operation that provides for the interleaving of two or more independent processes on one functional unit. Each process is unaware of the other since the computer services each on a regular and periodic basis.

Track The portion of a moving data medium, such as a drum, tape, or disk, that is accessible to a given reading head position.

Transaction file A file containing relatively transient data that, for a given application, is processed together with the appropriate master file. Synonymous with detail file.

Transaction processing Immediate and direct inputting of transaction data into the computer for processing. Sometimes called on-line processing. The opposite of batch processing, where processing is delayed until a series of transactions have been accumulated.

Truncation The deletion or omission of a leading

or trailing portion of a string in accordance with specified criteria.

*TTY *Telety*pewriter equipment.

*Unit record A card containing one complete record; a punched card.

Update To modify a master file with current information according to a specified procedure.

Validation The checking of data for correctness, or compliance with applicable standards, rules, and conventions.

Variable In computer programming, a character or group of characters that refers to a value and, in the execution of a computer program, corresponds to an address.

Verify To determine whether a transcription of data or other operation has been accomplished accurately.

VLSI Very Large Scale Integration.

Volatile storage A storage whose content is lost when the power is removed.

Waiting time See *latency*.

Word A character string or a binary element string that it is convenient for some purpose to consider as an entity.

Write To make a permanent or transient recording of data in a storage device or on a data medium.

Zone punch A hole punched in one of the upper three card rows of a 12-row punch card.

ACKNOWLEDGMENTS

American National Standards Institute—for material adapted from "The Origins of COBOL," *American National Standard Programming Language Cobol*, X 3.34—1974. Used by permission.

Laboratory for Computer Graphics & Spatial Analysis—for the map, "U.S. Population Densities, 1970," drawn by the SYMVU Program of the Harvard Laboratory for Computer Graphics & Spatial Analysis. Reproduced by permission.

G. P. Putnam's Sons—for "The Curse" from *Son of the Great Society* by Art Buchwald. Reprinted by permission of G. P. Putnam's Sons.

Scan-Tron Corporation—for their form 2065-INT. Reprinted by permission of Scan-Tron Corporation, U.S. Patent Nos. 3 800 349 and 3 900 961.

Wayne Foote of Foote's Florist, Auburn, CA—for the material in Figures 15–1, 15–5, 15–6, 15–7. Used by permission.

Jim Williams of Williams and Paddon, Roseville, CA—for material used in Figure 9–1. Used by permission.

COMPUTER NEWS SECTIONS

Chapter 1 The Wall Street Journal—for the article "Supreme Court Decides to Join Computer Age" by Stephen Wermiel. Reprinted by permission of *The Wall Street Journal*, © Dow Jones & Company, Inc. (1981). All rights reserved.

Chapter 2 Datamation—for the article "Movies by Computer: No Actors, No Cameras." Reprinted with permission of DATAMATION ® magazine, © copyright by TECHNICAL PUBLISHING COMPANY, A DUN & BRADSTREET COMPANY (1979)—all rights reserved.

Chapter 3 The Wall Street Journal—for the article "Software Makers Lose Sales to Influx of Program Pirates" by Richard A. Shaffer. Reprinted with permission of *The Wall Street Journal*, © Dow Jones & Company, Inc. (1981). All rights reserved.

Chapter 4 The Redding Record Searchlight—for the article "Computer: Moore's Is Not Less." Reprinted by permission.

Chapter 5 The Argus—for the article "The Computer Learns Shorthand" by Steve Wright. Reprinted by permission.

Chapter 6 Computer Decisions—for the article "System Provides Sales Data." Reprinted from COMPUTER DECISIONS, May 1981, page 164. Copyright 1981, Hayden Publishing Company.

Chapter 7 Time—for the article "The Smash Hit of Software." Reprinted by permission from TIME, The Weekly Newsmagazine; Copyright Time Inc. 1981.

Chapter 8 Hitchcock Publishing Company—for the article "How to Be a Superprogrammer" by Edward Yourdon. Reprinted from *Infosystems*. Copyright Hitchcock Publishing Company. Used by permission.

Chapter 9 Associated Press—for the article in the *Sacramento Bee*, "Computer Commuter." Reprinted by permission from Wide World Photos Inc.

Chapter 10 Hitchcock Publishing Company—for the article "Magic Wand Comes of Age with New Uses." Reprinted from *Infosystems*, July 1981. Copyright Hitchcock Publishing Company. Used by permission.

Chapter 11 Popular Science—for the article "How Magnetic Bubbles Work" by Ray Pioch. Reprinted with permission from *Popular Science* © 1979, Times Mirror Magazines, Inc.

Chapter 12 Business Week—for the article "IBM Drops the Other Shoe—and the Industry Relaxes." Reprinted from the Dec. 1, 1980, issue of *Business Week* by special permission, © 1980 by McGraw-Hill, Inc., New York, N.Y. 10020. All rights reserved.

Chapter 13 Business Week—for the article "A Mainframe on Three Chips." Reprinted from the March 2, 1981, issue of *Business Week* by special permission, © 1981 by McGraw-Hill, Inc., New York, N.Y. 10020. All rights reserved.

Chapter 14 Business Week—for the article "AMOCO Credit Card Billing Coup." Reprinted from the May 14, 1979, issue of *Business Week* by special permission, © 1979 by McGraw-Hill, Inc., New York, N.Y. 10020. All rights reserved.

Chapter 15 Output—for the article "Systems Houses: An Option for Success." Reprinted by permission.

Chapter 16 Data Management—for the article "Electronic Copy Boy." Copyright DATA MANAGEMENT Magazine. ALL RIGHTS RESERVED.

Chapter 17 Business Week—for the article "Voice Mail Arrives in the Office." Reprinted from the June 9, 1980, issue of *Business Week* by special permission, © 1980 by McGraw-Hill, Inc., New York, N.Y. 10020. All rights reserved.

Chapter 18 Time—for the article "Small Computer Shootout." Reprinted by permission from TIME, The Weekly Newsmagazine; copyright Time Inc. 1981.

Chapter 19 Business Week—for the article "The Latest Robots Who's Who." Reprinted from the June 9, 1980, issue of *Business Week* by special permission, © 1980 by McGraw-Hill, Inc., New York, N.Y. 10020. All rights reserved.

Chapter 20 Associated Press—for the article in the *Sacramento Bee*, "Computer Codes Get Censors Edgy." Reprinted by permission from Wide World Photos, Inc.

Chapter 21 Computerworld—for the article "Accused Embezzler Had Record of DP Crime." Copyright 1982 by CW Communications Inc. Framingham, MA 01701—Reprinted from COMPUTERWORLD.

Supplement B Associated Press—for the article "Social Security's Decrepit Computers." Reprinted by permission from Wide World Photos, Inc.

Supplement D Business Week—for the article "A Company That Works at Home." Reprinted from *Business Week* by special permission, © 1981 by McGraw-Hill, Inc., New York, N.Y. 10020. All rights reserved.

PHOTOGRAPHS

Cover Melvin L. Prueitt/Los Alamos National Laboratory. Work performed under the auspices of the Department of Energy. **Page 1** Lawrence Livermore National Laboratory **2 top** Dunn Instruments **2 bottom** Photos courtesy of NASA **3 top** Edwin Strickland/U.S. Geological Survey **3 bottom** National Center for Atmospheric Research **4** Photos courtesy of Dunn Instruments, using a Dunn camera, Model 631 **5 top** ASEA, Inc. **5 bottom left** American Telephone & Telegraph **5 bottom right** Photo courtesy of IBM **6 top left** Melvin. L. Prueitt/Los Alamos National Laboratory. Work performed under the auspices of the Department of Energy. **6 top right** Courtesy of Bell Laboratories **6 bottom** Lawrence Livermore National Laboratory **7 top left** Melvin L. Prueitt/Los Alamos National Laboratory. Work performed under the auspices of the Department of Energy. **7 top right** Robert Langridge, Ph.D/Computer Graphics Laboratory, University of California, San Francisco **7 bottom** Melvin L. Prueitt/Los Alamos National Laboratory. Work performed under the auspices of the Department of Energy. **8 top left** Photo courtesy of IBM **8 center top** American Telephone & Telegraph **8 top right** Photo courtesy of IBM **8 bottom** American Telephone & Telegraph **12 top** Photo courtesy of IBM **12 center** Honeywell, Inc. **12 bottom** Photo courtesy of IBM **13 left** Photo courtesy of Hewlett-Packard **13 top right** Courtesy of Apple Computer Inc. **13 bottom right** Photo courtesy of IBM **14** Historical Pictures Service **22** Data General **23 top left** Photo courtesy of IBM **23 top right** Photo courtesy of IBM **23 bottom left** Photo courtesy of Texas Instruments Incorporated **23 bottom right** Photo courtesy of IBM **25** Photo courtesy of Hewlett-Packard **26** Honeywell, Inc. **40** Courtesy of Apple Computer Inc. **52** Melvin L. Prueitt/Los Alamos National Laboratory. Work performed under the auspices of the Department of Energy. **53 left** Lawrence Livermore National Laboratory **53 right** Courtesy of Aydin Controls, A division of Aydin Corporation **63** United Press International **90** Courtesy of Dartmouth College **134 top** Courtesy of John Backus **134 bottom** Courtesy of Irving Ziller **176** United Press International **200** Courtesy Trilogy Systems Corporation **209** Wide World Photos **210 top** Courtesy of Intel Corporation **210 center left** Courtesy of Bell Laboratories **210 bottom** Courtesy of Bell Laboratories **211 top right** Courtesy of Bell Laboratories **211 bottom right** Courtesy of Intel Corporation **219** Photo courtesy of IBM **221** Photo courtesy of Wang Laboratories, Inc. **222** NCR Corporation **225** Courtesy of Sperry Univac **226** Photo courtesy of IBM **228** Historical Pictures Service **230 233 top** NCR Corporation **233 bottom** Chatsworth Datacorp **234** Tektronix, Inc. **235** © Emilio Mercado/Jeroboam **236 top** The Teletype Corporation **236 bottom** Burroughs Corporation **238** Photo courtesy of IBM **239** NCR Corporation **240** NCR Corporation **241** Threshold Technology **263** Iowa State University Information Services **265** Courtesy of Intel Corporation **266** Courtesy of Intel Corporation **267** Courtesy of Intel Corporation **273** Courtesy of Sperry Univac **276** Photo courtesy of IBM **278** Photos courtesy of IBM **283** Photo courtesy of IBM **295 top** Photo courtesy of IBM **295 bottom** Photo courtesy of Hewlett-Packard **296** Courtesy of Intel Corporation **298** Photo courtesy of Texas Instruments Incorporated **299 top** Courtesy of Intel Corporation **299 bottom** Radio Shack, A division of Tandy Corporation **300** Photo courtesy of Hewlett-Packard Company **301** Courtesy of Intel Corporation **303** Photo courtesy of Hewlett-Packard Company **304 top** Digital Equipment Corporation **304 bottom left** Honeywell, Inc. **304 bottom right** Photo courtesy of Wang Laboratories, Inc. **306** Photo courtesy of Texas Instruments Incorporated **324 top** Tektronix, Inc. **324 bottom left** Photo courtesy of Hewlett-Packard Company **324 bottom right** Control Data Corporation **327 top left** Photo courtesy of IBM **327 top right** NCR Corporation **327 bottom** NCR Corporation **330 top** © Robert Vernon Wilson **330 bottom left** © Robert Vernon Wilson **330 bottom right** Photo courtesy of IBM **333** Printa Color Corporation **335** Photo courtesy of Xerox Corporation **336** Photos courtesy of Xerox Corporation **340** © Robert Vernon Wilson **342** Photos courtesy of Calcomp **350 top** NEC Informations Systems, Inc. **350 bottom** American Telephone & Telegraph **351 top left** American Telephone & Telegraph **351 center left** American Telephone & Telegraph **351 top right** American Telephone & Telegraph **351 bottom** NASA **378** Photo courtesy of IBM **379 top** Photo courtesy of IBM **379 bottom** National Center for Atmospheric Research **384** National Center for Atmospheric Research **388** © Robert Vernon Wilson **389** © Robert Vernon Wilson **390** © Robert Vernon Wilson **391 top** American Telephone & Telegraph **391 bottom** American Telephone & Telegraph **393** American Telephone & Telegraph **416 top** Courtesy of Bell Laboratories **416** Photos courtesy of IBM **424** Joan Sydlow/Business Week **447 top** Photos by Nixdorf Computer Corporation **447 bottom** TASS from Sovfoto **452 top** Wide World Photos **452 bottom** Wide World Photos **452–453 center** Courtesy of Lucasfilm Ltd., © Lucasfilm Ltd. 1977. **453 top** Chrysler Corporation **453 bottom** Advanced Robotics Corporation **457** NASA **458 top** The DeVilbiss Company **458 bottom** Photo courtesy of Texas Instruments Incorporated **490** Wide World Photos **491** Wide World Photos **506 top** © Dan MCoy/Rainbow **506–507 center** Centre de Recherches Biologiques Néonatales de l'Hôpital de Port-Royal à Paris/World Health Organization **506 bottom** © Leonard Freed/Magnum **507 top right** Dunn Instruments **507 center right** Photo courtesy of IBM **507 bottom** T. Farkas/World Health Organization

INDEX

General Index

The page number on which a term is defined is set in **boldface**.

ABA (American Bankers Association), 226
ABC (Atanasoff-Berry Computer), 263
Absolute privacy, 474
Absolute value function, 547
ABS(X), 139, 547
Abuses to computers and data, 495–497
Access, random, 278–284
Access time, 277
Accident, 496
Accounts receivable, **354**, 366
Acoustic coupler, **388**
Accumulator, **20**, 31, 61, 296
ACM, 188, 486
Action entry, **534**, 542
Action stub, **532**, 542
ADA language, 25, 421
Address, **198**–201, 254
Addressable memory locations, 254
Address register, 296
Ad Hoc Committee on The Triple Revolution, 464
Advanced Study, Institute of, 63
Advisory Committee on Automated Personal Data Systems, 484
AFIPS, 486
Agreements, 60
Aiken, Howard, 436
Albus, James S., 464
Alcohol, Tobacco & Firearms, Bureau of, 477
Algebra, Boolean, 14
ALGOL, 171
Algorithm, 56
  hashing, **284**, 289
  See also Flowchart
Alienation of workers, 466
Alphanumeric characters, **91**, 106, 126
Alphanumeric data, **11**, 91, 106, 126
Alphanumeric terminal, 320
ALU, **20**, 193

Amdahl, Carl, 434
Amdahl, Gene, 200, 434
Amdahl Corporation
  electron beam accessed memory development, 417
  470/V and 580 series—IBM compatibles, 200, 364, 434
  mainframe manufacturer, 200, 292, 311, 433
American Civil Liberties Union (ACLU), 486–487
American Council on Education, 491
American Federation of Information Processing Societies, 486
American Management Association (AMA), seminars on privacy, 486
American National Standard for Minimal BASIC, 546
American National Standards Committee X3J2, 546
American National Standards Institute (ANSI), 171, 172
American Telephone and Telegraph, 316, 434
Ames Research Center, 399
Amoco Oil Company, 347
Ampex, 434
Analyst, systems, **355**, 366
Analytic engine, 19, 24
AND, 118, 133
Anderson, Howard, 429
ANS, 172
ANSI. *See* American National Standards Institute
ANSI Minimal BASIC, 546–550
Aperature cards, 338
APL, 38
Apple computer, 13, 22, 40, 50, 302, 438, 450
Application packages, 440
Application programmer, 558, 561

Applied Data Research, 441
APT, 170
Archival memory, 268
Arctangent function, 547
Argument, **138**, 165
Arithmetic, 194
  parallel, **260**
  serial, **260**
Arithmetic/logic unit (ALU), **20**, 193, 195, 295, 373
Arithmetic operators, 87
Arizona State Finance Center, inadvertent destruction of data, 497
ARPA network, 399
Array, **118**, 145, 165, 510
  declaration, 106, 549
  double, **145**, 165
  single, **145**, 165
  triple, **145**, 165
Arrest records, 480
Ascending sort, 12
ASCII-8, 273. *See also* 8-bit ASCII notation
ASEA Inc., 457
Assembler languages, 37–38
Assembly robot, 471
Association for Computing Machinery (ACM), in-service education, 486
Asterisk (*), 87
Asynchronous modems, 387
Atanasoff-Berry Computer (ABC), 263
Atanasoff, John, 263
Atari computer, 438, 450
Atlantic Richfield Corporation, 334
ATM. *See* Automated teller machine
ATN(X), 139, 547
ATP. *See* Automatic telephone payments
Attrition, 461
Audio responder, **343**
Audio response devices, **342**
Auditing, 366

582

Auditing procedures, 500
Auditor, 561
Audit trail, 500
AUTOCODER, 38
Automated clearinghouses, 243
Automated Data Processing, Inc., 440, 444
Automated teller machine (ATM), **237**
Automated warehouse, 456
Automatic telephone payments (ATP), 237
Automation
   coping of businesses, 468
   coping of educational institutions, 468
   coping of government, 468
   coping of labor groups, 468
   Diebold, John, 456
   economic impact of, 460
   feedback, 456
   Harder, D. S., 456
   impact on employment, 457–462
   impact on lifestyles, 467
   instructions, 456
   and productivity, 464
   sociopsychological impact, 465
   worker attitude, 465
   worker experience, 466

Babbage, Charles, 24, 35
Background memory, **380**
Backup, **280,** 289
Backus, J. W., 135
Baker, Michael A., 486
BAL, **38**
Bal, Subhash, 317
Ball printers, **329**
Band printer, **327**
Bank of America, 444
Bar code, 246
   Universal Product Code (UPC), 239
Bar graph, 117
Barron, C. B., 435
Barton, William, 450
Base, **256**
BASIC, **26**–31, 82–165, 546–550
   statement, 82
   See also DEF; DIM; FOR; GOSUB; GOTO; IF; LET; NEXT; PRINT; READ; THEN
Batch processing, **214,** 372
   job control language, **374**
   remote job entry, **375**
Bates, Keith G., 102
Bauer, William E., 347
Baxter, Norman, 412
BCD. *See* Binary Coded Decimal
Beeby, Patrick, 348
Beginners Allpurpose Symbolic Instruction Code. *See* BASIC
Bell, Alexander Graham, 392
Bell Telephone Co. of Pennsylvania, 428
Bell Telephone Laboratories, 267, 316, 392
   development of fiber optics, 425
Berry, Clifford, 263
BESM-6 Soviet computer, 446
Best, David P., 316
Bias magnetic, 270
Bifurcated, **534,** 542

Billings, Major John Shaw, 228
Binary, 254
Binary Coded Decimal (BCD), **258**
   4-bit notation, **259**
Binary digit (bit), **254**
Binary number system, **254**
Binary synchronous communications protocol (bisynch), **397**
Bisynch, **397**
Bit (binary digit), 14, 21, 254
Bits per word, 297, 303, 308
Blackjack, 80
Blauner, Robert, 466
Block, **274**
Block diagram. *See* Flowchart
Blocking factor, **275,** 289
Blue collar workers, 461
Bobeck, Andrew H., 267
Boeing Computer Services, 307, 442, 444
Bohn, Corrado, 106
Boole, George, 14, 21
Boolean operator, **118,** 133
Booz, Allen, and Hamilton, telecommunication traffic study, 459
BOT (beginning of tape), **274**
BPI, **273,** 289
Bradford National Corp., 444
Brain, human, 252
Brainerd, Captain, 494
Bricklin, Daniel, 168
Browstein, Neill H., 429
Bubble generator, 270
Bubble memory. *See* Magnetic bubble memory
Buchsbaum, Solomon J., 316
Buffers, memory, **253**
Bunker Ramo Corp., 444
Bureau of Labor Statistics, 361
Burkhardt, G. William, 428
   character recognition, 348
   flat panel display, 324
Burks, Arthur W., 68
Burroughs Corporation, 13
   B6805, 199
   B6900, 364
   mainframe manufacturer, 307, 311
   market share, (*table*) 433
   microcomputer manufacturer, 438
Bus; address, data, control, 295
Busicom Corp., 301
BYE, 92
Byte, **21,** 254
Byte Shop computer stores, 444
Bytes per inch (BPI), **273,** 289

Caesar, Julius, 159
Calculation, **11,** 16
Calendar, Gregorian, 159
   Julian, 159
California Law Enforcement Telecommunication System (CLETS), 402
Cambridge University, development of the EDSAC computer, 415
Captions, printing, 88, 93, 95
CARD, **12**
Card magnetic strip, 237
Card, punched, **216**
Card reader, **23**
Cards per minute (CPM), 22, 218

Career ladder, 556
Carnegie Technological Institute, 399
Carrier, communication, **391**
Carter administration, blocked IRS system, 476
Cartridge disk, 278
CAT, 92
Cathode ray tube (CRT), **25,** 235
   advantages, 236
   alphanumeric, **320**
   functional parts, 320
   terminal, 236
CCD. *See* Charged-coupled device
CCITTV24 Standard, 390
Cenco, Inc., fraud case, 495
Censorship of encryption theories, 489
Census Bureau, U.S., 288, 497
Central Intelligence Agency (CIA), exclusion from disclosure of record systems, 485
Central processing units (CPU), **20**–22, 373
Centralization, **552,** 561
Centronics Corp., 434
Chain file, **284,** 289
Chain printers, **284,** 289, 327
Channel allocating mechanism, 399
Channel communication, 391
Character-at-a-time printers, 331
Character recognition system, 347
Characters
   in ANSI Minimal BASIC, 546
   per second (CPS), **220,** 327
Charged-coupled device (CCD), **266**
   trends and development, 417
Check bit. *See* Parity check bit
Check characters, **397**
Check digits, 498
Cheh, Mary, 490
Chief programmer, 188
Chip, **264**
CII-HB, 445, 446
Cincinnati Milachron T-3 robot, 457
Cincom Systems, Inc., 440, 441
Circle, 88
Clearinghouse automation, 243
CLETS, 402
CMC. *See* Computer Machinery Corporation
Coast Guard, U.S., 477
Coaxial cable, 391
COBOL, 26, 38, 82, **171**–176, 558
   comparison with other languages, 180–185
   sample program, 174–175
   structured program, 173
CODASYL, 176
Code, Hollerith, 217
Codes, 498
Coding
   form, 83, 85
   program writing, 199
COGO, 171
Columns
   on 80-column card, 217
COM. *See* Computer output microfilm
Comma, 88, 90, 112
Command, System, **91,** 546
Commodore International, Ltd., 302, 438, 450

INDEX 583

Commodore International, Ltd., *(continued)*
  PET personal computer, 449
Common Business Oriented Language. *See* COBOL
Communication controller, 223
Communication media capacities, *(table)* 394
Communications protocol, 396
COMPASS, 38
Comparison, **195**
  of micro, mini, and mainframe computers, 312
Compiler, **39,** 46, 171
Compressing tables, 537–540
Compression Labs Inc., 430
CompuServe Inc., 424
Computer assisted fraud (CAF), 495
Computer cook, 414
Computer data notation systems, 258
Computer industry in United States, 432–445
  computing services, 440
  dominated by IBM, 433
  exodus of manufacturers, 433
  facilities management, 443
  mainframe computer manufacturers, 433
  market shares, *(table)* 433, 438, 439, 441
  microcomputer manufacturers, 438
  minicomputer manufacturers, 434
  network information services, 339, 441
  number of computers in use, 432
  percent of GNP, 432
  peripheral device manufacturers, 434
  semiconductor manufacturers, 438
  service bureaus, 440
  software services, 439
  utilities, 441
Computer industry in USSR, 446
Computerized Criminal History (CCH) file, arrest records, 480
Computerized files, *(table)* 475
Computerized robot, 471
Computerland retail store, 444
Computer logic and storage trends, 415
Computer Machinery Corporation, 434
Computer maid, 414
Computer memory, addresses, 193. *See also* Memory
Computer network. *See* Networks
Computer-on-a-chip, 13, 298
Computer operator, **559,** 561
Computer output microfilm (COM), **337**
  advantages and disadvantages, 340
  trends and developments, 418
Computer programming, 26–32
  decision tables, 532–542
Computers
  personal, 422
  See also Central processing unit; Disk; Flowchart; Hardware instructions; Hobby computer; Input, device; Language, programming; Output, devices; Secondary storage; Tape; Terminal
Computer Sciences Corporation, software services, 307, 442, 444
Computer security, 494
  improvements, 497

Computer stores, 444
Computer-Tabulating-Recording Company, 228, 436
Computer terminals. *See* Terminal
Computer utilities. *See* Network information services.
Computerworld, 561
Computing services, 440
Comshare Inc., 424
Conditional transfer, 94, 100
Condition entry, **533,** 542
Condition name, **534**
Condition stub, **532,** 542
Conference on Data System Languages (CODASYL), 176
Connector symbol, **67, 88**
Connector, 25,
  pin, 389
Constants in BASIC, 547
Continue, 171
Continuous form paper, 326
Contract programming, 440
Control break, 126
Control card and file specification, 177–181
Control characters, 396
Control Data Corporation (CDC), 13, 38, 437, 444
  computer stores, 445
  electron beam accessed memory development, 417
  imports a Soviet Ryad, 446
  mainframe manufacturer, 307, 311
  market share, *(table)* 433
  PLATO, 324
Controller, cathode ray tube, 25, 360
Control statements in BASIC, 548
Control structure, 106–108
Control unit, **20,** 193–203, 295, 373
  CRT, 321
Conversion
  direct, **366**
  parallel, **366**
Conversion methods
  binary to decimal, 257
  decimal to binary, 257
Coping with automation; business, education, government, labor groups, 468
Core, 34
Cornwell, George, 435
Corwin, Ed, 436
Cosine function, 547
Cost mix of hardware and software, trends and developments, 422
Cost of loss vs. cost of security, 497
Cost of programming, 180–185
COS(X), 139, 547
Counter, 29, **63,** 126
CPM. *See* Cards per minute
CPS. *See* Characters per second
CPU, **20**
Cray Research, Inc., mainframe manufacturer, 311, 433
Creative Strategies International, 316
CRT, 25, 360. *See also* Cathode ray tube
CRT control unit, 320
Cryogenic memory, 267
Cryptography, 489
CU, **20.** *See also* Control unit
Cullinane Corp., 307, 441

Cursor, 321
Cylinder, **277,** 289

Daisy wheel printer, 329
Dartmouth College, 82, 90, 101, 392
Data, **11,** 28, 86, 87, 108–111
  alphanumeric, **11**
  collection, 360
  division, **173**
  files, 43, 374
  name, **173**
  numeric, **11**
  random access, 275–288
  sequential access, 272–275, 279, 280
Databanks, 476
  impact on individual privacy, 476
Database, **284,** 286–288, 363, 364
Database administrator, **557,** 561
Database Management System. *See* DBMS
Database services, 424
Datachecker Co., 247
Data communications
  alternatives, 399–401
  devices, 423
  terminals, 385
  trends and developments, 424, 562
Data division, **173,** 186
Data entry operator, **559,** 561
Data flow line, 374
Data flow systems, 404
  off line, **405**
  on line, **407**
  real time, **407**
Data General, 13, 22, 437
Data notation systems, 258
Datapoint Corp., 428
Data preparation
  with cassettes/cartridges, 221
  devices, 221–224
  error minimizing, 216
  validation, **94,** 118, 221, 279
  verification, **94,** 118, 221, 279
Data processing, **11**
  applications. *See* "Index of Business Applications"
  data, **11,** 28
  information, **11,** 28
  See also Computers
Data Processing Management Association (DPMA), inservice education, 486
Dataproducts Corp., 434
Dataquest Inc., 316
Data register, 295
Data statement, 86, 100, 108–111
DATA Terminal Systems, 247
Datotek Corporation, encoding system, 498
Davida, George, 490
DBMS (Data Base Management System), **284,** 286–288, 300, 305, 310, 364, 420
DEC (Digital Equipment Corporation), 13
Decentralized, **553,** 555, 561
Decimal-binary gap, 256
Decimal point, 256
Decimal systems, 256

584 INDEX

Decision
  flowchart symbol, **65**
  IF, **94,** 100, 112–118, 141, 148, 163
Decision making in validation, **94,** 118, 279
Decision table, **532–542**
Declaration section, **176**
DEF, **140,** 165
Default options, **177**
Defense, Department of, 496
Defense Advanced Research Project Agency (ARPA), 399
Defense-Intelligence Agency, 477
Delaware Port Authority, 247
Delta Air Lines, 247
Demodulation, 387
Density, **272,** 289
Descending sort, 12
Destructive input, **199**
Developer, microfilm, 340
Diebold, John, 414
Digital Equipment Corp., 9, 13, 301, 302, 368, 437, 445
Digitizer, 233
DIM, **119,** 133, 140, 165, 549
Direct access, **283,** 289
  memory, 262
  in virtual memory system, 384
Direct conversion, **366**
Direct costs, 216
Directory, 281
Disclosure of personal data, under Fair Credit Reporting Act, 482, 484
Disk, 25, 272, 275–278, 289
  fixed, **276,** 289
  floppy, **277,** 289
  head per track, **277,** 289
  pack, 223, 276
  removable, **276,** 289
  sector, **275,** 289
  time sharing/swapping, 380
  track, **275,** 289
  virtual memory system, 384
Display devices, visual, 320
Distributed processing, 306, 403
Divisions (COBOL), **173,** 186
Documentation, **112,** 173, 366, 499
Document reader/sorter, OCR, 230
Document symbol, **57**
Documents, human-readable, 216
DO loop, 171
Dot matrix printer, **328**
Double arrays, **145,** 165
Dow Jones Databank, 442
DPMA. *See* Data Processing Management Association
Drum, 278
  plotter, **342**
  printers, **328**
Dummy argument, **138**–140, 165
Duplicator, microfilm, 340
Dymo Industries, 347
Dynamic partitioning, **379**

Eastern bloc countries, computer manufacturing, 446
Eastman Kodak, 434
Easton, A. Terrence, 428
EBAM. *See* Electron beam accessed memory

EBCDIC. *See* Extended Binary Coded Decimal Interchange Code
Eckert, J. Presper, 264, 436
Editing command, **91**
EDP (electronic data processing), 189
EDSAC, 36, 415
Education, U.S. Department of, 477
Educational attainment of employed persons, 461
EDVAC, 63
EFT. *See* Electronic funds transfer
Egoless programming, 188
EIA, 389
8-bit ASCII notation (ASCII-8), **259**
8-bit EBCDIC notation, 260
Electron beam accessed memory (EBAM), 267, 417
Electronic Communications Systems, Inc., 428
Electronic data processing. *See* EDP
Electronic funds transfer (EFT), 241
Electronic Funds Transfer Act, 242
Electronic Industries Association (EIA), 389
Electronic information services, 424
Electronic mail, 428
Electrostatic printer, 333
Eliminating redundancy, 537, 542
ELSE, **539,** 542
Employment projections, through 1985, 462
Encoder, magnetic ink, 226
END, **88,** 91, 100, 171, 548
End-of-data sentinel, **72,** 108, 125
ENIAC, 264, 301, 436, 494
Entry
  action, **534,** 542
  condition, **534,** 542
Environment division, **173**
EOT (end of tape), **274**
Equifax credit rating bureau, 479
Equity Funding Life Insurance Company, fraud case of, 495
Error checking, 385
Error minimizing, 216
Errors in credit data, 479
Espionage, 496
  vulnerable areas, 496
Ethical controls, 500
Evaluation, 87
Even parity, 259
Execute, **30,** 91, 100, 142
  cycle, **202,** 206
  program, **201,** 202
Exponential function, 547
Exponents, **87,** 88, 100
Expressions, in BASIC, 547
EXP(X), 139, 547
Extended BASIC, 93
Extended Binary Coded Decimal Interchange Code (EBCDIC), 260, 261, 273
Extended entry, **538,** 542
External storage, **12,** 25, 196. *See also* Secondary storage
Exxon Corporation, 324

Facilities management (FM), 443
Faggin, Frederico, 301
Fail safe computer, 477

Fairchild, microcomputer manufacturer, 438
Fair Credit Reporting Act of 1970 (FCRA), 479, 482
Fair information practices, 484
Farmworkers employment, 461
Federal Aviation Agency, 477
Federal Bureau of Investigation (FBI)
  personal data files, 476, 477, 480
  surveillance, 482
Federal Computer System Protection Act proposal, 502
Federal Law Enforcement Assistance Administration (LEAA), 474
Feedback phase of automation, 456
Fetch, **202,** 206
Fiber optics, 424
Field, **43,** 47, 217, 252
File, **285,** 287, 363
  chain, **284,** 289
  creation, 149–158
  hierarchical, **284,** 289
  list, **284,** 289
  master, 45, **280,** 289
  merging, 149, **541,** 542
  section, 173
  sequential, **279,** 289
  sorting, 150
  transaction, 43, **280,** 289
  update, 156–158
File extension, 181, 186
Filmware, trends and developments, 419
Fixed disk, **276,** 289
Fixed-word-length computer, **254**
  notation, 260
Flatbed plotters, 372
Flat panel display, 322–325
Flexible magnetic disk, 221
Floating point, **118.** *See also* Real number
Floppy disk, 221, **277,** 289
Florida Crime Information Center (FCIC), 478
Flowchart, **56**
  control break, 130
  decision table, **532–542**
  discounting, 98
  pseudocode, 58, 60
  rules, 67
  symbolic, **59**
  system, **45,** 364
  template, **70**
  validation, 94
Flowchart symbols
  connector, **67,** 88
  decision, **65,** 92, 94
  disk, 281
  document, **57,** 88
  flowline, **57**
  input/output, **57,** 88, 92
  manual input, 92
  preparation, **63,** 84–86
  processing, **57,** 83, 87
  tape, 45, 279
  terminal, **57,** 83, 90
  system, 43–47
Flow diagrams, 63
Flowline, **57**
FOR, **28,** 84, 100, 107, 548
  loops, 89, 100
  multiple 89, 100
  nested, 89, 100

INDEX   585

FOR (*continued*)
   single, 89, 100
Foreground memory, **380**
FORMAT, 171
FORTH, 170
FORTRAN, **26,** 38, 82, 135, 170, 186
   comparison with other languages, 180–185
   sample program, 172
   statements, 171
4-bit notation, **258,** 261
Frame, **273,** 289
   microfilm, 338
Frankstone, Robert, 168
Fraud, 495
   Cenco Inc. case, 495
   Equity Funding Life Insurance Company case, 495
Freedom of Information Act (FOIA), 485
Free form, 177–186
Friedman, Georges, 466
Fujitsu, 267, 445
Full duplex, 392
Function, **138,** 165, 547
Functional parts, **20,** 192

Gains and losses in occupational groups, (*table*) 462
Gantt chart, 365
General Accounting Office (GAO), 476
General Electric Corporation, 399, 417, 434, 442, 444
   electron beam accessed memory development, 417
   networks information services, 444
G.E. time share, 399
Ghertman, Jean, 436
Gilchrist, Bruce, 456
Godlike image of computer, 477
Goldstine, Herman, 63, 264
GOSUB, 548
Gotleib, Calvin, 468
GOTO, **94,** 100, 458
GPSS, **177**
Grange Mutual Insurance Co., 338
Graphics display, 32, 332
Graphics terminals, 320, 322
Gray-bar, 325
Gregorian calendar, **159,** 165
Gross national product (GNP), projections by James S. Albus, 464

Half duplex, 393
Handler, tape, 273
Hard copy, 325
Harder, D. S., 456
Hardware instructions, **197,** 206
Hardwired, 386
Hashing algorithm, **284,** 298
HDLC, 397
Head per track, 277, 289
Header, **532,** 542
Health, Education, and Welfare Department. *See* U.S. Department of Health, Education, and Welfare
Hewlett Packard Corporation, 302, 316, 450
   bar code reader, 248

CRT, 25
   personal computer, 438
   3000 computer, 13, 277, 364, 437
Hexadecimal number system, 257
Hierarchical DBMS, **286,** 289
   file, **284,** 289
Hierarchy chart, 107, 177
Highest value determination, 75
High-level languages, **38,** 170–183
History of computers, 14, 24, 40, 63, 90, 135, 166, 176, 200, 228, 263, 264, 283, 301, 392, 435
Hitachi, 445, 451
Hobby computer, 13, 22, 40, 50, 93
Hoerrman, Oskar, 436
Hoff, Marcian Edward "Ted," Jr., 301
Hoffman, L. P., 466
Hollerith code, 216, 217
Hollerith, Herman, 228, 436
Home computer, 13, 22, 40, 50, 93
Honeywell Corporation, 13, 292, 437
   mainframe manufacturer, 307, 311, 364
   market share, (*table*) 433
Hoos, Ida, 466
Hopper, Captain Grace, 176
Household computer, 414
Houston Chronicle, 410
Human brain, contrasted with computer memory, 252

IBG (interblock gap), **274,** 289
IBM (International Business Machines Corp.), 13, 25, 188, 247, 450
   bisynch protocol, 397
   computer stores, 445
   H-series, 291
   laser electrophotographic printer, 335
   magnetic bubble memory, 267
   market share, (*table*) 307, 311
   SDLC communication protocol, 397
   Selectric typewriter, 330
   64K-bit chip, 295
   System 1, 437
   System 3, 178
   System 32, 178
   System 34, 178
   System 38, 178
   System 305, 283
   System 704, 262, 415
   System 360/370, 36, 197, 200, 277, 415
   System 3030, 12, 91, 136, 291, 364, 434
   System 4300, 291
   029 keypunch, 219
Identification division, **173,** 186
Identifier
   standard universal, 481
   universal, 481
IF
   BASIC, **94,** 100
   COBOL, 173
   FORTRAN, 171
   Pascal, 178
   PL/1, 177, 179
IMAGE, 120, 133, 171, 369, 530
Impact printers, 325–330
Implementation, 364
Increment, 28, 84, 100, 107

Independent computer peripheral equipment manufacturers (ICPEMs), 434
Index, 63, **119,** 133, 145, 157, 159
Indexed sequential, **281,** 282, 289
Index page, microfiche, 339
Indicator, **195,** 206
Individual privacy, 474, 475
Industrial robots, 471
Infallibility, aura of, 478
Information, **11,** 16
   privacy, 475
   retrieval service, 442
   revolution, 476
   See also Data
Initialize, **61, 120,** 133
Input, **12**
   BASIC, **92,** 100, 141, 549
   circuit, **199,** 206
   device, **12,** 16
Input buffer, **253**
Input control, 385
Input device, **12,** 16, 215
   selection criteria, 214
Input/output devices, **22,** 31, 214, 374
   trends, 417
Input/output, flowcharting symbol, 57
Input specification, **179,** 186
Institute for Advanced Studies, Princeton University, 63
Instruction, **197,** 202
   execute, **202**
   fetch, **202**
   macro, **203**
   micro, **203**
Instruction phase of automation, 456
INT, **138,** 157, 165
Integer, **138,** 157, 165
Integer function, 547
Integrated circuit, 294
Intel Corporation, 40
   computer on a chip, 301
   mainframe on 3 chips, 315
   microcomputer manufacturer, 438
Intelligent terminals, **304**
Interactive
   terminal, 236
   programming, 320
Interblock gab, **274,** 289
Interface device, 223, 303, 388
Internal Revenue Service (IRS)
   personal data files, 476
   proposed network, 476
Internal security mechanisms
   check digits, 498
   documentation, 499
   encoding, 498
   sequence checks, 499
International Business Machines. *See* IBM
International computer industry, 445
International Telephone and Telegraph Consultative Committee (CCITT), 390
Interpreter, **39,** 47
Interrupt, **380**
INT(X), 547
Invasion of privacy, **474**
Inverted file, **285,** 289
I/O, **25,** 31
Iowa State College, 263

IRS. *See* Internal Revenue Service
ISAM (Index Sequential Access Method), **281,** 282, 289

Jackets, microfilm, 338
Jacopini, Guiseppe, 106
Jacquard, Joseph Marie, 228
JCL (Job Control Language), **91,** 100, 374
Job description, **554,** 561
Jobs, Steve, 40, 450
Johnson, Lyndon B., 464
Josephson, Brian, electrical flow theory, 415
JOVIAL, 171
Julian calendar, **159**–165

KB (kilobytes or thousands of bytes), **21,** 31
Kemeny, John G., 90
Key-disk. *See* Key-to-flexible disk
Keypunch, **22,** 217
Keystation, 223
Key-to-cartridge, 221
Key-to-cassette, 221
Key-to-flexible disk, 221
Key-to-tape, 221
Keyword, **82**
KILL, 91
King, Dr. Martin Luther, surveillance by FBI, 482
KOPS, 308, 312
KSAM (Key Sequential Access Method), 282
Kurtz, Thomas E., 90

Labor Statistics, Bureau of, 461
Language, programming
 assembler, **37,** 47
 comparison of, 170–186
 high-level, **38,** 47
 machine, **36,** 201
 object, **201,** 206
 problem-oriented, **38**
 selection, 180–186
 See also ALGOL; APL; ATS; AUTO-CODER; BAL; BASIC; COBOL; COGO; COMPASS; FORTRAN; GPSS; JOVIAL; NEAT/3; PLATO; RPG; SIMSCRIPT; SPS
Languages, trends and developments, 420
Language translators
 assembler, **37,** 47
 compiler, **39,** 47, 171
 interpreter, **39,** 47
Large-scale integrated circuits (LSIC), 264, **294**
Large-scale integration (LSI), 264
Laser beam memory, 268
Laser electrophotographic printer, 335
Laser printer, 335
Latency, 276
LEAA. *See* Federal Law Enforcement Assistance Administration
Leader, **274,** 289
LEN, 139
LET, **28,** 83, 87, 100, 140, 548

Library function, **138,** 165
Life-styles of worker, 466
Light pen,
 OCR, 230
Limit checks, 65
Limited entry, **538,** 542
Line-at-a-time printers, 12, 23, **25,** 325, 331
Line configurations, 394, 396
Line number, **82,** 100
Lines per minute (LPM), 12
 contrasted with characters per second (CPS), 327
List, **284,** 289
Little, Arthur D., Inc.
 electronic funds transfer study, 243
 forecast of DBMS structure, 420
Loading, **201**
Load point. *See* BOT
Locations, memory, **59,** 197, 254
LOG(X), 139, 547
Loneliness of workers, 467
Loop, **62,** 84, 107, 510
 counter, **63,** 85
 multiple, 89
 nested, 89
 overlapping, 89
Looping, **62,** 510
Loss of privacy, **474**
Lovelace, Ada, 24, 34, 494
LPM. *See* Lines per minute
LSIC. *See* Large-scale integrated circuits
Luke, Hugh D., 466

Machine codes, 214
Machine dependent, 36, 47
Machine independent, **38,** 47
Machine language, **36,** 47, 201
Macroinstruction, **203,** 206
Macroprogramming, **203**–206
Magnetic bubble memory **266,** 270
 trends and developments, 417
Magnetic cartridge. *See* Tape
Magnetic cassette. *See* Tape
Magnetic core memory. *See* Core, planar memory
Magnetic disk. *See* Disk
Magnetic drum, 278
Magnetic ink character reader, 226
Magnetic ink character recognition (MICR), 225, 226
Magnetic ink encoder, 226
Magnetic media, 221
Magnetic printers, 333
Magnetic strip card, 237
Magnetic tape. *See* Tape
Magnovox Corporation, PLATO, 324
Magnuson Corp., 311, 434
Mail sorter, 241
Mainframe computer, 291, 307, 315, 433
Manager of computer services department, **556,** 561
Mann, F. C., 466
Marconi, Guglielmo, 392
Mark I, 436
Marker, **274,** 289
Market share, minicomputer manufacturers, 438
Markkula, A. C., 40

Massachusetts criminal history file, 480
Mass storage unit, **278,** 289
 in time sharing swapping, 380
Master Card, computer output microfilm, 338
Master file, **45,** 154, 156, 165
Master file update, **45,** 149, 280, 289, 527, 530
 random, **280**–287
 sequential, **272**–280
Matrix printer, **328**
Mauchly, John, 264
Memorex
 independent computer peripheral manufacturer, 434
Mean time between failures (MTBF), **215**
 IBM 704, 415
Mechanization, **456**
Media readers, 225
Medium, **214,** 320
Memory, **12,** 20, 193, 197, 373
 access time, 12
 addresses, 198–201, 254
 archival, 268
 background, 380
 charged-coupled device (CCD), 226
 circuitry, 192–199
 core, 34
 cryogenic, 267
 electron beam accessed memory (EBAM), 267
 foreground, 380
 interleaving, 308
 locations, 59
 magnetic bubble, 266, 270
 magnetic core, 34
 read only, **205,** 206
 semiconductor, **21,** 23
 types, 263
 under development, 267, 268, 415
 virtual, 384
Memory of computer, contrasted with human brain, 252
Merging, 149, **541,** 542
Message, 199–206
Michael, Donald N., 456
MICR. *See* Magnetic ink character recognition
Microcode, 419
Microcomputer, 13, 22, 80, 294, 355, 415
 configurations, 298
 industry, 438
 memory capacity, 298
 personal computer, 13, 22, 40, 50
 prices, 300
 processor speed, 299
 software, 299
 sources, 300
 uses, 300
Microcomputer system, **298**
Microfiche, **338**
Microfilm, 337
 forms overlay, 341
 projection recording technologies, 340
 recorder, 341
Micromainframe computer, 315
Microprocessor, **294,** 295, 315
Microprogramming, **203**–206
Microwave relay, 391
Millions of instructions per second, 308, 312

Minicomputer, **13,** 93, 302
  bits per word, 303
  configurations, 303
  costs, 305
  data base management systems, 305, 364
  HP 3000, 13
  manufacturers, 13, 307, 364
  memory capacities, 304
  processor speed, 304
  sales, 437
  software, 305, 306
  uses, 307
Mini-floppy disk, 298
Minimal BASIC, 545
Minus (−), **87**
MIPS, 308, 312
Mitsubishi Electric, 451
Mixed entry, **538,** 542
Mnemonic, **37,** 47
Modem, 371, 386
Modes of processing, 372–408
Modulation, 387
Module, **107,** 173
Monitor, display unit, 321
Monotony of workers, 466
Moore School of Electrical Engineering, 264
Morse, Samuel, 392
Mostek, microcomputer manufacturer, 438
Motorola, microcomputer manufacturer, 438
Moving, **194,** 206
MTBF. *See* Mean time between failures
Multics computer, 496
Multiple loops, 89, 510
Multiplexing, 393, 399
Multiprocessing, **383**
Multiprogramming
  background memory, **380**
  foreground memory, **380**
  interrupt, **380**
  segments or overlays, **380**
  spooling, **383**
Multistation data preparation devices, **223**
Multistation devices, 392

Nanodata, 434
National Advanced Systems, 433
National Cash Register (NCR)
  and Thomas Watson, 435
  mainframe manufacturer, 433
  market share, (*table*) 433
National Crime Information Center (NCIC), 402
National Data Corp., 444
National Mutual Fund (NMF) proposed, 464
National Retail Merchants Association (NRMA), 240
National Science Foundation electronic funds transfer study, 243
National Security Agency, 489
National Semiconductor Corp.
  micros, 438
  speech synthesis, 249
Natural logarithm function, 547
Naville, Pierre, 466

NCIC. *See* National Crime Information Center
NCR (National Cash Register Corporation), 13, 36, 247, 307, 311, 433, 437, 444
  8200, 12
NEAT/3, 38
NEC. *See* Nippon Electric
Nested loops, **89,** 100, 107–111
Network communication
  channels, **399**
  circuits, **399**
  links, **399**
Network information services (NIS), 441
Networks, 399
  ARPA, 399
  California Law Enforcement Telecommunication System (CLETS), 402
  channel allocating mechanism, 399
  DBMS, **286,** 289
  G.E. time share, 399
  multiplexer, 399
  National Crime Information Center (NCIC), 402
  nodes, **399**
  Tymnet, 399
NEW, 92
NEXT, **29,** 88, 100, 548
Nippon Electric, 445, 451
Nixdorf, 445
Non-destructive output, **199,** 206
Nonimpact printers, 325–335
Nonvolatile storage, **262**
NOT, 108, 113
Notation systems, 254, 257
Noyce, Robert N., 301
Numeric data, **11,** 16, 216

Object language, **201**–206
Object program, **36,** 47, 201, 206
Obsolete credit data, 484
Occupational groups, gains and losses 1960–1976, (*table*) 462
Occupational mobility, **462**
OCR. *See* Optical character recognition
OCR-A, 22
  type font, 230
Odd parity, 259
Office of the future, 459
Off-line processing, **405**
OMR. *See* Optical mark recognition
ON, 548
On-line
  processing, 214, 407
  storage device, 374
Op code, **199,** 206
Open ended, **539,** 542
Operand, **36**
Operating system (OS), 373, 384
  programs, 254
  trends and developments, 420
Operation, **36,** 47
Operational and procedural security measures, 499
Operators
  arithmetic, **87,** 100
  boolean, **118,** 133
  relational, **94,** 100
Optical character recognition (OCR), **227**
  document reader/sorter, 230

  trends and developments, 417
  type fonts, 230
Optical mark recognition (OMR), **232**
  reader, 233
Option, 549
OR, 113, 118
  control, 385
  requirements, 359
  selection criteria, 320
OS (operating system), 373
Output, **12,** 199
  devices, **12,** 23, 214, 320
  specification, **179,** 186
Oval, 83
Overlays, **380**
  forms, 341
Owens-Illinois Glass Company, PLATO, 324

Pack, disk, 276
Paper tape. *See* Punched paper tape
Parallel arithmetic, **260**
Parallel conversion, **366**
Parallelogram, 86
Parallel transmission, 295
Parenthesis, 87
Parity, **259**
  even, 259
  odd, 259
Parity check bit, **259,** 273, 289
Parker, Donn, prudent person theory, 497
Partitioning, **379**
Pascal, 38, 176, 186
PDP. *See* Digital Equipment Corporation
PERFORM, 173
Personal computer, 13, 40, 50, 300, 422
Personal data in federal files, 477
PET computer, 450
Photodigital memory, **268**
Photoelectric cells, OCR reader, 227
Physical security, 497
Place value, 256
Plasma display, 324
PLATO. *See* Programmed learning and teaching operation
PL/1, 38, **177,** 186
Plotters, 342
  digital increment, **342**
  drum, **342**
  flatbed, **342**
  pen movement, 343
Plug-to-plug compatible devices, 292, 434
Plus (+), **87**
Pointer, **284,** 289
Point-of-sale (POS) terminals, 238
  advantages and disadvantages, 240
  in France and Switzerland, 447
POL. *See* Problem-oriented language
Portable terminals, 410
POS. *See* Point-of-sale terminals
Positional value, 256
Powers, James, 228
Powers Tabulating Company, 228
Precedence order, 57, **87,** 100
Preparation symbol, **63**
  for looping, 84, 85, 107, 108
Primary memory, **12,** 16
Prime computer, 13

PRINT, **28,** 88, 100, 146, 549
Print media
   continuous form card stock, 326
   continuous form paper, 325
   multi-part paper, 326
   no-carbon-required (NCR) paper, 326
   preprinted forms, 325
   stock tab, 325
Print using, 120, 133
Printer characteristics, (*table*) 331
Printer comparisons, (*table*) 331
Printer output, 325
Printer output devices
   advantages and disadvantages, 336
   character-at-a-time printers, 331
   image transfer methods, 326
   impact printers, 326–331
   line-at-a-time printers, 12, 23, 331
   nonimpact, 332–337
   printing terminals, 236
   serial printer, 331
   spacing chart, 359
Printing terminals, 236
Privacy, 473–491
   absolute, **474**
   Act of 1974 (PA74), 484
   individual, **474**
   of information, **475**
   invasion of, **474**
   loss of, **474**
   protection, **482**
   publications, **486**
   relative, **475**
   self-regulation by business, **486**
   social, **474**
   threats to, **475**
Privacy Act of 1974, 484
Privacy Protection Study Commission, 485
   recommendations for improvements, **485**
Problem oriented language, **38**
Problem statement, 41, 56
Procedure division, **173,** 186
Process control system, 407
Processing, 11, 17
Processing symbol, **57**
Processing transactions, **214**
Processor, **20**
Productivity, 459
Program, **14**–16, 56, 546
   coding form, 85
   flowchart, **45,** 47
   operating system, 254
   user, 254
   See also Flowchart; Language, programming
Programmed learning and teaching operation (PLATO), 324
Programmer, **14,** 16, 188
Programming, 199
   body section, **176**
   contract, 440
   cost increases, 422
   languages. *See* Language, programming
   macro, 203
   maintenance, 190
   micro, 203
   top-down hierarchy, 190, 421
   trends, 451

Programs
   in BASIC, **14,** 16
   building a master file, 154
   building a transaction file, 148
   computer, **14,** 16, 364
   documentation, **112**
   master file update, 156
   object, **36**
   operating system, 254
   simulation, 160
   sorting, 150
   structural, **106,** 421
   theft of, 496
   user, 254
   utility, **149**
Proposal, **358,** 366
Protection of privacy. *See* Privacy, protection
Protocol, **215,** 396
Prudent person theory, 497
Pseudocode, **58**
Punched card, 12, 22, 216
   80-column card, 12, 22, 216
   field, 43, 47
Punched card input device, 12, 22, 374
Punched card input/output, advantages and disadvantages, 218, 220
Punched card reader, **12,** 22, 217
Puritan work ethic, **465**

Question mark, 92, 93
Quotation marks, 89, 90
   INPUT, 141
   strings, 140–142

Radio Shack computer, 450
Radix, **256**
   point, **256**
RAMAC, 283
Rand Corp., 32, 399
Random access, **272,** 280–289
Randomize, 550
Range, John, 435
RCA
   microcomputer manufacturer, 438
READ, **28,** 86, 92, 100, 139
Reading, **12,** 16
Reading station, 23
Read-only memory (ROM), **205**–206, 295
Read/write head, **275,** 289
Real number, 120–123
Real-time processing, **407**
Rearrange, **12,** 16
Record, **43,** 47
   blocking, 274
   disk, 275–276
   merging, 149, 541, 542
   sorting, 12, 44
   tape, 272–275
Recorder, microfilm, 340,341
Red Cross, 361
Redundancy, 377, 382
Reel, 272
Register
   accumulator, 20, 31
   address, 198–201
   storage, 36
Relational DBMS, 286–289, 420

Relational operators, **94,** 286, 289
Relative privacy, 475
REM, **28,** 83, 112, 133, 550
Remington Rand Corporation, 229
   See also Sperry Rand Corporation
Remote job entry, **375**
Remote job entry station (RJES), **375**
Remote storage of files, 336
Removable disk, **276,** 289
Repetition, **107**
Replacement of data, **62**
Replicator, 123
Report generators, 422
Report program generator. *See* RPG
Reserved words
   BASIC, 82, 84
   COBOL, **173,** 186
   FORTRAN, 171
Restore, 549
Return, 548
Right to Financial Privacy Act of 1978, 485
RND, 139, 157, 165, 547
Robotics, 457, 471
ROM. *See* Read-only memory
Rosenberg, Jerry M., 465
Rotary switch, 374
Rows
   on 80-column card, **216**
   microfiche, 339
RPG, 26, 38, 173, 177
   coding forms, 181
   comparison, 180–186
   sample program, 182
RPG-II, 38, 177, 180
RS232C standard, 214, 389
Rule, decision table, **534,** 542
RUN, **30,** 91, 100, 142
RYAD Soviet computer, 446, 447
Ryan, Captain, 494

Sabotage, **496**
   U.S. Department of Defense, **496**
SAVE, 92
Scanners, bar code, 246
SCR, 92
Scratch tape, **280,** 289
Secondary storage, **12,** 25, 272–278, 417
   data cell, 278
   history, 283
   magnetic disk, 275–278
   magnetic drum, 278
   magnetic tape, 272–275
   mass storage unit, 278
   on personal computer, 277, 289
   random access, **272,** 280–289
   sequential access, 272–275
Sectors, **275,** 289
   flexible disk, 277, 289
Secure computer, 496
Seek, 276
Segments, 380
Selection, **106**
Self-documenting, **173**
Self-regulation by business, 486
Semicolon, 88, 112
Semiconductors
   cost per bit projections, 418
   memory, **21,** 23, 263

Semiconductors (*continued*)
   miniaturization, 264
Sentinel, end-of-data, **72**
Separation of responsibilities, 499
Sequence checks, 499
Sequence numbers, 82, 83
Sequence, simple, **106**
Sequential file processing, **272,** 279, 289
Serial arithmetic, **260**
Serial printers, 331
Serial transmission, **295**
Service bureaus, 355
SGN(X), 547
Shepard, Jon M., 466
Siemens, 445, 446
Simple sequence, **106**
SIMSCRIPT, 170
Simulation, **157,** 165
Single array, **145,** 165
Single-board computer, 298
SIN(X), 139, 458
Slash (/), 87
Small business computer, 306
Smithsonian Institution, 264
SNOBAL, 170
Social privacy, **474**
Social Security Administration, personal data files, 436, 476, 477
Social Security program, 361
Software, 50
   assemblers, **37,** 38, 47
   compilers, **39,** 47, 171
   cost trends, 422
   interpreters, **39,** 47
   operating systems, 440
   proprietary, 440
   sales growth, 439
   trends, 419
   See also Language, programming
Software industry
   major firms, 441
   sales mix, 439, 442
Software trends and developments, 419
Sort, **12,** 31, 44, 146, 279
   ascending, **12,** 16
   descending, **12,** 16
   rearrange, **12,** 16
Source, The, information service, 424, 451
Source program, **39,** 47, 91
Soviet computer
   BESM-6, 446
   RYAD, 446
Specifications (RPG), **179**
Speech synthesis. *See* Voice synthesis
Sperry Gyroscope, 229
Sperry Rand Corporation, 229, 292
Sperry-Univac, 13, 229, 292
   mainframe manufacturer, 292, 307, 311
   market share, (*table*) 433
Spooling, 383
SPS, 38, 170
SQR, 138, 165, 547
Standardized access methods: SDLC and HDLC, 397
   cabling, RS232C, 215
Standard universal identifier (SUI), features, **481**
Start, **83**
Start bit, 388

Statement categories, 28, **82,** 84, 354
   BASIC, 28, 82, 84, 548
Statements, in ANSI minimal BASIC, 548
STEP, **85,** 86
Stibitz, George, 392
Stop bit, 388
STOP statement, 171, 175, 548
Storage, **12,** 16, 20. *See also* Memory; Secondary storage
Storage location. *See* Address
Stored program concept, 63
String, 91, 133, 140–145, 159
   in ANSI minimal BASIC, 546
Structural unemployment, 461
Structured programming, **106,** 133, 173, 190, 421
   repetition, **107,** 133
   selection, **107,** 133
   sequence, **106,** 133
Stub
   action, **532,** 542
   condition, **532,** 542
Subscript, 119
Substring, 142, **159**
Super BASIC, 93
Superprogrammer, 188–190
Surveillance
   of activists by FBI, 482
   daily sheet, 482
Swapping, 380
Symbolic flowchart, 59
Symbols, flowchart. *See* Flowchart symbols
Synchronous modems, 385, 387
System command, **91,** 100, 546
Systems analysis, **354,** 366
Systems analyst, **355,** 366
Systems design, top-down hierarchy, 348, **354,** 358, 366
Systems flowchart, **45,** 364
Systems houses, 300, 302
Systems implementation, **354,** 366
Systems management software, trends and developments, 420
System/3. *See* IBM

TAB, 112, 133, 139
Tab card. *See* Punched card
Table
   array, **118,** 145
   decision, **532**–**542**
   one-dimensional, **145,** 165
   three-dimensional, **145,** 165
   two-dimensional, **145,** 165
Table header, **532,** 542
Tabulating Machine Company, 228, 436
Take-up reel, 274
TAN(X), 139, 548
Tandy Corp., 51, 438, 450
Tape
   beginning of, 274
   drive, 273
   label, 275
   magnetic, 272–275, 289
   mark, 274
Tape reader
   magnetic, 273
Tax Reform Act of 1976 (TRA76), 485

Teleconferencing, 460
Telephone tag, 428
Teletype Corporation, 235
Telex, independent computer peripheral manufacturer, 434
Teller machines. *See* Automated teller machine
Template, **70**
Terminal, 25, 235, 360
   alphanumeric, 320
   data communications, 385
   graphics, 320
   intelligent, **236,** 304
   interactive, **236**
   nonbuffered, 388
   plasma screen, **324**
   portable, 410
   symbol, 57
   trends and developments, 418
Testing, 127, 365, 366
Texas Instruments, 302, 450
   magnetic bubble memory, 267
   microcomputer manufacturer, 438
   T1765 terminal, 410
   voice synthesizer, 343
Theft, 495
THEN, 94, 171
Thimble printer, 329
Third generation computers, 415
Thousands of operations per second, 308, 312
Threats to privacy
   meeting them, 485–487
   of information, 475–485
3M Company, 428, 434
TIME, 139
Time sharing
   dynamic partitioning, **379**
   partitioning, **379**
   swapping, **380**
   time slice, **379**
Top-down programming, 107, 421
Totaler, 29–31, 61, 84, 87, 126–133
Tracks, 275, 289
   flexible disk, 273, 289
Training, 365
Train printers, 327
Transaction file, **45,** 146, **214,** 280, 289
Transaction processing
   cost, (*table*) 242
   from source documents, 238
   via keyboard, 234
Transfer
   conditional, 94, 100
   unconditional, 94, 100
Transfer rate, **274,** 289
Transistor, **21**
Translation, 36
Transmission modes, 392
Tree, **286,** 289
Trilogy Corp., 200
Triple arrays, **145,** 165
TRS-80 computer, 450
TRW, Credit Data Division, 479
Turnkey systems, 307
12-edge, of punched card, 217
Tymeshare, network information services, 399, 440, 442, 444
Tymnet, 399
Type fonts, OCR, 230

UCSD, 176
Unbundling, 439
Unconditional transfer, 94, 100
Underemployment, 461
Unit record, **221**
Unit record system. *See* Punched card
UNIVAC. *See* Sperry Univac
UNIVAC computer, 176, 229, 436
Universal identifier, 481
Universal Product Code (UPC), **239**, 246
University of Illinois, PLATO, 324
UPC. *See* Universal Product Code
Update, master file, 149, 279
U.S. Department of Defense
   security standards, 496
U.S. Department of Health, Education, and Welfare (HEW)
   Automated Personal Data Systems, Advisory Committee on, 484
   records, computers, and the rights of citizens, 481
User-defined function, **139**, 165, 550
User programs, **254**
U.S. Supreme Court, ruling on privacy, 485, 487, 490
Utilities. *See* Network information services
Utility program, **149**, 165

Validation, **65**, 94, 118, 216, 279
Van Tassel, Dennie, 482
Variable name, **59,** 60, 83, 112

Variables
   alphanumeric, 112
   in BASIC, 82, 83, 547
   cost, 184
   numeric, 82, 83
Variable-word-length computer, **254**
VAX, 364
Verification, 221
Verifying, **94,** 118, 279
Very large scale integration (VLSI), 294
Video display terminal. *See* CRT
Virtual memory, 384
Virtual storage. *See* Virtual memory
VISA credit card, 27, 83, 108, 138, 146, 252
VISICALC, 50, 168
Visual display devices, 320
Visual display media, 25, 360
Voice mail, 428, 429
Voice recognition system (VRS), **241**
Voice response devices, 249, **342**
Volatile storage, **262**
Von Neumann, John, 62
VRS. *See* Voice recognition system

Wand, 246
   OCR, 230
WATBOL, 135
WATFOR, 135
Watson, Dick, 436
Watson, Jeannette, 435

Watson, Thomas
   collection of intelligence data, 436
   concern for loyal employees, 436
   "Old Man" of IBM, 435–437
Watson, Thomas, Jr., 436
WHILE, 107
Wiener, Norbert, 456
Wirth, Niklaus, 176
Word, **254**
Word computer. *See* Fixed-word-length computer
Word processing, 17, 320, 460
   reserved, **176**
Worker experience with automation, 466
Workers' attitudes toward automation, 465
Work ethic, **465**
Working storage, 173, 253
Wozniak, Steve, 40, 450
WRITE, 12, 171

Xerox, 18, 41, 434, 444
   computer store, 445
   laser printer, 335
   personal computer, 438
Xerographic printers, 333

Ziller, Irving, 135
Zone rows, on 80-column card, **216**
Zone punching positions, **216**
Zuboff, Shooshana, 466

Index of Business Applications

Accounting, 15
Account numbers, 308
Accounts payable, 15
Accounts receivable, 15, 41–45, 272, 354, 366, 552
ACM, 188
Accused embezzler, hiring of, 504
Addressograph Multigraph Corp., 18
Aging of accounts, 360, 361
Alternatives, 355
Amoco Oil Co., credit card billing by, 347
Amortization, 513, 516
Annuity, 416, 514
Application programming, 208
Applied System Inc., program theft of, 496
Arizona State Finance Center file loss, 497
Atlantic Richfield Corp., use of xerographic printing by, 334
Auditing, 366
Automated clearinghouses, 243

Balance forward, 354, 366
Balance only, 354, 366
Balances, 146
Bank Americard, 26
Banking, 552
Bank of America, 41

Bar code scanner users, 247, 248
Bay Area Rapid Transit, 146–147
Billing, 11, 26, 347, 368, 517, 524
Board of directors, 553
Brewery, use of Apple II by, 449
Business data, 369

Cash flow, 94
Cashier, 13
Cenco Inc., computer fraud of, 495
Census Bureau, $7 million loss of, 497
Charge, 149
Check, 528
COM. *See* Computer output microfilm
Commission process examples, 126
Compound interest, 513
Computer networks, 399
Computer output microfilm (COM), Grange Mutual Insurance Company and, 338
Computing services, 552–556
Control break, 126
Conversion, 366
Cost analysis, 358
   direct, 355
   fixed, 183
   indirect, 355
   one time, 355
   programming, 183
   variable, 184, 355

County Seat Stores, 135
Court reporting, 102
Credits, 136

Data factory, 168
Dealership, 368
Decision table, 531–544
Depreciation exercise, 515, 522
Direct cost, 355
Discount, 94, 98, 521

Effective interest rate, 513
Electrical billing, 524
Engineering, 15
Equity Funding Life Insurance Company, fraud case of, 495
Exxon card, 41

Fare, 147
F International Ltd., 562
Financial trends, 168
Fire, destruction of computer center by, 496
Fixed cost, 183
Flowers by Foote, 355
Fraud, 495, 497, 504
Fringe benefit, 183

Gantt chart, 365
General Dynamics, use of robots by, 457
General ledger, 15, 168, 368
General Motors, use of robots by, 458
Grange Mutual Insurance Company, computer output microfilm (COM) and, 76
Gross pay exercise, 525–528

Indirect cost, 355
Interest, 413
Interest exercise, 512–520
International Business Machines (IBM), 291, 292
Interstate calls, 536
Intrastate calls, 536
Inventory, 15, 136, 368, 523, 530, 562
Invoice, 41, 368

J. C. Penney Co., privacy safeguards of, 486
Job description, 554, 561

Leasing, 291, 368
Ledger, 15, 168, 368
Ledger card, 355–358
Levi Strauss & Co., 298, 456
Liberty National Bank, 208
Loans, 417, 516, 519

Maintenance, 292
Manufacturers, 552
    of general purpose computers, 13
    of minicomputers, 13
Marginal propensity, 525
Marketing strategies, 291
Market share, 291
Master Card, 26, 338
Mechanization, 368
Microcomputers, 13
Microfilm users, 338
Monsanto Co., use of voice recognition by, 241
Monthly payments, 513, 515

National BankAmericard Inc. *See* VISA

Oklahoma City Bank, 208
One time cost, 355
Open ended, 539, 542
Open item AR, 354, 366
Operator, computer, 559, 561
    data entry by, 559, 561
Optical character recognition (OCR), 240
Order form, 356
Order processing, 536–539
Organization chart, 552, 561

Pacific Gas & Electric Co., 41
Payment, 149
Payroll, 14, 15, 32, 368, 525–528, 541, 552
Portable terminals, 410
Posting, 140
Pricing, 292
Profits, 292
Programming applications, 208
Programs, theft of, 504
Projection, 168
Proposal, 358, 366

Readability, Fleisch, 522
Register, payroll, 528
Remittance stub, 359
Rental, 358, 368
Retirement plan, 514
Robots, 457, 458
Rule of 78s, 518

Sales, 292
Sears Roebuck & Company, 41
Service bureaus, 355
Shipping, 536–540
Simulation, 157, 165, 510
Social Security, 544
Software services, 562
Sorting, 527, 529, 530
Soundex code, 520
Squibb & Sons, theft case of, 496

Standards, 523
Star Wars, 33
Statement, 26, 361, 524
Stock analysis, 449
Stockholders, 553
Superprogrammer, 188
Super Valu Stores Inc., 135
Supreme Court, 17
Systems, 354, 366
    analysis, 354, 366
    analyst, 355, 557, 561
    programmer, 558, 561

Telecommuting, 562
Telephone tag, 428
Terminal, portable, 410
Theft, 504
Transcription, 102
Travel cost, 516, 519
Trial balance, 360

Universal Product Code, 247
UPC. *See* Universal Product Code
Utility billing, 517, 524

Validating, 94, 96, 535
Value exchange system. *See* VISA
Variable cost, 355
VISA, 26, 27, 36, 83, 108, 138, 141, 146, 252, 272–289, 354
VISICALC, 50, 168
Voice mail at 3M Co., 428

Waiting cost, 516
Wand reader, data collection by, 246
Want ad, 517
Warehouse, 536–540
Water billing, 517
Wells Fargo Bank, theft case of, 495
Word processing, 17

Xerographic printing, 334